LIBRARY OF SECOND TEMPLE STUDIES

95

formerly the Journal for the Study of the Pseudepigrapha Supplement Series

Editor
Lester L. Grabbe

Founding Editor
James H. Charlesworth

Editorial Board
Randall D. Chesnutt, Jan Willem van Henten, Judith M. Lieu,
Steven Mason, James R. Mueller, Loren T. Stuckenbruck,
James C. VanderKam

A HISTORY OF THE JEWS AND JUDAISM IN THE SECOND TEMPLE PERIOD

Volume 3

The Maccabaean Revolt, Hasmonaean Rule, and Herod the Great (175–4 BCE)

Lester L. Grabbe

t&tclark

LONDON · NEW YORK · OXFORD · NEW DELHI · SYDNEY

T&T CLARK
Bloomsbury Publishing Plc
50 Bedford Square, London, WC1B 3DP, UK
1385 Broadway, New York, NY 10018, USA
29 Earlsfort Terrace, Dublin 2, Ireland

BLOOMSBURY, T&T CLARK and the T&T Clark logo
are trademarks of Bloomsbury Publishing Plc

First published in Great Britain 2020
This paperback edition published in 2021

© Lester L. Grabbe, 2020

Lester L. Grabbe has asserted his right under the Copyright, Designs and Patents Act, 1988,
to be identified as the Author of this work.

Cover design: Charlotte James
Cover image: 753. Coins of Herod the Great 40–4 BC
© www.BibleLandPictures.com / Alamy Stock Photo

All rights reserved. No part of this publication may be reproduced or transmitted in any form
or by any means, electronic or mechanical, including photocopying, recording, or any information
storage or retrieval system, without prior permission in writing from the publishers.

Bloomsbury Publishing Plc does not have any control over, or responsibility for, any third-party
websites referred to or in this book. All internet addresses given in this book were correct at the
time of going to press. The author and publisher regret any inconvenience caused if addresses have
changed or sites have ceased to exist, but can accept no responsibility for any such changes.

A catalogue record for this book is available from the British Library.
A catalog record for this book is available from the Library of Congress.

ISBN: HB: 978-0-5676-9294-8
       PB: 978-0-5677-0378-1
     ePDF: 978-0-5676-9295-5

Series: Library of Second Temple Studies, volume 95

Typeset by: Forthcoming Publications Ltd

To find out more about our authors and books visit www.bloomsbury.com and sign up
for our newsletters.

To my sisters

Ina Lou

Birdie Susan

Ronda Glen

CONTENTS

Preface	xiii
Abbreviations	xv

Part I
INTRODUCTION

Chapter 1	
INTRODUCTION	3
1.1. The Reconstruction of Jewish History	3
1.2. The Question of Jewish Identity and Appropriate Terminology	5
1.2.1 Terminology	6
1.2.2. The Question of Jewish Identity	7
1.2.3. Ethnic Group or Religion?	9
1.3. Chronology	13
1.3.1. Introductory Comments	14
1.3.2. Babylonian, Egyptian and Seleucid Dates	15
1.3.3. The Dating System in 1 Maccabees	16
1.3.4. Dates of Major Events in 1 Maccabees	21
1.3.5. Herodian and Roman Dating	26
1.3.5.1. Fall of Jerusalem to Pompey in 63 BCE	26
1.3.5.2. Appointment as King	26
1.3.5.3. Conquest of Jerusalem	27
1.3.5.4. Herod's Death	29
1.3.6. The Sabbatical Year	32
1.3.7. Table of Some Important Dates	35
1.4 Terminology and Other Technical Matters	36

Part II
SOURCES

Chapter 2	
ARCHAEOLOGY, INCLUDING COINS AND INSCRIPTIONS	41
2.1. Unwritten Remains and Material Culture	41
2.1.1. Individual Sites	42
2.1.1.1. Paneas (Paneion, Banias)	42
2.1.1.2. Tel Anafa	42

2.1.1.3. Tel Dan	43
2.1.1.4. Tel Kedesh	43
2.1.1.5. Ptolemais/Akko (Tell Fukhar)	44
2.1.1.6. Capernaum (Talḥum)	44
2.1.1.7. Sepphoris	45
2.1.1.8. Shiqmona	46
2.1.1.9. Atlit (Adarot, Arados/Adoros, Boucolonpolis)	46
2.1.1.10. Philoteria (Beth Yeraḥ, Khirbet el-Kerak)	46
2.1.1.11. Tel Dor	47
2.1.1.12. Tel Mevorakh	47
2.1.1.13. Straton's Tower/Caesarea Maritima	48
2.1.1.14. Beth-Shean/Scythopolis	48
2.1.1.15. Apollonia (Arsuf; Tell Arshaf)	49
2.1.1.16. Tel Michal (Makmish)	49
2.1.1.17. Tel Dothan	50
2.1.1.18. Samaria/Sebaste	50
2.1.1.19. Shechem (Tell Balâtah) and Mt Gerizim	51
2.1.1.20. Jaffa (Joppa)	52
2.1.1.21. Bethel	52
2.1.1.22. Jericho (Tell es-Sultan, Tulul Abu el-'Alayiq)	53
2.1.1.23. Gezer (Tell Jezer)	53
2.1.1.24. Jamnia (Yavneh, Yavneh-Yam, Minet Rubin)	54
2.1.1.25. Jerusalem and Vicinity	55
2.1.1.26. Qumran	57
2.1.1.27. Ashdod (Azotus)	57
2.1.1.28. Ashkelon (Ascalon)	57
2.1.1.29. Beth-Zur	57
2.1.1.30. Gaza (Tell Ḥaruba/Tell 'Azza, Tall al-Ajjul)	58
2.1.1.31. En-gedi (Tel Goren, Tell el-Jurn)	58
2.1.1.32. Tel Maresha (Tell eṣ-Ṣandaḥanna)	59
2.1.1.33. Beersheba (Tel Sheva; Tell es-Saba')	60
2.1.1.34. Gamala (Gamla)	60
2.1.1.35. Hippos (Sussita, Qasl'at el-Ḥusn)	61
2.1.1.36. Gadara (Umm Qeis)	61
2.1.1.37. Pella (Ṭabaqaṭ Faḥl)	61
2.1.1.38. Gerasa (Jerash)	62
2.1.1.39. Philadelphia (Rabbath-Ammon)	62
2.1.1.40. 'Iraq al-Amir	63
2.1.1.41. Desert Fortresses	64
2.1.2. Surveys and Synthesis	64
2.1.2.1. Introductory Comments	66
2.1.2.2. Regions	67
2.1.2.3. Topics	71
2.2. Inscriptions	74
2.3. Coins and Seals	75

Contents ix

Chapter 3

JEWISH LITERATURE 79
3.1. 1 and 2 Maccabees 79
3.2. Letters and Documents in 1 and 2 Maccabees 83
    3.2.1. Treaties with Rome 84
    3.2.2. Alleged Kinship with the Spartans 85
    3.2.3. The Letters in 2 Maccabees 1–2 85
    3.2.4. The Letters in 2 Maccabees 9 and 11 85
3.3. Daniel 88
3.4. Josephus 91
3.5. 1 Enoch 83–108 96
3.6. Book of Jubilees 97
3.7. Judith 99
3.8. 1 Baruch 101
3.9. Testament of Moses (Assumption of Moses) 102
3.10. Letter of (Pseudo-)Aristeas 103
3.11. Pseudo-Hecataeus 106
3.12. Psalms of Solomon 106
3.13. Wisdom of Solomon 108

Chapter 4

GREEK AND LATIN SOURCES 111
4.1. Appian 111
4.2. Cicero 112
4.3. Cassius Dio 112
4.4. Diodorus Siculus 113
4.5. Livy 113
4.6. Nicolaus of Damascus 114
4.7. Justin/Pompeius Trogus 114
4.8. Pliny the Elder 115
4.9. Plutarch 115
4.10. Polybius 115
4.11. Porphyry 116
4.12. Posidonius 117
4.13. Strabo 118
4.14. Suetonius 118
4.15. George Syncellus 118

Part III
SOCIETY AND INSTITUTIONS

Chapter 5

ECONOMICS 123
5.1. The Economy under Hasmonaean Rule 123
5.2. Economic Changes with the Coming of the Romans 127

x   Contents

5.3. The Economy of Judaea under Herod   129
5.4. Conclusions   132

Chapter 6
SECTS AND MOVEMENTS   134
6.1. Hasidim   135
6.2. Sadducees and Boethusians   137
    6.2.1. Sources   138
    6.2.2. Analysis and Conclusions   141
6.3. Pharisees   143
    6.3.1. Josephus   145
    6.3.2. Conclusions about Josephus   150
    6.3.3. The New Testament   152
    6.3.4. Conclusions about the New Testament   156
    6.3.5. Rabbinic Literature   157
    6.3.6. Summary with Regard to Tannaitic Literature   159
    6.3.7. 4QMMT and the Temple Scroll (11QT)   160
    6.3.8. Analysis in the Context of Recent Study   160
    6.3.9. Summary and Conclusions   163
6.4. 'The Scribes'   165
    6.4.1. 'Scribes' in Jewish Literature   166
    6.4.2. 'Scribes' in the Gospels   168
    6.4.3. Summary and Conclusions   169
6.5. Essenes   170
    6.5.1. Sources   170
    6.5.2. Conclusions   172
6.6. Synthesis   173

Chapter 7
QUMRAN AND THE DEAD SEA SCROLLS   176
7.1. The Archaeology   178
7.2. Identity   181
    7.2.1. Are the Scrolls to Be Associated
           with the Settlement at Qumran?   182
    7.2.2. Some Recent Theories about the Origin
           of the Qumran Site   184
    7.2.3. The Essene Hypothesis   186
7.3. Some Historical Data   190
7.4. Conclusions   192

Chapter 8
THE SAMARITANS: FROM SANBALLAT TO VESPASIAN   194
8.1. The Samaritan Literary Sources   196
    8.1.1. Samaritan Pentateuch and Translations   196

8.1.2. Samaritan Chronicles	197
8.1.3. Samaritan Writings in Greek	201
8.2. Historical Overview of the Samaritans	202
8.2.1. Persian Period and Earlier	202
8.2.2. Early Hellenistic Period (335–175 BCE)	203
8.2.3. Time of the Maccabees and the Hasmonaean Kingdom	205
8.2.4. The Samaritans under Roman Control	209
8.3. Other Topics	213
8.3.1. Archaeology	213
8.3.2. The Origins of the Samaritan Sect and Their Cult	213
8.3.3. Relationship with the Judaeans	214
8.3.4. The Question of Hellenization	216
8.4. Conclusions	217

Chapter 9
THE IDUMAEANS, ARABS AND PARTHIANS

	220
9.1. Idumaeans	220
9.2. Nabataeans	222
9.3. Ituraeans	225
9.4. Parthians	226

Chapter 10
THE DIASPORA: JEWISH COMMUNITIES OUTSIDE JUDAH
FROM ALEXANDER TO HEROD (330 BCE TO 4 BCE)

	231
10.1. Ideology of the Land and the Concept of Exile	231
10.2. Jews in Various Areas	234
10.2.1. Egypt	234
10.2.1.1. Jewish Generals under Cleopatra III	235
10.2.1.2. Alleged 'Persecution' under Ptolemy IV (3 Maccabees)	235
10.2.1.3. Temple at Leontopolis	236
10.2.2. Syria, Asia Minor and Greece	238
10.2.3. Rome	241
10.2.4. Babylonia	244
10.3. Conclusions	246

Chapter 11
CAUSES OF THE MACCABAEAN REVOLT

	248
11.1. Ancient Views	249
11.2. Hellenization of Antiochus's Empire	250
11.3. Antiochus's Promotion of the Cult of Zeus	251
11.4. Thesis of E. J. Bickerman	252
11.5. Thesis of V. A. Tcherikover	253
11.6. Thesis of J. A. Goldstein	254

xii   *Contents*

11.7. Thesis of K. Bringmann   255
11.8. Thesis of Erich Gruen   257
11.9. Thesis of Anathea Portier-Young   257
11.10. Thesis of Steven Weitzman and Sylvie Honigman   258
11.11. Socio-Economic Causes   259
11.12. Conclusions   259

Chapter 12
RELIGION:
TEMPLE, SCRIPTURE, BELIEF AND PRACTICE   262
12.1. The Temple and Synagogues   262
12.2. Development of the Biblical Texts   263
12.3. Beliefs and Practice   268
    12.3.1. Circumcision   268
    12.3.2. Ritual Purity and Mikva'ot   269
    12.3.3. Angelic Beings   270
    12.3.4. Eschatology and Ideas of Salvation   272
    12.3.5. Messiah   275
    12.3.6. Martyrdom   280
12.4. Apocalyptic and Prophecy   281
    12.4.1. Did Prophecy Cease in the Second Temple Period?   283
    12.4.2. Conclusions about Prophecy and Apocalyptic   285
12.5. Revelation from Textual Interpretation   287
12.6. Chronography   287
12.7. Conclusions   289

Part IV
HISTORICAL SYNTHESIS

Chapter 13
BACKGROUND: THE PTOLEMIES, THE SELEUCIDS AND THE ROMANS   295
13.1. The Ptolemaic Realm   296
    Outline of Ptolemaic History   296
13.2. The Seleucid Empire   298
    Outline of Seleucid History   299
13.3. The Rise of Rome   304

Chapter 14
EVENTS PRECEDING THE MACCABAEAN REVOLT (175–168 BCE):
A NEW CONSTITUTION FOR JERUSALEM   310
14.1. The First 25 Years of Seleucid Rule   311
14.2. Antiochus IV (175–164 BCE)   312
14.3. The Problem of Sources:
    Different Accounts of How the Revolt Began   315

Contents xiii

14.4. A New Constitution for Jerusalem 318
14.4.1. Jason Displaces Onias as High Priest 319
14.4.2. Who Were the 'Hellenizers'? 324
14.4.3. Jason and his Hellenistic Jerusalem in Perspective 328
14.4.4. Menelaus Takes the Office of High Priest 334
14.5. Conclusions 338

Chapter 15
THE MACCABAEAN REVOLT TO THE DEATH OF JUDAS (170–161 BCE) 340
15.1. The Sixth Syrian War 341
15.2. The Judaean 'Revolt' and Its Consequences 345
15.2.1. Critical Analysis of the Reports on the Revolt 345
15.2.2. Two Recent Theories to Explain Antiochus's Actions 349
15.2.3. The 'Alien Cult' Set up in the Temple 356
15.3. The Beginnings of the Revolt 358
15.3.1. The Initial Resistance 358
15.3.2. The Question of Mattathias 359
15.4. Judas Maccabaeus 360
15.4.1. Judas Maccabee's Initial Campaigns 361
15.4.2. Concessions by the Seleucids to the Jews 366
15.4.3. Temple Retaken and Returned to Service 370
15.4.4. Final Military Activities of Judas 371
15.4.5. The Embassy to Rome 378
15.4.6. The Death of Judas 380
15.4.7. Achievements of Judas Maccabaeus 383
15.5. Conclusions 385

Chapter 16
THE HASMONAEAN KINGDOM:
FROM JONATHAN TO ALEXANDRA SALOME (161 TO 67 BCE) 388
16.1. Jonathan Maccabee (161–143 BCE) 389
16.1.1. Jonathan Takes Over But Is on the Run 389
16.1.2. Gains Made by Jonathan 391
16.1.3. Appointed High Priest by the Seleucids 392
16.1.4. Seventh Syria War (147–145 BCE) 395
16.1.5. Jonathan Makes Further Gains for Judah 396
16.1.6. The Embassies Allegedly to Rome and Sparta 398
16.1.7. Death of Jonathan 401
16.2. Simon (143–135 BCE) 402
16.2.1. Initial Actions 402
16.2.2. Independence for Judah and Praise of Simon 403
16.2.3. Treaty with Rome 405
16.2.4. Main Accomplishments of Simon 407
16.2.5. Death of Simon 409

xiv *Contents*

16.3. John Hyrcanus I (135–104 BCE)	409
16.3.1. Beginning of Hyrcanus's Reign	410
16.3.2. Eighth Syrian War (ca. 128–122 BCE)	411
16.3.3. Territorial Expansion and Conquests	413
16.3.4. Contacts with Rome	414
16.3.5. The Rest of John Hyrcanus's Reign	415
16.4. Judah Aristobulus I (104–103 BCE)	417
16.5. Alexander Jannaeus (103–76 BCE)	419
16.6. Alexandra Salome (76–67 BCE)	424
16.7. Conclusions	426

Chapter 17
END OF THE HASMONAEAN KINGDOM
AND THE BEGINNING OF ROMAN DOMINATION (67–40 BCE)

AND THE BEGINNING OF ROMAN DOMINATION (67–40 BCE)	429
17.1. The Roman Republic in the First Century BCE to the Roman Civil War (100–49 BCE)	429
17.2. Aristobulus II and Hyrcanus II (67–63 BCE)	431
17.3. Pompey's Settlement in Judaea and the Region	433
17.4. Jews under Roman Administration: Scaurus, Gabinius, Crassus and Cassius	435
17.5. First Phase of the Roman Civil War to the Death of Caesar (49–44 BCE)	438
17.6. Judah during the First Phase of the Roman Civil War: Julius Caesar (49–44 BCE)	439
17.7. Next Phase of the Roman Civil War: Octavian and Antony (44–40 BCE)	440
17.8. Relationship of Antipater and Hyrcanus	441
17.9. Early Career of Herod	442
17.9.1. Ancestry of Herod	442
17.9.2. Governor of Galilee	444
17.9.3. Death of Antipater	445
17.10. Conclusions	447

Chapter 18
THE REIGN OF HEROD THE GREAT (40–4 BCE)

THE REIGN OF HEROD THE GREAT (40–4 BCE)	449
18.1. Last Phase of the Roman Civil War: Octavian and Antony (40–31 BCE)	450
18.2. First Phase of Herod's Reign (40–30 BCE)	451
18.2.1. The Parthians Take Palestine	451
18.2.2. Retaking of Jerusalem	452
18.2.3. Troubles with Cleopatra	455
18.2.4. Actium: On the Losing Side	457
18.3. Reign of Augustus (31 BCE–14 CE)	459

18.4. The Rest of Herod's Reign (30–4 BCE)	461
18.4.1. Administration under Herod	461
18.4.2. Magnificent Buildings	464
18.4.3. From Actium to the Death of Agrippa (30–14 BCE)	467
18.4.4. Conflicts with the Arabs	469
18.4.5. Family Quarrels and Problems	472
18.4.6. Death of Herod	478
18.4.7. Assessment of Herod's Reign	482
18.5. Conclusions	487

Part V
CONCLUSIONS

Chapter 19
JUDAISM FROM ONIAS III TO HEROD THE GREAT:
A HOLISTIC PERSPECTIVE 493

Bibliography	509
Index of References	564
Index of Authors	581
Index of Subjects	589

PREFACE

The present volume has been too long in coming, for which I apologize. Having done two volumes of this work (2004, 2008), I expected to finish the next two volumes promptly after retiring. Unfortunately, after being free from day-to-day teaching and administration, I accepted a number of invitations, mostly for short pieces, all worthwhile and interesting but time consuming. Then it dawned on me that I was letting these many articles distract me from my main projects. But there was also a lot of necessary editing, as well as a long-planned monograph on evolution and creation. So, a decade after volume 2, here is volume 3, though I hope that the 4th and final volume will not be long delayed.

One of the obstacles to completing this volume was the many recent studies on the Maccabaean period, a good number of which have appeared since the year 2000. They have taken time to digest but have also paid rich dividends in new ideas and interpretations, for which I am immensely grateful. Those of us who do not live near major research libraries often find access to necessary publications, especially secondary studies, a difficulty. For this and other reasons, I am particularly grateful to individuals who have kindly made their studies available to me or otherwise been helpful in researching this volume. Andrea Berlin very kindly invited me to a conference on the Middle Maccabean Period in June 2018 and also supplied one of her articles at short notice. Sylvia Honigman gave me a copy of her ground-breaking, *Tales of High Priests and Taxes: The Books of the Maccabees and the Judean Rebellion against Antiochos IV*, which has been a major stimulus. Edward Dąbrowa generously passed on a copy of *The Hasmoneans and their State: A Study in History, Ideology, and the Institutions*, which is otherwise not easy to access. Menahem Mor sent me a copy of the volume, *Jews and Gentiles in the Holy Land in the Days of the Second Temple, the Mishnah and the Talmud: A Collection of Articles*, that he co-edited. Reinhard Pummer, whose work is so important for Samaritan studies, very kindly made a gift of his *Samaritans in Flavius Josephus*. There are no doubt others whom I have overlooked, for which I profusely apologize. But I am grateful for these generous gifts and thank the givers for the fruit of their scholarly labours. I am also profoundly grateful to those predecessors and colleagues who have done so much work in elucidating this period in history. I just hope my own work building on and interacting with their studies does justice to their efforts.

Lester L. Grabbe
Kingston-upon-Hull
1 May 2019

ABBREVIATIONS

AASOR	Annual of the American Schools of Oriental Research
AAWG	Abhandlungen der Akademie der Wissenschaften zu Göttingen
AB	Anchor Bible
ABD	David Noel Freedman (ed.) (1992) *Anchor Bible Dictionary* (vols 1-6)
AfO	*Archiv für Orientforschung*
AGAJU	Arbeiten zur Geschichte des antiken Judentums und des Urchristentum
AIEJL	T. C. Vriezen, and A. S. van der Woude (2005) *Ancient Israelite and Early Jewish Literature*
AJA	*American Journal of Archaeology*
AJAH	*American Journal of Ancient History*
AJBA	*Australian Journal of Biblical Archaeology*
AJP	*American Journal of Philology*
AJS Review	*American Jewish Studies Review*
AJSL	*American Journal of Semitic Languages*
ALD	*Aramaic Levi Document*
ALGHJ	*Arbeiten zur Literatur und Geschichte des hellenistischen Judentums*
A.M.	*anno mundi*, a dating system which begins with the supposed date of the world's creation
AnBib	Analecta biblica
AncSoc	*Ancient Society*
ANET	J. B. Pritchard (ed.) (1969) *Ancient Near Eastern Texts relating to the Old Testament*
AnOr	Analecta orientalia
ANRW	*Aufstieg und Niedergang der römischen Welt*
Ant.	Josephus, *Antiquities of the Jews*
Arav	R. Arav (1989) *Hellenistic Palestine: Settlement Patterns and City Planning, 337–31 B.C.E.*
ASORAR	American Schools of Oriental Research Archaeological Reports
ASTI	*Annual of the Swedish Theological Institute*
ATR	*Anglican Theological Review*
AUSS	*Andrews University Seminary Studies*
AUSTIN	M. M. Austin (2006) *The Hellenistic World from Alexander to the Roman Conquest: A Selection of Ancient Sources in Translation*

Abbreviations

BA	*Biblical Archeologist*
BAGNALL AND DEROW	R. S. Bagnall and P. Derow (eds.) (2004) *The Hellenistic Period: Historical Sources in Translation*
BAR	*Biblical Archaeology Review*
BASOR	*Bulletin of the American Schools of Oriental Research*
BCE	Before the Common Era (= BC)
BCH	*Bulletin de Correspondance Hellénique*
BETL	Bibliotheca Ephemeridum Theologicarum Lovaniensium
BHS	*Biblia Hebraica Stuttgartensis*
Bib	*Biblica*
BibOr	Biblica et orientalia
BiOr	Biblica et orientalia
BJRL	*Bulletin of the John Rylands Library*
BJS	Brown Judaic Studies
BO	*Bibliotheca Orientalis*
BSOAS	*Bulletin of the School of Oriental and African Study*
BTB	*Biblical Theology Bulletin*
BURSTEIN	S. M. Burstein (1985) *The Hellenistic Age from the Battle of Ipsus to the Death of Kleopatra VII.*
BZ	*Biblische Zeitschrift*
BZAW	Beihefte zur *ZAW*
BZNW	Beihefte zur *ZNW*
CAH	*Cambridge Ancient History* (1st edition)
CAH²	*Cambridge Ancient History* (2st edition)
CBQ	*Catholic Biblical Quarterly*
CBQMS	*Catholic Biblical Quarterly* Monograph Series
CBR	*Currents in Biblical Research*
CC	Corpus Christianorum
CCTC	Cambridge Classical Texts and Commentaries
CE	Common Era (= AD)
CEJL	Commentaries on Early Jewish Literature
CHCL	P. E. Easterling et al. (eds) (1982–85) *Cambridge History of Classical Literature*
CHI	*Cambridge History of Iran*
CHJ	W. D. Davies and L. Finkelstein (eds) (1984–2017) *Cambridge History of Judaism* (vols 1-8)
CIJ	Corpus Inscriptionum Judaicarum
ConBNT	Conjectanea biblica, New Testament
ConBOT	Conjectanea biblica, Old Testament
CP	*Classical Philology*
CPJ	V. A. Tcherikover et al. (1957–64) *Corpus Papyrorum Judaicarum*
CQ	*Classical Quarterly*
CR: BS	*Currents in Research: Biblical Studies*
CRAIBL	*Comptes rendus de l'Académie des inscriptions et belles-lettres*
CRINT	Compendia rerum iudaicarum ad Novum Testamentum

CSCT	Columbia Studies in Classical Texts
DDD^2	K. van der Toorn, B. Becking, and P. W. van der Horst (eds) *Dictionary of Deities and Demons in the Bible*: 1st edition 1995 (= *DDD*); 2nd edition 1999 (= *DDD²*)
DJD	Discoveries in the Judaean Desert
DSD	*Dead Sea Discoveries*
EI	*Eretz-Israel*
ESHM	European Seminar in Historical Methodology
ET	English translation
FAT	Forschungen zum Alten Testament
FoSub	Fontes et Subsidia ad Bibliam pertinentes
FOTL	Forms of Old Testament Literature
FRLANT	Forschungen zur Religion und Literatur des Alten und Neuen Testaments
FS	Festschrift
GCS	Griechische christliche Schriftsteller
GLAJJ	Menahem Stern (1974–84) *Greek and Latin Authors on Jews and Judaism* (vols 1-3)
GRBS	*Greek, Roman, and Byzantine Studies*
HAT	Handbuch zum Alten Testament
HdA	Handbuch der Archäologie
HdO	Handbuch der Orientalisk
HJJSTP 1	Lester L. Grabbe (2004) *A History of the Jews and Judaism in the Second Temple Period 1: Yehud: A History of the Persian Province of Judah*
HJJSTP 2	Lester L. Grabbe (2008) *A History of the Jews and Judaism in the Second Temple Period 2: The Coming of the Greeks: The Early Hellenistic Period (335–175 BCE)*
HJJSTP 3	The current volume.
HJJSTP 4	Forthcoming volume on the Roman period.
HR	*History of Religions*
HSCP	*Harvard Studies in Classical Philology*
HSM	Harvard Semitic Monographs
HSS	Harvard Semitic Studies
HTR	*Harvard Theological Review*
HUCA	*Hebrew Union College Annual*
IAA	Israel Antiquities Authority
ICC	International Critical Commentary
IDB	G. A. Buttrick (ed.) (1962) *Interpreter's Dictionary of the Bible* (vols 1-4)
IDBSup	Supplementary volume to *IDB* (1976)
IEJ	*Israel Exploration Journal*
INJ	*Israel Numismatic Journal*
INR	*Israel Numismatic Research*
Int	*Interpretation*
IOS	*Israel Oriental Studies*

xxii Abbreviations

ITQ	*Irish Theological Quarterly*
JAAR	*Journal of the American Academy of Religion*
JAJ	*Journal of Ancient Judaism*
JAJSup	Supplements to *Journal of Ancient Judaism*
JANES	*Journal of the Ancient Near Eastern Society of Columbia University*
JAOS	*Journal of the American Oriental Society*
JBL	*Journal of Biblical Literature*
JCH	Lester L. Grabbe (1992) *Judaism from Cyrus to Hadrian* (2 vols with continuous pagination)
JCS	*Journal of Cuneiform Studies*
JEA	*Journal of Egyptian Archaeology*
JES	*Journal of Ecumenical Studies*
JHS	*Journal of Hellenic Studies*
JJS	*Journal of Jewish Studies*
JLBM	George W. E. Nickelsburg (2005[2]) *Jewish Literature between the Bible and the Mishnah*
JNES	*Journal of Near Eastern Studies*
JQR	*Jewish Quarterly Review*
JR	*Journal of Religion*
JRS	*Journal of Roman Studies*
JSHRZ	Jüdische Schriften aus hellenistisch-römischer Zeit
JSJ	*Journal for the Study of Judaism*
JSJSup	Supplements to *Journal for the Study of Judaism*
JSNT	*Journal for the Study of the New Testament*
JSOT	*Journal for the Study of the Old Testament*
JSOTSup	*Journal for the Study of the Old Testament*—Supplementary Series
JSP	*Journal for the Study of the Pseudepigrapha*
JSPSup	*Journal for the Study of the Pseudepigrapha*—Supplementary Series
JSS	*Journal of Semitic Studies*
JTS	*Journal of Theological Studies*
JWSTP	Michael E. Stone (ed.) (1984) *Jewish Writings of the Second Temple Period*
KAT	Kommentar zum Alten Testament
LCL	Loeb Classical Library
LSTS	Library of Second Temple Studies
LXX	Septuagint translation of the Old Testament
MGWJ	*Monatschrift für Geschichte und Wissenschaft des Judentums*
ms(s)	manuscript(s)
MT	Masoretic textual tradition (only the consonantal text is in mind when reference is made to pre-medieval mss)
NEAEHL	Ephraim Stern (ed.) (1992) *The New Encyclopedia of Archaeological Excavations in the Holy Land* (4 vols); (2008) *5 Supplementary Volume*

NIGTC	New International Greek Testament Commentary
NovT	*Novum Testamentum*
NovTSup	Novum Testamentum, Supplements
NTOA	Novum Testamentum et Orbis Antiquus
NTS	*New Testament Studies*
OBO	Orbis Biblicus et Orientalis
OCD	Simon Hornblower, A. Spawforth, and E. Eidinow (eds) (2012) *The Oxford Classical Dictionary* (4th edn)
OEANE	Eric M. Meyers (editor-in-chief) (1997) *The Oxford Encyclopedia of Archaeology in the Near East* (5 vols)
OEBA	D. M. Master (ed.) (2013) *The Oxford Encyclopedia of the Bible and Archaeology* (2 vols)
OGIS	W. Dittenberger (1903–5) *Orientis graeci inscriptiones selectae*
OLA	*Orientalia Lovaniensia Analecta*
OTG	Old Testament Guides
OTL	Old Testament Library
OTP 1-2	James H. Charlesworth (ed.) (1983–85) *Old Testament Pseudepigrapha*
OTS	*Oudtestamentische Studiën*
PAAJR	*Proceedings of the American Academy of Jewish Research*
PVTG	Pseudepigrapha Veteris Testamenti graece
PW	Georg Wissowa and Wilhelm Kroll (eds) (1894–1972) *Paulys Real-Encyclopädie der classischen Altertumswissenschaft*
PWSup	Supplement to *PW*
RC	C. B. Welles (1934) *Royal Correspondence in the Hellenistic Period: A Study in Greek Epigraphy*
REB	*Revised English Bible*
REG	*Revue des études grecs*
REJ	*Revue des études juives*
RevB	*Revue biblique*
RevQ	*Revue de Qumran*
RSR	*Religious Studies Review*
RSV	Revised Standard Version
SANE	Studies on the Ancient Near East
SAWH	*Sitzungsbericht der Akademie der Wissenschaften zu Heidelberg*
SBL	Society of Biblical Literature
SBLASP	SBL Abstracts and Seminar Papers
SBLBMI	SBL Bible and its Modern Interpreters
SBLDS	SBL Dissertation Series
SBLEJL	SBL Early Judaism and its Literature
SBLMS	SBL Monograph Series
SBLRBS	SBL Resources for Biblical Study
SBLSBS	SBL Sources for Biblical Study
SBLSCS	SBL Septuagint and Cognate Studies
SBLSPS	Society of Biblical Literature Seminar Papers Series
SBLTT	SBL Texts and Translations

xxiv   *Abbreviations*

SBT	Studies in Biblical Theology
SC	Sources chrétiennes
SCHÜRER	Emil Schürer (1973–87) *The Jewish People in the Age of Jesus Christ* (rev. G. Vermes, et al)
SCI	*Scripta Classica Israelica*
ScrHier	*Scripta Hierosolymitana*
SE	Seleucid era year
SEG	Supplementum epigraphicum graecum
SFSHJ	South Florida Studies in the History of Judaism
SFSJH	South Florica Studies in Jewish History
SHERK	Robert K. Sherk (1984) *Rome and the Greek East to the Death of Augustus*
SJLA	Studies in Judaism in Late Antiquity
SJOT	*Scandinavian Journal of the Old Testament*
SJLA	Studies in Judaism in Late Antiquity
SHAJ	*Studies in the History and Archaeology of Jordon*
SNTSMS	Society for New Testament Studies Monograph Series
SP	Samaritan Pentateuch
SPA	*Studia Philonica Annual*
SPB	Studia postbiblica
SR	*Studies in Religion/Sciences religieuses*
SSAW	Sitzungsbericht der sachischen Akademie der Wissenschaften
STDJ	Studies on the Texts of the Desert of Judah
SUNT	Studien zur Umwelt des Neuen Testaments
SVTP	Studia in Veteris Testamenti pseudepigrapha
TAD 1-4	Bezalel Porten and Ada Yardeni (1986–99) *Textbook of Aramaic Documents from Ancient Egypt. Volumes 1-4*
TAPA	*Transactions of the American Philological Association*
TDNT	G. Kittel and G. Friedrich (eds) (1964–76) *Theological Dictionary of the New Testament*
TLZ	*Theologische Literaturzeitung*
Trans	*Transeuphratène*
TSAJ	Texte und Studien zum antiken Judentum
VC	*Vigiliae Christianae*
VT	*Vetus Testamentum*
VTSup	*Vetus Testamentum*, Supplements
War	Josephus, *War of the Jews*
WBC	Word Bible Commentary
WHJP	*World History of the Jewish People*
WMANT	Wissenschaftliche Monographien zum Alten und Neuen Testament
WUNT	Wissenschaftliche Untersuchungen zum Neuen Testament
YCS	*Yale Classical Studies*
ZA	*Zeitschrift für Assyrologie*
ZAW	*Zeitschrift für die Alttestamentliche Wissenschaft*
ZDMG	*Zeitschrift der Deutschen Morganländischen Gesellschaft*

ZDPV	*Zeitschrift des Deutschen Palästina-Vereins*
ZNW	*Zeitschrift für die Neutestamentliche Wissenschaft*
ZPE	*Zeitschrift für Papyrologie und Epigraphik*
§	Cross reference to numbered section or sub-section elsewhere in the book; in a citation from Josephus, it refers to paragraph numbers in the text

Part I

INTRODUCTION

Chapter 1

INTRODUCTION

The previous volume (*HJJSTP 2*) began with a history of the Jews during and after the Greek conquest and went down to the beginning of Seleucid rule. The present volume continues with Jewish history under Hellenistic rule, taking it to the coming of the Romans. This Introduction covers several areas of importance for the book, specifically the questions of reconstructing Jewish history, Jewish identity and the appropriate terminology, and chronology.

1.1. *The Reconstruction of Jewish History*

L. L. Grabbe (2017) *Ancient Israel: What Do We Know and How Do We Know It?*

As always, the emphasis will be given to the primary sources (archaeology and inscriptions, and Jewish, Greek and Roman historians), but these sources have to be interpreted. Putting the data of the sources together from a critical perspective is the principal aim. But a simply narrative description is not always possible: a critical discussion of the sources, especially when they contradict each other, will often be required. The amount of data is basically the same for all historians of this period, but reconstructions of the history differ because of different ways of reading these data. This is why we begin, in Part II, with a survey of the available sources. If a 'fact' (more correctly a 'datum') is cited, where does it come from? It is always important to keep in mind the question, how do we know what we know?

General principles of historical methodology and trying to write a history of events in antiquity were outlined in *HJJSTP 1* (2–19) and *HJJSTP 2* (8–24; cf. also Grabbe 2017: 4–38). Some points that supplement the comments there are the following:

- The principles of historical methodology established in Classical Studies are very important. The sources for the present study of a section of Jewish history are a part of the sources for the history of the Graeco-Roman world. They have the same value and problems that have been faced by classical historians for centuries. The fact that they are written by Jews or are about Jews does not change this.

- Primary sources – meaning mainly archaeology, including coins, and inscriptions – should provide the backbone of any historical research for this period. Unfortunately, archaeology of Palestine for the Hellenistic and Roman periods has not had the same priority as that of the Iron Age in recent years. Thus, while many syntheses exist for aspects of Iron Age archaeology and for ancient Israel in general, the studies of the Hellenistic period (which are indeed multiplying at present) are still mostly available in scattered studies, without a good, up-to-date synthesis (on this problem, see further §2.1). It is expected that this will change in the next few years, but at the present time we have to deal with what we have. In some ways, we are much better supplied with numismatic studies, with collections not only of Hellenistic and Roman coins but also Jewish coins from the Greek and Roman periods (see further §2.3). As for inscriptions, classical scholars have been diligent in collecting these, and much work has gone into editing collections and also into translating and commenting on them. For Palestine and for the Jewish community in the diaspora, the amount of inscriptional material until recently was small, but the past few years have seen the launch of several collections that should give us a veritable *embarras de richesses* (on all inscriptions, see §2.2).

- In spite of the desire to depend on primary sources, for most of the details of ancient history we are still dependent on narratives sources, usually written long after the events and often written for a specific ideological purpose. This applies to Josephus who remains the main source for narrative history of the Jews in the Greek and early Roman periods (see §3.4). The books of Maccabees were written much closer to the time of the events they allegedly describe, with 1 Maccabees perhaps as early as the 120s or even 130s, and 2 Maccabees about the same time. Both are still followed closely, even more or less paraphrased, by many histories of the period. Yet both 1 and 2 Maccabees have specific purposes, and the credibility of their data is evaluated quite diversely by different specialists of this period. Their aims and biases need careful consideration and critical scrutiny: it is not sufficient simply to paraphrase them, as if they were eye-witness accounts by neutral observers (see further at §3.1).

1.2. The Question of Jewish Identity and Appropriate Terminology

F. Barth (ed.) (1969) *Ethnic Groups and Boundaries: The Social Organization of Culture Difference*; **G. Bohak** (1997) 'Good Jews, Bad Jews, and Non-Jews in Greek Papyri and Inscriptions', in B. Kramer et al. (eds), *Akten des 21. Internationalen Papyrologenkongresses*, 105–12; **M. G. Brett (ed.)** (1996) *Ethnicity and the Bible*; **W. Clarysse** (1994) 'Jews in Trikomia', in A. Bülow-Jacobsen (ed.), *Proceedings of the 20th International Congress of Papyrologists*, 193–203; **S. J. D. Cohen** (1983) 'Conversion to Judaism in Historical Perspective: From Biblical Israel to Postbiblical Judaism', *Conservative Judaism* 36: 31–45; **idem** (1985) 'The Origins of the Matrilineal Principle in Rabbinic Law', *AJS Review* 10:19–53; **idem** (1986) 'Was Timothy Jewish (Acts 16:1-3)? Patristic Exegesis, Rabbinic Law, and Matrilineal Descent', *JBL* 105: 251–68; **idem** (1999) *The Beginnings of Jewishness*; **B. Eckhardt** (2013) *Ethnos und Herrschaft*; **B. Eckhardt (ed.)** (2012) *Jewish Identity and Politics between the Maccabees and Bar Kokhba*; **C. Geertz** (1973) *The Interpretation of Cultures*; **D. Goodblatt** (2006) *Elements of Ancient Jewish Nationalism*; **idem** (2012) 'Varieties of Identity in Late Second Temple Judah (200 BCE–135 CE)', in B. Eckhardt (ed.), *Jewish Identity and Politics between the Maccabees and Bar Kokhba*, 11–27; **J. M. Hall** (1997) *Ethnic Identity in Greek Antiquity*; **J. Hutchinson and A. D. Smith (eds)** (1996) *Ethnicity*; **S. Jones** (1997) *The Archaeology of Ethnicity*; **K. A. Kamp and N. Yoffee** (1980) 'Ethnicity in Ancient Western Asia during the Early Second Millennium B.C.: Archaeological Assessments and Ethnoarchaeological Prospectives', *BASOR* 237: 85–104; **C. F. Keyes** (1997) 'Ethnic Groups, Ethnicity', in T. Barfield (ed.), *The Dictionary of Anthropology*, 152–54; **A. E. Killebrew** (2005) *Biblical Peoples and Ethnicity*; **R. Kletter** (2006) 'Can a Proto-Israelite Please Stand Up? Notes on the Ethnicity of Iron Age Israel and Judah', in A. M. Maeir and P. de Miroschedji (eds), *'I Will Speak the Riddles of Ancient Times'*, 573–86; **S. Mason** (2007) 'Jews, Judaea, Judaizing, Judaism: Problems of Categorization in Ancient History', *JSJ* 38: 457–512; **D. Mendels** (1992) *The Rise and Fall of Jewish Nationalism*; **S. Moore** (2015) *Jewish Ethnic Identity and Relations in Hellenistic Egypt: with Walls of Iron?*; **E. Regev** (2013) *The Hasmoneans: Ideology, Archaeology, Identity*; **D. R. Schwartz** (2007)

'"Judaean" or "Jew"? How Should We Translate *ioudaios* in Josephus?', in J. Frey, D. R. Schwartz and S. Gripentrog (eds), *Jewish Identity in the Greco-Roman World*, 3–27; **S. Schwartz** (2010) *Were the Jews a Mediterranean Society?*; **S. J. Shennan (ed.)** (1989*) Archaeological Approaches to Cultural Identity*; **S. Sokolovskii and V. Tishkov** (1996) 'Ethnicity', in A. Barnard and J. Spencer (eds), *Encylopedia of Social and Cultural Anthropology*, 190–93; **K. L. Sparks** (1998) *Ethnicity and Identity in Ancient Israel*; **S. Weitzman** (2008) 'On the Political Relevance of Antiquity: A Response to David Goodblatt's *Elements of Ancient Jewish Nationalism*', *Jewish Social Studies* 14: 165–72; **M. H. Williams** (1995) 'Palestinian Jewish Personal Names in Acts', in R. Bauckham (ed.), *The Book of Acts in its First Century Setting, Volume 4*, 79–113; **idem** (1997) 'The Meaning and Function of *Ioudaios* in Graeco-Roman Inscriptions', *ZPE* 116: 249–62.

1.2.1 *Terminology*

The word 'Jew' has been used in English for many centuries and has also been the standard term in Jewish studies, but it has recently become customary in some circles (primarily among some New Testament scholars but also some scholars of Judaica) to use the term 'Judaean' and avoid the term 'Jew' (e.g., Mason 2007). There are two problems that we face immediately:

- In English 'Judaean' means someone associated with the territory (province, kingdom, nation etc.) of Judaea (cf. the survey in D. R. Schwartz 2007). It is of course possible to change usage, as has been done in recent biblical scholarship (e.g., with regard to gender matters), but there is the potential for confusion, since many readers would still see 'Judaean' as being a geographical designation.
- Ancient Hebrew/Aramaic, Greek and Latin have only the one word יהדי/יהודי/*Ἰουδαῖος*/*Iudaeus* for both 'Jew' (referring to religion and/or ethnicity) and 'Judaean' (referring to someone who lives in or is from Judaea).

A survey of the use of the Greek word *Ioudaios* comes to the conclusion that, in a non-Jewish context, 'the basic function of *Ioudaios* is always the same – to draw an explicit distinction between Jews and non-Jews. But what exactly was the epithet meant to convey?... [It] is hard to believe that the epithet...is doing any more than reflecting an awareness of ethnic difference' (Williams 1997: 254–55). Williams goes on to note that the matter of religious orientation does not usually seem to be a concern in the various contexts where the usage occurs.

1. *Introduction* 7

In previous volumes of the present history, I have generally used the term 'Jew' and reserved 'Judaean' for those who lived in Judaea. I propose to continue this practice in this and the final volume. The reasons for doing so are justified by the discussion above, in my opinion. Therefore, I shall, as usual, use

- 'Jew/Jews' for those belonging to the Jewish community or the Jewish ethnic group;
- 'Judaean' will be reserved for people living or at least originating in Judaea.

The important matter of the place of religion will be discussed in the next section.

1.2.2. *The Question of Jewish Identity*

E. Bloch-Smith (2003) 'Israelite Ethnicity in Iron I: Archaeology Preserves What Is Remembered and What Is Forgotten In Israel's History', *JBL* 122: 401–25; **L. L. Grabbe** (2000a) 'Hat die Bibel doch recht? A Review of T. L. Thompson's *The Bible in History*', *SJOT* 14: 117–39; **I. Finkelstein** (1997) 'Pots and People Revised: Ethnic Boundaries in the Iron Age I', in N. A. Silberman and D. B. Small (eds), *The Archaeology of Israel: Constructing the Past, Interpreting the Present*, 216–37; **E. S. Gruen** (2018b) 'Kinship Relations and Jewish Identity', in *The Construct of Identity in Hellenistic Judaism: Essays on Early Jewish Literature and History*, 95–111; **T. L. Thompson** (1999) *The Bible in History: How Writers Create a Past*.

The question of Jewish identity has been much discussed in recent scholarship, with the above bibliography being only a sample of some of the more important recent works. This view has been challenged. For example, it has been suggested that what began as an ethnic and/or geographical designation changed to a religious one in the early centuries BCE or CE (e.g., Thompson 1999: 254–66; cf. Cohen 1999, but see Grabbe 2000a). We can begin by noting that the question of identity was not normally a problem for most people. You were a Jew because you were born a Jew, and part of your identity was living by Jewish customs, including Jewish religious law. Jewish identity was being part of the Jewish community or Jewish people. Like most religions at this time, Judaism was primarily an ethnic religion.

How was Jewishness defined in antiquity? It seems clear that both the people themselves and outsiders saw a group identity that we would call ethnic. To be a Jew was (and indeed remains) an ethnic identity but one in which religion is a major ethnic identifying feature. Even today many Jews are identified not only by religion but also by descent (one born of a Jewish mother), which can only be ethnic. The question of ethnicity has been a much-debated area of modern social anthropology, and so a brief survey of the discussion might be helpful.

There have been different approaches to ethnicity, extensively in anthropological study (Shennan [ed.] 1989; Hutchinson and Smith [eds] 1996; Sokolovskii and Tishkov 1996; Keyes 1997), but also in biblical scholarship (Brett 1996; Sparks 1998; Killebrew 2005: 8–16). A view that ethnicity should be seen mainly in biological terms (ethnic groups have a common ancestry or kinship or genetic pool) is widely rejected in modern study. Yet it has contributed the important insight that ethnic groups generally define themselves in kinship or quasi-kinship terms. This was also true in antiquity, including in the Hellenistic period (cf. Gruen 2018b; Eckhardt 2013). Others have seen the question in terms of distinct cultures, but this was problematic in that cultural groups do not always develop an ethnic identity or group consciousness, nor do some ethnic groups have specific cultural features (especially those that show up in archaeology). There is also the fact that there is a 'primordial' quality to ethnic identity in which the group's distinctiveness – 'we/they' – is essential (Geertz 1973: 255–310; Keyes 1997).

For anthropologists and others, the classic study is that of F. Barth (1969), who pointed to the importance of inter-group boundary mechanisms: ethnic groups define themselves in contrast with other groups ('self-ascription'), often by a minimum of explicit (even trivial, at least to an outsider) differences. He explicitly rejected the use of an inventory of cultural traits, but there has been a good deal of discussion since Barth (Kamp and Yoffee 1980; Shennan [ed.] 1989; Hutchinson and Smith [eds] 1996; Finkelstein 1997; Jones 1997; Bloch-Smith 2003; Kletter 2006). Because our knowledge of groups in antiquity is based on texts rather than a direct study of living peoples, we are limited by what the texts tell us. This means that the task of penetrating to identity and ethnicity is often very complicated.

Trying to find a definition of an ethnic group is still not easy. Recent treatments tend to recognize the fluidity of ethnic identity (an insight from Barth), and any definition must recognize that. Kamp and Yoffee have stated that most sociologists and anthropologists see an ethnic group as 'a number of individuals who see themselves as being alike by virtue of a common ancestry, real or fictitious, and who are so regarded by others' (1980: 88). Kletter follows A. D. Smith in identifying an ethnic group as:

> ...a group of people who share most – but not necessarily all – of the following: (1) a collective proper name; (2) a myth of common ancestry; (3) historical memories; (4) one or more differentiating elements of common culture; (5) an association with a specific homeland (which may be symbolic, without physical control of the homeland); and (6) a sense of solidarity among at least parts of the group. (Kletter 2006: 574)

Sokolovskii and Tishkov give a similar definition, and suggest that it 'opens further avenues for integration of anthropological, political and psychological knowledge in understanding of ethnic phenomena' (1996: 192). Of particular interest is that self-identity may be strongly based on religion, myth and law, areas which have traditionally been studied with regard to early Judaism.

Coming back to the Jews in the Second Temple period it seems clear that both the people themselves and outsiders saw a group identity that we would call ethnic. Benedikt Eckhardt (2013) has recently pointed out that Greek sources often refer to the Jews as an *ethnos*, which can be variously translated as 'nation', 'people', 'ethnic group', or the like. He emphasizes that this is the term in the ancient texts, which varies in meaning according to the context (see further in the next section).

1.2.3. *Ethnic Group or Religion?*

What was involved in being or becoming a Jew? Personal Jewish identity was usually bound up with certain specific elements, and these elements would often be part of what we today would call 'religion'. In antiquity the matter was not so clear-cut because religion was a part of daily life and not a separate sphere as it often is today. (This does not mean that Graeco-Romans could not easily distinguish matters relating to God/the gods, the sacred and temples.) Similarly, characteristics seen as peculiar to an ethnic group in antiquity might be those that we today would call religion. This applies especially to the Jews: the customs, views and practices that set them apart as a distinctive people or *ethnos* were heavily on the religious side (as seen from the perspective of a modern observer). When Greek and Roman writers refer to Jews, they often mention characteristics that we today associate with religion. Yet it is also true that their descriptions of other 'barbarians' also often listed customs and practices that we would call religious.

Two points will be made here. First, the definition can be in part clarified by considering those Jews who are reported to have abandoned their Judaism in antiquity. Only a few are known, but we shall examine the two most prominent ones. One is Dositheus son of Drimylus in the

10   *A History of Jews and Judaism in the Second Temple Period, Volume 3*

third century BCE, 'a Jew by birth [τὸ γένος 'Ιουδαῖος] who later changed his religion [νόμιμα] and apostatized from the ancestral traditions [τῶν πατρίων δογμάτων]' (*3 Macc.* 1.3). We now know from papyrological information that there was indeed an individual named Dositheus son of Drimylus (Δοσίθεος τοῦ Δριμύλου [*CPJ* 1.127a-e]). He was one of the two heads of the royal scribal system (ὁ ὑπομνηματογράφος [*CPJ* 1.127a line 24]) and also priest of 'Alexander and the gods Adelphoi and the gods Euergetai', i.e., the deified Alexander and the current Ptolemy and his wife (*CPJ* 1.127d-e). He is nowhere identified as Jewish in the surviving documentation, but his name makes it highly probable, since few non-Jews bore the name 'Dositheus' (*CPJ* 1, p. 231).

It is interesting that the author of 3 Maccabees, in spite of his venomous antipathy to Dositheus, does not deny that he is a Jew. He seems to toy with the idea that Dositheus and those like him who had transgressed against God and the law were not really members of the Jewish people, but in the end he still calls them 'Jews' (*3 Macc.* 7.10: τοὺς ἐκ τοῦ γένους τῶν Ιουδαίων). The same applies to the other main example, Tiberius Julius Alexander, the son of the Alexandrian alabarch Alexander and nephew of Philo of Alexandria in the first century CE (*JCH* 438–39; to be discussed in *HJJSTP 4*). Josephus states that the father was superior to his son in the matter of piety toward God (πρὸς τὸν θεὸν εὐσεβείᾳ), for the son was 'not faithful to the ancestral customs' (*Ant.* 20.5.2 §100: τοῖς πατρίοις οὐκ ἐνέμεινεν ἔθεσιν). We have a number of contemporary documents mentioning Tiberius Alexander (*CPJ* 2, pp. 188–98). None of them refers to Alexander as a Jew, but upper-class individuals seldom have their ethnic identity remarked on. Josephus does not deny Alexander's identity as a Jew, but he does not use the term to refer to him. These two examples are not definitive, but they suggest that abandoning the Jewish religion did not make them cease to be Jews. While religion was a part of ethnic identity, it was not the sole criterion, apparently, even among the Jews.

The second point relates to conversion. At this time we have a most unusual situation: as well as perhaps a few wanting to join the Jewish community, we have the forceable conversion of large groups of people by Hasmonaean rulers. The question of conversion in general will be discussed in *HJJSTP 4*; however, a few words will be said here (see also §9.1 and §12.3.1 on the conversion of the Idumaeans and Ituraeans and on the issue of circumcision).

Two recent studies, both appearing about the same time and evidently making their points independently of each other, discuss Jewish identity during the last two centuries BCE. Both emphasize the importance of ideology, legitimation and power in the rule of Judaea in this period.

First, as already noted, B. Eckhardt (2013) had examined the relationship between ethnicity and the type of government in power, looking at both Hasmonaean and Herodian rule. The resistance to the measures of Antiochus IV began a new ethnos or identity figuration. For Hasmonaean rule he notes the emphasis on several entities relating to the Jewish population (Eckhardt 2013: 60–127): Hebrew language as their own language; freedom as sovereignty over their own land; centralization; religious rituals; history; festivals; and alternative belief systems. With Hasmonaean rule new festivals and religious rituals were introduced or given new emphasis, as was the Hebrew language. They also began to take responsibility for the Jews in the diaspora. This in turn provoked the rise or growth of variant groups ('sects') within the Jewish community. With regard to the traditional dual legitimation of the ruler – merit and genealogy – both the Hasmonaeans and Herod emphasized the matter from the 'merit' perspective; that is, they ruled because of their deeds, not necessarily their descent. One emphasis that arose under the Hasmonaeans but continued under Herod was that of circumcision (see further §12.3.1). On the analogy of ruler legitimation, circumcision was a means of becoming Jewish by 'merit' rather than descent.

E. Regev (2013) has argued that under the Maccabees/Hasmonaeans a new political system was introduced but also Jewish identity changed: 'identity was based on commitment to the Torah and hatred toward the idolatrous Gentiles. A new, "nationalistic" sense of Jewish collective identity was created' (2013: 16). To support his view, he points to a number of innovations under Hasmonaean rule. These innovations were not necessarily completely new, but a new emphasis was given to them. They included the celebration of Hanukkah as a religious and 'political' festival, the centrality of the temple, the Hasmonaean 'national' monarchy, the political discourse on Hasmonaean coinage, the architecture of Hasmonaean palaces and the introduction of ritual baths. They embraced Hellenistic culture but primarily as a means of furthering their ideological and political aims. For example, the domestic layout and life within their palaces were mainly simple and conformed to Jewish law, yet they also provided gardens and swimming pools that sent conforming cultural messages to the wider Hellenistic world. The *mikva'ot* or ritual baths seem to be a new creation at this time, at least judging from the archaeological finds thus far known (see further §12.3.2).

Yet a note of caution should be injected here. There is a tendency to assume that Jews of that time saw their life and identity primarily in religious terms. In most cases, though, we do not know one way or the other. The writings preserved are mainly religious literature and show us what was important to the writer, but we cannot assume that Philo was the model for Alexandrian Jews or that the apocalypses show us where most Jews of Palestine concentrated their energies. If we look at a writer such as Josephus, we see an interesting mixture. His writings contain a large religious element, but they are not just religious. He certainly saw his identity in the broad context of Judaism but also in Jewish history and ethnicity. It would be wrong to define Josephus's view of himself in purely religious terms. Indeed, his outlook is very much parallel to that which we find in many Graeco-Roman writers of the time, such as Cicero or Plutarch. Religion and personal piety were very important, but they evidently did not dominate the lives of most Jews. As noted above, Jews then did not make a sharp distinction between religion and other aspects of life such as politics and profession. However, that outlook was not unique to the Jews – no self-respecting Roman or Greek gentleman would have regarded himself as 'secular' in the modern sense. To be thought of as an 'atheist' was a serious stigma. This was why the charge of 'atheism' against Socrates, for example, was so serious.

Indeed, religion meant different things to different Jews, and to assume that all took the same view is to misapprehend. For the average Jew – farmer, day labourer, craftsman, beggar – making a living was not easy. Getting enough for food, as well for clothing and housing, was sufficient concern for many. This would not make them irreligious, for most were probably quite pious by their own lights; it is simply a matter of emphasis. The piety of the sectarian was not that of most Israelites, and what was slackness or impiety in the eyes of the sect member might be normal accepted behaviour for other Jews. Some individuals had the means and the leisure to practise a strenuous form of religion; most did not. Of course, poverty was no barrier to intense devotion, so that even those living on the edge of subsistence might well turn to religion for solace and hope.

In sum, Jewish identity at this time was usually ethnic. Although many of the characteristics of Jews – as seen both within the Jewish community and by outsiders – would be labelled religious from a modern point of view, various ethnic groups were identified by outsiders by traits that we would call religious. The distinction between religious and other customs was not necessarily made at that time. The question of religious conversion, especially individual conversion, does become an issue especially in the 1st century CE and will be discussed in *HJJSTP 4*. However, for our period conversion comes up primarily with regard to the supposed forced conversion of Idumaeans and Ituraeans under John Hyrcanus and Aristobulus I (see §9.1; §9.3).

1.3. Chronology

B. Bar-Kochva (1976) *The Seleucid Army: Organization and Tactics in the Great Campaigns*; **idem** (1989) *Judas Maccabaeus: The Jewish Struggle against the Seleucids*; **J. C. Bernhardt** (2017) *Die jüdische Revolution: Untersuchungen zu Ursachen, Verlauf und Folgen der hasmonäischen Erhebung*; **E. J. Bickerman** (1937a) *Der Gott der Makkabäer: Untersuchungen* über *Sinn und Ursprung der makkabäischen Erhebung*; **idem** (1979) *The God of the Maccabees: Studies on the Meaning and Origin of the Maccabean Revolt*; **idem** (1980) *Chronology of the Ancient World*; **K. Bringmann** (1983) *Hellenistische Reform und Religionsverfolgung in Judäa: Eine Untersuchung zur jüdisch-hellenistischen Geschichte (175–163 v. Chr.)*; **W. H. Brownlee** (1962) 'Maccabees, Books of', *IDB* 3:204; **M. B. Dagut** (1953) 'II Maccabees and the Death of Antiochus IV Epiphanes', *JBL* 77: 149–57; **K. Ehling** (2008) *Untersuchungen zur Geschichte der späten Seleukiden (164–63 v. Chr.): Vom Tode des Antiochos IV. bis zur Einrichtung der Provinz Syria unter Pompeius*; **J. A. Fitzmyer and D. J. Harrington** (1978) *A Manual of Palestinian Aramaic*; **D. Gera and W. Horowitz** (1997) 'Antiochus IV in Life and Death: Evidence from the Babylonian Astronomical Diaries', *JAOS* 117: 240–52; **J. A. Goldstein** (1976) *I Maccabees: A New Translation with Introduction and Commentary*; **L. L. Grabbe** (1991) 'Maccabean Chronology: 167–164 or 168–165 BCE?' *JBL* 110: 59–74; **E. S. Gruen** (1984) *The Hellenistic World and the Coming of Rome*; **R. Hanhardt** (1964) 'Zur Zeitrechnung des I und II Makkabäerbuches', in A. Jepsen and R. Hanhardt (eds), *Untersuchungen zur israelitisch-jüdischen Chronologie*, 53–96; **A. Houghton, C. Lorber and O. Hoover (eds)** (2008) *Seleucid Coins: A Comprehensive Catalogue, Part II: Seleucus IV through Antiochus XIII, Volumes I and II*; **W. Huß** (2001) *Ägypten in hellenistischer Zeit: 332–30 v. Chr.*; **F. X. Kugler** (1922) *Von Moses bis Paulus*; **H. Lichtenstein** (1931–32) 'Die Fastenrolle, eine Untersuchung zur jüdisch-hellenistischen Geschichte', *HUCA* 8–9: 257–351; **P. F. Mittag** (2006) *Antiochos IV. Epiphanes: Eine politische Biographie*; **O. Mørkholm** (1966) *Antiochus IV of Syria*; **A. T. Olmstead** (1937) 'Cuneiform Texts and Hellenistic Chronology', *Classical Philology* 32: 1–14; **R. A. Parker and W. H. Dubberstein** (1956) *Babylonian Chronology 626 B.C.–A.D. 75*; **P. W. Pestman** (1967) *Chronologie égyptienne d'après les textes démotiques (332 av. J.-C.-453 ap. J.-C.)*; **J. D. Ray** (1976) *The Archive of Hor*; **A. J. Sachs** (1952) 'Babylonian Horoscopes', *JCS* 6: 49–75; **A. J. Sachs and D. J. Wiseman** (1954) 'A Babylonian King List of the Hellenistic Period', *Iraq* 16: 202–11; **A. E. Samuel** (1962) *Ptolemaic Chronology*; **K.-D. Schunck** (1954) *Die Quellen des I. und II. Makkabäerbuches*; **T. C. Skeat** (1961) 'Notes on Ptolemaic Chronology: II. "The Twelfth Year which is also the First": The Invasion of Egypt by Antiochus Epiphanes', *JEA* 47: 107–12; **A. E. Steinmann** (2009) 'When Did Herod the Great Reign?'

NT 51: 1–29; **H. Volkmann** (1924-25) 'Demetrios I. und Alexander I. von Syrien', *Klio* 1: 373–412; **B. Z. Wacholder** (1984) 'The Beginning of the Seleucid Era and the Chronology of the Diadochoi', in F. E. Greenspahn, E. Hilgert and B. L. Mack (eds), *Nourished with Peace: Studies in Hellenistic Judaism in Memory of Samuel Sandmel*, 183–211; **F. W. Walbank** (1957–79) *A Historical Commentary on Polybius*.

1.3.1. *Introductory Comments*

One might think that with the abundance of Greek, Roman, Babylonian and Egyptian sources, the chronology for this period would be straightforward. Sadly, often not, especially in the realm of Jewish history. For example, books around the turn of the century, when giving the time for the 'abomination of desolation' during the Maccabean revolt, would usually specify the dates as 168–165 BCE. However, E. J. Bickerman, after accepting this, then changed his mind in his study, *Der Gott der Makkabäer*, arguing for a revision to 167–164 BCE (1937a: 155–68//1979: 101–11). This position has been widely accepted and is found in many standard references (e.g., Schürer 1973–87: 1:155). However, several recent researchers have still argued for 168–165 (Schunck 1954: 16–31. Brownlee 1962: 3:204; Bringmann 1983: 15–28; cf. also Bernhardt 2017: 222, 540 [168–164 BCE]). Similarly, the standard date for the death of Herod as 4 BCE has been questioned in recent years (see below). Thus, it is important to discuss general questions of chronology but also to make clear which system or systems are used in the present book.

The main sources will be discussed below, but a comment should be made at this point about the Jewish writing, the 'Scroll of Fasting' (*Megillat Ta'anit*), which is often cited as a source in discussions on chronology; however, there is a tendency to quote it when it seems to match their reconstruction and dismiss it when it does not. The original Aramaic text, dating from perhaps the first century CE, is only a bare list of dates on which fasting is forbidden, with a brief explanation (Fitzmyer and Harrington 1978: text 150 [pp. 184–87, 248–50]). The information given could often fit a variety of historical situations. The accompanying Hebrew commentary is from a much later time and generally recognized to be of little historical value (Lichtenstein 1931–32 has both the Aramaic text and the Hebrew commentary). Some of the dates probably do reflect genuine events in Hasmonaean times. The problem is that only month and day dates are given, but not year. This means that for many questions of Hasmonaean chronology, the writing gives little help, but there are too many uncertainties to use it as anything but minor evidence.

1.3.2. *Babylonian, Egyptian and Seleucid Dates*

Recent studies in Babylonian cuneiform records and Egyptian papyri have clarified a good deal about chronology in the Hellenistic Near East through astronomy and other exact methods, though this has not eliminated all problems by any means: many dates cannot be related to the astronomical data and must be worked out from literary sources. This is especially true of dates in Jewish history.

In the past few decades, a number of new finds have allowed a refinement of certain aspects of the chronology of the second century BCE. These new sources include dated cuneiform documents (Parker and Dubberstein 1956), a cuneiform king list of the first Seleucid kings (Sachs and Wiseman 1954), astronomically dated Egyptian records (Samuel 1962; Pestman 1967) and Seleucid coins (Houghton, Lorber and Hoover [eds] 2008). For example, some of the dates for Antiochus IV are from the cuneiform Seleucid king list (Sachs and Wiseman 1954) and are extremely valuable (note that the Seleucid era reckoning is Babylonian, from spring 311 BCE).

- – Seleucus IV takes throne: 125 SE (187 BCE) and rules 12 years.
- – Seleucus IV dies: year 137 SE, month 6, day 10 (175 BCE, 2 or 3 Sept.).
- – Antiochus IV takes throne: year 137 SE, month 6 (175 BCE, Aug.–Sept.).
- – Antiochus IV rules jointly with Antiochus, son of Seleucus IV: year 137 SE, month 8 (175 BCE, Oct.–Nov.).
- – Antiochus IV executes Antiochus, son of Seleucus IV: year 142 SE, month 5 (170 BCE, 30 July to 30 Aug.).
- – Antiochus IV's death reported in Babylon: [year 148 SE], month 9 (164 BCE, 19 Nov.–19 Dec.).

Yet there are still questions. For example, the beginning of the Sixth Syrian War is still debated and placed anywhere from late 170 to early 169 BCE – only two or three months different but not exact. The date for Daphne has conventionally been given as summer or autumn of 166 BCE. B. Bar-Kochva (1989: 466–73) has gone against the generally agreed date by arguing for 165 BCE, but there are good reasons for favouring the consensus (Mørkholm 1966: 166–67; Mittag 2006: 296–97; Bernhardt 2017: 239 n. 102). Demetrius took the throne late in the year 162 BCE, probably in the autumn since the latest date known for Antiochus V is 18 VII 150 SE Babylonian (= 16 October 162 BCE) and the earliest for

16   *A History of Jews and Judaism in the Second Temple Period, Volume 3*

Demetrius I is 22 II 151 SE (= 14 May 161 BCE). (For these dates, see Kugler 1922: 330, 334; cf. Parker and Dubberstein 1956: 23.) These are just a few examples to illustrate the remaining uncertainty.

Some of the problems revolve around the use of the Seleucid era in dates in many documents from the Seleucid period, including 1 and 2 Maccabees (*HJJSTP 2*: 272–73). During the wars of the Diadochi, Seleucus I (with the help of Ptolemy I) defeated Antigonus at Gaza in the summer of 312 BCE. This opened the way for Seleucus to retake Babylon. At some point, Seleucus introduced the Seleucid era (commonly abbreviated SE) which was calculated to begin with his retaking of Babylon (Wacholder 1984). This was an important innovation because it imposed a common dating system over a wide area, one which continued in use in some areas until well into the Common Era. The problem is that since different calendars were used in different areas of the Seleucid empire, the Seleucid era was calculated differently from one place to another. Two major systems were in use: the *Babylonian*, which counted year 1 SE as beginning with Nisan (spring) 311 BCE, and the *Syro-Macedonian*, which began year 1 SE with Tishri (autumn) 312 BCE. A major question is which system was used in 1 and 2 Maccabees. J. C. Bernhardt (2017: 525–45) has recently argued that the main dating system used in 1 and 2 Maccabees is the latter: from autumn 312 BCE. This seems to be correct for the most part, though a complication will be discussed below (§1.3.3).

For the purposes of the present book, most of the available evidence is nicely summarized in Ehling 2008 and Huß 2001. They will generally be followed for Seleucid and Ptolemaic dates, unless other sources are cited. Dates in Jewish sources will usually be discussed where they are crucial. Some of the principles for reconstructing Jewish chronology are given in the following sections.

1.3.3. *The Dating System in 1 Maccabees*

It was already argued by Bickerman (1937a: 155–58//1979: 101–3) that two systems of dating are used in 1 Maccabees, one according to the normal Syro-Macedonian year which began in the autumn (Tishri); the other beginning with spring (Nisan). K.-D. Schunck (1954: 16–31) makes the important point that 'Jewish' dates in 1 Maccabees (i.e., those that include not only the year but also the month and sometimes even the day) begin with spring 312, whereas dates with only the year may well be Syro-Macedonian, using the autumn of 312 BCE as the starting date. This needs to be kept in mind when reading a date in 1 Maccabees. Indications for a Nisan reckoning are the following:

- 1 Maccabees 7.1 is dated to 151 SE. The defeat of Nicanor took place on 13 Adar (v. 43), presumably in the same year. After Demetrius heard of the defeat, he dispatched a new army to oppose Judas (1 Macc. 9.1-3). Since the army reached Jerusalem in the 'first month' (Nisan), this is almost certainly only a month or so after the original defeat (if there was an intercalary Adar II, up to two and half months could have intervened between Nicanor's defeat and the arrival of the new army). Yet the time is stated to be 152 SE (1 Macc. 9.3), showing a year change with 1 Nisan.
- 1 Maccabees 10.1-21 describes the initial activities of Alexander I Balas in the late summer or early autumn of 160 SE (1 Macc. 10.1). These included conferring the office of high priest on Jonathan Maccabee. At the Feast of Tabernacles (beginning 15 Tishri), Jonathan donned the high priestly robes, but this was still the year 160 SE (v. 21), showing that the year had not changed at 1 Tishri and indicating a Nisan-to-Nisan reckoning. Some (e.g., Bernhardt [2017: 544] want to put Jonathan's donning of the robes a full year later, in autumn 159 SE, but there is no reason to do so).

Yet the normal reckoning in documents and coins from Syria is an autumn-to-autumn one (beginning Tishri 312 BCE), and one would expect this to be the usual dating. These data confirm a widespread opinion among scholars that more than one form of the Seleucid era is found in 1 Maccabees (Bickerman 1937a: 155–58//1979: 101–3; Schunck 1954: 16–31; Goldstein 1976: 22–25; Bar-Kochva 1989: 562–65). It is generally thought that the reckoning from Tishri was used for the dating of external events (often those with only a year dating) and the version from Nisan for internal events (usually including month and day as well as year). But this has been challenged by Bringmann (1983: 15–28) who thinks that all dates in both 1 and 2 Maccabees fit an era beginning with Tishri 312 BCE. In order to do this, he must dispose of the two arguments mentioned above. However, he gets rid of the first one by postulating – without argument – that a full year intervened between 1 Macc. 7.1-43 and 9.1-3 (Bringmann 1983: 28). He simply refers to B. Bar-Kochva (1976: 14, 210–11 n. 29), but Bar-Kochva does not actually discuss the point there, though he does assume Jewish dating from Nisan 311 BCE. Bar-Kochva does take up the subject in his more recent book (1989: 373–75, 385) but is trying to get rid of a difficulty by the hypothesis of a year's intervention. On Bringmann's own terms, Bar-Kochva gives little support. The second problem he tries to dispose of is by an ingenious if unconvincing argument (Bringmann 1983: 24–25). He notes that an

18   *A History of Jews and Judaism in the Second Temple Period, Volume 3*

intercalary month in the Syro-Macedonian year might cause the Jewish Feast of Tabernacles (in the month of Tishri) to fall before the beginning of Tishri (i.e., a new Seleucid year) according to the Syro-Macedonian calendar. But this is more ingenious than convincing. It seems unlikely that 1 Macc. 10.1 was given according to the Syro-Macedonian system while 10.21 was according to a Jewish system, which differed from it by only a month. Also, we do not know how the Jewish calendar correlated with the Syro-Macedonian calendar at this time. It may well have been kept parallel with it by the priests, so that intercalary months were inserted in the Jewish liturgical calendar to correspond with those in the Macedonian calendar. Thus, while the Jewish calendar may have been out of phase with that used in Syria, we cannot assume so in the absence of relevant data. The simplest explanation is a calendar beginning with Nisan. It seems to me that the arguments for a dual system in 1 Maccabees still stand.

The question is the starting point for each system. The Syro-Macedonian system is almost universally agreed on as beginning with Tishri 312. The problem is when the Nisan era begins. Most handbooks now list year 1 SE as beginning with Nisan 311 BCE, just as in Babylon. Yet older writers, including Bickerman at one point, argued for Nisan 312 BCE (1930: 14:781–84; Schunck 1956: 16–31; Kugler 1922: 344, 352–53). Are there internal reasons for seeing Nisan 312 BCE as a starting point for some of the dates in 1 Maccabees? In fact, many of the dates proposed as fitting the Syro-Macedonian reckoning would also fit a system beginning with Nisan 312 BCE. Similarly, the spring-to-spring reckoning could fit either with 311 or 312 BCE in most cases because of the sparseness of data. However, several dates in 1 Maccabees do not seem to fit with the normal calculation from either Tishri 312 or Nisan 311 BCE:

- According to 1 Macc. 6.20, Judas besieged Jerusalem shortly after the death of Antiochus. This would seem to be sometime in the spring or early summer of 163 BCE, since Antiochus died about November 164. This event is dated to 150 SE. Neither the dating from Tishri 312 nor Nisan 311 BCE fits; dating from Nisan 312 BCE does, however. This dating is also confirmed by the autumn 163–162 sabbatical year (cf. §1.3.6 below) mentioned in 1 Macc. 6.49. Bickerman (1937a: 156–58//1979: 102–3) admitted that this fits only a calculation from Nisan 312 BCE; therefore, he had to assume an error on the part of the author to get rid of the problem. Similarly, Bringmann (1983: 27 n. 50).

1. *Introduction* 19

- Demetrius I began his reign in 151 SE (1 Macc. 7.1) or 162–161 BCE, usually dated to the autumn of 162 BCE. The battle instigated by him in Adar (1 Macc. 7.43) would appear to be shortly after his taking the throne, i.e., spring 161 BCE, since no new date is given. However, a new date occurs for the very next month (first month of 152 SE or 161–160 BCE: 1 Macc. 9.3). Only reckoning from Nisan 312 BCE fits these data. This simplest understanding of the passage represents a problem for many scholars who attempt to explain it away by rather dubious means. Goldstein (1976: 341–43) accepts that the battle in Adar was in the spring 161 BCE but then attempts to place the reengagement a full year later. Bringmann (1983: 28) does likewise. Why? The real reason appears to be that it does not fit their thesis about the Seleucid era in 1 Maccabees. Some use the mission sent to Rome (1 Macc. 8) as an excuse to insert an entire year (Bringmann 1983: 28; Bar-Kochva 1989: 374), but this is a red herring. A mission to Rome could have set out in early 161 but need not have returned and reported before the battle with Bacchides. (Nothing in the report of 1 Macc. 8.22-32 requires the mission to have reported to Judas before the battle.) But most importantly, this thesis ignores the chronological data given by 1 Maccabees itself. The events leading up to the battle on 13 Adar could have taken place in the three or four months to spring.
- When 1 Maccabees is compared with the few dates in 2 Maccabees, it is clear that there are differences, but these are instructive. 1 Maccabees 6.20 puts the siege of the Acra and its relief by Lysias in 150 SE, whereas 2 Macc. 13.1 makes it 149 SE. It is often thought that one gives a reckoning from Tishri and the other from Nisan, a reasonable explanation, but which is which? The answer seems to be found in a comparison of 1 Macc. 7.1-25 (in which Alcimus is made high priest in 151 SE) with 2 Macc. 14.3-4 (also 151 SE). Since Alcimus became high priest after Demetrius took the throne in the autumn of 162 BCE and before Nisan 161 BCE, the only reckoning which fits is for 1 Macc. 7.1 to be reckoned from Nisan 312 and 2 Macc. 14.4 from Tishri 312. The siege of the Acra (which I have put in spring/summer 163) would be dated 150 SE if counting from Nisan 312 (= Nisan 163–162 BCE) but 149 from Tishri 312 (= Tishri 164–163 BCE). Thus, in both cases 1 Maccabees is using an era reckoned from Nisan 312, while 2 Maccabees has the standard Syro-Macedonian system from Tishri 312.

- 1 Maccabees 14.1-3 refers to the campaign of Demetrius II against the Parthians in which he was taken captive. If the interpretation of a fragmentary cuneiform text is correct, there is reason to think that Demetrius was himself taken captive in the summer of 141 BCE. Since 1 Macc. 14.1 puts this in the year 172 SE, only an era counted from Nisan 312 would agree with the actual date. Demetrius II was on the Babylonian throne in March 142 (= XII 169 SE Babylonian) according to a horoscope published by A. B. Sachs (1952: especially 62–63). Another text (Text SH 108, discussed but only partially published in Kugler 1922: 339–43), indicates that Arsaces (Mithradates I) defeated Demetrius and took the throne of Babylon in July 141 BCE (cf. also Olmstead 1937: 12–13). A little further on in a passage difficult to read but dated to September 141 BCE, it appears that the capture of (Demetrius) Nicator is referred to.

But the next question is whether there are passages which oppose using Nisan 312 BCE? There seems to be only one problematic passage: 1 Maccabees 10, in which Jonathan is granted the high priesthood by Alexander I Balas. If this is the year 152 BCE as is often assumed, there is no way that a Syro-Macedonian date in 1 Macc. 10.1 (= autumn 160 SE) would fit with a spring 312 reckoning in 1 Macc. 10.21. Several modern scholars take this point as decisive against a Nisan 312 era (Bringmann 1983: 20; Hanhart 1964: 60–61). However, modern discussions often vacillate between 153 and 152 BCE (cf. Volkmann 1924–25: 403–4, who puts the arrival of Alexander in Ptolemais in the summer of 153).

F. W. Walbank (1957–79: 3:42, 557, 560) puts the date as 152 for the following reasons: (1) Based on the collection of excerpts of Polybius in the Constantinian *De legat. gent.* he assumes that 33.15.1-2 should be dated to Olypiad 156,3 = 154–153 BCE. (2) He then dates to 153 the embassy of Heracleides, bringing the alleged children of Antiochus IV (Alexander Balas and Laodice), which seems to have arrived near the summer solstice. (3) The embassy itself was not likely to have been heard until the beginning of 152 BCE according to the normal practice of the Senate (33.18.1-14). All this is solid work by a major scholar, but the state of our information is too uncertain to be dogmatic. Bar-Kochva (1989: 470–71, 548) has already questioned how reliable the position of fragments in the Constantinian collection can be considered. If Alexander arrived in Ptolemais in late summer of 153 BCE, the two dates in 1 Maccabees 10 (10.1 and 10.21) would fit a reckoning from Nisan 312 (i.e., 160 SE would equal spring 153–52). The date in 1 Macc. 10.1 is often assumed to be given according

1. *Introduction*   21

to the Syro-Macedonian system (= autumn 153–152), but it is a date important for events within Judah itself. Thus, there is nothing against its being calculated by the spring-to-spring system, which would fit Nisan 312 but not Nisan 311. If future study shows that Alexander definitely arrived in Ptolemais in the summer of 152, this would be a serious problem to any thesis about a system beginning in Nisan 312. But from the data presently known, the summer of 153 seems equally possible and the proposal for a dating from Nisan 312 a viable one.

Finally, counting from Nisan 312 has often been dismissed with the statement that no such era is known (e.g., Bickerman 1937a: 157//1979: 103). But since most of what we know about the use of the Seleucid era among the Jews comes from 1 Maccabees and Josephus, it seems that we have too little information to make such a negative judgment at this point. There is no discussion about the Seleucid era in any ancient Jewish source. Most of what we know has been determined by simply working with the data. The data have demonstrated that an era reckoned from Nisan 312 is sometimes used in 1 Maccabees.

1.3.4. *Dates of Major Events in 1 Maccabees*

Having established some preliminary positions and problems, we can now look at the major dates in 1 Maccabees itself, some of which can be established precisely (for further detail on some of these points, see Grabbe 1991). Antiochus came to the throne in 137 SE (1 Macc. 1.10). According to the cuneiform Seleucid king list, Seleucus IV died 10 VI 137 SE (= 3 Sept. 175 BCE), and Antiochus IV came to the throne in VI 137 SE (= Sept. 175 BCE) (Sachs and Wiseman 1954: 208). 1 Maccabees 1.16-28 describes Antiochus's attack on Egypt and associates it with the plundering of the Jerusalem temple. There are some problems here because Antiochus twice invaded Egypt; however, the date is given as 143 SE (170–169 BCE), which fits only the first invasion. It is now established that this invasion almost certainly occurred in late 170 BCE or early 169 BCE (Nov. 170 BCE seems a strong possibility: Skeat 1961). The problem is that 1 Macc. 1.20-28 seems to associate the taking of Jerusalem by force with the first invasion of Egypt, whereas 2 Maccabees 5 appears to make the use of force against the city and the despoiling of the temple a product of the second invasion. Although some doubt whether Daniel is sufficiently clear, others argue that Dan. 11.25-31 refers to both invasions of Egypt but associates a peaceful despoiling of the temple with the first, and the violent taking of the city with the second (Bringmann 1983: 36–40; Bickerman 1937a: 160–68//1979: 104–11; Mørkholm 1966: 142–45).

'Two years later' (μετὰ δύο ἔτη ἡμερῶν) Antiochus sent a force to take Jerusalem, enslave many of the people, establish a garrison, and defile the temple (1 Macc. 1.29-40). From when are these two years counted? If dating from the beginning of the first invasion, they take us to the autumn of 168 BCE. It is not completely clear whether the 'abomination of desolation' took place at this time or slightly later (1 Macc. 1.54-64), but the actual defiling of the temple is dated to 15 Kislev 145 SE. Although the 'two years later' may be intended only as an approximate figure, it could also be understood as pointing to November–December 168 BCE for the institution of pagan sacrifice in the temple. This indeed fits with 2 Maccabees 5, which has Antiochus attack Jerusalem on his way back from his second invasion of Egypt, followed shortly afterward by the suppression of the temple cult. The precise date of Antiochus's retreat from Egypt is now known to be 30 July 168 BCE (Ray 1976: 14–20, 124–30). Again, the natural sequence of events suggests that the Jerusalem cult was stopped toward the end of 168 BCE.

The next event is the death of Mattathias, the father of the Maccabaean brothers, in 146 SE (1 Macc. 2.70). By this time the Maccabaean resistance had begun. Antiochus is said to be angry on hearing about this opposition to his measures and to set about gathering an army, only to find that he has no money to pay for it. So he had to launch a campaign to the East to gain funds. This naive picture must be rejected. The Jewish resistance was a minor problem at this time, and Antiochus had probably long planned an eastern campaign (Gruen 1984: 660–63; cf. also Mørkholm 1966: 95–101). But the significant datum in 1 Maccabees is that this march east took place in 147 SE (1 Macc. 3.37). The beginning of this campaign is usually dated to the spring or summer of 165 BCE, but in the light of present knowledge it could have begun in late 166 BCE (cf. Mørkholm 1966: 98 n. 37). Although Bar-Kochva (1989: 466–73) has tried to redate the celebrations at Daphne to the summer of 165 (rather than 166 as is usually done), he also makes them the immediate prelude to marching east, one reason being that this would have saved paying the mercenaries for a year of idleness. His arguments could be used just as well to put Daphne in the summer of 166 and make the actual expedition begin straight afterward in the autumn of 166. Antiochus had left the subduing of the Jewish rebels to his lieutenants, and a number of battles are described (1 Macc. 3.38–4.35). This culminates with Judas and his group retaking the temple and purifying it on 25 Kislev 148 SE (1 Macc. 4.36-59). If the date of 168 BCE given above for the start of the desolation is correct, this would make the restoration in November–December 165 BCE.

The fighting was not yet over, and Judas' battles against the surrounding nations are described in 1 Maccabees 5. Meanwhile, after suffering a major reversal Antiochus heard about the retaking of Jerusalem and died shortly afterward in 149 SE (1 Macc. 6.1-16). This sequence of events is often ignored or explained away: Antiochus died *after* the temple was retaken and cleansed. We know that his death was reported in Babylon sometime between 20 November and 18 December 164 BCE, so he most likely died in November or possibly early December 164 (Sachs and Wiseman 1954: 208–9).

In the year 150 SE, Judas besieged the Acra at Jerusalem, which was in the hands of the Seleucid troops (1 Macc. 6.17-47). The new king Antiochus V, who was still a minor and had Lysias as his guardian, dispatched an army to relieve the garrison in the Acra. Judas met them and a series of pitched battles took place. At one point the Syrians 'showed the juice of grapes and mulberries' to the war elephants to excite them to fight (1 Macc. 6.34). The precise meaning of this passage is uncertain, but it does suggest a time of the year when grapes and mulberries would have been in season, viz., summer or early autumn. Bar-Kochva (1989: 312) denies that this indicates the time of year of the battle since wine could be given to the elephants at any time. But his objection fails to explain why the phrase, 'the blood of grapes and mulberries' (suggesting fresh juice) is mentioned rather than just 'wine'. To make the elephants drunk could be as dangerous to themselves as to the enemy (cf. J. Goldstein 1976: 320).

When Judas' army was temporarily routed, the Seleucid army was able to gain Beth-zur. This city surrendered because the inhabitants had no food to withstand a long siege, since it was a sabbatical year (1 Macc. 6.49-50). According to the pattern established (see §1.3.6 below), this sabbatical year would have been 164–163 BCE. Because the shortage of food would be felt toward the latter part of the sabbatical year, the city probably capitulated sometime in the summer or early autumn of 163, a point confirmed by the statement about the juice of grapes and mulberries. Bar-Kochva (1989: 339–42, 544–46) states that the siege was in the spring of 162, at a time when the effects of the sabbatical year would still have been felt. It is true that the Jews would have been relying on stores even after the end of the sabbatical year until the spring harvest. But the harvest could have begun as early as Nisan in some areas, whereas Nisan is the earliest time that the siege would have begun according to Bar-Kochva's reckoning (since it could only have begun with the new year). As noted, he also rejects any significance in the mention of the 'blood of grapes and mulberries'. But the most important objection to his thesis is that 1 Macc. 6.49, 53 plainly states that the siege

24   *A History of Jews and Judaism in the Second Temple Period, Volume 3*

was *during* the sabbatical year, not after it as Bar-Kochva thinks (cf. Bringmann 1983: 20 n. 18; Schunck 1956: 28).

This dating is also supported by the event which ended the siege (1 Macc. 6.55-63). When Lysias heard that Philip had returned from the East to Antioch and was attempting to take over, he made a hasty peace with the Jews and hurried north to regain control. It is likely that Philip would have returned to Antioch at the earliest opportune moment after Antiochus's death if he wanted to make a play for power. The summer of 163 is a reasonable time for him to do so (Gera and Horowitz 1997: 249–52). The later dating, to the spring/summer of 162, well over a year after Antiochus's death, advocated by some scholars is not (Goldstein 1976: 167; Hanhart 1964: 94; Bar-Kochva 1989: 339–42, 544–46, 551). As Bickerman (1937a: 156–57//1979: 102) already noted, 'the general [Philip] certainly did not wait a whole year before he started the struggle for the regency'.

It becomes very clear that the aforementioned year 150 SE could not be given according to the Babylonian reckoning (= Nisan 162–161 BCE) nor according to the normal Syro-Macedonian Seleucid year (= Tishri 163–162 BCE). The only reckoning for this date which fits is a Seleucid era which counts year 1 from Nisan 312 BCE, i.e., Nisan 163–162 BCE. This conforms with the Seleucid dates of the defilement and purification of the temple suggested by the sequence of events noted above: Kislev 145 SE (equivalent to Nov.–Dec. 168) and Kislev 148 SE (Nov.–Dec. 165 BCE). This dating also fits the actual narrative of 1 Maccabees which puts the restoration of the temple before the death of Antiochus (cf. 1 Macc. 4.36-59 with 6.5-7).

The normal dating of 'the abomination of desolation' to Kislev 167–164 BCE has actually caused a good deal of trouble to scholars because they have had to explain away the most straightforward reading of 1 Maccabees. Some do this by following 2 Maccabees, which gives a slightly different order of events, even though there is general agreement that 1 Maccabees is more trustworthy. For example Bar-Kochva (1989: 165, 276–82) seems to feel it necessary to explain at length how the author of 1 Maccabees made an error in the sequence of events. This is clearly an embarrassment because elsewhere Bar-Kochva frequently shows how 1 Maccabees is the more trustworthy, often representing an eyewitness account of the actual events (cf. 1989: 153–55, 160–62). However, the reason he has this difficulty is that he assumes the temple must have been restored in 164 BCE.

On the other hand, it has been argued that 2 Maccabees *originally* had the same sequence of events as 1 Maccabees but that this was altered by

1. Introduction   25

the epitomizer (Dagut 1953: 152–54; Hanhart 1964: 73–76). Other explanations are even more fanciful (Goldstein [1976: 165] has to postulate that the calendar was two months out of phase with the solar year because of lack of two required intercalations of a month each; see especially the table in 1976: 165). This is purely hypothetical since the sources say nothing about any calendrical problems, and becomes completely absurd when one realizes that he dates the purification of the temple as early as mid-October 164. Bar-Kochva (1989: 279 n. 7) takes him to task on this but then himself suggests a calendar difference as well.

All the data seem to fit this explanation, with one possible exception. The difficulty is 1 Macc. 4.28. According to the narrative, Antiochus crossed the Euphrates in 147 SE, leaving Lysias in charge of Antioch (1 Macc. 3.32-37). Lysias sent an army against Judas, which was defeated at Emmaus (1 Macc. 3.38–4.27). Then, 'the next year' (ἐν τῷ ἐχομένῳ ἐνιαυτῷ) Lysias sent another army, after the defeat of which Judas cleansed the temple (1 Macc. 4.28-59). If Antiochus's march occurred in the summer of 165, as often dated, my explanation would require the two defeats to have taken place between the spring or summer of 165 and December 165, which does not easily allow for 'the next year' of 4.28. But the difficulty is not a great one since at least two considerations are relevant: (1) As already noted above, it is very possible that Antiochus left on his eastern campaign in 166, making the first defeat at Emmaus possibly as early as the autumn of 166. (2) Alternatively, the 'next year' might be a loose expression meaning that a new year had begun even though a full calendar year had not actually passed. With regard to the second point, Bar-Kochva (1989: 283–84) states that if this were the case, the expression would have been ἐν τῷ ἐρχομένῳ ἔτει. Bar-Kochva's retroversions to the original Hebrew are the work of solid scholarship and often compelling, but that is not to say that this particular case is a decisive argument. The following considerations demonstrate the difficulties involved: (1) The reading ἐχομένῳ (instead of ἐρχομένῳ) is preferred by many scholars, which might affect the meaning or phrasing of the idiom; (2) the two words for 'year' (ἔτος and ἐνιαυτός) are often interchangeable in Greek usage; (3) there are major problems with retroverting from the present Greek text back to the (presumed) Hebrew when no portion of the original has survived to act as a control.

All the relevant data in 1 Maccabees and the few relevant dates in 2 Maccabees have now been taken care of. The dates of the letters in chap. 11 are problematic and have often been debated, but they form a separate question (on these, see §3.2 and §15.4.2).

1.3.5. *Herodian and Roman Dating*

T. D. Barnes (1968) 'The Date of Herod's Death', *JTS* 19: 204–9; **P. M. Bernegger** (1983) 'Affirmation of Herod's Death in 4 B.C.', *JTS* 34: 526–31; **J. van Bruggen** (1978) 'The Year of the Death of Herod the Great', in T. Baarda et al. (eds), *Miscellanea Neotestamentica*, 1–15; **O. Edwards** (1982) 'Herodian Chronology', *PEQ* 114: 29–42; **W. E. Filmer** (1966) 'The Chronology of the Reign of Herod the Great', *JTS* 17: 283–98; **B. Mahieu** (2012) *Between Rome and Jerusalem: Herod the Great and his Sons in their Struggle for Recognition*; **A. K. Marshak** (2006) 'The Dated Coins of Herod the Great: Towards a New Chronology', *JSJ* 37: 212–40; **M. Stern** (1974b) 'Chronology', in S. Safrai and M. Stern (eds), *The Jewish People in the First Century*, 1:62–77.

Most of the dates after the Hasmonaean period relate to Herod, but a number are of important events in Roman history. The table gives the more important dates relating to Herod's reign. However, the exact date of every aspect of Herod's reign cannot be determined for certain nor is it always important to do so for general purposes. There are several dates, however, which are crucial not only to the framework of his own reign but also to the correct chronology of the later history of Judah.

1.3.5.1. *Fall of Jerusalem to Pompey in 63 BCE*

The first date to consider is actually pre-Herodian. According to Josephus (*Ant.* 14.4.3 §66), the temple fell to Pompey's forces in the 3rd month on the fast day (τῆς νηστείας ἡμέρα) in the 179th Olympiad (Sept. 64–Sept. 63: Bickerman 1980: 119), the Roman consuls being G. Antonius and M. Tullius Cicero: 63 BCE (Bickerman 1980: 151). But what time of year? The 'fast day' can refer to the Day of Atonement, which was the 10th of Tishri, the 7th month. Yet Greek and Latin writers often refer to the sabbath as a fast day, for some reason, perhaps because many Jews would not light a fire to cook on that day (Strabo 16.2.40; Suetonius, *Div. Aug.* 76.2); Cassius Dio (37.16) explicitly refers to the sabbath. Marcus (LCL *Josephus*, vol. VII: 481 n.) states that it was 'probably…about July 63 BC'. This problem of the 'fast day' also comes up later.

1.3.5.2. *Appointment as King*

The basic data for the time of Herod's appointment as king are the following: (1) it was during the consulships of Domitius Calvinus (second time) and Asinius Pollio (*Ant.* 14.14.5 §389), which was 40 BCE (Bickerman 1980: 151); (2) Mark Antony and Octavian were in cooperation, but there had been a good deal of friction between them for several years until the pact of Brundisium in September/October 40 BCE;

(3) according to Appian (*Bell. Civ.* 5.75.319) Herod was made king of the Idumaeans and Samaritans in 39 BCE.

The last point might seem to contradict the dating of 40 BCE (Filmer 1966: 285). However, the first two points appear to be conclusive for the year 40, even though Josephus has been known to make a mistake in his dating by consulships (e.g., *Ant.* 14.1.2 §4). The last point can probably be reconciled with these since it relates to activities of Mark Antony after leaving Rome, whereas Herod's appointment was earlier while he was still there; furthermore, the statement in Appian is about Herod as ruler over Samaria and Idumaea, not Judah. This could be interpreted as a reference to territories added to Herod's realm once Antony came to the region (Stern 1974b: 1:63–64).

1.3.5.3. *Conquest of Jerusalem*

This has traditionally been placed in 37 BCE, though with considerable discussion about the time of year in which it occurred. Recently, it has been argued that the date should be 36 BCE (Mahieu 2012: 60–99; Steinmann 2009: 8–11; Filmer 1966: 285–91; see the counter arguments of Barnes 1968: 204–9; Bernegger 1983: 526–31; Bruggen 1978). The problem with Steinmann is that he ignores all the solid data and depends on the figure of 27 years since Pompey's conquest of Jerusalem, as well as on a sabbatical year reckoning, which is, unfortunately, incorrect (see §1.3.6). In a very confusing discussion, Mahieu begins the siege in Tishri 37 and ends it on Adar 13, 36 BCE; the reasons are not at all clear, though she also uses an incorrect sabbatical year. To resolve the problem of the siege of Jerusalem, we must first enumerate the basic data, which are the following:

- During the consulships of Marcus Agrippa and Caninius Gallus (*Ant.* 14.16.4 §487), which was 37 BCE, or of Claudius and Norbanus (Cassius Dio 49.23.1), which would make it 38 BCE (though Mahieu [2012: 61] may be correct that Dio is referring only to Sosius's appointment as being in that consular year). (Note that Steinmann [2009: 11] misleadingly quotes Dio, inserting a bracketed '37 BCE' for the year following the siege, as if it were the proposed year of the siege.)
- In the 185th Olympiad (*Ant.* 14.16.4 §487), which covered 1 July 41 to 30 June 37 BCE.
- 27 years from the capture of the city under Pompey in 63 BCE (*Ant.* 14.16.4 §487); one must keep in mind that this may be inclusive reckoning or even a possible miscalculation on Josephus's part.

28 *A History of Jews and Judaism in the Second Temple Period, Volume 3*

- In the 'third month' (*Ant.* 14.16.4 §487; 14.4.3 §66) or the 'fifth month' (*War* 1.18.2 §351). According to *Ant.* 14.16.2 §473 the city fell sometime in the summer (θέρος). It may be that the 'third month' refers to a siege of three months, while the 'fifth month' meant the fifth month of the calendar, i.e., the month of Av. Or (less likely) possibly a siege of five months, ending in the month of Sivan (the third month of the Jewish calendar), though this would better fit the Olympiad. But the 'third month' could simply be an error (see below).
- On the 'Fast Day' (*Ant.* 14.16.4 §487) or the sabbath day (Cassius Dio 49.22.4; 37.16.4). The 'fast day' as the Day of Atonement does not fit with the other data in the passage, while a capitulation of Jerusalem on the Day of Atonement exactly 27 years after its fall to Pompey seems stylized and rather suspect. But as noted above, non-Jewish sources often referred to the sabbath as a fast day, which agrees with Dio's statement.
- During a 'sabbatical year' (*Ant.* 14.16.2 §475). The summer of 137 BCE was getting toward the end of a sabbatical year, which would have exacerbated the problem with lack of food for the besieged.

We must distinguish between those data that Josephus probably took from sources and those based on his own calculations. References to consuls, Olympian dates, 'third/fifth month' and the sabbatical year were probably in his sources. The 27 years since Pompey's taking of Jerusalem may well have been his own (mis?)calculation. Despite the contrary arguments of Mahieu, Steinmann and Filmer, the date 37 BCE seems to be firm, not only because the consuls (as given by Josephus) are correct but also because Mark Antony invaded Parthia with a large army in the spring of 36 BCE (though Mahieu wants to make the fall of Jerusalem before Antony's invasion of Parthia). Since a large Roman force also aided Herod during his siege, it is unlikely that such would have been available in 36 BCE (Stern 1974b: 1:67; *GLAJJ* 2:361–62). Also, from what is known of the sabbatical year cycle at that time, the sabbatical year mentioned by Josephus would have been autumn 38 to autumn 37 (§1.3.6 below).

More difficult is the time of year. The Olympic year assignation of Josephus suggests the siege would have been finished by the end of June; however, a number of Josephus's Olympic-year datings are incorrect in this part of the *Antiquities*, if he counted from summer to summer as is normally done; however, there was no consistent reckoning for the start of the Olympic year in antiquity, and some authors counted from the autumn instead of the summer (cf. Bickerman 1980: 76). Also, the start of the siege was definitely in the 185th Olympiad, even if counted from June, which could also be a source of confusion. What does the 'third month' mean, and what about the 'fifth month' mentioned elsewhere? The 'third month' may actually be an error, since it correctly belongs to Pompey's siege and may well have been accidentally inserted here (Stern 1974b: 1:66). The siege would thus have begun at the end of winter and have lasted five months, which would put it sometime in mid-summer of 37 BCE.

Puzzling is Josephus's statement that the fall of Jerusalem was on the 'day of the fast'. While this normally refers to the Day of Atonement in his usage, the 'fifth month' just noted does not accord with this. It has been widely accepted that Josephus has mistakenly interpreted his source here (probably Strabo). Among pagan writers it was common to refer to the sabbath as a fast day. That the city fell on a weekly sabbath is stated by Dio Cassius. If Strabo or another source referred to the sabbath by the designation 'fast day', it would be perfectly understandable that Josephus misunderstood this as Yom Kippur. Thus, a sabbath in midsummer 37 BCE seems to be the correct time of the city's capture.

Finally, Josephus states that the siege of Jerusalem by Herod fell during a sabbatical year (*Ant.* 14.16.2 §§475). Since the siege took place at least partly during the summer (§473), this would put it close to the end of the sabbatical year, which would come with late summer or autumn. In spite of some contrary views, it is now almost universally accepted that Herod's siege of Jerusalem ended in 37 BCE, even though the exact month is still debated.

1.3.5.4. *Herod's Death*
Although Herod's death has generally been placed in 4 BCE just before Passover, this has not been accepted by everyone. Both Edwards (1982) and Bernegger (1983) have recognized some of the difficulties with the figures in Josephus, while Mahieu (2012), Steinmann (2009) and Filmer (1966) have attempted to redate it to 1 BCE. The data are as follows:

- Herod had ruled 37 years since being declared king or 34 years over Jerusalem (*War* 1.33.8 §665; *Ant.* 17.8.1 §191).
- After a certain number of activities relating to attempts to cure his ailment, he died just before Passover (*War* 2.1.3 §10; *Ant.* 17.9.3 §213);
- An eclipse of the moon occurred shortly before Herod's death (*Ant.* 17.6.4 §167).
- The subsequent reigns of Herod's sons were definitely counted from about 4 BCE (Edwards 1982; Bruggen 1978).

Much of the discussion has centred around the placing of the eclipse and the Passover that followed. It has been common to accept the eclipse on 13 March 4 BCE, but the major problem has been to fit all the activities after the eclipse in the time before the Passover, which came one month later. Indeed, it is because of the argument that it was not possible to do so that Filmer tried for another dating (but cf. Bruggen 1978: 6–8). Two arguments have now been advanced against this eclipse. The first is that other lunar eclipses seem to have been more spectacular (Steinmann 2009: 12):

- 23 March 5 BCE, total eclipse a month before Passover
- 15 September 5 BCE, total eclipse, seven months before Passover
- 13 March 4 BCE, partial eclipse, a month before Passover
- 10 January 1 BCE, total eclipse, three months before Passover

It is then argued that the eclipse in 1 BCE is not only a 'better' candidate by being a total eclipse but that it gives more time for all the activities to do with Herod's death to have taken place. Unfortunately, these arguments are a complete red herring.

Josephus does not appear to refer to the lunar eclipse as a chronological indicator. He mentions it only in passing but in a context in which he lists the punishment of individuals named Matthias. One was a high priest by this name whom Herod removed from office; the other was an individual seen as instigating rebellion whom Herod had burnt alive. The context suggests that the lunar eclipse is mentioned as a heavenly portent, which would have been the normal reaction of people at that time when astronomical events coincided with spectacular events on the human plane (cf. Plutarch, *Aemilius Paullus* 17.7-10, where a lunar eclipse was interpreted by soldiers as sign of the eclipse of their king). A partial lunar eclipse could well have been remembered by the source that Josephus used for those events. However, it is not clear that the deposition of the high priest happened on that date. In the immediate context, it was the burning of the other Matthias that happened on the day of the eclipse. This could have been the carrying out of a sentence that had been pronounced earlier, possibly even after Herod's death.

As for the time for the events before Passover, Josephus is not very clear about the chronology of these last days of Herod. After the reference to the eclipse, he talks about the progress of his illness, various other events, his death and the funeral march that took his body for burial in Herodium (*Ant.* 17.6.5–8.3 §§168-99). There is no reason to assume that all of this happened between the lunar eclipse and the Passover. The focus on the eclipse has skewed the discussion.

1. *Introduction*

On the other hand, the other data all point to 4 BCE. The 37 years since Herod's accession as king and the 34 years since he had Antigonus executed (after retaking Jerusalem) both fit 4 BCE, if reckoned inclusively. Similarly, Archelaus's rule of 9 or 10 years ended in 6 CE (*War* 2.7.3 §§111; *Ant.* 17.13.2 §342; 18.2.1 §26), which is ten years reckoned inclusively. Steinmann (2009: 22) proposes that Archelaus began to rule before Herod's death, so that his 9 or 10 years overlapped with the last part of Herod's rule. This is pure speculation to get them out of a difficulty. Mahieu (2012: 397–98) explains it away by speculating that the figure is based on Josephus's 'reconstruction', rather than the number in his source(s). Again, this is speculation for which there is no supporting evidence.

Philip ruled 37 years until his death, in the 20th year of Tiberius (*Ant.* 18.4.6 §106), which would be about 34 CE. Some have wanted to read Tiberius's '22nd' year, based on a reading in a Latin manuscript (Steinmann 2009: 23–24; Mahieu 2012: 399). But the Latin is only a translation, whereas so far all the extant Greek manuscripts read '20'. Steinmann suggests the reading '22nd' is the *lectio difficiliar*, and in textual criticism the most difficult reading is often to be preferred (though no text critical rule is absolute; each must be weighed against other considerations). In this case, however, '22nd' in the Latin translation is easily explained. In the general context, Josephus tells us that Tiberius died after ruling 22 years and some months (*War* 2.9.5 §180; cf. *Ant.* 18.6.10 §225). The '22nd' for Philip's reign looks like an assimilation to this. This date also tells us something else: Josephus reckons Tiberius's reign from 14 CE (not 12 CE, as could be argued). It also seems unlikely that Josephus would record Philip's death as Tiberius's 22nd year without associating it with Tiberius's own death, but he clearly separates them.

As for Herod Antipas, we have coinage minted by him in the year 43 (Hendin 2010: 254–55; cf. Mahieu 2012: 274–78). Again, this poses a serious difficulty for Mahieu, because there is no way that Antipas could fit 43 years between 1 BCE and his being deposed in 39 CE. Again, she resolves the difficulty by speculation: 'Antipas may be responsible for the coins of 24, 33, 34, and 37, while those of the year 43 would have emanated from a different authority' (Mahieu 2012: 275). Why a 'different authority' would have continued to issue Antipas's coins long after he was deposed is not clarified, nor is any evidence for such a different authority provided.

In sum, in spite of some recent doubts, the length of Herod's reign from known dates and the reigns of his successors all point to 4 BCE as the date of Herod's death. The only concrete datum that might go against this is the '22' years of Philip's rule in the Latin translation, but it is not supported by any Greek manuscript and looks like simply a cross contamination from Tiberius's length of reign.

1.3.6. *The Sabbatical Year*

P. Benoit et al. (eds) (1961) *Discoveries in the Judaean Desert II: Les grottes de Murabba'ât*; **D. Blosser** (1981) 'The Sabbath Year Cycle in Josephus', *HUCA* 52: 129–39; **G. Dalman** (1932) *Arbeit und Sitte in Palästina*; **B. Kanael** (1971) 'Notes on the Dates Used During the Bar Kokhba Revolt', *IEJ* 21: 39–46; **M. R. Lehmann** (1963) 'Studies in the Murabba'at and Nahal Hever Documents', *RevQ* 4: 53–81; **P. Schäfer** (1981) *Der Bar Kokhba-Aufstand: Studien zum zweiten jüdischen Krieg gegen Rom*; **B. Z. Wacholder** (1973) 'The Calendar of Sabbatical Cycles during the Second Temple and the Early Rabbinic Period', *HUCA* 44: 153–96; **idem** (1975) 'Chronomessianism: The Timing of Messianic Movements and the Calendar of Sabbatical Cycles', *HUCA* 46: 201–18; **idem** (1983) 'The Calendar of Sabbath Years during the Second Temple Era: A Response', *HUCA* 54: 123–33; **R. Yaron** (1960) 'The Murabba'at Documents', *JJS* 11: 157–71; **S. Zeitlin** (1918–19) 'Megillat Taanit as a Source for Jewish Chronology and History in the Hellenistic and Roman Periods', *JQR* o.s. 9: 71–102; **idem** (1919–20) 'Megillat Taanit as a Source for Jewish Chronology and History in the Hellenistic and Roman Periods', *JQR* o.s. 10: 49–80; **B. Zuckermann** (1866) *A Treatise on the Sabbatical Cycle and the Jubilee.*

Many discussions on Maccabean and Herodian chronology have made some reference to the sabbatical year (שמטה *šĕmiṭṭāh* or שביעית *šĕvî'ît*) described in Lev. 25.1-7 and Deut. 15.1-11. The sabbatical year is still observed by Orthodox Jews in the land of Israel, based on a consistent cycle. This cycle was established in the Middle Ages by the authority of Maimonides (see the discussion by Zuckermann 1866; his tables list the sabbatical years from 535 BCE to 2239 CE). According to this, the next sabbatical year will be autumn (Tishri) 2021 to autumn 2022. This cycle has been accepted by many authors, some thinking it sufficient to project back into the Second Temple period without further argument (e.g., S. Zeitlin 1918–19: 71–102; 1919–20: 49–80, 237–90). Although there is broad agreement that the sabbatical year was observed during the Second Temple period, it is not infrequently asserted that the exact timing of it cannot be ascertained or that there was no consistent cycle (Bernhardt 2017: 529; Dagut 1953: 156 n. 42; Bickerman 1979: 114).

Some scholars, however, have wanted to go with B. Z. Wacholder's calculations. He has claimed that the cycle of Orthodox Jews is wrong, advancing a proposal which puts the sabbatical year one year later in each case (Wacholder 1973: 153–96; cf. also 1975: 201–18). A criticism of part of Wacholder's study was given by Blosser (1981: 129–39), to which Wacholder replied (1983: 123–33). Wacholder was also criticized by J. A. Goldstein (1976: 315–18). Was there a consistent cycle and, if so,

1. *Introduction* 33

can it be determined with reasonable assurance? The answer in both cases is yes: the data to determine the question are not extensive but they seem to be decisive.

Josephus states that the siege of Jerusalem by Herod fell during a sabbatical year (*Ant.* 14.16.2 §475). Since the siege took place at least partly during the summer (§473), this would put it close to the end of the sabbatical year, which would come with late summer or autumn. It is now almost universally accepted that Herod's siege of Jerusalem ended in 37 BCE, even though the exact month is still debated (Stern 1974b: 64–68; *GLAJJ* 2:361–62, on Cassius Dio 49.23.1; Bruggen 1978: 13–14). Although Wacholder (1973: 165–67; 1983: 127–28) mentions some problems with determining the time of the capitulation to Herod, he nevertheless seems to accept the year 37 BCE. O. Edwards (1982: 29–42), while attempting to give a new dating for Herod's death, similarly still accepts the year 37 for the fall of Jerusalem. Until recently the only one who seems to have attempted a redating was W. E. Filmer (1966: 285–91), but now A. E. Steinmann (2009) and B. Mahieu (2012) have done so, albeit unconvincingly (see further the previous section, §1.3.5.3).

Another date of importance is the sabbatical year around the beginning of the Bar Kokhva revolt. A rental contract (Mur 24) is dated to 'the 20th of Shevat, year 2 of the redemption of Israel' (באשרין לשבת שנת שתים לגאלת ישראל: Benoit et al. [eds] 1961: 124). This puts the dating of the document itself to about February 134 according to the conventional dating of the revolt (132–35 CE). The dating of the revolt is a whole study in itself, but it is widely accepted among specialists that coins and other documents now confirm the beginning of the revolt in the spring or summer of 132 (P. Schäfer 1981; Kanael 1971). The document states that five full years are being reckoned until the beginning of the sabbatical year. Since the contract is dated about February, how are the six months remaining before Tishri counted? (Wacholder does not discuss this problem.) A study of agriculture in Palestine shows that even grain could be planted as late as the month of Shevat, and late planting of other sorts of crops was common (Dalman 1932: 2:130–39, 176–79, 205–18). Thus, Hillel ben Grys, who rented the field to Yehuda ben Raba in Mur 24, expected the months until Tishri to count as the first year because a full cropping was possible. This puts the sabbatical year in 138–39 CE.

A final question concerns the sabbatical year mentioned in a document from the early part of Nero's reign. A deed of sale of land (Mur 18) is dated to the second year of Nero Caesar (the exact date is lost), which is said to be a sabbatical year, at least as some scholars have translated the passage in question (J. T. Milik in Benoit et al. [eds] 1961: 100–104). Mur 18.7

34   *A History of Jews and Judaism in the Second Temple Period, Volume 3*

reads ושנת שמטה דה, which has sometimes been understood to mean 'this (year) is the sabbatical year', i.e., the document was written in a sabbatical year. Since Nero became emperor on 13 October 54 CE, his second year would have been 55–56 CE. This would seem to put the sabbatical year in 55–56 CE and thus contradict the cycle established above. However, there are two arguments against this. One would reconcile the data of the document with the established cycle of sabbatical dates. Lehmann (1963: 56–57) proposed the following solution: on the basis of a passage in the Babylonian Talmud (*b. B. Bat.* 164a-b), he argued that tied documents such as Mur 18 always count the ruler's first year as his second out of respect. Although this interpretation is disputed by Wacholder (1973: 170–71), he only doubts it rather than attempting to disprove it, and Lehmann's interpretation has become widely accepted. The other resolves the problem by rendering the disputed phrase as a conditional clause, making it have no direct bearing on the date of the sabbatical cycle (cf. the translation of Mur 18.6-7 by J. A. Fitzmyer and D. J. Harrington (1978: 139): 'I will reimburse you with (interest of) a fifth and will settle in en[tirety], even if this is the Year of Release.' This interpretation was already given by the original editor J. T. Milik (in Benoit et al. [eds] 1961: 102–3) and accepted by R. Yaron (1960: 158). Thus, Mur 18 does not refute the cycle already established by more solid data.

The only real difficulty in this interpretation of the sabbatical year is found in Josephus. *Antiquities* 13.7.4-8.1 §§228-35 states that sometime during John Hyrcanus's siege of Ptolemy, the sabbatical year came around. According to the cycle established above, the sabbatical year would have been 136–135 BCE, but this does not fit 1 Macc. 16.14, which puts Simon's death in Shevat at 177 SE. Since Hyrcanus's siege began shortly after Simon's death, one cannot state that a sabbatical year beginning with Tishri 136 'came on' (ἐνίσταται – §234). Even reckoning Simon's death by using the earliest dating (Nisan 312, as proposed above) means that the sabbatical year was already well underway by the time of his death in January or February 135. Counting from Tishri 312 or Nisan 311 would put Simon's death even later). But there are also other problems with this passage. The statement about the sabbatical year seems copied from a non-Jewish source which did not fully understand it. Contrary to the statements in the passage, the sabbatical year was not analogous to the sabbath in forbidding work, and there is no reason why the siege could not have continued despite the onset of the sabbatical year (for example, Judas fought in a sabbatical year: 1 Macc. 6.48-53). Also, the sabbatical year is normally expected to affect the besieged, not the besiegers. The whole passage is peculiar and so far inexplicable.

1. Introduction 35

Some uncertainty is always the case with historical matters. Nothing more than probability can be established in the light of very incomplete data. Nevertheless, certain reasonably firm dates can give us confidence that the sabbatical year fell according to a regular pattern during the time under consideration. The sabbatical year can thus be used as another source of chronological data. Indeed, the sabbatical year cycle is no more uncertain than many other matters of dating or even the course of events at this time. That is the nature of historical study. But the data about the sabbatical year are too pressing to be simply dismissed as some do. We have a right – indeed, a duty – to consider it alongside other information about dating in our sources for the Hasmonaean period.

1.3.7. *Table of Some Important Dates*

The following are some of the main dates relating to Jewish history, especially those that might be controversial. It should be noted that even when the calculations here differ from those found in many handbooks, they differ only by a year. In the following table, some of the Seleucid era dates are given according to what are regarded here as dates by 'Jewish reckoning' (using a SE date from Nisan 312 BCE) but some are clearly given by 'Babylonian reckoning' (using a SE date from Nisan 311 BCE).

Julian Date (BCE)	Seleucid Date year (mo., da.)	Subject	Source
175 (Aug.–Sept.)	137 (6, –) BR	Antiochus IV takes throne	Sachs and Wiseman 1954
170 (July–Aug.)	142 (5, –) BR	Executes son of Seleucus IV	Sachs and Wiseman 1954
168 (July)		Antiochus leaves Egypt	Ray 1976
168 (Dec.)	145 (11, 25) JR	'Abomination of desolation' set up	1 Macc. 1.19
165 (Dec.)	148 (11, 25) JR	Temple cult resumed	1 Macc. 4.52
164 (Nov.–Dec.)	148 (9, –) BR	Antiochus IV's death reported	Sachs and Wiseman 1954
161 (Mar.–Apr.)	152 (1, –) JR	Death of Judas Maccabee	1 Macc. 9.3
143–142	170 JR	Simon's 1st year: freedom for Israel declared	1 Macc. 13.41

141 (Aug.–Sept.)	172 (6, 18) JR	Decree of people regarding Simon (his 3rd year)	1 Macc. 14.27
135 (Jan.–Feb.)	177 (11, –) JR	Simon's assassination	1 Macc. 16.14
63 (summer)	Gaius Antonius and Marcus Tullius Cicero, consuls	Pompey takes Jerusalem	*Ant.* 14.4.3 §66
40 (Dec)	Gnaeus Domitius Calvinus and Gaius Asinius Pollio, consuls	Herod declared king by Romans	*Ant.* 14.14.5 §389
38–37 (autumn)		Sabbatical year	*Ant.* 14.16.2 §475
37 (summer)	Marcus Agrippa and Caninius Gallus, consuls	Herod takes Jerusalem	*Ant.* 14.16.4 §487
31 (2 Sept)		Battle of Actium	
4 (spring?)	37 years since appointed king	Death of Herod	*Ant.* 17.8.1 §191

JR = Jewish reckoning of Seleucid area (§1.3.3 above)
BR = Babylonian reckoning of Seleucid era

1.4 *Terminology and Other Technical Matters*

Readers should be aware of several points:

- The transliteration of Hebrew will be clear to scholars who work in that language, generally following the standard forms; however, I have used *v* and *f* for the non-*daghesh*ed forms of *bet* and *pe*, while *w* is always used for *waw* (or *vav*, even though now pronounced *v* by most modern users of Hebrew). An exception is *mikva'ot* because this is the way it usually occurs.
- Proper names generally follow the conventional forms used in English Bibles or by classicists where they are not biblical names.
- Translations are normally my own, unless the source of the translation is explicitly given.
- The terms 'apocalyptic' and 'apocalypticism' are used interchangeably here; some North American scholars object to 'apocalyptic' as a noun, but it has a long and respectable history of such usage and is still so used on this side of the Atlantic.

- As set out above (§1.2.1), the term 'Judaean' is normally restricted to those who live in Judaea or were at least born there. Otherwise, the term 'Jew' is used for anyone in the Jewish ethnic community or who is labelled יהודי/יהדי/Ἰουδαῖος/*Iudaeus* in the historical sources.
- 'Palestine' is purely a geographical term, used because it has been widely accepted for many years and because it is sometimes difficult to find a suitable substitute.

Part II

SOURCES

Chapter 2

ARCHAEOLOGY, INCLUDING COINS AND INSCRIPTIONS

2.1. *Unwritten Remains and Material Culture*

ARAV = R. Arav (1989) *Hellenistic Palestine*; **M. Avi-Yonah** (1974) 'Archaeological Sources', *The Jewish People in the First Century* 1:46–62; **A. M. Berlin** (1997) 'Between Large Forces: Palestine in the Hellenistic Period', *BA* 60: 2–51; **idem** (2005) 'Jewish Life before the Revolt: The Archaeological Evidence', *JSJ* 36: 417–70; **G. M. Cohen** (2005) *The Hellenistic Settlements in Syria, the Red Sea Basin, and North Africa*; **I. Finkelstein** (2010) 'The Territorial Extent and Demography of Yehud/Judea in the Persian and Early Hellenistic Periods', *RevB* 117: 39–54; **R. P. Goldschmidt-Lehmann** (1981) 'The Second (Herodian) Temple: Selected Bibliography', *Jerusalem Cathedra* 1: 336–59; **M.-C. Halpern-Zylberstein** (1989) 'The Archeology of Hellenistic Palestine', *CHJ* 2: 1–34; **A. Kasher** (1988) *Jews, Idumaeans, and Ancient Arabs*; **H.-P. Kuhnen** (1990) *Palästina in griechisch-römischer Zeit*; **L. I. Levine** (1981) 'Archaeological Discoveries from the Greco-Roman Era', in H. Shanks and B. Mazar (eds), *Recent Archaeology in the Land of Israel*, 75–88; **O. Lipschits and O. Tal** (2007) 'The Settlement Archaeology of the Province of Judah', in O. Lipschits et al. (eds), *Judah and the Judeans in the Fourth Century B.C.E.*, 33–52; **J. Magness** (2012) *The Archaeology of the Holy Land: From the Destruction of Solomon's Temple to the Muslim Conquest*; **E. M. Meyers** (1994) 'Second Temple Studies in the Light of Recent Archaeology: Part I: The Persian and Hellenistic Periods', *CR:BS* 2:25–42; **E. Meyers and M. A. Chancey** (2012) *Alexander to Constantine: Archaeology of the Land of the Bible, volume 3*; **D. W. Roller** (1998) *The Building Program of Herod the Great*; **R. H. Smith** (1990) 'The Southern Levant in the Hellenistic Period', *Levant* 22: 123–30.

A number of Seleucid and Maccabaean sites are known (see the general surveys given by Kuhnen 1990 and Arav 1989; also the articles of Berlin 1997, 2005, and Lipschits and Tal 2007). Although the ceramic evidence

42   *A History of Jews and Judaism in the Second Temple Period, Volume 3*

does not usually show sharp breaks for the Hellenistic period, dating is generally easier for this period because of the destructions during the Maccabaean revolt, as well as coins (Kuhnen 1990: 38–42). The building programme of Herod is summarized in several recent works, but a survey of the archaeology, with a bibliography up to the mid-1990s is in Roller (1998: 125–238).

2.1.1. Individual Sites

Southern Phoenicia and the Galilee

2.1.1.1. Paneas (Paneion, Banias)

> **A. M. Berlin** (1999) 'The Archaeology of Ritual: The Sanctuary of Pan at Banias/Caesarea Philippi', *BASOR* 315: 27–45; *NEAEHL* 1:136–43; 5:1587–94; *OEANE* 1:270–71; **V. Tzaferis and S. Israeli (eds)** (2008) *Paneas Volume 1: The Roman to Early Islamic Periods Excavations in Areas A, B, E, F, G and H.*

It is assumed that cultic rites at the base of Mt Hermon to the god Pan took place already in the 3rd century BCE, possibly originated by Ptolemy II but perhaps only by soldiers or merchants. A series of temples and open-air cult platforms extended along the cliff base. Stratum VIa was early Hellenistic, with local pottery and 'spatter ware' from the Hula Valley. Stratum VIb was late Hellenistic: pottery associated with the second ramp wall included local ware and also Eastern terra sigillata A. Stratum Va is that of Herod who founded the Augusteum, the first temple at the site, in 19 BCE. He might also have built a colonnated pool, depicted on coins, though no remains have been found.

2.1.1.2. Tel Anafa

> **ARAV** 100–102; **S. C. Herbert (ed.)** (1994) *Tel Anafa I,i and ii: Final Report on Ten Years of Excavation at a Hellenistic and Roman Settlement in Northern Israel*; **idem (ed.)** (1997) *Tel Anafa II, i: The Hellenistic and Roman Pottery: The Plain Wares and the Fine Wares*; *NEAEHL* 1:58–61; *OEANE* 1:117–18;

The site has extensive Hellenistic remains that mostly relate to the 'Late Hellenistic era' (Herbert [ed.] 1994: 10, 12). It seems to have been originally a small, poor community, though there is artefactual evidence for cloth making. This settlement seems to have ended sometime in the

3rd century BCE. By the last part of the 2nd century BCE there were new settlers, who built a large ornamented residential building ('Late Hellenistic Stuccoed Building'). This housed a bath complex and a large quantity of luxury goods. It was extensively remodelled about 100 BCE, though the population seems to have remained the same. Punic parallels suggest Phoenician influence, and most of the coins were from Tyre or Sidon. The site was and remained non-Jewish. This was probably why it was abandoned (not destroyed) by about 75 BCE (Berlin 1997: 40, 43).

2.1.1.3. *Tel Dan*

> **ARAV** 166; **A. Biran** (1994) *Biblical Dan*; **idem (ed.)** (1996) *Dan I: A Chronicle of the Excavations, the Pottery Neolithic, the Early Bronze Age and the Middle Bronze Age Tombs*; **idem (ed.)** (2002) *Dan II: A Chronicle of the Excavations and the Late Bronze Age 'Mycenaean' Tomb*; *NEAEHL* 1:323–32; 5:1696–89; *OEANE* 2:107–12;

The site of Tel Dan is well known because of the 'house of David' inscription found there from the 9th century BCE. It continued to serve as a cultic site through the Hellenistic period. Extensive renovation occurred in the Hellenistic period, though most of it seems to be in the early Hellenistic; however, a fountain house seems to date from the early Roman period. Particularly interesting is the bilingual inscription in Greek and Aramaic: the Greek reads, 'To the god which is in Dan Zoilus makes a vow', while the Aramaic (partially destroyed) apparently read, 'The vow of Zoilus to the g[od in Dan]'. The inscription cannot be dated precisely in the Hellenistic period, but it indicates a non-Jewish cultic site at the time.

2.1.1.4. *Tel Kedesh*

> **D. T. Ariel and J. Naveh** (2003) 'Selected Inscribed Sealings from Kedesh in the Upper Galilee', *BASOR* 329: 61–80; **S. C. Herbert and A. M. Berlin** (2003) 'A New Administrative Center for Persian and Hellenistic Galilee: Preliminary Report of the University of Michigan/University of Minnesota Excavations at Kedesh', *BASOR* 329: 13–59; *NEAEHL* 3:855–59; 5:1905–6; *OEBA* 2:373–81.

This city is well known from the Hebrew Bible (Josh. 12.22, etc.), and a nearby man-made cave has Middle Bronze artefacts. Hellenistic literary sources mention it (e.g., 1 Macc. 11.63, 73), and Josephus associates it with Tyre (*War* 2.18.1 §459; 4.2.3 §104; *Ant.* 13.5.6 §154). Much of the

44   *A History of Jews and Judaism in the Second Temple Period, Volume 3*

material culture relates to Phoenicia. One of the main Hellenistic finds was a large building (46 × 40 m) that was identified as an administration building. More than 2,000 clay seal impressions seem to be mostly Seleucid, though some are Phoenician. They indicate some sort of archive. The building seems to date from the early 2nd century BCE but was apparently abandoned about the middle of the 2nd century for a short period, perhaps as a result of Jonathan Maccabee's victory on the Hazor plain against Demetrius II (1 Macc. 11.63-74); if so, the archive might have been burnt by the Tyrians rather than Jonathan (Herbert and Berlin 2003: 54). In the last part of the 2nd century BCE it was reoccupied, probably as a residence, but was abandoned again in the early 1st century BCE. There is no evidence of Roman period occupation of the building (though a nearby temple is Roman).

2.1.1.5. *Ptolemais/Akko (Tell Fukhar)*

ARAV 16–20; *NEAEHL* 1:16–31; 5:1554–61; *OEANE* 1:54–55.

This was originally a Phoenician site. In the 2nd century BCE it minted tetradrachmas on the Phoenician standard, and Phoenician semi-fine ceramics and Eastern Sigillata A tableware appeared there (as with other coastal areas). Its main function in the Hellenistic period was as a harbour. The southern breakwater and the Tower of the Flies in the harbour to the east of it (marking off the port entrance between them) seem to have been built during the Hellenistic period (though some have argued for the Persian period). The pottery and metal objects found indicate flourishing trade during this period. The coinage indicates that the city became independent of Seleucid rule about 107/106 BCE.

2.1.1.6. *Capernaum (Talḥum)*

NEAEHL 1:291–96; *OEANE* 1:416–19; **V. Tzaferis** (1983) 'New Archaeological Evidence on Ancient Capernaum', *BA* 46: 198–204; **idem** (1989) *Excavations at Capernaum, Volume 1: 1978–1982.*

The site was settled perhaps as early as the Early Bronze Age, but there was a gap during the Iron Age before it was resettled in the 5th century BCE and reached its peak in the Roman period. It was primarily a fishing settlement, though it remained one of the most important towns of the Sea of Galilee for many centuries. The synagogue, which is now the focus of the site, is from the 4th–5th centuries CE, long after our period. Whether there is a 1st-century synagogue under it, as speculated, remains to be demonstrated. The village apparently increased hugely in population with the consolidation of Hasmonaean rule, perhaps suggesting an immigration of Jews from other areas. The indications from the material culture is that the population was mainly Jewish.

2.1.1.7. *Sepphoris*

E. M. Meyers and C. L. Meyers (eds) (2013) *The Pottery from Ancient Sepphoris*; **R. M. Nagy, C. L. Meyers, E. M. Meyers and Z. Weiss (eds)** (1996) *Sepphoris in Galilee – Crosscurrents of Culture*; *NEAEHL* 4:1324–28; 5:2029–35; *OEANE* 4:527–36; *OEBA* 2:336–48; **J. F. Strange, D. E. Groh and T. R. W. Longstaff** (1994) 'Excavations at Sepphoris: The Location and Identification of Shikhin, Part I', *IEJ* 44: 216–27; **idem** (1995) 'Excavations at Sepphoris: The Location and Identification of Shikhin, Part II', *IEJ* 45: 171–87.

Sepphoris was perhaps already settled during the Iron Age, as indicated by some pottery finds. Much of what we know about the early history is from literary sources. From Josephus it was probably in existence about 100 BCE (*Ant.* 13.12.5 §338), and was the site of one of Garbinius's five synods after the Roman conquest (§17.4). It seems to have been the capital of Jewish Galilee. The ancient city was dominated by the citadel, which was sited on the summit of the hill, but evidently extended over all the slopes. Yet the Hellenistic remains are few, and it is mainly the Roman city that is preserved. Stone quarries on the western slope indicate the earliest evidence for what became a residential quarter. The earliest layers of the residential area seem to be Hellenistic, and there are some reasonably preserved late Hellenistic remains near the citadel, including the remains of a building with thick walls and two ritual baths. No certain remains of a palace supposedly built there by Herod (*War* 2.4.1 §56; *Ant.* 17.10.5 §271) have been found, though some fragments of frescoes might possibly point in this direction. After Herod's death, the city rebelled in the 'War of Varus' (§18.4.6) and was allegedly burnt (*War* 2.5.1 §68; *Ant.* 17.10.9 §289). The scattered remains suggest that Josephus's destruction may not have been as great as he describes: settlement seems to be continuous during this period. The site of Shikhin, often referred to as Asochis (Ἀσωχις) in Greek sources, seems to be established nearby to the north (Strange et al. 1994, 1995).

2.1.1.8. *Shiqmona*

ARAV 28–30; **J. Elgavish** (1976) 'Pottery from the Hellenistic Stratum at Shiqmona', *IEJ* 26: 65–76; *NEAEHL* 4:1373–78; *OEANE* 5:36–37.

The position of this site would have given it strategic importance. As noted in *HJJSTP 2* (29) a destruction of the town in the early 5th century BCE (perhaps by earthquake) led to the central mound being abandoned for a time, with the town apparently rebuilt in the surrounding fields. Finds from the site suggest it was under Phoenician control during the Persian and Hellenistic periods. At first the excavator argued for a Seleucid camp on the mound in the mid-2nd century BCE (ARAV 29), but more recently he writes (*OEANE* 5:36) that a fortress was erected on the mound in the late Persian period but destroyed (perhaps during the fighting of the Diadochi), followed by another in the Greek period. There seems to be a single level of Hellenistic remains. Multi-roomed stone buildings that had been destroyed by fire suggest a military intervention. The latest dated object (a stamped jar handle), as well as coins, suggest the incident occurred in 133/132 BCE (Elgavish 1976: 67). ARAV (29) suggested a residential quarter in the Hippodamian pattern; in any case, the quality of the building was not great. As well as strong Phoenician influence, the ceramic assemblage suggests that there was not a Jewish population.

2.1.1.9. *Atlit (Adarot, Arados/Adoros, Boucolonpolis)*

ARAV 25–27; *NEAEHL* 1:112–22.

This site had natural port facilities and was on the Via Maris. The town plan was apparently set out to be integrated into the design of the harbour. The pre-Hellenistic harbour was evidently Phoenician. The finds from the Hellenistic harbour indicate that it had quays and breakwaters, with two towers at the end of the breakwaters to mark the harbour entrance. The port seems to have allowed substantial marine traffic.

2.1.1.10. *Philoteria (Beth Yeraḥ, Khirbet el-Kerak)*

ARAV 97–98; *NEAEHL* 1:255–59; 5:1649–51; *OEANE* 1:312–14.

The buildings of the Hellenistic period were oriented differently from the earlier settlements, set parallel to the Sea of Galilee shoreline. The settlement ended in the second half of the 2nd century BCE, which does not fit the statement that Alexander Jannaeus conquered it about 100 BCE

2. Archaeology, Including Coins and Inscriptions

(Syncellus, *Chron.* 355, possibly borrowed from Josephus); however, the settlement of his time might have been on an unexcavated part of the mound. Pre-Byzantine Roman finds have only been sporadic.

2.1.1.11. *Tel Dor*

> ARAV 12–15; **D. Ariel et al.** (1985) 'A Group of Stamped Hellenistic Storage-Jar Handles from Dor', *IEJ* 35: 135–52.; **D. Gera** (1985) 'Tryphon's Sling Bullet from Dor', *IEJ* 35: 153–63; *NEAEHL* 1:357–72; 5:1695–1703; *OEANE* 2:168–70; **E. Stern** (1994) *Dor, Ruler of the Seas*; **E. Stern (ed.)** (1995a) *Excavations at Dor, Final Report, Volume IA: Areas A and C: Introduction and Stratigraphy*; **idem** (1995b) *Excavations at Dor, Final Report, Volume IB: Areas A and C: The Finds.*

This was originally a Phoenician site (a rectangular lead weight had the sign of Phoenician Tanit-Astarte on one side and the club of Hercules [= Baal Melqart] on the other), though ceramic finds indicate it had become a Greek city by the Hellenistic period. The plan of the city continued much as it had been during the Persian period (Hippodamian pattern), though a different building technique was used. It apparently had two construction phases. The remains of three temples may date to the Hellenistic period (though they continued to be used into the Roman period). There was a large affluent residential district (Berlin 1997: 5). A large public building apparently marked the entrance to the city's governmental centre. Oil presses and Herodian and early Roman coins were also found. The would-be Seleucid emperor Tryphon held Dor for a number of years during the time of Jonathan Maccabee. Although there is no evidence of military destruction at that time, four lead sling projectiles have 'Dor Year 5' on one side and 'For the victory of Tryphon' on the other (Gera 1995). There are also a set of stamped jar handles that mention 'year 2'; the stratigraphic position and the Ptolemaic style of dating suggest this is also a reference to Tryphon's reign (Ariel et al. 1985).

2.1.1.12. *Tel Mevorakh*

> ARAV 27–28; *NEAEHL* 3:1031–35; **E Stern (ed.)** (1978) *Excavations at Tel Mevorakh (1973–1976) Part One: From the Iron Age to the Roman Period.*

This was a small site with room for only one substantial building on the mound. This was on a square platform of unusual construction, showing Phoenician architectural elements. As indicated in *HJJSTP 2* (30–31),

48   *A History of Jews and Judaism in the Second Temple Period, Volume 3*

stratum III seems to have two phases. The earlier phase (IIIb), dated by the editor to 201–80 BCE (Stern [ed.] 1978: 85), contains a number of walls, with apparently a single large building. Incorporated into one of the walls was a limestone block originally interpreted as a dye vat (Stern [ed.] 1978: 24–25), but was more likely the remains of an olive press (ARAV 1989: 28). A mausoleum seems to have been built in the Roman period. The town was apparently subordinate to both Dor and Straton's Tower.

2.1.1.13. *Straton's Tower/Caesarea Maritima*

ARAV 20–25; **L. I. Levine** (1975) *Roman Caesarea*; *NEAEHL* 1:270–91; 5:1656–84; *OEANE* 1:399–404; **A. Raban (ed.)** (1989) *The Harbours of Caesarea Maritima, Volume I: The Site and the Excavations.*

Straton's Tower was a Phoenician harbour town, apparently first attested in the Zenon papyri (*P.Cairo Zenon* 59004). Third- and second-century ceramic remains, a section of fortified wall and some foundation walls are about all that is left of Straton's Tower, except for some harbour remains. Straton's Tower apparently had two closed harbours, with artificial breakwaters. The low number of 1st-century sherds have been interpreted to mean that the town was in decline when Herod took it over. Herod's city included a circus for chariot racing (though called an 'amphitheatre' by Josephus: *Ant.* 15.9.6 §341), a theatre and a temple to Augustus. His harbour construction was apparently one of the most sophisticated examples of marine engineering in antiquity.

2.1.1.14. *Beth-Shean/Scythopolis*

ARAV 99–100; **Y. Landau and V. Tzaferis** (1979) 'Tel Iṣṭabah, Beth Shean: The Excavations and Hellenistic Jar Handles', *IEJ* 29: 152–59; **A. Mazar** (2006) *Excavations at Tel Beth-Shean 1989–1996, Volume I: From the Late Bronze Age IIB to the Medieval Period*; *NEAEHL* 1:214–35; 5:1616–44; *OEANE* 1:305–9; *OEBA* 1:118–29.

Coins and pottery indicate that the mound was inhabited continually from the third to the mid-1st century BCE (Mazar 2006: 39). At one point it was called Nysa by the Greeks, though whether this came before the name Scythopolis is uncertain. The settlement was expanded in the first quarter of the 2nd century BCE, then Antiochus IV founded a well-planned Hippodamian city at Tel Iztabba, apparently with primarily a Greek population, as indicated by an inscription of about 145 BCE listing the priests of Zeus Olympius (*SEG* 8:33). The city was surrendered to

John Hyrcanus about 108/107 BCE, who is said to have burnt it and exiled its citizens (*Ant.* 13.10.3 §280). Whether this is confirmed by the archaeology is disputed (*OEBA* 1:120 vs. Berlin 1997: 31). In any case, stamped amphora handles indicate that the settlement survived at least until after 100 BCE (Landau and Tzaferis 1979). It was refounded by Gabinius about 55 BCE and became the largest of the Decapolis cities.

2.1.1.15. *Apollonia (Arsuf; Tell Arshaf)*

ARAV 32–34; *NEAEHL* 1:72–75; **I. Roll and O. Tal** (1999) *Apollonia-Arsuf, Final Report of the Excavations, Volume I: The Persian and Hellenistic Periods.*

There was general continuation from the Persian into the Hellenistic period of settlement. A 'straightened reef' (apparently dating from the Hellenistic period) appears to have served as a breakwater for a harbour, which enhanced the town's position as a trading site (as did the presence of the Via Maris which passed close by). It seems to have served as a central civilian town for the region, 'twinned' with Tel Michal (4 km away), which was the military site. Most of the Area D finds were Hellenistic, though the settlement could have been renewed either in the Persian or the Hellenistic period. A refuse pit in the same area was used up to the late 2nd or early 1st century BCE. The town may have been taken by John Hyrcanus but more likely Alexander Jannaeus (latest ceramic assemblage from the late 2nd or early 1st century BCE). Resettlement by Gabinius seems mainly an administrative matter. The abundant sheep, goat and cattle remains suggest that animals were herded in the area.

2.1.1.16. *Tel Michal (Makmish)*

ARAV 31–32; **Z. Herzog, G. Rapp, Jr and O. Negbi (eds)** (1989) *Excavations at Tel Michal, Israel*; *NEAEHL* 3:1036–41; *OEANE* 4:20–22.

The Hellenistic period seems to have four strata. On the tell was a sequence of fortresses, though some residential areas also existed alongside them. A large winepress and other artifacts suggest a shift from grain production to viticulture. Judging from coins, there was a Seleucid settlement that ended when John Hyrcanus conquered Jaffa. One fortress may have been built by Alexander Jannaeus, as indicated by coins. It has been suggested that it was part of the 'Jannaeus line' (or 'Yannai line'), but this has been disputed (see §16.5).

Samaria

2.1.1.17. *Tel Dothan*

ARAV 94–96; **D. M. Master et al. (eds)** (2005) *Dothan I: Remains from the Tell (1953–1964)*; *NEAEHL* 1:372–74.

As indicated in *HJJSTP 2* (31) the excavation of this site was unsatisfactory according to the accepted standards of the time. It was initially only a small site on the summit of the mound. After a settlement gap since the 7th century, Dothan was resettled in the Hellenistic period, and several Hellenistic occupation levels have been identified. A large building in the northwestern corner of area A (on the south side of the mound) might be a family dwelling. Adjacent is an insula (area of several dwellings). Among the finds were a number of bread ovens, several silos, a coin of 'Antiochus the king' (probably Antiochus VII) and a group of 16 Rhodian stamp seals.

2.1.1.18. *Samaria/Sebaste*

ARAV 88–91; **J. W. Crowfoot, K. M. Kenyon and E. L. Sukenik (eds)** (1942) *The Buildings at Samaria*; **J. W. Crowfoot, G. M. Crowfoot and K. M. Kenyon (eds)** (1957) *The Objects from Samaria*; *NEAEHL* 4:1300–10; *OEANE* 4:463–67; *OEBA* 2:329–36; **G. A. Reisner, C. S. Fisher and D. G. Lyon (eds)** (1924) *Harvard Excavations at Samaria 1908–1910*.

In the early Hellenistic period the Iron Age walls had been strengthened by round towers. Then in the 2nd century the citadel got a new wall, and a further city wall was built around the lower city. The fortifications in general were strengthened. Some 2,000 stamped jar handles are dated to this period in Hasmonaean history. There is evidence of a comprehensive conflagration, which seems to fit with the destruction by John Hyrcanus about 110 BCE (Berlin 1997: 31). With the coming of the Romans, the city under Roman and then Herodian rule was rebuilt as a Roman fortress. The city seems to have been expanded and the wall of the lower city considerably strengthened, including by regular round towers that projected out to protect both the wall and the gates. New buildings are dated to the early Roman period by coins. This included a new temple in the centre of the city to honour Augustus, with the city now renamed Sebaste.

2. Archaeology, Including Coins and Inscriptions

2.1.1.19. Shechem (Tell Balâtah) and Mt Gerizim

ARAV 92–94; **E. F. Campbell** (1991) *Shechem II: The Shechem Regional Survey*; **E. F. Campbell and G. R. H. Wright** (2002) *Shechem III: The Stratigraphy and Architecture of Shechem/Tell Balâṭah*; **Y. Magen** (2007) 'The Dating of the First Phase of the Samaritan Temple on Mount Gerizim in Light of the Archaeological Evidence', in O. Lipschits et al. (eds), *Judah and the Judeans in the Fourth Century B.C.E.*, 157–211; **Y. Magen, H. Misgav and L. Tsfania** (2004) *Mount Gerizim Excavations, Volume I: The Aramaic, Hebrew and Samaritan Inscriptions*; *NEAEHL* 2:484–92; 5:1742–48; *OEANE* 4:407–9, 469–72; **R. Pummer** (1989) 'Samaritan Material Remains and Archaeology', in A. D. Crown (ed.), *The Samaritans*, 166–75; **idem** (1997) 'Samaritans', in E. M. Meyers (ed.), *The Oxford Encyclopedia of Archaeology in the Near East*, 4:469–72; **E. Stern and Y. Magen** (2002) 'Archaeological Evidence for the First Stage of the Samarian Temple on Mount Gerizim', *IEJ* 52: 49–57; **G. E. Wright** (1964) *Shechem: The Biography of a Biblical City*.

With regard to Mt Gerizim, the recent archaeological excavations found only a temple to Zeus from the Roman period (begun in 160 CE) on the site known as El Ras. On the highest peak, where the Church of Mary was built in the late 5th century CE, a Samaritan temple seems to have been established in the Persian period, dated by the excavator to the mid-fifth century BCE (Magen 2007: 162–64, 176–83; Stern and Magen 2002; cf. the discussion in *HJJSTP 1*: 31–32; *HJJSTP 2*: 32–33). Both pottery and coins indicate that there was no break between the Persian and Greek periods, suggesting that the rebellion in Samaria in 331 BCE (*HJJSTP 2*: 276–78) did not affect the temple on Gerizim. Indeed, the settlement around the temple seems to have grown in the 4th century, perhaps expanded by refugees from Samaria after Alexander had it resettled by Macedonians. The Persian-period temple continued until the rule of Antiochus III after his conquest of the region, as indicated by both pottery and coins (Magen 2007: 182–83). A Hellenistic city, with residential quarters, was built around the sacred precinct.

In the early 2nd century BCE the temple and compound were built and the city expanded. A new temple with ashlars replaced the Persian-period one, though it was evidently not modelled on the Jerusalem temple but had elements of Greek architecture. The six-chambered gate was replaced by a four-chambered one. A number of large public buildings were built, apparently to help accommodate pilgrims to the cult site. The domestic dwellings of the settlers were mainly on the west and south sides, though a

52   *A History of Jews and Judaism in the Second Temple Period, Volume 3*

main road came up the steep east side, with steps leading from it up to the east entrance of the sanctuary. But there is no evidence of urban planning, and the settlement seems to have grown without any direction.

The temple and settlement were evidently destroyed by Hyrcanus I about 110 BCE. Since there was no defensive wall, evidence can be found of barricades being thrown up and the gate structures and citadel blocked off, apparently at the time of Hyrcanus's siege. After this destruction the site remained abandoned until the 4th century CE, when a sacred precinct was reconstructed and the mountain became a place of pilgrimage, until the Church of Mary was begun in 484 BCE. However, there is some evidence of sacrifices on the site during the Crusader period.

Judah (including Philistia and the Shephela) and the Coast

2.1.1.20. *Jaffa (Joppa)*

> Arav 38–41; **J. Kaplan** (1972) 'The Archaeology and History of Tel Aviv-Jaffa', *BA* 35: 66–95; *NEAEHL* 2:655–59; *OEANE* 3:206–7.

Jaffa seems to mark the most southern extent of Phoenician control, as *HJJSTP 2* (34) indicated. An abundance of Greek imported objects have been found. Pottery and coins show that the earlier buildings continued in use into the later Hellenistic period. In area A, level IB contained the remains of a square fort dated to the Ptolemaic and Seleucid period, while level IA from the Hasmonaean period contained an altar. Judas apparently tried to attack the city (2 Macc. 12.3-7). Jonathan (with Simon's help) took Jaffa when they opened their gates to his army (1 Macc. 10.74-76). Simon installed a Jewish garrison, expelled the non-Jewish population and brought in Jewish settlers, finally gaining a harbour for Judaea (1 Macc. 12.33-34; 14.5, 34). A horde of 800 coins from the time of Alexander Jannaeus has been found.

2.1.1.21. *Bethel*

> **W. F. Albright and J. L. Kelso (eds)** (1968) *The Excavation of Bethel (1934–1960)*; *NEAEHL* 1:192–94; *OEANE* 1:300–301; *OEBA* 1:98–104.

According to Albright and Kelso ([eds] 1968: 38–39), Hellenistic remains were found, but later excavations found none. There were apparently two Hellenistic phases. The second one is associated with Bacchides who is said to have refortified the site (1 Macc. 9.50), with the tumulus Rujm Abu 'Ammar thought to be part of this (surface pottery is from the 2nd century BCE).

2. Archaeology, Including Coins and Inscriptions 53

2.1.1.22. *Jericho (Tell es-Sultan, Tulul Abu el-'Alayiq)*

ARAV 75–78; **R. Bar-Nathan (ed.)** (2002) *Hasmonean and Herodian Palaces at Jericho: Final Reports of the 1973–1987 Excavations, Volume III: The Pottery* ; **R. Bar-Nathan and J. Gärtner (eds)** (2013) *Hasmonean and Herodian Palaces at Jericho: Final Reports of the 1973–1987 Excavations, Volume V: The Finds from Jericho and Cypros*; *NEAEHL* 2:674–81; 5:1798–1800; **E. Netzer** (1975) 'The Hasmonean and Herodian Winter Palaces at Jericho', *IEJ* 25: 89–100; **idem** (1977) 'The Winter Palaces of the Judean Kings at Jericho at the End of the Second Temple Period', *BASOR* 228: 1–13; **E. Netzer (ed.)** (2001) *Hasmonean and Herodian Palaces at Jericho: Final Reports of the 1973–1987 Excavations, Volume I: Stratigraphy and Architecture*; **E. Netzer and R. Laureys-Chachy (eds)** (2004) *Hasmonean and Herodian Palaces at Jericho: Final Reports of the 1973–1987 Excavations, Volume II: Stratigraphy and Architecture*; *OEANE* 3:220–24; *OEBA* 2:1–9; **S. Rozenberg (ed.)** (2008) *Hasmonean and Herodian Palaces at Jericho: Final Reports of the 1973–1987 Excavations, Volume IV: The Decoration of Herod's Third Palace at Jericho.*

As noted in *HJJSTP 2* (35) Hellenistic and Roman Jericho seems to have centred on Tulul Abu el-'Alayiq, a different site (ca. 2 km distance) from the Tell es-Sultan of the Israelite and Canaanite city. During the Hellenistic period, however, residences were evidently found up and down the Jericho valley, while fortifications occupied the hilltops. Jericho was very important for its climate and also for the balsam produced there, which attracted enormous revenues (usually for the current ruler of Judaea). For this and other reasons, it became the site of Hasmonaean palaces: first was work under the rule of Alexander Jannaeus, with palaces and recreational areas, but also always with defence in mind. Building did not stop with Alexander's death but continued under Alexandra Salome, with new buildings, pools, and gardens. The Hasmonaean palaces, with their exquisite grounds, were later transformed by Herod.

2.1.1.23. *Gezer (Tell Jezer)*

W. Ameling et al. (eds) (2018a) *Corpus Inscriptionum Iudaeae/Palaestinae, Volume IV: Iudaea/Idumaea*; ARAV 41–43; **W. G. Dever et al.** (1971) 'Further Excavations at Gezer, 1967–1971', *BA* 34: 94–132; **W. G. Dever, H. D. Lance and G. E. Wright** (1970) *Gezer I: Preliminary Report of the 1964–66 Seasons*; **W. G. Dever (ed.)** (1974) *Gezer II: Report of the 1967–70 Seasons in Fields I and II*; **S. Gitin** (1990) *Gezer III: A Ceramic Typology of the Late Iron II, Persian and Hellenistic Periods at Tell Gezer*; *NEAEHL* 2:496–506; *OEANE* 2:396–400; *OEBA* 1:468–74 **R. Reich** (1981) 'Archaeological Evidence of the Jewish Population at Hasmonean

Gezer', *IEJ* 31: 48–52; **idem** (1990) 'The "Boundary of Gezer" Inscriptions Again', *IEJ* 40: 44–46; **B. Z. Rosenfeld** (1988) 'The "Boundary of Gezer" Inscriptions and the History of Gezer at the End of the Second Temple Period', *IEJ* 38: 235–45; **J. Schwartz** (1990) 'Once More on the "Boundary of Gezer" Inscriptions and the History of Gezer and Lydda at the End of the Second Temple Period', *IEJ* 40: 47–57.

Simon besieged the city but accepted its surrender; he then expelled the non-Jewish population, 'cleansed' it of its idolatry and settled a Jewish population (1 Macc. 13.43-48; 14.34). He refortified it and also built a house there for himself (an inscription seems to mention Simon's 'palace' [Ameling et al. [eds] 2018a: 196–98 = *CIJ* 2:1184]). There is a late Hellenistic destruction layer that could be associated with his siege, as well as archaeological evidence for the refortification (Berlin 1997: 29). Many of the houses are said to have *miqva'ot*. There are also 11 boundary stones, most of which have 'boundary of Gezer' inscriptions in Hebrew; some also have Greek inscriptions with reference to 'Alkios, Archelaus, Alexa' (Reich 1990). The suggestion is that these boundary stones separated the agricultural territory of Gezer from lands owned by Alkios, Archelaus, and Alexa (for a different interpretation, see Rosenfeld 1988, but also the criticisms of his thesis by Reich 1990 and Schwartz 1990).

2.1.1.24. *Jamnia (Yavneh, Yavneh-Yam, Minet Rubin)*

B. Isaac (1991) 'A Seleucid Inscription from Jamnia-on-the-Sea: Antiochus V Eupator and the Sidonians', *IEJ* 41: 132–44; **R. Kletter et al. (eds)** (2010) *Yavneh 1: The Excavation of the 'Temple Hill' Repository Pit and the Cult Stands*; *NEAEHL* 4:1504–6; 5:2071–72; *OEANE* 5:374–5.

The original site of Yavneh is 8 km from the coastal site, which was known as Yavneh-Yam, and Iamnia in the Hellenistic period. Yavneh-Yam apparently served as a harbour but also a fort. The original square enclosure is now partly under the sea, but part of it is preserved on land. According to a partially preserved inscription (Isaac 1991), Sidonians held the site in the time of Antiochus V (164–162 BCE). Iamnia was attacked by Judas Maccabaeus in defence of the Jews among its population; he set ships on fire in the harbour (2 Macc. 12.8-9). Cendebaeus, Antiochus VII's commander-in-chief for the region, seems to have made Iamnia his base for attacking Judaea about 137 BCE (1 Macc. 15.38-40). The site was under Jewish control under Alexander Jannaeus (*Ant.* 13.15.4 §395). Herod was evidently given the city and then willed it to his sister Salome on his death (*War* 2.6.3 §98).

2. *Archaeology, Including Coins and Inscriptions* 55

2.1.1.25. *Jerusalem and Vicinity*

ARAV 71–75; **D. T. Ariel (ed.)** (1990) *Excavations at the City of David 1978–1985 Directed by Yigal Shiloh, Volume II*; **idem** (2000a) *Excavations at the City of David 1978–1985 Directed by Yigal Shiloh, Volume V*; **idem** (2000b) *Excavations at the City of David 1978–1985 Directed by Yigal Shiloh, Volume VI*; **D. T. Ariel and A. De Groot (eds)** (1996) *Excavations at the City of David 1978–1985 Directed by Yigal Shiloh, Volume IV*; **N. Avigad** (1983) *Discovering Jerusalem* (1983); **idem** (1985) 'The Upper City', *Biblical Archaeology Today*: 469–75; **M. Ben-Dor** (1986) 'Herod's Mighty Temple Mount', *BAR* 12, no. 6 (Nov.–Dec.): 40–49; **A. De Groot and D. T. Ariel (eds)** (1992) *Excavations at the City of David 1978–1985 Directed by Yigal Shiloh, Volume III*; **L. Dequeker** (1985) 'The City of David and the Seleucid Acra in Jerusalem', *OLA* 19: 193–210; **Y. Gadot and Y. Shalev** (forthcoming) 'New Evidence for Persian and Hellenistic Jerusalem and the Implications for the Location of the City', in Andrea M. Berlin (ed.), *The Period of the Middle Maccabees: From the Death of Judas through the Reign of John Hyrcanus (ca. 160–104 BCE)*; **K. Galor and H. Bloedhorn** (2013) *The Archaeology of Jerusalem: From the Origins to the Ottomans*; **H. Geva** (1981) 'The "Tower of David' – Phasael or Hippicus?' *IEJ* 31: 57–65; **H. Geva (ed.)** (1994) *Ancient Jerusalem Revealed*; **idem** (2000) *Jewish Quarter Excavations in the Old City of Jerusalem Conducted by Nahman Avigad, 1969–1982: Volume I: Architecture and Stratigraphy: Areas A, W and X–2 Final Report*; **idem** (2003) *Volume II: The Finds from Areas A, W and X–2 Final Report*; **O. Lipschits and O. Tal** (2007) 'The Settlement Archaeology of the Province of Judah', in O. Lipschits et al. (eds), *Judah and the Judeans in the Fourth Century B.C.E.*, 33–52; **B. Mazar** (1978) 'Herodian Jerusalem in the Light of the Excavations South and South-West of the Temple Mount', *IEJ* 28: 230–37; *NEAEHL* 2: 698–804, especially 717–29; *OEANE* 3:224–38; **Y. Tsafrir** (1975) "The Location of the Seleucid Akra," *RB* 82: 501–21; **A. D. Tushingham** (1987) 'The Western Hill of Jerusalem: A Critique of the "Maximalist" Position', *Levant* 19: 137–43; **J. Wilkinson** (1975) 'The Streets of Jerusalem', *Levant* 7: 118–36; **Y. Yadin (ed.)** (1975) *Jerusalem Revealed*; **A. Zilberstein** (forthcoming) 'The Hellenistic Sequence from Givati Parking Lot – Ben-Ami and Tchekhanovets Excavations', in Andrea M. Berlin (ed.), *The Period of the Middle Maccabees: From the Death of Judas through the Reign of John Hyrcanus (ca. 160–104 BCE)*.

As the only major city in Judaea, Jerusalem was often the scene for great events in the history of the region. It was also the location of the temple, which was the context for many episodes in Jewish history at this time. Hellenistic remains from Jerusalem are rather scarce despite the extensive excavations, probably because later building activities tended to obliterate the earlier. One question concerns the area of settlement of Jerusalem at this time. The 'maximalist' position assumes that the Western Hill (the Upper City) was already inhabited and a part of the city by the time of the Maccabees (Avigad 1985), whereas the 'minimalist' position thinks that it was only during Hasmonaean rule that the Western Hill became incorporated into the city boundary (Tushington 1987). It now looks likely that settlement had begun there by the 2nd century BCE: the excavations in the Jewish Quarter produced mainly finds from the Hasmonaean period or later (Geva [ed.] 2000: 24; also Lipschits and Tal 2007: 34, 38, 40; Berlin 1997: 16).

Under Hasmonaean rule Jerusalem expanded considerably, with public buildings, fortifications and aqueducts. A palace was also built. Alexander Jannaeus seems to have finished the fortifications around the residential area of the southwestern hill that had begun under Simon and John Hyrcanus (Berlin 1997: 40–41). This included lengthy stretches of walls and the lower courses of rectangular towers (built of ashlars with rough bosses laid as headers and stretchers). The Hasmonaean wall appears to have followed the Iron Age 'First Wall'. The 'Second Wall' was apparently built by Hyrcanus II, or at least before Herod's time. John Hyrcanus apparently built a fortress or Baris on the north side of the temple mount (Galor and Bloedhorn 2013: 75–76). Herod later extensively rebuilt this to make the Antonia fortress.

One problem which has exercised archaeologists is the location of the Akra, which played such an important role in the Maccabean crisis. According to Josephus, the Akra itself was destroyed and even the hill on which it stood was levelled by Simon Maccabee. However, the statement of Josephus that the hill was levelled seems to be a legendary touch, for the hill on which the temple was erected was evidently always higher than that on which the City of David was located. Despite a fierce debate over the decades, there has been no agreement on its location. Recent excavations in the Gavati parking lot have produced a large fortress tower west-southwest of the temple mount, and some think this is the remains of the Akra, but others remain unconvinced (Gadot and Shalev forthcoming; Zilberstein forthcoming). The finds include fortification walls, a watchtower measuring 4 by 20 metres and a glacis. Ongoing excavations might clarify the matter.

Herod made extensive changes and improvements to the city, many of which are still in evidence. Most of these are listed in the discussion of his building programme (§18.4.2).

2.1.1.26. *Qumran*

For archaeological and other information, as well as bibliography, see Chapter 7 (especially §7.1).

2.1.1.27. *Ashdod (Azotus)*

> ARAV 37–38; *NEAEHL* 1:93–102; 5:1573–75; *OEANE* 1:219–20; **OEBA** 1:67–72.

The Greek name for Ashdod was Azotus, and it has a rich history in the Maccabean period. The Persian-period layer (stratum 4) was destroyed by the Hellenistic constructions. Stratum 3 was Hellenistic, with coins and sherds on the floors. The Hellenistic city shows careful town planning. There was a stone-built water channel. Five furnaces for ceramics suggest an industrial area. The stone walls were laid on foundations of mud brick. A destruction toward the end of the 2nd century has been ascribed to the Hasmonaeans. Only meagre remains are found in the early Roman period when the city was apparently less important.

2.1.1.28. Ashkelon (Ascalon)

> ARAV 45–47; *NEAEHL* 1:103–12; *OEANE* 1:220–23; *OEBA* 1:73–82.

The excavations by Garstag in the 1920s produced little from the Hellenistic period. A 2nd-century cistern held Rhodian and Italic amphorae, tableware from Greece and Italy and other ceramics. Phoenician connections were clearly in evidence. It was a major banking centre and hosted a mint in the Hellenistic and Roman periods. It was autonomous from the late 2nd century BCE and not a part of the Hasmonaean kingdom. Coins of Cleopatra VII show that she took refuge there when at war with Ptolemy XIII (her brother and husband). Herod funded building projects there, including a palace in honour of Augustus. It was an important trading city, with pottery vessels showing imports from Spain, Italy, North Africa and the Black Sea.

2.1.1.29. *Beth-Zur*

> ARAV 67–71; **R. W. Funk** (1958) 'The 1957 Campaign at Beth-Zur', *BASOR* 150: 8–20; *NEAEHL* 1:259–61; *OEANE* 1:314; **O. R. Sellers** (1933) *The Citadel at Beth-Zur*; **idem** (1958) 'The 1957 Campaign at Beth-Zur', *BA* 21: 71–76; **O. R. Sellers (ed.)** (1968) *The 1957 Excavation at Beth-Zur*.

Although the history of Beth-Zur is known in some detail from the books of Maccabees, coordinating this knowledge with the stratigraphy has been a problem, with a variety of different interpretations (cf. Arav 1989: 67–71). Stratum I seems to be the Second Temple period. The citadel shows three phases. Opinion has gone mainly with that of R. Funk who put phase 1 of the citadel in the 3rd century BCE (*NEAEHL* 1:261). The city reached its zenith in the 2nd century BCE. It was a peaceful, prosperous town under Antiochus IV, with bathrooms, a marketplace and many cisterns. In phase 2 the citadel was rebuilt (by Judas?), while most have agreed that phase 3 was carried out by the Syrian general Bacchides (1 Macc. 9.52). Simon took the city and expelled the Seleucid garrison, as one would expect (1 Macc. 14.33), but he apparently resettled it, as the archaeology shows a later 2nd-century settlement outside the walls. The ceramics are utilitarian and without decoration, and there is no imported pottery (Sellers 1968: 75–77). There was a decline in the population in the later 2nd century BCE, and the city was abandoned about 100 BCE (as indicated by coins).

2.1.1.30. *Gaza (Tell Ḥaruba/Tell ʿAzza, Tall al-Ajjul)*

Arav 49; **A. Kasher** (1982) 'Gaza during the Greco-Roman Era', *Jerusalem Cathedra* 2: 63–78; *NEAEHL* 1:464–47; *OEANE* 1:38–41 (Tall al-Ajjul); *OEBA* 1:451–53.

Gaza was an important coastal city over many centuries. It was once thought that Tall al-Ajjul was the site of ancient Gaza, but this is now generally rejected for Tell Ḥaruba/Tell ʿAzza. Unfortunately, most of our information comes from literary sources, while there is little archaeological evidence, and no Hellenistic remains of much significance. The reason is two-fold: the modern city of Gaza covers much of the ancient site, and later building seems to have destroyed much of the earlier remains. The city came under Seleucid rule with the conquest of Antiochus III in 200 BCE. Jonathan Maccabee then attacked it about 145 BCE (1 Macc. 11.61-62), after which Alexander Jannaeus destroyed it shortly after 100 BCE (*Ant.* 13.3 §§358-64). It was rebuilt by Gabinius about 57 BCE, came under Herod's control, but was taken over by the Romans after Herod's death.

2.1.1.31. *En-gedi (Tel Goren, Tell el-Jurn)*

Arav 83–85; **B. Mazar, T. Dothan and I. Dunayevsky** (1966) *En-Gedi: The First and Second Seasons of Excavations 1961–1962*; *NEAEHL* 2:399–409; *OEANE* 2:222–23.

B. Mazar seems to assign the extensive fortifications to the Hasmonaean period (*NEAEHL* 2:403–4), while E. Stern agrees with this interpretation (*OEANE* 2:222). Similarly, Lipschits and Tal (2007: 43 n. 8) argue that the fort of Stratum III is of early Hasmonaean date (John Hyrcanus?). Some had wanted to date the fortifications to the Ptolemaic period. The citadel of stratum II was assigned by Mazar et al. (1966: 44–46) to the Hasmonaeans, either John Hyrcanus or Alexander Jannaeus, while its destruction was connected to the Parthian invasion and Herod's wars with the last of the Hasmonaeans. A cistern was assigned to stratum III, though it continued to be used during stratum II, which was associated with the later Herodian rulers.

Idumaea and the Negev

2.1.1.32. *Tel Maresha (Tell eṣ-Ṣandaḥanna)*

ABD 4:523–25; **ARAV** 52–57; **G. Horowitz** (1980) 'Town Planning of Hellenistic Marisa: A Reappraisal of the Excavations after Eighty Years', *PEQ* 112: 93–111; **D. M. Jacobson** (2007) *The Hellenistic Paintings of Marisa*; **A. Kloner (ed.)** (2003) *Maresha Excavations Final Report I: Subterranean Complexes 21, 44, 70*; **A. Kloner et al.** (2010) *Maresha Excavations Final Report III: Epigraphic Finds from the 1989–2000 Seasons*; *NEAEHL* 3:948–57; 5:1918–25; *OEANE* 3:412–13; **E. D. Oren and U. Rappaport** (1984) 'The Necropolis of Maresha – Beth Govrin', *IEJ* 34: 114–53; **N. Sagiv and A. Kloner** (1996) 'Maresha: Underground Olive Oil Production in the Hellenistic Period', in D. Eitam and M. Heltzer (eds), *Olive Oil in Antiquity*, 255–92.

As noted in *HJJSTP 1* (43) and *HJJSTP 2* (39–40), the city of Maresha was especially important in the Hellenistic period, and much of the archaeological evidence dates from that period. The original site consisted of a central mound or upper city, surrounded by a lower city. Both upper and lower cities apparently date from the 3rd century BCE, with the earlier structures displaced. It was an important economic centre, and the inhabitants of both cities seem to have enjoyed a high standard of living. The artefacts from the lower city represent some of the richest Hellenistic assemblages so far in the Levant. The subterranean complexes have been thoroughly explored by A. Koner (2003). The fifteen family tombs date mainly from the 2nd century BCE; many contain Greek inscriptions and demonstrate the practice of secondary burial. The city was taken by John Hyrcanus about 110 BCE (*Ant.* 13.9.1 §257) and finally destroyed by the Parthians in 40 BCE (*Ant.* 14.13.9 §364).

2.1.1.33. Beersheba (Tel Sheva; Tell es-Saba')

> **Y. Aharoni (ed.)** (1973) *Beer-Sheba I: Excavations at Tel Beer-Sheba 1969–1971 Seasons*; *NEAEHL* 1:167–73; *OEANE* 1:287–91; *OEBA* 1:90–98.

As noted in *HJJSTP 2* (41) Beersheba was always a key site in the defence of Judah's southern border, and it seems to have fulfilled a similar role in the Hellenistic period. The Hellenistic occupation may have been more intensive than even the Roman (Aharoni [ed.] 1973: 7–8). Many of the coins were Seleucid or minted under John Hyrcanus. With three distinct floor levels, a fortress may have been founded as early as the Persian period. A large Hellenistic fortress was constructed by first bringing in a large amount of fill material to level the site. The final fortress on the site was dated to the Roman period. The remains of two broad parallel walls, found under the Roman fortress, were probably external walls of the Hellenistic fortress. There was also a large Herodian palace with bathhouse. Evidence of courtyards, grain silos, ovens and the like occurred nearby.

Transjordan and the Golan (including the Decapolis)

2.1.1.34. *Gamala (Gamla)*

> **ARAV** 114; **A. M. Berlin** (2006) *Gamla I: The Pottery of the Second Temple Period*; *NEAEHL* 2.459–63; 5:1739–42; *OEANE* 2:382; *OEBA* 1:434–43.

Gamala was already settled in the Early Bronze Age but then abandoned, followed by a long habitation gap until about 200 BCE when the site was resettled, perhaps as a military garrison (more than 600 coins, from Antiochus III to Demetrius II, were found) and the Early Bronze layer was built over. Civilian inhabitants seem to have settled there by the 1st century BCE at the latest (350 coins of John Hyrcanus and Aristobulus I). Gamala could have been a pilgrim station for travellers from Babylonia. One of the prominent buildings has been identified as a synagogue, with an adjoining room that was labelled a study area. A water channel took water through the synagogue into a basin on the west side, but then on into a *miqveh* further on. These were probably not built until the very late 1st century BCE (not earlier than the end of Herod's reign), though an earlier building on the same site cannot be ruled out at the moment. It was probably a 'Hellenizing Jewish village' until Jannaeus's conquest about 80 BCE, after which it continued to flourish (Berlin 1997: 40).

2. *Archaeology, Including Coins and Inscriptions* 61

2.1.1.35. *Hippos (Sussita, Qasl'at el-Ḥusn)*

NEAEHL 2:634–36; 5:1782–87.

Hippos was one of the Decapolis cities (Pliny, *Nat. Hist.* 5.15.74), along with Scythopolis, Pella and others. Judging from literary sources, a town was founded there by the Seleucids. Although Alexander Jannaeus is said to have conquered it about 100 BCE (Syncellus 355), little of the Hellenistic settlement is preserved. According to Josephus (*Ant.* 14.4.4 §75), Pompey conquered it, then rebuilt it along Hippodamian lines, which remained evident in the later city. Of the building remains, a compound or temenos arose in the Hellenistic period, probably 2nd century BCE, and continued to function as a cult site into the Roman period. The forum and monumental building and the east gate (probably also the west gate) are later than our period (as are, of course, the churches).

2.1.1.36. *Gadara (Umm Qeis)*

Arav 113–14; **Y. Hirschfeld (ed.)** (1997) *The Roman Baths of Hammat Gader: Final Report*; **A. Hoffmann** (2001) 'Hellenistic Gadara', *SHAJ* 7:391–97; *NEAEHL* 2:565–73 (Ḥammat Gader only); *OEANE* 5:281–82.

Gadara was a well-known city of the Decapolis and, according to literary sources, already existed in the 3rd century BCE (Polybius 5.71.3). It was widely known in antiquity for a number of poets and philosophers who were born there. Sited on a plateau east of the Sea of Galilee, it is identified with Umm Geis but is near to Ḥammat Gader on the Yarmuk river which contained hot springs (Strabo 16.2.29). Much of the remains date from the Roman period. However, the archaeology suggests that, after the Seleucid conquest in 200 BCE, it was refortified to a high technical level (Hoffmann 2001: 392). Hellenistic remains include the first city wall and a temple to Zeus. The city wall seems to have been destroyed by the Maccabees. Pompey took the city and added it to the Decapolis. It later came under Herodian control.

2.1.1.37. *Pella (Ṭabaqaṭ Faḥl)*

Arav 112; *NEAEHL* 3:1174–80; 5:1862; *OEANE* 4:256–59; **R. H. Smith** (1973) *Pella of the Decapolis, Volume I: The 1967 Season of the College of Wooster Expedition to Pella*; **R. H. Smith and L. P. Day (eds)** (1989) *Pella of the Decapolis, Volume 2: Final Report on the College of Wooster Expeditions in Area IX, The Civic Complex, 1979–1985*; **R. H. Smith and A. W. McNicoll** (1983) 'The 1980 Season at Pella of the Decapolis',

BASOR 249: 45–77; **idem** (1986) 'The 1982 and 1983 Seasons at Pella of the Decapolis', *BASOR, Supplementary Studies* 24: 89–116; **R. H. Smith, A. W. McNicoll and J. B. Hennessy** (1981) 'The 1980 Season at Pella of the Decapolis', *BASOR* 243: 1–30; **J. Tidmarsh** (2004) 'How Hellenised Was Pella in Jordan in the Hellenistic Period?' *SHAJ* 8: 459–68.

The present evidence suggests that the site was habited continually throughout the 1st millennium BCE, though extensive rebuilding means that earlier buildings were often destroyed. Much of the Hellenistic material relates to the 2nd and early 1st centuries BCE, since the city expanded and grew throughout the 2nd century, after coming under Seleucid rule. Ceramic lamps and a bronze coin of Ptolemy IV suggest that a small fortress or garrison existed from no later than the 3rd century on the Tall al-Ḥuṣn mound (Tidmarsh 2004: 460). Signs of a massive conflagration on the main mound is thought to be archaeological evidence of Jannaeus's demolition of Pella about 82 BCE (*War* 1.4.8 §104; *Ant.* 13.15.3-4 §§393-97). Pompey gave it nominal independence as one of the Decapolis cities, but recovery was apparently slow. Remains of fortresses on the mounds of Jabal al-Ḥammah and Sarṭaba are, unfortunately, not certainly dated as yet.

2.1.1.38. *Gerasa (Jerash)*

Arav 113; *NEAEHL* 2:470–79; 5:1859–60; *OEANE* 3:215–19.

The city may have been founded by Perdiccas, Alexander's general, as a settlement for Macedonian soldiers. It became an important fort in the chain built by Hellenistic kings to guard their eastern border. It contained a temple of Zeus from about 200 BCE. There is evidence of Nabataean influence, because of its position on various trade routes, including coins, a Nabataean inscription and cults of the so-called Arab god. A tomb from the late 2nd or early 1st century BCE was found under the Roman-period city wall. The town came under the control of Philadelphia in the 2nd century BCE, but was then taken by Alexander Jannaeus about 82 BCE, though without a battle (*Ant.* 13.15.3 §393). Pompey removed it from Judaean control and made it part of the Decapolis.

2.1.1.39. *Philadelphia (Rabbath-Ammon)*

Arav 110–11; *NEAEHL* 4:1243–52; 5:1868–69; *OEANE* 1:98–102.

The site has a long history as Rabbath-Ammon, and the name seems to have stuck, even after it was refounded as Philadelphia by Ptolemy II

2. Archaeology, Including Coins and Inscriptions

(about the middle of the 3rd century). The 2nd century BCE seems to have been dominated by the Nabataeans. Refortifications in the middle of the 2nd century, with the Iron Age bastion of the acropolis rebuilt as a curved casemate wall, were perhaps the work of Zeno Cotylas who took Philadelphia about 134 BCE. Pottery within the rubble was dated to the second half of the 2nd century BCE. The masonry was very much like that of the earlier section of the east wall of the Temple Mount in Jerusalem. Alexander Jannaeus may have tried to take it about 80 BCE (though only the region and not the city is named [*Ant.* 13.15.3-4 §§393-97]); if so, he did not succeed. When Pompey conquered the region, he gave the city nominal autonomy as one of the Decapolis cities. Because a good deal of the construction blocks seems to have been reused in the Roman build, little of the Hellenistic city survives. Remains of several Hellenistic structures have apparently been found: a cistern and water system at the north end of the acropolis and repair of the bastion in the southeastern corner of the lower city, as well as pottery and coins. Dry construction of the acropolis walls with polygonal blocks is thought to be a building technique of the Hellenistic period.

2.1.1.40. *'Iraq al-Amir*

J. M. Dentzer, F. Villeneuve and F. Larché (1982) 'Iraq el Amir: Excavations at the Monumental Gateway', *SHAJ* 1: 201–7; **C. C. Ji** (2001) "Irāq al-'Amīr and the Hellenistic Settlements in Central and Northern Jordan', *SHAJ* 7: 379–89; **C.-H. Ji and J. K. Lee** (2004) 'From the Tobiads to the Hasmoneans: The Hellenistic Pottery, Coins, and History in the Regions of 'Irāq al-Amīr and the Wādi Ḥisbān', *SHAJ* 8: 177–88; **N. L. Lapp (ed.)** (1983) *The Excavations at Araq el-Emir, Vol. 1*; **C. C. McCown** (1957) 'The 'Araq el-Emir and the Tobiads', *BA* 20: 63–76; **B. Mazar** (1957) 'The Tobiads', *IEJ* 7: 137–45, 229–38; *NEAEHL* 2: 646–49; *OEANE* 3:177–81; **E. Will** (1982) 'Un Monument Hellénistique de Jordanie: Le Qasr el 'abd d''Iraq al Amir', *SHAJ* 1: 197–200; **E. Will and F. Larché (eds)** (1991) *'Iraq al Amir: Le Château du Tobiade Hyrcan*.

This site was discussed at length in *HJJSTP 2* (41–42), with an eye to its Tobiad background. It was of course associated with the Tobiad family, but according to literary sources its history continued well into the 2nd century BCE. Two inscriptions on cave facades that bore the name 'Tobiah' (טוביה) have been variously dated, from as late as the 3rd to the 2nd century (*NEAEHL* 2:647), to even as early as the 5th century BCE (Mazar 1957: 141–42; cf. *OEANE* 3:177). Only small portions of the site were available for excavation, which means there are still many unanswered questions. Of the six strata uncovered in soundings, stratum

III was dated to the 2nd century BCE, following the 11th-century stratum IV, which meant a gap of 900 years. The buildings, including the main Qaṣr al-'Abd, however, seem to have been built perhaps as early as the 3rd century BCE, though possibly a bit later. The material evidence led to the conclusion that this first phase of Hellenistic settlement consisted of 'flourishing settlements', including 'cities, villages, military fortresses, and watchtowers' (Ji and Lee 2004: 183); this phase apparently came to an end in the second quarter of the 2nd century BCE. Some of the buildings (e.g., the 'Square Building') are Byzantine, and the later occupations of the Qaṣr al-'Abd were in the Late Roman period (3rd to 4th centuries CE) or later.

2.1.1.41. *Desert Fortresses*

> **E. Netzer** (1981) *Greater Herodium*; **S. Rocca** (2008b) *The Forts of Judaea 168 BC–AD 73: From the Maccabees to the Fall of Masada*; **D. W. Roller** (1998) *The Building Program of Herod the Great*; **Y. Tsafrir** (1982) 'The Desert Fortresses of Judaea in the Second Temple Period', *Jerusalem Cathedra* 2: 120–45.

The important desert fortresses better known from the time of Herod (Machaerus, Alexandrium, Masada, Hyrcania) were actually Hasmonaean foundations in most cases, as was the palace at Jericho (Tsafrir 1982). Much of the defensive building was done by Alexander Jannaeus: he was responsible for the fortress line along the eastern border of the hill country that incorporated both existing and new fortified hills (Berlin 1997: 41). The Jordan valley was a vulnerable area that would allow an invasion by an enemy army, but the new line of forts would help protect against any such incursion. The fortresses of Dok and Hyrcania and possibly also Masada were already in existence, but Jannaeus constructed Alexandrium and Machaerus. Herod took over these and renovated them. He also built Herodium as a new site.

2.1.2. *Surveys and Synthesis*

> **S. Applebaum** (1986) 'The Settlement Pattern of Western Samaria from Hellenistic to Byzantine Times: A Historical Commentary', in S. Dar (ed.) *Landscape and Pattern*, 257–69; **idem** (1989a) *Judea in Hellenistic and Roman Times: Historical and Archaeological Essays*; **idem.** (1989b) 'The Beginnings of the Limes Palaestinae', in *Judaea in Hellenistic and Roman Times*, 132–42; **A. M. Berlin** (2002) 'Power and its Afterlife: Tombs in Hellenistic Palestine', *NEA* 65: 138–48; **S. Dar** (1986) *Landscape and Pattern: An Archaeological Survey of Samaria, 800 B.C.E.–636 C.E.*;

D. R. Edwards and C. T. McCollough (eds) (1997) *Archaeology and the Galilee: Texts and Contexts in the Graeco-Roman and Byzantine Periods*; **D. A. Fiensy and J. R. Strange (eds)** (2014) *Galilee in the Late Second Temple and Mishnaic Periods, Volume 1: Life, Culture, and Society*; **idem** (2015) *Galilee in the Late Second Temple and Mishnaic Periods, Volume 2: The Archaeological Record from Cities, Towns, and Villages*; **I. Finkelstein** (1988–89) 'The Land of Ephraim Survey 1980–1987: Preliminary Report', *TA* 15–16: 117–83; **I. Finkelstein and Z. Lederman (eds)** (1997) *Highlands of Many Cultures: The Southern Samaria Survey: The Sites*; **M. Gichon** (1967) 'Idumea and the Herodian Limes', *IEJ* 17: 27–42; **R. Hachlili** (2005) *Jewish Funerary Customs, Practices and Rites in the Second Temple Period*; **B. Isaac** (1991) 'A Seleucid Inscription from Jamnia-on-the-Sea: Antiochus V Eupator and the Sidonians', *IEJ* 41: 132–44; **A. Kloner** (1980) 'A Tomb of the Second Temple Period at French Hill, Jerusalem', *IEJ* 30: 99–108; **I. Kreimerman and D. Sandhaus** (forthcoming) 'Political Trends as Reflected in Material Culture: A New Look at the Transition between the Persian and Early Hellenistic Periods', in S. Honigman et al. (eds), *Judah and Judeans in the Long Third Century*; **H.-P. Kuhnen** (1990) *Palästina in griechisch-römischer Zeit*; **A. Lichtenberger** (1999) *Die Baupolitik Herodes des Großen*; **Y. Magen** (2002) *The Stone Vessel Industry in the Second Temple Period: Excavations at Ḥizma and the Jerusalem Temple Mount*; **C. L. Meyers, E. M. Meyers and J. F. Strange (eds)** (1974) 'Excavations at Meiron, in Upper Galilee, 1971, 1972: A Preliminary Report', *BASOR* 214: 2–25; **E. M. Meyers** (1971) *Jewish Ossuaries: Reburial and Rebirth: Secondary Burials in Their Ancient Near Eastern Setting*; **idem** (1976) 'Galilean Regionalism as a Factor in Historical Reconstruction', *BASOR* 221: 93–101; **E. M. Meyers, J. F. Strange and D. E. Groh** (1978) 'The Meiron Excavation Project: Archaeological Survey in Galilee and Golan, 1976', *BASOR* 230: 1–24; **E. A. Myers** (2010) *The Ituraeans and the Roman Near East: Reassessing the Sources*; *NEAEHL* 2:449–58, 525–46; 3:815–16; 4:1310–18; **E. Netzer** (1999) *Die Paläste der Hasmonäer und Herodes' des Großen*; **idem** (2008) *The Architecture of Herod the Great Builder*; **E. Netzer et al.** (1981) 'Symposium: Herod's Building Projects', *Jerusalem Cathedra* 1: 48–80; **L. Y. Rahmani** (1967) 'Jason's Tomb', *IEJ* 17: 61–100; **idem** (1981a) 'Ancient Jerusalem's Funerary Customs and Tombs: Part One', *BA* 44: 171–77; **idem** (1981b) 'Ancient Jerusalem's Funerary Customs and Tombs: Part Two', *BA* 44: 229–35; **idem** (1982a) 'Ancient Jerusalem's Funerary Customs and Tombs: Part Three', *BA* 45: 43–53; **idem** (1982b) 'Ancient Jerusalem's Funerary Customs and Tombs: Part Four', *BA* 45: 109–19; **E. Regev** (2013) *The Hasmoneans: Ideology, Archaeology, Identity*; **P. Richardson** (1985) 'Religion and Architecture: A Study in Herod's Piety, Power, Pomp and Pleasure', *Bulletin of the Canadian Society of Biblical Studies* 45: 3–29; **idem** (1986) 'Law and Piety in Herod's Architecture', *SR* 15: 347–60; **idem** (2004) *Building Jewish in the Roman East*; **S. Rocca** (2008b) *The Forts of Judaea 168 BC–AD 73: From the Maccabees to the*

Fall of Masada; **I. Roll and O. Tal** (1999) *Apollonia-Arsuf, Final Report of the Excavations, Volume I: The Persian and Hellenistic Periods*; **D. W. Roller** (1982) 'The Northern Plain of Sharon in the Hellenistic Period', *BASOR* 247: 43–52; **idem** (1998) *The Building Program of Herod the Great*; **D. Sandhaus** (forthcoming) 'Drawing Borders at the Fringe: The Shephelah from the Fourth to the First Century BCE', in Andrea M. Berlin (ed.), *The Period of the Middle Maccabees: From the Death of Judas through the Reign of John Hyrcanus (ca. 160–104 BCE)*; **N. Shalom et al**. (forthcoming) 'Judah in the "Long Third Century B.C.E." – An Archaeological Perspective', in S. Honigman (ed.), *Judah in the "Long Third Century B.C.E."*; **D. Syon** (forthcoming) 'The Hasmonean Settlement in Galilee – A Numismatic Perspective', in A. M. Berlin (ed.), *The Period of the Middle Maccabees: From the Death of Judas through the Reign of John Hyrcanus (ca. 160–104 BCE)*; **Y. Zelinger** (forthcoming) 'The Settlements Patterns in the Plain of Sharon during the Hellenistic and Hasmonean Periods', in Andrea M. Berlin (ed.), *The Period of the Middle Maccabees: From the Death of Judas through the Reign of John Hyrcanus (ca. 160–104 BCE)*.

2.1.2.1. *Introductory Comments*

The problem with describing the later Hellenistic period is that there are no destruction layers between the early 6th and the mid-2nd century BCE, which makes distinguishing different periods difficult (Shalom et al. forthcoming; also Kuhnen 1990: 40; ARAV 7–8). Many surveys had trouble distinguishing between Persian and early Hellenistic pottery. There is also the fact that the Hellenistic period is poorly represented at many sites.

The transition between the late Persian and the early Hellenistic period has generally been seen as basically a smooth one, based on survey results, but Igor Kreimerman and Debora Sandhaus have now challenged that (Kreimerman and Sandhaus, forthcoming). Drawing on the finds of recent excavations, they argue that the transition was 'by no means a smooth one' and 'call into question the notion of a proliferation of sites in the Early-Hellenistic period'. If there was a proliferation of sites in the Hellenistic period, it was not necessarily in the early part of this period. They identify sites that were rebuilt according to a new plan in the transition period or later as including Shechem, Gezer, Khirbet Qeiyafa and Tel 'Eton, and probably Samaria and Mt Gerizim. Sites abandoned during the transition and suffering violent destruction include Wâdī ed-Dâliyeh, Ramat Raḥel, Jabel Nimra, En-Gedi, and possibly Samaria. These sites all seem to have had an administrative function.

One of the first things to notice about the Palestinian area in the Hellenistic period, especially the areas of Jewish settlement, is the extent to which it is rural. There were some major cities along the coast (a number only later falling into Jewish hands) and a few inland (e.g., the Decapolis), but the only real city in Judah proper was Jerusalem (Berlin 1997: 16; 2002: 141). Most Jews living in the land at this time seem to have been agriculturalists of one sort or another, tilling the soil, growing vines or olive trees or herding livestock – often more than one of these. Many of the archaeological sites in the later Hellenistic period are villages or even individual farmsteads.

In the Hellenistic period the coast shows a division between continued Phoenician domination and Greek cultural influences. Just as in the Persian period, we still find a pattern of core settlements surrounded by dependent satellites (Rolls and Tal 1999: 253–55). Core settlements include Apollonia-Arsuf, Tell Michal and Joppa, with satellite settlements reaching from the border with Idumaea to the Yarkon river to the river Poleg not far south of Carmel. Apollonia and Tel Michal seem quite close (only 4 km apart) for both to be core settlements, but it may be that Apollonia was the civil settlement and Tel Michal the military (though Apollonia was probably dominant overall). The Yarkon seems to have been the centre for many small settlements, both north and south, including urbanized settlements, farmsteads and military outposts.

A number of constructions were evidently intended for purposes of commerce, including depots, customs houses and storage at places as widely dispersed as Pelusium, Gaza, Maresha, Khirbet el-Qôm and Akko (Berlin 1997: 4–6), though some storehouse sites (such as Tell Jimmeh and Tell el-Hesi) decline through the 3rd century. Signs of prosperity are indicated by affluent residences in towns such as Gaza, Ashkelon, Tel Mor (Ashdod) and Dor, about which A. M. Berlin waxes eloquent:

> The city's residents enjoyed a particularly rich material culture: their tables were set with fine imported dishes; their pantries were filled with wine amphoras from Rhodes and Knidos; and their personal effects included earrings and rings of gold and silver and pendants of faience and bone in an Egypto-Phoenician style. (Berlin 1997: 5)

While she is speaking specifically of Dor, her words might be extrapolated to some of the other residences noted above.

2.1.2.2. *Regions*
Upper Galilee is better known than Lower Galilee for the Hellenistic period. Western parts of the region tended to be Phoenician dominated throughout the Hellenistic and Roman periods, but the Jewish areas are now more easily identified. Settlement was evidently concentrated in small

68   *A History of Jews and Judaism in the Second Temple Period, Volume 3*

villages. Jewish settlement begins to displace the earlier (non-Jewish?) small sites from about 100 BCE. In some cases, the Seleucid-period settlements were abandoned, but often the settlement is continuous though the population seems to have changed to Jewish. Akko-Ptolemais controlled the region in the earlier Hellenistic period but was eventually replaced by Sepphoris as capital of the Jewish parts. Just under a hundred Hellenistic sites have been identified in Upper Galilee. Upper Galilee had a cultural continuum with the Golan area (see below) under Hasmonaean expansion to the north. Tyre seems to have kept control of the western region, even after Alexander Jannaeus's conquests.

The influence on Lower Galilee was more from the Greek side, mainly from the Decapolis and coastal cities. Yet in the eastern region both the areas of Upper and Lower Galilee were thoroughly Judaized and remained so well into the Roman period. Thus, there was not a major divide between Upper and Lower Galilee with regard to lifestyle and material culture. Alexander Jannaeus took over sections of the coast from Mt Carmel to as far south as Gaza, but also Galilee and the Golan (the cities of Akko-Ptolemais, Straton's Tower, Dor, Gaza, Gadara and Gerasa; also Samaria), as indicated by the sudden appearance of his coins in these areas; however, he did not conquer the whole region: Ashkelon and Akko/Ptolemais retained their independence, and Tel Anafa remained under Tyrian control (Applebaum 1989: 21 n. 51; Berlin 1997: 37, 40). The Hasmonaean conquest did not extend north of the Hula valley.

In northern Samaria the population dropped considerably during the Hellenistic period (*NEAEHL* 4:1312). The same seems to have happened in western Samaria, with a decline in the number of sites in the early part of the Hellenistic period. But then about the beginning of the 2nd century BCE a significant expansion in agricultural settlement took place. Exactly the opposite is found for southern Samaria, where a sharp decline in the Persian period is then countered by a return to prosperity in the Hellenistic (*NEAEHL* 4:1314).

Under Hasmonaean rule encouragement of agriculture continued, though there seems to have been an attempt to 'Judaize' the population. A number of farms and agricultural villages have been identified (though not necessarily excavated). One site excavated was Khirbet el-Ḥammam, a fortified town that existed from the Iron II period, but was rebuilt and refortified in the later Hellenistic period (*NEAEHL* 2:563–65). It has been identified with Arubboth and Narbata. Few of the Roman-type *villa rustica* have survived, probably because the social and economic conditions did not encourage the Roman villa culture here (Dar 1986: 249).

There may have been some military settlers, suggested by some large fortified towers. Forts were established in a number of key points during the Hellenistic period.

The mountains of Samaria were relatively densely populated. Even though most families lived on small holdings, grain production was sufficient to feed the farming family, with a small surplus; however, the main exports from the region were wine and oil. A network of rural roads criss-crossed the region from an early time and was in use during the Hellenistic period (it was later integrated into the Roman road system). Settlements in the northern central hills from the early Hellenistic period seem to be confined to Samaria and Shechem (including Gerizim) (Berlin 1997: 11). A feature of western Samaria is the small stone field towers, of which about 1,200 have been catalogued (Dar 1986: 88–125). They seem to have had a function primarily in wine production, which was the main product of this region. They served as temporary dwellings and also places of storage. It has been suggested that they are a mark of the 'king's land' which has been identified with this region and portions of the Galilee (Applebaum 1986; Berlin 1997: 12–14). Whatever the merits of the 'king's land' arguments, these towers seem to be confined to a specific area of the northern hill country (for further on 'king's land', see §5.1).

For the purposes of describing the archaeology, Judah can be divided into four regions: (1) Benjamin District, between the Soreq Valley and Bethel, as far east as Jericho; (2) Jerusalem District and Beth-Hakkerem District, south of the Soreq Valley and including the Raphaim Valley, Bethlehem and Tekoa; (3) Beth-Zur District, the central Judaean Hills between Bethlehem and Hebron, including the western shore of the Dead Sea; (4) Qe'ila District, the northern Shephelah from the Ayalon Valley to the Elah Valley (Shalom et al. forthcoming). Settlement increased considerably over the whole of Judah during the Hellenistic period: the sites nearly doubled from 192 documented sites in the Persian period to 383. This increase continued until about 100 CE. The number of sites fell slightly, but the settled area total increased considerably. For the Judaean hills the main centres were Hebron, Ziph and Adoraim (Dura) (*NEAEHL* 3:816). The literary sources for the Hasmonaean conquests seem to reflect the archaeology which indicates a number of rapid phases of military activity that radiate out from Judaea in the mid- to late 2nd century BCE (Zilberstein forthcoming). For example, the plain of Sharon near Lod and Pegai was conquered, with a dense network of Jewish villages settled in the area (by Simon?).

70   *A History of Jews and Judaism in the Second Temple Period, Volume 3*

The lowland area of the Shephelah was mainly rural settlements, with the major economic activity the production of olive and wine. There seems to be a clear division between the northern (mostly rural) area, and the southern, which included the city of Maresha (Sandhaus forthcoming). The former was more conservative and ethnocentric, while the latter was much more open to cultural influences and trade from across the Mediterranean, not just the cities but even the countryside.

Settlements in the Idumaean region also appear to have a border defence function, at least in some cases. Some new settlements that also functioned as road stations were established on the northern border of the Negev (Berlin 1997: 6). But more explicit defences were organized across the southern border of the region (Berlin 1997: 7–8; Kuhnen 1990: 43–47). Maresha was at one end of a line that stretched to the Dead Sea, with other sites including Beth-Zur and Arad. Although John Hyrcanus destroyed Maresha about 110 BCE (*Ant.* 13.9.1 §257), most Idumaean sites continued to be inhabited without a break (e.g., Tel 'Ira, Tel Ḥalif); indeed, new settlements were established, such as Ḥorvat Rimmon (Berlin 1997: 31). Maresha itself was evidently rebuilt, since its final destruction came only about three-quarters of a century later, by the Parthians (*Ant.* 14.13.9 §364). The Phoenician presence continued in the form of Sidonian settlements such as we find at Maresha (also in Iamnia [Isaac 1991]).

The Golan does not seem to have been settled until the 2nd century BCE (with some small exceptions), but then it grew rapidly, with a hundred settled sites by the 1st century CE. The earlier settlers were the Ituraeans, judging not only from literary sources but also material culture. An important artefact was the so-called 'Golan ware'. Of 67 Ituraean sites identified, 33 were dated to the Hellenistic period (and 38 to the early Roman: *NEAEHL* 2:535). Two sites have had a considerable influence on the interpretation of the archaeology, because they have been excavated: Gamala and Ḥorvat Kanaf. Ḥorvat Kanaf has helped to establish the stratigraphic sequence for the region (*NEAEHL* 3:847–50). Scythopolis was the last or next to the last (Josephus's chronology is muddled) territorial conquest of John Hyrcanus (*War* 1.2.7 §66; *Ant.* 13.10.3 §280).

The Transjordanian region is now much better known for the archaeology than even two or three decades ago, with extensive excavation and survey work (see the summary in Ji 2001; Ji and Lee 2004). This has included a good deal of work in the Hellenistic period. Earlier reports had tended to see a gap in the early Hellenistic period (Ji 2001: 379; Ji and Lee 2004: 177), but now sufficient information on the early Hellenistic has become available to call this interpretation into question (Ji 2001: 379 and *passim*). The eastern and southern part of Transjordan in the Hellenistic period was under Nabataean control, as indicated by their coins. South of the Golan the main Jewish area was Peraea, extending down the eastern side of the Jordan Valley and south along the northeastern shore of the Dead Sea.

'Judaization' of Peraea had begun under John Hyrcanus and Alexander Jannaeus. A major site in the Transjordan was 'Iraq al-Amir. Apart from it the archaeology of the Transjordan in the Hellenistic period was dominated by the Greek cities of the Decapolis (including Philadelphia-Amman, Pella, Gerasa-Jarash, Gadara). Rabbat-Ammon had a long history but was made into the Greek foundation of Philadelphia by Ptolemy II. Excavations of it and Gerasa-Jerash have taken place; however, the archaeological remains of the other cities are skimpy. Settlement as a whole seems to have been scattered, with subsistence agriculture being the main means of surviving. Various Hasmonaean excursions were directed at Transjordan, such as the attacks by John Hyrcanus against Madeba, Samega et al. (*Ant.* 13.9.1 §§254-58); however, there is no archaeological evidence to confirm these (Berlin 1997: 31). On the other hand, it has been argued these may have been sites near Samaria (with perhaps names corrupted in the manuscript tradition.

2.1.2.3. *Topics*

The progress of Hasmonaean expansion (especially under Hyrcanus I and Jannaeus) is well represented in the archaeology. This policy of taking over Gentile areas and opening them to Jewish settlers is sometimes referred to as 'colonization' (Applebaum 1989a: 44). The evidence for this are the many new Hellenistic sites in Judaea and Samaria. Some seem to combine agricultural villages with strategic outposts, such as the Samarian sites of 'Azoun and Qarawat bene Hassan (Dar 1986; Berlin 1997: 28). The negative side seems to be the driving out of non-Jews, at least in some cases. Possible examples include the destruction of the military farm at Tirat Yehuda and the agricultural village at Tel Dothan (Berlin 1997: 28).

Architectural projects are characteristic of Hasmonaean rule (Berlin 1997: 40–42), though many of these seem concerned foremost with defence. Some of this happened under Simon and Hyrcanus, at least in Jerusalem, but the main instigator seems to have been Alexander Jannaeus. He was responsible for the fortress line along the eastern border of the hill country, which included the older forts of Dok and Hyrcania (and perhaps Masada) and the new builds of Alexandrium and Machaerus. The masonry dressing is the same as the Hasmonaean walls in Jerusalem. Jericho was an important focus for building, especially palaces and recreational areas,

72   *A History of Jews and Judaism in the Second Temple Period, Volume 3*

but also always with defence in mind. The building there continued under Alexandra Salome, with new buildings, pools, and gardens.

Evidence of this expansion of Jewish settlement is clearly evident in the Galilee. Yet this did not happen everywhere that the literary sources allege. One area where the native peoples were said to have been compelled to convert, to avoid expulsion, was that of Ituraea (for a discussion of this region, see §9.3). According to Josephus (*Ant.* 13.11.3 §318) the Ituraeans, like the Idumaeans, were forced to accept circumcision and to follow Jewish laws. Yet the archaeology of the Ituraean area shows no evidence of military attack, conquest or Jewish religious practice. The archaeology does not support the assertions of the text.

With regard to Jewish burials, from about 100 BCE Jews began to differ from Phoenicians, with whom they had shared a common tradition for family or clan burials in discreet tombs. By the late 2nd century BCE and into the 1st CE, many publicly visible tombs with ostentatious exteriors were built (Hachlili 2005; Berlin 2002; Rahmani 1981a, 1981b, 1982a, 1982b). This was in keeping with the general Hellenistic practice. A good example are the tombs of the Hasmonaeans, beginning with elaborate monuments allegedly raised up by Simon for his parents and brothers (1 Macc. 13.27-29), though it must be said that no archaeological evidence for these has been found. Another is 'Jason's tomb' in the Kidron valley (Rahmani 1967; Berlin 1997: 32–33).

Another issue relating to death and burial is the employment of ossuaries, or bone boxes used for secondary burial (i.e., to collect the bones of the dead after the flesh had decayed). They are first attested about the end of the Hasmonaean period or the beginning of the Herodian (Magen 2002: 135–36). They are not found in Samaria or non-Jewish areas, and they ceased to be used about the time of the Bar-Kokhva revolt. The suggestion is that the use of ossuaries related to belief in the resurrection of the dead. However, the bones of the dead were often collected in tombs after the flesh had decayed to make room for further burials, a practice that goes back long before the Second Temple period.

The appearance and disappearance of chalk vessels (Magen 2002), which seem to be related to matters of purity, coincides largely with that of ossuaries. Most vessels for food or drink were subject to impurity and could not be reused once they had become polluted. Stone vessels did not acquire impurity, however, and it became a widespread custom to use chalk for cups, bowls, basins and jars to avoid impurity. They are widely found in this period in Jewish areas but not in non-Jewish settlements. These chalk vessels seem to appear toward the end of the 1st century BCE and mainly ceased after the destruction of Jerusalem in 70 CE, though a few are associated with the Jewish refugees at the time of the Bar-Kokhva revolt (Magen 2002: 162). Their use suggests a connection with the temple, since questions of purity and impurity mainly related to the temple. However, the suggestion that the chalk vessels and ossuaries originated with Pharisees is without foundation. There is no evidence for such a connection. If the ossuaries relate to belief in the resurrection, as has been speculated, it must be remembered that many Jews other than the Pharisees believed in resurrection.

One of the features of Jewish culture under Hasmonaean rule is its plainness – its lack of luxury, ornamentation and ostentation. Even the Hasmonaean palaces, while having an outward show that would have been well appreciated in the upper-class Hellenistic world, were plain and functional in the living areas (cf. Regev 2013: Chapter 6, especially 263–65). As Berlin (1997: 39) puts it:

> Now [in the reign of Jannaeus], however, the balance shifted, with those who defined themselves by religious affiliation controlling more territory, more resources, and more power, than those whose lives were oriented towards commerce and material comforts. The archaeological record of early first century BCE Palestine revealed fundamental changes. With a few exceptions (e.g., Ashkelon), the Mediterranean-facing culture of the Graeco-Phoenician coastal plain and Idumaea diminished or disappeared. Jewish settlements established in previously Gentile areas largely contained household products made only in Judea and other Jewish areas (e.g., Lower Galilee). Imports and luxury items were rare or absent, a phenomenon most obviously reflected by the dearth of Aegean wine amphoras and ESA [Eastern Sigillata A ware]. Architecture was plain; industry was confined to the production of wine and oil for local use.

For example, Eastern Sigillata A ware, certainly a luxury item, is found widely in the Phoenician dominated areas and also in Idumaea and in the Galilee, Golan heights and northern Transjordan. Yet in the century preceding Pompey's conquest of Judah, this ware is not to be found in Judaea or Samaria. This indicates a deliberate boycotting of such goods; a reasonable guess for this gap in the material culture is that the populations of these central regions adhered to their local produce and pots for religious reasons. The curious situation was that as the Jewish settlement expanded into other areas of the region, such as the coastal plain and Idumaea, they seem to have exported their outlook on the material culture: rather than the expected diversity, 'the long entrenched economic isolation of the central hills came to characterize the formerly cosmopolitan regions brought into its realm' (Berlin 1997: 36).

74   *A History of Jews and Judaism in the Second Temple Period, Volume 3*

By the end of Hasmonaean rule, the area controlled included Palestine, Gaulanitis and much of Transjordan (Berlin 1997: 42–43). Much of the settlement was concentrated in Judaea and Samaria (especially the hill country), the lower Galilee and the Golan. The regions on the perimeter, however, had been largely depopulated, with many sites abandoned (Tel Anafa, many homesteads in the Ptolemais region, Straton's Tower, Ashdod, Gezer, Maresha). From an archaeological perspective, the Hellenistic period had come to an end with the struggles between Hyrcanus II and Aristobulus II. As Berlin (1997: 42) notes:

> The material remains of this core area [Judaea, Samaria, lower Galilee, Golan] included mainly locally produced, utilitarian goods, with few imports and little influence from Phoenician or Mediterranean cultures. Palestine was now in effect Hasmonean: religiously defined, inwardly focused, with a population settled largely in farmsteads and small villages, and organized around the single city of Jerusalem.

Pompey's invasion changed that, decentralizing the settlement pattern (with many of the old Greek cities given their independence – under Roman control, of course! – some of them being rebuilt after having been abandoned for a time) and reverting to a situation much like in the Persian and early Hellenistic periods.

2.2. *Inscriptions*

W. Ameling (ed.) (2004) *Inscriptiones Judaicae Orientis, Volume II: Kleinasien*; **W. Ameling et al. (eds)** (2014) *Corpus Inscriptionum Iudaeae/ Palaestinae, Volume III: South Coast: 2161–2648*; **idem** (2018a) *Corpus Inscriptionum Iudaeae/Palaestinae, Volume IV: Iudaea/Idumaea, Part 1: 2649–3324*; **idem** (2018b) *Corpus Inscriptionum Iudaeae/Palaestinae, Volume IV: Iudaea/Idumaea, Part 2: 3325–3978*; **Austin**; **Bagnall and Derow**; **K. Brodersen, W. Günther and H. H. Schmitt (eds)** (1997) *Historische griechische Inschriften in Übersetzung: Band II, Spätklassik und früher Hellenismus (400–250 v. Chr.)*; **idem** (1999) *Historische griechische Inschriften in Übersetzung, Band III: Der griechische Osten und Rom (250–1 v. Chr.)*; **Burstein**; **H. Cotton et al. (eds)** (2011) *Corpus Inscriptionum Iudaeae/Palaestinae, Volume I: Jerusalem, Part 1: 1–704*; **idem** (2012) *Corpus Inscriptionum Iudaeae/Palaestinae, Volume I: Jerusalem, Part 2: 705–1120*; **CPJ**; **W. Horbury and D. Noy (eds)** (1992) *Jewish Inscriptions of Graeco-Roman Egypt. With an Index of the Jewish Inscriptions of Egypt and Cyrenaica*; **B. Isaac** (1983) 'A Donation for Herod's Temple in Jerusalem', *IEJ* 33: 86–92; **D. Noy (ed.)** (1993) *Jewish Inscriptions of Western Europe, Volume 1: Italy (excluding the City of Rome), Spain* *and Gaul*; **idem** (1995) *Jewish Inscriptions of Western Europe, Volume 2: The City of Rome*; **D. Noy and H. Bloedhorn (eds)** (2004) *Inscriptiones Judaicae Orientis, Volume III: Syria and Cyprus*; **D. Noy, A. Panayotov and H. Bloedhorn (eds)** (2004) *Inscriptiones Judaicae Orientis, Volume I Eastern Europe*; SHERK; **J. F. Strange** (1975) 'Late Hellenistic and Herodian Ossuary Tombs at French Hill', Jerusalem', *BASOR* 219: 39–67.

Although they are not so important in the present volume, see *HJJSTP 2*: 54–55 for a list of some of the main Egyptian papyri collections relevant for the background and some of the events of our period. The three volumes of *CPJ* cover the late Hellenistic period, as well as the early. For many of the Greek and Roman inscriptions useful for the last two centuries BCE, see AUSTIN, BAGNALL AND DEROW, BURSTEIN, and SHERK; also *Historische griechische Inschriften in Übersetzung*. A number of collections of Jewish inscriptions have appeared in recent years, several of them still in progress: *Corpus Inscriptionum Iudaeae/ Palaestinae, Inscriptiones Judaicae Orientis*, and *Jewish Inscriptions* edited by Horbury and Noy.

2.3. *Coins and Seals*

D. T. Ariel (2018) 'Coins from the Renewed Excavations at Qumran', in Y. Magen and Y. Peleg (eds), *Back to Qumran: Final Report (1993–2004)*, 403–29; **D. T. Ariel and J.-P. Fontanille** (2012) *The Coins of Herod: A Modern Analysis and Die Classification*; **D. T. Ariel and J. Naveh** (2003) 'Selected Inscribed Sealings from Kedesh in the Upper Galilee', *BASOR* 329: 61–80; **N. Avigad** (1975) 'A Bulla of Jonathan the High Priest', *IEJ* 25: 8–12; **N. Davis and C. M. Kraay** (1973) *The Hellenistic Kingdoms: Portrait Coins and History*; **K. Ehling** (2008) *Untersuchungen zur Geschichte der späten Seleukiden (164–63 v. Chr.): Vom Tode des Antiochos IV. bis zur Einrichtung der Provinz Syria unter Pompeius*; **T. Fischer** (1975) 'Johannes Hyrkan I. auf Tetradrachmen Antiochos' VII.?' *ZDPV* 91: 191–96; **G. Finkielsztejn** (1998) 'More Evidence on John Hyrcanus I's Conquests: Lead Weights and Rhodian Amphora Stamps', *Bulletin of the Anglo-Israel Archaeological Society* 16: 33–63; **idem** (2007) 'Poids de plomb inscrits du Levant: une réforme d'Antiochos IV?' *Topoi* Supplement 8: 35–60; **R. S. Hanson** (1974) 'Toward a Chronology of the Hasmonean Coins', *BASOR* 216: 21–23; **D. Hendin** (2010) *Guide to Biblical Coins*; **idem** (2013) 'Current Viewpoints on Ancient Jewish Coinage: A Bibliographic Essay', *CBR* 11: 256–301; **A. Houghton, C. Lorber and O. Hoover (eds)** (2008) *Seleucid Coins: A Comprehensive Catalogue, Part II: Seleucus IV through Antiochus XIII, Volumes I and II*; **D. Jeselsohn** (1974) 'A New Coin Type with Hebrew Inscription', *IEJ* 24: 77–78; **idem** (1980) 'Hever Yehudim –

A New Jewish Coin', *PEQ* 112: 11–17; **A. Kindler** (1954) 'The Jaffa Hoard of Alexander Jannaeus', *IEJ* 4: 170–85; **idem** (1968) 'Addendum to the Dated Coins of Alexander Janneus', *IEJ* 18: 188–91; **A. J. M Kropp** (2013) *Images and Monuments of Near Eastern Dynasts, 100 BC–AD 100*; **Y. Meshorer** (1982) *Ancient Jewish Coinage, Volume I: Persian Period through Hasmonaeans; Volume II: Herod the Great through Bar Kokhba*; **idem** (1986) 'Jewish Numismatics', in R. A. Kraft and G. W. E. Nickelsburg (eds), *Early Judaism and its Modern Interpreters*, 211–20; **idem** (1990–91) 'Ancient Jewish Coinage: Addendum I', *INJ* 11: 104–32; **idem** (2001) *A Treasury of Jewish Coins*; **J. Naveh** (1968) 'Dated Coins of Alexander Janneus', *IEJ* 18: 20–25; **U. Rappaport** (1970) 'Gaza and Ascalon in the Persian and Hellenistic Periods in Relation to their Coins', *IEJ* 20 (1970) 75–80; **idem** (1976) 'The Emergence of Hasmonean Coinage', *AJS Review* 1: 171–86; **R. Reich and E. Shukron** (2007) 'The Yehud Stamp Impressions from the 1995–2005 City of David Excavations', *TA* 34: 59–65; **O. R. Sellers** (1962) 'Coins of the 1960 Excavation at Shechem', *BA* 25: 87–95; **A. Spaer** (1977) 'Some More "Yehud" Coins', *IEJ* 27: 200–203; **D. Sperber** (1965) 'A Note on Hasmonean Coin-Legends: Heber and Rosh Heber', *PEQ* 97: 85–93; **D. Syon** (2006) 'Numismatic Evidence of Jewish Presence in Galilee before the Hasmonean Annexation', *INR* 1: 21–24: **Y. Zlotnik** (2010) 'Mattathias Antigonus Coins – The Last Kings of the Hasmonean'; **idem** (2011a) 'Alexander Jannaeus' Coins and their Dates'; **idem** (2011b) 'The Beginning of Hasmonean Coinage', *The Celator* 25, no. 3: 20–28; **idem** (2012) 'Minting of Coins in Jerusalem during the Persian and Hellenistic Periods'.

Important catalogues of Jewish coins are given by Y. Meshorer (1982, 2001), D. Hendin (2010, 2013), and D. T. Ariel and J.-P. Fontanille (2012). There are also many individual studies (e.g., Zlotkin 2010, 2011a, 2011b, 2012). Also important for this study is the Seleucid coinage. The standard collection is Houghton, Lorber and Hoover ([eds] 2008), though it is not always easy to get access to. Many of the relevant Seleucid coins, however, are treated by Ehling (2008). Coins will be referred to here and there in the chapters of this book. Only a few miscellaneous points will be discussed here.

According to 1 Macc. 15.6 Simon was given the right to mint his own coins; however, the actual finds have the names of Johanan, Judah, Jonathan and Mattathias in paleo-Hebrew script, with no archaeological evidence for coins minted under Simon. The problem of identifying the extant coins is that more than one ruler may have borne some of these names: Johanan was the name of Hyrcanus I but also possibly of Hyrcanus II; and Judah of Aristobulus I but possibly also of Aristobulus II. It was once argued that the minting of coins only began with Alexander

2. *Archaeology, Including Coins and Inscriptions* 77

Jannaeus, and all the Johanan and Judah coins were those of Hyrcanus II and Aristobulus II (Hendin 2013: 18–19). Now, however, it is generally agreed that John Hyrcanus minted the first coins, and it can even be questioned whether Hyrcanus II and Aristobulus II ever minted coins (Hendin 2010: 204).

One puzzle about the 'Jonathan' and 'Johanan' coins is the phrase 'congregation/council of the Jews' (חבר יהודים *hbr yhwdym*). This sometimes appears as 'so-and-so, high priest and *hever* of the Jews'. Sperber (1965) has argued that it refers to John Hyrcanus's taking over a title because of the opposition of the Pharisees; however, he accepts the reports in the much later rabbinic literature as reliable for this early period. Jeselsohn (1980) has drawn attention to the new find of a coin with the legend '*hever* of the Jews' alone, with no ruler's name. He also ties this in with the Pharisaic opposition to the Hasmonaeans, this time to the reign of Alexander Jannaeus, and thinks that these coins were issued by the opposition to Jannaeus. Again, one of the major questions is whether the opposition to Jannaeus was led by Pharisees: from all we see the Pharisees were only one element within this opposition (§16.5). Yet one could accept his suggestion that the *hever* was an institution abolished by Jannaeus without having to tie this in with the Pharisees. Some coins have 'Johanan head of the *hever* of the Jews' (יחנן ראש חבר יהודים *yhnn rʾs hbr yhwdym*). According to Meshorer (1982: 1:66–67), Hyrcanus II adopted this title when he was designated 'ethnarch of the Jews' under Julius Caesar.

For a detailed study of Herodian coinage, see especially D. T. Ariel and J.-P. Fontanille (2012; also Hendin 2010, 2013; Meshorer 2001; 1982: 2:5–34). Bronze coins were issued throughout Herod the Great's reign, though only one series was dated, that with 'year 3' on it. These differ from the undated coins in having various symbols taken from Roman coins. Meshorer has now argued that 'year 3' does not refer to the 3rd year of Herod's kingship but rather to the 3rd year counting from when he became tetrarch in 42 BCE, thus dating the coins to 40 BCE when he still had not ousted Antigonus from Jerusalem. In Meshorer's view, the good quality of the coins and the Roman symbols were meant as a propaganda device against Antigonus who was also issuing his own coins; that is, they served as ideological weapons in the struggle of the two individuals for the control of the Judaean people. Once Herod was in control, he no longer used the Roman symbols and left the coins undated; the quality of the coins also deteriorated.

A further question is why Herod did not issue silver coins. Some have used the absence of these as evidence of his subservience to Rome; however, other client kingdoms of rather lesser standing in Roman eyes (e.g., the Nabataeans) issued silver coinage, so why not Herod? Meshorer argues that he did indeed coin in silver but that these were the Tyrian shekels. The Tyrian-style coins were minted in silver of a very pure type. With the introduction of Roman coins of a lesser quality, these ceased to be issued by Tyre. Yet we find that Tyrian coins continue to be issued to the year 66 CE, though from 18 BCE they show certain differences from the previous minting, including an inferior style. Meshorer has proposed the following explanation: the Tyrian shekels were the official coinage used in the Jerusalem temple. When Tyre ceased to mint them, Herod obtained permission to continue issuing them internally to meet the needs of the temple. Thus, Herod took over the Tyrian model (with some slight modifications) beginning in 18 BCE, and his successors continued to issue them until the war with Rome broke out in 66 CE. Herod's coins, even the early issue with Roman symbols, have no human representations on them. The inscriptions are in Greek only, with the simple designation '(belonging to) Herod the king' (ηρωδου βασιλεως, ηρωδης βασιλευς).

Chapter 3

JEWISH LITERATURE

Several writings and writers important for this period have already been surveyed in earlier volumes. In such cases, reference is made back to the earlier treatment, though points relevant for the last centuries BCE will be discussed. This includes Josephus and *1 Enoch*. Note that the 'documents' in 1 and 2 Maccabees are included here, although as often letters from Seleucid or other non-Jewish officials, they could have been included in the chapter on Greek and Latin Literature (Chapter 4).

3.1. *1 and 2 Maccabees*

AIEJL 554–60; **F.-M. Abel** (1949) *Les libres des Maccabées*; **B. Bar-Kochva** (1989) *Judas Maccabaeus: The Jewish Struggle Against the Seleucids*, 151–85; **J. R. Bartlett** (1973) *The First and Second Books of the Maccabees*; **T. A. Bergren** (1997) 'Nehemiah in 2 Maccabees 1.10–2.18', *JSJ* 28: 249–70; **J. C. Bernhardt** (2017) *Die jüdische Revolution*, 41–57; **E. J. Bickerman** (Bikermann) (1930) 'Makkabäerbucher', *PW* 14:779–800; **idem** (1937) *Der Gott der Makkabäer*; **idem** (1979) *The God of the Maccabees*; **F. Borchardt** (2014) *The Torah in 1 Maccabees: A Literary Critical Approach to the Text*; **J. C. Dancy** (1954) *A Commentary on First Maccabees*; **R. Doran** (1981) *Temple Propaganda: The Purpose and Character of 2 Maccabees*; **idem** (2012) *2 Maccabees: A Critical Commentary*; **J. A. Goldstein** (1976) *I Maccabees*; **idem** (1983a) *II Maccabees*; **C. Habicht** (1976a) *II. Makkabäerbuch*; **J. W. van Henten** (1997) *The Maccabean Martyrs as Saviours of the Jewish People: A Study of 2 and 4 Maccabees*; **S. Honigman** (2014) *Tales of High Priests and Taxes: The Books of the Maccabees and the Judean Rebellion against Antiochos IV*; *JLBM* 102–10; *JWSTP* 171–83; **A. Momigliano** (1975) 'The Second Book of Maccabees', *Classical Philology* 70: 81–88; **G. O. Neuhaus** (1974) 'Quellen im 1. Makkabäerbuch? Eine Entgegung auf die Analyse von K.-D. Schunck', *JSJ* 5: 162–75; **K.-D. Schunck** (1954) *Die Quellen des 1 and II Makkabäerbuches*; **idem** (1980) *Jüdische Schriften aus hellenistisch-römischer*

80   *A History of Jews and Judaism in the Second Temple Period, Volume 3*

Zeit: Band I Historische und legendarische Erzählungen: Lieferung 4 I. Makkabäerbuch; **SCHÜRER** 3:180–85, 531–7; **D. R. Schwartz** (2008) *2 Maccabees*; **S. Schwartz** (1991) 'Israel and the Nations Roundabout: 1 Maccabees and the Hasmonean Expansion', *JJS* 42: 16–38; **S. Tedesche and S. Zeitlin** (1950) *The First Book of Maccabees*; **M. Tilly** (2015) *1 Makkabäer*; **D. S. Williams** (1999) *The Structure of 1 Maccabees*.

The two books of Maccabees are our main sources for what happened to Judaea under Antiochus IV and the next quarter of a century or so until the founding of the Hasmonaean state. Without them we would know extremely little. They are thus important sources for this study. Most of the secondary literature to the time of publication, including information on critical editions of the Greek text, are found in Goldstein's commentaries (1976, 1983a); however, since he does not attempt to represent all points of view, other commentaries still need to be consulted for older interpretations which differ from his. Especially well done of the older commentaries is Abel. Two recent commentaries on 2 Maccabees are by Schwartz (2008) and Doran (2012); cf. also van Henten 1997 (17–57). Unfortunately, 1 Maccabees has not been as well served, but see the recent commentary by Tilly (2015).

1 Maccabees was most likely written by an anonymous author some time during John Hyrcanus's reign (135–104 BCE), probably before 125 BCE (Bar-Kochva 1989: 162–64). Although the original was presumably in Hebrew, only the Greek version is extant. It is the most extensive source for the events in Judaea for the 40 years from about 175 to 135 BCE. Of the sources for the Maccabaean revolt, it has often been judged also the most trustworthy. This is mainly because of its matter-of-fact narrative, without any overt elements of miracle or supernatural intervention. More recently, however, scholars have recognized the underlying *Tendenz* of the writing and consider the appearance of straightforwardness as one of the arts of the narrator. It is now generally accepted that 1 Maccabees was to some extent the official version of the Hasmonaean dynasty and thus a one-sided account from the Maccabaean point of view.

The precise sources of the author are not clear. Schunck (1954) gave a detailed source analysis, but this has been criticized by Neuhaus (1974), who reflects the current move away from confident identification of multiple sources. On the other hand, several recent attempts at source analysis have been made (Williams 1999; Borchardt 2014). No doubt Neuhaus is correct in dismissing the idea that one can find a different source for practically every episode within the book, but some source proposals may be more widely accepted than others. For example, the use of a Seleucid chronicle of some sort has long been accepted in scholarship, suggested for example by the presence of date formulae at various points which differ from those normally found in Jewish sources (Schunck 1954; Bickerman 1937: 17–21, 155–58//1979: 9–12, 101–3). Bar-Kochva has argued that the author was an eyewitness to a number of the battles described and was able to obtain reports from participants in others (1989: 158–62, but see the objections of S. Schwartz [1991: 37 n. 64]).

According to the preface to the book itself (2 Macc. 2.19-32), 2 Maccabees is an epitome of a much larger work by Jason of Cyrene, a writer otherwise unknown. The account is parallel in part to 1 Maccabees; on the other hand, it covers a much briefer period of time (ca. 175–161 BCE), is more detailed about the events preceding the suppression of the Jewish religion, and often gives a different perspective on various issues. Because of the explicit appeal to the supernatural at various points in the account, scholars in the past often considered 2 Maccabees much inferior to 1 Maccabees. Recent scholarship sees a much more nuanced picture. 2 Maccabees is more overtly theological in its aim, and its chronology is often confused and less trustworthy than 1 Maccabees. The long descriptions of martyrdom in chap. 7 is suspect in certain details (though some religious executions apparently did occur). On the other hand, the information about the events during the 'Hellenistic reform' are much more detailed than in 1 Maccabees, and there are other data at various points not found elsewhere.

S. Honigman (2014: 65–94) gives an interpretation that differs from many other commentators. She first of all argues that the author was not a diaspora figure but an inhabitant of Jerusalem itself. She also argues that the aim of 2 Maccabees is to support the Hasmonaean dynasty, i.e., functions as a 'Dynastic History', thus not differing in basic purpose from that of 1 Maccabees. This proposal for the main intent of the work is important for her interpretation of 2 Maccabees. Some have countered, however, that while Judas is treated heroically, Simon has a rather negative presentation; therefore, the book could not be a defence of the Hasmonaean family as a whole. Yet although the presentation of Simon is not as adulatory as that of Judas, by any means, he is generally shown in a positive light. It seems plausible that 2 Maccabees was supportive of the Hasmonaean leaders who followed Judas.

As with 1 Maccabees, the sources used (other than the documents explicitly quoted) are not clear. A number of scholars (most recently Goldstein [1976: 90–103; 1983a: 37–41]) have suggested that a common source underlies both 1 and 2 Maccabees. However, the disagreements seem to be rather striking and many of the agreements can be explained

82   *A History of Jews and Judaism in the Second Temple Period, Volume 3*

as due to knowledge of the actual events rather than a common source. Thus, the theory of a *Grundschrift* for both books seems to require a good deal more argument to be accepted as cogent. Some of the main points about using the books as historical sources can be summarized as follows:

- The two books are parallel to a certain extent, though the amount of material each devotes to particular events varies considerably. 2 Maccabees is much fuller on the events preceding the Sixth Syrian War (beginning 170 BCE), but it breaks off with the victory over Nicanor and thus avoids recounting Judas's death which took place shortly afterward. Both record various military engagements of the Maccabees and their followers but often with different details. The chronology of 2 Maccabees is generally not as reliable as that of 1 Maccabees.
- Both works represent a pro-Hasmonaean bias, exaggerating the achievements of the Maccabees, ignoring the other elements of the anti-Seleucid resistance and vilifying the 'Hellenists' who are all lumped together without distinction between them.
- Both works centre on a dispute within the priesthood over religious leadership of the nation; because religious leadership also entailed political leadership at this time, victory in one also led to victory in the other. It is not quite this neat, of course, because the Maccabees did not originally take action to pursue either of these goals, at least as mentioned by the sources, but religious and political leadership was always at stake in the revolt against the Seleucids.
- Both books make the temple and its service the centre of Jewish religion and give no hint of any shift away from this. No indication is given of the existence of synagogues and the like. However, mention is made of scrolls of the law (1 Macc. 1.56-57), and some sort of collection of official writings (ascribed to Nehemiah) is assumed (2 Macc. 2.13-15).
- Both books attest directly and indirectly the extent to which Jews within Palestine were a broader part of the Hellenistic world. Neither book speaks of a resistance to cultural Hellenization; indeed, both books circulated widely in Greek and also present the Hasmonaeans as fully at home in the Hellenistic world.
- A somewhat enigmatic group called the *Hasidim* (Greek *Asidaioi*) is mentioned in both books. Whether they are as important as some have alleged is a moot point, but they are likely to continue to be discussed (see further §6.1).

3. Jewish Literature

- A feature of both books, but especially of 2 Maccabees, is that of martyrdom. This seems to be a new concept in Jewish theological thinking (§12.3.6).
- The letters in 2 Maccabees 1–2 have a complicated tradition history, though one or more authentic letters may lie at the base of this section (van Henten 1997: 37–50). This section attests to the new festival celebrating the purification of the temple (later called Hanukkah, though not here) and also promotes its celebration among Jewish communities outside Palestine. The Nehemiah story may have been a way of legitimating both the Second Temple cult and also Judah Maccabaeus (cf. Bergren 1997).

Of particular importance are a number of Jewish, Seleucid and Roman documents quoted at various points in the text. These are discussed in the next section (§3.2).

3.2. *Letters and Documents in 1 and 2 Maccabees*

B. Bar-Kochva (1989) *Judas Maccabaeus: The Jewish Struggle against the Seleucids*, 516–42; **E. J. Bickerman** (1980) 'Une question d'authenticité les privilèges Juifs', in *Studies in Jewish and Christian History*, 2:24–43; **K. Bringmann** (1983) *Hellenistische Reform und Religionsverfolgung in Judäa*; **R. Doran** (2012) *2 Maccabees: A Critical Commentary*; **L. Feldman** (1984) *Josephus and Modern Scholarship*; **T. Fischer** (1980) *Seleukiden und Makkabäer: Beiträge zur Seleukidengeschichte und zu den politischen Ereignissen in Judäa während der 1. Hälfte des 2. Jahrhundersts v. Chr.*; **J.-D. Gauger** (1977) *Beiträge zur jüdischen Apologetik*; **E. S. Gruen** (1984) *The Hellenistic World and the Coming of Rome*; **C. Habicht** (1976b) 'Royal Documents in Maccabees II', *Harvard Studies in Classical Philology* 80: 1–18; **A. Momigliano** (1975) 'The Second Book of Maccabees', *Classical Philology* 70: 81–88; **idem** (1982) Review of Gauger, *Beiträge zur jüdischen Apologetik*, *Classical Philology* 77: 258–61; **V. L. Parker** (2007) 'The Letters in II Maccabees: Reflexions on the Book's Composition', *ZAW* 119: 386–402; **D. R. Schwartz** (2008) *2 Maccabees*; **J. Sievers** (1990) *The Hasmoneans and their Supporters: From Mattathias to the Death of John Hyrcanus I*.

A number of documents, mostly in the form of letters, are quoted in 1 and 2 Maccabees. These are valuable original sources, if authentic, as is confirmed by the fact that they sometimes contradict the narrative in which they are embedded. The question of the authenticity of these has been the subject of much debate, however. Most of these are now widely

84   *A History of Jews and Judaism in the Second Temple Period, Volume 3*

accepted as genuine documents, though it must be recognized that in many cases they were translated from Greek into Hebrew and then back into Greek which may cause changes or potential misunderstandings. The main dispute has centred round the treaty with Rome under Judas and the letter from the Spartan king Areus. The letters are as follows:

1 Maccabees:

8.23-32:	treaty with Rome.
10.18-20:	from Alexander Balas to Jonathan.
10.25-45:	from Demetrius I to Jonathan.
11.30-37:	from Demetrius II to Jonathan.
11.57:	from Antiochus VI to Jonathan.
12.6-18:	from Jonathan to the Spartans.
12.20-23:	from king Areus of Sparta to the high priest Onias.
13.36-40:	from Demetrius II to Simon.
14.20-23:	from the Spartans to Simon.
15.2-9:	from Antiochus VI to Simon.
15.16-24:	circular letter from Roman consuls

2 Maccabees:

1.1-10a:	from Palestinian Jews to Egyptian Jews on the observance of Hanukkah.
1.10b–2.18:	from Judas to the Egyptian Jews.
9.19-29:	from Antiochus IV to the Jews.
11.16-21:	from Lysias to the Jews (#1).
11.22-26:	from Antiochus V to Lysias (#2).
11.27-33:	from Antiochus IV to the Jewish *gerousia* and 'the other Jews' (#3).
11.34-38:	from the Roman ambassadors to 'the Jewish people' (#4).

We can group the letters into three areas of inquiry, since the supposed letters in each case are our major basis for information on the events. The first two topics relate mainly to letters in 1 Maccabees, while the third is mostly based on letters in 2 Maccabees. The main groups are discussed below, though engagement with some of the individual documents is found in §15.4.2 below.

3.2.1. *Treaties with Rome*

These have been much debated, especially the one alleged for Judas. For discussion and secondary studies, see §15.4.5 (for Judas), §16.1.6 (Jonathan), §16.2.3 (Simon) and §16.3.4 (John Hyrcanus).

3.2.2. *Alleged Kinship with the Spartans*

This topic is discussed, with secondary literature, at §16.1.6.

3.2.3. *The Letters in 2 Maccabees 1–2*

T. A. Bergren (1997) 'Nehemiah in 2 Maccabees 1.10–2.18', *JSJ* 28: 249–70; **E. J. Bickerman** (1933) 'Ein jüdischer Festbrief vom Jahre 124 v. Chr. (II Macc 1₁₋₉)', *ZNW* 32: 233–54; **J. A. Goldstein** (1983a) *II Maccabees: A New Translation with Introduction and Commentary*, 154–88; **V. A. Tcherikover** (1959) *Hellenistic Civilization and the Jews*; **B. Z. Wacholder** (1978) 'The Letter from Judah Maccabee to Aristobulus: Is 2 Maccabees 1.10b–2.18 Authentic?' *HUCA* 49: 89–133.

Of the two letters prefacing 2 Maccabees, the first (1.1-10 [Eng. 1.1-9]) is generally taken to be genuine. More of a problem is the one allegedly from Judas (1 Macc. 1.10–2.18) since it seems to reflect the situation sometime after the retaking of the temple (Momigliano 1975: 84; Goldstein 1983a: 154–88; Sievers 1989: 6–7). Goldstein has also pointed out the chronological problems relating to hearing the news of Antiochus's death and sending the letter to Egypt. Although Wacholder has more recently argued for its authenticity, it seems most likely a forgery (Schwartz 2008: 144 suggests a core may go back to Judas), often thought to be an attack on the temple at Leontopolis (Bickerman 1933: 250; Parker 2007: 389 n. 7).

Schwartz (2008: 129–69, 519–29) argues convincingly that the two letters are integral to the book, the authors of both knowing the (more or less) completed book but the author of the first also editing the book to some extent to achieve agreement on the Hanukkah festival. For example, although the climax of 2 Maccabees comes with the defeat and death of Nicanor, 2 Macc. 10.1-8 was added in to shift the focus toward the rededication of the temple and its celebration in Hanukkah. The second letter uses a story about liquid fire to connect Judas's rededication not only to the fire in the time of Nehemiah but also to Jeremiah and even backward to the original fire from heaven at the time of Solomon. Schwartz also resolves the problem of the date in 2 Macc. 1.10 by following the variant reading 'year 148' (of the SE), so that the passage refers to the rededication of the temple in 165–164 BCE. The letter itself is dated to year 169 SE (2 Macc. 1.7) which seems to coincide more or less with the declaration of national independence under Simon in 143–142 BCE (§16.2.2).

3.2.4. *The Letters in 2 Maccabees 9 and 11*

The letter of Antiochus IV in 2 Macc. 9.19-27 has been accepted by a number of scholars because it does not prove what it is alleged to prove by the narrative in which it is set. Although it is introduced as a confession of sin by Antiochus, it in fact gives no such admission. Bickerman (1980: 35), for example, considers the title changed and perhaps the presence of interpolations (1930: 790) but otherwise accepts it. Nevertheless, Momigliano is bothered because 'the king puts his hope in heaven..., writes a prescript which is impossible for a king, and takes no account of the real situation in Judaea' (1975: 84). Therefore, he considers it modelled on an authentic document, perhaps a genuine letter to Antioch. Habicht (1976: 5–7) also argues that it is a forgery.

The letters in 2 Maccabees 11 are almost universally considered genuine (Habicht 1976: 12). However, Momigliano (1975: 84–85) has pointed out that the letter of Antiochus V to Lysias (#2, 11.22-26) is suspect because there is no reason for it to have been sent to the Jews. It could have come as a copy, but then it should have had a covering letter. Why was the covering letter not quoted? Also, why does 1 Macc. 6.57-59 show no knowledge of it, and why does it not seem to have affected subsequent events? There are plenty of those who defend it (cf. Bar Kochva 1989: 523), but it is probably the most questionable of those in 2 Maccabees 11.

One of the major problems with these letters concerns their dates and relationship to events, since they seem to have little to do with the context into which they have been inserted in 2 Maccabees 11. Although three of the letters are dated, letters #3 and #4 both have the same date. This suggests that a copyist has accidentally copied the date of one for the other as well, but which one is original is debated. A further complication is that the month named in letter #1 is otherwise unknown. Thus, the sequence of the letters is placed differently by different scholars (e.g., Habicht 1976: 3,1,4,2; Tcherikover 1959: 1,4,3,2; Fischer 1980: 3,4,2,1; Bringmann 1983: 1,3,4,2; Bar-Kochva 1989: 1,4,3,2; the order supported at §15.4.2 below is 3,1,4,2). Here is a brief analysis of each letter:

Letter #1 (11.16-21): The year 148 SE would put it in autumn of the year 165–164 BCE. The month 'Dios Corinthios' is not otherwise known; however, the month Dios is the first month of the Macedonian calendar (October–November). Since it is thought that Antiochus may have added some extensions to month names, several scholars accept that this is dated to the month Dios, or about October 165 BCE (Bringmann 1983: 44; Bar-Kochva 1989: 522–23). If so, it is most likely the earliest of the four letters. Those such as Habicht (1976) who put it later must assume a corruption beyond restoration in the name. There are also those who reconstruct it as Dystros, about February–March (Tcherikover 1959: 482 nn. 21, 22).

3. *Jewish Literature*   87

A second problem is that of the addressees: only the 'multitude' (*plēthos*) of the Jews. Thus, it seems to have gone to an unofficial group with whom Lysias wanted reconciliation. It has been argued that it was addressed to the 'Hellenizers' or to Jews not primarily supporters of Judas (Tcherikover 1959: 216–18). Several reasons have been given as to why this was Judas's group (Habicht 1976: 10; Bar-Kochva 1989: 521–22), for example, that it was unlikely that Menelaus and his followers would have wanted religious rights restored; however, none of their points make it Judas's group exclusively. They have especially not answered the arguments of Tcherikover (1959: 216–18) that it was Menelaus's group which initiated the decrees, to be addressed to the mass of the Jews who were not necessarily supporters of Judas, in order to weaken the hold of the Maccabaean leadership. (Because Menelaus could not be certain he would be listened to, he also enlisted the aid of a Roman delegation in the region.)

Letter #2 (11.22-26): Since this comes from Antiochus V, it must be after December 164, making it probably the latest of the four (assuming it is genuine, which most do).

Letter #3 (11.27-33): Sent from Antiochus IV, this letter gives 'until the 30th Xanthikos' as the deadline for Jews to benefit from a general amnesty, i.e., until sometime in March. This date within the body of the letter does not seem to be disputed. The letter itself is dated 15 Xanthikos 148 SE, or about the beginning of March 164 BCE. This date fits well with Antiochus's own life, since he died less than a year later in about December 164. The problem is that the date of the letter is the same as letter #4; further, if Antiochus wrote a letter on 15 Xanthikos from somewhere in the eastern provinces, it could hardly have reached Palestine and its intended recipients in time for them to do anything about the amnesty. A number of scholars think that the date '15 Xanthikos 148' has been accidentally copied from letter #4 (Bringmann 1983: 45–46). If so, the letter itself would probably have been issued toward the end of 165, or about the same time as the letter #1. Others see the reverse of the argument (Tcherikover1959: 215; Bar-Kochva 1989: 528–29), that is, that the date on letter #3 is correct but accidentally displaced that on #4. The problem with this is that it assumes the date was when the letter left Antioch, which does not address the problem of Antiochus's presence across the Euphrates.

Letter #4 (11.34-38). This comes from a Roman embassy which happened to be in the region. One problem is the date, which has just been discussed. The other is that the individuals named as making up the embassy are not otherwise known. Data on the embassies for this particular period are rather skimpy, however, and it is hardly surprising that

88   *A History of Jews and Judaism in the Second Temple Period, Volume 3*

the named persons are not otherwise attested; attempts to see the names as corruptions of known Romans in the area should probably now be dismissed (Gruen 1984: 746 n. 7; Bringmann 1983: 47–50; Bar-Kochva 1989: 532–33).

For a discussion of how the letters fit into Judaean history, see §15.4.2.

3.3. *Daniel*

AIEJL 472–83; **M. Broshi and E. Eshel** (1997) 'The Greek King Is Antiochus IV (4QHistorical Text=4Q248)', *JJS* 48: 120–29; **J. G. Bunge** (1973) 'Der "Gott der Festungen" und der "Liebling der Frauen": Zur Identifizierung der Götter in Dan. 11,36–39', *JSJ* 4: 169–82; **R. H. Charles** (1929) *A Critical and Exegetical Commentary on the Book of Daniel*; **J. J. Collins** (1977) *The Apocalyptic Vision of the Book of Daniel*; **idem** (1993) *A Commentary on the Book of Daniel*; **J. J. Collins and P. W. Flint (eds)** (2001) *The Book of Daniel: Composition and Reception*; **P. R. Davies** (1985) *Daniel*; **T. Fischer** (1980) *Seleukiden und Makkabäer: Beiträge zur Seleukidengeschichte und zu den politischen Ereignissen in Judäa während der 1. Hälfte des 2. Jahrhunderts v. Chr.*; **A. Frisch** (2017) *The Danielic Discourse on Empire in Second Temple Literature*; **J. E. Goldingay** (1989) *Daniel*; **L. L. Grabbe** (2001) 'A Dan(iel) for All Seasons: For Whom Was Daniel Important?', in J. J. Collins and P. W. Flint (eds), *The Book of Daniel: Composition and Reception*, 1:229–46; **L. F. Hartman and A. A. Di Lella** (1978) *The Book of Daniel*; **W. L. Humphries** (1973) 'A Life-Style for Diaspora: A Study of the Tales of Esther and Daniel', *JBL* 92: 211–23; *JLBM* 22–27, 77–83; **K. Koch** (1995) *Die Reiche der Welt und der kommende Menschensohn: Studien zum Danielbuch*; **idem** (1997) *Europa, Rom und der Kaiser vor dem Hintergrund von zwei Jahrtausenden Rezeption des Buches Daniel*; **J. C. H. Lebram** (1974) 'Perspektiven der Gegenwärtigen Danielforschung', *JSJ* 5: 1–33; **idem** (1975) 'König Antiochus im Buch Daniel', *VT* 25: 737–72; **J. A. Montgomery** (1927) *A Critical and Exegetical Commentary on the Book of Daniel*; **C. A. Moore** (1977) *Daniel, Esther and Jeremiah: The Additions*; **C. A. Newsom** (2014) *Daniel: A Commentary*; **P. L. Redditt** (1999) *Daniel, Based on the New Revised Standard Version*; **H. H. Rowley** (1935) *Darius the Mede and the Four World Empires in the Book of Daniel*; **SCHÜRER** 3:245–50; **O. H. Steck, R. G. Kratz and I. Kottsieper (eds)** (1998) *Das Buch Baruch; Der Brief des Jeremia; Zusätze zu Ester und Daniel*; **J. Ziegler** (1999) *Susanna, Daniel, Bel et Draco* (2nd edn).

The scholarship and secondary literature on Daniel is enormous, but it is not the purpose of this section to survey all the scholarship on Daniel (for this, see Koch 1995 and 1997 and recent commentaries, especially Collins 1993). Rather, it will focus on Daniel's importance as a historical source

3. *Jewish Literature*

for this part of Seleucid and Jewish history. A number of recent commentaries are helpful, especially the commentary by Collins (1993) and the most recent one by Newsom (2014); however, the older ones of Charles and Montgomery still have much value.

Although some have argued that all of Daniel should be assigned to Maccabaean times (e.g., Rowley 1935), many would now propose that the material of Daniel 1–6 grew up over a period of time and was already in essentially its present form before the Maccabaean revolt (Collins 1977: 7–11). Thus, the 'tales of Daniel' (Dan. 1–6) are of a different character and probably originated in a different time and place from the 'apocalypse of Daniel' (Dan. 7–12). That is, they are tales about a heroic figure in an ancient Near Eastern court who is adviser to the king. They picture a series of contests and conflicts which demonstrate his wisdom and piety and, ultimately, serve as a model for Jews of the diaspora (Humphries 1973). The Maccabaean author did not compose these chapters but simply took them over and added his material to them.

This means that our concern is primarily with Daniel 7–12. Scholarship has long recognized that these chapters were written during the Maccabaean revolt but before the Jews retook the temple area, i.e., about 166–165 BCE (Fischer [1980: 140] is a notable exception in arguing for ca. 160/159 BCE). Various elements within this section of the book clearly represent the period around the time of the Maccabaean revolt, and Dan. 11.45 predicts the death of Antiochus IV in a way that did not actually occur, showing that it forms a genuine prediction which failed. The importance of the book is that it represents the view of a writer contemporary with the events. Where it can be checked, it seems to record them accurately (if briefly) and in correct order. The problem is that the symbolic language of the book often makes it difficult to interpret its allusions and to determine the actual happenings behind the symbols.

It is often asserted that Daniel 7–12 owes its authorship to Hasidic circles. However, not only is not a lot known about the Hasidim (§6.1) but also some elements within the book seem to be at variance with the views of this group. Especially important is its attitude toward active resistance to persecution. We know that the Hasidim were willing to fight against the Seleucids. Indeed, they are referred to as 'mighty warriors' (1 Macc. 2.42), but the author of Daniel believed in passive resistance only, with martyrdom being the way of fighting against the forces of evil. In this he has some affinities with the *Testament of Moses* (Collins 1977: 198–210). Also, contrary to the way the author is often depicted, it seems likely that he was an upper-class individual who had obtained a Hellenistic education and was someone like the Eupolemus known from 2 Macc. 4.11 (Grabbe 2000). One reason is that Daniel 11 is almost certainly based on a

Hellenistic source, which is unlikely to have been available in Hebrew. As suggested by M. Broshi and E. Eshel (1997), 4Q248 might be the source of the events under Antiochus IV, especially since the author was contemporary with these events (though other explanations are possible). But for the earlier history, his source was almost certainly in Greek.

The importance of Daniel 11 is that it seems based on an accurate portrayal of the interactions between the Seleucid and Ptolemaic rulers, though given under the guise of prophecy. It is generally assumed that some sort of chronicle made during Ptolemaic times underlies this chapter. Although the historical description is in symbolic language, it is generally clear what event is being referred to. It still provides useful information, especially when used in conjunction with the lost account of Porphyry, which is often quoted or paraphrased in Jerome's commentary on Daniel (see further at §4.11).

Points to be kept in mind with regard to Daniel include the following:

- The book is a significant source for certain events during the Maccabaean revolt. It is, in fact, the only real contemporary source, since even the books of Maccabees were written some decades later.
- Although not the earliest apocalypse, Daniel 7–12 is one of the best examples of the genre. The book forms a vital link in the development of apocalyptic in general, as well as serving as a source for later apocalyptic speculation.
- The book well illustrates the practice of *ex eventu* prophecy which serves to interpret the significance of the Maccabaean period for at least one segment of the Jewish community. These prophecies also became a vehicle for reinterpretation and further attempts to discern the future in both subsequent Judaism and in Christianity. Attempting to present history as a series of kingdoms leading up to a final empire (the Greek, in this case) is one that became common in apocalyptic writings.
- Other eschatological aspects of the book include new developments, especially the idea of a resurrection (Dan. 12.1-3).
- Martyrdom is one theological theme, expressed as a means of resistance to the Greek oppression. This idea of passive resistance is different from the military stance taken in other books (such as 1 and 2 Maccabees) but parallel to that in the *Testament of Moses* (§3.9).
- Daniel 1–6 provides a model of Jewish apologetic and self-identity. It even gives a model of how Jews in the diaspora were meant to conduct themselves among their Gentile neighbours: not that most

3. Jewish Literature

Jews would have moved in royal circles, but it shows the proper attitude toward putting the Jewish law first even to the point of risking one's life.

- Wisdom is a key concept in the book, representing both wisdom which comes from study and learning and wisdom which is revealed by God, thus uniting what might be called 'proverbial wisdom' and 'mantic wisdom'. There is evidence that the author was an educated member of the upper classes in Jerusalem, probably someone much like Eupolemus son of John, rather than a member of a disaffected sect (Grabbe 2000).

3.4. Josephus

J. M. G. Barclay (2007) *Flavius Josephus, Volume 10:* Against Apion*: Translation and Commentary*; **S. J. D. Cohen** (1979) *Josephus in Galilee and Rome: His Vita and Development as a Historian*; **J. Edmondson, S. Mason and J. Rives (eds)** (2005) *Flavius Josephus and Flavian Rome*; **J. A. Goldstein** (1976) *I Maccabees: A New Translation with Introduction and Commentary*; **idem** (1983a) *II Maccabees: A New Translation with Introduction and Commentary*; **J. W. van Henten** (2014) *Flavius Josephus, Volume 7b:* Judean Antiquities *15: Translation and Commentary*; **J. Klawans** (2012) *Josephus and the Theologies of Ancient Judaism*; **R. Laqueur** (1920) *Der jüdische Historiker Flavius Josephus*; **S. Mason** (2001) *Flavius Josephus, Volume 9:* Life of Josephus*: Translation and Commentary*; **idem** (2008) *Flavius Josephus, Volume 1b:* Judean War *2: Translation and Commentary*; **idem** (2014) 'The Priest Josephus Away from the Temple: A Changed Man?' *RevQ* 26: 375–402; **A. Momigliano** (1934a) 'Josephus as a Source for the History of Judaea', *CAH* 10:884–87; **É. Nodet** (2018) *The Hebrew Bible of Josephus: Main Features*; **W. Otto** (1913) '14) Herodes I', *PW Supp.* 2:1–202; **J. Pastor, P. Stern and M. Mor (eds)** (2011) *Flavius Josephus: Interpretation and History*; **M. Pucci Ben Zeev** (1998) *Jewish Rights in the Roman World: The Greek and Roman Documents Quoted by Josephus Flavius*; **T. Rajak** (1984) 'Was There a Roman Charter for the Jews?' *JRS* 74: 107–23; **Z. Rodgers (ed.)** (2007) *Making History: Josephus and Historical Method*; **R. J. H. Shutt** (1961) *Studies in Josephus*; **S. Swoboda** (2014) *Tod und Sterben im Krieg bei Josephus: Die Intentionen von* Bellum *und* Antiquitates *im Kontext griechisch-römischer Historiographie*.

For a general introduction to Josephus and his writings (with an extensive bibliographical guide), and his value as a historian, see *HJJSTP 2* (68–75). The bibliography is not repeated here, only more recent items listed or those omitted from the earlier list. Josephus is of course our main historical source for the history of the Jews during Hasmonaean

92   *A History of Jews and Judaism in the Second Temple Period, Volume 3*

and Roman times to about 75 CE. His importance for religion is on a different order. Although he is writing mainly as a historian in most of his writings, he still says a good deal about Jewish religion. Also his book *Against Apion* (*Contra Apionem*) contains a variety of material of relevance to religious issues.

In the *War* (1.1.1–2.2 §§31-53) Josephus has a brief account of the Maccabaean revolt. Although short and evidently muddled to some extent, it is nevertheless valuable in that it seems to be independent of our other extant sources. The tendency among scholars has been to ignore the picture of the *War* as confused. Undoubtedly, there is truth to this since his picture of Onias, Jason and Menelaus as all being brothers (and Menelaus also bearing the name Onias) is less credible than the more complicated picture of 2 Maccabees. But he is the one who explicitly notes the involvement of the Tobiads in the machinations to obtain the high priesthood, a point ignored by both 1 and 2 Maccabees. Also, any independent evidence is useful in countering the systematic bias of the two major sources. Josephus's information is probably from Nicolaus of Damascus (§4.6).

Antiquities (12.5.1 §237–13.7.4 §229) provides a much longer account of the Maccabaean revolt and Hasmonaean rule to the coming of the Romans. His primary source for the Maccabean conflict was 1 Maccabees, which he closely paraphrased; however, he shows frequent minor differences which are usually due to his own reworking of the data, including his own surmises and inferences (for discussion and bibliography, see Cohen 1979: 44–47). However, he added additional information at several places (e.g., 12.5.5 §§257-64; 13.2.4-3.4 §§59-79; 13.4.5-9 §§103-22), which came from another source or sources, one probably being Nicolaus of Damascus and another Strabo's (now lost) history. It seems evident (as most scholars generally agree) that he did not know either Jason of Cyrene or 2 Maccabees (despite the different opinion of Goldstein [1976: 55–61; 1983a: 26–27 nn. 79–80, 549]). Since Josephus's account no longer closely parallels 1 Maccabees after 13.42 (*Ant.* 13.7.6 §214), it has been suggested that his version did not have 13.43–16.24, though other explanations are also possible. Once he ceased to use 1 Maccabees, Josephus's main source appears to have been Nicolaus of Damascus for the *War* and Nicolaus and Strabo for the *Antiquities*. For this part of Josephus's history, there is considerably more text in the *Antiquities* than in the *War*, but the actual data are not usually significantly greater, suggesting that the greater bulk of the *Antiquities* represents rhetorical expansion rather than further information. However, new sources of information are occasionally drawn upon and thus supplement the data from *War*.

There is a strong consensus that Josephus's main source for the reign of Herod the Great was Nicolaus:

- He quotes him by name occasionally (e.g., *Ant.* 14.1.3 §9; 14.6.4 §104), and once takes him to task for excessive praise of Herod (*Ant.* 16.7.1 §§183-86), hinting at his own dependence on him. But there are other indications as well:
- Josephus's account is detailed for that period for which Nicolaus gave a thorough account, viz., the lives of Antipater and Herod the Great. At precisely the point at which Nicolaus ceased his history of the Jews (shortly after Herod's death), Josephus suddenly becomes very skimpy.
- The account in the *War* is often quite favourable to Antipater, Herod's father, as well as to Herod for the early part of his reign. It is in the *Antiquities* where other sources are also cited and clearly used that greater criticism of Herod comes to the fore.
- Josephus is generally antagonistic to Antigonus (son of Aristobulus II) who was a rival to Herod.
- Of the possible successors to Herod, he is hostile to Antipater, as Nicolaus is said to have been.
- The attitude and interest taken is sometimes more characteristic of a Greek writer than of a Jewish one (e.g., benefactions of Herod for the Olympic games [*War* 1.21.12 §426]).

Although the *War* is definitely the shorter account, the narrative in the *Antiquities* is generally closely parallel for the earlier part of Herod's life down to his submission to Augustus in 30 BCE; after that, however, there are often substantial differences in arrangement and bulk but sometimes also in the actual outline of events (e.g., the circumstances of the execution of Mariamme). This makes it difficult to determine precisely what Josephus got from Nicolaus and what comes from other accounts and from his own embellishments. Many feel that the *War* more directly relied on Nicolaus and is therefore closer to the Damascene's history. Laqueur developed the theory that the *War* is more favourable to Herod and thus more directly reliant on Nicolaus whereas the *Antiquities* represents a thorough-going anti-Herodian revision, a view combatted by Marcus (see the discussion at §17.8).

Whereas the *War* seems to rely on Nicolaus almost entirely, the *Antiquities* also makes abundant use of the lost history of Strabo (§4.13). Strabo's history is quoted several times (e.g., *Ant.* 14.3.1 §35-36; 14.7.2 §§111-18) but probably also serves as the source of certain additional information found in the *Antiquities* but not in the earlier work. Nevertheless, Josephus himself indicates that both Strabo and Nicolaus were quite similar for the history of much of this period (*Ant.* 13.12.6 §347; 14.6.4 §104), not because of one borrowing from the other but because of use of some of the same basic sources (SCHÜRER 1:26).

In the last century and the earlier part of this century, it was quite common to argue that Josephus took much of his material not directly from Nicolaus, Strabo, etc., but from an intermediary source (cf. the survey in Otto 1913: 6–15; Laqueur 1920). Such an approach is not very popular now for several reasons: (1) such intermediate sources are usually hypothetical rather than historically attested; (2) there is no reason why Josephus could not have known some of his major sources directly; (3) the theory assumes that contradictions, diversity of opinions and differences of evaluation must come from the source rather than being Josephus's own individual contributions to his historical writing; (4) the lack of consensus among scholars about these supposed intermediate sources did not inspire confidence in the attempts to identify them. This is not to say that Josephus always knew his quoted sources directly since he clearly referred to certain writers known only second hand (e.g., *Ant.* 1.3.9 §108).

Although the account of Herod's reign in books 15–17 of the *Antiquities* is much longer than that in the *War*, most of this does not appear to be due predominantly to additional information. That is, much of the greater length has the character of rhetorical embellishment and dramatic expansion, often referred to as 'novelistic elements': descriptions of the thoughts of the characters, additional dialogue and speech, expansion by inessential detail, which may come from the imagination rather than a greater knowledge, and Josephus's own personal views. It is certainly possible that Josephus had conversed with Hasmonaean descendants and thus had more anecdotal information available. But most of the additional bulk does not increase the actual factual content of the narrative, and consequently gives the impression of being his own literary invention. The other chief difference is that the *War* tends to be topical in this section, whereas *Antiquities* 15–17 gives a basically chronological narrative. For example, the accounts of Herod's building projects and of his territories are a unit in the *War* whereas they are split up and presented in chronological fashion in the *Antiquities*.

Since Josephus is cited continually throughout this book, it would be both difficult and superfluous to try to describe his contribution in detail, but some of the main areas where he makes a contribution can be summarized as follows:

3. *Jewish Literature*

- He claims to be a priest and consequently to have special knowledge of the religious laws. Judging from the *Life* (2 §9), where he alleges to have been consulted as an expert already by age 14, some of his claims are certainly exaggerated. Nevertheless, he would have had some training while growing up, whether formal or just from contact with family members, and he would certainly have been familiar with the temple and its cult before the destruction in 70. There are many passages that mention the temple and cult in passing.
- A section on the Jewish law (*Ant.* 4.8.1-46 §§176-314) gives an insight into how some of the biblical laws were interpreted and applied. This does not mean that we can always accept Josephus's presentation as evidence of actual practice since he also has an apologetic aim in his description. At times his interpretation is at variance with other sources, but his writings at least give one particular view of the time.
- His information on Judaean society, including its religious aspects, is very valuable. For example, he is one of the main sources on the various sects and groups which moved briefly across the field of historical vision before being lost to view forever. Whether he claimed to have been a Pharisee or not (*Life* 2 §12; see the discussion at §6.3.1), there is no evidence that he ever was. Nevertheless, he knew prominent Pharisees and members of other Jewish sects of the time.
- Two of his writings (*Antiquities* and *Against Apion*) are particularly important for showing us the sort of attacks made on Jews by some Graeco-Roman writers and the type of defences used in return by Jewish writers (see Rajak 1984, Pucci Ben Zeev 1998 and further in *HJJSTP 4*). Josephus is very important for illustrating the complexities of outlook on the Jews and their laws held among the educated members of Greek and Roman society during the Second Temple period.
- Josephus gives information on the biblical canon, especially in the important passage in *Against Apion* (1.8 §§37-43), but also in the biblical books used as the basis of some of his own writings. See further the next point and §12.2.
- He also provides information on the state of the biblical text. This is mainly through the various texts used as the basis for parts of his own writings which are by and large paraphrases of the biblical text (see further at §12.2). He alleges that the text had been fixed since

96   *A History of Jews and Judaism in the Second Temple Period, Volume 3*

Persian times (*Ag. Ap.* 1.8 §42), but this is belied by his own use of texts other than the Hebrew, and by the different versions of the Greek text which served as the basis of his discussion.

3.5. *1 Enoch 83–108*

AIEJL 592–602; **F. Dexinger** (1977) *Henochs Zehnwochenapokalypse und offene Probleme der Apokalyptikforschung*; *JLBM* 83–86, 110–14; **G. W. E. Nickelsburg** (2001) *1 Enoch: A Commentary on the Book of 1 Enoch, Chapters 1–36, 81–108*; **L. T. Stuckenbruck** (2007) *1 Enoch 91–108*; **P. A. Tiller** (1993) *A Commentary on the Animal Apocalypse of* 1 Enoch.

A general introduction and bibliography to *1 Enoch* as a whole is given in *HJJSTP 2* (81–84). The various sections of *1 Enoch* 83–108 are likely to have been composed between the Maccabaean revolt and the Roman conquest (ca. 168–63 BCE). This section of *1 Enoch* is probably made up of two separate writings: (1) The *Dream Visions of Enoch* (83–90) which contain two visions of Enoch about the future: the first vision predicting the great flood to come on the earth (83–85); the second containing a review of history beginning with Adam and Eve and extending to the time of Judas Maccabaeus in the form of the *Animal Apocalypse* (86–89). (2) The *Epistle of Enoch* (90–105), which contains a diversity of material, including the *Apocalypse of Weeks* (93; 91.12-17) and material from a *Book of Noah* (105–7), with 'another Book of Enoch' at the very end (108). The main points about Judaic religion include the following:

- The apocalyptic vision of history is very much in evidence. The *Animal Apocalypse* and the *Apocalypse of Weeks* both contain *ex eventu* prophecies which lead into genuine predictions about the near future. The two writings suggest that the authors expected the end time to come about in their lifetimes, both of which were about the time of the Maccabaean revolt.
- This is further evidence of a lost 'Book of Noah', which also appears to be drawn on in the *Parables of Enoch* (*1 En.* 37–72).
- The *Animal Apocalypse* views the temple and cult set up in the Persian period as polluted and the post-exilic period as a time of religious blindness and poor leadership (89.73–90.5).
- There is a positive attitude to the Maccabaean revolt and to Judas in particular (90.6-15). There is no indication that the author formed part of a group that supported the revolt actively, but he regarded Judas as God's instrument. Because the revolt ends with the direct

intervention of God, we find no indication of how the group represented by the author might have related to the new leadership after
165 BCE.

- One of the Qumran manuscripts (4QEn^c) shows that the *Apocalypse
of Weeks* has suffered textual displacement in the Ethiopic tradition
and confirms the emendation long made by scholars to correct this.
Apparently, the *Apocalypse of Weeks* envisaged that the present age
was to end with the seventh week, and weeks eight to ten refer to
a time of judgment and to a new age.
- A good deal of the *Epistle* is taken up with paraenetic material
either condemning certain activities or encouraging others. Much
of this is worded in very general terms, though some of the things
condemned are those familiar from the prophets and other early
Jewish writings, such as the rich and those who oppress the poor,
and pagan worship. Other items are that men will wear more
bodily decoration than women (98.2), abortion and abandonment
of children (99.5).
- A major theme is judgment. The spirits of the dead, whether
righteous or wicked, are apparently already undergoing some sort
of reward or punishment (102.5-11), but there would be a resurrection for a final judgment of all the dead (103–104). The final
reward of the righteous is to 'shine like the lights of heaven',
sometimes referred to as 'astral immortality' (104.2), and to sit on
thrones of honour (108.11-12).
- There is a hint of disputes about Scripture, with the charge that the
wicked have altered or invented words in the Scriptures, but the
righteous will be given proper books (104.10-12).

3.6. *Book of Jubilees*

AIEJL 575–81; **M. Albani et al. (eds)** (1997) *Studies in the Book of
Jubilees*; **R. H. Charles** (1902) *The Book of Jubilees or the Little Genesis*;
R. Doran (1989) 'The Non-Dating of Jubilees: Jub 34–38; 23.14–32 in
Narrative Context', *JSJ* 20: 1–11; **J. C. Endres** (1987) *Biblical Interpre-
tation in the Book of Jubilees*; **J. A. Goldstein** (1983b) 'The Date of the
Book of Jubilees', *PAAJR* 50: 63–86; **L. L. Grabbe** (2009) 'Jubilees and
the Samaritan Tradition', in G. Boccaccini and G. Ibba (eds), *Enoch and
the Mosaic Torah: The Evidence of Jubilees*, 145–59; **B. Halpern-Amaru**
(1999) *The Empowerment of Women in the* Book of Jubilees; *JLBM* 69–74;
JWSTP 97–104; **M. A. Knibb** (1989) *Jubilees and the Origins of the
Qumran Community*; **J. L. Kugel** (1994) 'The Jubilees Apocalypse', *DSD*
1: 322–37; **idem** (2012) *A Walk through* Jubilees*: Studies in the* Book of

98   *A History of Jews and Judaism in the Second Temple Period, Volume 3*

> Jubilees *and the World of its Creation*; **R. Pummer** (1979) 'The *Book of Jubilees* and the Samaritans', *Eglise et Théologie* 10: 147–78; SCHÜRER 3:308–18; **M.** Segal (2007) *The Book of* Jubilees: *Rewritten Bible, Redaction, Ideology and Theology*; **J. C. VanderKam** (1977) *Textual and Historical Studies in the Book of Jubilees*; **idem** (1981a) 'The Putative Author of the Book of Jubilees', *JSS* 26: 209–17; **idem** (1994b) 'Genesis 1 in Jubilees 2', *DSD* 1: 300–321; **J. C. VanderKam (ed.)** (1989) *The Book of Jubilees*.

This book presents itself as a revelation to Moses on Sinai. In fact it is a paraphrase of much of Genesis 1 to Exodus 12, but with many different details and interpretations. All events are dated according a 49-year jubilee cycle (hence the name), and a solar calendar is presupposed. In a list of Sabbath instructions and regulations (*hĕlākôt*) in 50.6-13, a number of parallels are found to similar instructions in the Damascus document (CD 10.14–11.18) at Qumran. The main interest of the work for the historian is its interpretation of the biblical text and additional material which give an insight into the state of Judaism—or one sort of Judaism—at that time.

There is general agreement that the work dates from the 2nd century BCE, but precise dating is uncertain. VanderKam (1977: 207–85) argues for 161–140 BCE, based on battles of the patriarch Judah which he argues are thinly veiled descriptions of battles during the Maccabaean revolt. Goldstein (1983b) correctly notes that the alleged parallels are far from obvious but then uses the same dubious method to date the book to 169–167 on the basis of presumed (but less-than-obvious) parallels with the 'Hellenistic reform'. Nickelsburg (*JLBM* 73–74) similarly agrees that it comes from about 168 BCE. Granted that though many passages in the book can be associated with the period immediately preceding, during or soon after the Maccabaean revolt, most of them could also fit other times. Doran (1989) has pointed out the uncertainty of some of the most important proposed historical allusions and how easily they can be differently interpreted. Beyond a general 2nd-century date, no precise time of composition can be said to have been established (cf. also SCHÜRER 3:311–13). The book of *Jubilees* tells us a number of things about Jewish religion during the period of what was probably the 2nd century BCE:

- The book is a prime example of 'rewritten Bible', a means of interpreting the biblical text by paraphrasing and rewriting it. It seems almost certain that the writer has drawn on the canonical version of Genesis 1 to Exodus 12 (though it has been speculated that he was trying to write a book to replace the present books of Genesis and Exodus).

- The author has a schematic view of history in which all major events happen according to a jubilee cycle of 49 years (versus the 50 years of Lev. 25). All the events of the patriarchs' lives are marked according to these cycles, and the reader is left with the impression that all history fits this same scheme.
- The book proclaims the observance of a 364-day solar calendar and polemicizes against use of a lunar calendar (6.32-38).
- A good deal of emphasis is placed on proper observance of the law which did not come about only with the mission of Moses. On the contrary, many Jewish beliefs and practices normally associated with Moses and later were already in effect or presaged in the lives of the patriarchs according to *Jubilees*. For example, the main annual festivals (Feast of Firstfruits = Pentecost: 6.17-31; 15.1-4; 22.1-9; Feast of Booths: 17.20-31; 32.27-29; 44.1-4; Day of Atonement: 34.17-19) arose in commemoration of events in the lives of Abraham, Isaac and Jacob (even though the Pentateuch strongly indicates their origins at or after the exodus). Also, Levi was already appointed priest through a vision from God during his own lifetime (30.18-20; 31.11-17).
- One of the earliest detailed descriptions of the Passover observance is given in *Jubilees* 49. There are also detailed regulations relating to sabbath observance (2.25-33; 50).
- Belief in the resurrection of the spirit is evidently a concept found in the book (23.31); if so, this is important evidence of the diversity of eschatological views.

3.7. *Judith*

AIEJL 524–28; **A. Brenner (ed.)** (1995) *A Feminist Companion to Esther, Judith and Susanna*; **T. Craven** (1983) *Artistry and Faith in the Book of Judith* (1983); *JLBM* 97–102; *JWSTP* 46–52; **C. A. Moore** (1985) *Judith*; Schürer 3:216–22; **C. Schedl** (1965) 'Nabuchodonosor, Arpaksad und Darius: Untersuchungen zum Buch Judit', *ZDMG* 115: 242–54; **M. Stocker** (1998) *Judith: Sexual Warrior, Women and Power in Western Culture*.

The setting of Judith is the time of Nebuchadnezzar. The story itself recounts the deliverance of an Israelite town besieged by Nebuchadnezzar's general Holophernes. Judith, a pious widow, volunteered to enter the enemy camp, then seduced Holophernes and cut off his head to end the siege. The actual time of writing is difficult, since there are historical remembrances which point to the early Persian period (Shedl 1965), the time of Artaxerxes III or the Maccabean revolt (cf. Moore 1985: 38–49, 67–70). The Maccabaean/Hasmonaean period is probably the most favoured dating. There is little that the book would add to our knowledge of actual events, even if its precise historical setting could be determined. Its contribution is rather on the side of Jewish religious and social history during the Greek period. The book is often associated with Pharisaism (cf. Moore 1985: 60–63, 70–71) but without good reason. The characteristic piety of the book (fasting, prayer, almsgiving) is by no means unique to Pharisaism; indeed, there seems a tendency to add the adjective 'Pharisaic' to any occurrence of 'piety' in early Jewish literature. On the other hand, none of the traits unique to what is known of the Pharisees occurs in the book (§6.3). There is in fact nothing particular in the book to associate it with any of the known sects of early Judaism (cf. Craven 1983: 120–21). The exact date of Judith is uncertain, though the 2nd century BCE seems reasonable. Some of the main points about Judaism as a religion are the following:

- Judith demonstrates without a doubt that historical 'facts' can be used quite inaccurately to bolster theological narratives. The historical setting, with Nebuchadnezzar as king of the Assyrians, bears no resemblance to history, though there is some evidence that some historical remembrances of the Babylonian rebel Artaxerxes III in the early Persian period may be found in the book (Shedl 1965).
- The book has been quite popular for feminist interpreters because it features a heroine, which is somewhat rare in Jewish literature, especially her direct action in slaying Holophernes, a deed not normally associated with a woman. This episode has been of much interest to artists through the ages (cf. Brenner 1995).
- One of the main messages is that when threatened, the Jewish people must trust in God. This does not exclude militant means, however, as Judith's own attack on Holophernes shows. There are indications that the story is to be understood symbolically: the eponymous name of the heroine Judith (= 'Jewess'); the name of the town Bethulia (= bĕtulāh 'virgin'?) and so on.
- The book places a great deal of emphasis on prayer (9; 12.6-8). This is one of the chief means for Judith to express her piety.
- Judith's strict observance of dietary laws, including her argument that violation of them would cause the city to fall, is an important theme in the book (11.12-15; 12.1-4, 17-19).

3. Jewish Literature

- A new attitude to fasting is attested here, perhaps for the first time: regular fasting as an act of piety. In the Hebrew Bible fasting was primarily a thing to do in a crisis, though a late passage such as Isaiah 56 makes fasting a means of expressing humility. Fasting and wearing sackcloth also occur in Judith in the old sense when Jerusalem is threatened (4.11–15); however, before this crisis arose Judith fasted all the days except for the sabbaths and holidays and the preparation day ('eve') before each festival (8.6) as a normal part of her lifestyle. Another possible ascetic act is her remaining unmarried, despite many opportunities to remarry (16.22). This might be simply out of loyalty to her first husband, but it may also be another element of her ascetic lifestyle.
- The book does not seem to represent a 'democratization' of Jewish worship as such, however, since the temple, cult and priesthood are taken for granted and in no way slighted (4.2-3, 12, 14-15; 8.21, 24; 9.8, 13; 11.13; 16.16-20). The high priest also acts as the leader of the nation (4.6-8), though a reference is also made to the *gerousia* 'council of elders' in Jerusalem, which is able to make important decisions (11.14).

3.8. *1 Baruch*

AIEJL 538–42; *JLBM* 94–97; *JWSTP* 140–46; **A. Kabasele Mukenge** (1998) *L'unité littéraire du livre de Baruch*; **C. A. Moore** (1977) *Daniel, Esther and Jeremiah: The Additions*; **SCHÜRER** 3:734–43; **O. H. Steck** (1993) *Das apokryphe Baruchbuch: Studien zu Rezeption und Konzentration 'kanonischer' Überlieferung*; **O. H. Steck, R. G. Kratz and I. Kottsieper (eds)** (1998) *Das Buch Baruch; Der Brief des Jeremia; Zusätze su Ester und Daniel*; **E. Tov** (1976) *The Septuagint Translation of Jeremiah and Baruch: A Discussion of an Early Revision of the LXX of Jeremiah 29–52 and Baruch 1:1-38.*

This takes the form of a letter, written by Jeremiah's scribe Baruch in exile, to those remaining in Jerusalem. The exact purpose of the book is unclear since it seems to be made up of disparate sections on the situation of the exile (1.1-14), a prayer of confession over sins (1.15–3:8), the figure of wisdom (3.9–4.4) and a poem on Zion (4.5–5.9). The precise dating is also uncertain. A number of scholars have seen Antiochus IV and the high priest Alcimus behind the images of Nebuchadnezzar and the high priest Jehoiakim (e.g., Kabasele Mukenge 1998); if so, that puts the book fairly precisely to about 150 BCE. However, this interpretation is by no means certain, and the dating of the book still remains unclear. E. Tov (1976) connects the book with the translation of LXX Jeremiah, which he argues was done about 116 BCE. Among points to be gleaned from the book are the following:

- The theme of exile and return is strong in the book. The 'letter' of Baruch should be compared with Jeremiah 24 (which compares the exiles to good figs and those remaining in the land to bad) and Jeremiah 29 (which contains a letter in the name of Jeremiah encouraging the exiles to settle and make the best of it). The focus of 1 Baruch is on the return from exile as a sort of second exodus (cf. Isa. 51.10-11).
- A good portion of the book is a prayer (1.15–3.8), apparently based on or having much in common with Dan. 9.4-19. Although a literary prayer, it may well tell us something of prayer of the time.
- The image of wisdom (3.9–4.4) is an indication of how the figure was being developed at the time (to be discussed in *HJJSTP 4*). Like Ben Sira 24, wisdom is equated with the Torah (4.1), though much of the poem seems to draw on Job 28.12-28 about the inaccessibility of wisdom.

3.9. *Testament of Moses (Assumption of Moses)*

AIEJL 605–9; **J. J. Collins** (1977) *The Apocalyptic Vision of the Book of Daniel*; *JLBM* 74–77, 247–48; *JWSTP* 344–49; **G. W. E. Nickelsburg (ed.)** (1973) *Studies on the Testament of Moses*; **A. Schalit** (1989) *Untersuchung zur 'Assumptio Mosis'*; SCHÜRER 3:278–88; **J. Tromp** (1993) *The Assumption of Moses: A Critical Edition with Commentary*.

Although this book was probably completed between 4 BCE and about 30 CE (because it mentions the death of Herod the Great but does not know of that of his sons Archelaus, Philip, or Herod Antipas: 6.2-9), it appears that a substantial portion (or a first edition) was written not long after the Maccabaean revolt. Its review of history has a significant section relating to the Maccabaean revolt (chs. 8–9), which has led Nickelsburg to argue that an original was composed during Hasmonaean times which was then updated in the early 1st century CE (1973: 34–37). The recent edition and commentary by Tromp is an important tool for study, especially since the book survives only in a single manuscript in Latin translation (probably translated from a Hebrew original). The book is significant for a number of reasons:

- It is a good example of a testament but also has all the features of an apocalypse (though some would see these as mutually exclusive, mistakenly in my view).
- The book contains (or apparently contained in its original form) some significant interpretative traditions about Moses. Unfortunately, both the beginning and ending are lost, but the ending once evidently included a dispute between Michael and Satan over Moses' body and the ascension of Moses' soul to heaven (Jude 9; cf. Origen, *De Princ.* 3.2.1, and see the discussion in Tromp 1993: 270–85).
- A good portion of the book is taken up with a review of history, much of which relates to biblical history, though its section on the Maccabaean revolt is a quite valuable historical source (suggesting to some [e.g., Nickelsburg 1973: 34–37] that an original work was produced about that time and only subsequently updated in the 1st century).
- The book seems to calculate the world as ending about 4000 A.M. and is a good example of the works for which chronography was an important issue (§12.6).
- *Testament of Moses* 9 exhibits a variant attitude toward the Antiochene persecution, that of passive resistance and martyrdom rather than active military measures against the oppression. In this it shows clear affinities with the book of Daniel and may well have originated in similar circles (Collins 1977: 198–210); these circles were not necessarily those which supported the Maccabaean cause.
- The book contains some negative references to the temple and its sacrifices (5.1–6.1). These are difficult to interpret, since the author is not anti-temple as such. Whether it is a critique of the past or current priesthood, whether it merely notes that the Second Temple was inferior to the First Temple or whether it has another purpose is unclear.

3.10. *Letter of (Pseudo-)Aristeas*

AIEJL 571–75; **J. J. Collins** (2000) *Between Athens and Jerusalem* 97–103; **M. Hadas** (1951) *Aristeas to Philocrates*; *JLBM* 196–99; *JWSTP* 75–80; **E. Matusova** (2015) *The Meaning of the Letter of Aristeas*; **H. M. Orlinsky** (1975) 'The Septuagint as Holy Writ and the Philosophy of the Translators', *HUCA* 46: 89–114; **A. Pelletier** (1962) *Lettre d'Aristée à Philocrate*; Schürer 3:677–87; **V. A. Tcherikover** (1958) 'The Ideology of the Letter of Aristeas', *HTR* 51: 59–85; **M. Tilly** (1997) 'Geographie und Weltordnung im Aristeasbrief', *JSJ* 28: 131–53; **B. G. Wright, III** (2015) *The Letter of Aristeas: 'Aristeas to Philocrates' or 'On the Translation of the Law of the Jews'.*

This work ostensibly tells about how the Pentateuch came to be translated into Greek: Ptolemy II wanted copies of all the important works of literature among the non-Greeks to be included in his famous library at Alexandria. Aristeas brought the Jewish Law to the notice of Ptolemy's minister Demetrius and recommended that such a 'famous' book be translated and included in the library. Messengers were dispatched to Jerusalem for copies of the Law and for skilled translators. After a lengthy description of Jerusalem and the temple, the letter tells how the high priest Eleazar sent beautiful copies of the Scriptures along with 72 translators allotted to the task of rendering them into Greek. At the Egyptian court they were elaborately entertained and their wisdom tested and found superior by Ptolemy. They did the job of translation, and the Pentateuch in Greek was accepted by the Jewish community in a public ceremony.

The letter is a fake, as far as the surface level is concerned: It was not written by an official of the minister Demetrius nor, as most specialists agree, does it tell the true origins of the Greek Old Testament. Rather, it is a piece of clever Jewish apologetic, probably on behalf of the LXX version, and likely written after the reign of Ptolemy II. Exactly when it was written is a matter of debate. Perhaps the most popular date is the last decades of the 2nd century, i.e., during Hasmonaean times. However, some scholars would put it during the Ptolemaic period, while others would date it just before the Maccabaean revolt. The dating is important in that it affects the question of whether the work has authentic material for Ptolemaic times in its description of Judah and Jerusalem. It obviously presents an idealized picture, Judaea as a utopian state; also, some of its description of the temple appears to be based on the LXX Pentateuch. On the other hand, elements of the narrative may represent a genuine remembrance of the pre-Maccabaean state. More specific study needs to be done on this question, though it would be difficult to check its information in detail. If it was written in the late 2nd century, one would need solid reasons for having confidence that it contained accurate information about Judah and the temple in Ptolemaic times, though it might be useful for the Hasmonaean state. Some of the points about Jewish religion are the following:

- The whole story of LXX origins is meant to strengthen the importance and accuracy of the translation (*HJJSTP 2*: 253–54, 305–6). Not only its alleged royal origins but also the fact that the Jewish community publicly accepted it when it was read out (cf. Orlinsky 1975) is an impressive attempt to give authority to the text, which was evidently becoming widely used among Greek-speaking Jews but was perhaps also being criticized or questioned by some.
- Judah is presented as a utopian state, with ideal geography, climate, organization and buildings (83–120; cf. Tilly 1997).
- The description of the sages who come to translate the Pentateuch emphasizes not only their knowledge of both Jewish and Greek culture but also their astuteness of mind, cleverness and other attributes of the Hellenistic and Jewish sage. The representation of these 72 Jews from Palestine fits very well into both the oriental and the Hellenistic wisdom traditions, reminding one of both Ahiqar and some of the traditions in Artapanus (*HJJSTP 2*: 89–90). The claim that six came from each of the twelve tribes is symbolic of the connection seen with ancient Israel.
- One of the most interesting parts of the book is the apologetic for the Jewish law, including why certain animals were not eaten by the Jews (128–71). It is defended not just on the grounds of being a command of God but as being rational according to normal Greek thinking. On the other hand, the author is in no way embarrassed about Jewish beliefs, including belief in one God and rejection of images, and the general refusal of the Jews to mix freely with others (134–43).
- Presented as a letter from a Greek official, the book is another example of a pseudepigraphic writing designed to gain respect and admiration for the Jews in the Greek world. The fact that Ptolemy II is pictured as seeing his library as incomplete without a copy of the Jewish law and the other references are designed to boost support for the Jewish law (9–40), though whether in the Jewish community or among non-Jews might be debated.
- The emphasis on a translation of the law so that any Jews literate in Greek would have access to it is a sign of the growing importance of the written law at least among diaspora Jews, probably sometime during the 2nd century CE.

3.11. *Pseudo-Hecataeus*

B. Bar-Kochva (1996) *Pseudo-Hecataeus,* On the Jews: *Legitimizing the Jewish Diaspora*; **M. Pucci Ben Zeev** (1993) 'The Reliability of Josephus Flavius: The Case of Hecataeus' and Manetho's Accounts of Jews and Judaism: Fifteen Years of Contemporary Research (1974–1990)', *JSJ* 24: 215–34; *OTP* 2:905–19.

It has long been debated whether the quotations ascribed to Hecataeus of Abdera in the *Contra Apionem* by Josephus are genuine or not. Whether the study by Bar-Kochva will settle the matter remains to be seen (cf. Pucci Ben Zeev 1993), but if nothing else it considerably strengthens the case for considering them the work of a Jewish forger. Bar-Kochva dates the book to about 100 BCE, by a moderately conservative Jew living in Egypt who wrote to justify Jewish residence in Egypt. He also argues that the Ezechias who supposedly led the Jews to Egypt is not to be identified with 'Hezekiah the governor' (*HJJSTP 1*: 149; *HJJSTP 2*: 282–83) as has often been argued. There was no such high priest; rather, the writer changed the governor into a high priest, and a forced deportation of Jews to Egypt by Ptolemy I was transformed into a voluntary immigration. A number of the studies on Hecataeus (*HJJSTP 2*: 113–19) also discuss these alleged quotations. The following points about Judaism of the time arise from the quotations.

* The Jewish population in Egypt is said to date from the time of Ptolemy I and to have been a voluntary immigration led by Ezechias, a high priest.
* Jews were supposed to have fought in Alexander's army.
* The Jewish adherence to the law and the willingness to defend it to the death are emphasized.
* The Jewish population, both in and outside of Palestine, is quite large, and their land, city and temple are beautiful and admirable.
* Divination (or at least pagan divination) is rejected.
* About 1,500 priests were supposed to be serving at the time of writing.

3.12. *Psalms of Solomon*

AIEJL 584–87; **K. Atkinson** (1998a) 'Towards a Redating of the Psalms of Solomon: Implications for Understanding the *Sitz im Leben* of an Unknown Jewish Sect', *JSP* 17: 95–112; **idem** (1998b) 'On the Herodian Origin of Militant Davidic Messianism at Qumran: New Light from *Psalm of*

3. Jewish Literature

Solomon 17', *JBL* 118: 435–60; **idem** (2004) *I Cried to the Lord: A Study of the Psalms of Solomon's Historical Background and Social Setting*; **E. Bons and P. Pouchelle (eds)** (2015) *The Psalms of Solomon: Language, History, Theology*; **S. P. Brock** (1984) 'The Psalms of Solomon', in H. F. D. Sparks (ed.) *The Apocryphal Old Testament*, 649–82; **R. R. Hann** (1982) *The Manuscript History of the Psalms of Solomon*; **idem** (1988) 'The Community of the Pious: The Social Setting of the Psalms of Solomon', *SR* 17: 169–89; *JLBM* 238–47; *JWSTP* 573–74; *OTP* 2:639–70; **J. Schüpphaus** (1977) *Die Psalmen Salomos: Ein Zeugnis jerusalemer Theologie und Frömmigkeit in der Mitte des vorchristlichen Jahrhunderts*; **Schürer** 3:192–97; **J. L. Trafton** (1985) *The Syriac Version of the Psalms of Solomon: A Critical Evaluation*; **idem** (1986) 'The Psalms of Solomon: New Light from the Syriac Version?' *JBL* 105: 227–37; **idem** (1992) 'Solomon, Psalms of', *ABD* 6:115–17; **idem** (1994) 'The *Psalms of Solomon* in Recent Research', *JSP* 12: 3–19.

A group of 18 psalmic writings have come down to us in Greek and Syriac, though the original language is generally agreed to be Hebrew (now lost). Arguments have now been made that both the Greek and the Syriac versions were translated directly from the original (Hann 1982; Trafton 1985, 1986). The language is often general, covering themes familiar from the canonical Psalms. However, there are historical allusions which put the general date for the collection as a whole in the period following Pompey's conquest of Jerusalem in 63 BCE, probably about the middle of the first century BCE. The *Psalms* have a number of points relating to Judaism of the time:

- The attitude to Rome, and especially the subordination of Judaea by the Romans, is clear. The destruction of Jerusalem is seen as a punishment for the sins of the Jews (2.1-14; 8.1-22; 17.5-18), but God in turn punished the arrogant Pompey with death at the hands of Caesar (*Pss. Sol.* 2.15-31).
- The *Psalms* are critical of what was being done in the temple and by the leadership in Jerusalem (1.4-8; 2.2-5; 8.11-22; 17.5-15, 22). This seems to be anti-Hasmonaean criticism. A criticism of 'profane' Jews is found in *Psalm* 4.
- *Psalms* 17–18 describe an idealized king like David who is a larger-than-life character but still very much on the human plane. These chapters are obviously important for the question of messianic expectations during this general period of time (§12.3.5).
- The righteous will be resurrected, apparently to an ideal form of existence on the earth, in contrast to the wicked who are destroyed (2.31; 3.11-12; 14.3-5, 9-10). Nothing is said of an immortal soul.

3.13. *Wisdom of Solomon*

AIEJL 529–32; **N. Calduch-Benages and J. Vermeylen (eds)** (1999) *Treasures of Wisdom: Studies in Ben Sira and the Book of Wisdom: Festschrift M. Gilbert*; **S. Cheon** (1997) *The Exodus Story in the Wisdom of Solomon*; **J. J. Collins** (2000) *Between Athens and Jerusalem*, 195–202; **H. Engel** (1998) *Das Buch der Weisheit*; **F. Focke** (1913) *Die Entstehung der Weisheit Salomos: Ein Beitrag zur Geschichte des jüdischen Hellenismus*; **D. Georgi** (1980) *Weisheit Salomos*, 391–478; **M. Gilbert** (1973) *La critique des dieux dans le Livre de la Sagesse (Sg 13–15)*; **idem** (1986) 'Sagesse de Salomon (ou Livre de la Sagesse)', in J. Briend and E. Cothenet (eds), *Supplément au Dictionnaire de la Bible*, 11:58–119; **L. L. Grabbe** (1997e) *Wisdom of Solomon*; **K. M. Hogan** (1999) 'The Exegetical Background of the "Ambiguity of Death" in the Wisdom of Solomon', *JSJ* 30: 1–24; **H. Hübner** (1999) *Die Weisheit Salomons*; *JLBM* 205–12; *JWSTP* 301–13; **M. Kolarcik** (1991) *The Ambiguity of Death in the Book of Wisdom 1–6*; **C. Larcher** (1969) *Etudes sur le Livre de la Sagesse*; **idem** (1983–85) *Le Livre de la Sagesse ou la Sagesse de Salomon*; **B. L. Mack** (1973) *Logos und Sophia: Untersuchungen zur Weisheitstheologie im hellenistischen Judentum*; **L. Mazzinghi** (2019) *Wisdom*; **J. M. Reese** (1970) *Hellenistic Influence on the Book of Wisdom and Its Consequences*; **J. Reider** (1957) *The Book of Wisdom*; SCHÜRER 568–79; **U. Schwenk-Bressler** (1993) *Sapientia Salomonis als ein Beispiel frühjüdischer Textauslegung: Die Auslegung des Buches Genesis, Exodus 1–15 und Teilen der Wüstentradition in Sap 10–19*; **D. Winston** (1979) *The Wisdom of Solomon: A New Translation with Introduction and Commentary*; **J. Ziegler** (1980) *Sapientia Salomonis*.

The Wisdom of Solomon is one of the main representatives (along with Philo) of what is often referred to as 'Hellenistic Judaism'; it is certainly one of the most important writings that can be said with a great deal of assurance to have an origin outside Palestine. The book was almost certainly written in Alexandria in the early Roman empire. Although it has recently been argued by some important interpreters that the book was written during the crisis under Caligula (Winston 1979: 20–25; Cheon 1997), it seems more likely to stem from some decades earlier in the reign of Augustus (Gilbert 1986: 91–93; Grabbe 1997e: 102–5). There is a strong consensus among modern scholars that the book is a literary unity and thus probably the product of a single author who, nevertheless, drew strongly on the Jewish wisdom and biblical traditions. He is likely to have had a good education in the Greek language and was knowledgeable in Hellenistic literary culture.

The book itself falls well into one of the main Hellenistic genres, being probably either an *encomium* or a *logos protrepticus* (Latin, from the Greek *logos protreptikos*). The encomium is a well-known genre in which the writer or orator praises a particular thing, often a person but sometimes something more abstract such as a particular course of action or way of life. As for the protreptic discourse, this was not primarily aimed at persuasion on a course of action but at encouraging listeners to admire someone or something. On the other hand, if the admired thing was a value of some sort, the praise would have the ultimate aim of convincing one to adopt it, thus forming a protreptic. It is evident that the encomium and the protreptic are closely related in many ways, and both fit Wisdom to a large degree.

The prime audience most likely in the mind of the author was the educated Jewish youth of Alexandria who found the surrounding Hellenistic culture attractive, including the various Hellenistic religious cults (e.g., Isis worship), and might be tempted to abandon Judaism altogether. That such might happen can be exemplified from even the very family of the upper-class Philo whose nephew Tiberius Alexander had abandoned his ancestral religion (at least, according to Josephus, *Ant*. 20.5.2 §100). Except for the matter of religion, there was little to prevent educated young Jewish men from partaking of the delights of Greek culture glittering all round them. The book was also likely to have been intended as encouragement to the Jewish community, not only in opposing the attractions of the larger Graeco-Roman society but also the antagonism and sometimes even oppression from that same society. (The problem of oppression would have been a particularly important factor if the book was written during the rule of Caligula, though the book does not dwell on oppression.)

It cannot be ruled out that the author also wanted to reach a Graeco-Roman readership, as some have suggested, but this would have been a secondary aim at best. Non-Jews would have had a difficult time understanding some aspects of the book, which drew heavily on Jewish tradition. The book touches on a number of issues about Judaic religion, especially as manifested in the diaspora:

- The figure of wisdom is significant in the book, culminating a long tradition beginning with Proverbs 1–9 (to be discussed in *HJJSTP 4*). The importance of seeking and gaining wisdom is emphasized.
- The writer combines a good Greek education (evidenced in the rhetoric and literary forms) with Jewish tradition, almost half the book being a midrash on the exodus from Egypt (Wis. 11–19).

- The writer devotes a good deal of space contrasting the righteous and wicked, with a clear moral aim. Although these are not explicitly identified with the Jews and Gentiles respectively, this seems to be implied for the most part. Presumably some Jews could be considered wicked (primarily those seen as apostates), but whether some Gentiles could be seen as righteous is unclear. However, in the last part of the book, the righteous are represented by the Israelites, and the wicked by the Egyptians.
- The book is an important witness to a Jewish eschatology which focused on the soul and its fate after death, with no hint of a resurrection. The text is deliberately ambiguous about the sort of death meant in some passages, referred to by some modern scholars as the 'ambiguity of death' in the book (Kolarcik 1991). The soul is not naturally immortal, however, with only the souls of the righteous having immortality bestowed upon them. The reward of the righteous is to become like the stars, what is sometimes called 'astral immortality' (Wis. 3.7-9; cf. §12.3.4). Whether the author believed in transmigration of souls is unclear, though 8.19-20 might imply that.
- An important theme is opposition to polytheism and, especially, to the use of images in worship (12.24–13.19); however, worship of animals (ascribed to the Egyptians) was considered even lower than idol worship (15.18-19).

Chapter 4

GREEK AND LATIN SOURCES

T. S. Brown (1973) *The Greek Historians* (1973); **H. Cancik, H. Schneider et al. (eds)** (1996–2003) *Der Neue Pauly: Enzyklopädie der Antike*; ***CHCL***; **R. Drews** (1973) *The Greek Accounts of Eastern History* (1973); ***GLAJJ***; ***LCL***; ***OCD***; ***PW***.

The following give general information on the history of the period, though Jewish history specifically is seldom mentioned. All the listed authors are found in the Loeb Classical Library (LCL), except Nicolaus of Damascus, Justin/Pompeius Trogus, Porphyry and Syncellus (editions and translations are listed for them). The LCL generally provides a convenient text and translation. An up-to-date introduction with bibliography can be found in the recent *Der Neue Pauly*. Although out of date, the entries in the old *PW* were often of better quality than its more recent counterpart, and can still be usefully consulted. See also *CHCL* and *OCD*. The specific passages on Jews and Judaea are collected in *GLAJJ*.

4.1. *Appian*

K. Brodersen (1989) *Appians Abriss der Seleukidengeschichte (*Syriake *45,232–70,369) Text und Kommentar*.

An introduction to Appian was given in *HJJSTP 2* (121). Writing in Greek, Appian (fl. 150 CE) produced a history of Rome down to Trajan. For our period, book 11 of the *Syriakē* is very important because it covers events in the eastern Mediterranean that had relevance for Jewish history. The treatise on the (Roman) *Civil Wars* is extremely valuable for events during this period of time (see *Bell. Civ.* 13–18). It includes history from the death of Julius Caesar to the eventual triumph of Augustus, with many references to events in Judaea from the end of Hasmonaean rule to the rise

112 *A History of Jews and Judaism in the Second Temple Period, Volume 3*

of Herod the Great. For example, he mentions the conquest of Jerusalem by Pompey, his procession in a chariot studded with gems, and the imprisonment of Aristobulus II. He also knows of the special tribute required of Judaea and other eastern countries under Mark Antony.

4.2. *Cicero*

M. Gelzer (2014) *Cicero: Ein biographischer Versuch*; **C. Habicht** (1990) *Cicero the Politician*; **A. Lintott** (2008) *Cicero as Evidence: A Historian's Companion*; **T. N. Mitchell** (1979) *Cicero, the Ascending Years*; **idem** (1991) *Cicero, the Senior Statesman*; **D. R. Shackleton Bailey** (1971) *Cicero*.

As a member of the Roman Senate, Marcus Tullius Cicero (106–43 BCE) was not one of the old Roman aristocracy. Rather, he was a 'new man' (*homo novum*), a member of a family only recently wealthy enough to enter the Senate. His fame was mainly as an orator, who made his reputation by defending or prosecuting a number of prominent Romans. He was consul in 63 BCE. Because of the quantity of publications from his pen, Cicero's life is well known, as evidenced by the fictionalized biography by Robert Harris: *Imperium* (2009), *Lustrum* (2010) and *Dictator* (2016). He was caught up in the final throes of the Roman Republic, which he wanted to save. This put him in opposition to Julius Caesar, though he was not among Caesar's assassins. He was condemned by Mark Antony, with Octavian's approval, and was assassinated in 43 BCE. Although Cicero mentions the Jews only a few times, his extant speeches, essays and extensive collections of letters have a great deal of value for the historical context of the time.

4.3. *Cassius Dio*

F. Millar (1964) *A Study of Cassius Dio*; **M. Reinhold** (1988) *From Republic to Principate: An Historical Commentary on Cassius Dio's* Roman History *Books 49–52 (36–29 B.C.)*; **J. W. Rich (ed.)** (1990) *Cassius Dio: The Augustan Settlement (*Roman History *53–55.9)*.

Dio began his history of Rome (in Greek) in 229 CE and eventually included events up to that date. Where extant he is often a useful source, since he sometimes had access to the works of important writers which have been lost (e.g., portions of Tacitus's writings). Unfortunately, many of Dio's books are known only from fragments or the epitome of the Byzantine writer Joannes Zonaras, including those which cover most of the Maccabaean and Hasmonaean period. However, the years 68–10 BCE are complete (books 36–54), while book 55 (9 BCE–8 CE) is preserved in abbreviated form. Thus, it is evident that much of Roman history for the early Roman and Herodian periods of Jewish history is covered by the portion of Dio's history which has been preserved in full, a fortunate accident of history.

4.4. *Diodorus Siculus*

C. E. Muntz (2017) *Diodorus Siculus and the World of the Late Roman Republic*.

A general introduction to Diodorus of Sicily was given in *HJJSTP 2* (112–20). He makes a number of references to Jews and Judaism, especially in the Hasmonaean period and at the time of Pompey's conquest. Unfortunately, it is often not possible to identify the source of his statements about the Jews. Some of them come from Hecataeus of Abdera (see *HJJSTP 2*: 113–19), but others are unidentified. One of the most important is his general description at 40.3 (discussed in *HJJSTP 2*: 283–86). The wonders of the Dead Sea are described (2.48.6-9; 19.98-99). He also relates the story that Antiochus IV, when he entered the temple, found a statue of a man seated on an ass with a book in his arms, a story which recurs in other writers (34/35.1.3).

4.5. *Livy*

J. A. Briscoe (1973) *A Commentary on Livy, Books XXXI-XXXIII* (1973); **G. B. Miles** (1995) *Livy: Reconstructing Early Rome*; **R. M. Ogilvie** (1965) *A Commentary on Livy, Books 1–5*; **H. Tränkle** (1977) *Livius und Polybios*; **P. G. Walsh** (1961) *Livy: His Historical Aims and Methods*.

The history of Rome by Livy (64 BCE–17 CE) covered from its beginnings down to 9 BCE. Along with Tacitus, he is one of the best Roman historians, but also like him much of his work has perished. Of the original 142 books, only 35 have survived (and these not always complete): 1–10 of the early history and 21–45 on the Second Punic War and the Macedonian and Syrian wars. For our period, complete are books 41–45, which cover the period 178–167 BCE, an important period for Jewish history. However, he is often thought to be an important source for Cassius Dio and thus a source at second hand for the Herodian period. There are also extensive fragments and summaries of the lost books. In quality of historical writings, many would rank him alongside Tacitus though behind Ammianus Marcellinus, Polybius and Thucydides.

4.6. Nicolaus of Damascus

GLAJJ 1.227–60; **F. Jacoby** (1926–58) '90. Nicolas von Damascus', *Die Fragmente der griechischen Historiker* 2A; **É. Parmentier and F. P. Barone** (2011) *Nicolas de Damas: Histoires, Recueil de coutumes, Vie d'Auguste, Autobiographie*; **R. J. H. Shutt** (1961) *Studies in Josephus*, 79–92; **M. Stern** (1974a) 'The Greek and Roman Literary Sources', in *The Jewish People in the First Century*, 1:18–36; **B. Z. Wacholder** (1962) *Nicolas of Damascus*.

Nicolaus of Damascus was a secretary to Herod the Great. If not of Greek origin, he was certainly trained in the Greek rhetorical tradition, which skill he used in arguing the case of Archelaus before Augustus after Herod's death. He wrote a universal history in 144 books, most of which has perished. Since he had access to documents in Herod's archives, however, his work evidently had a good deal on Jewish history and was thus a valuable source for Josephus for the Hasmonaean and Herodian periods. Most of what survives from Nicolaus is known through Josephus, but some portions of his works are known through other sources (see Parmentier and Barone 2011; *FGH*; *GLAJJ*).

For the period of Hasmonaean rule, Nicolaus seems to be Josephus's main source, both in the *War* and the *Antiquities*. Although Josephus used 1 Maccabees for the Maccabaean revolt and the period down to the rulership of Simon in the *Antiquities*, Nicolaus was probably his source for this period in the *War* (which does not seem to use 1 Maccabees) as well as for the information in the *Antiquities*, which does not agree with 1 Maccabees. The use of Nicolaus by Josephus is universally agreed, but when it comes to a detailed picture of exactly how, there is wide diversity of opinion. The reason for this is the fact that the few fragments of Nicolaus's original work preserved make it difficult to compare the original with Josephus's version.

4.7. Justin/Pompeius Trogus

B. Mineo and G. Zecchini (eds) (2016) *Justin, Abrége des* Histoires Philippiques *de Trogue Pompée, Tome I, Livres I-X*; **idem** (2018) *Justin, Abrégé des* Histoires Philippiques *de Trogue Pompée, Tome II: Livres XI – XXIII*; **O. Seel (ed.)** (1956) *Pompei Trogi Fragmenta*; **idem** (1985) *M. Iuniani Iustini Epitoma Historiarum Philippicarum Pompei Trogi*; **J. C. Yardley and R. Develin (ed. and trans.)** (1994) *Justin: Epitome of the Philippic History of Pompeius Trogus*.

In the Augustan age Trogus wrote in Greek a universal history in 44 books called the *Historiae Philippicae*. Unfortunately, the original work is lost apart from a few fragments. The Greek work was summarized in the Latin epitome of Justin about the 3rd century CE which survives. The epitome is not normally very detailed and shows considerable confusion in certain areas; nevertheless, it has some useful information to supplement other historians of the period and to fill in gaps in their narratives.

4.8. *Pliny the Elder*

Of equestrian rank Pliny (ca. 23–79 CE) served in Germany and wrote a (now lost) work, *Bellorum Germaniae*, that was used by Tacitus. He was a prolific writer and produced a number of other works, all now lost. The one work preserved is his 37-book treatise on natural history (*Naturalis Historia*). This covered many technical fields, including astronomy and cosmology, geography, zoology, agriculture, medicine and metallurgy. It drew on an enormous number of sources and preserves a great deal of ancient knowledge that would otherwise be lost.

4.9. *Plutarch*

A priest of Delphi for several decades of his life, and devoted to his hometown of Chaeronea in Boeotia, Plutarch (ca. 50–120 CE) found time to write a voluminous set of volumes. The *Moralia* contains essays on a diversity of topics, some of them of considerable interest for religion in antiquity. Of more direct value for political history are his *Parallel Lives* of noble Greeks and Romans. The quality of his sources for these varies, and his concern is usually more moralistic than historical. Nevertheless, in some cases they provide valuable information on certain individuals. For the Hellenistic and early Roman period, his lives of Pompey, Cato (Minor), Crassus, Julius Caesar, Cicero, Brutus and Antony are extant.

4.10. *Polybius*

C. B. Champion (2004) *Cultural Politics in Polybius's* Histories; **P. Derow** (1979) 'Polybius, Rome, and the East', *JRS* 69: 1–15; **idem** (2015) *Rome, Polybius, and the East*; **A. M. Eckstein** (1995) *Moral Vision in* The Histories *of Polybius*; **B. Gibson and T. Harrison (eds.)** (2013) *Polybius and his World: Essays in Memory of F. W. Walbank*; **B. McGing** (2010) *Polybius'*

116   *A History of Jews and Judaism in the Second Temple Period, Volume 3*

Histories; **M. G. Morgan** (1990) 'The Perils of Schematism: Polybius, Antiochus Epiphanes and the "Day of Eleusis"', *Historia* 39: 37–76; **K.-E. Petzold** (1969) *Studien zur Methode des Polybios und zu ihrer historischen Auswertung*; **C. Smith and L. M. Yarrow (eds)** (2012) *Imperialism, Cultural Politics, and Polybius*; **H. Tränkle** (1977) *Livius und Polybios*; **F. W. Walbank** (1957–79) *A Historical Commentary on Polybius*; **idem** (1972) *Polybius*.

In the opinion of many historians, the quality of Polybius's historical writing is second only to Thucydides among ancient historians (on his principles of writing history, see *HJJSTP 2*: 14–15); however, he has a serious bias against Antiochus IV. He was a Greek (ca. 200 to post-118 BCE) who spent many years in Rome as a hostage and thus got to know the Romans well. He wrote a history of the Hellenistic world and the rise of Rome from the First Punic War to the Roman conquest of Greece (264–146 BCE). It is thus unfortunate that just Books 1–5 are preserved intact while the rest survive only in fragments or extracts made by Byzantine writers. Where he is extant, though, Polybius is a very important source. With regard to the 2nd century, he is a major source for the historical narrative of events for the first half of it. He describes many of the major occurrences in the eastern Mediterranean, including events in Syro-Palestine. Walbank's commentary (1957–79) is a valuable resource on Polybius's text.

4.11. *Porphyry*

G. L. Archer (1958) *Jerome's Commentary on Daniel*; **M. Becker** (2016) *Porphyrios,* Contra Christianos: *Neue Sammlung der Fragmente, Testimonien und Dubia mit Einleitung, Übersetzung und Anmerkungen*; **J. Braverman** (1978) *Jerome's Commentary on Daniel*; *FGH* 260; *GLAJJ* 2:444–75; **A. von Harnack (ed.)** (1916) *Porphyrius, "Gegen die Christen", 15 Bücher: Zeugnisse, Fragmente und Referate*; **Hieronymus (Jerome)** (1964) *Commentariorum in Danielem.*; **A. Magny** (2010) 'Porphyry in Fragments: Jerome, Harnack, and the Problem of Reconstruction', *Journal of Early Christian Studies* 18: 515–55.

Porphyry was a neo-Platonist philosopher (ca. 234–305 CE). One of his main works was *Against the Christians*. Although the work as a whole has been lost, it was extensively quoted by other writers in antiquity. Especially important for the Maccabaean period were his comments on Daniel, which were extensively quoted or cited by the church father

4. *Greek and Latin Sources* 117

Hieronymus or Jerome (ca. 342–420 CE) in the latter's commentary on Daniel. This provides important historical background to this period in Jewish history (Hieronymus 1964); for example, Porphyry's comments on Daniel 11 give important information on the interaction between the Seleucids and Ptolemies in the 3rd and 2nd centuries BCE. Exactly what Porphyry's source was is uncertain, but it seems to have been basically a reliable one. The standard collection, with text, German translation and commentary is Becker 2016. The older collections of Harnack 1916 and *FGH* 260 sometimes give a different view of which fragments can be reliably ascribed to Porphyry. A convenient English translation of Jerome's commentary is given by Archer (1958, though using the old Migne text rather than the more reliable one in CCL; see also *GLAJJ* 2: 444–75).

4.12. *Posidonius*

L. Edelstein and I. G. Kidd (eds) (1989) *Posidonius: Volume I, The Fragments*; ***GLAJJ*** 141–47; **I. G. Kidd** (1988) *Posidonius: Volume II, The Commentary, (i) Testimonia and Fragments 1–149*; **idem** (1988) *Posidonius: Volume II, The Commentary, (ii) Fragments 150–293*; **idem** (1999) *Posidonius: Volume III, The Translation of the Fragments*.

Although a polymath who wrote many works during his lifetime, none of the writings of Posidonius (ca. 150–51 BCE) has survived intact: only fragments and quotations have come down to us. He was a Greek who grew up in Apamea. As a Stoic philosopher, he wrote commentaries on Plato and much on physics, ethics and logic but also on various aspects of science: mathematics, astronomy, geography, the ocean, seismology, geology, biology, as well as history. He is named by Josephus (*Ag. Ap.* 2.7–8 §§79–96) as making anti-Jewish statements quoted by Apion. It is not clear, however, whether Posidonius was actually the source of Apion's alleged statements, especially since the story that may come from Posidonius seems to differ from the statement about Jewish worship cited by Josephus. As well as the collected fragments (Edelstein and Kidd [eds] 1989), Posidonius may have been the source of many other passages in writers of the time. For example, he may have been the source of Diodorus 34/35.1.1-5 on Antiochus VII's siege of Jerusalem under John Hyrcanus (§16.3.1).

118   *A History of Jews and Judaism in the Second Temple Period, Volume 3*

4.13. *Strabo*

Strabo (ca. 64 BCE to after 21 CE) wrote an important history which has now been lost. However, his *Geography* survives and provides some useful information on Palestinian history as well as geography (16.2.28-46 §§759-65). The source from which he drew his information may have been describing the situation before Alexander Jannaeus, for he refers to the destruction of the city Gaza by Jannaeus (16.2.30) but says nothing about its being rebuilt, which it was in 61 BCE. The extant *Geography* of Strabo has a lengthy section on Judaea, including a bit of its history, in book 16. His *History* was an important source for Josephus, from whom most of the quotations of it come (§3.4). According to Josephus (*Ant.* 13.12.6 §347; 14.6.4 §104), Strabo and Nicolaus of Damascus generally told the same story, suggesting that the two depended on a common source.

4.14. *Suetonius*

Suetonius (ca. 69 to after 122 CE) is mainly known for his *Lives of the Twelve Caesars* (Julius to Domitian), which often provide valuable information. Unfortunately, many of his data are given typologically rather than chronologically, and he was too fond of filling up his space with scandalous anecdotes. As a long-time civil servant, he had the opportunity to gather first-hand information on the Roman emperors. Where he quotes actual documents, as in the life of Augustus, he is extremely important. However, none of the later lives show this use of original documents in the same way, suggesting that he no longer had access to such information after finishing his life of Augustus. (He was dismissed from his post by Hadrian in 121/22 CE.) Although he often serves as an important source, it is not always easy to evaluate his material, and what he says should be carefully compared with other writers such as Tacitus where extant.

4.15. *George Syncellus*

W. Adler (1989) *Time Immemorial: Archaic History and its Sources in Christian Chronography from Julius Africanus to George Syncellus*; **W. Adler and P. Tuffin (ed. and trans.)** (2002) *The Chronography of George Synkellos: A Byzantine Chronicle of Universal History from the Creation*; **A. A. Mosshammer (ed.)** (1984) *Georgii Syncelli Ecloga chronographica.*

George Syncellus (died after 810 CE) was a Christian monk who lived much of his life in Palestine, before going to Constantinople. He became secretary to Tarasius, Patriarch of Constantinople. In about 810 CE he wrote the work, *Extract from Chronography*, that traced the history of the world from creation to the beginning of Diocletion's reign (ca. 284 CE). After his death it was finished by his friend Theophanes, though most of the material is Syncellus's. Much of his work is taken from known and extant sources, such as Josephus and Julius Africanus. Now and then, however, he has some unique information that supplements the earlier classical historians.

Part III

SOCIETY AND INSTITUTIONS

Chapter 5

ECONOMICS

S. Applebaum (1976) 'Economic Life in Palestine', in S. Safrai and M. Stern (eds), *The Jewish People in the First Century*, 2:631–700; **idem** (1977) 'Judaea as a Roman Province: The Countryside as a Political and Economic Factor', *ANRW II*: 8:355–96; **F. M. Heichelheim** (1938) 'Roman Syria', in T. Frank (ed.), *An Economic Survey of Ancient Rome*, 4:121–257; **H. G. Kippenberg** (1982) *Religion und Klassenbildung im antiken Judäa*: 78–110; **J. Pastor** (1997) *Land and Economy in Ancient Palestine*; **A. Schalit** (1969) *König Herodes: Der Mann und sein Werk*; **F. E. Udoh** (2005) *To Caesar What Is Caesar's: Tribute, Taxes, and Imperial Administration in Early Roman Palestine (63 B.C.E.–70 C.E.)*.

This chapter will focus on the economy of Judaea from the beginning of Seleucid rule to the reign of Herod. Although the discussion here begins with an overview that considers the wider horizons of the economy, a general discussion about the debate concerning economic study of the Graeco-Roman world and more information on the Ptolemaic and Seleucid economies can be found in *HJJSTP 2* (205–24). For a general discussion on the Roman economy, see the discussion to be given in *HJJSTP 4*.

5.1. *The Economy under Hasmonaean Rule*

A. M. Berlin (1997) 'Between Large Forces: Palestine in the Hellenistic Period', *BA* 60: 2–51; **S. Dar** (1986) *Landscape and Pattern: An Archaeological Survey of Samaria, 800 B.C.E.–636 C.E.*; **S. Honigman** (2014) *Tales of High Priests and Taxes: The Books of the Maccabees and the Judean Rebellion against Antiochos IV*; **H. Kreissig** (1962) 'Der Makkabäeraufstand zur Frage seiner Socialökonomischen Zusammenhänge und Wirkungen', *Studii Clasice* 4: 143–75; **A. Mittwoch** (1955) 'Tribute and Land-tax in Seleucid Judaea', *Bib* 36: 352–61.

124   *A History of Jews and Judaism in the Second Temple Period, Volume 3*

With the conquest of Antiochus III and the reversion of Palestine to Seleucid rule, there does not seem to have been any major change in the economic sphere initially. The basic tribute was probably the same under the Seleucids as under the Ptolemies. This is implied in the decree of Antiochus III, which allowed the Jews to continue under their native laws but also remitted taxes for a period of time because of help which they provided for the Seleucid army. A similar conclusion can be drawn from later concessions made by Seleucid rulers to Hasmonaean leaders (1 Macc. 10.18-45; 11.30-37; 13.36-40). We get some idea of the annual tribute when we see the money offered by Jason for the high priesthood: the figure of 360 talents of silver (2 Macc. 4.8) was probably a raising of the normal annual tribute of about 300 talents (Bringmann 1983: 115). Jason offered another 80 talents as well, plus a further 150 to make Jerusalem into a *polis*, giving a total tribute payment of 440 talents (plus another 150, for 590 in all, if the 150 was annual).

Recently, however, Sylvie Honigman has presented another far-reaching proposal. She argues that Seleucus IV had begun a reform of the tax system, and it was left up to Antiochus to finish it off (Honigman 2014: 316–61). According to her reconstruction, 1 Maccabees 3 and the episode with Heliodorus was a fictionalized account of Seleucus's attempt to regulate the temples and taxes more closely in Coele-Syria and Phoenicia. Simon's dispute with Onias III (2 Macc. 3.2-6) was over Simon's response to an imperial request for a report that may have included the money in the temple deposited there by Hyrcanus Tobiad. In her view, Antiochus IV was continuing this dispute (since Heliodorus had been somehow thwarted in his attempt to take Hyrcanus's money). Having Jason replace Onias was the simplest way of dealing with the problem. According to this interpretation the extra tribute payment was not something that Jason offered freely but was part of Antiochs's new tax demand.

With regard to the demand for extra tribute, Antiochus had only begun his reign when the encounter with Jason took place; it is unlikely that he had already initiated a particular tax system, with his own plan to increase taxes this early. If that is the case, Jason's petition would have still fallen right into Antiochus's long-term plans and needs. What seems clear is that in spite of the large increase in annual tribute (from 300 to 440 talents), Judaea was able to bear this amount of taxation (and even the further 150 talents, if this was an annual requirement; possibly it was a one off payment). On the other hand, this was not the case with the amount that Menelaus was contracted to pay, a doubling of the annual tribute that Jason was paying. Antiochus and his tax collectors knew what the province could deliver and were unlikely to have made the mistake of over-taxing the inhabitants. On the other hand, if Menelaus came to Antiochus with promises of greater contributions to the royal coffers, Antiochus would no doubt have accepted his offer. But the amount was more than the province could raise, as became clear, because Menelaus could not pay it, i.e., he could not gather sufficient funds from the tax payers to meet this annual amount.

As noted in *HJJSTP 2* (220–21), the economic position of Judah seems to have improved considerably from the middle of the 3rd century BCE (when the province seems to have paid 20 talents annually in tribute) to the paying of 300 talents and then 440 talents in the first part of the 2nd century. When Jerusalem became a *polis*, there were no doubt many advantages in having a Greek foundation and in being a citizen of it. An obvious one, though, is that it also seems likely that the new status would make Jerusalem more attractive for trade.

A major question about the Maccabaean revolt is to what extent socio-economic matters played a part. No doubt they played an important role after it developed, but were they the cause? Was it, for example, a peasant's revolt? Although the idea of a peasants' revolt has been argued by Kreissig (1962) and also seems to be endorsed by Kippenberg (1982: 88–90), the sequence of events shows that there was no resistance to the 'Hellenizers' until Lysimachus began to sell the temple vessels, and then this came from the *gerousia* and the people of Jerusalem. If there was a general revolt during the Antiochus's second campaign in Egypt, as some propose (§15.2.1), there is no reason to think it was a 'peasant revolt'. With the religious suppression, opposition was led by the Maccabees who were hardly peasants. Of course, peasant revolts may be led by members of the upper classes, and many of the Maccabaean supporters may have been peasants. Once the Seleucids were willing to withdraw the measures and allow religious freedom again, the support for further resistance fell away. A genuine peasant's revolt would probably not have been stopped by such concessions.

This does not mean that support for the revolt did not arise from a number of motives. The Maccabean movement at some point became one of independence, and many of their supporters may have been motivated at least in part by hope of improving their socio-economic position (cf. Mittwoch 1955). But one must keep in mind that there was little popular support for the independence movement for many years. When the Maccabaean leadership eventually took control and achieved its goal, it no doubt became clear that the socio-economic position of many Jews was going to be improved. However, in the years following the return to religious freedom, many seem to have doubted that such resistance had

126   *A History of Jews and Judaism in the Second Temple Period, Volume 3*

any hope of success, and present peace was more important and secure than the vague hope of improved conditions following the ravages of a prolonged and unpromising war against Seleucid rule.

What about the economy under Hasmonaean rule? F. E. Udoh (2005: 5) refers – quite rightly – to 'the Hasmonean independent system of taxation, about which we know nothing'. We are given no real data in the sources. We are told several things in passing, but figures and numbers do not usually accompany them. We know that as time went on, the Maccabaean movement was able to obtain tax concessions from the Seleucid rulers (1 Macc. 10.18-45; 11.30-37; 13.36-40) which were no doubt welcome. With independence the Hasmonaean state still required finances. It is not clear how these were collected and on whom they fell. Not only the state apparatus but the standing army that was kept to protect the ever-expanding borders of Judah would have been a considerable cost (and eventually led to the hiring of mercenaries toward the end of Hasmonaean rule). On the other hand, the revenues from the newly conquered territories no doubt brought in substantial wealth. Also, many Jews would have been settled on land in the new territories. The result was almost certainly that the average Jew was better off now than under Seleucid rule, even the peasants and others on the lowest level of the socio-economic plane. The summary of Simon's reign in 1 Maccabees thus had a large degree of truth, despite the utopian language borrowed from Scripture: 'They worked their soil in peace, the land gave its increase... Everyone sat under his vine and fig tree' (1 Macc. 14.8, 12).

Under Jonathan and Simon there are archaeological indications that the inhabitants of Judaea seem to have separated themselves economically from the wider world (Berlin 1997: 29–30):

> The material remains found at Jewish sites both in and just outside Judea consisted almost exclusively of Judean-produced household pottery. This region's ceramic assemblages contained no Phoenician E[astern]S[igillata] A, nor any Phoenician semi-fine vessels, Aegean wine amphoras, Hellenistic decorated wares such as West Slope-style plates and cups, Alexandrian white-painted lagynoi, nor southern Italian table wares and wine amphoras. The wholesale uniformity of the household inventories of Jewish settlements bespeaks a deliberate policy of economic independence.

As discussed further at §2.1.2.3, this segregation seems to have had a religious motivation, at least to some extent. Even as Jewish settlement expanded into other Palestinian regions with the various Hasmonaean conquests, this approach to the material culture seems to have been extended into those areas as well. That is, the economic isolation characteristic of the central hill country came to characterize regions that were formerly quite cosmopolitan (Berlin 1997: 36).

Whatever their sacrifices and deprivations initially, the Hasmonaean family eventually benefitted financially from their position. One area which contributed to this seems to be their control of 'royal lands' or 'king's land'. The Hellenistic kings, like their Oriental predecessors, had royal lands as a matter of course. Although in theory the king may have owned all the land under his rule, this was never the case in practice, since private ownership was the situation with most of the land in a king's territory. When Hasmonaean rule replaced Seleucid rule over Judaea, the Hasmonaeans seem to have inherited the former royal lands. It is clear that Jonathan and Simon owned estates (Pastor 1997: 64, 66–68).

'The Mountain of the King', a large central section of Samaria, has been identified as royal land (Dar and Applebaum in Dar 1986: 88–125, 257–69). One of the indicators is the series of field towers that have been found in the region of Samaria. Applebaum's reconstruction of the territory of the 'King's Mountain' has to be taken with a grain of salt, however, though the material evidence of the field towers is well documented and perhaps the strongest support for the hypothesis. Applebaum makes the case partially but is hampered by the use of sources that are widely scattered in time and knowledge of the situation in Palestine; for example, there might be a memory in late rabbinic literature (to which Applebaum appeals), but the data are hardly likely to be reliable or of good quality, especially such sources as the medieval scholia to the *Megillat Ta'anit* (cf. §1.3.1).

One of the prime areas to have been in the possession of the Hasmonaeans (and later under Herod – see below) was the oasis of Jericho, in particular the balsam groves that produced a large revenue (1 Macc. 16.11-12). The lucrative produce of the date palms and other agricultural products of the oasis should also not be overlooked. More on this below (§5.3).

5.2. *Economic Changes with the Coming of the Romans*

The return of Judaea to foreign domination was no doubt demoralizing to many Jews, but this was paled by the practical consequences on the socio-economic level. Although the Hasmonaean policy of expansion placed burdens of taxation on the people, and certain traditional 'royal lands' had probably been reappropriated by the later Maccabaean rulers,

128   *A History of Jews and Judaism in the Second Temple Period, Volume 3*

this was more than offset by the land made available in the newly annexed territories (Schalit 1969: 171–72, 702–3). Fertile farmland in the areas of the Transjordan, the coastal plain and especially the Galilee was a real boost to the Jewish population even though the native populations were not generally ousted. Also, the sphere of commerce had been boosted by the ports now in Jewish possession.

Much of this was lost in the Pompeian settlement. The Greek cities were restored to nominal independence, and whole tracts of land were removed from Judaean rule. Although statements on the subject are rare, there are hints that many Jewish small farmers were affected. Those who had been given appropriated lands in the conquered territories under the Hasmonaeans were now turned out. It would have been a hardship for them as well as for their relatives and companions who had to accommodate their return and resettlement in their old homes. Some probably had to make their living as landless tenants or day labourers. Again, we have little in the way of figures.

It has also been suggested that this was a time when the Jewish population had reached a peak (Applebaum 1977: 361–62). If so, such a glut of unemployed workers suddenly dumped on the market would have created enormous hardships for a certain stratum of the population. There is no way of confirming this – or at least quantifying it – so it remains no more than speculative, but such might have been one of the causes of the popular military support which Aristobulus and his sons were able to muster in the series of revolts instigated by them after 63 BCE. For example, Josephus writes that right after taking Jerusalem, Pompey reinstated Hyrcanus as high priest. The reason was Hyrcanus's support during the siege, particularly in detaching from Aristobulus large numbers of 'the rural population' who were anxious to join his standard (*War* 1.7.6 §153). Roman rule also brought in a war indemnity, as well as various taxes and other expropriations to help finance the Roman military endeavours.

The exact rate of tax imposed by Pompey is uncertain but seems to have been to some extent relieved by a decree of Julius Caesar in 48 BCE, as quoted by Josephus (*Ant.* 14.10.6 §§202-3): Julius Caesar ruled that a tax had to be paid for the city of Jerusalem (= Judaea?) every year except in the seventh year. Since Joppa is excluded from the tax, this may have referred to the whole province. In the second year they were to pay the tribute at Sidon at the rate of a fourth of the produce. The problem is to know from Caesar's phraseology precisely what the tax rate was. Heichelheim (1938: 235) concluded that it was a tax of 25 percent paid every second year of a sabbatical cycle, that is, 12.5 percent for six years out of seven. Schalit (1969: 779–81), however, argues that the normal tax was 20 percent most years, with no tax in the seventh year, with the tax for the year after the sabbatical being 25 percent. This illustrates the difficulties in determining firm figures from the data preserved in our literary sources.

Thus, the Romans laid tribute on the Judaeans but, as Udoh points out (2005: 12, 22, 30), they were often not in a position to collect it because of the fluid military situation in the 25 years or so between Pompey's conquest and Herod's becoming king. In these troubled times, however, the Romans resorted to a cruder way of tribute: simply taking whatever wealth was available. According to Josephus (*Ant.* 14.7.1 §§105-6) when Crassus was about to march against the Parthians, he took 2,000 talents from the temple treasury, then stripped 8,000 talents of gold from the temple (even though Pompey had not looted the temple when he took Jerusalem). Elsewhere Josephus (*Ant.* 14.4.5 §78) states that Rome extracted more than 10,000 talents in a short space of time after Pompey's conquest. Whether this is to be equated (partially or wholly) with Crassus's confiscation or is completely separate is not clear. During the Roman Civil War, Cassius was arrayed against the friends of Caesar, Mark Antony and Octavian. In about 134 BCE he decided to raise 700 talents from Judaea and commissioned the local governors to collect the funds (*War* 1.11.1-2 §§218-22; *Ant.* 14.11.2 §§271-76). Herod showed his mettle by being the first to collect that allotted to him, 100 talents. This was from the area of the Galilee and suggests what it might have been able to pay in tribute.

What seems clear is that the Romans took what funds they could from Judaea as the needs and opportunities arose. But whether a fixed tribute was regularly collected is not at all clear (cf. further the discussion in Udoh 2005: 9–112).

5.3. *The Economy of Judaea under Herod*

S. Applebaum (1989c) 'The Troopers of Zamaris', in *Judaea in Hellenistic and Roman Times*, 47–65; **D. Braund** (1984) *Rome and the Friendly King: The Character of Client Kingship*; **M. Broshi** (1987) 'The Role of the Temple in the Herodian Economy', *JJS* 38: 31–37; **E. Gabba** (1990) 'The Finances of King Herod', in A. Kasher, U. Rappaport and G. Fuks (eds), *Greece and Rome in Eretz Israel: Collected Essays*, 160–68; **A. Momigliano** (1934b) 'Richerche sull' organizzazione della Giudea sotto il dominio romano (63 a. C.–70 d. C.)', *Annali della Scuola Normale Superiore di Pisa*, Classe di Lettere 3: 183–221; **W. Otto** (1913) '14) Herodes I', *PW Supp.*: 2:1–202; **J. Pastor** (2003) 'Herod, King of Jews and Gentiles: Economic

Policy as a Measure of Evenhandedness', in M. Mor, A. Oppenheimer, J. Pastor and D. R. Schwartz (eds), *Jews and Gentiles in the Holy Land in the Days of the Second Temple, the Mishnah and the Talmud: A Collection of Articles*, 152–64.

The quarter century between Pompey's and Herod's kingship would have been difficult at the best of times, but it was further complicated by the wars and fightings in the area through this time. The establishment of Herod's rule was therefore not a totally unwelcome event from an economic point of view. While he collected his share of taxes, he ended the long period of fighting and brought in an extended time of peace. He also brought back under his own rule most of the areas which had been under Hasmonaean control, including the ports and commercial centres.

The real gains came in 30 BCE and later. At this time the coastal cities, temporarily lost to Cleopatra under Mark Antony's governorship, were restored by Octavian, along with certain Greek cities. He also gained other territories north of Galilee and developed new territories by settlements in unpopulated areas. With the reign of Herod we finally start to find some data that might be sufficient to work out the economic situation of Judaea under him. We can begin with propositions that go against many treatments of Herod's reign:

- Herod's kingdom was not taxed by the Romans under his reign. That is, the Judaeans were not in effect paying double taxes as so often alleged.
- Herod's building programmes did not overburden the economy and cause excessive hardship on the people because of his tax burden.
- Under Herod the country prospered, and the people as a whole were generally in a reasonable financial situation, judging by the standards of the time.

Books on Herod's rule generally emphasize the crushing burden of taxation placed on the inhabitants of Judaea (e.g., Applebaum 1976: 2:664–67; 1977: 8:377). Granted, the weight of taxation was not evenly distributed, and some felt it much more acutely than others. But this was the general situation of that time (and many other times); the question is whether people were worse off under Herod than under other forms of rule, such as Hasmonaean? What we find is that there have been other evaluations of the economic situation under Herod, even given his enormous building program (Momigliano 1934: 351–57; Gabba 1990; Pastor 2003; Udoh 2005: 113–206).

First, the income from his territories was about 1,000 talents per year (*Ant.* 17.11.4 §§317-20), not necessarily that large a sum when compared with the size of the territory and such economically productive elements as ports and trade centres. For example, one source of income was the oasis of Jericho, with its date palms and especially its balsam production. This territory was taken from Herod by Mark Antony and given to Cleopatra. Herod then leased Jericho back from Cleopatra for 200 talents (*War* 1.18.5 §§361-62; *Ant.* 15.4.2 §§96-103). Considering that Herod had to bear maintenance costs, it is likely that the actual yield from this oasis was probably at least twice this 200 talents annually. Agrippa I also had an income of equal size or perhaps even larger from a territory slightly smaller than Herod's (*Ant.* 19.8.2 §352), yet he was said to have been popular with the people.

Secondly, Herod did a great deal to increase the economic prosperity of the region. This was especially true in the new areas which he opened up to cultivation. For example, in 23 and 20 BCE new territories north of Galilee were added to Herod's domain. These were an important boost to the economy because of Herod's policy of developing some of the sparsely populated areas in these new territories by bringing in settlers and opening up the land to cultivation. For instance, he founded the city of Phasaelis in a wilderness area which was then reclaimed by irrigation projects (*Ant.* 16.5.2 §145; cf. Schalit 1969: 324–25). Later, when he acquired the territory of Trachonitis, he again brought in new settlers (*Ant.* 17.2.1-2 §§23-27). The original settlers were from Babylon, but many other Jews joined them (Applebaum 1989c).

Thirdly, the building program within the country was itself a stimulus to the economy by providing work for many Jews. Indeed, when work on the Jerusalem temple ceased in the 60s CE, it created a problem by making so many unemployed all at once (*Ant.* 20.9.7 §§219-23).

Fourthly, it has been suggested that a large part of Herod's building programme was paid out of the revenue from the annual half-shekel contribution from each Jew in the diaspora, which brought in large sums each year (Broshi 1987). The question is whether such money would be available to Herod for such projects; however, it should be noted that Agrippa II evidently used temple funds to pave Jerusalem when he alleviated the unemployment caused by the end of work on the temple (*Ant.* 20.9.7 §222). Thus, Schalit (1969: 322–28) can with good reason argue that the Jews were better off economically at the end of Herod's reign than at the beginning.

The opposition to Herod may be due more to social than economic factors. As Kippenberg has noted, the Roman administration already began a taxation process which bypassed the traditional aristocracy (1982: 113–15). Under the Seleucids, the aristocracy had been responsible for collecting and paying taxes to the Seleucid administration. During Hasmonaean rule any taxes were still bound tightly to the high priestly aristocracy. Roman control took away this traditional power base by leaving them out of the process altogether, and Herod's method of collecting taxes continued the same arrangement. In addition, he took away the power of the aristocratic Sanhedrin (cf. §17.9.2; §18.4.1). Although it probably continued in name, it seems to have had little practical power because nothing more is heard of it during his reign. Thus, not only were those on whom fell the heaviest weight of taxation disenchanted with Herodian rule but also the (priestly) aristocracy, the class which in previous times had always been a part of the government.

One of the vexed questions is whether Herod paid tribute to Rome, that is, whether the Jews had to shoulder additionally a Roman tax as well as those paid to Herod's own treasury. Well-known scholars have argued that regular tribute to Rome was paid (Momigliano 1934: 348–51; Schalit 1969: 161–62; Applebaum 1976: 2:661–62; 1977: 373), but others have opposed the idea (Udoh 2005: 148; SCHÜRER 1:317; Otto 1913: 55). The study by D. Braund has added considerable weight to the argument against any Roman taxation under Herod. Braund (1984: 63–66) argues that client kings did not generally pay regular tribute, though some were required to pay a fixed war indemnity, and all could be called upon to supply provisions and auxiliaries when needed for the Roman army in their area. Although he admits that the case of Judaea is a problematic one, he feels that the argument from silence is important: there is plenty of material where such tribute would logically have been mentioned, yet no reference is made to such after Herod became king. Further, the

> absence of conclusive evidence is made all the more significant by the fact that certain non-royal states – notably the Macedonian and Illyrian republics – are definitely known to have paid tribute to Rome. (Braund 1984: 66)

5.4. Conclusions

Determining economic situations in ancient societies is not always easy to do. Often there is little or no data, or the data are in literary sources and might be of dubious reliability. The following summarize some of the main points made in this chapter:

- The economic situation of Judaea in the early 2nd century BCE seems to have been much better and more prosperous than it was a century earlier. Becoming a *polis* was also likely to be advantageous for trade and the economy in general.
- The amount of tribute that Jason agreed to pay (440 talents plus possibly 150 additional, though the latter might have been a one-off payment) was within the means of the province – there is no indication that he did not pay it. On the other hand, the amount of tribute agreed by Menelaus (double Jason's amount) was impossible, which is shown by his failure to pay.
- Other data for Hasmonaean rule are hard to come by, but the territorial expansion was no doubt beneficial for many Jews and probably attracted new settlers from Judaea into those areas.
- The Hasmonaeans themselves seem to have benefitted personally and to have amassed a considerable fortune out of the royal lands and other sources of income.
- The coming of Roman rule brought the reduction of Judaea to its old boundaries and the loss of conquered territory. There were also assessments of tribute, but the troubled situation seems to have made it difficult to collect on a regular basis. Instead, the standard procedure was to seize money regarded as necessary at the moment, when the Romans had the opportunity to do so.
- The reign of Herod brought stability and also prosperity. Far from overtaxing the people and impoverishing the country, the indication is that Judaeans were generally better off at the end of his reign than at the beginning. The amount of income from his realm was not excessive, and his building programme provided work for many people in the country. The argument that the country was 'double taxed' by both Herod and the Romans seems to be incorrect: since Herod was regarded as a 'friendly king', the Romans did not collect taxes in his territory.

Chapter 6

SECTS AND MOVEMENTS

A. I. Baumgarten (1997) *The Flourishing of Jewish Sects in the Maccabean Era: An Interpretation*; **S. J. D. Cohen** (1986a) 'The Political and Social History of the Jews in Greco-Roman Antiquity: The State of the Question', in R. A. Kraft and G. W. E. Nickelsburg (eds), *Early Judaism and its Modern Interpreters*, 33–56; **idem** (2014) *From the Maccabees to the Mishnah*; **L. L. Grabbe** (1989) 'The Social Setting of Early Jewish Apocalypticism', *JSP* 4: 27–47; **idem** (1999b) 'Sadducees and Pharisees', in J. Neusner and A. J. Avery-Peck (eds), *Judaism in Late Antiquity: Part Three. Where We Stand: Issues and Debates in Ancient Judaism: Volume 1*, 35–62; **idem** (1999c) Review article: A. I. Baumgarten, *The Flourishing of Jewish Sects in the Maccabean Era*, *JSJ* 30: 89–94; **H. Maccoby** (1989) *Judaism in the First Century*; **G. F. Moore** (1927–30) *Judaism in the First Three Centuries of the Christian Era*; **G. G. Porton** (1986) 'Diversity in Postbiblical Judaism', in R. A. Kraft and G. W. E. Nickelsburg (eds), *Early Judaism and its Modern Interpreters*, 57–80; **A. J. Saldarini** (1986) 'Reconstructions of Rabbinic Judaism', in R. A. Kraft and G. W. E. Nickelsburg (eds), *Early Judaism and its Modern Interpreters*, 437–77; **idem** (1988) *Pharisees, Scribes and Sadducees in Palestinian Society*; **A. Segal** (1986) *Rebecca's Children*; **M. Smith** (1956) 'Palestinian Judaism in the First Century', in *Israel: Its Role in Civilization*, 67–81; **G. Stemberger** (1995) *Jewish Contemporaries of Jesus: Pharisees, Sadducees, Essenes*; **M. E. Stone** (1988) 'Enoch, Aramaic Levi and Sectarian Origins', *JSJ* 19: 159–70; **idem** (2018) *Secret Groups in Ancient Judaism*; **S. Talmon** (1986) 'The Emergence of Jewish Sectarianism in the Early Second Temple Period', in *King, Cult and Calendar in Ancient Israel*, 165–201; **B. R. Wilson** (1973) *Magic and Millennium*; **idem** (1990) *The Social Dimensions of Sectarianism*.

The various groups, sects and movements in Second Temple Judaism have sometimes been given an undue emphasis in attempts to sketch a history of this period. The little information we have – which is mainly from literary sources – tends to indicate that the sects were small, only a minority of the population even when their numbers are combined. As elsewhere in this volume, the aim is to focus on the primary sources, though various scholarly interpretations will be engaged with where appropriate.

First of all, it is important not to become entangled in terminology. Terminology should be a means of discussion and clarity, not of scholastic debate and hair splitting. For some the term 'sect' creates difficulties. The word is obviously used in a variety of ways in scholarly discussion. As B. R. Wilson has pointed out, usage of the term has too often been influenced by the situation and bias of the Christian tradition (1973: 11–16). It is often used in a pejorative sense, but some who use it neutrally still confine it to groups which withdraw from or reject the values of the wider society (cf. Cohen 2014: 124–26). This may fit many Christian sects but is not necessarily transferable to other societies (Wilson 1990: 1–3). Borrowing from Wilson's insights, I use the term 'sect' here in a neutral and more encompassing sense to mean a minority religious movement (Wilson 1973: 11–18; cf. Greek *hairēsis*). Thus, it does not imply a 'church' as its counterpart, nor does it assume that the group in question rejects the wider society. The problem with using organization as a criterion has been well discussed by Wilson. The problem with using ideology is that we often do not know enough about the ideology to make distinctions. Most of the groups we know of, including the Pharisees, were minority religious movements within the Jewish temple state of the time. In the usage here, they are all sects, and trying to separate some (e.g., the Pharisees) off from the others is already a question-begging exercise.

Earlier sectarianism, associated with the Persian period, was discussed in *HJJSTP 1* (256–61). The present chapter discusses only the three 'primary' sects – Sadducees, Pharisees and Essenes – and their possible predecessors and related groups (although Qumran is discussed in Chapter 7, cross-references will be given here). There will necessarily be some repetition in the presentation of the Sadducees and Pharisees, since some of the same literary passages describe both. Other groups and movements, especially those arising in the first century CE, will be dealt with in *HJJSTP 4*. This includes the 'brigands' (λῇσται), sometimes referred to as 'social bandits', even though we have some references to them for the early Roman period.

6.1. *Hasidim*

J. J. Collins (1977) *The Apocalyptic Vision of the Book of Daniel*, 201–6; **P. R. Davies** (1977b) '*Hasîdîm* in the Maccabean Period', *JJS* 28: 127–40; **J. Kampen** (1988) *The Hasideans and the Origins of Pharisaism*; **J. N. Lightstone** (1983) 'Judaism of the Second Commonwealth: Toward

136 *A History of Jews and Judaism in the Second Temple Period, Volume 3*

> a Reform of the Scholarly Tradition', in H. Joseph et al. (eds), *Truth and Compassion*, 31–40; **J. Sievers** (1990) *The Hasmoneans and their Supporters*, 38–40.

The first group to consider here are the *Asidaioi* (οἱ Ασιδαῖοι) of the Greek texts of Maccabees, a name which is generally assumed to reflect the Hebrew *Ḥăsîdîm* (חסידים 'the pious'). They are mentioned only in a few passages in 1 and 2 Maccabees:

1 Macc. 2.39-42: When Mattathias and his associates learned of the massacre of some who refused to fight on the Sabbath, they decided that they would fight if they were attacked on the sabbath. Shortly afterward 'there joined with them an assembly (συναγωγή) of Hasidim, mighty warriors (ἰσχυροὶ δυνάμει) of Israel, every one of whom acted voluntarily for the law' (1 Macc. 2.42).

1 Macc. 7.12–16: A 'company of scribes' (συναγωγὴ γραμματέων) came to Alcimus and Bacchides to ask for terms. The passage goes on to say that 'the Hasidim were the first among the sons of Israel to seek peace' from Alcimus and Bacchides because the former was 'a priest from the seed of Aaron'. They trusted them, but Bacchides took captive sixty of them and killed them.

2 Macc. 14.6: In a speech to the Seleucid king Demetrius I, the high priest Alcimus states, 'The Jews called Hasidim, to whom Judas the Maccabee serves as leader, maintain a warlike policy and are rebelling, not permitting the kingdom to secure tranquillity'.

Most of the relevant passages have been critically studied in the seminal article by Davies (1977; cf. also Collins 1977: 201–6; Lightstone 1983: 36–40; Saldarini 1988: 251–54). About all we are told is that they were a group of 'mighty warriors' who joined the Maccabees (1 Macc. 2.39–42), that they were the first to seek peace after Alcimus was made priest (1 Macc. 7.12-16) and that they were a group led by Judas Maccabaeus (2 Macc. 14.6). There are many questions; in any case, these few data already contradict some assumptions, but they tell us next to nothing about the group.

Thus, the one concrete thing we are told is that this group was composed of 'mighty warriors'. Far from being pacifist, they were fighters and thus to be disassociated from those who allowed themselves to be martyred (Davies 1977: 134–35; Collins 1977: 215–18). This means that such individuals should not be considered as authors of the book of Daniel which encourages passive resistance through martyrdom rather than active armed resistance to persecution (Davies 1977: 129–30;

Collins 1977: 198–210). Another point is that the statement of Alcimus to Demetrius (2 Macc. 14.6) makes Judas the leader of the Hasidim. Either this is an error of identification by Alcimus, or it is another indication that the term was used only generally, or that – heaven forefend – Judas was an entirely different leader from his picture in 1 and 2 Maccabees! For example, Alcimus's statement is often labelled an error or misunderstanding. But as one of the few passages providing actual data on the Hasidim, it should not be dismissed lightly.

The Hasidim are also alleged to have been the ancestors of both the Pharisees and the Essenes. For example, J. Kampen (1988) has argued for a connection with the Pharisees; however, one of the main reasons is the supposition that the Hasidim formed a unified movement, and another is that the Pharisees had a position in Jewish society and religion which will be argued against below (§6.3.8). They have also been described as the 'orthodox' who opposed the 'Hellenizers' under the Hellenistic reform of Jason and Menelaus. The list of their characteristics goes on and on, little if any of it based on the actual original data. The Greek translator undoubtedly understood the term *hăsîdîm* in his source to be a name, but this does not mean that the original Hebrew text of 1 Maccabees pointed to anything more than a miscellaneous group of 'pious individuals'. That is, since *hăsîdîm* was ambiguous in the Hebrew text of 1 Maccabees, it may well be that to read this as an organized group is a misunderstanding. While either interpretation is possible, it further weakens the confidence with which one attempts to reconstruct the history of the alleged Hasidim. As Collins (1977: 201) noted:

> The party of the Hasideans has grown in recent scholarship from an extremely poorly attested entity to the great Jewish alternative to the Maccabees at the time of the revolt. There has been no corresponding growth in the evidence.

The only appropriate conclusion at the moment is one of agnosticism. We do not know for certain that the Hasidim were a definite organized group; but even if only one particular group is in mind, we know little about it other than that it was not the author of Daniel 7–12 and that its relationship – if any – to the Essenes and Pharisees is unknown.

6.2. *Sadducees and Boethusians*

D. Daube (1990) 'On Acts 23: Sadducees and Angels', *JBL* 109: 493–97; **M. Goodman** (2008) 'The Place of the Sadducees in First-Century Judaism', in F. E. Udoh (ed.), *Redefining First-Century Jewish and Christian Identities: Essays in Honor of Ed Parish Sanders*, 139–52; **J. LeMoyne** (1972)

Les Sadducéens; **R. Leszynsky** (1912) *Die Sadduzäer*; **J. Lightstone** (1975) 'Sadducees versus Pharisees', in *Christianity, Judaism and Other Greco-Roman Cults*, 3:206–17; **E. Main** (1990) 'Les Sadducéens vus par Flavius Josèphe', *RevB* 97:161–206; **W. Poehlmann** (1992) 'The Sadducees as Josephus Presents Them, or The Curious Case of Ananus', in A. J. Hultgren et al. (eds), *All Things New: Essays in Honor of Roy A. Harrisville*, 87–100; **A. Schremer** (1997) 'The Name of the Boethusians: A Reconsideration of Suggested Explanations and Another One', *JJS* 43: 290–99; **B. T. Viviano and J. Taylor** (1992) 'Sadducees, Angels, and Resurrection (Acts 23:8–9)', *JBL* 111: 496–98.

The main problem with the Sadducees is that we have not a line of their own writings or thoughts – as far as we know – and the sources we do possess are generally hostile. Even their name might be a punning creation of their enemies (cf. Schremer 1997, though he suggests the same might be true for the Boethusians and even the Pharisees). Thus, the Sadducees have tended to be the whipping boys of most writers, whether Jewish or Christian. In addition, the little information extant is very skimpy and tends to be overinterpreted by most who write on them. We have three main sources: Josephus, the New Testament, and some scattered references in rabbinic literature.

6.2.1. *Sources*

We begin with Josephus as our first source. As will be evident, several of his statements show an anti-Sadducaean (and a pro-Pharisaic) bias. He gives two general descriptions of the Sadducees and their beliefs, the first in *War* 2.8.14 §§164-66:

- The Sadducees reject the concept of Fate.
- With regard to evil, they believe God is incapable not only of committing it but even thinking about it.
- Humans have the free choice of doing good or evil, and it is up to each individual which he chooses.
- They reject the continuation of the soul after death, including any penalties or rewards in the underworld.
- The Pharisees are affectionate towards each other and promote harmony within the community. On the other hand, the Sadducees are uncouth toward each other, behaving toward their fellows as if they would to strangers.

This last statement is often taken at face value, but it is clearly biased. Most historians would quickly seize on a statement that Democrats/ Labour party members/Christian Socialists are affectionate to each other, but Republicans/Tories/Christian Democrats are boorish and rude. Yet the number who have accepted this statement by Josephus without question is surprising. His next statement is in *Ant*. 18.1.4 §§16-17 (also 13.5.9 §§171-72, which seems to add nothing):

- They believe that the soul dies when the body dies.
- They observe only the (written) laws.
- They consider it a virtue to dispute with their philosophy teachers.
- Although there are only a few who follow this teaching, they are men of the greatest reputation.
- Yet they do not accomplish anything because when they become officials, they must accede to what the Pharisee says; otherwise, the multitude would not put up with them.

As will be seen, Josephus himself gives no evidence for his last point about the Sadducees submitting to Pharisaic rule. Not only is the statement incredible in itself, but there are other data which oppose it.

Apart from these general descriptions, Josephus refers to individual Sadducees and activities of the Sadducees hardly at all. One major episode relates to the reign of John Hyrcanus (*Ant*. 13.10.6 §§293-98). Josephus tells the story of a feast given by John Hyrcanus in which the Pharisees were present. On asking them to speak frankly, one Eliezar was critical of him. When Hyrcanus took counsel as to how he should punish Eliezer, Jonathan (a friend of Hyrcanus and belonging to the party of Sadducees) suggested that the king let the Pharisees sentence Eliezer. When they chose flogging and imprisonment, rather than capital punishment, this was seen as siding with one of their own against the king. Jonathan supposedly talked Hyrcanus into leaving the Pharisees and joining the Sadducees for the rest of his reign. But in this episode Josephus makes some more statements, giving information but also showing anti-Sadducaean and pro-Pharisaic prejudice:

- The Pharisees have such force with the multitude that even when they speak against a king or high priest, they are immediately believed.
- Hyrcanus abolished customs which the Pharisees had established for the people and punished those who observed them; from this arose the hatred of the multitude for Hyrcanus and his sons.

140   *A History of Jews and Judaism in the Second Temple Period, Volume 3*

- The Pharisees had given to the people certain customs transmitted by former generations but not written in the laws of Moses. These were rejected by the Sadducaean group who considered valid only the written customs but believed that the tradition of the fathers need not be kept.
- The Sadducees have only the trust of the well-off but no following from the populace, while the Pharisees have the multitude as allies.

Opposition to the Pharisees supposedly continued under Alexander Jannaeus, though nothing further is said about the Sadducees at this point, nor about them in the reign of Alexandra Salome when the Pharisees became the dominant influence in her government (§16.6). Much later, just before the war with Rome, the high priest Ananus is said to have been one of the Sadducees, 'who are more fierce in judgment than any of the other Jews' (*Ant.* 20.9.1 §199), another prejudiced statement. He managed to have James the brother of Jesus and some others condemned to death by the Sanhedrin. As pointed out by W. Poehlmann (1992) this somewhat negative picture of Ananus here is exceptional, since in the *War* and also in the *Life* Ananus is presented in a very positive manner. Otherwise, no other specific persons are said to be Sadducees.

For the New Testament, Acts associates the Sadducees with the high priest (ostensibly about 33 CE): 'But the high priest rose up and all who were with him, that is, the party of the Sadducees' (Acts 5.17; also Acts 4.1). They are evidently the dominant group on the Sanhedrin even though there are also Pharisees, such as Gamaliel. According to the picture in Acts 23.6-10 (dated by the author to about 59 CE) the Sanhedrin seems more evenly divided; nevertheless, the Sadducees are able to enforce their will to keep Paul under arrest. They are also said not to believe in angels or the resurrection (Acts 23.8; but cf. Daube [1990] on the question of angels). The Sadducees are mentioned in the gospels as well, but without much specificity. They may be little more than ciphers to fill out the quota for 'opponents of Jesus' (cf. §6.3.4).

Rabbinic literature is uniformly hostile to the Sadducees. There is also a further problem in that the term seems to be interchangeable (at least at times) with 'Boethusian' and even occasionally with 'Samaritan'. The latter is clearly an assimilation to later opponents. The question of 'Boethusian' is more difficult (LeMoyne 1972: 101–2, 337–40; Schremer 1997). It is often explained as a reference to the family of Boethus which provided a number of the high priests from the time of Herod on. If so, the association of Sadducees and Boethusians is explicable without assuming a precise identity (Saldarini feels, however, that since we know so little, the two groups should be kept apart [1988: 227–28]). Some even want to identify them with the Essenes (see the references in Schremer 1997), though the beliefs ascribed to them in the sources do not fit the Essenes. A few religious beliefs are mentioned as coming up in debates between Pharisees and Sadducees/Boethusians, including the following:

- They reckoned Pentecost as being the Sunday following the seventh weekly Sabbath after the wavesheaf day (LeMoyne 1972: 177–90). That is, they interpreted the term 'Sabbath' in Lev. 23.15-16 as the weekly Sabbath, whereas the Pharisees took it to mean the annual holy day. The Sadducaean Pentecost always fell on a particular day of the week (Sunday), while the Pharisaic view would assign it to a particular day of the month (either 5, 6 or 7 Sivan on a calendar determined by observation). The most natural reading of the Hebrew text is that of the Sadducees, a conclusion confirmed by the practice of other Jewish sects (Samaritans; Karaites; cf. Qumran).
- They rejected the concept of the *eruv*, which was a means of extending the limits of a Sabbath day's journey (LeMoyne 1972: 201–4).
- They may also have objected to the popular customs of pouring water and beating with willow branches at the Feast of Tabernacles (LeMoyne 1972: 192–95, 283–89).
- It is often asserted that they accepted only the Pentateuch as canonical, but this is only a deduction from their supposed rejection of beliefs in angels and spirits (on this, see Daube 1990). It may be that a late book such as Daniel, with an elaborate angelology and the resurrection, was not accepted, but it is not clear that the Old Testament canon was closed at this time in any case. The Sadducees may well have accepted the Pentateuch, Prophets and some of the Writings just as apparently many other Jews did (cf. LeMoyne 1972: 357–79).

6.2.2. *Analysis and Conclusions*

The following are the beliefs and characteristics of the Sadducees, according to our sources:

- The Sadducees reject the concept of Fate.
- With regard to evil, they believe God is incapable not only of committing it but even of thinking about it.
- Humans have the free choice of doing good or evil, and it is up to each individual which he chooses.

142 *A History of Jews and Judaism in the Second Temple Period, Volume 3*

- They reject the continuation of the soul after death, including any penalties or rewards in the underworld.
- They believe that the soul dies when the body dies.
- They observe only the (written) laws.
- They consider it a virtue to dispute with their philosophy teachers.
- Although there are only a few who follow this teaching, they are men of the greatest reputation.
- They are evidently the dominant group on the Sanhedrin.
- Said not to believe in angels or the resurrection.

The Boethusians are said to have the following views, which are taken here as most likely the same as the Sadducees:

- They reckoned Pentecost as being the Sunday following the seventh weekly Sabbath after the wavesheaf day.
- They rejected the concept of the *eruv*, which was a means of extending the limits of a Sabbath day's journey (LeMoyne 1972: 201–4).
- They may also have objected to the popular customs of pouring water and beating with willow branches at the Feast of Tabernacles

Evaluation of the data we have is very difficult. The earliest references to the Sadducees (in Josephus) indicate that they are a political party with the Pharisees as their primary rivals, but no particular religious beliefs are indicated. Otherwise, they tend to be characterized by particular religious positions, but these have a rather miscellaneous character about them: they do not form a coherent set of beliefs. We could take individual points from a variety of sources and create an artificial system, but this takes little account of the nature of our evidence. The best we can do is advance cautiously from the surest conclusions to the less certain to attempt some sort of hypothesis, recognizing however that it is only a reconstruction whose tentative nature has always to be acknowledged:

1. The most certain conclusion is that the group first appeared as a political entity (whatever its origin and other characteristics) and continued to exist in some form until after the fall of Jerusalem, possibly even into the 2nd century CE (Lightstone 1975).
2. Several bits of information suggest some sort of connection with the priestly establishment: (a) The name Sadducees is often thought to be derived from 'Zadok', the name associated with the altar priests. If the 'Boethusians' are to be associated in some way with

the Sadducees, their name is also suggestive (assuming it derives from the family of Boethus which provided a number of high priests). (b) Several beliefs connect them with the older Israelite religion, such as their rejection of the afterlife (on whether they rejected angels, see Daube 1990). These would be compatible with the conservatism of the priesthood. (c) Restricting themselves to the authority of the written word seems also a priestly characteristic (however, even the priests were likely to have their own tradition of interpretation [cf. Saldarini 1988: 303–4]). (d) Their method of reckoning Pentecost is not only the most natural one from the biblical text (cf. the Karaites) but also coincides with that of the Samaritans. This points to a priestly practice. (e) Other beliefs associated with them seem to concern rituals relating to the temple (e.g., objections to certain popular practices at Sukkot). (f) Acts 5 makes them the high priestly party and gives them a majority on the Sanhedrin which was dominated by the high priest; Josephus also notes that one high priest in the 60s was a Sadducee but does not seem to be suggesting that this was unique.

3. Josephus states that they were to be identified with the upper socio-economic class (and thus not popular with the masses). This is not confirmed in other sources, but it is compatible with an association with the priestly establishment and membership on the Sanhedrin. However, this is not to suggest that the two were co-extensive: not all Sadducees were necessarily priests or perhaps even wealthy, nor were all priests or upper-class individuals Sadducees.

6.3. *Pharisees*

A. I. Baumgarten (1983) 'The Name of the Pharisees', *JBL* 102: 411–28; **idem** (1984) 'Josephus and Hippolytus on the Pharisees', *HUCA* 55: 1–25; **idem** (1984–85) '*Korban* and the Pharisaic *Paradosis*', *JANES* 16–17: 5–17; **idem** (1987) 'The Pharisaic *Paradosis*', *HTR* 80: 63–77; **idem** (1991) 'Rivkin and Neusner on the Pharisees', in P. Richardson and S. Westerholm (ed.), *Law in Religious Communities in the Roman Period: The Debate over* Torah *and* Nomos *in Post-Biblical Judaism and Early Christianity*, 109–26; **S. J. D. Cohen** (1984) 'The Significance of Yavneh: Pharisees, Rabbis, and the End of Jewish Sectarianism', *HUCA* 55: 27–53; **R. Deines** (1997) *Die Pharisäer: Ihr Verständnis im Spiegel der christlichen und jüdischen Forschung seit Wellhausen und Graetz*; **J. A. Fitzmyer** (1998) *The Acts of the Apostles: A New Translation with Introduction and Commentary*; **M. Goodman** (1999) 'A Note on Josephus, the Pharisees and Ancestral Tradition', *JJS* 50:

17–20; **L. L. Grabbe** (1994) Review of S. Mason, *Flavius Josephus on the Pharisees*, *JJS* 45: 134–36; **idem** (1997a) 'The Current State of the Dead Sea Scrolls: Are There More Answers than Questions?' in S. E. Porter and C. A. Evans (eds), *The Scrolls and the Scriptures: Qumran Fifty Years After*, 54–67; **idem** (1997c) '4QMMT and Second Temple Jewish Society', in M. Bernstein, F. García Martínez and J. Kampen (eds), *Legal Texts and Legal Issues: Proceedings of the Second Meeting of the International Organization for Qumran Studies*, 89–108; **idem** (1999c) review article: A. I. Baumgarten, *The Flourishing of Jewish Sects in the Maccabean Era*, *JSJ* 30: 89–94; **idem** (2000e) 'The Pharisees – A Response to Steve Mason', in A. Avery-Peck and J. Neusner (eds), *Judaism in Late Antiquity: Part Three: Where We Stand: Issues and Debates in Ancient Judaism, Volume 3*, 35–47; **idem** (2018) 'What Did the Author of Acts Know about Pre-70 Judaism?', in J. H. Ellens et al. (eds), *Wisdom Poured Out Like Water: Studies on Jewish and Christian Antiquity in Honor of Gabriele Boccaccini*, 450–62; **H. K. Harrington** (1995) 'Did the Pharisees Eat Ordinary Food in a State of Ritual Purity?' *JSJ* 26: 42–54; **M. Hengel and R. Deines** (1995) 'E. P. Sanders' "Common Judaism", Jesus, and the Pharisees', *JTS* 46: 1–70; **S. Mason** (1988) 'Priesthood in Josephus and the "Pharisaic Revolution"', *JBL* 107: 657–61; (1989) 'Was Josephus a Pharisee? A Re-Examination of *Life* 10–12', *JJS* 40: 31–45; **idem** (1991) *Flavius Josephus on the Pharisees: A Composition-Critical Study*; **idem** (1994) 'Method in the Study of Early Judaism: A Dialogue with Lester Grabbe', *JAOS* 115: 463–72; **idem** (1999) 'Revisiting Josephus's Pharisees', in A. Avery-Peck and J. Neusner (eds), *Judaism in Late Antiquity: Volume 4, Part II*, 23–56; **A. J. Mattill, Jr** (1978) 'The Value of Acts as a Source for the Study of Paul', in C. H. Talbert (ed.) *Perspectives on Luke-Acts*, 76–98; **J. Neusner** (1971) *The Rabbinic Traditions about the Pharisees before 70*; **idem** (1973) *From Politics to Piety*; **idem** (1981) *Judaism: The Evidence of the Mishnah*; **J. Neusner and C. Thoma** (1995) 'Die Pharisäer vor und nach der Tempelzerstörung des Jahres 70 n. Chr.', in S. Lauer and H. Ernst (ed.) *Tempelkult und Tempelzerstörung (70 n. Chr.): Festschrift für Clemens Thoma zum 60. Geburtstag*, 189–230; **R. I. Pervo** (2009) *Acts: A Commentary*; **J. C. Poirier** (1996) 'Why Did the Pharisees Wash their Hands?' *JJS* 47: 217–33; **E. Rivkin** (1972) 'Defining the Pharisees: The Tannaitic Sources', *HUCA* 43: 205–40; **A. J. Saldarini** (1992) 'Pharisees', *ABD* 5:302; **Y. Sussmann** (1989–90) 'The History of *Halakha* and the Dead Sea Scrolls: A Preliminary to the Publication of 4QMMT', *Tarbiz* 59: 11–76 (Heb.)// **idem** (1994) partial ET in E. Qimron and J. Strugnell (eds), *Qumran Cave 4: V Miqṣat Maʿaśe ha-Torah*, 179–200; **J. C. VanderKam** (1992) 'The People of the Dead Sea Scrolls: Essenes or Sadducees?' in H. Shanks (ed.), *Understanding the Dead Sea Scrolls: A Reader from the Biblical Archaeology Review*, 50–62, 300–302; **H.-G. Waubke** (1998) *Die Pharisäer in der protestantischen Bibelwissenschaft des 19. Jahrhunderts*.

6. Sects and Movements

Because of limits of space, this section looks only at the major sources which have been suggested as potentially important for the Pharisees by recent studies and considers whether they seem to be relevant. However, no potential sources have been consciously rejected without discussion. The sources are contained essentially in three collections: the writings of Josephus, the New Testament and rabbinic literature. It has also recently been suggested that some Qumran writings represent Sadducaean viewpoints and, by implication, give an insight into the development of the Pharisaic movement.

6.3.1. *Josephus*

The writings on Josephus are extremely important because he lived at a time when the Pharisaic movement was active and had personal knowledge of some prominent Pharisees. One of his earliest references is in *War* 1.5.2-3 §§110-14, which relates to Alexandra Salome (76–67 BCE):

> Beside Alexandra, and growing as she grew, arose the Pharisees, a body of Jews with the reputation of excelling the rest of their nation in the observances of religion, and as exact exponents of the laws. To them, being herself intensely religious, she listened with too great deference; while they, gradually taking advantage of an ingenuous woman, became at length the real administrators of the state, at liberty to banish and to recall, to loose and to bind, whom they would. In short, the enjoyments of royal authority were theirs; its expenses and burdens fell to Alexandra... But if she ruled the nation, the Pharisees ruled her... Thus they put to death Diogenes, a distinguished friend of Alexander, accusing him of having advised the king to crucify his eight hundred victims. They further urged Alexandra to make away with the others who had instigated Alexander to punish those men; and as she from superstitious motives always gave way, they proceeded to kill whomsoever they would.

War 1.29.2 §571 relates to Herod's accusations against Pheroras's wife. He accused her before a council of friends and relatives, among other things, of encouraging the Pharisees to oppose the king. It is in *Ant.* 17.2.4-3.1 §§41-47 that a more detailed account of what seems to be the same episode is recounted:

> They were a group of Jews priding itself on its adherence to ancestral custom and claiming to observe the laws of which the Deity approves, and by these men, called Pharisees, the women (of the court) were ruled. These men were able to help the king greatly because of their foresight, and yet they were obviously intent upon combating and injuring him. At least when the whole

Jewish people affirmed by an oath that it would be loyal to Caesar and to the king's government, these men over six thousand in number, refused to take this oath, and when the king punished them with a fine, Pheroras' wife paid the fine for them. In return for her friendliness they foretold – for they were believed to have foreknowledge of things through God's appearances to them – that by God's decree Herod's throne would be taken from him, both from himself and his descendants, and the royal power would fall to her and Pheroras and to any children that they might have. These things... were reported to the king, as was the news that the Pharisees had corrupted some of the people at court. And the king put to death those of the Pharisees who were most to blame... He also killed all those of the household who approved of what the Pharisees said... After punishing the Pharisees who had been convicted of these charges, Herod held a council of his friends and made accusations against Pheroras' wife... The fine that had been imposed by him (on the Pharisees) had been evaded, thanks to the payments that she had made, and nothing was now being done without her help.

One of the main passages that describes the beliefs of the Pharisees is *War* 2.8.14 §§162-66. Later, in *Ant.* 18.1.3 §§4-23 Josephus gives another description, which repeats some of this but also adds to the image:

War 2.8.14 §§162-66	*Ant.* 18.1.3 §§4-23
•The leading sect and considered the most accurate interpreters of the laws.	•Extremely influential among the city dwellers, who practise their beliefs and pay tribute to their virtue (*aretē*). •All prayers and sacred rites of divine worship are carried out according to their views.
•Attribute everything to fate and to God; i.e., conduct is mostly determined by the individual but in each action fate cooperates.	•Assume everything comes through fate, though there is still a place for free will. •Live simply and make no concessions to luxury.
•Every soul is immortal: the soul of the good goes into another body (transmigration?), but the soul of the wicked suffers eternal punishment.	•Believe that souls survive death and are rewarded or punished under the earth: evil souls suffer eternal imprisonment, but good souls go into a new life (transmigration?). •Follow traditional doctrinal teachings of their circle.

•The Pharisees are affectionate towards each other and promote harmony with the community. On the other hand, the Sadducees are uncouth toward each other, behaving toward their fellows as they would to strangers.	•Show respect to their elders, deferring to them and not contradicting them.

A similar statement about fate is given in *Ant.* 13.5.9 §171-72: according to the Pharisees some events happen due to fate, but other events depend on the individuals themselves; on the other hand, the Sadducees reject fate and argue that all things lie within our own power and are our individual responsibility.

War 2.17.2-3 §§410-11: At the beginning of the 66–70 revolt the principal citizens, the chief priests and the most notable Pharisees assembled to consider the situation, since they were faced with disaster.

Ant. 13.10.5-7 §§288-99 is extremely important because it asserts a number of things about the Pharisees. Josephus now tells the story of a feast given by John Hyrcanus in which the Pharisees were present. On asking them to speak frankly, one Eliezar was critical of him. When Hyrcanus took counsel as to how he should punish Eliezer, Jonathan (a friend of Hyrcanus and belonging to the party of Sadducees) suggested that the king let the Pharisees sentence Eliezer. When they did not sentence him to death, Jonathan made Hyrcanus angry by insinuating that the Pharisees gave a 'mild' punishment because they agreed with Eliezer's views. The result was that Hyrcanus joined the Sadducaean party and deserted the Pharisees. According to Josephus, he also abrogated certain regulations that the Pharisees had established for the people (see below). Here are some of the points this passage makes about the Pharisees:

- The people, especially the Pharisees, were hostile to Hyrcanus because of envy at the successes of himself and his sons. The influence of the Pharisees is so great with the masses that even when they speak against a king or high priest, they are believed.
- The Pharisees had passed on to the people certain regulations handed down by former generations and not recorded in the Laws of Moses. It was apparently some of these that the Pharisees had established for the populace that Hyrcanus abrogated. The Sadducaean group opposed these because they held that only

148   *A History of Jews and Judaism in the Second Temple Period, Volume 3*

those regulations written down (in Scripture) were to be observed and not the traditions of former generations. The two groups had serious controversies over this point.

- While the Sadducees had the confidence only of the wealthy, the Pharisees had the support of the masses.

Now, if the *Antiquities* is to be believed, Hyrcanus was faced with a revolt which was caused by his breach with the Pharisees. The *War* says nothing about the Pharisees but ascribes the revolt to the 'successes' (*eupragia*) of Hyrcanus and his sons, which is also how the *Antiquities* actually begins the passage. Despite supposedly not having the people behind him, Hyrcanus put down the revolt, and the rest of his reign was peaceable (both the *War* and the *Antiquities* give the same picture). So much for the power of the Pharisees. The actual events described by Josephus contradict his allegations about the power and influence of the Pharisees. Indeed, the *War* knows nothing about the place of the Pharisees in all this, which suggests that the part they played was a rather small one.

Ant. 13.15.5-16.5 §§401-23: The context of this is Alexander Jannaeus on his deathbed and the instructions he gives to his wife Alexandra. He tells her to yield some of her executive power to the Pharisees, with the hope that they might then influence others favourably toward her. Jannaeus states that this is because they had the confidence of the ordinary people and could persuade them to be hostile or friendly to persons in power, as they chose. Alexandra did as instructed, including placing Jannaeus's body at their disposal. The result was that they gave him a magnificent funeral and became her friends. However, this was because she allowed them the power to put in place regulations depending on Pharisaic tradition. The result was that 'while she had the title of queen, the Pharisees had the power' (*Ant.* 13.16.2 §409). But the country was peaceful for the most part, except that the Pharisees tried to convince her to kill those who had advised Jannaeus to put his opponents to death. As a consequence, Aristobulus used fear that the Pharisees might rule their family after her death, and tried (unsuccessfully) to seize power.

Ant. 15.1.1 §3: Herod especially honoured Pollion the Pharisee and his disciple Samais because these men had advised the citizens to admit Herod during the siege of Jerusalem. When Herod was on trial for his life, Pollion had also foretold that if Herod's life was spared, he would persecute Hyrcanus and the judges, as indeed happened.

Ant. 15.10.4 368-71: This describes the oath of loyalty that Herod compelled everyone to take. Some refused, including the Pharisees and the Essenes. Herod imposed a fine on most of the Pharisees; however, he excused the Essenes, and also tried to persuade Pollion the Pharisee and Samais and most of their disciples to take the oath. When they refused, though, he did not punish them, because of his regard for Pollion.

Life 2 §§10–12: This is a crucial passage. Josephus claims that at age 16 he decided to experience the various sects for himself, with the aim of finally selecting the one that he thought best to follow. So he submitted to the various entry requirements, which meant that he 'passed through' (διῆλθον) the training courses of the three main sects. He then spent three years with a hermit named Bannus. At age 19, 'I began to govern my life (πολιτεύεσθαι) by the rules of (κατακολουθῶν) the Pharisees' (*Life* 2 §12).

Mason (1989; 1991: 342–56) has written at length to argue that Josephus does not claim here to have joined the Pharisees at age 19, as this passage is normally taken to say. He states that those who say Josephus became a Pharisee are dependent on the phrase, τῇ Φαρισαίων αἱρέσει κατακολουθῶν, but if so, 'he has chosen an excruciatingly circuitous way of saying it' (1991: 355–56). Mason is right about the round about way of speaking, but Hellenistic historians were often more interested in rhetoric and literary style than in being straightforward and clear. The fact is that the predominant judgment does not depend on just that phrase but also on the entire context: in the context, the most natural way of understanding Josephus's statement is that at age 19 he became a Pharisee. Mason rightly points out that there is no evidence elsewhere that Josephus was a Pharisee, but that is beside the point – Josephus often makes claims according to the circumstances, not necessarily according to the reality.

Life 5 §21: Josephus goes on to comment that when Menahem and his brigand chiefs had been executed, he came out of his refuge in the temple and associated again with 'the chief priests and the leading Pharisees'.

Life 38 §191: Josephus refers to Simon son of Gamaliel, who was a Jerusalem native from a distinguished family, and a member of the sect of the Pharisees, who have a reputation for being experts in their 'country's laws' (τὰ πάτρια νόμιμα).

Life 39 §§196-98: When Josephus was the military commander in Galilee, the leadership in Jerusalem were unhappy with him and sent a four-man delegation to investigate. Two of them were from the ordinary class of people, but both Pharisees. A third came from a priestly family but was also a Pharisee. The final member was from a family of high priests. The idea was to be able to examine Josephus from a variety of angles. For example, if Josephus was defended with regard to his expertise in the laws, they could reply that they were also knowledgeable in 'the customs of their fathers' (ἔθη τὰ πάτρια).

6.3.2. *Conclusions about Josephus*

There are a number of points we can draw from the data just presented:

- Josephus himself had personal acquaintance with the Pharisaic and Sadducaean movements and knew or had knowledge of prominent figures in the movements. However, there is no evidence that he was himself ever a member of either movement. (Mason has rightly pointed this out, but he was not the first to do so; cf. Grabbe 1992: 5.)
- His attitude toward both movements is ambivalent. Toward the Pharisees he is sometimes favourable, sometimes neutral and occasionally negative. Toward the Sadducees there are positive points in his descriptions, but he often has an edge to his presentation and never seems completely favourable or even neutral. To what extent he follows his sources in individual passages is debatable. Although in typical Hellenistic manner he usually rewrote his sources, this does not mean that he imposed a consistent view on them and could have (or has) in some cases allowed the viewpoint of the original source to stand.
- According to his presentation, both the Pharisees and Sadducees have political aspirations much of the time. Although so little is said about the Sadducees that it is difficult to draw certain conclusions, one has the impression that the Sadducees – or at least certain individual Sadducees – were significantly involved in government. They number the wealthy and prominent among their number or their sympathizers. The Pharisees are often pictured as seeking political power, sometimes exercising it as a group (as under Alexandra Salome), and sometimes having individuals with a prominent position. The only time Josephus depicts them as actually in power, however, is under Alexandra Salome.

- Both groups are portrayed as having religious beliefs, but very little is actually said as to what these are. Apart from the somewhat irrelevant question of fate, the Pharisees are characterized by having 'traditions from the fathers' (though what these were is never spelled out in detail) and respect for the teachings of the elders. They also believe in reward and punishment after death. They have a reputation for accurate interpretation of the Scriptures and are influential among the common people. The Sadducees do not accept anything not written in the Scriptures and allow younger members to argue with elders. They reject reward and punishment after death. In several passages the Pharisees have a reputation for being able to predict the future.
- In one passage (*Ant.* 18.1.3 §§12-17), the Pharisees are alleged to be able to enforce their views on the Sadducees and cause public worship to be conducted according to their rites (whatever these are – we are never told). However, this passage is not supported by the rest of Josephus's statements on the two groups except in the nine-year reign of Alexandra. The Pharisees are kept under control by Alexander Jannaeus and by Herod and not even mentioned for other rulers. The priests are in charge of the temple (e.g., *Ag. Ap.* 2.21 §184-87; 2.23 §§193-94; cf. also Mason 1988).
- In the later *Antiquities* Josephus has the Pharisees in some passages where they do not appear in the earlier *War*, especially with regard to John Hyrcanus and Alexander Jannaeus. Why this is so is not completely clear. However, in one of his latest writings he also *claims* (falsely) to have become an adherent of the Pharisees at an early age in *Life* 2 §§10-12. Putting these together suggests that he is trying to gain favour from contemporary Pharisees toward the end of his life, for whatever reason. This could also explain his statements about the alleged power and popularity of the Pharisees.

The Hasmonaeans, Romans and Herodians rule the country; only under Alexandra do the Pharisees have sufficient influence to get their way. As far as we can tell, this influence came to an end when Alexandra died; there is no evidence that it continued after her. Some 'notable Pharisees' (such as Simon son of Gamaliel) are involved in the leadership at the time of the revolt, but they are only a part of it and do not necessarily dominate (or at least do not do so because of their Pharisaic membership). After all, Simon was subordinate to the high priest Ananus who was a Sadducee (*Life* 38 §§189-94). Nowhere does Josephus give any evidence to support the view that the Pharisees controlled the temple

152   *A History of Jews and Judaism in the Second Temple Period, Volume 3*

or were able to manipulate the Jewish ruler (except under Alexandra Salome) or could enforce their own tradition in the form of legal regulations on society.

6.3.3. *The New Testament*

The one individual claiming to be a Pharisee whose actual words we seem to have is the apostle Paul. Information about his Pharisaic background is given in two sources: the genuine letters of Paul and the Acts of the Apostles (on use of the latter source, see below.) In Phil. 3.4-6, Paul gives his Jewish 'credentials', including being a Pharisee according to the law. The problem is that Paul's Christian teachings in some cases represent a reaction against his Jewish background. It is difficult, therefore, to determine which (if any) of Paul's views or beliefs or teachings show a Pharisaic influence. His being a Pharisee is associated with observance of the law. Beyond that it is difficult to go.

In the gospels there are many references to the Pharisees. The following parallels in the Synoptic Gospels show the opponents of Jesus in the various pericopae:

Mark	Matthew	Luke
2.1-12: Jesus is brought a paralytic; the scribes criticize him	9.1-8: scribes	5.17-26: Pharisees and teachers; scribes
2.16-17: scribes of Pharisees criticize him for eating with sinners/ tax collectors	9.11-13: Pharisees	5.30-32: Pharisees and their scribes
2.18: John's disciples and Pharisees fast	9.14: disciples of John	5.33: disciples of John and disciples of Pharisees
2.23-24: Pharisees criticize Jesus for letting disciples pluck grain on the Sabbath	12.1-2: Pharisees	6.1-2: Pharisees
3.1-6: Pharisees criticize Jesus for healing on the Sabbath, then plot with Herodians	12.9-14: Pharisees	6.6-11: scribes and Pharisees
3.22: scribes say Jesus is possessed by Beelzebul	9.32-34: Pharisees say he casts out demons by Beelzebul//12:22-24: Pharisees	11.14-15: some

6. Sects and Movements

153

7.1-5: Pharisees and some scribes criticize disciples for eating with unwashed hands	15.1-3: Pharisees and scribes	11.37-39: a Pharisee/the Pharisees
7.14-23: disciples ask about the saying on what defiles a person	15.12: Pharisees offended at his saying	
8.11: Pharisees seek a sign from Jesus to test him	16.1-4: Pharisees and Sadducees//12.38: some of the scribes and Pharisees	11.16: others
8.15: Jesus says beware the leaven of the Pharisees and the leaven of Herod	16.5-12: Pharisees and Sadducees	12.1: Pharisees
10.2: Pharisees ask Jesus about divorce to test him	19.3: Pharisees	16.14-18: Pharisees
11.27-33: chief priests, scribes and elders ask Jesus about his authority	21.23-27: chief priests and elders of the people	20.1-8: chief priests and scribes with elders
12.12: they tried to arrest him	1.45-46: chief priests and Pharisees	20.19: scribes and chief priests
12.13: Pharisees and some of the Herodians sent to entrap him	22.15-16: Pharisees and Herodians	20.20: they (scribes and chief priests?)
12.18-27: Sadducees ask him about resurrection	22.23-33: Sadducees	20.27-40: Sadducees
12.28: one of the scribes asks about the first commandment	22.34-35: Pharisees, one of them a lawyer	10.25: lawyer
12.35: scribes teach about the Christ	22.41-42: Pharisees	20.41: they
12.37-40: Jesus says, 'Beware of the scribes'	23.1-12: scribes and Pharisees sit in Moses' seat	20.45-47: beware of scribes
14.3: Jesus eats at the house of Simon the leper	26.6: Simon the leper	7.36-39: Pharisee's house

Mark	Matthew	Luke	John
14.43-52: Judas comes from chief priests, scribes and elders	26.47-56: chief priests and elders of the people	22.47-53: –	18.2-12: chief priests and the Pharisees

The Q Document

Luke	Matthew
3.7-9: John excoriates multitudes when they come for baptism 7.30: Pharisees and lawyers rejected God's purpose	3.7-10: Pharisees and Sadducees (11.7-19 is parallel to Lk. 7.24-35, but there is no exact parallel to this verse)
– – 11.39: Pharisees cleanse outside of cup 11.42: Pharisees tithe small herbs 11.43: Pharisees love best seats in synagogues and salutations 11.44: you are like graves 11.47: you build tombs of prophets 11.52: lawyers (*nomikoi*) prevent entering kingdom	23.15: scribes and Pharisees 23.25: " 23.23: " – – 23.27: " 23.29: " 23.13: "

Matthew (No Parallels)

5.20:	righteousness must exceed that of scribes and Pharisees
27.62:	chief priests and Pharisees gather to ask for Jesus' tomb to be guarded

Luke (No Parallels)

13.31:	Pharisees threaten Jesus with Herod
14.1-3:	Jesus dines at house of Pharisee; speaks to lawyers and Pharisees
15.1-3:	scribes/Pharisees grumble because he eats with sinners (Mt. 18.12: teaching disciples)
17.20-21:	Jesus asked by Pharisees about the kingdom of God
18.10-11:	a Pharisee and a tax collector pray in the temple
19.39:	Pharisees criticize Jesus for not rebuking disciples

Fourth Gospel

1.24:	Jews send priests and Levites; sent by the Pharisees
3.1:	a Pharisee named Nicodemus comes to Jesus secretly by night
4.1:	Jesus knows that the Pharisees have heard he baptized more disciples than John
7.32-52:	chief priests and Pharisees try to arrest Jesus; Nicodemus defends him
[8.3:	Pharisees bring woman caught in adultery to Jesus]
8.13:	Pharisees debate with Jesus
9.1-41:	Jesus heals blind beggar; Pharisees refuse to accept the miracle and cast the healed man out ('the Jews' had agreed that anyone professing Jesus would be put out of the synagogue)
11.46-47:	chief priests and Pharisees plot against Jesus because of his raising of Lazarus from the dead
11.57:	chief priests and Pharisees plot to arrest Jesus
12.19:	Pharisees astonished at the crowds who meet Jesus on his entry into Jerusalem
12.42:	authorities who believed in Jesus do not confess him out of fear because the Pharisees would cast them out of the synagogue

(On 18.3, see above under Mark and parallels.)

Book of Acts

There is considerable disagreement among New Testament scholars on the extent to which Acts is a credible historical source (on this point, see some recent commentaries, such as Fitzmyer 1998 and Pervo 2009; also Mattill 1978; Grabbe 2018).

Acts 4.1-2: While Peter and John were speaking to the people in the temple, 'the priests, the captain of the temple and the Sadducees' arrived and were upset about their teaching.

Acts 5.17-39: This chapter describes the arrest of the apostles because of their teaching in the temple. This was done by the high priest and 'all who were with him (that is, the sect of the Sadducees)' (Acts 5.17). They convened the Sanhedrin and the elders and threatened the apostles with the death penalty. But a member of the Sanhedrin, named Gamaliel, who was a Pharisee and also a 'teacher of the law' (Acts 5.34: νομοδιδάσκαλος) made a speech, urging clemency. The Sanhedrin is said to have gone along with his recommendation.

156 *A History of Jews and Judaism in the Second Temple Period, Volume 3*

Acts 22.3: Paul defends himself before the Sanhedrin, with the statement, 'I am a Jewish man, born in Tarsus of Cilicia, but educated in this city at the feet of Gamaliel, taught with precision according to our ancestral law, being zealous for God, just as all of you are today'.

Acts 22.30–23.10: The military tribune in Jerusalem wanted to find out what Paul was being accused of by the Jews. So he ordered the chief priests and the Sanhedrin to meet. At some point in the proceedings, Paul noticed that some of the members were Sadducees and others were Pharisees. He therefore stated, 'I am a Pharisee, a son of Pharisees' (Acts 23.6). This caused a disagreement between the Pharisees and the Sadducees, because Paul had alleged he was on trial for belief in the resurrection, whereas 'the Sadducees say that there is no resurrection, or angel, or spirit' (Acts 23.8: the Pharisees believe in all three.)

Several points emerge in these passages:

- The Sadducees are associated with the high priest.
- They form an important part of the Sanhedrin. There are also Pharisees on the Sanhedrin, though the Sadducees are dominant even in the 60s, according to Acts 23.
- The Pharisee Gamaliel is usually identified with Gamliel the Elder, and the portrayals of him in Acts and in rabbinic literature are remarkably parallel (see Neusner 1971: 1:347, 373–76). The statement that Paul studied under Gamaliel has no confirmation in the genuine Pauline writings, nor in rabbinic literature.

6.3.4. *Conclusions about the New Testament*

- The gospel traditions are difficult because of their tradition history and the question of their interrelationships. The two earliest sources of the gospel tradition are, by a strong consensus, Mark and Q. There is very little Q information on the question, the main parallel being Q 11.39-52 (Q is conventionally cited according to Luke chapter and verse numbering). The most valuable source of information is therefore Mark (usually considered the earliest gospel, written around 70 or not long afterward) with its synoptic parallels.
- There is also the problem that certain groups and individuals seem only to be ciphers set up as Jesus's opponents simply for the sake of being knocked down. Yet despite this some patterns do emerge. The

6. Sects and Movements

opponents of Jesus most frequently cited in Mark are the Pharisees, but they appear in only slightly more than half the pericopae; on the other hand, they often appear accompanied by others (scribes, Herodians, John's disciples), and there are quite a few others (e.g., scribes) cited alone. (Interestingly, the Herodians found three times in Mark disappear except for Mt. 22.15-16.)

- There is a tendency to add the Pharisees or to change from another name to the Pharisees in the synoptic parallels where Mark does not have them.
- The teachings of the Pharisees include agricultural law, the sabbath, washing and ritual purity in general. They also ask Jesus about the messiah and Roman rule.
- The pericopae which imply special religious authority for the Pharisees are in the later sources (Mt. 23.2; Jn 9.22-35; 12.42).
- According to Acts, the Sadducees are associated with the high priest. They also form an important part of the Sanhedrin. Although there are also Pharisees on the Sanhedrin (e.g., the Pharisee Gamaliel, usually identified with Gamliel the Elder), the Sadducees are dominant even in the 60s.

6.3.5. *Rabbinic Literature*

Ṣaddûqîm and Pěrûšîm in Tannatic Sources
A number of passages in Tannaitic literature which mention the *Ṣaddûqîm* and *Pěrûšîm* have been taken at one time or another to refer to the Sadducees and Pharisees of the Greek sources (Rivkin 1972). Here is a brief list of the main ones:

m. Ḥag. 2.7: This compares the relative purity of the clothes of different groups: the *'am hā'āreṣ*, the *Pěrûšîm*, those who eat heave offerings, those dealing with the water of the sin offering.

m. Sota 3.4: a saying of various things that wear out the world, including a foolish saint, a clever fool, a hypocritical woman and the wounds of the *Pěrûšîm*.

m. Mak. 1.6: differences between the *Ṣaddûqîm* and sages on the question of executing false witnesses.

m. Menaḥ. 10.3: the Boethusians (*Baitôsîm*) and the wavesheaf (*'ōmer*) day.

m. Tohor. 4.12: cleanness of the *pěrîšût*.

m. Parah 3.7: the *Ṣaddûqîm* and the *ṭěvûl yôm*.

158   *A History of Jews and Judaism in the Second Temple Period, Volume 3*

m. Nid. 4.2: daughters of *Ṣaddûqîm* are like the daughters of the Samaritans (with regard to menstrual impurity) unless they separate and follow the 'Israelites'.

m. Yad. 4.6-8: differences between the *Ṣaddûqîm* and *Pĕrûšîm* on various matters of halaka.

t. Berak. 3.25: the 'blessing' of the Eighteen Benedictions about the *minim* includes that against the *Pĕrûšîm*.

t. Šab. 1.15: a *zav* of the *Pĕrûšîm* does not eat with a *zav* of the *'am hā'āreṣ*.

t. Roš ha-Šanah 1.15: the Boethusians (*Baitôsîm*) hire witnesses to mislead the sages about the new moon because of the counting of Shavu'ot.

t. Yoma 1.8: a Boethusian (*Baitôsîm*) (high priest) prepares the incense for the Holy of Holies, contrary to the opinion of the sages, and dies as result.

t. Suk. 3.1: the Boethusians (*Baitôsîm*) attempt to prevent the beating of the willows on the Sabbath, contrary to the halaka, which permits it.

t. Ḥag. 3.35: the *Ṣaddûqîm* laugh at the *Pĕrûšîm* for immersing the menorah after the festival.

t. Sanh. 6.6: Judah b. Tabbai wants to root out the false notion of the Boethusians (*Baitôsîm*) about the execution of false witnesses.

t. Sota 15.11-12: the rabbis taught that the *Pĕrûšîm* multiplied in Israel after the temple was destroyed.

t. Parah 3.8: high priest of the *Ṣaddûqîm*, about to burn the red heifer, made unclean by Yohanan b. Zakkai.

t. Yad. 2.20: debates between the *Pĕrûšîm* and the Boethusians (*Baitôsîm*).

Other Rabbinic Traditions

The relevant sources have been collected and analyzed by Jacob Neusner (1971). The traditions about the named pre-70 sages and the houses of Hillel and Shammai have often been drawn on for evidence about the Pharisees. The problem is that these figures are not labelled Pharisees. The Tannaitic pericope that talk about the *Pĕrûšîm* never associate them with the named sages or their schools. The might lead one to conclude that there was no connection. Yet this does not settle the matter because we have the additional complication that two of the pre-70 sages *are* called Pharisees in other sources: Gamliel the Elder looks very much like the individual called Gamaliel in Acts 5.34; similarly, Šim'on b. Gamliel of the rabbinic traditions seems to be the Simon son of Gamaliel known from Josephus (*Life* 38 §§190-91).

6.3.6. *Summary with Regard to Tannaitic Literature*

- The terminology of *Pĕrûšîm* and *Ṣaddûqîm* is already problematic. *Pĕrûšîm* could be used in the sense of 'separatists' or 'abstainers/ asetics' as well Pharisees. Cf. the translation of Herbert Danby (1933), which generally renders 'Pharisee', with that of Jacob Neusner (1988), which often uses 'abstainer' to interpret the Hebrew word. *Ṣaddûqîm* was sometimes inserted in manuscripts in place of an original *minîm* or similar expression.
- It is difficult to take all references to the *Pĕrûšîm* as a reference to the same entity (whether Pharisees or something else). Although the teachings of the *Pĕrûšîm* seem to agree with those of the sages most of the time, it is interesting to see that none of the pre-70 figures is designated as one of the *Pĕrûšîm*.
- The pericopae about the 'debates' (it is not even clear that these were real debates) between the *Pĕrûšîm* and *Ṣaddûqîm* are given with a bias toward the former. But what emerges is that the *Pĕrûšîm* are interacting with equals or near equals. In other words, despite the pro-*Pĕrûšîm* flavor of the pericopae's present form, the *Ṣaddûqîm* are able to hold their own or to be treated as serious rivals. There is no evidence that the views of the *Pĕrûšîm* prevail without further ado. One does not get the impression that the *Pĕrûšîm* are in charge of religious belief or practice or of societal norms.
- There are several possibilities with regard to the historical reality about the debates between the *Pĕrûšîm* and *Ṣaddûqîm*. They could be (1) a memory of actual pre-70 debates; (2) a memory of debates between post-70 groups; or perhaps (3) an artificial construct to reflect a contemporary debate by using old or traditional names. There may also be other possibilities, and determining which is the correct evaluation is not easy.
- The dating of the pericopae is very difficult. Only two of those with both the *Pĕrûšîm* and *Ṣaddûqîm* concern matters relevant only to the pre-70 situation (*t. Hag.* 3.35 on the immersion of the menorah; cf. also *m. Parah* 3.7 on the *Ṣaddûqîm* and 'the elders'). Another with the *Ṣaddûqîm* alone concerns matters which relate to a time when the temple still stood (*t. Parah* 3.8); the same applies to the pericope about the Boethusians who seem especially to be associated with the temple. Most of the others give no indication that they are supposed to be related to Second Temple times.

160   *A History of Jews and Judaism in the Second Temple Period, Volume 3*

- Whether the Boethusians (*Baitôsîm*) are to be equated with the *Ṣaddûqîm* is a moot point. No explicit equation is made in rabbinic literature, yet there are indications that the Boethusians may be closely related to the *Ṣaddûqîm*. Neither seems to believe in the *ṭĕvûl yôm*, and the debates between the *Pĕrûšîm* and *Ṣaddûqîm* in *m. Yad.* 4.6-8 are said to be between the *Pĕrûšîm* and the Boethusians in *t. Yad.* 2.20. Sometimes the high priest is identified with the *Ṣaddûqîm* and sometimes with the Boethusians.

6.3.7. *4QMMT and the Temple Scroll (11QT)*

It has recently been argued that some of the regulations in 4QMMT and also the *Temple Scroll* represent Sadducaean halakha and specifically oppose Pharisaic rulings. I have dealt with the question in detail elsewhere. There are problems with interpretation (Grabbe 1997; cf. also VanderKam 1992). Out of the seventeen separate *halakot* in 4QMMT, only four have been suggested as agreeing with the Sadducees. Of these four only two are really possibilities. If one or two of these regulations coincide with the views of the *Ṣaddûqîm* alleged by rabbinic literature, this is a long way from saying that the author(s) of 4QMMT were Sadducees and opposed the Pharisees. See further Chapter 7 on Qumran.

6.3.8. *Analysis in the Context of Recent Study*

The most important fact to notice about the sources is that we have no statement from anyone who seems to be a Pharisee or a Sadducee. The Christian Paul claims to have been a Pharisee, but this is also a part of his past. Although late in his life Josephus seems to claim to have become a Pharisee at age 19, this is belied by his own account of his activities and his descriptions of the Pharisees. The rabbinic sources refer to individuals who may have been Pharisees, but these are either in the past or, possibly, a contemporary but separate group. Thus, all our information is from external sources. Some of those mentioning the Pharisees appear to identify with them or at least to be friendly. With regard to the Sadducees, we have neutral sources at best, while in a number of cases the sources are plainly hostile. It is from the Greek sources that the name 'Pharisees' and 'Sadducees' are taken; we must therefore begin there.

Josephus is our best source because (a) he knew individual Pharisees (and possibly a Sadducee) and had the opportunity to know of the groups firsthand; (b) he gives descriptions of the various Jewish 'philosophies'; (c) his accounts claim to speak of the Pharisees and Sadducees before the 66–70 revolt. With regard to the Pharisees his attitude seems to have varied (whether because of his own views or those of his sources), from very friendly to quite critical. Although he refers to Pharisees in a variety of passages, he makes two essential points: first, he states that they have traditions of the fathers not written in the Scripture; secondly, he presents them as a group trying to gain political power and advantage. Unfortunately, he gives very little information about the special Pharisee tradition (*paradosis*), confining his observations to the question of fate and what happens after death.

The main question is what place the Pharisees had in society. Few individual Pharisees are named, the main one being Simon son of Gamaliel, who was a prominent individual at the time of the 66–70 revolt. Two other named individual Pharisees (Pollion and Samais) are not described in such a way as to suggest their social or economic background, except that Pollion was able to speak with Hyrcanus II and other prominent people. Pharisees also had access to the women of Herod's court. However, religious teachers may have an entrance into circles far above their socio-economic status. One individual Pharisee is identified as a priest. It has been suggested that the Pharisees belonged to the 'retainer' class, meaning those 'whose roles in society were military, governing, administrative, judicial and priestly...mostly townspeople who served the needs of the governing class as soldiers, educators, religious functionaries, entertainers and skilled artisans' (Saldarini 1988: 37–38; 1992: 5:302). This has a prima facie cogency, but there is little evidence to resolve the question one way or the other. Their supposed popularity with the common people does not settle the question, either, since popular leaders may come from any class. The few data we have suggest Pharisees came from a variety of socio-economic strata.

The power of the Pharisees has been a major area of debate. In one oft-cited passage Josephus says that they are believed if they speak against a king or high priest (*Ant.* 13.10.5 §288), and religious rituals are conducted according to their dictates even if the Sadducees are in office (*Ant.* 18.1.3 §§15-17). Although several episodes show the Pharisees in the process of seeking political power, the only time that the Pharisees are shown to operate as de facto head of state and as supreme religious authority is under Alexandra Salome. In other passages, Josephus emphasizes the place of the priests in carrying out the cult and in teaching the people (see §6.3.2 above).

Josephus speaks of the Sadducees on three occasions: as a group in competition with the Pharisees in the time of John Hyrcanus, as having one of the main 'philosophies' with certain beliefs (on fate, dependence on the written word and lack of an afterlife) and of an individual high

162   *A History of Jews and Judaism in the Second Temple Period, Volume 3*

priest who was a Sadducee. Josephus says that although they are few in number, they include 'men of the highest standing' (*Ant.* 18.1.4 §17: τοὺς μέντοι πρώτους τοῖς ἀξιώμασι). This is the only indication he gives of the socio-economic identity of the Sadducees.

The gospels are hostile to a variety of groups who are seen as opponents of Jesus. In many cases one suspects the various opponents are mere straw figures to be knocked down by Jesus, and use of a particular name has no specific content or significance. This is certainly the impression one has with the synoptic parallels to Mark, where the groups named in Mark are often different in Matthew and Luke. Also, the Pharisees tend to appear in the two later gospels where they do not occur in Mark. In John 'the Jews' have ceased to be the Jewish people and become simply an opponent of Jesus; that epithet seems to alternate with 'Pharisee'. In Mark and Q the Pharisees are not said to have special religious authority; it is in Mt. 23.2 that they sit in Moses's seat (along with the scribes) and in John (9.22-35; 12.42) that they have authority to expel people from the synagogue.

The one statement by Paul about his Pharisaic past does not give any real information on the group. Acts is especially difficult to evaluate, often being untrustworthy yet at times seeming to have some reliable information. It associates the Sadducees with the party of the high priest and makes them dominant on the Sanhedrin. It also mentions Gamaliel, who has some remarkable parallels to Gamliel the Elder in rabbinic literature (cf. Neusner 1971: 3:291). Its description of the Sadducees as not believing in angels or the resurrection also coincides with information in Josephus (see further Grabbe 2018).

The beliefs of the Pharisees as described in the gospels coincide in part with the interests of the Mishnah and Tosephta, especially on traditions not found directly in the written Scripture, and its concern with details of tithing, ritual purity and sabbath observance. The Pharisees are also pictured as wanting to rid themselves of Jesus, who is seen as a rival and as being interested in the question of Roman and Herodian rule; Josephus has statements on the Pharisees which fit reasonably well with this. The one belief without parallel is that of the messiah, which occurs in the New Testament but not in the other sources.

The rabbinic literature is the hardest to evaluate. The pericopae mentioning the *Pĕrûšîm* and *Ṣaddûqîm* are taken by some as the key to the historical Pharisees and Sadducees, whereas others regard them as practically useless for the subject. Even if one regards them as reflecting actual pre-70 groups, few would see every reference to the *Pĕrûšîm* as referring to Pharisees, or every reference to the *Ṣaddûqîm* as to the Sadducees. Some would see the decisive criterion for the historical sects of pre-70 times in those passages which mention a debate between the two groups, yet only two such passages have a definite pre-70 setting. Even if one assumes that we are dealing with actual historical debates between the Pharisees and Sadducees, could these be references to *post*-70 groups?

It is the general assumption that named figures such as Hillel, Shammai, Gamaliel and Simon were Pharisees. One cannot help feeling that there must be a connection between Hillel, Shammai and their houses, and the Pharisees, but definite proof is lacking. After all, the rabbinic tradition was quite capable of 'rabbinizing' all sorts of historical figures. However, there is some evidence in other sources that Gamaliel I and his son Simon were Pharisees, and it may be that the family of Gamaliel is an important link between the Pharisees and the later rabbinic movement (cf. Neusner and Thoma 1995: 198–99.

A significant connection may be found in the New Testament, which centres the interests of the Pharisees around Sabbath observance, tithing, ritual purity and other halakhic matters. Although this is only a brief catalogue in comparison with the entire Mishnah/Tosephta, considering the brevity of the gospel passages, there is an interesting coincidence between the Pharisaic concerns and those of the Mishnah. Sadly, Josephus, who mentions the importance of the 'traditions of the fathers' on several occasions, in fact gives little information on the content of the Pharisaic tradition.

6.3.9. *Summary and Conclusions*

We have essentially three sources, each one with problems of dating, *Tendenz* and reliability. In many cases, the sources are so problematic, one wonders whether we can know anything about the Pharisees and Sadducees. Yet the main sources all seem to be independent of each other, which makes coincidences between their different pictures of potential significance. Whatever our conclusions, though, they can only be tentative at best; we simply do not know a great deal about these groups.

Josephus is the most valuable source: he knew certain individual Pharisees and had access to information on the group before 70; he wrote while they were in existence or during the time that they were transforming themselves; his biases are probably the easiest to analyse and to take into account. The New Testament writings cover a considerable span of time and are characterized by a general hostile attitude to the various Jewish groups. Although post-70, both Mark and Q seem to have had some pre-70 traditions and show a more nuanced description than the synoptic parallels and the Fourth Gospel. Acts is very difficult to evaluate. Rabbinic literature is the latest and most problematic to use. Even the

164   *A History of Jews and Judaism in the Second Temple Period, Volume 3*

Tannaic writings were redacted long after 70 CE, and the extent to which genuine pre-70 data are preserved is not easy to determine. References to the *Pĕrûšîm* and *Ṣaddûqîm* may or may not have the historical pre-70 Pharisees and Sadducees in mind; on the other hand, those figures most often designated as Pharisee in modern treatments are not so identified in rabbinic literature. Keeping in mind these major difficulties with using and evaluating the sources, some tentative concluding observations can be made:

- The Greek sources (and possibly rabbinic literature) make both the Pharisees and the Sadducees important at least some of the time, beginning about the reign of John Hyrcanus (135–104 BCE). They also make the Sadducees and Pharisees rivals, both seeking political power at the expense of the other.
- There may have been certain socio-economic differences between the groups, in that the Sadducees are said to have the support of the wealthy and prominent persons, whereas the Pharisees had the support of the masses (Josephus); on the other hand, popular leaders do not necessarily come from the lower social strata, and some priests are said to be Pharisees.
- The Sadducees and Pharisees are also alleged to differ on a number of religious beliefs. The Pharisees are especially characterized by the traditions of the fathers, whereas the Sadducees do not accept as authoritative anything not in the written Scripture (Josephus). The Pharisees believe in the survival of the soul and rewards and punishments in the afterlife; the Sadducees reject this. (If the Boethusians are to be associated with the Sadducees, the two groups also differ on the counting of the wavesheaf day and the celebration of the Feast of Weeks.) According to Josephus, the Pharisees (like the Essenes) have a reputation for knowing the future.
- Two of our sources seem to make the Pharisees especially concerned about halakic matters. The gospels have them particularly exercised about tithing, ritual purity (washings), Sabbath observance and the like. According to rabbinic literature, the *Pĕrûšîm* and *Ṣaddûqîm* also have certain halakic differences. The Pharisaic agenda according to the Gosepls – as far as one can determine it from the few brief references – accords well with the contents of the Mishnah/Tosephta (with the exception of the gospels debates about the messiah and the question of the government of Judaea).
- Those sources which give the Pharisees a general dominance of religious belief and practice are those which come later in relation to parallel sources. Thus, it is only two later passages in the

Antiquities which state that public worship is carried out according to Pharisaic regulations and that the Sadducees are required to follow them even when they hold office. This is not stated in the *War* and is not borne out in Josephus's other passages on the Pharisees. The one exception is the reign of Alexandra; indeed, the statement of Josephus about the Pharisees controlling the king and high priest fits well with her reign. Similarly, although the gospels give considerable prominence to the Pharisees as opponents of Jesus, it is only the late Fourth Gospel which suggests that they can cast people out of the synagogues. It is also the later passages in the book of Acts which suggest that the Pharisees make up a significant part of the Sanhedrin (though they are still not dominant). It is the Ushan stratum of Tannaitic literature which begins to assert that Hillel controlled the temple (Neusner 1971: 3:255–59).

- An important question is whether the Boethusians of rabbinic literature represent another group or are identical with (or a sub-division of) the Sadducees. There is no clear answer on this, but the Boethusians are associated with the priesthood and their teachings seem to be closer to those of the Sadducees. The argument that the term is derived from the high priestly family of Boethus is plausible and seems more likely than the theory that they are the Essenes (cf. Sussmann 1989–90: 40–60; 1994: 111–21).

Finally, the tentativeness of our knowledge about the Pharisees and Sadducees must be emphasized. Despite the vast amount of literature written over the past couple of centuries, we have few data, and what data we do have are often contradictory or problematic. We know little about the structure, aims or beliefs of these two groups and can only make intelligent guesses about their place in Judaean society at the turn of the era. It is perfectly legitimate to attempt to make historical reconstructions involving them, but these must take account of all the data (unfortunately, those which do not fit are too often ignored) and can never be more than theories to be tested continually.

6.4. *'The Scribes'*

A. Yarbo Collins (2007) *Mark: A Commentary*; **M. J. Cook** (1978) *Mark's Treatment of the Jewish Leaders*; D. Ellenson (1975) 'Ellis Rivkin and the Problems of Pharisaic History: A Study in Historiography', *JAAR* 43: 787–802; **L. L. Grabbe** (1995) *Priests, Prophets, Diviners, Sages: A Socio-historical Study of Religious Specialists in Ancient Israel*; **idem** (2015) 'Penetrating the Legend: In Quest of the Historical Ezra', in

M. C. A. Korpel and L. L. Grabbe (eds), *Open-Mindedness in the Bible and Beyond: A Volume of Studies in Honour of Bob Becking*, 97–110; **D. J. Harrington** (1980) 'The Wisdom of the Scribe According to Ben Sira', in J. J. Collins and G. W. E. Nickelsburg (eds), *Ideal Figures in Ancient Judaism*, 181–88; **J. Jeremias** (1969) *Jerusalem in the Time of Jesus*; **J. S. Kloppenborg** (2008) *Q, the Earliest Gospel: An Introduction to the Original Stories and Sayings of Jesus*; **D. Lührmann** (1987) 'Die Pharisäer und die Schriftgelehrten im Markusevangelium', *ZNW* 78: 169–85; **J. Neusner** (1981) *Judaism: The Evidence of the Mishnah*: 230–48; **E. Rivkin** (1978) 'Scribes, Pharisees, Lawyers, Hypocrites: A Study in Synonymity', *HUCA* 49: 135–42; **A. J. Saldarini** (1988) *Pharisees, Scribes and Sadducees in Palestinian Society: A Sociological Approach*, 144–87, 241–76; **C. Schams** (1998) *Jewish Scribes in the Second-Temple Period*; **D. R. Schwartz** (1992) *Studies in the Jewish Background of Christianity*; **H. Stadelmann** (1980) *Ben Sira als Schriftgelehrter: einer Untersuchung zum Berufsbild des vor-makkabäischen Sofer unter Berücksichtigung seines Verhältnisses zu Priester-, Propheten- und Weisheitslehrertum.*

The word 'scribe' (*grammateus*) is widely used in Greek literature to refer to a professional, someone trained to write, copy, keep accounts and otherwise carry out the functions we now associate with being a clerk or secretary. The position could vary from a rather lowly individual keeping records in a warehouse to a high minister of state whose office was an important one in the established governmental bureaucracy. One thinks of the analogy of our modern English usage of the word 'secretary', which can refer to someone whose essential job is typing or word processing but can also mean an administrative official who holds high office as 'secretary of this or that', even 'secretary of state'. A parallel usage is found in Jewish literature. Josephus frequently applies it to a public official or a secretary: village clerks (*War* 1.24.3 §479); the secretary to Herod (*War* 1.26.3 §529); the secretary of the Sanhedrin (*War* 5.13.1 §532); the scribes of the temple (*Ant.* 12.3.3 §142). The same sort of usage occurs in other Jewish literature (cf. 1 Macc. 5.42; Ben Sira 10.5).

6.4.1. *'Scribes' in Jewish Literature*

Another function carried out by some scribes – probably only a very few – was that of literary activity and wise counsel. The legendary scribe Ahiqar was said to be an advisor to the king of Assyria and the composer of wise sayings. In *The Words of Ahiqar* he is described as 'a wise and rapid/skilful scribe' (*TAD* C1.1:1; cf. line 35) and as 'the wise scribe and master of good counsel' (*TAD* C1.1:42; cf. lines 12, 18). In general, scribes were an important part of the intellectual scene during the Second Temple period (Schams 1998; Grabbe 1995: 152–76). In the Jewish texts, there are hints that another usage might also be developing: one learned in the Jewish law. 1 Macc. 7.12-13 speaks of a delegation of scribes who appeared before Alcimus to ask for terms. While these may have represented the learned among the anti-Seleucid opposition (the scholars among the Hasidim? [7.13]), it is also possible that they were professional scribes (it is not clear that they had anything to do with the Hasidim). 2 Maccabees 6.18-31 describes the martyrdom of Eleazar. Again, his title possibly comes from his knowledge in divine law, but he may have been a scribe in the normal sense (4 *Macc.* 5.4 states that he was a priest).

The biblical Torah scribe *par excellence* is Ezra (also referred to as a 'rapid/skilful scribe' [ספר מהיר: Ezra 7.6]). The presentation of him in the book of Ezra may be primarily as a literary construct rather than as a historical figure (cf. *HJJSTP 1*: 324–31). Nevertheless, if we concentrate on the literary construct in Ezra 7 and Nehemiah 8, the designation of 'scribe' for Ezra seems to be primarily in association with his bringing the book of the law. He promulgates the law, propounds it and interprets it. One could also infer that he wrote it, though this is not explicitly stated. It is also significant that the first point made in the story (Ezra 7.1-6, 11) is that Ezra is a priest. It is hardly surprising, then, that a priestly figure is the one associated with the genesis of the Torah. In spite of problems with the Ezra tradition, it would not be a surprise if some such figure was indeed associated with the writing, editing, and/or promulgating of the five books of Moses in the Persian period (cf. Grabbe 2015).

Next, we can consider Ben Sira, who is a bridging character: he provides another model of the scribe and he is also associated with the Torah. He provides perhaps the most famous passage in Jewish literature on the scribe (Sir. 38.24–39.11). He emphasizes the importance of leisure in order to cultivate wisdom and pursue the knowledge of the ancients. But the main issue is to devote time to focusing on the law of God. Although the word 'scribe' is not used at this point, it is the obvious antecedent from 38.24, which begins the passage by referring to the 'wisdom of the scribe'. This is no doubt an idealized image of the scribe, which makes the scribe responsible for knowledge and study of God's law. It should be kept in mind, however, Ben Sira's close association with the temple (some have argued that he was himself a priest; cf. Stadelmann 1980). It is not clear that Ben Sira was suggesting that everyone with scribal training was to be an expert in the law, but evidently in his mind this was the pinnacle of the scribal profession. He no doubt saw himself as suited to this role.

6.4.2. 'Scribes' in the Gospels

Apart from Ezra and Ben Sira, this usage of 'scribe' to mean one learned in the sacred law is best known from the New Testament. In some New Testament texts 'scribe' seems to have almost a sectarian meaning, as if they were a religious group alongside the Sadducees, Pharisees and others. Thus, Mk 7.1-23 mentions both Pharisees and scribes together, as do Mt. 12.38, 23.2 and Lk. 5.21 (see further at §6.3.3). Is this a new and different identity for the 'scribes'? Is there now a religious sect known as 'the scribes'? The answer is not an easy one and needs to take into account recent study of the gospel writers, their knowledge and their intent.

Several attempts at investigating the question have been made, with rather different conclusions (cf. Cook 1978: 71–73). E. Rivkin (1978) has identified the scribes with the Pharisees, arguing that the terms are mutually interchangeable, but his use of the New Testament passages is uncritical (cf. Saldarini 1988: 228–34; Ellenson 1975). Also, Josephus never associates the two. One possible explanation is that by the time Mark (usually thought to be the earliest of the evangelists) wrote, the Pharisees were the only group really known, and references to other groups was not made on the basis of proper knowledge. Yet scribes as such seem to be referred to in the pre-Markan tradition and in Q. Q was the 'sayings source', a collection of Jesus' sayings, that many New Testament scholars think was one of the sources used by Matthew and Luke. The presumption of many is that material in the pre-Markan tradition and in Q is more likely to go back to the historical Jesus (on Q, see Kloppenborg 2008). D. R. Schwartz has noted that since the temple personnel were often drawn on for their scribal skills, the 'scribes' of the gospels may in many cases be Levites (Schwartz 1992: 89–101).

The key may lie in passages that some scholars have dismissed as secondary. The most likely reading of Mk 2.16 is 'scribes of the Pharisees', which suggests that scribes were not a separate party but certain professionals among them. Acts 23.9 likewise speaks of 'scribes of the Pharisees' party'. If this is historical, it suggests that these 'scribes' were not to be identified with the Pharisees but constituted those learned in the Torah, regardless of their sectarian affiliation. This would indicate that other parties (e.g., the Sadducees) also had their own scribes, perhaps individuals with special expertise in the law or legal interpretations of the sect in question (cf. Jeremias 1969). If so, this usage would be in line with that of Ben Sira and Ezra, in which the 'ideal' of the scribe is not only one with professional knowledge and skills but also knowledge and understanding of God's law. Also, this explanation need not contradict D. R. Schwartz's argument, since some of the Levites may well have belonged to various of the sects extant at the time.

M. J. Cook (1978) argued that the phrase, 'scribes of the Pharisees' (Mk 2.16), is unusual and probably the correct reading, but then dismisses it as Mark's creation. This is unlikely since Mark's contribution would be 'scribes *and* the Pharisees', and the phrase 'scribes *of* the Pharisees' is thus likely to be pre-Markan. Mark 2.16, then, suggests that the Pharisees had their scribes but that the two were not co-extensive. To this may be added a passage in Luke: the 'lawyers' (*nomikoi*) and Pharisees (Lk. 7.30 = Q?). Finally, the scribes who occur in the passion narrative could be non-Pharisees. Saldarini (1988: 266–68, 273–76) concludes that the scribes of the gospels are indeed professional scribes, but the difficulty arises because the New Testament presents them as a unified group, which they were not. When this is recognized, the usage falls into line with what we know of scribes generally in the world of that time.

6.4.3. *Summary and Conclusions*

The discussion has thus led to the following possibilities and conclusions:

- The term 'scribe' was widely used in the Hellenistic world, including Palestine, to refer to personal secretaries and to public officials who functioned as village clerks, recorders and registrars, and scribes of the temple.
- While the term was also used of those skilled in Jewish law, they seem normally to have held the professional scribal office mentioned above. The scribes of the gospels are an exception to this, since they appear as almost a sectarian grouping. However, this seems to be only an artificial construct created by the gospel writers. In reality the scribes were probably professional scribes, and the impression of unity of belief is due to the theological aims of the Christian tradents and writers.
- Scribes as such seem to be referred to in the pre-Markan tradition and in Q. If this is historical, it suggests that they were not to be identified with the Pharisees but constituted those learned in the Torah, regardless of their sectarian affiliation. This would lead to the conclusion that those who postulate Sadducaean and other scribes, as well as Pharisaic scribes, have some justification for their view. But we need to recognize that scribalism generally represented a profession, and those labelled 'scribes' in these sources are not to be confused with the later rabbinic figures for whom knowledge of the Torah was an avocation rather than a public office.

6.5. *Essenes*

J. Kampen (1986) 'A Reconsideration of the Name "Essene" in Greco-Jewish Literature in Light of Recent Perceptions of the Qumran Sect', *HUCA* 57: 61–81; **J. Murphy-O'Connor** (1974) 'The Essenes and their History', *RevB* 81: 215–44; **idem** (1985) 'The *Damascus Document* Revisited', *RevB* 92: 223–46; **J. E. Taylor** (2007) 'Philo of Alexandria on the Essenes: A Case Study on the Use of Classical Sources in Discussions of the Qumran-Essene Hypothesis', *SPA* 19: 1–28; **idem** (2012) *The Essenes, the Scrolls, and the Dead Sea*; **G. Vermes** (1960) 'The Etymology of "Essenes"', *RevQ* 2: 427–43; **G. Vermes and M. D. Goodman** (eds) (1989) *The Essenes according to Classical Sources*.

This section will focus on the Essenes, which are known to us almost entirely from classical and Jewish literary sources. The question of Qumran is not discussed here but in Chapter 7, at which point the identity of Qumran and its inhabitants will be discussed.

6.5.1. *Sources*

Most of what we know about the Essenes comes from the statements made by such contemporary or near-contemporary authors as Pliny, Philo and Josephus. A detailed discussion of the classical sources is given by J. E. Taylor (2012: 22–201; also Vermes and Goodman 1989).

Of the ancient descriptions of the Essenes, one of the most important comes from the Roman writer, Pliny the Elder (ca. 24–79 CE), who describes them in his *Natural History* (5.73). He states that 'the tribe of the Essenes' (*Esseni...gens*) live on the west side of the Dead Sea. They are remarkable because they renounce sexual intercourse and have no women. They also have no money and keep only palm trees for company. Then 'below' (*infra*) the Essenes was the former site of En-gedi and after that, Masada. The approximate location of the Essenes' habitation is made clear by Pliny's geographical description. The meaning of the term *infra* has been much discussed, but there is a fair consensus that in this context he means 'south', since the sequence of listing is from north to south. Thus, the Essenes evidently lived on the northern part of the west coast of the Dead Sea, north of En-gedi. The exact spot is not clarified, though the description potentially includes the area where Khirbet Qumran is found.

Our most detailed sources are Philo and Josephus. The accounts which Philo gives in *Quod omnis probus* (75–87) and *Hypothetica* (as quoted by Eusebius, *Praep. evang.* 8 [LCL 9.437-43]) are both very close to those in *Josephus* (*War* 2.8.2-13 §§120-61; *Ant.* 18.1.5 §§18-22). This leads to the supposition that the two used a common earlier source, at least in part, rather than actually employing personal knowledge in their description of the Essenes (despite Josephus's claim to have been initiated into the sect [*Life* 2 §§10–11]). Both Josephus and Philo (one or more accounts) agree on a number of points about the Essene community:

- Number about 4,000 males (*Ant.* 18.1.5 §20; *Probus* 75).
- Live in many towns and villages (*War* 2.8.4 §124; *Probus* 76; *Hyp.* 11.1).
- No wives, women or marriage (*War* 2.8.2 §§120-21; *Ant.* 18.1.5 §21; *Hyp.* 11.14-17).
- Community of goods and communal meals (*War* 2.8.3 §122; *Ant.* 18.1.5 §20; *Probus* 85-86; *Hyp.* 11.4-5).
- Work at agriculture and crafts (*Ant.* 18.1.5 §19; *Probus* 76; *Hyp.* 11.6, 8-9).
- No swearing of oaths (*War* 2.8.6 §135; *Probus* 84).
- No changing of clothes (*War* 2.8.4 §126; *Hyp.* 11.12).
- No slaves (*Ant.* 18.1.5 §21; *Probus* 79).

The following points are found in the *War* and the *Antiquities* but not in either of Philo's accounts:

- Election of overseers and officials (*War* 2.8.3 §123; *Ant.* 18.1.5 §22).
- Belief in the immortality of the soul (*War* 2.8.11 §§154-58; *Ant.* 18.1.5 §18).

The *War* makes a number of points which do not occur in the *Antiquities* or in Philo:

- Oil defiling (*War* 2.8.3 §123).
- Prayers to the sun (*War* 2.8.5 §128).
- Daily schedule of work (*War* 2.8.5 §§128-32).
- Bathing before eating (*War* 2.8.5 §129) and if touched by an outsider (*War.* 2.8.10 §150).
- Speaking in turn (*War* 2.8.5 §132).
- Study of the writings of the ancients and medicines (*War* 2.8.6 §136).
- Regulations for admission to (*War* 2.8.7 §§137-42) and expulsion from the order (*War* 2.8.8 §§143-44).
- Preservation of angels' names (*War* 2.8.7 §142).

172   *A History of Jews and Judaism in the Second Temple Period, Volume 3*

- No spitting in company or to the right (*War* 2.8.8 §147).
- Strictness in observing the sabbath (*War* 2.8.8 §147).
- Foretelling the future (*War* 2.8.12 §159).
- Also a group which marries (*War* 2.8.13 §160).

Philo's two accounts are very moralizing, and most of what he gives is paralleled in Josephus and thus has already been listed.

Josephus also mentions a few individual Essenes: Judas who was noted for his successful foretelling of events in the time of Aristobulus I (*Ant.* 13.11.2 §311); Manaemus who predicted Herod's rise to rule and was rewarded by him (*Ant.* 15.10.5 §373); Simon who interpreted a dream of Archelaus (*Ant.* 17.13.3 §§347-48); John who was one of the commanders during the war against Rome (*War* 2.20.4 §567; 3.2.1 §11).

6.5.2. *Conclusions*

Although the Essenes are in many ways the best attested of the ancient Jewish sects, many questions remain unanswered. Even the name 'Essene' has not been satisfactorily explained. It has often been explained as from the Aramaic *ḥăsayyā'/ḥāsîn* 'pious', related to the Hebrew *ḥăsîdîm*, but this has been strongly influenced by various assumptions about the Hasidim (§6.1 above). Also, the root *ḥsy* is known from Syriac but is not attested in Jewish Aramaic. G. Vermes (1960; SCHÜRER 2:559–60) suggested that the name was from *'āsyā'*, an Aramaic word for 'healer', connecting the name with that of the Therapeutae (to be discussed in *HJJSTP 4*), which means 'healers' in Greek; however, this explanation does not seem to have attracted many adherents. These and other suggestions have usually assumed a Semitic etymology of some sort, but Kampen (1986) has argued for a Greek origin, from *essēn*, the name for a cultic official of Artemis.

Although Pliny mentions only one settlement of Essenes, both Philo and Josephus indicate Essene communities in towns and villages around Judaea. Even though Pliny and Philo indicate a celibate group, Josephus states explicitly that some Essenes (or groups of Essenes) marry and bring up children. They are a closed group, with rules about probation, admission and expulsion. They seem to support themselves primarily by agriculture. They have a number of beliefs that differ from many other Jews, with regard to such matters as dress, swearing of oaths, slavery and spitting. Some of them study the writings of the ancients and medicine. Some have a reputation for being able to foretell the future.

6.6. *Synthesis*

Religion among the Jewish people in the late Second Temple period has often been seen in terms of the 'sects', especially the Pharisees and Sadducees. Writers on the subject have tended to give a somewhat more nuanced picture in recent years, but the old emphasis on the Pharisees and Sadducees has by no means gone away. Although focusing on the various groups is likely to distort our understanding of Second Temple Judaism, there is no question that they are important (some of which arose in the 1st century BCE and are to be treated in *HJJSTP 4*). They are also extremely difficult to come to grips with, despite the frequent statements made with great confidence about them. One problem with a number of recent treatments is their concentration on the Pharisees rather than recognizing that the Sadducees are as prominent in the sources as the former. The Essenes dominate the discussion for others, primarily because of the Qumran texts. Such a narrow focus leads to a skewed discussion because of concentrating on one or the other group in isolation.

We cannot afford to take anything for granted. Any study of the different sects has to go back to the basics, looking first of all at the sources and the problems with using them with as few preconceptions as possible. This is what I have attempted to do in my earlier article on the Sadducees and Pharisees (Grabbe 1999b) and my summaries of the different groups here. What I hope I have made clear is the basis of any positive statement made about the different groups, as well as the uncertainties in our knowledge.

The question of the different groups in society is an important one and well addressed in the recent study by Baumgarten (1997; cf. the review in Grabbe 1999c). Some interesting proposals about how groups originate (e.g., an attempt to return to an idealized past, a product of the growth of literacy, a consequence of urbanization) must be considered hypothetical, if sometimes plausible. On the other hand, the conventional mentality of assigning all sectarian origins to some sort of crisis situation ignores the fact that one cannot necessarily draw a sharp distinction between a sect and other forms of the religion. Sects are not just 'crisis cults', and ideology and theology can also be significant social drivers (cf. Grabbe 1989; 1999c: 91; Baumgarten 1997: 152–66).

We know that in during the Maccabaean revolt there was a group called the Hasidim. Then, sometime around 100 BCE, the three groups of Sadducees, Pharisees and Essenes are said by our sources to be in existence, but we know nothing of their origins. The fact that the Sadducees and Pharisees are first mentioned when Josephus is talking about the reign of Jonathan Maccabee is hardly evidence that they already existed at that time; on the contrary, he first connects their activities with John Hyrcanus (135–104 BCE) some decades later. If this is correct (and there are some problems), they *might* have originated in the post-Maccabean-revolt situation, but they could be earlier or even later. The Essenes are first connected with the reign of Aristobulus I (104–3 BCE). The following are some overall conclusions:

- Sects and movements have a long history in Judaic religion, perhaps going back to pre-exilic times but, in any case, most likely being present already in the Persian period. They become well attested in post-Maccabaean times, though some of the 'schools of thought' known or postulated from earlier writings could well be in the nature of sects (e.g., the 'Deuteronomistic School', the 'wise' of Daniel).
- Although much has been ascribed to the Hasidim, we actually know little about them. It is unclear that they are a unified movement, and a number of recent scholars have argued that the term is applied to a diversity of groups in the books of Maccabees. *A fortiori*, we do not know that they have any connection with the later sects.
- The Sadducees seem to have been in existence by the end of the second century BCE. We first encounter them as a group seeking political power with the Hasmonaean ruler John Hyrcanus. There is only sporadic evidence after this, though some prominent individuals are said to have been Sadducees. They are associated with the upper classes and the priesthood, and certain religious beliefs are ascribed to them, some of which also point to a priestly or temple group.
- The Pharisees also seem to have been around by about 100 BCE and first appear as seeking political power, with the Sadducees as their rivals. They gain actual power under Alexandra Salome but then appear only sporadically in history to 70. A few prominent Pharisees are known, and some Pharisees seem to have been priests. They are supposed to have been interested in their own particular 'traditions of the fathers' not written in the law of Moses, though exactly what these traditions are is never described. The family of Gamaliel seems to have been an important Pharisaic 'school' which bridged the gap between the Second Temple and rabbinic periods, with some members of the family in prominent civic positions. If Hillel and Shammai were Pharisees, as often alleged, they seem to have been concerned mainly with basic laws relating to agricultural matters, purity and the sabbath and festivals;

there is little evidence that they held positions in civic society or the temple administration. On the other hand, their 'schools' were probably the core making up the religious reconstruction at Yavneh after 70 (to be discussed in *HJJSTP 4*).

- The Essenes are also attested as early as 100 BCE. In contrast to the Sadducees and Pharisees, they seem to have withdrawn – at least to some extent – from ordinary society and developed a communal life based on religious ideals of common property and careful observance of the law (as they interpreted it). Some of the communities appear to have been celibate, though not all. (Whether they are to be related to Qumran is discussed in Chapter 7.)

- From all we can tell, the numbers of Jews belonging to a sect were few. Each individual sect was small, and even if the sectarian membership was all totalled together, they would still constitute very much a minority of the population. In some cases their influence may have significantly exceeded their size, but it is one thing to influence and another to control. Sometimes a sect would seize a position of power (e.g., the Pharisees under Alexandra Salome; the Zealots in the 66–70 revolt [*HJJSTP 4*]), but this did not last. The place of sects in the religious picture of the time must be kept in proportion.

Chapter 7

QUMRAN AND THE DEAD SEA SCROLLS

M. Abegg, P. Flint and E. Ulrich (eds) (1999) *The Dead Sea Scrolls Bible*; M. Bernstein et al. (eds) (1997) *Legal Texts and Legal Issues: Proceedings of the Second Meeting of the International Organization for Qumran Studies, Cambridge 1995, Published in Honour of Joseph M. Baumgarten*; K. Berthelot and D. Stökl Ben Ezra (eds) (2010) *Aramaica Qumranica: Proceedings of the Conference on the Aramaic Texts from Qumran in Aix-en-Provence, 30 June–2 July 2008*; G. J. Brooke (2005) *The Dead Sea Scrolls and the New Testament: Essays in Mutual Illumination*; G. J. Brooke, with F. García Martínez (eds) (1994) *New Qumran Texts and Studies: Proceedings of the First Meeting of the International Organization for Qumran Studies, Paris 1992*; G. J. Brooke and C. Hempel (eds) (2016) *T&T Clark Companion to the Dead Sea Scrolls*; P. R. Callaway (1988) *The History of the Qumran Community*; R. R. Cargill (2009) *Qumran through [Real] Time, A Virtual Reconstruction of Qumran and the Dead Sea Scrolls*; J. H. Charlesworth (ed.) (2006) *The Bible and the Dead Sea Scrolls, Volumes 1–3*; J. H. Charlesworth et al. (eds) (1994–) *The Dead Sea Scrolls: Hebrew, Aramaic, and Greek Texts with English Translations. I–*; E. G. Chazon and M. E. Stone (eds) (1999) *Pseudepigraphic Perspectives: The Apocrypha and Pseudepigrapha in Light of the Dead Sea Scrolls: Proceedings of the International Symposium of the Orion Center for the Study of the Dead Sea Scrolls and Associated Literature, 12–14 January, 1997*; J. J. Collins (1997) *Apocalypticism in the Dead Sea Scrolls*; idem (2009) *Beyond the Qumran Community: The Sectarian Movement of the Dead Sea Scrolls*; J. J. Collins and R. Kugler (eds) (2000) *Religion in the Dead Sea Scrolls*; F. M. Cross (1961) *The Ancient Library of Qumran*; F. H. Cryer and T. L. Thompson (eds) (1998) *Qumran between the Old and New Testaments*; P. R. Davies (1982a) *Qumran*; idem (1983) *The Damascus Covenant: An Interpretation of the 'Damascus Document'*; idem (1987) *Behind the Essenes: History and Ideology in the Dead Sea Scrolls*; P. R. Davies et al. (2002) *The Complete World of the Dead Sea Scrolls*; D. Dimant (ed.) (2012) *The Dead Sea Scrolls in Scholarly Perspective: A History of Research*;

D. Dimant and **U. Rappaport (eds)** (1992) *The Dead Sea Scrolls: Forty Years of Research*; **H. Eshel** (2015) *Exploring the Dead Sea Scrolls: Archaeology and Literature of the Qumran Caves*; **D. K. Falk** (1998) *Daily, Sabbath, and Festival Prayers in the Dead Sea Scrolls*; **A. Feldman et al. (eds)** (2017) *Is There a Text in this Cave? Studies in the Textuality of the Dead Sea Scrolls in Honour of George J. Brooke*; **M. Fidanzio (ed.)** (2017) *The Caves of Qumran: Proceedings of the International Conference, Lugano 2014*; **J. A. Fitzmyer** (1990) *The Dead Sea Scrolls: Major Publications and Tools for Study*; **P. W. Flint and J. C. VanderKam (eds)** (1998) *The Dead Sea Scrolls after Fifty Years: A Comprehensive Assessment, vol. 1*; **idem** (1999) *The Dead Sea Scrolls after Fifty Years: A Comprehensive Assessment, vol. 2*; **F. García Martínez** (1992) *Qumran and Apocalyptic: Studies on the Aramaic Texts from Qumran*; **F. García Martínez and E. J. C. Tigchelaar** (ed. and trans.) (1997–98) *The Dead Sea Scrolls Study Edition, Volume One: 1Q1–4Q273; Volume Two: 4Q274–11Q31*; *JLBM* 119-89; *JWSTP* 483-550; **Z. Kapera (ed.)** (1996) *Mogilany 1993: Papers on the Dead Sea Scrolls Offered in Memory of Hans Burgmann*; **idem** (1998) *Mogilany 1995: Papers on the Dead Sea Scrolls Offered in Memory of Aleksy Klawek*; **M. A. Knibb** (1987) *The Qumran Community*; **R. A. Kugler and E. M. Schuller (eds)** (1999) *The Dead Sea Scrolls at Fifty: Proceedings of the 1997 Society of Biblical Literature Qumran Section Meetings*; **A. Lange** (2009) *Handbuch der Textfunde vom Toten Meer, Band 1: Die Handschriften biblischer Bücher von Qumran und den anderen Fundorten*; **A. Lange, E. Tov and M. Weigold (eds)** (2011) *The Dead Sea Scrolls in Context: Integrating the Dead Sea Scrolls in the Study of Ancient Texts, Languages, and Cultures*; **T. H. Lim and P. S. Alexander** (1997) *The Dead Sea Scrolls Electronic Reference Library*, vol. 1; (no ed.) (1999) *The Dead Sea Scrolls Electronic Reference Library, 2, including the Dead Sea Scrolls Database (Non-Biblical Texts) Edited by Emanuel Tov*; **T. H. Lim and J. J. Collins (eds)** (2010) *The Oxford Handbook of the Dead Sea Scrolls*; **G. de Looijer** (2015) *The Qumran Paradigm: A Critical Evaluation of Some Foundational Hypotheses in the Construction of the Qumran Sect*; **S. Metso et al. (eds)** (2010) *The Dead Sea Scrolls: Transmission of Traditions and Production of Texts*; **J. T. Milik** (1959) *Ten Years of Discovery in the Wilderness of Judaea*; **J. Murphy-O'Connor** (1974) 'The Essenes and their History', *RevB* 81: 215–44; **D. W. Parry and E. Tov (eds)** (2014) *The Dead Sea Scrolls Reader, Volumes 1–2*; **D. W. Parry and E. Ulrich (eds)** (1999) *The Provo International Conference on the Dead Sea Scrolls: Technological Innovations, New Texts, and Reformulated Issues*; **A. D. Roitman et al. (eds)** (2011) *The Dead Sea Scrolls and Contemporary Culture: Proceedings of the International Conference Held at the Israel Museum, Jerusalem (July 6–8, 2008)*; **L. H. Schiffman and J. C. VanderKam (eds)** (2000) *Encyclopedia of the Dead Sea Scrolls*; SCHÜRER 2:575–83; 3:380–469; **H. Stegemann** (1998) *The Library of Qumran: On the Essenes, Qumran, John the Baptist, and Jesus*; **D. Stökl Ben Ezra** (2016) *Qumran:*

Die Texte vom Toten Meer und das antike Judentum; **M. E. Stone and E. G. Chazon (eds)** (1998) *Biblical Perspectives: Early Use and Interpretation of the Bible in Light of the Dead Sea Scrolls: Proceedings of the First International Symposium of the Orion Center for the Study of the Dead Sea Scrolls and Associated Literature, 12–14 May, 1996*; **J. E. Taylor** (2012) *The Essenes, the Scrolls, and the Dead Sea*; **J. C. VanderKam** (1994) *The Dead Sea Scrolls Today*; **idem** (1998) *Calendars in the Dead Sea Scrolls: Measuring Time*; **G. Vermes** (1977) *The Dead Sea Scrolls: Qumran in Perspective*; **idem** (2011) *The Complete Dead Sea Scrolls in English*.

The finds from the caves on the northwestern shores of the Dead Sea, near the ruins known as Khirbet Qumran, have revolutionized our understanding of certain aspects of Jewish history in the late Second Temple period. For a recent survey of scholarship on Qumran, which also discusses some of the main writings, see Brooke and Hempel 2016; also Lim and Collins 2010. Some of the older introductions and also many of the collections of essays on Qumran are listed in the bibliography above. The official publication is the *Discoveries in the Judaean Desert* series (OUP), but the text of the Scrolls, with English translation, is also readily available in Parry and Tov 2014 and García Martínez and Tigchelaar 1997–98; English translation only in Vermes 2011.

The Scrolls contain several different types of writings: fragments of every book of the Hebrew Bible except Esther (some of these important for the development of text are discussed at §12.2); portions of the Apocrypha and Pseudepigrapha; other Jewish writings heretofore unknown; and writings which seem to be a product of the sectarian community itself (sometimes referred to as Qumran 'sectarian writings'; for a discussion of its identity, see §7.2 below). Some of these will be considered at various points in this volume for their relevance to the wider history of the Jewish people. But others will be important in the present chapter because of information they have that may be important to the identity of the community and trying to reconstruct its history. This chapter will consider the archaeology of the Qumran site, the question of the relationship (if any) of the Scrolls with the site, the identity of those living at Qumran and finally the more explicit references made in the Scrolls to events in Judaea in the Hasmonaean and Herodian periods.

7.1. *The Archaeology*

P. Bar-Adon (1977) 'Another Settlement of the Judean Desert Sect at 'En el-Ghuweir on the Shores of the Dead Sea', *BASOR* 227: 1–25; **P. R. Davies** (1988) 'How Not To Do Archaeology: The Story of Qumran', *BA* 51: 203–7;

Y. Hirschfeld (2004) *Qumran in Context: Reassessing the Archaeological Evidence*; **J.-B. Humbert (ed.)** (2003) *Khirbet Qumran et 'Ain Feshkha / The Excavations of Khirbet Qumran and Ain Feshka II: Etudes d'anthropologie, de physique et de chimie / Studies of Anthropology, Physics and Chemistry*; **M. and K. Lönnqvist** (2002) *Archaeology of the Hidden Qumran: The New Paradigm*; **Y. Magen and Y. Peleg (eds)** (2007) *The Qumran Excavations, 1993–2004: Preliminary Report*; **J. Magness** (1995) 'The Chronology of the Settlement at Qumran in the Herodian Period', *DSD* 2: 58–65; **idem** (2002) *The Archaeology of Qumran and the Dead Sea Scrolls*; **idem** (2012) *The Archaeology of the Holy Land: From the Destruction of Solomon's Temple to the Muslim Conquest*, 108–32; **D. Mizzi** (2011) '60 Years of Qumran Archaeology', *Strata: Bulletin of the Anglo-Israel Archaeological Society* 29: 31–50; **idem** (2014) 'Qumran Period I Reconsidered: An Evaluation of Several Competing Theories', *DSS* 22: 1–42; **idem** (2017) 'Qumran at Seventy: Reflections on Seventy Years of Scholarship on the Archaeology of Qumran and the Dead Sea Scrolls', *Strata: Bulletin of the Anglo-Israel Archaeological Society* 35: 9–45; **D. Mizzi and J. Magness** (2016) 'Was Qumran Abandoned at the End of the First Century BCE?' *JBL* 135: 301–20; **D. Stacey and G. Doudna** (2013) *Qumran Revisited: A Reassessment of the Archaeology of the Site and its Texts*; **R. de Vaux** (1973) *Archaeology and the Dead Sea Scrolls*.

Very important for both the history of the community and for its general contribution to the archaeological picture of Judaea is the archaeological survey carried out at Qumran (de Vaux 1973; cf. Davies 1982a: 36–69). However, one must be careful to distinguish between the actual data and the interpretation placed on them by the archaeologists and others. First, de Vaux's original archaeological scheme can be outlined as follows:

Qumran was inhabited off and on for almost a millennium. Discounting evidence of prehistoric occupation in some of the caves, the first major occupation took place during the time of the Israelite monarchy. The site is probably referred to in some biblical passages (such as perhaps the 'City of Salt' in Josh. 15.61-62) but the precise identification is disputed. It was most likely a fortress or military installation only. The site was abandoned at some point in the late Iron Age, probably toward the end of the monarchy, and left vacant for several centuries.

The main periods of occupation are contained in phases Ia, Ib and II (using de Vaux's terminology). Phase Ia was a very small settlement, comprising only a few dozen individuals at most. It cannot be dated precisely, but both coins and pottery indicate the last part of the 2nd century BCE, though the beginning of the 1st century BCE cannot be excluded. Ib represents a considerable expansion in building, without any break in habitation. The community came to include perhaps up to 200 inhabitants. The dating of this phase depends on that of phase Ia which was probably of only a short duration. Coins suggest that Ib covered the first two-thirds of the 1st century (i.e., about 100–31 BCE). The reason for this last date is the evidence of an earthquake and conflagration, followed by a period of abandonment. Since Josephus mentions a major earthquake in 31 BCE, this dating is usually accepted.

Phase II began about the turn of the era and seems to have been brought to an end by the Romans, as evidenced by Roman arrow heads associated with a burn layer (i.e., about 1–68 CE). The size of the community seems to have been about the same as in Ib. The layout of the buildings was basically the same, with some modifications. These and other indications suggest that the community of phase II was a continuation of that of Ib. This was followed by phase III, which represents a short occupation by Roman forces, probably only until about 73 or 74 with the fall of Masada. Some coins also suggest a brief occupation during the Bar-Kokhva revolt, probably by Jewish fighters.

De Vaux's interpretation has remained widely accepted but with some significant modifications. The modified scheme of J. Magness (1995, 2002) has been very influential. She has pointed out that the evidence for phase Ia is very skimpy and pretty much eliminates it: there is little or no 2nd-century pottery, and coins are mainly from Alexander Jannaeus or later. In any case, she sees the rehabitation of the site (several centuries after the Iron Age occupation) in the early 1st century BCE, which she associates with a religious community (essentially de Vaux's phase Ib). This was not ended by the earthquake of 31 BCE (though there was some damage to the site), but continued to about 9/8 BCE. There was a brief abandonment of the site and then a resumption of habitation by the same group (about 4 BCE to 68 CE, de Vaux's phase II). More recently this has been slightly modified (Mizzi and Magness 2016): the only clear evidence for the site's abandonment would be about 68 CE. As already noted the earthquake of 31 did not cause a break in habitation, and there appears to be evidence only of localized incidents of damage in the 1st century BCE and CE. Thus, there was no occupation break between Periods Ib and II. In their opinion, the (sectarian) settlement at Qumran probably experienced one long, continuous occupation from the early 1st century BCE to 68 CE.

Others have given a fairly similar reconstruction (see the tables in Stökl Ben Ezra 2016: 104; Mizzi 2014: 18). Some still wish to see a short period of occupation in the late 2nd century BCE (Hirschfeld 2004; Cargill 2009), but most accept Magness's arguments that the first clear evidence for habitation is the early 1st century BCE. The differences tend to be about what sort of settlement Qumran was. These other views are discussed in the next section (§7.2.2).

7.2. Identity

G. Boccaccini (1998) *Beyond the Essene Hypothesis: The Parting of the Ways between Qumran and Enochic Judaism*; **M. Broshi** (1999) 'Was Qumran at Crossroads?', *RQum* 19: 273–76; **J. J. Collins** (1989) 'The Origin of the Qumran Community: A Review of the Evidence', in M. P. Horgan and P. J. Kobelski (eds), *To Touch the Text: Biblical and Related Studies in Honor of Joseph A. Fitzmyer, S.J.*, 159–78; **F. M. Cross and E. Eshel** (1997) 'Ostraca from Khirbet Qumran', *IEJ* 47: 17–29; **F. H. Cryer** (1997) 'The Qumran Conveyance: A Reply to F. M. Cross and E. Eshel', *SJOT* 11: 232–40; **P. R. Davies** (1982b) 'The Ideology of the Temple in the Damascus Document', *JJS* 33: 287–301; **idem** (1995a) 'Was There Really a Qumran Community?' *CR: BS* 3: 9–36; **G. R. Driver** (1965) *The Judaean Scrolls: The Problem and the Solution*; **R. Eisenman** (1983) *Maccabees, Zadokites, Christians and Qumran*; **F. García Martínez** (1988) 'Qumran Origins and Early History: A Groningen Hypothesis', *Folio Orientalia* 25: 113–36; **N. Golb** (1995) *Who Wrote the Dead Sea Scrolls?*; **M. Goodman** (1995) 'A Note on the Qumran Sectarians, the Essenes and Josephus', *JJS* 46: 161–66; **L. L. Grabbe** (1997a) 'The Current State of the Dead Sea Scrolls: Are There More Answers than Questions?' in S. E. Porter and C. A. Evans (eds), *The Scrolls and the Scriptures: Qumran Fifty Years After*, 54–67; **idem** (1997b) Review of N. Golb, *Who Wrote the Dead Sea Scrolls?*, *DSD* 4: 124–28; **idem** (1997c) '4QMMT and Second Temple Jewish Society', in M. Bernstein, F. García Martínez and J. Kampen (eds), *Legal Texts and Legal Issues: Proceedings of the Second Meeting of the International Organization for Qumran Studies, Cambridge 1995, Published in Honour of Joseph M. Baumgarten*, 89–108; **T. H. Lim** (1993) 'The Wicked Priests of the Groningen Hypothesis', *JBL* 112: 415–25; **J. Magness** (2013) 'Was Qumran a Fort in the Hasmonean Period?' *JJS* 64: 228–41; **J. Murphy-O'Connor** (1985) 'The *Damascus Document* Revisited', *RevB* 92: 223–46; **C. Roth** (1958) *The Historical Background to the Dead Sea Scrolls*; **L. H. Schiffman** (1990b) 'The New Halakhic Letter (4QMMT) and the Origins of the Dead Sea Sect', *BA* 53: 64–73; **J. E. Taylor** (2007) 'Philo of Alexandria on the Essenes: A Case Study on the Use of Classical Sources in Discussions of the Qumran-Essene Hypothesis', *SPA* 19: 1–28; **J. L. Teicher** (1951) 'The Dead Sea Scrolls, Documents of the Jewish-Christian Sect of the Ebionites', *JJS* 2: 67–99; **B. Thiering** (1992) *Jesus & the Riddle of the Dead Sea Scrolls: Unlocking the Secrets of His Life Story*; **J. C. VanderKam** (1992) 'The People of the Dead Sea Scrolls:

Essenes or Sadducees?' in H. Shanks (ed.), *Understanding the Dead Sea Scrolls: A Reader from the* Biblical Archaeology Review, 50–62, 300–302; **G. Vermes and M. D. Goodman (eds)** (1989) *The Essenes according to Classical Sources*; **A. S. van der Woude** (1990) 'A "Groningen" Hypothesis of Qumran Origins and Early History', *RevQ* 14: 521–42; **A. Yardeni** (1997) 'A Draft of a Deed on an Ostracon from Khirbet Qumrân', *IEJ* 47: 233–37.

When considering what sort of site Qumran was, we need to take into account not only the archaeology but also the contents of the Scrolls themselves and the statements made by such contemporary or near-contemporary authors as Pliny, Philo and Josephus. The main points of these classical sources are surveyed at §6.5.1. The archaeology has already been considered in the previous section (§7.1). Any thesis about Qumran and those who lived there must make use of all three sources.

7.2.1. *Are the Scrolls to Be Associated with the Settlement at Qumran?*

This has been a much-debated question but one answered in the affirmative by the vast majority of Qumran scholars: the Scrolls were at least in part copied in the community, though some of them are older than the settlement itself. This means that at least these writings, and perhaps some others, were copied elsewhere and brought to the site. Some of the reasons are the following:

- All of the eleven Scroll caves are near the site of Qumran. Some can only be reached through the site.
- Some of the Scrolls were found in cylindrical jars that are practically unique for Qumran and the surrounding area (a few have been found in Jericho). None of these jars have been found in other caves around the Dead Sea or in the Judaean Desert. The clay for many of the jars comes from the local area (though some were made from clay imported from the area of Jerusalem).
- Although none of the Scrolls turned up in the Qumran site itself, ink pots were found, showing that writing went on there. Also, apparently rolls of blank parchment were mixed in with some of the caches of Scrolls, again indicating that copying was taking place near where the Scrolls were stored.

A number of specialists have argued that the Scrolls were not the product of Qumran but were brought there from elsewhere, perhaps to hide them from the advancing Romans. One suggestion is that the Scrolls represent the library of the Jerusalem temple. One of those advancing this argument was N. Golb, in a series of articles, with most of his arguments summarized in his book (Golb 1995). He has argued that the Scrolls are from a Jerusalem library or libraries, and were brought to the caves during the 66–70 revolt. Ultimately, the thesis that the Scrolls were brought from elsewhere has greater problems than the theory it is meant to replace (see Grabbe 1997a: 60–63; 1997d). Note the following points:

- Dismissal of the location of the Scrolls around the Khirbet Qumran site is a weakness. At least the Scrolls were found physically near to Qumran, whereas there is nothing specifically to tie the Scrolls to Jerusalem. There is also the matter of the jars in which some of them were stored, and the indication that writing took place at Qumran.
- If the Scrolls were originally housed in Jerusalem, it would have made more sense to store them there where many potential hiding places existed. Many people managed to hide even when the Romans took the city, until they were forced out by hunger.
- The keepers of the Scrolls would have been aware that the area of Qumran was precisely a geographical area through which the Romans could well march when coming to Jerusalem. They would have been putting the Scrolls in the line of fire, as it were, by transporting them from Jerusalem to Qumran.
- The idea that the Scrolls could have been transported to Qumran during the siege of Jerusalem is unrealistic when the situation is considered. The city was surrounded by the Romans and getting in and out would have been very difficult. A vehicle would have been required, and the Romans would have noticed any such activity, whether getting the Scrolls out of Jerusalem, transporting them over the roads to Qumran, or carrying them up or down to the various caves.
- Before the Romans invested Jerusalem, some of the various Jewish factions guarded the gates to prevent anyone going out without their permission (*War* 4.4.3 §236). A few people managed to escape with their lives, but they were hardly carrying wagon loads of manuscripts. A careful reading of Josephus shows that this aspect of the theory is fatally flawed.

One attempt to connect the Scrolls with the site of Qumran has been the find of the so-called '*Yaḥad* ostracon' (Cross and Eshel 1997). This was interpreted as the record of a donation to the community (*yaḥad*) living at Qumran. Cross and Eshel read line 8 as, 'when he fulfils (his oath) to the community' (וכ[מ]לותו ליחד). That interpretation was immediately challenged by Cryer (1997). However, it was the study by A. Yardeni, who certainly had no axe to grind against Cross, which fatally undermined the *Yahad* interpretation. She accepted that the text was probably a gift deed, but she read it somewhat differently (Yardeni 1997). She read the crucial line 8 as, 'and every oth[er(?)] tree[…]' ([ר]וכולאילנ אח). Thus, the '*yahad* hypothesis' seems to be unproven.

7.2.2. *Some Recent Theories about the Origin of the Qumran Site*

The first identification made of the Qumran community (and also the ones who copied the 'sectarian' scrolls) was that it was Essene. This suggestion, apparently first made by E. Sukenik but about the same time by W. H. Brownlee and A. Dupont-Sommer, became widely adopted (Mizzi 2017: 34 n. 6). This became the dominant thesis, though other connections were suggested (cf. below). Then, as more of the Qumran writings began to be published after 1990, new suggestions began to come forth, some with more plausibility than others. Some of these include the following, along with objections that have been made with regard to them (Stökl Ben Ezra 2016: 133–48; Mizzi 2014):

- In the early days of Scrolls research both C. Roth (1958) and G. R. Driver (1965) argued that the Qumran community, at least in the 1st century CE, was Zealot. The Teacher of Righteousness was Menahem, who was killed in 66 CE. The thesis gained little in the way of a following. It especially lacks a fit with the historical Zealots, who will be discussed in *HJJSTP 4*.
- The Scrolls were a Christian product. This seems to have been first proposed by J. L. Teicher (1951), who argued that the Scrolls come from Ebionite Christians, with Paul as the Wicked Priest. More recently, R. Eisenman (1983) has also argued that these texts are Christian, but arising from the circle of James the Just. About the same time as Eisenman's thesis, B. Thiering (1992) claimed that the Scrolls were the product of rivalry between the supporters of John the Baptist (who is the 'Teacher of Righteousness') and Jesus (the 'Man of the Lie'). Qumran scholarship has been almost unanimous in rejecting the Christian identification.
- The community was Sadducean (Schiffman 1990b). This identification was based primarily on 4QMMT, which was interpreted to show that the author of the letter (believed to be a leader at Qumran) was promoting certain religious practices that opposed Pharisaic views. The problem is that halakhic matters alleged to be Pharisaic were not actually Pharisaic or rabbinic for the most part

(Grabbe 1997c; VanderKam 1992). As the discussion about the Sadducees demonstrates (§6.2), the group associated with the 'sectarian scrolls' differs at certain essential points from the Sadducees, as far as our evidence for Sadducean beliefs presently indicates.

- Qumran was a fortress (Hirschfeld 2004; Magen and Peleg [eds] 2007; cf. Cargill 2009). One of the features of Qumran was the fortified tower on the north side of the site. Two considerations immediately put a question mark by this identification: most fortresses were on top of inaccessible mountain peaks, and the walls of the fortified tower at Qumran were rather thinner than normal for fortresses. J. Magness (2013) has now challenged this connection, using two main arguments: the lack of similarities between the known Hasmonaean forts and Qumran, and the absence of archaeological evidence that Qumran was inhabited before 100 BCE. As noted above (§7.1), Magness does not entirely reject the idea of Phase Ia, but she has severe doubts about its existence.
- Qumran was a rustic villa or perhaps a winter residence of the Hasmonaeans (Humbert [ed.] 2003; Hirschfeld 2004). Two considerations militate against this, First is the climate: the excessive heat would have made it very unpleasant for upper-class visitors wanting a luxurious experience, especially in the summer; secondly, such villas normally were very conspicuously decorated, but this is not the case for Qumran (Mizzi 2014: 30–40). For example, the *opus sectile* tiles found at the site are probably Herodian, not Hasmonaean, in date; also, they seem never to have been laid.
- Qumran was a trade centre or caravansary, perhaps manufacturing pottery for export. Pottery was indeed made on the site, but it seems doubtful that it was a manufacturing centre for pottery for sale. In any case, Qumran was not on a major trade route (Broshi 1999). If a trade centre was needed, it would have been sited elsewhere.

These various theories all offer some insight into either the archaeology or the content of the Scrolls or both. It was not before time that the Essene hypothesis was treated sceptically and subjected to extended scrutiny. Too often one read statements such as, 'the Essenes at Qumran', as if this were an unquestionable fact. As with all historical work, we can only deal in probabilities, and some historical reconstructions are more probable than others. What most of these theories do not explain are the abundance of ritual baths, the animal bones buried in jars or under pot sherds, or the vast number of scrolls with a connection to a small community of 200 at most (some argue for many fewer).

As this section indicates, the evidence such as we presently have it supports some sort of connection between Qumran and the Essenes. This still seems the most probable hypothesis, but it must always be kept in mind that new evidence will almost certainly modify it and might even overturn it. It is now time to look at the question of Qumran and the Essenes.

7.2.3. *The Essene Hypothesis*

The thesis still most widely favoured among scholars of this period is the Essene hypothesis, though this takes different forms. Although in the early days after the discovery of the Scrolls, the group producing them was identified with one or the other of most of the ancient sects, the suggestion of the Essenes became widely accepted. The question of whether the Scrolls themselves are to be associated with the ancient habitation at Qumran is discussed above (§7.2.1), but this question is also relevant for the identity of the group in the Scrolls, since it is generally agreed that some of the Scrolls have sufficient points in common (characteristic vocabulary, peculiar terminology and theological outlook) to be considered as related, i.e., as forming a core of 'sectarian scrolls'. This includes the *Damascus Document* (CD; 4Q266–273; 5Q12; 6Q15), the *Community Rule* (1QS), the *Rule of the Congregation* (1QSa), the *Habakkuk Commentary* (4QpHab), the *Hodayot* (1QH), and the *War Scroll* (1QM).

As noted in §7.2.1, it has been proposed that the Scrolls had diverse origins (e.g., Golb 1995; cf. the review in Grabbe 1997b), but the real question is not whether some of the Scrolls originated in another context and were simply taken over by the Qumran community (as was probably the case) but whether the clearly identified core of 'sectarian' writings have any connection with what we know of the Essenes. To discuss this question, only two writings will be drawn on: the *Damascus Document* and the *Community Rule*. The reason is that both of these contain regulations about the organization of a community and are generally agreed to be related to each other. They will be compared with the classic statements on the Essenes by Philo and Josephus.

- *Settlements of the Essenes*. Philo (*Probus* 76; *Hyp.* 11.1) and Josephus (*War* 2.8.4 §124) indicate communities in a variety of towns and villages; this also seems to be the view of the *Damascus Document* about its own communities (CD 7.6; 12.19–14.16; 19.2). The statement of Pliny the Elder, on the other hand, indicates only one settlement: on the northwest shore of the Dead Sea, though the exact spot is not indicated. We do not know what Pliny's source was, though he probably did not obtain his information personally. In any case, he was primarily interested in the philosophical aspects of the group, even if he had information on Essene groups other than those at Qumran or other than celibate males.

- *Community of goods*. Philo (*Probus* 85–86; *Hyp.* 11.4), Josephus (*War* 2.8.3 §122; *Ant.* 18.1.5 §20) and 1QS (1.11-12; 5.1-22; 6.16-23) agree that property was held in common. All new entrants turned over their property to the community on attaining full membership. However, certain passages in the *Damascus Document* can be interpreted as allowing at least some private ownership (CD 9.10-16; 14.12-16).
- *Common meals, preceded by bathing* (*Probus* 86; *Hyp.* 11.5, 11; *War* 2.8.5 §129; CD 10.10-13; 1QS 3.4-5; 5.13-14; 6.2, 25; 7.2-3).
- *Regulations for assemblies*. The members were to sit according to a particular order (*Probus* 81; 1QS 6.8-10), to speak in turn (*War* 2.8.5 §132; 1QS 6.10-13) and not to spit (*War* 2.8.8 §147; 1QS 7.13).
- *Procedures for entry*. The sources agree that a period of probation was required. Josephus (*War* 2.8.7 §§137-42) describes it in three stages, each lasting a year. 1QS 6.13-23 mentions two stages, each of a year, though a further, less formal stage preceding these is not incompatible with Josephus's data.
- *Rigour in keeping the Sabbath*. Josephus (*War* 2.8.9 §147) states that the community was more particular in their Sabbath observances than any other group. This seems to be confirmed by such regulations as those found in CD 10.14–11.18.

More controversial are some other points, though many would see them as also showing a connection:

- *Worship at the temple*. Overall, the Qumran documents seem to oppose the Jerusalem cult as polluted (e. g., CD 6.11-20). Also, Philo indicates that Essenes had no interest in physical sacrifice (*Probus* 75); however, Josephus (*Ant.* 18.1.5 §19) says that the Essenes would send votive offerings to the temple, though he then immediately adds that they had their own cultic rites. Certain passages would appear to support the view that some offerings were allowed (CD 11.18-21; 12.1-2; 16.13). One explanation is that the Essenes as a whole (including the pre-Qumran community) allowed a minimal amount of participation in the temple cult, but that the Qumran group forbade even that (cf. Davies 1982b; 1983: 134–40; Murphy-O'Connor 1985).

- *Women and marriage*. The ancient sources agree that the Essenes were celibate, except that Josephus asserts there was one group who married for purposes of procreation. The Scrolls present a diverse picture: the *Community Rule* is silent on the subject. However, the *Damascus Document* (CD 7.6-7; 12.1-2; 15.5; 16.10-12; 7.6-7// 19.2-3), the *War Scroll* (1QM 7.3) and 1QSa 1.4, 9-11 all indicate the presence of women; the *Damascus Document* also seems to have in mind the intention of procreation (CD 4.10–5.2; cf. Davies 1987: 73–85). On this particular question, the archaeology is also relevant. The burial excavations so far carried out at the Qumran cemetery have complicated matters: on the one hand, in what was only a sampling of the graves, skeletons of women and children were found; on the other hand, these were few and on the outskirts of the cemetery rather than in the main part of it, which might suggest women were not generally present (DeVaux 1973: 47–48). Various suggestions have been made to explain this: one is that the women and children were visitors who died on the site; another is that a few women worked at the site but were not a part of the Qumran community. The important thing is that future excavations may change the picture so far obtained.

How valid are these arguments? It is clear that there are some important disagreements between the sources, especially with regard to the location of the place where the Essenes lived and whether they were celibate. It is for this reason that the Essene hypothesis needs careful scrutiny at this time (cf. the cautions of Goodman 1995). If identity requires exact correspondence, then this is clearly not found; nevertheless, there are some striking correspondences that go beyond common Jewish practices. It is also methodologically unsound to require such identity in every detail. There are various reasons why some discrepancy might occur:

- The natural differences between the perceptions of observers who are describing the same thing, especially an entity outside their normal experience.
- The differing amount of completeness in the description, with one source emphasizing certain aspects, and another source giving most weight to other details.
- Sources that describe the same entity but at different points in its development.
- The amount of variety or division within the movement, so that a description fits only one particular faction or perhaps excludes the differences nursed in certain factions.

All of these points may be involved in our sources on the Essenes. A Graeco-Roman writer such as Pliny would have interpreted his source (even if it was Jewish) from his own perspective; also his source may have been quite an old one. Although both Philo and Josephus were probably using detailed Jewish sources, they still interpret them. Philo in particular is making a theological point in his description, while Josephus wants to make the Essenes a philosophical school whose character will be admired by a Graeco-Roman audience. On the other hand, there is no reason to assume that the Essenes were a rigidly organized group with no internal factions or developments over time. Both the questions of celibacy and place of settlement could be explained at least in part on this basis.

Whether one wishes to invoke such explanations depends on how likely one thinks the evidence is of a connection. In this case, most scholars find it difficult to believe that the agreements between Pliny, Philo, Josephus and a certain group of the Scrolls can be mere coincidence. These agreements are on peculiar points, not on customs and practices likely to have been common to a wide range of Jewish groups. The view is that either we must postulate another unattested group at Qumran that had certain unique characteristics in common with the Essenes or we must assume that Qumran is somehow related to the Essenes. The first alternative goes against the natural principle of parsimony in argument; however, the latter would still leave open at least four possibilities:

1. Qumran served as a sort of headquarters for a larger movement.
2. Qumran was a celibate community where Essenes could go if they chose to adopt a more monastic style of life (temporarily or permanently), as opposed to other communities that lived more directly in Jewish society.
3. Qumran was simply one of the many Essene groups which happened to live in the desert rather than in towns or villages.
4. Qumran was a breakaway group, founded by the Teacher of Righteousness.

This last case would suggest that Qumran had renounced the parent movement and, despite still having much in common with it, cultivated some different beliefs and practices which it focused on as evidence of corruption of the parent group. At the present, the last possibility looks most appealing, but the evidence does not seem sufficient to suggest any of the possibilities can be ruled out. There is also a modified form of the Essene thesis advanced in the 'Groningen Hypothesis' (García Martínez 1988; van der Woude 1990; criticized by Lim 1993), as well as by Boccaccini (1998). Overall conclusions are given below (§7.4).

7.3. Some Historical Data

J. M. Baumgarten, E. G. Chazon and A. Pinnick (eds) (2000) *The Damascus Document: A Centennial of Discovery*; **G. J. Brooke** (1985) *Exegesis at Qumran*; **G. J. Brooke (ed.)** (1989) *Temple Scroll Studies*; **M. Broshi and E. Eshel** (1997) 'The Greek King Is Antiochus IV (4QHistorical Text=4Q248)', *JJS* 48: 120–29; **W. H. Brownlee** (1982–83) 'The Wicked Priest, the Man of Lies, and the Righteous Teacher—the Problem of Identity', *JQR* 73: 1–37; **M. Chyutin** (1997) *The New Jerusalem Scroll from Qumran: A Comprehensive Reconstruction*; **P. R. Davies** (1977a) *1QM, the War Scroll from Qumran: Its Structure and History*; **H. Eshel** (2008) *The Dead Sea Scrolls and the Hasmonean State*; **L. L. Grabbe** (2000b) 'Warfare', in L. H. Schiffman and J. C. VanderKam (eds), *Encyclopedia of the Dead Sea Scrolls*, 961–65; **D. J. Harrington** (1997) *Wisdom Texts from Qumran*; **M. P. Horgan** (1979) *Pesharim: Qumran Interpretations of Biblical Books*; **J. K. Lefkovits** (2000) *The Copper Scroll (3Q15): A Reevaluation*; **B. A. Levine** (1978) 'The Temple Scroll: Aspects of its Historical Provenance and Literary Character', *BASOR* 232: 5–23; **S. Metso** (1997) *The Textual Development of the Qumran Community Rule*; **D. Pardee** (1972–73) 'A Restudy of the Commentary on Psalm 37 from Qumran Cave 4', *RQum* 8: 163–94; **N. Rizzolo** (2017) *Pesher: L'interpretazione della Parola per la fine dei giorni: Studio sul genere letterario dei Pesharym*; **L. H. Schiffman** (1990a) '*Miqsat Ma'aseh Ha-torah* and the *Temple Scroll*', *RevQ* 14: 435–57; **A. Steudel** (1994) *Der Midrasch zur Eschatologie aus der Qumrangemeinde (4QMidrEschat*[a.b]*): Materielle Rekonstruktion, Textbestand, Gattund und traditionsgeschichtliche Einordnung des durch 4Q174 ('Florilegium') und 4Q177 ('Catena A') repräsentierten Werkes aus den Qumranfunden*. **D. D. Swanson** (1995) *The Temple Scroll and the Bible: The Methodology of 11QT*; **Y. Yadin (ed.)** (1962) *The Scroll of the War of the Sons of Light against the Sons of Darkness*; **idem** (1983) *The Temple Scroll*.

We appear to find two sorts of historical data in the Scrolls: those relating to the internal history of the sect, and those referring to events in the wider world. It is this latter that are of particular interest, but there are not many such references. Most of them are covered by H. Eshel (2008), though some of his interpretations are more convincing than others. Here are the ones that seem to be well established:

- Several Hasmonaean figures are apparently mentioned by name in texts on the priestly courses (4Q331-33): Alexandra Salome (שלמציון,שלמצון), John Hyrcanus (יוחנן), Hyrcanus II (הרקנוס) the Roman governor Marcus Aemilius Scaurus (אמליוס).

- The Jewish leader Peitholaus (פותלאיס) seems to be mentioned in 4Q468e (Eshel 2006: 142–43 and the references there; also §17.4).
- The Nahum commentary (4QpNah) says that a King Demetrius came against a 'furious young lion' (1.5) who also 'hangs men alive' (1.7-8). All this strongly suggests Alexander Jannaeus and the incident during his rule involving Jewish opponents (some of whom he crucified) and the Seleucid king Demetrius III (§16.5). There seems also to be a reference to Antiochus IV (אנתיכוס).
- The 'Kittim' (1QpHab 2.12, 14; 3.4, 9; 1QM 1.2, 4, 6, 9, 12, etc.: כתיים, כתיאים) are now almost universally identified with the Romans.
- The *War Scroll* (1QM) describes an eschatological military campaign between the forces of good and the forces of evil. Not only human beings but also angelic powers take part, with the eventual triumph of good over evil. Although the fighting itself is very stylized and unworldly for the most part, the work also reflects a genuine knowledge of military matters (Yadin [ed.] 1962; Grabbe 2000b).
- The 'Historical Text' 4Q248 appears to make reference to Antiochus IV's invasions of Egypt in 170/169 and 168 BCE and the capture of Jerusalem (Broshi and Eshel 1997).

Most of the historical references in the Scrolls appear to involve some aspects of the history of the Qumran sect itself. For example, a figure mentioned in a number of passages is the 'Wicked Priest'. This has generally been taken to refer to one of the Hasmonaean priest-rulers, such as Simon (Cross 1961: 149–52) or Jonathan (Vermes 1977: 31), or even a succession of Hasmonaean rulers (Brownlee 1982–83). Also featured is the 'Man of Lies'. Is he to be identified with the Wicked Priest, as is often thought, or is he someone else? He might be an individual within the movement. The founder and leader of the sect is called the 'Teacher of Righteousness' (מורה הצדק *môrēh haṣṣedek*). A number of passages have been widely interpreted as referring to the internal development of the sect (e.g., CD 1.1–2.1) or to interaction between the community and the Hasmonaeans (especially the Habakkuk commentary [1QpHab]). Certain groups are referred to as 'the wicked of Ephraim and Manasseh' (4QpPs^a 2.18), which have been widely identified with the Sadducees and Pharisees, yet these were hardly the only movements extant in the 1st century BCE. Similarly, the 'Seekers after Smooth Things' (4QNah 2.2) are often taken to be the Pharisees. However, one should be cautious since these are stereotyped terms which could be applied to a variety of enemies (Pardee 1972–73);

192   *A History of Jews and Judaism in the Second Temple Period, Volume 3*

it would certainly be a mistake to use such data to reconstruct the history of the Pharisaic movement. As Davies (1987: 87–105) has pointed out, the Hymns (1QH) may have been a source for stereotyped expressions which had different meanings at different times and in different contexts, even if a particular passage seems to have a clear referent.

There is thus not even sufficient information for a history of the sect itself, much less a significant contribution to particular events in the wider world of Judaea or even further afield. The contribution of the Scrolls is primarily in the areas of Jewish belief, practice, theology, Scripture and culture. These are of course part of history as well. In these areas the Scrolls and the settlement at Qumran are very important.

7.4. *Conclusions*

Although the Essenes are in many ways the best attested of the ancient Jewish sects, many questions remain unanswered. Even the name 'Essene' has not been satisfactorily explained (see §6.5.2). The dominant 'Essene hypothesis' has rightly been questioned; however, questioning it does not mean that it is wrong, only that it should receive proper scholarly scrutiny. In spite of some recent doubts, the balance of the evidence still favours some sort of relationship between a group of 'sectarian' documents among the Scrolls and the Essenes, though this relationship may not be a simple one. Also, the most likely explanation is that the settlement at Khirbet Qumran used and hid many of the scrolls found in the surrounding caves, even if this connection is not without some problems. One initial point seems clear from the archaeology: the Qumran settlement took place in the early 1st century BCE. The original community was only about 50 individuals, though later it seems to have expanded to about 200.

Whatever the group at Qumran was, it was very small and certainly not the 4,000 Essenes given by Philo and Josephus. It was evidently founded by an individual called the 'Teacher of Righteousness' (despite many suggestions, no consensus about his identity has emerged). The group was opposed by the 'wicked priest' (הכוהן הרשע *hakkôhēn hārāšā'*), usually equated with the high priest in the Jerusalem temple; most have identified him with one of the Hasmonaean priest-kings, but the range of suggestions has been wide: Jonathan, Simon, John Hyrcanus, Alexander Jannaeus or even a succession of Hasmonaean figures. Another opponent was the 'Seekers after Smooth Things', who are often confidently asserted to be the Pharisees, but this is not at all certain: it could be a general term for a succession of 'enemies' or competitors of the community (Grabbe 1997a: 58–60).

The most likely explanation is that the Qumran group began within the Essene movement but broke away. Several references to the 'Man of Lies' looks like an internal reference to the leader of the parent group, but we must keep in mind that a sect's bitterest attacks may be against those closest to it ideologically. No history of the larger movement can be traced (unless some hints of it are given in CD 1.1-11//4Q266 2.1-11; cf. Murphy-O'Connor 1974; Davies 1982a). The 390 years (CD 1.5-6) has sometimes been used to calculate the beginnings of the group, but this is likely to be a stylized number borrowed from Ezekiel (4.5) and not historically useful. The Qumran group survived the (real or imagined) attacks of the 'Wicked Priest' and the death of the Teacher, continued to flourish, perhaps with only one short break in settlement—or perhaps none at all—until the destruction by the Romans who overran the area of Qumran about 68 CE. The group is not likely to have survived these events.

The problem is that many widely accepted interpretations depend on several assumptions about the nature of the evidence and the associated methodological problems, assumptions which have been strongly challenged in recent years. New debates have arisen and new suggestions for solutions proposed. These will no doubt continue, as much work remains to be done on this rich treasure of material from Second Temple Judaism.

Chapter 8

THE SAMARITANS:
FROM SANBALLAT TO VESPASIAN

Z. Ben-Hayyim (1957–77) *The Literary and Oral Tradition of Hebrew and Aramaic amongst the Samaritans, Vols I–V* (Heb.); **idem** (1971) review of J. D. Purvis, *The Samaritan Pentateuch and the Origin of the Samaritan Sect*, *Bib* 52: 253–55; **J. Bowman** (1977) *Samaritan Documents Relating to their History, Religion and Life*; **R. J. Coggins** (1975) *The Samaritans and Jews*; **idem** (1987) 'The Samaritans in Josephus', in L. H. Feldman and G. Hata (eds), *Josephus, Judaism, and Christianity*, 257–73; **A. D. Crown (ed.)** (1989) *The Samaritans*; **A. D. Crown, R. Pummer and A. Tal (eds.)** (1993) *A Companion to Samaritan Studies*; **R. Egger** (1986) *Josephus Flavius und die Samaritaner*; **L. L. Grabbe** (1987a) 'Josephus and the Reconstruction of the Judean Restoration', *JBL* 106: 231–46; **idem** (2002b) 'Betwixt and Between: The Samaritans in the Hasmonean Period', in P. R. Davies and John M. Halligan (eds.), *Second Temple Studies III: Studies in Politics, Class and Material Culture*, 202–17; **B. Hensel** (2016) *Juda und Samaria: Zum Verhältnis zweier nach-exilischer Jahwismen*; **S. J. Isser** (1976) *The Dositheans: A Samaritan Sect in Late Antiquity* (1976); **J. Macdonald** (1964) *The Theology of the Samaritans*; **idem** (1971) 'Samaritans', *EJ* 14:728–32; **Y. Magen** (2008a) *The Samaritans and the Good Samaritan*; **idem** (2008b) *Mount Gerizim Excavations: Volume II, A Temple City*; **Y. Magen et al.** (2004) *Mount Gerizim Excavations: Volume I, The Aramaic, Hebrew and Samaritan Inscriptions*; **J. A. Montgomery** (1907) *The Samaritans: The Earliest Jewish Sect*; **R. Pummer** (1976) 'The Present State of Samaritan Studies [1]', *JSS* 21: 39–61; **idem** (1977) 'The Present State of Samaritan Studies [2]', *JSS* 22: 27–47; **idem** (1979) 'The *Book of Jubilees* and the Samaritans', *Eglise et Théologie* 10: 147–78; **idem** (1982a) 'Antisamaritanische Polemik in jüdischen Schriften aus der intertestamentarischen Zeit', *BZ* 26: 224–42; **idem** (1982b) 'Genesis 34 in Jewish Writings of the Hellenistic and Roman Periods', *HTR* 76: 177–88; **idem** (1987a) *The Samaritans*; **idem** (1987b) 'Ἀργαριζιν: A Criterion for Samaritan Provenance?' *JSJ* 18: 18–25; **idem** (2009) *The Samaritans in Flavius Josephus*; **idem** (2016) *The Samaritans: A Profile*; **J. D. Purvis**

(1968), *The Samaritan Pentateuch and the Origin of the Samaritan Sect*; **idem** (1986) 'The Samaritans and Judaism', in R. A. Kraft and G. W. E. Nickelsburg (eds), *Early Judaism and its Modern Interpreters*, 81–98; **L. H. Schiffman** (1984–85) 'The Samaritans in Tannaitic Halakhah', *JQR* 75: 323–50.

The Samaritan community, with its cult on Mt Gerizim, is one of the most important religious communities in Palestine besides the Jews, not least because it has continued to exist even to the present. To get at the history of the community is not a simple matter, and we must begin with the basics: What are the sources? What are the problems with extracting their data? What do they tell us about the history of the community?

In much Jewish polemic of antiquity, the Samaritans are out and out pagans. Yet in the Samaritans' own writings, they are simply Israelites who have faithfully preserved the ancestral religion of Moses. And indeed in various references in rabbinic literature, this is tacitly recognized, in that the Samaritans are regarded as observing most of the Torah (*b. Qid.* 76a; cf. Schiffman 1984–85). Unfortunately, other passages make them non-Jews at best and even pagans at their most uncomplimentary (Pummer 2016: 66–73). Tracing the history of the Samaritans has been bedeviled by two main problems: (1) much of our data from early sources comes from hostile witnesses; (2) the Samaritan writings themselves are generally very late in both the manuscript witnesses and in their current literary form. Also, because of the small number of Samaritan specialists, relatively little work has so far been done on the traditio-historical analysis of the literature. Although a number of older surveys have long been available (e.g., Montgomery 1907; Macdonald 1964; Bowman 1977), they can be unreliable in parts because of faulty methodology in attempting to reconstruct Samaritan history and should be read in the light of studies by Coggins (1975), Pummer (1987, 2009, 2016), Hensel (2016) and several edited collections (Crown 1989; Crown et al. 1993). Only the briefest of introductions to Samaritan studies can be given here, and that will relate mainly to the historical question for the period from about 200 BCE to about 70 CE. The archaeology of Samaria and of Mt Gerizim is discussed in Chapter 2.

Unless otherwise qualified, the term 'Samaritan(s)' will be used of the community whose religious centre was the cult on Mt Gerizim and which produced the community still in existence. How large and extensive that community was, and how much of the population in the old region of Samaria it embraced, has yet to be determined. This chapter makes no a priori assumptions about them. 'Samarian(s)' refers to the inhabitants of the province or region of Samaria, whether Samaritan, Jewish or Greek.

8.1. The Samaritan Literary Sources

This section deals only with Samaritan sources. Other relevant historical sources are discussed in the historical survey itself, in the time period to which they relate.

8.1.1. Samaritan Pentateuch and Translations

J. Joosten (2014) 'The *Samareitikon* and the Samaritan Tradition', in W. Kraus and S. Kreuzer (eds), *Die Septuaginta – Text, Wirkung, Rezeption*: 346–59; **S. Schorch (ed.)** (2018) *The Samaritan Pentateuch: A Critical Editio Maior: III Leviticus*; **H. Shehadeh** (1989–2002) *The Arabic Translation of the Samaritan Pentateuch*; **A. Tal (ed.)** (1980) *The Samaritan Targum of the Pentateuch: A Critical Edition, Part I: Genesis, Exodus*; **idem** (1981) *The Samaritan Targum of the Pentateuch: A Critical Edition, Part II: Leviticus, Numeri, Deuteronomium*; **idem** (1983) *The Samaritan Targum of the Pentateuch: A Critical Edition, Part III: Introduction*; **idem** (1994) *The Samaritan Pentateuch Edited according to MS 6 (C) of the Shekhem Synagogue*; **E. Tov** (1989) 'Proto-Samaritan Texts and the Samaritan Pentateuch', in A. D. Crown (ed.), *The Samaritans*, 397–407; **idem** (2011) *Textual Criticism of the Hebrew Bible*, 80–100; **B. K. Waltke** (1965) *Prolegomena to the Samaritan Pentateuch*; **idem** (1970) 'The Samaritan Pentateuch and the Text of the Old Testament', in J. B. Payne (ed.), *New Perspectives on the Old Testament*, 212–39.

It is widely accepted that the Samaritan Pentateuch is a community (sectarian) recension of a previously existing non-sectarian text-type, sometimes referred to as proto-Samaritan (Tov 1989; 2011: 80–100). If we accept this position, the question remains: When did this sectarian recension take place? Purvis has argued that it followed shortly after Hyrcanus's destruction of Samaria and Shechem in the late 2nd century BCE (Purvis 1968). This suggestion is plausible, but is there actual evidence? Purvis argues primarily from the script and orthography, which he claims indicate an origin in the Hasmonaean period. None of his arguments seem to preclude a recension as much as two or three centuries after 100 BCE, however (see, for example, the doubts expressed by Z. Ben-Hayyim 1971). Indeed, a recension before 100 BCE cannot be excluded, though it is not so far attested. Thus, the Samaritan scriptures do not provide us with any certain data on when or whether a major break occurred between the Jewish and Samaritan communities. For some of the contents of the chronicles, however, see the next section (§8.1.2).

One of the problems with the Samaritan Pentateuch was the lack of a critical edition. One is now in progress, edited by S. Schorch (2018). An earlier text, based on a single manuscript, was issued by A. Tal (1994).

Like the Jewish scriptures, the Samaritan Pentateuch was eventually translated into Aramaic, the Samaritan Targum (Tal 1980, 1981, 1983). There was also a later Arabic translation (Shehadeh 1989–2002). There is also the question of a Greek translation, the *Samareitikon*, though the answer is not straightforward (Joosten 2014). We should also not overlook Z. Ben-Hayyim's transcription of a traditional oral reading of the Samaritan Pentateuch (Ben-Hayyim 1957–77: 4:353–554).

8.1.2. Samaritan Chronicles

E. N. Adler and M. Seligsohn (1902a) 'Une nouvelle chronique samaritaine [1]', *REJ* 44: 188–222; **idem** (1902b) 'Une nouvelle chronique samaritaine [2–3]', *REJ* 45: 70–98; 223–54; **idem** (1903) 'Une nouvelle chronique samaritaine [4]', *REJ* 46: 123–46; **Z. Ben-Hayyim** (1942–43) ספר אסטיר, *Tarbiz* 14: 104–90; **idem** (1943–44) ספר אסטיר, *Tarbiz* 15: 71–87; **J. Bowman** (1954) *Transcript of the Original Text of the Samaritan Chronicle Tolidah* [text only, using a different manuscript from Neubauer]; **J. M. Cohen** (1981) *A Samaritan Chronicle: A Source-Critical Analysis of the Life and Times of the Great Samaritan Reformer, Baba Rabba*; **O. T. Crane** (1890) *The Samaritan Chronicle or the Book of Joshua, the Son of Nun*; **A. D. Crown** (1966) *A Critical Re-examination of the Samaritan Sepher Yehoshua*; **idem** (1971–72) 'New Light on the Inter-relationships of Samaritan Chronicles from Some Manuscripts in the John Rylands Library [1]', *BJRL* 54: 282–313; **idem** (1972–73) 'New Light on the Inter-relationships of Samaritan Chronicles from Some Manuscripts in the John Rylands Library [2]', *BJRL* 55: 86–111; **M. Florentin** (1999) *The Tulida: A Samaritan Chronicle: Text, Translation Commentary*; **M. Gaster** (1908) 'Das Buch Josua in hebräisch-samaritanischer Rezension, endeckt und zum ersten Male herausgegeben', *ZDMG* 62: 209–79, 494–549; **idem** (1925–28) 'The Chain of Samaritan High Priests', *Studies and Texts*, 1:483–502 (English translation), 3:131–38 (text); **idem** (1927) *The Asatir: The Samaritan Book of the 'Secrets of Moses' together with the Pitron or Samaritan Commentary and the Samaritan Story of the Death of Moses*; **J. Macdonald** (1963) *Memar Marqah: The Teaching of Marqah*; **idem** (1969) *The Samaritan Chronicle No. II*; **A. Neubauer** (1869) 'Chronique samaritaine, suivie d'un appendice contenant de courtes notices sur quelques autres ouvrages samaritains', *Journal asiatique* 14: 385–470 [text and French translation]; **P. Stenhouse** (1985) *The Kitāb al-Tarīkh of Abū 'l-Fath, Translated into English with Notes*.

The Samaritan writings preserved by the present-day Samaritan community give a quite different picture from that found in Jewish and Christian sources. This information is found mainly in their chronicles, all of which seem interrelated despite some difference of detail. For our purposes here, the chronicles to be mentioned are the following. The relationship between them is complicated; for an attempt to sort them out, see Crown (1971–72, 1972–73):

– *The Asatir (Chronicle 1)*. This is a paraphrase and expansion of the Samaritan Pentateuch, with legendary and other interpretative material. It is structured around the four figures of Adam, Noah, Abraham and Moses. For text and translation, see Ben-Hayyim (1942–43, 1943–44) and Gaster (1927).

– *Chronicle 2*. Published only in part by J. Macdonald (1969), and with another section by J. M. Cohen (1981), the entire chronicle apparently extends from the death of Moses to medieval times. The section on the Hasmonaean period has not been published. For a summary of the entire contents, see Macdonald (1971). From his description, the contents sound very similar to Abu 'l-Fath.

– *Tulidah (Chronicle 3)*. This is a simple list of the Samaritan high priests. The best edition is by M. Florentin (1999; cf. also Bowman 1954, which has errors; Neubauer 1869). Bowman has argued that it is the earliest and most original source, but studies by Crown (1971–72, 1972–73) have suggested that it is in fact an abbreviation of the fuller chronicle(s) which lie(s) behind Chronicle 7.

– *Samaritan Book of Joshua (Chronicle 4)*. While about half of this is a paraphrase of the MT Joshua, the rest of the book takes the story down as late as the time of Baba Rabba (about the 4th century CE). See especially A. D. Crown (1966; cf. also Crane 1890; Gaster 1908).

– *The Shalshalah (Chronicle 5)*. This is the shortest of the chronicles, even shorter than the Tulidah, being a bare list of the high priests with the lengths of reign correlated with various world eras. It goes from Adam to the 19th century in its present form. Text and English translation are given by M. Gaster (1925–28: 1:483–502 [English translation], 3:131–38 [text]).

– *Abu'l Fath (Chronicle 6)*. This differs from the other chronicles in being a composite history composed in the 14th century in Arabic by a single individual. Much of it is based on the Arabic version of the Samaritan book of Joshua, though at times the author seems to have had better manuscripts than those now available. For the rest, he had a chronicle similar to the Tulidah and the Adler Chronicle (below) but often much more expansive than these. An English translation is given by

P. Stenhouse (1985), though Stenhouse's own critical text of the Arabic original is still unpublished; partial translation in J. Bowman (1977: 114–213).

– *Adler Chronicle (Chronicle 7)*. This is similar to the Tulidah in being mainly a list of the high priests, but most of the figures are accompanied by a small block of material relating the events of his term of office. While its present form is late, the core of the work seems to have a respectable antiquity (Crown 1971–72; 1972–73, contra Bowman 1977: 87). The text and translation were given by Adler and Seligson (1902a, 1902b, 1903).

In addition to the chronicles, two other writing are sometimes of importance, especially for the development of theology. These are the *Defter*, an early liturgical collection, and the *Memar Marqa*. This latter is hard to characterize but is mainly a midrashic collection from the 4th century CE. Macdonald has produced an edition and translation (1963), but there are evidently some problems with it (Pummer 1976: 57).

In spite of differences in detail between the various chronicles, they all agree on an overall picture which is considerably different from that found in the non-Samaritan (mostly Jewish and anti-Samaritan) sources. According to their version of events, a parting of the ways came in the time of Eli. He became a renegade, moving the ark from it proper place at Gerizim to Shiloh. The Jerusalem priesthood was descended from this breakaway faction of Eli, while the true Aaronic line continued at Gerizim. Although there were several captivities and exiles, as well as much persecution, the true Israelite priesthood continued as a pure line through the centuries and remains true to the faith at Shechem (Nablus) and God's holy mountain Gerizim today. Far from having a pagan or synchretized worship, they are descendants of Joseph and Levi who have preserved the true worship.

The Samaritan Chronicles of potential value for the history of the sect are Chronicle 2, the Tulidah (Chronicle 3), the Shalshalah (Chronicle 5), Abu 'l-Fath (Chronicle 6) and the Adler Chronicle (Chronicle 7). The Chronicles are a minefield of problems. On the one hand, they claim to trace the Samaritan religion back to Moses and to give an account of their history independently (at least, in part) of the Old Testament. On the other hand, all the Chronicles are late, some of them from the 19th or even 20th century in their present form. Study of them is not far advanced, and Samaritan specialists have reached no consensus on their interrelationships. It seems that each specialist prefers a different Chronicle as the most basic. Bowman thinks Tulidah is earliest. P. Stenhouse concentrates on Abu 'l-Fath (1989). A. D. Crown (1971–72, 1972–73) has argued that the basis of all the Chronicles is the Samaritan Book of Joshua (Chronicle 4) and a *Sefer ha-Yamim* (of which the Adler Chronicle and Chronicle 2 are late examples), with the former being incorporated into the latter at some point.

Where the Chronicles relate Samaritan history to external events, there is often confusion. In addition, some of the events which Jewish literature recounts with reference to the Jews is claimed for the Samaritans by the Chronicles. For example, where Josephus and other Jewish sources have Alexander the Great doing obeisance to the Jewish high priest, the Chronicles (Adler; Tulidah; Abu 'l-Fath; Chronicle 2, *apud* Macdonald) make him do it to the Samaritan high priest (for a discussion of this event, its sources and historicity, see *HJJSTP 2* [274–78]). For the Hasmonaean period, the only event mentioned is the reign of 'King John', evidently John Hyrcanus though possibly Alexander Jannaeus. The story is found in Abu 'l-Fath (Stenhouse 1985: 140–42; Bowman 1978: 134–35) and apparently also in Chronicle 2 (so Macdonald in his summary). According to their version, however, John destroys Samaria but not Shechem. Eventually, he acknowledges its claim and attempts to go on a pilgrimage to Gerizim! The source of this account is uncertain, though it seems remarkably close to that of Josephus; one could argue that it is his version with a deliberate twist.

Another account is more problematic. It concerns a king of the Jews named Simeon and his son 'Arqiah (Abu 'l-Fath) or Hilqiyah (Adler). This sounds very much like Simon Maccabee and his son (John) Hyrcanus, but the episode is dated to the Persian period, and their reigns are followed by a captivity of the Jews. Simeon is said to have caused great hostility between the Jews and Samaritans because the Jews persecuted the Samaritans and forbade them to worship. Finally, the Samaritans called their diaspora brethren from Babylon and attacked Jerusalem, destroying it and the temple, though Simeon got away. King Darius heard of this and supported the Jews, whereupon many Samaritans emigrated, while those that remained again had their religion proscribed. Under 'Arqiah/ Hilqiyah a quarrel that arose between 'the sons of Ithamar and the sons of Manasseh' appears to be an inner-Samaritan quarrel. After that 'the nations' besieged Jerusalem and exiled the Jews, allowing the Samaritans to return with thanks and praise to God.

Can anything of historical value be gleaned from these accounts? This seems doubtful in the present state of knowledge. The most one can say is that Josephus's account of the destruction of the Gerizim temple has no memory in the Samaritan sources.

Bowman makes the surprising claim that both these events confirm the accounts of Josephus (see the notes to his translation). Against it are the following points: if the incident relating to 'King John' is borrowed from Josephus, it has no independent value; if not, it specifically denies the destruction of Shechem by Hyrcanus I. Similarly, the quarrel between the sons of Ithamar and the sons of Manasseh cannot be dated (is it the Persian period or the time of John Hyrcanus?) nor does it make any allusion to the supposed defection of Manasseh, a son of the high priest, to Gerizim. On this last event and its historicity, see *HJJSTP 1* (157–58).

8.1.3. *Samaritan Writings in Greek*

J. J. Collins (2000) *Between Athens and Jerusalem*; **C. A. Holladay** (1983) *Fragments from Hellenistic Jewish Authors, Volume I: Historians*; **idem** (1989) *Fragments from Hellenistic Jewish Authors, Volume II: Poets: The Epic Poets Theodotus and Philo and Ezekiel the Tragedian*; **D. Mendels** (1987) *The Land of Israel as a Political Concept in Hasmonean Literature*.

Pseudo-Eupolemus is the name given to two fragments preserved among the Fragmentary Jewish Greek writers. For an edition and translation, with a summary of scholarship up to the time of writing, see C. A. Holladay (1983: 157–87; cf. also Collins 2000: 38–39). One of these is preserved in the name of Eupolemus, the other as 'anonymous'; the consensus of scholarship is that they are both by an anonymous Samaritan who wrote sometime during the 3rd or 2nd centuries BCE. R. Doran (in *OTP* 2:873–82) suggests the first fragment is from Eupolemus himself. Among the Fragmentary Writers is also Theodotus. He too has often been identified as a Samaritan, but the weight of evidence seems against it; he is more likely a Jewish writer (Holladay 1989: 2:51–68; Pummer 1982a). F. Fallon (in *OTP* 2:785–93) sees no clear evidence to decide the matter. D. Mendels (1987: 110–16), however, argues that Theodotus was Samaritan.

Even with the small amount of preserved text, Pseudo-Eupolemus tells several things. He evidently had a good Greek education, showing that such opportunities were available for Samaritans as well as other Orientals. Pseudo-Eupolemus was quite happy to interpret biblical tradition in the light of Greek mythology. Sometimes this is called 'syncretism', but inaccurately. Pseudo-Eupolemus gives no indication of diluting the Samaritan cult or other aspects of the religion with pagan elements; rather, the biblical tradition is only put in the Greek context, showing how the native tradition fits in with Greek legend and myth. Far from engaging in compromise, Pseudo-Eupolemus is actually strengthening his people's tradition by showing that the Greeks have a memory of it, if perhaps only a dim and inaccurate one. He is using his Greek knowledge for apologetic purposes, with the aim not of diminishing his own tradition but of defending it.

Pseudo-Eupolemus is thus very much like contemporary Jewish writers in Greek. These, too, made use of Greek knowledge and literary techniques to extend, update, interpret and defend their religious tradition. But to do so required a knowledge of Greek language, literature and culture. This shows that such knowledge was available and that a Samaritan could gain a Greek education but also remain loyal to his native people.

8.2. *Historical Overview of the Samaritans*

As has already been indicated, trying to write a history of the Samaritan community around Mt Gerizim is fraught with many difficulties. The Samaritan sources (mainly the chronicles) cannot be said to give such a history, and the question of how much actual historical data are available in them is a major question. Many are suspicious of them and generally discount their value for reconstructing a history of the community (e.g., Pummer 2016: 241–42). The sceptical approach is probably the right one, but here and there might be some genuine memories; however, this will become determined only when much more thorough study of the chronicles and other Samaritan literature has taken place. For the present survey, the standard historical sources will be used, especially Josephus. Yet because the sources are by outsiders and are often hostile to the Samaritan community, they must be used with caution.

8.2.1. *Persian Period and Earlier*

– *2 Kings 17*. This has been the locus of much of the early Jewish comment on the subject and has even been accepted as normative by many modern scholars. The burden of the chapter is that all the inhabitants of the Northern Kingdom (except for some of the very poor) were deported and replaced with pagans from various parts of the Assyrian empire. Yahwism was introduced only as a superstitious gesture, and then only by an illegitimate priest from one of the forbidden northern shrines. The polemical nature of this account becomes clear when other Old Testament passages and the Assyrian records are consulted, for only a small portion of the population (some of the upper class) was deported and the bulk of the population remained in the land (Coggins 1975: 13–18).

– *Ezra/Nehemiah*. The inhabitants of Samaria are consistently presented as hostile to the returnees from the Exile. Sanballat in particular is taken as an enemy, specifically to Nehemiah (see further *HJJSTP 1*: 298–302).

Josephus, Ant. 11.7.2-8.7 §§302-47. Josephus reports that at the time of Alexander, the Samaritan priesthood was founded by a renegade priest from Jerusalem. While Josephus may have had some independent information, the whole of the story is pervaded by anti-Samaritan bias (Coggins 1975: 93–99; 1987; Grabbe 1987; cf. *HJJSTP 2*: 157–58).

8.2.2. Early Hellenistic Period (335–175 BCE)

> **J. C. Greenfield and M. E. Stone** (1979) 'Remarks on the Aramaic Testament of Levi from the Geniza', *RB* 86: 214–30; **E. M. Schuller** (1990) '4Q372 1: A Text about Joseph', *RevQ* 14, no. 55: 349–76; **G. Stemberger** (1996) *Introduction to the Talmud and Midrash*; **idem** (2011) *Einleitung in Talmud und Midrasch*.

– *Quintus Curtius 4.8.9-11.* Shortly after Syro-Palestine submitted to Alexander and after he had carried his campaign further east, Samaria revolted against the Greek-appointed governor and killed him. Alexander had the city of Samaria attacked, the inhabitants massacred or sold into slavery and the city razed. There are problems with this report in that it has no confirmation elsewhere in the Alexander material and is not considered reliable by some classical scholars (Coggins 1975: 106–9). However, it has a certain confirmation in the Wadi Daliyeh papyri (*HJJSTP 2*: 276–78).

Various scholars of the past and present have claimed to find anti-Samaritan polemic in a number of early Jewish writings. For the most part these do not stand up (see especially Pummer 1977, 1982a, 1982b). Although Genesis 34, with its massacre of the inhabitants of Shechem by Jacob's sons, is treated by several documents, *Jubilees* and Judith are not clearly anti-Samaritan. The author of *Testament of Levi* 5–7 is plainly polemicizing against the Shechemites of his own time; however, the date and provenance of the Greek writing are disputed. The main debate about the *Testaments of the Twelve Patriarchs* is whether these are Christian documents which make use of Jewish material or are Jewish writings with Christian intervention. Some Aramaic fragments of *Testament of Levi* are known from the Cairo Genizah and Qumran. One of the Genizah fragments (Cambridge T-S 16.94) seems to contain a version of the story in Genesis 34, though it does not correspond to the extant Greek text of *Testament of Levi*. (For recent scholarship on the question, see Greenfield and Stone 1979; SCHÜRER 3:767–81; Collins 2000: 57–60; *JWSTP* 325–55.)

According to the editor of *4QApocryphon of Joseph*[b] (4Q372), this scroll about Joseph also reflects anti-Samaritan views (Schuller 1990). This interpretation is based primarily on lines 11–14, which speak of 'building a high place for themselves on a high mountain to arouse the jealousy of Israel'. This interpretation may, of course, be correct, but it is not at all certain.

Ben Sira 50.25-26 makes the enigmatic statement, 'Two nations my soul abhors, and the third is not a people: Those who live on Mount Seir, and the Philistines, and the foolish people that dwell in Shechem'. The precise meaning is difficult, though it looks anti-Samaritan on the face of it (Coggins 1975: 82–86). But not everyone agrees. There is some question as to whether these verses were written by Ben Sira himself or were from another source, whether before his time or a later insertion (cf. Coggins 1975: 83–86; Pummer 1982a: 232 plus n. 45; Egger 1986: 85–93). They do not fit well into the context. The sentiment expressed seems clear, but how early it arose is more problematic. Purvis (1986) has attempted to suggest a historical background for the statement, but the evidence offered is extremely scanty. The only data he seems to offer are *Ant.* 12.4.1 §156 and the scholia of the *Megillat Taanit*. The first is problematic because its dating is very uncertain, and it does not necessarily have anything to do with Shechem (see below). His use of the scholia of the *Megillat Taanit* is surprising since these are commonly acknowledged to be post-Talmudic in origin, not like the *Megillat Taanit* itself which is usually dated to the 1st or 2nd century CE (on this writing and the scholia, see Stemberger 1996, 2011). We can have no confidence that the scholia are likely to contain any reliable information for the 2nd or 3rd century BCE. Nevertheless, the statement in Ben Sira is likely to have originated no later than the 2nd century BCE, since it is found in the Greek translation of Ben Sira's grandson about 132 BCE.

Josephus relates another incident on the Samaritans in *Ant.* 12.4.1 §156:

> Now at this time the Samaritans [Σαμαρεῖς] were in a flourishing condition and much distressed the Jews by cutting off parts of their land and carrying off slaves. This happened when Onias was high priest.

The first question is when this took place. It is dated to the time of Ptolemy V Epiphanes (204–180 BCE) and the high priest Onias, son of Simon the Just. This Simon the Just is often identified with Simon II who lived around 200 BCE and is mentioned in Ben Sira 50.1-24. That would date the event to the early 2nd century. Yet various other episodes in this context, mainly those relating to the Tobiads, are misdated and should be put earlier. The activities of Joseph Tobiad could have taken place only during Ptolemaic rule over Palestine; therefore, their dating to the reign of Ptolemy V must be mistaken. Ptolemy III (246–221 BCE) is more likely the person intended, though Josephus might have misunderstood his source. Therefore, we cannot be confident that Josephus has correctly placed the incident.

Secondly, who were those doing the enslaving? Although Josephus is not consistent in his terminology, the term *Samareis* is often used generically for the inhabitants of the region of Samaria (see Pummer 2009: 4–7; also Egger 1986; but see the review by R. Pummer 1988).

We do not know if Josephus's source understood the raiders to be members of the community on Mt Gerizim, and Josephus does not make this specific identification. They could have been inhabitants of Samaria who had nothing to do with the Gerizim cult, but neither can we rule this possibility out. Therefore, the relevance of this event to the main question is uncertain.

8.2.3. *Time of the Maccabees and the Hasmonaean Kingdom*

> **G. Alon** (1977) 'The Origin of the Samaritans in the Halakhic Tradition', in idem, *Jews, Judaism and the Classical World: Studies in Jewish History in the Times of the Second Temple and Talmud*: 354–73; **D. Barag** (1992–93) 'New Evidence on the Foreign Policy of John Hyrcanus I', *INJ* 12: 1–12; **E. J. Bickerman** (1937b) 'Un document relatif a la persécution d'Antiochos IV Epiphane', *RHR* 115: 188–223; **K. Bringmann** (1983) *Hellenistische Reform und Religionsverfolgung in Judäa: Eine Untersuchung zur jüdisch-hellenistischen Geschichte (175–163 v. Chr.)*; **M. Delcor** (1962) 'Vom Sichem der hellenistischen Epoche zum Sychar des Neuen Testamentes', *ZDPV* 78: 34–48; **R. Doran** (1983) '2 Maccabees 6:2 and the Samaritan Question', *HTR* 76: 481–85; **G. Finkielsztejn** (1998) 'More Evidence on John Hyrcanus I's Conquests: Lead Weights and Rhodian Amphora Stamps', *Bulletin of the Anglo-Israel Archaeological Society* 16: 33–63; **A. Schalit** (1970–71) 'Die Denkschrift der Samaritaner an König Antiochos Epiphanes zu Beginn der Großen Verfolgung der jüdischen Religion im Jahre 167 v. Chr. (Josephus, *AJ* XII, §§258-264)', *ASTI* 8: 131–83.

Josephus is clearly prejudiced against the Samaritans, which seems plain from many passages (despite R. Egger 1986: esp. 310–13; she may well be right that there are passages where his approach is more neutral, but quite a few simply cannot be explained away; see also Pummer 2009). When Josephus mentions the Samaritans, he often takes the opportunity to disparage the Samaritan community. Nevertheless, in some instances he may have had useful sources even if he has turned them to his own purposes. (One of these is the alleged letter from the Shechemites to Antiochus IV discussed below.) In one of his more notorious statements (*Ant.* 9.14.3 §291; similarly, 11.8.6 §341), he claims that they change their approach according to circumstance. When they see the Jews doing well, they claim to be related to them with a common descent from Joseph. On the other hand, when the Jews are having difficulties, they say that they have nothing in common with them and are themselves from a different ethnos. This may strike one initially as only another expression of prejudice. Undoubtedly, Josephus intended no less, but in fact the statement may describe a genuine state of affairs. Those who have had the experience of sectarian infighting know well that a group may emphasize or disavow resemblances to other groups, depending on the circumstances. It would hardly be surprising if the Samaritans did the same.

Josephus quotes a letter, allegedly written at the time of Antiochus IV, which claims to be from a group of Sidonians at Shechem (*Ant*. 12.5.5 §§258-61). They argue, first, that they observe the sabbath because it originated long before in response to droughts within their country. They have a temple on Mt Gerizim and offer sacrifices there. The Jews are quite properly being punished, but the king's officers treat them (the 'Sidonians') in the same way in the mistaken belief that they are related to the Jews, whereas they are Sidonians. They call on Antiochus IV to instruct his officers Apollonius and Nicanor not to molest them. They also ask that their temple be called after Zeus Hellenios. Antiochus allegedly replies (*Ant*. 12.5.5 §§262-64) that because the 'Sidonians' have elected to live according to Greek practices, they are absolved of any charges and their temple is permitted to be dedicated to Zeus Hellenios.

The first question is whether these two documents are authentic. Although the question was widely debated in the past, with eminent names on both sides of the argument, most writers have accepted authenticity since Bickerman's study (1937b; more or less accepting Bickerman's conclusions are Schalit 1970–71; Egger 1986: 280–81). Both the alleged petition and its reply bear the characteristics expected of Seleucid documents from the period. Just as persuasive is the argument that no clear reason can be found as to why a Jewish forger would have written the documents in their present form (Bickerman 1937b). Also in the surrounding context, Josephus makes statements which are contradicted by the documents (e.g., the origin of the Samaritans as colonists from the Medes and Persians). The one difficulty which Bickerman did not deal with is whether we might have original documents which have nevertheless been tampered with in some way (also noted by R. J. Coggins 1975: 98–99; G. Alon 1977: 369; R. Pummer 1982a: 239 n. 94). Such documents are likely to be found elsewhere in Josephus and, despite Bickerman, it seems that this possibility cannot be ruled out here.

If authentic, this letter and the Seleucid response give an important message about the Samaritans, especially when read in the light of 2 Macc. 6.1-2. Should we conclude, as many have, that the Samaritans gave themselves over to allow their cult to be Hellenized? A closer inspection does not lead to this conclusion. The actual religious practices of the Jews and Samaritans were very similar: the same sabbath observance, the same food laws, much the same purity laws, the same requirement of circumcision. The primary distinction between them was the question of God's chosen place for his temple. To an outsider, especially, they must have looked indistinguishable. Antiochus's order suppressing Jewish worship must therefore have delivered the same blow to the Shechemites as to the Jews. The religion to which they adhered with equal fervour was about to be abolished. But they had done nothing to anger Antiochus or to attract this abolition; it was simply a side effect of the Jewish situation. Therefore, it would hardly be surprising if the community of Shechem attempted by diplomacy to have the decree lifted with regard to themselves.

But in so doing, they do not deny keeping the sabbath; instead, they emphasize an origin which might sound rational to a Greek and also appears to have a different basis from that of the Jews. This does not suggest they are abandoning the sabbath but rather are intending to continue observing it. As another means of defence, they could stress that they have a different ethnic origin from the Jews. Although the precise significance of the phrase, 'Sidonians of Shechem' is still not clear, it had a useful function in attempting to distance the community from the Jews. Bickerman (1937b) took the phrase as a synonym for 'Phoenician', which, in turn, was only the Greek term for 'Canaanite'. Schalit (1970–71: 149–56) seems to agree, though his position is not completely clear. But this view is based on assumptions about the origins of the Samaritans which no longer stand up. There is no reason to think that the Samaritans would have any more willingly identified themselves as Canaanites than the Jews.

The term Sidonians is known for a group in the Hellenistic Edomite city of Marissa, and it has been proposed that there was a Sidonian colony at Shechem who wrote this letter (Delcor 1962, followed by Pummer 1982b: especially 184–86; Egger 1986: 266–80). This is unlikely. One can hardly expect a Phoenician colony to be sabbath keepers, and the explanation that they had picked up some practices from the Samaritan community or were loosely associated with its cult is merely an attempt to explain away a difficulty. Pummer (1982b: 184–86) correctly notes that nothing is said about circumcision, implying that it was being kept; if so, this says little for their being a Sidonian colony but much for the Samaritan community. The best explanation to me is that the Samaritan community itself wrote the letter and that, whatever the origin of the designation, it was trying to distance itself from the Jews. None of this suggests an intent to change their cult. On the contrary, it would be a useful means of defending it (Bickerman 1937b; Bringmann 1983: 142–43).

There is nothing in 1 Maccabees which clearly bears on the question of the Samaritans. 1 Maccabees 3.10 says that Apollonius 'gathered the Gentiles and a large force from Samaria to fight against Israel'. If Apollonius was governor of Samaria (so *Ant.* 12.5.5 §261; 12.7.1 §287), he would have had a military force at his disposal, no doubt in part recruited locally. Since this need not imply that the Samaritans as a nation or community sided with Apollonius against the Jews, the incident has no clear bearing on our question. 2 Maccabees may have been written at a time when relations between Jews and Samaritans were deteriorating. Yet even if this was so, two passages give information not necessarily detrimental to the Samaritans:

> [22]But he left overseers to maltreat the people: in Jerusalem Philip of the tribe of Phrygians, having a manner more barbarous than his appointer; [23]in Mt Gerizim Andronicus; but with them Menelaus who treated the citizens worse than the others, since he was hostilely disposed toward his Jewish countrymen. (2 Macc. 5.22-23)

The context and wording indicate that the Samaritans were put under the same restrictions, even religious persecution, which affected the Jews. Another passage supports and supplements this:

> [1]Shortly afterward the king sent out Geron the Athenian to force the Jews to turn away from the ancestral laws and not to live according to the laws of God, [2]and also to defile the temple in Jerusalem and to rename it for Zeus Olympius, and the one in Mt Gerizim, for Zeus Xenio ['Zeus Who Protects the Rights of Strangers'], just as those dwelling there requested. (2 Macc. 6.1-2)

What are the implications of this? Did the Samaritans accept the Hellenization of their cult? Some translations suggest that the Samaritans themselves requested that their temple be given a Greek name. The problem is the final phrase: καθὼς ἐτύγχανον οἱ τὸν τόπον οἰκοῦντες, Διὸς Ξενίου. Some take it to refer to the practice of the community, i.e., to be hospitable. Others interpret it to mean that the inhabitants requested that their temple be renamed. The former interpretation seems more likely (Pummer 1982a: 238–39; Doran 1983).

An event of considerable significance took place under John Hyrcanus. This was the capture and destruction of the city of Samaria and also Shechem and the temple on Mt Gerizim (*War* 1.2.6-7 §§63-65; *Ant.* 13.9.1 §255-56; 13.10.2-3 §§275-81). The two may not be related: we know that the Samaritan sect built and maintained the temple on Gerizim, whereas the city of Samaria may have been primarily descendants of a Macedonian colony settled there by Alexander (*HJJSTP 2*: 276–78). On the other hand, many Samaritans may now have lived in Samaria; we just do not know (cf. the discussion in Pummer 2009: 208). As noted elsewhere (§16.3.3), Hyrcanus turned the siege of Samaria over to his sons Aristobulus and Antigonus. The inhabitants of the city called on a Seleucid ruler for help, which was given, but Aristobulus's forces defeated the Seleucid troops. Resistance was resumed in the form of Seleucid guerrilla action, but Samaria fell after a year. This was apparently about the year 112/111 BCE (Finkielsztejn 1998: 49). It is not clear why Hyrcanus attacked Samaria. Contrary to Josephus it was unlikely to be because the people of Samaria had attacked the Idumaean city of Marisa at the instigation of the Syrians (*Ant.* 13.10.2 §275). It may be that 'Marisa' is a corruption of 'Garizim', which would mean that Hyrcanus was actually defending the Samaritans from the Macedonian colonists at Samaria. More likely, however, is that Hyrcanus took the city for strategic reasons, since it seems to have been an important stronghold. In that case, the siege of Samaria had nothing to do with the Samaritans at Shechem/Gerizim.

The siege and capture of Shechem and Mt Gerizim was a different matter. Why Hyrcanus took the Samaritan temple is an interesting question on which the sources throw no light. Although there had been friction between the Samaritans and Jerusalem, there had also clearly been a lot of social and cultural interchange. As noted above, the Samaritans apparently distanced themselves from the Jews in the time of Antiochus IV, which might have created long-term resentment if there were other such acts not recorded in the extant sources. There is also the question of when he carried out this siege. It was once suggested that there were two conquests, one in 128 BCE and a later one, but archaeology does not support this thesis (Magen 2008: 27). Coins found at the site suggest it was probably about 112/111 BCE (Pummer 2009: 202–4; Barag 1992–93); in other words, perhaps about the same time as the fall of Samaria.

8.2.4. *The Samaritans under Roman Control*

J. Naveh (1982a) 'An Ancient Amulet or a Modern Forgery?' *CBQ* 44: 282–84; **idem** (1982b) 'Some Recently Forged Inscriptions', *BASOR* 247: 53–58; **J. Strugnell** (1967) 'Quelques inscriptions samaritaines', *RBib* 74: 555–80.

The Samarian area came under Roman control at the same time as Judaea did, with the advance of Pompey into the region. The Samarians are not specifically mentioned by Josephus, however, except in passing and alongside other regions neighbouring Judaea. The province of Samaria was apparently attached to Judah. Some have suggested that Herod particularly favoured the Samarians, though the evidence is rather thin. The main datum is that he married a Samaritan wife, Malthace, who was the mother of both Archelaus and Herod Antipas.

One of the most bizarre incidents occurred during the governorship of Coponius (ca. 6–9 CE) at the time Judaea had reverted to being a Roman province. According to Josephus (*Ant.* 18.2.2 §§29-30), when the gates of the temple were opened at midnight at Passover time, some Samarians polluted the temple by scattering human bones in it. At first the account looks straightforward until one begins to look more closely at the details (see the analysis of Pummer 2009: 222–30). First, it is not clear whether those polluting the temple were members of the Samaritan sect (Samaritans) or simply people from the region of Samaria (Samarians). It is difficult to understand why Samarians would have had any reason to pollute the Jerusalem temple. On the other hand, Samaritans normally held the Passover about the same time as the Jews: if Samaritans had scattered human bones in the temple, they would have been themselves polluted and unable to partake of the Passover. Since the Samaritan calendar was reckoned independently of the Jewish (though evidently following the same general calendrical principles), their Passover could have been a month different if an intercalary month was inserted in one calendar but not the other. This might have allowed time for purification, but it would have required considerable animosity for Samaritans to carry out such a deed. Yet Josephus suggests no motivation.

Secondly, the temple guards would probably have quickly intervened and prevented any widespread pollution (the text refers to the 'porticoes' [στοαῖς] initially but then says 'through all the temple' [διὰ παντὸς τοῦ ἱεροῦ]). Also, Josephus does not say what happened to the culprits: surely they would have been caught and punished! Thirdly, why did the perpetrators come 'secretly' (κρύφα) to Jerusalem? There was no prohibition on Samaritans/Samarians entering Jerusalem. Even if they had human bones with them, these could have been hidden without the bearers having to be secretive in their journey to Jerusalem. Finally, the text is corrupt (Pummer 2009: 223–25). Attempts at reconstruction have often involved the restorer's particular understanding of the passage.

The difficulties of reading and interpretation led Pummer to conclude, 'it is doubtful whether there is a historical basis to Josephus' narrative'

(2009: 229). It may well be that a minor incident has been blown up into a major event by popular retelling. In any case, we certainly cannot be sure that it involved members of the Samaritan community. In spite of his general hostility to the Samaritans, even Josephus himself makes nothing of this incident.

Another episode, one more important and also explicable, took place under the governor Pontius Pilate (*Ant*. 18.4.1-2 §§85-89). A man promised to show the Samaritans the sacred vessels of the tabernacle, which according to Samaritan tradition had been buried in a hidden site on Mt Gerizim. A large group gathered in a nearby village with the intention of climbing Mt Gerizim for the demonstration at a particular time. Whether it was anything more than a peaceful gathering is not indicated, but Pilate evidently interpreted it as the prelude to a revolt. That he was not wrong in this is suggested by the mention that some at least were 'in arms' (ἐν ὅπλοις). Before they could actually make the ascent of the mountain, they were intercepted by Roman troops sent by Pilate, who killed and captured many and scattered the rest. The main leaders and most prominent individuals among those captured were executed on Pilate's orders. This was too much for the Samaritan council, who protested to Vitellius, the governor of Syria; they also accused Pilate of more general persecution of their people. Exactly what the charges were or why Vitellius accepted the accusations is not clear, but he did, sending Marcellus to take over in Judaea and ordering Pilate to return to Rome and appear for trial before Tiberius (see further in *HJJSTP 4*). With a careful reading of this account, there is reason to see this incident as involving a messianic pretender.

Another episode took place during the time when Ventidius Cumanus was procurator of Judah, about 51–52 CE (*War* 2.12.3-7 §§232-46; *Ant*. 20.6.1-3 §§118-36; Tacitus, *Annales* 12.54). Some Samaritans attacked a group of Galilaeans on their way to Jerusalem for a festival and killed many (*Ant*. 20.6.1 §118) or only one (*War* 2.12.3 §232). When the Jews appealed to Cumanus he did nothing, allegedly because he had been bribed by the Samaritans (only in *Antiquities*; bribery was a common accusation to discredit an opponent). A mob of Jews took the law into their own hands and attacked some Samaritan villages, led by the 'brigand' (λῃστής) Eleazar son of Deinaeus (and also another unknown individual called Alexander). Josephus indicates the beginnings of a mass revolt since the Galilaeans urged their Jewish colleagues to assert their 'freedom' (ἐλευθερία: *Ant*. 20.6.1 §120). Cumanus intervened with troops, while the Jewish leaders attempted to persuade the rebels to return home; the two forms of persuasion eventually worked, but both Jews and Samaritans appealed to the Syrian governor Ummidius Quadratus.

Quadratus reserved judgment until he had a chance to examine the matter at first hand. After a preliminary investigation he executed some of the chief participants in the fighting (*War* 2.12.6 §§241-42 suggests those executed were all Jewish; Samaritans are not mentioned; *Ant.* 20.6.2 §129 says he crucified both Jews and Samaritans). Quadratus then sent Cumanus, the military tribune Celer, some of the Samaritan notables and the high priests Jonathan and Ananias and other Jewish leaders to Rome for trial before Claudius. The Jews were assisted by Agrippa II who petitioned Claudius on their behalf. Claudius found in favour of the Jews, executing three prominent Samaritans (*War* 2.12.7 §245) or even the whole Samaritan delegation (so *Ant.* 20.6.3 §136), and exiling Cumanus. The tribune Celer was taken back to Jerusalem and there publicly executed. As is evident, the account in *War* is more neutral and even handed, while *Antiquities* shows a more anti-Samaritan bias and a greater anti-Samaritan outcome. These differences must be recognized and taken account of. Yet in spite of differences in detail, the overall picture of the events is similar in both Josephus's accounts. Tacitus adds another perspective, with some differences, but confirms the basic events.

During the siege of Jotapata in 67 CE (see *HJJSTP 4*), Japha the largest village of Galilee revolted (*War* 3.7.31-32 §§289-315). This was attacked and taken in short order about the time that Jotapata fell. About this time a group of Samaritans assembled on Gerizim. The reasons are unclear, since Josephus states that they were conceited by their lack of power! This might suggest, however, that they were expecting divine intervention. Certainly, their contemplation of a revolt (so *War* 3.7.32 §308) seems strange, since the whole region was well garrisoned by the Romans. In any case, Vespasian clearly interpreted this as a threat and was taking no chances: he sent Cerealius who commanded the 5th Legion to the site. They surrounded the mountain and called on the Samaritans to surrender. It was very hot and there was no water on the mountain. Nevertheless, although some Samaritans went over to the Romans, most refused to lay down their arms. Finally, Cerealius sent in his troops and apparently most of the Samaritans were slain, the number said to be over 11,000. It has been suggested that this episode shows that the Samaritans joined the Jews in resisting Roman rule at this time (Egger 1986: 164–65; Pummer 2009: 265).

A Samaritan inscription preserved in casts in the École Biblique in Jerusalem has been published and discussed by J. Strugnell (1967: 561–70). It looks remarkably like the event described by Josephus: the emperor Trajan (98–117 CE, rather than the general Cerealis in 67 CE) besieged the Samaritans on Gerizim for a month. When they ran out of water, he slaughtered 10,000 of them. Judging from the statement, 'fountain of the Samaritan woman', on one of the casts, Strugnell thought it might have originally been placed at the site of Jacob's well. Although the original stone containing the inscription has disappeared, Strugnell was convinced the inscription was genuine. However, it has been pointed out that the script is strange, and J. Naveh (1982a, 1982b) has labelled some similar alleged Samaritan inscriptions as forgeries. Pummer (2009: 266–68) also argues that this inscription is probably not genuine. Thus, an apparent archaeological confirmation of Josephus's basic story (though not the chronology) seems too doubtful to be helpful at this point.

8.3. *Other Topics*

8.3.1. *Archaeology*

The archaeology of Mt Gerizim, Shechem and Samaria are discussed in Chapter 2 (§§2.1.1.18; 2.1.1.19).

8.3.2. *The Origins of the Samaritan Sect and Their Cult*

> **J. D. Purvis** (1981) 'The Samaritan Problem: A Case Study in Jewish Sectarianism in the Roman Era', in B. Halpern and J. D. Levenson (ed.), *Traditions in Transformation: Turning Points in Biblical Faith*, 323–50;
> **T. L. Thompson** (1992) *Early History of the Israelite People from the Written and Archaeological Sources*.

The origins of the community and cult are still uncertain. The origins according to interpretations of 2 Kings 17 (pagan foreigners brought in) and Josephus (dissident Jerusalem priests) are the product of considerable bias and cannot be taken at face value. For the origins of the Gerizim cult, Josephus gives two contradictory answers. First, he says that they were foreigners brought in from elsewhere in the ancient Near East (Mesopotamia, Media, Persia). Secondly, he claims they were made up of defected priests and Jews who left the Jerusalem cult for various nefarious reasons. Both claims have a polemical intent; neither is necessary. For present purposes, however, there is no need to settle the matter of origins of the cult; we shall proceed on the basis that the cult was Yahwistic, with no more foreign elements than contemporary Judaism – indeed, that in most respects it was very similar to the worship in Jerusalem at the time. There do not seem to be significant arguments against the idea that the cult was ultimately descended from the Yahwistic worship of the Northern Kingdom, which would explain its similarity to Second Temple Judaism but would also recognize a certain independence (cf. Coggins 1975: 162–65 and the later view of Purvis 1981: 337). Nevertheless, for present purposes it is not necessary to take a position on the question of origins.

Likewise, the ethnic diversity of Samaria is unknown. One could no doubt argue that ethnic outsiders were brought in at various times: T. L. Thompson (1992: 412–21) argues this. It appears that he exaggerates the amount of ethnic mixing since the deportation of peoples often involved a minority of the population. Also, where communities were deported, they frequently kept their identity in their new habitation, sometimes even for centuries, perhaps resisting ethnic mixing. There is little evidence that any population mixing had a significant impact on the Samaritan religion. If there were pagan groups in the region of Samaria, this may have created antagonism between them and the Samaritan community, just as between the latter and the Jews. Also, if there were other groups, some of the references to 'Samaritans' may have nothing to do with the Gerizim community.

8.3.3. *Relationship with the Judaeans*

Perhaps the most difficult area to investigate is that of Jewish and Samaritan relations. The actual religious practices of the Jews and Samaritans were very similar: the same sabbath observance, the same food laws, much the same purity laws, the same requirement of circumcision. The primary distinction between them was the question of God's chosen place for his temple. To an outsider, especially, they must have looked indistinguishable. If or when major Samaritan/Jewish hostility arose is uncertain. At least until about 100 BCE there was communication between the Jewish and Samaritan communities. Exactly when friction developed between them is unknown, though some friction could go back to an early time, as early as the time of Nehemiah or even pre-exilic times. But the existence of strained relations does not preclude communication and even good relations between some parts of the two communities. Evidently, these were best between the upper classes, such as the Tobiad family. As already noted, Joseph Tobiad borrowed money from friends in Samaria to fund his initial venture into Ptolemaic politics (*Ant.* 12.4.3 §168). This may well have been a continuation of contacts going back at least to the time of Nehemiah (Neh. 4.7; 6.1).

The animosity between the Samaritan and Jewish communities has often been taken for granted, though there has been debate over when it began. Yet we do not have to assume a severe breach before the first century CE and perhaps not even then. True, the episode in which Samaritans scattered bones in the Jerusalem temple (*Ant.* 18.2.2 §30), the attack on Jewish pilgrims from Galilee and the counter charge of Jewish attacks on Samaritan villages (*War* 2.12.3-6 §§232-44; *Ant.* 20.6.1-3 §§118-36), and the statement in John 4.9 all suggest major barriers between Jews and Samaritans. The first example suggests individuals who were hostile to the Jerusalem temple; the second is less clear but could also show religious hostility; the third definitely has differences of worship in mind. But these all relate to the first century CE. Counter to this are many examples showing contact between Jews and individuals from the region of Samaria: Herod's relations (*Ant.* 14.15.3 §408; 14.15.4 §413; 14.15.14 §467; 17.1.3 §20; 17.4.2 §69); joint delegation to complain against Archelaus (*Ant.* 17.13.2 §342); loan to Agrippa from a Samaritan freedman (*Ant.* 18.6.4 §167); Josephus's Samaritan friends (*Life* 52 §269). All of these can be explained away, but they indicate the matter is not straightforward.

If the two religious communities had little to do with each other in the first century, this situation could have had its roots in earlier periods. The enmity between Nehemiah and Sanballat might have been a foreshadow, but the text shows that many Jews did not agree with Nehemiah (Neh. 6.17-19; 13.4-7). The Tobiads, who were intermarried with the high priestly Oniad family, also seem to have had relations with and even relatives in Samaria, whether the city or the region (*Ant.* 12.4.3 §168). The Samaritan decision to protect their temple by disavowing the Jews may not have helped inter-community relations, but it need not have created a permanent breach. Hyrcanus's conquest of Samaria and Shechem could have strained relations seriously – and some scholars see this as the incident which closed the communities off from one another – but we cannot be sure of that. Hyrcanus is also supposed to have forcibly converted the Idumaeans, and most of them remained Jewish in their religion according to the later references to them.

There is some small evidence of intermarriage between the Jewish and Samaritan communities. What few data we have concern the upper classes: Joseph Tobiad, who had friends in Samaria who loaned him money; Herod, who married a wife from there; perhaps even Josephus himself, who admits to having friends in Samaria. Except for Herod, who may have married for diplomatic reasons, no explicit reference is made to relatives. Yet our sources may have been somewhat coy to admit actual intermarriage. If there was intermarriage, it illustrates a common sociological phenomenon in which the upper classes have a different standard from those at the bottom end of the scale.

The latest archaeological and other data still seem to bear up a destruction of the city in the time of Hyrcanus (§2.1.1.19). If the temple and cult were also destroyed at this time, it could have created great hostility. But destruction of the city does not require destruction of the cult. Against the interpretation that Shechem's conquest was the decisive point is the absence of polemic in Jewish literature until the first century. The only probable earlier example is Ben Sira 50.25-26 (§8.2.2 above). If the Samaritans were the ones to sever relations, Jewish writers as members of the dominant ethnic group may not have been interested in polemicizing against the Samaritans; that is, the Samaritans may not have been of sufficient interest to warrant attention. On the other hand, it is not necessary to assume a breach before the 1st century, and the literature would bear this out. The argument that the Samaritan Pentateuch shows redaction in the decades after the destruction of Shechem is based on too many uncertainties. Neither would such a redaction even require the assumption that the two communities had ceased to communicate.

8.3.4. *The Question of Hellenization*

> **D. Mendels** (1993) *The Rise and Fall of Jewish Nationalism*; **G. E. Sterling** (1992) *Historiography and Self-Definition: Josephos, Luke-Acts and Apologetic Historiography*.

The Samaritans were evidently as affected by Hellenization as the Jews. As argued elsewhere (§14.4.2), the dichotomy of 'Hellenized' versus 'faithful' Jews is a false one. Similarly, the idea that the Samaritans were more 'syncretistic' than the Jews is equally a caricature. Hellenization was a cultural phenomenon of the entire ancient Near East. No people was immune to it, though different peoples and different individuals may have responded in different ways. One response was what has been called apologetic historiography, the interpretation of the native history in such a way that it would commend itself to Greek readers (on the concept, see especially Sterling 1992). This was a common phenomenon of nationalism among nations under Greek and then Roman rule (Mendels 1993: 35–54). A good example of this is the 'Anonymous Samaritan' or Pseudo-Eupolemus who combines Samaritan tradition with material from Greek mythology.

The question of Hellenization has exercised a number of researchers on the Samaritans, often with unfortunate results. Part of the problem is that the situation in Jerusalem is misunderstood and then a false analogy imported to Shechem. The process of Hellenization was complex, but both the Jews and Samaritans were affected by it the same as other Near Eastern peoples. The question, with supporting data, is discussed at length in *HJJSTP 2* (Chapter 6). Therefore, it is hardly surprising to find works in Greek which seem to be by Samaritan authors (§8.1.3 above). If the situation in Judaea is anything to go by, there was likely a variety of attitudes toward Hellenistic culture within the Gerizim community. Those who propose a 'Hellenistic' party among the Samaritans have plausibility on their side.

Where the misconception lies is assuming a dichotomy of a 'Hellenistic' party on one side versus a 'loyal, pious' group on the other. The authors of the Hellenistic reform in Jerusalem were also loyal, pious individuals – many of them priests – who did not attempt to compromise the traditional temple cult. The Jewish cult and religion were, of course, eventually compromised and suppressed at the order of Antiochus IV, and some Jews seem to have had a hand in it. But there is no evidence that the authors of the Hellenistic reform, led by Jason, were involved. When opposition developed, it was not against Jason's Hellenistic reform, but against the alleged sale of temple vessels by Menelaus. Similarly, there is no reason to think that any Hellenistic party in Samaria would have compromised the temple cult there. As has already been noted (§8.2.3 above), the evidence available does not indicate that those who wrote to Antiochus IV were seeking a change to their traditional cult. Postulating that this letter was written by a 'Hellenistic party' at Shechem is, therefore, irrelevant to the question.

8.4. *Conclusions*

As with so much Samaritan history, we have very little information. There is considerable danger of over interpreting the data that we do have. The source which seems to give the most information is in many ways also our most problematic one: Josephus. In most passages, if perhaps not in all, he is openly prejudiced against the dwellers of Shechem. This does not mean that he does not give us historical data, but sorting it out from the negative polemic is not easy. Further, his terminology is not always consistent or clear. Sometimes he explicitly refers to the cult on Gerizim and its adherents, but at other times he may have had inhabitants of the entire region of Samaria in mind, and we cannot be sure that they necessarily had anything to do with the Gerizim cult and community. One has to proceed with a good deal of caution and scepticism. The following are some of the points summarizing our discussions on the Samaritans. At the risk of repetition, it is important to make again, as a summary of our discussion, some of the points made above:

- We often do not know precisely who is being referred to when the sources speak of 'Samaritans' and the like. Despite Egger's arguments (1986), Josephus does not use his terminology consistently, leaving us uncertain at least some of the time. Was it the community with worship centred on the Gerizim cult or was it some other group in the region of Samaria, perhaps with no connection to the Samaritan community of concern to us? The problem may even be more acute when no names are used, and we are left guessing from the context.
- The ethnic diversity of Samaria is unknown. If there were pagan groups in the region of Samaria – as there may have been (Samaria may have originated as an early Greek Macedonian settlement) – this may have created antagonism between them and the Samaritan community. But if there were other groups, some of the references to 'Samaritans' may have nothing to do with the Gerizim community.
- The origins of the community and cult are still uncertain. The interpretation that has them originate from pagan foreigners imported into Israel or that makes the cult originate with dissident Jerusalem priests shows considerable bias and cannot be taken at face value. There seems much to commend the view that the cult was Yahwistic, with no more foreign elements than contemporary Judaism – that it was ultimately descended from the Yahwistic worship of the Northern Kingdom has much to commend it. Yet there also seems to be considerable influence from later Judaism on the Samaritan religion as well.
- When major Samaritan/Jewish hostility arose is uncertain. It may well be that some friction goes back to as early as the time of Nehemiah or even pre-exilic times. But the existence of strained relations does not preclude communication and even good relations between some parts of the communities. It appears that we do not have to assume a severe breach before the 1st century CE and perhaps not even then. The Samaritan decision to protect their temple by disavowing the Jews may not have helped intercommunity relations, but it need not have created a permanent breach. Hyrcanus's conquest of Samaria and Shechem could have strained relations seriously. Indeed, some scholars see this as the incident which closed the communities off from one another, but we cannot be sure of that. Also, we have many examples showing contact between Jews and individuals from the region of Samaria: Herod's relations (*Ant.* 14.15.3 §408; 14.15.4 §413; 14.15.14

§467; 17.1.3 §20; 17.4.2 §69); joint delegation to complain against Archelaus (*Ant.* 17.13.2 §342); loan to Agrippa from a Samaritan freedman (*Ant.* 18.6.4 §167); Josephus's Samaritan friends (*Life* 52 §269). It is true, though, that incidents showing a breach between the two communities seem to be best illustrated by 1st century CE sources.

- The Samaritans were evidently as affected by Hellenization as the Jews, but as argued elsewhere, the dichotomy of 'Hellenized' versus 'faithful' is a false one. Likewise, we have no evidence that the Samaritans were more 'syncretistic' than the Jews. Hellenization was a cultural phenomenon of the entire ancient Near East and affected both Jews and Samaritans. We have examples of Samaritan literature in Greek that combines Samaritan and biblical tradition with Greek myth (e.g., Pseudo-Eupolemus), but we also have Jewish writers who do the same (e.g., Artapanus). The process of Hellenization was complex, but both the Jews and Samaritans were affected by it the same as other Near Eastern peoples.

Chapter 9

THE IDUMAEANS, ARABS AND PARTHIANS

G. W. Bowersock (1983) *Roman Arabia*; **G. Fisher (ed.)** (2015) *Arabs and Empires before Islam*; **A. Kasher** (1982) 'Gaza during the Greco-Roman Era', *Jerusalem Cathedra* 2: 63–78; **idem** (1988) *Jews, Idumaeans, and Ancient Arabs*; **J. Retsö** (2003) *The Arabs in Antiquity: Their History from the Assyrians to the Umayyads*.

This chapter attempts to give an overview of the history of several areas that are important for the history of the Jews during the Hasmonaean and Herodian periods. The sections on the Idumaeans and Nabataeans extend over the period of Hasmonaean rule and Roman control until the end of the Nabataean kingdom in the early 2nd century CE.

9.1. *Idumaeans*

The Idumaeans have already been extensively discussed in earlier volumes (*HJJSTP 1*: 49–53, 162–66; *HJJSTP 2*: 46–48, 176–82). As early as the early Greek period, we have evidence of Hellenization in certain areas of Idumaea, though this was probably most intensive in cities such as Marisa (Mareshah). It is during the Maccabaean period that the Idumaeans become frequently mentioned. They made up one of the 'surrounding nations' which harassed the rebel Jewish state under Judas Maccabee and against which he fought, taking Hebron and Marisa (1 Macc. 5.3, 65-68).

We then skip forward to the reign of John Hyrcanus and one of the strangest episodes, the conversion of the Idumaeans to Judaism (*Ant.* 13.9.1 §§257-58). Josephus states that he subdued them but then allowed them to stay in their country if they would adopt circumcision and also observe Jewish law. He goes on to say that they did this precisely because they were attached to their native land, but they had in essence become

Jews and continued with this identity, as will be made clear in subsequent events described below and especially in *HJJSTP* 4. This is puzzling, not so much about what was done by the Hasmonaeans, since they were trying to clear the borders of expanded Judah from idolatry, but because the effects of the conversion lasted.

That is, forced conversion does not usually represent a change of mind and, if possible, those compelled carry on their original religion covertly and revert to it openly as soon as they can. This did not happen with the Idumaeans. Although we know of the occasional individual who intended to return to the ancestral religion (e.g., Costobarus: *Ant.* 15.7.9 §§253-55), the Idumaeans as a whole supported the Jews in their later wars with the Romans. For example, in the 'war of Varus' (ca. 4 BCE) Idumaea revolted along with Jerusalem (*War* 2.5.2-3 §§72-79). Attested in even greater detail is the participation of several thousand Idumaeans in the defence of Jerusalem during the 66–70 war.

Why did the conversion of the Idumaeans succeed? According to the Greek historian and geographer Strabo (16.2.34), the Idumaeans 'joined the Jews and had their customary laws [τῶν νομίμων] in common with them', which sounds like a voluntary adoption of Jewish customs. A. Kasher (1982: 46–77) has dealt with the question at length (drawing on the work of a number of predecessors). While there are some problems with his argumentation in places (e.g., he attempts to use late talmudic and even post-talmudic sources to show the Jewish attitude toward conversion in the 2nd century BCE), he covers most of the important issues. His conclusion is that the Idumaeans were assimilated to Judaism voluntarily, perhaps by agreement between Hyrcanus and the Idumaean leadership. Part of this agreement was to place an Idumaean (the father of Antipater – Herod's grandfather) as governor of the territory. Of course, not all individual Idumaeans may have accepted willingly the decision made on their behalf by the leadership, so that forced conversion may have been the case for some. Nevertheless, the fact that the Idumaeans retained their Judaism is strong evidence that the conversion was more or less voluntary and did not represent a major change for most inhabitants of the area. Not all the following points are from Kasher, but he has further discussion on most of them:

- Circumcision was a normal practice for Idumaeans so that enforced circumcision would have been an irrelevancy for most of them (apart from perhaps a few Hellenized individuals who had foregone the traditional rite).

- Strabo (16.2.34) says nothing about forced conversion but only that the Idumaeans 'joined the Jews and shared with them the same customary laws'. See also below for a similar statement about the Ituraeans, suggesting in both cases not a compulsion by force but an agreed adoption.
- It may be that some Jews always remained living in the area of Idumaea and influenced the Edomites who settled there. It certainly seems that there was considerable Jewish influence – from whatever source – long before the activities of Hyrcanus I.
- Josephus's source for his statement that Hyrcanus compelled Idumaeans to accept circumcision was likely to have been Nicolaus of Damascus. As a non-Jew and no particular friend of the Hasmonaeans, Nicolaus may have interpreted the event – however achieved – in a negative way as if done under compulsion.

Kasher also argues that Hellenistic urbanization intensified under the Seleucids after Antiochus IV, and the Idumaeans felt hostility to this, which would have speeded up the assimilation process. Is this another example of blaming problems on that all-purpose scapegoat, Hellenization? The cogency of this argument is debatable. That the Idumaeans, like the Jews and other natives, may have felt treated as inferiors by the citizens of the Hellenistic cities would not be surprising, but whether that would create solidarity is another question. The Jews as a whole do not seem to have been drawn closer to neighbouring peoples as a result of this process.

Further information on the Idumaeans in their interaction with the Jews can be found at various points in Chapters 15–18.

9.2. Nabataeans

U. Hackl et al. (2003) *Quellen zur Geschichte der Nabatäer*; **A. J. M. Kropp** (2009) 'Nabataean Petra: The Royal Palace and the Herod Connection', *Boreas* 32: 43–59 + 15 tables; **Y. Meshorer** (1975) *Nabataean Coins*; **A. Negev** (1977) 'The Nabateans and the Provincia Arabia', *ANRW* II: 8:520–686; **C.-G. Schwentzel** (2013) *Juifs et Nabatéens: Les monarchies ethniques du Proche-Orient hellénistique et romain*; **R. Wenning** (1987) *Die Nabatäer – Denkmäler und Geschichte: Eine Bestandsaufnahme des archäologischen Befundes*; **idem** (1990) 'Das Nabatäerreich: seine archäologischen und historischen Hinterlassenschaften', in H. P. Kuhnen, *Palästina in griechisch-römischer Zeit*, 367–415; **idem** (1994) 'Die Dekapolis und die Nabatäer', *ZDPV* 110: 1–35.

9. The Idumaeans, Arabs and Parthians

The Arab tribe known as the Nabataeans first appears in historical records at the time of the Diadochi. About 312 BCE Antigonus attempted without success to subdue them (Diodorus 19.94-100). They were also alleged to engage in piracy during this and perhaps even later times (Diodorus 3.43.5; Strabo 16.4.8). Otherwise, little is known until the time of Antiochus IV and the wars of the Maccabees. The list of the Nabataean kings is as follows (Hackl et al. 2003: 63), though some of the dates are no more than approximate. It is also possible that one or two other names should be added to the list but their existence has only been suspected since they are not clearly attested in any historical sources:

- Aretas I (fl. 168 BCE)
- Aretas II (ca. 120/110–96 BCE)
- Obodas I (ca. 96–85 BCE)
- Rabbel I (ca. 85/84 BCE)
- Aretas III (84–[62/61?] 60/59 BCE)
- Obodas II (?) (62/61–60/59 BCE)
- Malichus I (59–30 BCE)
- Obodas III (II) (30–9 BCE)
- Šulla/Syllaius and Aeneas/Aretas IV (9 BCE)
- Aretus IV (9/8 BCE–39/40 CE)
- Malichus II (39/40–69/70 CE)
- Rabbel II (70/71–106 CE)
- Malichus III (?) (106 CE)

The Roman province of Arabia was created in 106 CE and brought the native kings to an end. The Maccabees had hostilities with a number of Arab tribes or families (e.g., 1 Macc. 9.36-42; 2 Macc. 12.10-12) but seem to have been on good terms with the Nabataeans for the most part (1 Macc. 5.25-26; 9.35). The Nabataean king at this time was Aretas I (2 Macc. 5.8). In the late 2nd century under Aretas II the Nabataeans began to assert themselves, as the Seleucid empire threatened to break up, pushing into Moab and Gilead. They had benefited from profits of the overland trade from southern Arabia (the *Arabia Felix* of the Romans) already at an early stage. Now, as they consolidated power, it became obvious to them (if it was not already so) that possession of certain territory would have given them greater control and profits. Not surprisingly, this brought them in conflict with the Hasmonaeans.

Most of the important references to the Nabataeans, Idumaeans, and Arabs in their interaction with Judaea and the Jews are discussed in Chapters 15–18, which should be consulted for details. Alexander Jannaeus already fought with Aretas II over Gaza, which would have been important as a centre for the caravan trade (*Ant.* 13.13.3 §360). Jannaeus was subsequently defeated by Obodas I, Aretas's successor, but still managed to control certain towns in Moab (*Ant.* 13.15.4 §397; 14.1.4 §18). However, under Aretas III things improved for the Nabataeans. He occupied Damascus for a time, defeated Jannaeus, included the title *philhellene* on his coins and was able to take advantage of the internecine struggles between Hyrcanus II and Aristobulus II. The intervention of Pompey in the region brought him difficulties, as it did many other small kingdoms. Scaurus the new governor of Syria was sent against the Nabataeans. The outcome was a large tribute payment to the Romans to retain their freedom, while Scaurus minted a coin alleging his victory over Aretas. The Nabataeans also gave up territories along the Phoenician coast but obtained some of the Ituraean area in compensation, the Romans no doubt creating a deliberate rivalry between the two Arab groups (Kasher 1988: 114–15). Malichus I supported the Parthians when they invaded the Syro-Palestinian area (40 BCE) and was punished by the Romans with an assessment of tribute. His refusal to pay this brought about a war with Herod. His death marks the end of the formative period of the Nabataean kingdom.

The so-called Middle Nabataean Period (30 BCE–70 CE) saw the northern Nabataean settlements in the Hauran become important. Little is known of the kings during this period, despite its importance for Nabataean history. The reign of Obodas II seems to have been generally prosperous. During his reign, the Romans sent an ill-fated expedition to Arabia under Aelius Gallus. One of the causes of the failure was alleged to be the treachery of Syllaeus (one of Obodas's ministers who acted as guide for the expedition), though this is disputed by Bowersock (1983: 47–48). Syllaeus was also a thorn in Herod's side. It was the next king, Aretas IV, who succeeded in getting rid of Syllaeus, with Herod's help. Some evidence suggests that there was a three-year period not long after Herod's death when Aretas's kingdom was annexed by Rome (Bowersock 1983: 54–57). If so, the Romans must have decided a client kingdom was preferable to a new province at this time. During Aretas's long reign, there is evidence of the flourishing of Nabataean culture and urbanization of the people (Bowersock 1983: 57–65). Hegra also shows evidence of development, perhaps with the thought in mind that Nabataea proper might have to be abandoned to the Romans. Aretas's daughter was married to Herod Antipas, which created a major conflict when Antipas divorced her. A final point is one of the apostle Paul's statements, which suggests that Aretas was in control of Damascus about 40 CE. While this is not otherwise known, it seems quite possible (Bowersock 1983: 68–69).

We know little of Malichus II except that he sent troops to help Titus against the Jewish rebels in 67 CE (*War* 3.4.2 §68). It has been suggested that Malichus's reign and that of Rabel II saw a marked decline in certain parts of the Nabataean kingdom, especially in the southern region, caused by encroaching nomadic Arab tribes who destroyed or reduced Nabataean settlements in the Negev and in Arabia (Negev 1977: 639–40). However, this interpretation has also been denied, with the claim that the prosperity of Aretas's reign continued (Bowersock 1983: 72–74). There was a shift of the balance of power to the northern parts of the kingdom, though, as indicated by the change of capital from Petra to Bostra. We also find that, for whatever reasons, the use of irrigation for agriculture climbed sharply under Aretas IV and Malichus, reaching a peak under Rabel.

The final event for the period of time covered here was the annexation of the Nabataean kingdom as the Roman province of Arabia in 106 CE. The exact reason for this is uncertain, but it seems part of the general policy of expansion under Trajan. Nabataea was about the only client kingdom remaining in the region. This annexation does not seem to have been all that important to the Romans, since the surviving sources make little of it. But Roman military units were sent to protect the southern border, as inscriptions in the region of Hegra and to the south show. Although Petra had the title of 'metropolis of Arabia', the actual capital and administrative centre seems to have been Bostra.

9.3. *Ituraeans*

A. M. Berlin (1997) 'Between Large Forces: Palestine in the Hellenistic Period', *BA* 60: 2–51; ***NEAEHL*** 2:535–37; **E. A. Myers** (2010) *The Ituraeans and the Roman Near East: Reassessing the Sources*.

The Arab tribe of the Ituraeans first appears on the scene approximately 200 BCE, at the time Antiochus III took over Coele-Syria from the Ptolemies. It is about this time that significant settlement began in the Golan, especially the more northern regions (there had been a few sites in southern Golan before then). The Ituraeans cleared the indigenous forest and built mostly small, unwalled settlements using roughly cut or uncut local stones. Sites excavated include Ḥorvat Zemel, Ḥorvat Namra and Bab el-Hawa.

The Ituraeans are said to have been converted to Judaism under Aristobulus I, like the Idumaeans under Hyrcanus I: Aristobulus 'forced the inhabitants to be circumcised and to live by Jewish laws, if they wished to remain in the land' (*Ant.* 13.11.3 §318). However, Josephus also quotes as his source Strabo (who is relying on Timagenes), who has a slightly different understanding: Aristobulus caused a 'part' (μέρος) of the Ituraean *ethnos* to be joined to them by circumcision (*Ant.* 13.11.3 §319). Thus, Strabo at least does not necessarily suggest compulsion.

The former Ituraean region was actually north of Upper Galilee, first in the interior of Lebanon, with their capital in Chalcis, then further south into the Mt Hermon region and the northern Golan Heights. This area has been thoroughly explored archaeologically (Myers 2010: 42–101; Berlin 1997: 36–37). Particularly characteristic of Ituraean settlement appears to be the so-called 'Golan ware', especially the large hand-produced pithoi or storage jars that seem to have been the main reservoir for water (cisterns do not appear in this region). As Berlin (1997: 37) notes, first, there is no evidence for attacks on or destruction of any of the Ituraean sites at this time; rather, settlement continued and even expanded. Secondly, no evidence for Jewish religious practice is found in the material culture; instead, the local cult sites continued.

In short, the archaeology appears to contradict Josephus's narrative. It is possible that some sort of conversion of *some* Ituraeans took place. But if so, it would appear to be those in Jewish territory, which was only a part of the tribe. And again, if so, it would appear to have been similar to that of the Idumaeans and not primarily under compulsion. As already noted, there is no evidence of Ituraean settlement in Galilee proper. But if there were some – perhaps only a few – settlements in Galilee they would have been among Jewish neighbours for a long time (since the Persian period, according to Kasher 1988: 80–83). This would probably have made acceptance of the required aspects of the Jewish lifestyle easy to adopt.

9.4. *Parthians*

A. D. H. Bivar (1983) 'The Political History of Iran under the Arsacids', in E. Yarshater (ed.), *Cambridge History of Iran, Volume 3, parts 1: The Seleucid, Parthian, and Sasanian Periods*, 100–115; **R. N. Frye** (1984) *History of Ancient Iran*; **D. Goodblatt** (1987) 'Josephus on Parthian Babylonia (Antiquities XVIII, 310-379)', *JAOS* 107: 605–22; **A. Keaveney** (1981) 'Roman Treaties with Parthia circa 95–circa 64 B.C.', *AJP* 102: 195–212; **E. Keitel** (1978) 'The Role of Parthia and Armenia in Tacitus *Annals* 11 and 12', *AJP* 99: 462–73; **R. P. Longden** (1931) 'Notes on the Parthian Campaigns of Trajan', *JRS* 21: 1–35; **G. J. P. McEwan** (1986) 'A Parthian Campaign against Elymais in 77 B.C.', *Iran* 24: 91–94; **S. P. Mattern-Parkes** (2003) 'The Defeat of Crassus and the Just War', *The Classical World* 96: 387–96; **J. M. Schlude and B. B. Rubin (eds)** (2017) *Arsacids, Romans and Local Elites: Cross-Cultural Interactions* *of the Parthian Empire;* **S. Sherwin-White and A. Kuhrt** (1993) *From Samarkhand to Sardis: A New Approach to the Seleucid Empire;* **J. Wiesehöfer (ed.)** (1998) *Das Partherreich und seine Zeugnisse: The Arsacid Empire: Sources and Documentation;* **J. Wiesehöfer and S. Müller (eds)** (2017) *Parthika: Greek and Roman Authors' Views of the Arsacid Empire / Griechisch-römische Bilder des Arsakidenreiches;* **J. Wolski** (1993) *L'empire des Arsacides;* **idem** (2003) *Seleucid and Arsacid Studies: A Progress Report on Developments in Source Research;* **E. Yarshater (ed.)** (1983) *Cambridge History of Iran, Volume 3, parts 1-2: The Seleucid, Parthian, and Sasanian Periods.*

The Parthians originated among the Parni, a group of Iranian-speaking tribes, nomadic horsemen who apparently originated in Central Asia. Much is still not known about the migration of the Parni into the region of Parthia. The general view has been that by about 240 BCE the Parthians had taken away the northeast part of the Seleucid empire once and for all. This historical reconstruction has severe weaknesses (Sherwin-White and Kuhrt 1993: 84–90). The earliest area occupied by the Parthians, under Arsaces I the founder of a new dynasty about 238 BCE, was in fact north of the Elburz and thus outside the Seleucid realm. Arsaces took control of the provinces of Parthia and Hyrcania. Seleucus II led a campaign against them ca. 230 BCE, but had to break off and return to put down a revolt in Asia Minor. The Parthians made raids into Seleucid territory, but occupation south of the Elburz did not take place until the middle of the second century. The Parthians were still vassals under Antiochus III (223–187 BCE) and seemed to recognize this status themselves.

Movement into Seleucid territory began after the death of Antiochus III. It was Mithradates I (170–134 BCE) who completed the process that had been started by his predecessors. By 140 BCE he had displaced the Seleucids from Iran and was making incursions into Babylonia. Demetrius II (145–140 BCE) marched east against the Parthians but was taken captive by them. His successor Antiochus VII (138–129 BCE) made major efforts against the Parthian incursions, but his defeat and death at the hands of Phraates II opened the way for Parthian occupation of Babylonia. The Seleucid ruler Demetrius III, known in Jewish history because of the battle between him and Alexander Jannaeus, was taken captive by the Parthians in 87 BCE, perhaps by Mithradates II (ca. 123–87 BCE).

Contact with Rome had been made toward the beginning of the first century BCE, but it was in 65–63 BCE that Pompey helped to broker a peace between Phraates III of Parthia and Tigranes II of Armenia. The new governor of Syria Crassus attacked the Parthians in 53 BCE but was defeated and killed. During the Roman Civil War Pompey attempted to form an alliance with the Parthians but was killed before it came to anything, while a plan by Julius Caesar to wage war against the Parthians also came to nothing because of his assassination. Against the backdrop of conflicts between the Hasmonaeans and other Jewish factions, the Parthians invaded Syria-Palestine in 40 BCE. Antigonus, the son of the Hasmonaean king Aristobulus II, was allied with them in hopes of re-establishing the Hasmonaean throne. Although the Parthians killed his brother, Herod escaped to Rome and gained Roman support to retake Palestine. However, the Parthians did not remain long in the region; perhaps they always intended their occupation of Syria-Palestine to be a temporary measure. In any case, they left Antigonus to face Herod and his Roman legions alone. In 39 BCE Mark Antony pushed the Parthians back beyond the Euphrates. With Cleopatra's financial support he then invaded Parthia in 36 in a disastrous campaign which cost him a third of his force. His successful invasion and capture of Armenia in 34 BCE hardly made up for this.

The Parthians were able to avert a war with Augustus by returning the captured standards of Crassus and Mark Antony in 20 BCE. The temporary peace established allowed trade to flourish between the two spheres of influence. But further treaties were signed between the two powers in 1 CE, in 18 or 19 CE, and in 37 CE. Parthia itself was riven by internal disputes over the throne (with Rome occasionally intervening for its own interests, usually to keep the region unstable). Armenia stayed mostly under the domination of Rome, though this continued to create tension between the Romans and the Parthians. In the mid-1st century CE, friction developed between Rome and Parthia over Armenia, since Rome traditionally had to approve any candidate for the throne of that country. The Roman commander Corbulo invaded and enthroned the Romans' own choice of candidate in 58 CE, Corbulo himself becoming the governor of Syria. A few years later the Roman puppet king provoked the Parthians and then requested Roman aid. The Roman commander sent by Nero in 62 was defeated and captured by the Parthians. When Corbulo came too late to rescue him, he was still able to negotiate a settlement in which both the Romans and Parthians would withdraw from Armenia, while the Parthian candidate would become king of Armenia but go to Rome to be crowned.

The treaty signed in 63 CE established a peace between Rome and Parthia that lasted the next half century. Yet a curious tradition developed that we find in several Jewish apocalyptic writings, with a similar idea taken up in Christian writings on the anti-Christ. This is the concept of

Nero redivivus ('Nero resurrected'). After the death of Nero in 69 CE, rumour had it that he had not actually died but was still alive and living secretly in the East. It was only a matter of time before he would gather an army of Parthian soldiers and return in triumph to take up his throne again. Originally, no actual 'resurrection' was envisaged – only the return of Nero who had not actually died – until after the time of Nero's expected lifespan.

In the early 2nd century CE, the Romans attempted to extend their border eastward, which once again brought them into conflict with the Parthians. In 106 the emperor Trajan annexed Arabia to form a new province, but this was only a prelude to his campaigns to the East. His invasion of Mesopotamia was undoubtedly undertaken primarily out of strategic motives, since developments in Parthia were problematic from the Roman point of view. When the Parthian king Pacorus II died in 109/110, the Parthian throne was taken by his brother Chosroes. Pacorus had intended that the throne of Armenia go to his younger son Axidares, with Roman approval, but Chosroes now supported Pacorus's other son Parthamasiris (Axidares's elder brother) who had seized the Armenian throne. Trajan set out in the spring of 114 for Armenia. Parthamasiris submitted, but the crown was removed from him, and Armenia – or at least the western part of it – was made into a Roman province.

In the autumn of 114 Trajan turned south into Mesopotamia. The precise course of events for the next year is uncertain, but he obtained the submission of various territories, including Nisibis, Edessa, Singra and even territory beyond the Tigris. He did not return until late in 115. There was now a new province of Mesopotamia, but Trajan was not finished. In the spring of 116 he set out for the conquest of Assyria and Babylonia. He took Adiabene, Seleucia and Ctesiphon by the summer, establishing the new province of Assyria. After Trajan moved to the site of ancient Babylon to spend the winter, a general revolt took place in the newly created provinces of Mesopotamia and Assyria. This appears to have included a Parthian counter-attack. The emperor effectively suppressed the revolt and most of the conquered areas remained under Roman control, but Trajan died soon afterward.

Although Hadrian (117–38 CE) had to put down revolts in the Mediterranean, under him relations between Rome and Parthia seem to have been peaceful. The same applied to his successor Antonius Pius (138–61 CE). Shortly after Marcus Aurelius (161–80 CE) began his reign, however, the Parthians broke the peace to attempt to remove the Roman-supported king of Armenia. The first Roman army sent against them was severely beaten. As usual, the Romans responded in force and made considerable advances eastward, taking the Parthian capital and replacing the Parthian king. The peace established in 166 CE lasted for a quarter of a century. In the civil turmoil that initiated the reign of Septimius Severus (193–211 CE), the Parthians took advantage of the situation and made advances into Roman-controlled territory. After Severus defeated his rival Pescennius Niger, he began his First Parthian War and won back territory in Mesopotamia, gaining the title *Parthicus Arabicus*. He launched his Second Parthian War in 197, capturing the Babylonian centre of Ctesiphon and creating a province of Mesopotamia, but he failed to take the city of Hatra. Severus's son Caracalla (officially Aurelius Antonius, 211–17 CE) managed to gain the throne and sought a pretext to attack the Parthians. When his request to marry a Parthian princess was refused, he invaded Mesopotamia. He was assassinated shortly afterward, and his successor Macrinus offered peace to the Parthians. They refused until the battle of Nisibis, at which point they concluded a treaty that required the Romans to pay an indemnity. Not long afterward, about 225 CE, the Sasanians overthrew the Parthians and established their own ruling dynasty.

For a tentative list of Parthian kings, with corrected dates, see Bivar (1983: 98–99).

Chapter 10

THE DIASPORA: JEWISH COMMUNITIES
OUTSIDE JUDAH FROM ALEXANDER TO HEROD
(330 BCE TO 4 BCE)

Discussing Jews in the diaspora is not easy. First, we often have little information and must piece together what few data there are to come up with any sort of picture. Secondly, trying to split up the history of each diaspora community between the various volumes of the current *History* creates some problems. Logically, the entire history of the various communities should be discussed all together in the present chapter. Yet some of the events, especially as they relate to the communities of Rome and Alexandria, more properly belong to the next volume (*HJJSTP 4*). Therefore, this chapter basically stops with the conversion of Judaea to a Roman province a decade after Herod's death, and will leave it for the next volume to continue the process. Also, the question of citizenship will be discussed in *HJJSTP 4* because it is thought to have become most acute during the 1st century CE.

10.1. Ideology of the Land and the Concept of Exile

K. Berthelot (2017) *In Search of the Promised Land? The Hasmonean Dynasty between Biblical Models and Hellenistic Diplomacy*; **W. D. Davies** (1974) *The Gospel and the Land: Early Christianity and Jewish Territorial Doctrine*; **idem** (1982) *The Territorial Dimensions of Judaism*; **I. M. Gafni** (1997) *Land, Center and Diaspora: Jewish Constructs in Late Antiquity*; **L. L. Grabbe (ed.)** (1998b) *Leading Captivity Captive: 'The Exile' as History and Ideology*; **J. Hausmann** (1987) *Israels Rest: Studien zum Selbstverständnis der nachexilischen Gemeinde*; **D. Mendels** (1987) *The Land of Israel as a Political Concept in Hasmonean Literature*; **idem** (1992) *The Rise and Fall of Jewish Nationalism: The History of Jewish* *and Christian Ethnicity in Palestine within the Greco-Roman Period (200 B.C.E.–135 C.E.)*; **J. M. Scott (ed.)** (1997) *Exile: Old Testament, Jewish, and Christian Conceptions*; **W. C. van Unnik** (1993) *Das Selbstverständnis der jüdischen Diaspora in der hellenistisch-römischen Zeit*.

We find two complementary views in Jewish biblical and later texts: the concept of the blessing of the land and the horror of exile from it (e.g., Lev. 26; Deut. 28; 1 Kgs 8.34, 46-53; Isa. 40.1-11; 51.9-23). Exile is a major theme, especially in the later biblical literature (Hausman 1987; Scott [ed.] 1997; Grabbe [ed.] 1998), no doubt in part because of the actual exile of many Judaeans by Nebuchadnezzar (though not the bulk of the population, contrary to statements in 2 Kgs 25.11-12; 2 Chron. 36.20-21). But some of these exiles or their descendants returned (as recounted in Ezra and Nehemiah), making the concept of exile and attachment to the land a strong ethnic memory. The biblical material has already been discussed in *HJJSTP 1* (244–47).

Apart from any possible biblical statements, we do not have much information on the subject from the first part of the Greek period. A book such as Tobit, which is likely to be from this time, suggests how those in the diaspora lived and thought, including how they continued to look toward Jerusalem, where the surviving Israelites will return to rebuild the temple (Tob. 14.4-7). Through the second and first centuries – moving from Seleucid rule to the Hasmonaean 'greater Israel' to subordination by Rome – we see a range of attitudes (see Mendels 1988 for a survey). Alongside the belief that the land belongs to Israel and all others should be eliminated (the view well known from many biblical texts) appear other beliefs. For example, *Jubilees* distinguishes between the 'Canaanites' who should be eliminated and the Edomites who are kin to Israel and, despite friction, can be accommodated by being brought under Israelite rule (*Jub.* 35–38); the same contrast applies to the Ishmaelites with whom they should also live in peace (*Jub.* 22.1-4).

Centrality of the land then became reinforced when an independent Jewish state was established under Hasmonaean rule. Under John Hyrcanus we start to see expansion of rule from Jerusalem, with what seems to be a programme to conquer neighbouring territories, including Idumaea, Samaria and Galilee (§16.3.3). Whether the doctrine of the land was used as an excuse for Hasmonaean expansion is a question, though *Jubilees* and the fragments of Eupolemus might suggest this. Certainly, some have suggested that this was because of a desire to imitate ancient Israel and expand to the old borders. Now, K. Berthelot (2018) challenges the 'paradigm of the reconquest of the promised land' – the idea that the Hasmonaeans were modelling themselves on the biblical conquests ascribed to Joshua and David – espoused by a number of scholars over the years. She concludes not only that there is no evidence that the Hasmonaeans saw their conquests as 'reconquering' land taken by Joshua (passages such as 1 Macc. 15.33-35 have been misunderstood or misapplied) but that this lack of a statement has to be explained in the light of their military activities and their writings. A better explanation is that the Hasmonaeans were only doing what was normal in the Hellenistic world – and they were well integrated into it (though this was not incompatible with observance of the Torah). In any case, it is not surprising: territorial expansion is common when a state and its ruler become ascendant in the region.

With the coming of the Romans and the loss of Judah's independence, we see reactions, with (a) attempts to justify this loss of independence and the continuing exile, and (b) a desire to regain lost territories. The sins of the Jews are seen as the cause of the new domination by foreigners (*Pss. Sol.* 2.1-14; 8.1-22; 17.5-18). A spiritualization of the concept of the land and exile is found in some literature (e.g., Philo, *Spec. Leg.* 4.178; *Somn.* 2.250). Others saw possession of the land in eschatological terms (e.g., *Pss. Sol.* 17–18; *Ant.* 18.1.1 §§4-8). It is likely that this strong theology of the land was a factor in the various revolts through the 1st century, culminating in the 66–70 revolt. Related to this was also the view that the 'Lost Ten Tribes' – the Northern Israelites taken captive about 720 BCE by the Assyrians – were still an entity settled on the other side of the Euphrates (2 Kgs 17) but would come to the aid of their brethren in Palestine in the end time (e.g., Josephus, *War* 1.Pref.2 §5; 6.6.2 §343; *Ant.* 11.5.2 §133; *4 Ezra* 13.39-47). A further indication of the land ideology has been seen in the practice of interment in the land of Israel of the bodies of those who died abroad; however, it seems that this did not develop until the 3rd century CE, long after the Second Temple period (Gafni 1996: 79–95).

Views about the land of Israel did not all go in only one direction, however (Gafni 1996: 27–40). Perhaps as a reaction to the terra-centric view of many Jews in Palestine, some of those in the diaspora came up with counter-proposals that helped to neutralize the land ideology by taking away any stigma of living outside the land. This is not surprising, since the majority of Jews were living in the diaspora by the turn of the era. One justification was that living abroad as 'colonists' was an honourable state, indicating God's blessings on Israel by widening its habitation (cf. *Ant.* 4.6.4 §115). Another was the Jewish witness or mission to Gentiles by living among them (cf. Tob. 13.6, though the evidence for this is mainly from later rabbinic statements).

Although the evidence is not always straightforward, some data point to Jews who maintained their Jewish identity but also regarded their local region as their 'fatherland' (*patris* [Gafni 1996: 41–57), a form of what might be called 'local patriotism'. There is even evidence that in the talmudic period, the Babylonian Jews developed a pro-Babylonian stance in which Babylonia was seen as Abraham's original home which had some of the same qualities as the land of Israel, though this was in part a response to a strong land ideology being developed among Palestinian rabbis (Gafni 1996: 58–78).

10.2. *Jews in Various Areas*

E. Gruen (2002) *Diaspora: Jews amidst Greeks and Romans*; **M. Pucci Ben Zeev** (1998) *Jewish Rights in the Roman World.*

10.2.1. *Egypt*

J. J. Collins (2000) *Between Athens and Jerusalem: Jewish Identity in the Hellenistic Diaspora*, 122–31; ***CPJ***; **S. R. Johnson** (2004) *Historical Fictions and Hellenistic Jewish Identity: Third Maccabees in its Cultural Context*; ***JWSTP*** 80–84; **E. Matusova** (2015) *The Meaning of the Letter of Aristeas: In Light of Biblical Interpretation and Grammatical Tradition, and with Reference to its Historical Context*; **H. R. Moehring** (1975) 'The *Acta pro Judaeis* in the *Antiquities* of Flavius Josephus', in J. Neusner (ed.), *Christianity, Judaism and Other Greco-Roman Cults*, 3:124–58; **F. Parente** (1988) 'The Third Book of Maccabees as Ideological Document and Historical Source', *Henoch* 10: 143–82; **V. A. Tcherikover** (1961) 'The Third Book of Maccabees as a Historical Source of Augustus' Time', *Scripta Hierosolymitana* 7: 1–26.

Already at the end of the monarchy period, we have stories of the migration of Jews to Egypt, including the prophet Jeremiah (Jer. 43–44). More importantly we have a good deal of information on an actual Jewish community in Egypt, viz., the settlement at Elephantine (*HJJSTP 1*: 54–55, 318–19), though it seems to have come to an end before the Greek period. Sources indicate a population already under the first Ptolemy: perhaps credible is the statement that a large number of Jews were settled in Egypt by Ptolemy I (*Aris.* 4, 12-14, though the figure of 100,000 is ridiculous – this would have been more than all the Jews in Palestine). Since our data have covered the whole of the Hellenistic and early Roman periods (especially in *CPJ*), little more can be said at this point specifically about the last two centuries BCE. The Jews and Jewish communities in Egypt during the Hellenistic period generally were discussed in *HJJSTP 2* (181–85, 193–204), while events in Alexandria under the Romans will be treated in *HJJSTP 4*. However, some events treated elsewhere in the present volume will be noted here:

10.2.1.1. *Jewish Generals under Cleopatra III*

Two of the sons of the Onias who built the temple at Leontopolis (below §10.2.1.3), Chelkias and Ananias (Strabo, as quoted in *Ant*. 13.10.4 §§284-87), were generals in the army of Cleopatra III (fl. 140–100 BCE). This was at a time when the Jews of Egypt and Cyprus were flourishing (*Ant*. 13.10.4 §§284-87). There was also an unnamed general of Cleopatra III who was executed by her (Justin 39.4): he might be one of the two sons; however, the Jewish sources give no hint of any friction between the queen and her Jewish generals. During the 'War of the Sceptres' (§16.5), Ptolemy IX came to the aid of Ptolemais on the Palestinian coast, which was being attacked by Alexander Jannaeus. At this point Cleopatra III intervened, concerned at the nearness of Ptolemy to Egypt, by sending a fleet and a land army under her two Jewish generals. Although Ptolemy attempted to seize Egypt behind the backs of the army, he failed, but the general Chelkias seems to have died in the fighting at this time. After Cleopatra drove Ptolemy out of Egypt and he had returned to Cyprus, Alexander Jannaeus approached Cleopatra with gifts. Her Jewish general Ananias also spoke on Jannaeus's behalf, and she made an alliance with him.

10.2.1.2. *Alleged 'Persecution' under Ptolemy IV (*3 Maccabees*)*

In the Fourth Syrian War Antiochus III was defeated by the Egyptians and forced to retire from Coele-Syria (*HJJSTP 2*: 298–301). This is the context of an incident regarding Ptolemy IV narrated in the book of *3 Macc*. 1.1-7. The next section of the book (1.8–2.24) tells of how Ptolemy came to Jerusalem and attempted to enter the Holy of Holies but was refused. He then returned to Egypt and initiated a persecution of the Alexandrian Jews who were, however, miraculously delivered (2.25–6.22), and the king repented of his plan and acknowledged the God of heaven (6.23-29). The Jews were allowed a festival, and the king issued a decree in their favour (6.30–7.23). Recent study has indicated that *3 Maccabees* is itself later than the reign of Ptolemy IV. Opinion is divided between a composition late in the Ptolemaic period, probably the predominant opinion (Johnson 2004: 129–41), and in the early Roman period (Collins 2000: 124–26; Tcherikover 1961; Parente 1988); a Ptolemaic composition that was updated in the Roman period is one way of explaining the later references.

In any case, *3 Maccabees* draws on some genuine Ptolemaic sources. Its account of the battle of Raphia (see *HJJSTP 2*: 298–301), though brief, seems to have a good source (Johnson 2004: 190–201; Tcherikover 1961: 2–3; Parente 1988: 147–48). The basis of the story about the persecution of the Jews may lie in actual events, but this is a moot point since there is no clear evidence of a Jewish persecution under Ptolemaic rule (Johnson 2004: 188; but Matusova [2015: 113–15] uniquely seems to accept that a coercion to worship Dionysus occurred). No doubt the persecutions of Antiochus IV would have been sufficient inspiration, though the assumption of threats to the Jewish community goes back even before that, as the book of Esther indicates. Just as there is no evidence that the Jews were menaced under Persian rule, so the alleged persecutions under the Ptolemies seem fantasy (contra Matusova). Although legendary in its present form (Tcherikover 1961: 7–8; *CPJ* 1:21–23) the story, if given its final editing in the Augustan age, could also reflect the situation at that time (Parente 1988).

10.2.1.3. *Temple at Leontopolis*

J. C. Bernhardt (2017) *Die jüdische Revolution: Untersuchungen zu Ursachen, Verlauf und Folgen der hasmonäischen Erhebung*, 593–603; **E. J. Bickerman** (1933) 'Ein jüdischer Festbrief vom Jahre 124 v. Chr. (II Macc 1_{1-9})', *ZNW* 32: 233–54; **G. Bohak** (1995) 'CPJ III, 520: The Egyptian Reaction to Onias' Temple', *JSJ* 26: 32–41; **idem** (1996) *Joseph and Aseneth and the Jewish Temple in Heliopolis*, 19–40, 63–74; **M. Delcor** (1968) 'Le temple d'Onias en Egypte', *RevB* 75: 188–205; **E. S. Gruen** (1997) 'The Origins and Objectives of Onias' Temple', *Scripta Classica Israelica* 16: 47–70; **C. T. R. Hayward** (1982) 'The Jewish Temple at Leontopolis: A Reconsideration', *JJS* 33: 429–43; **V. L. Parker** (2007) 'The Letters in II Maccabees: Reflexions on the Book's Composition', *ZAW* 119: 386–402; **S. H. Steckoll** (1967–69) 'The Qumran Sect in Relation to the Temple of Leontopolis', *RevQ* 6: 55–69; **J. E. Taylor** (1998) 'A Second Temple in Egypt: The Evidence for the Zadokite Temple of Onias', *JSJ* 29: 297–321.

An interesting episode in the history of Judaism is that in which no less than the hereditary high priest of the Jerusalem cult founded a breakaway temple in Egypt. The difficulty with analyzing what happened and why is the sometimes contradictory information found in the various accounts in Josephus (*War* 7.10.2-4 §§423-36; *Ant.* 12.5.1 §§237-38; 12.9.7 §387; 13.3.1-3 §§62-73). Notice the following regarding the temple:

- It was founded by Onias III, the high priest deposed by Jason, according to *War* (7.10.2 §423), but by his son Onias IV according to *Antiquities* (12.9.7 §387).
- It was in the nome of Heliopolis. This site is often identified with Tell el-Yehudieh and some of the remains there, though the archaeology is perhaps less than clearcut (cf. Taylor 1998: 313–20; SCHÜRER 3:146 n. 33).
- It was similar to that in Jerusalem, according to one passage (*Ant.* 13.3.3 §72). Elsewhere, however, it is said to be unlike the Jerusalem temple but instead in the form of a tower (*War* 7.10.3 §427). Although C. T. R. Hayward (1982) has suggested the two can be reconciled in that the Jerusalem temple was often compared to a tower, this contradicts Josephus's own statement that the one was different from the other.
- The new temple outside Jerusalem was justified from a prophecy of Isaiah (perhaps Isa. 19.18-22).
- According to *Antiquities* (13.3.2 §70) there was already a ruined temple on the site which Onias was allowed to cleanse and rebuild. The passage in *War* is silent on this.
- The temple was closed in 73 CE, '343 years' after its founding (*War* 7.10.4 §§433-36), though the figure should be nearer to 243 years for its existence (perhaps simply a scribal error or misreading).

In a far-reaching – but rather speculative – thesis, J. E. Taylor (1998: especially 308–10) has identified the Onias of the story with Onias III (who was deposed by his brother Jason), who was made to lead Jewish forces on the side of Ptolemy VI against Antiochus IV in the Sixth Syrian War, built the temple, then returned to Antioch to protest against Menelaus, and was executed there. She has pointed out the fact that Josephus is somewhat confused about Onias III and Onias IV, but her scenario agrees with neither Josephus nor 1 and 2 Maccabees, nor is there a hint that Onias III (or IV) fought against Antiochus IV (cf. Bernhardt 2017: 596 n. 20). Josephus also changed the founder from Onias III to Onias IV in his later writing. S. H. Steckoll (1967–69) proposed a connection between the Qumran community and the Leontopolis temple. This was criticized by M. Delcor (1968, and de Vaux in a post-script to Delcor's article). Hayward (1982) has made some cautious comparisons, though some of these resemblances could be due simply to the common situation of both being communities of worship viewed as 'heterodox' by the Jerusalem establishment. Taylor (1998: 311–13) suggests that the Oniad temple might have used the solar calendar. A number have suggested that the second introductory letter in 2 Maccabees (1.10–2.18) is an attack on the Leontopolis temple (Bickerman 1933: 250; Parker 2007: 389 n. 7).

E. S. Gruen (1997) argues that the Oniad temple (built in his view by Onias IV) was not intended as a rival to that of Jerusalem. At the time it was built, the high priesthood in Jerusalem was vacant, and the Jewish place of worship (the temple) was in jeopardy. He suggests that Onias even avoided the title 'high priest'. The aim was that the 'Jewish sanctuary in Egypt was a reinforcement, not a rival, of Jerusalem' (1997: 70). G. Bohak (1995) points to what he thinks may have been local Egyptian opposition to the temple. A fragmentary papyrus from the 2nd or 3rd century CE is identified as a prophetic text, which talks of 'Jews' (Ἰου[δαίοις]) who inhabit the 'Land of the Sun' (Heliopolis?) and make the city desolate. Bohak suggests that the prophecy was 'recycled' at a later time but that the original goes back to Egyptian priestly criticism of the Onias temple that was putting them out of employment. If so, the priests finally got their wish in 73 CE when the Onias temple was closed by the Romans.

10.2.2. *Syria, Asia Minor and Greece*

It is in the Greek period that we first begin to hear about Jewish communities in the cities of Syria, Asia Minor and even the Greek mainland. Already Antionchus III is said to have transported 2,000 Jews from Mesopotamia to places in Phrygia, to perform garrison duty and provide general protection for the Seleucids in Asia Minor (*Ant.* 12.3.4 §§147-53). However, much of what we know of Jews in these regions are the letters and decrees recorded by Josephus in *Ant.* 14.10.1-26 §§185-267, often relating to appeals to Roman officials from the various Jewish communities of these regions. These are currently taken as by and large authentic, though they are in some cases Greek translations of Latin originals, are often quoted only partially, and seem to have been copies of copies, with many copyist errors (Gruen 2002: 85; Pucci Ben Zeev 1998: 6–11, 357–73; despite Moehring 1975). The documents are a miscellaneous collection of decrees and communications relating to various Jewish communities in Asia Minor about their interactions with the cities or Roman officials (or both) with regard to their right to maintain and practise their ethnic traditions (including certain religious rights). They are all confined to the decade of the 40s BCE, though we shall also look at some later decrees in the last decade BCE from *Antiquities*, book 16.

The earliest of those documents collected here by Josephus relates to the consul Lucius Lentulus Crus, who was a supporter of Pompey against

Julius Caesar (*Ant.* 14.10.13, 16, 18-19 §§228-30, 234, 236-40; these quotations all seem to relate to the same decree or letter). In 49 BCE he set out to recruit a force for Pompey from among Roman citizens of Asia Minor. A few Jews were Roman citizens, but non-citizens could still be recruited into the auxiliary ranks. However, a request was made to Lentulus to excuse Jews from military service, and he did so in a letter directed specifically to Ephesus, which was apparently the chief city of Asia (*Ant.* 14.10.11 §224), though copies seem to have gone to other cities. One was by Lentulus's subordinates M. Piso, who sent the decree to the island of Delos (*Ant.* 14.10.14 §231-32).

A number of the documents relate to the short period when Caesar was in control, from 48 to 44 BCE. Perhaps the most important was Caesar's decree, which not only made Hyrcanus II the ethnarch of all Jews – those in the diaspora as well as the homeland – but also granted various rights and privileges to the Jews (*Ant.* 14.10.2-8 §§190-216). The corollary is that the Jews are exempt from military service, having troops billeted on them, money demanded of them, being taxed in the sabbatical year, and having sabbath observance restricted, and are generally to have their ancestral customs respected. These rights were confirmed by a *senatus consultum* and also reaffirmed after Caesar's death by a decree of the Senate (*Ant.* 14.10.9-10 §§217-22). These decrees by Caesar and the Senate were not because of special favour toward the Jews but because of aid that Hyrcanus and Antipater had provided to Caesar in his campaign against Egypt (*Ant.* 14.8.1-3 §§127-39; see §17.6); Caesar provided similar privileges to other allies (Gruen 2002: 88). Hyrcanus fulfilled his duties in the office by writing to the Roman governor of Asia, C. Rabirius, who sent letters to Laodicea and other cities detailing Jewish rights (*Ant.* 14.10.20 §§241-43).

After Caesar's assassination, Hyrcanus requested assurances that Caesar's decrees in favour of the Jews would continue to be respected, from the Senate (as noted above) but even from his assassins. In this fervent period, both pro-Caesar and anti-Caesar commanders and officials had other things on their mind than Jewish rights. Thus, it may have been a useful pro-active move on Hyrcanus's part about 43 BCE to contact the proconsul of Syria, P. Dolabella, and request that Jews continue to be exempt from military service (which was granted: *Ant.* 14.10.11-12 §§223-27). Shortly afterward, about 42 BCE (after Dolabella had taken his own life), the Jews of Ephesus themselves appealed to Marcus Brutus, the assassin of Caesar (if this is the right reading; there is some textual uncertainty), to guarantee their rights, especially with regard to the sabbath, which he did (*Ant.* 14.10.25 §§262-64). Yet Gruen (2002:

88-91) also notes that these Roman decrees and letters were a means for Hyrcanus to assert his authority and status before his own people, since a number of the letters indicate that the cities written to were not adverse to granting the Jews their ancestral rights. Indeed, only at Miletus and Delos are Jewish rights alleged to have been restricted (*Ant.* 14.10.8 §213-16; 14.10.21 §§244-46). Some of Hyrcanus's actions were part of inter-Jewish politics, not necessarily to provide relief for oppressed Jews! In some cases, Hyrcanus's attempt at throwing his weight around might have been counter-productive.

After the opponents of Caesar were defeated in 42 BCE, Mark Antony came to take over the eastern part of the empire. The high priest Hyrcanus met him in Ephesus to ask for assurances that the decrees in favour of the Jews would remain in force (*Ant.* 14.12.2-6 §§304-23). Antony issued three letters. The one to Hyrcanus (and the 'Jewish nation' [Ἰουδαίων ἔθνει] according to one reading) thanked him (them) for the Jewish loyalty to the Caesarian cause and also decreed that Jews enslaved by Pompeians should be freed. Two others were sent to Tyre, commanding that the Jewish rights be restored to them, including release of any Jews sold into slavery under Cassius and return of any Jewish possessions taken from them. Similar letters were said to be sent to Sidon, Antioch and Aradus. Apparently, Jewish property had been taken by Tyrians, though there is no evidence of a general policy against the Jews in the Greek cities, while the Romans were not out to champion the Jews but simply to be honest brokers in any dispute (cf. Gruen 2002: 96).

From the time of the late 40s BCE to late in Herod's reign we hear of nothing to indicate troubles for the Jewish communities in this region. Marcus Agrippa was sent to Asia Minor in 14 BCE, and Herod persuaded him to visit Jerusalem (§18.4.3). Then, the next spring Herod sailed to the Pontus to join him, and they made a lengthy return journey by land together. It was at this point that the Jews of Ionia appealed to Herod for help with regard to certain local infringements on their practice of religion. He made representation to Agrippa about the matter and gained a hearing for the Jews' petition. The result was that Agrippa confirmed their traditional religious rights. Note, however, that the original complaint was about the Jews' being a part of the *politeia*, which seems to mean the political processes of the Ionian cities. Why this should have led to curtailment of Jewish religious rights is not clear at this time, since the region seems to have been flourishing, but it may have been a desire to restrict benefits conferred by Rome to a small circle of citizens; the Jews were not the only ones being kept out (cf. Gruen 2002: 97–100).

Yet in spite of Agrippa's careful decision that Jewish rights were to be respected, the insistence from the Greek side for Jews to exercise full civic duties (including public honour of the gods) or to lose their privileges continued (*Ant.* 16.6.1 §§160-61). The Jews complained directly to Augustus, which led him sometime after the death of Agrippa (in 12 BCE) to issue an edict reasserting Jewish rights in general, with specific reference to sending money to the Jerusalem temple, the inviolability of synagogues and their property and permission for Jews to observe the sabbath with regard to court appearances (*Ant.* 16.6.1-2 §§161-65). August also wrote to the proconsul of Asia, Gaius Norbannus Flaccus, who in turn wrote to various cities, including Sardis (*Ant.* 16.2.3-7 §§166-73) and apparently Ephesus (Philo, *Gaium* 314-15). We also know that the proconsul Julius Antonius also wrote to Ephesus, asserting Jewish rights, though we do not know the exact date (sometime between his consulship in 10 BCE and his death in 2 BCE). This seems to have solved the problem, at least for the time being, since no more incidents are recorded by Josephus.

10.2.3. *Rome*

> **E. Baltrusch** (2002) *Die Juden und das Römische Reich: Geschichte einer konfliktreichen Beziehung*; **E. J. Bickerman** (1958) 'Altars of Gentiles: A Note on the Jewish *Ius Sacrum*', *Revue internationale des droits de l'Antiquité* (3rd ser.) 5: 137–64; **E. Haenchen** (1971) *The Acts of the Apostles*; **E. N. Lane** (1979) 'Sabazius and the Jews in Valerius Maximus: A Re-Examination', *JRS* 69: 35–38; **H. R. Moehring** (1959) 'The Persecution of the Jews and the Adherents of the Isis Cult at Rome A.D. 19', *NovT* 3: 293–304.

We cannot be sure when Jews first settled in Rome, though we know there was a community there by 139 BCE. In that year, according to Valerius Maximus (1.3.3), the praetor (chief magistrate) Cn. Cornelius Scipio Hispanus expelled the 'Chaldeans', i.e., the astrologers, from Rome and Italy (text and commentary in *GLAJJ* §147). He also expelled the 'Jews, who had tried to corrupt the Roman customs with the cult of Jupiter Sabazius' (*Iudaeos, qui Sabazi Iovis cultu Romanos inficere mores conati erant*). One of the accounts contains a rather puzzling statement that the praetor also overthrew the 'private altars' (*aras privatas*) of the Jews in public places. Although one or two temples/altars other than in Jerusalem are known at this time (see above, §10.2.1.3; cf. *HJJSTP 1*: 217–18), multiple altars in the various diaspora communities are not so far attested. It has been suggested that this might be a reference to synagogues, but it is difficult to think of a part of a synagogue at this time that would be compared to an altar. Bickerman (1958) suggested that it was a reference to altars raised up by Romans honouring the Jewish God, which is possible but speculative.

There are several problems with Valerius Maximus's accounts (for details, see Lane 1979). The first is that we do not have the original continuous text as such but only extracts and summaries in some late manuscripts. Two manuscripts contain excerpts made by Julius Paris about 400 CE, plus a third manuscript with the complete epitome by Julius Paris. There is also another manuscript containing an epitome made in the 6th century CE by Januarius Nepotianus. Lane argues cogently that there is confusion in the manuscripts, and that Valerius Maximus originally referred to the expulsion of at least three groups from Rome in 139 BCE: the astrologers, the worshipers of the Sabazius cult and the Jews. That is, there was no connection of the Jews with the cult of Sabazius. While a Sabazius later became identified with Jupiter, this was not the case originally, and confusion with the Jews (because of the resemblance of the deity's name to the word 'sabbath') came much later. Thus, if Lane is right, a whole infrastructure of interpretation of the Jews and 'Jupiter Sabazius' has been built on a confused manuscript tradition.

Basically, all we know is that an expulsion of Jews took place in 139 BCE. It seems clear from the consuls named by Valerius Maximus (Cn. Calpurnius Piso and M. Popillius M.f. Laenas) that a substantial Jewish community had grown up in Rome no later than 139 BCE but was expelled at this time. It has been suggested that there might have been a connection between Simon Maccabee's embassy to Rome in 143–142 BCE and some sort of religious activity by Jews there that was unacceptable to the Roman authorities (cf. Baltrusch 2002: 117). Perhaps, but it seems a rather short period of time for such a situation to develop that the Roman officials felt it necessary to take action. In any case, it would have taken longer than three years for the sort of Jewish community suggested by Valerius Maximus – of a significant size and influence – to have been established in the city. Once a link with Sabazius is eliminated – as it apparently should be – we are left with no clear reason for the expulsion of the Jews. E. S. Gruen notes that during the 2nd century BCE a number of decrees were issued against various groups as posing a risk to Roman customs, morals and thinking. Generally these did not work and were repeated in a few years, mostly as a gesture: 'Rome's *principes* [leaders] paraded their protection of the nation's values against too much contamination from abroad. Symbolic significance rather than any systematic expulsion held primacy' (Gruen 2002: 19). There is no evidence of particular Roman hostility toward the Jews at this time.

It seems clear that Jews soon returned (as was evidently the case with other groups expelled from the capital). Philo tells us that many Jews in Rome lived over the Tiber, whose ancestors had been brought there as slaves but then freed (cf. Philo, *Gaium* 155-56; Josephus, *Ant.* 14.4.5 §78; Plutarch, *Pompeius* 45.1-2; Appian, *Mithr.* 117, 571). As is evident, many Jews who were settled there were slaves or descendants of slaves. However, a major increase in the Jewish population seems to have come about after the conquest of Jerusalem by Pompey in 63 BCE. For example, according to Josephus, 3,000 Jewish opponents were made captive when Alexander was recaptured (*War* 1.8.3 §163; *Ant.* 14.5.2 §85); during the Roman civil war Cassius made slaves of 30,000 Jews of Tarichaeae (*War* 1.6.9 §180); and so on. We can speculate about how accurate these figures are, but in any case, at the beginning of Roman rule large numbers of Judaeans seem to have been enslaved, with some of them taken to Rome. As was the custom, slaves were often manumitted after years of service, or perhaps the children or descendants of slaves were allowed to go free. Romans were quite liberal in their freeing of slaves and then in according them rights, even citizenship (Gruen 2002: 23).

In his defence of Flaccus in 59 BCE, the orator and statesman Cicero says some derogatory things about Jews, though many scholars have pointed out that he said what the occasion demanded (cf. *GLAJJ* §68; Gruen 2002: 19–23): we should not assume this represented his real underlying views of Jews. Cicero was answering the charge against Flaccus that he had prevented Jewish communities from sending gold (derived from the temple contribution) to Jerusalem but had confiscated it for the state in some cases. If we ignore the invective against the Jews (whose function was to put the jury in sympathy with Flaccus), Cicero's speech shows us several things. First, it supports other passages (see below) that indicate the Jewish communities in Asia Minor and elsewhere were collecting the temple contribution and regularly dispatching it to Jerusalem. Secondly, it shows us there was a certain solidarity among the scattered Jewish communities, because the Roman community turned out to support their brethren in Asia Minor who had suffered from Flaccus's measures. Thirdly, it indicates that the Jewish community in Rome could throw around a certain amount of political weight when it felt the need to do so. It is clear that they were not all slaves or recently freed slaves, or Cicero would have pounced on this fact to support his cause. Silence on Cicero's part is as important as what he does say.

According to Suetonius (*Julius* 84) a large number of Jews (apparently both local and foreign) attended Julius Caesar's funeral. Under Augustus, a Jewish lad from Sidon claimed to be Herod's son Alexander (*War* 2.7.1-2 §101-10; *Ant.* 17.12.1-2 §§324-38). He first gained a following in Crete and Melos, but evidently many Jews of Rome also supported him when he came there (until Augustus condemned him to the galleys). Also under Augustus, Philo tells us that Jews of Rome were eligible for grain distribution (Philo, *Gaium* 155-58, which apparently meant that they were citizens). Because they could not receive the distribution on the sabbath, August decreed that a portion be reserved for them, to be distributed the day after the sabbath. As recounted elsewhere (§18.4.6), the death of Herod brought a number of his descendants to Rome; it also brought a delegation from Jerusalem claiming to represent the people (who petitioned Augustus unsuccessfully to abolish Herodian rule). This delegation was allegedly supported by 8,000 local Jews from Rome itself.

Finally, there is the question of the *collegia*, voluntary associations that were often religious (perhaps relating to funerary celebrations) but also like trade guilds or that had other social functions. Because there was the potential of political strife involving them (the membership often heavily freedmen or slaves), they were banned several times in the late Republic or early Empire, beginning in 64 BCE. For example, Julius Caesar banned all *collegia* except for old, established ones. Sometimes it is asserted that Jewish synagogues were exempt from this ban, but it seems unlikely that a specific Jewish exemption was ever a part of such decrees. Rather, synagogues were simply not classified as *collegia*: they did not fit the definition (Gruen 2002: 24–26).

10.2.4. *Babylonia*

J. Neusner (1984) *A History of the Jews in Babylonia 1: The Parthian Period*; **D. R. Schwartz** (2008) *2 Maccabees*.

Our first incident is the exile of some of the population of Northern Israel by the Assyrians about 720 BCE (2 Kgs 17). The text makes it the total population, with another population from Mesopotamia being brought in to replace them. Archaeology (as well as certain other biblical passages) suggests that only a section of the population was removed and replaced by migrants (discussed with bibliography in Grabbe 2017: 161, 191–92). Nevertheless, since those deported apparently did not return, the concept of the 'Lost Ten Tribes' persisted in later centuries (*War* 1.Pref.2 §5; 6.6.2 §343; *Ant*. 11.5.2 §133; *4 Ezra* 13.39-47).

Jews from the Southern Kingdom were first taken to Babylonia as captives in 597 BCE when Jehoiachin surrendered to Nebuchadnezzar (2 Kgs 24.8-16; for more information on this captivity and the subsequent return of some Jews from Babylonia to Palestine, see Grabbe 2017: 232–33, 252–55; *HJJSTP 1*: 271–85). What is clear is that most of those taken to

Babylonia and their descendants did not return to Palestine but continued to make up a large diaspora community in Babylonia (*HJJSTP 1*; 317–18). The problem from our point of view is that they more or less dropped out of sight for several hundred years until the Parthian period. Even then our knowledge of them is often based on rabbinic literature (Neusner 1984). Not only was this literature written long after the events allegedly being described, but the focus is on religious matters and religious figures rather than on the Babylonian Jewish community as a whole. This was already commented on in detail by Neusner in trying to develop a historical method to deal with rabbinic literature (see *HJJSTP 4* forthcoming), including in the 'Introduction to the Third Printing' of volume 1 of his history of the Jews in Babylonia (Neusner 1984: xix–xxxvi).

Most of what we know from Josephus is not the history of the Jewish community(ies) in Babylonia, but the interaction of Hasmonaean rulers with Seleucid rulers who were leading campaigns against Parthia: e.g., Hyrcanus I allied with Antiochus VII; the interaction with the Parthians during attempts at hegemony of Syria and Palestine; temporary conquest of Palestine by the Parthians (40–38 BCE); the settlement of Zamaris and those with him in Trachanaea by Herod (see further at §9.4).

We have evidence that Jews lived in a variety of cities in the Babylonian region. A problem is that our information is sometimes from inscriptions or archaeology of the late Roman or early Byzantine period. A prime example is Dura Europus, where a good deal of iconographic and other aspects of Jewish culture were found in abundance, but none of it is attested earlier than the late 2nd century CE (SCHÜRER 3:10–13). We have evidence of Jewish settlement in a number of the Greek and other cities in the region: Seleucia on the Tigris, Susa, Charax-Spasinu, Bet Adini, Nisibus, Nicephorium, Carrhae, Edessa, Gundashapur, Gazaca, and Hyrcania (Neusner 1984: 10–14; SCHÜRER 3:5–15). Tannaitic sources apparently also mention Nehardea, Nehar, Pekod, Kifri and Huṣal, though how early we find evidence is not clear (Neusner 1984: 14 n. 2). Unfortunately, the list in Acts 2.9-11 cannot be taken at face value since the writer may have simply listed all the areas to the east that he was aware of.

The Parthians began to take over the eastern part of the Seleucid empire about the middle of the 3rd century BCE and had taken Babylonia by the middle of the 2nd century BCE (see further §9.4 on Parthian history). Greek influence continued in the eastern part of the old Seleucid empire even after it was lost to Seleucid rule (cf. *HJJSTP* 2: 289). This meant that the Jews even in Mesopotamia in some cases were influenced by Greek culture and some evidently had a Greek education. Very little is known about the Jews and Jewish communities in Mesopotamia between the Persian period and the 1st century BCE (Neusner 1984: 11). 2 Maccabees

8.20 reports an incident in which Jews were part of a military force who fought against the Galatians (Gauls) in Babylonia; exactly when this took place is not stated, possibly under Antiochus III, but the occasion remains obscure (cf. Schwartz 2008: 337–38). We also know of an incident under Tigranes II the Great of Armenia (ca. 95–55 BCE), that he deported a large number of Jews to his country (Neusner 1964: 231, citing native Armenian sources).

Under Herod there was considerable interaction with the Parthians, who now controlled the various areas around Babylon. We have several references to the Babylonian Jewish community from Josephus's accounts of Herod's reign. When Hyrcanus II was taken captive in 40 BCE (§18.2.1), the Parthians had allowed him to settle in the Jewish community in Babylon where he was greatly honoured. (He wanted to return to Palestine, however, and Herod invited him to come back.) Later on Herod appointed a priest named Ananel from a Babylonian family to be high priest in the Jerusalem temple, though he eventually replaced him (*Ant.* 15.3.1 §§39-41).

About 10 BCE Herod sought to accomplish the dual aims of giving protection to the pilgrims journeying from Babylonia through the northern part of his kingdom to Jerusalem and also to the inhabitants of the region. The problem was in the area of Trachonitis (*Ant.* 17.2.1-2 §§23-28), which was in danger of being overrun by brigands because of the low population. So Herod set about creating a buffer zone in Batanaea (War 2.17.4 §421; *Ant.* 17.2.1-3 §§23-32; *Life* 1.11 §§46-61). He settled there a community of 600 Jews who had come to Antioch from Babylonia under their leader Zamaris (§18.4.4). Herod offered Zamaris land, fortresses, and a village free of taxes and tribute by the name of Bathyra. Over several generations the people of this settlement not only fulfilled their original function but also served as a royal body guard, up to the time of Agrippa II.

10.3. *Conclusions*

An Israelite diaspora could be said to have begun as early as the 8th century BCE, under the Assyrians when they conquered the Northern Kingdom. Certainly many from the Kingdom of Judah were taken captive to Babylonia in the last days of the monarchy. The Jewish community in Babylonia continued to grow and flourish, even as a few returned to Palestine at various times in the Persian period. Unfortunately, apart from some cuneiform tablets about the 'city of Judah' in Mesopotamia and the presence of some Jewish names in the Murashu documents, we have little in the way of direct evidence for the large Jewish population in Babylonia.

There are sporadic references to the Jews of the region in the literary sources of the Hellenistic period, especially in Josephus, but little data. The talmudic material focuses on some rabbinic figures allegedly under Arsacid rule, but this material is long after the actual individuals lived and of uncertain quality.

With regard to Egypt, some biblical references (e.g., Jeremiah) suggest Jews living there from the end of the monarchy. More concretely, the Jewish colony at Elephantine might have begun during the time of the monarchy but, in any case, it was well in place during the 5th century BCE, though it then evidently disappears. We have evidence of a large Jewish population in Egypt from at least the early Greek period and well attested in the papyri during the 2nd and 1st centuries BCE (discussed in *HJJSTP 2*). During the Hasmonaean period the temple at Leontopolis was founded perhaps as early as the mid-2nd century BCE, but we also have literary references to Jewish generals serving the Ptolemaic rulers in the later 2nd century.

References are made to Jews in Asia Minor at least as early as 200 BCE, but much of our information belongs to the mid-1st century BCE with a series of letters to and from Roman officials about Jewish rights in the region. About 14 BCE Augustus's friend Agrippa was also asked to adjudicate on a petition from the Jews of Ionia.

There was already a Jewish community in Rome by 139 BCE, because they were expelled about that time. But they quickly returned, and we know a large population lived there by the 1st century BCE because they are mentioned by Cicero. A large number attended Julius Caesar's funeral and were also attested at the time of Herod's death. Many of those living in Rome might have been descendants of those sold into slavery under Pompey and after subsequent rebellions of Alexander and Antigonus. But many such slavers were freed, with their descendants becoming citizens of Rome. The Jewish community in Rome was not by and large made up of slaves.

The story of these various communities will be taken forward in *HJJSTP 4*.

Chapter 11

CAUSES OF THE MACCABAEAN REVOLT

B. **Bar-Kochva** (1989) *Judas Maccabaeus*; J. C. **Bernhardt** (2017) *Die jüdische Revolution*; E. J. **Bickerman** (1937a) *Gott der Makkabäer*; **idem** (1979) *God of the Maccabees*; K. **Bringmann** (1983) *Hellenistische Reform und Religionsverfolgung in Judäa: Eine Untersuchung zur jüdisch-hellenistischen Geschichte (175–163 v. Chr.)*, 103–11; J. G. **Bunge** (1973) 'Der "Gott der Festungen" und der "Liebling der Frauen": Zur Identifizierung der Götter in Dan. 11,36-39', *JSJ* 4: 169–82; J. A. **Goldstein** (1976) *I Maccabees*; **idem** (1983a) *II Maccabees*; E. **Gruen** (1993) 'Hellenism and Persecution: Antiochus IV and the Jews', in P. Green (ed.), *Hellenistic History and Culture*, 238–74; C. **Habicht** (1989) 'The Seleucids and their Rivals', *CAH*[2] 8:324–87; I. **Heinemann** (1938) 'Wer veranlasste den Glaubenszwang der Makkabäerzeit?', *MGWJ* 82: 145–72; M. **Hengel** (1974) *Judaism and Hellenism*; S. **Honigman** (2014) *Tales of High Priests and Taxes: The Books of the Maccabees and the Judean Rebellion against Antiochos IV*; J. **Ma** (1999) *Antiochos III and the Cities of Western Asia Minor*; P. F. **Mittag** (2006) *Antiochos IV. Epiphanes*; O. **Mørkholm** (1966) *Antiochus IV of Syria*; A. E. **Portier-Young** (2011) *Apocalypse Against Empire: Theologies of Resistance in Early Judaism*; K. J. **Rigsby** (1980) 'Seleucid Notes', *TAPA* 110: 233–54; C. **Seeman** (2013) *Rome and Judea in Transition: Hasmonean Relations with the Roman Republic and the Evolution of the High Priesthood*; V. **Tcherikover** (1959) *Hellenistic Civilization and the Jews*; S. **Weitzman** (2004) 'Plotting Antiochus's Persecution', *JBL* 123: 219–34.

As the discussion at §14.3 indicates, the exact course of events in the period 170–164 BCE is not certain, thus making any attempt to explain the events – or *alleged* events, since some are disputed by some of the theories discussed below – under Antiochus more difficult. The facile explanations so often found, especially in older handbooks, frequently do not even note correctly the sequence of events leading up to the suppression of the temple sacrifices (e.g., failing to note that the 'abomination of desolation' was not immediately associated with Antiochus's taking of Jerusalem but rather an event some time later). Although the suppression of Judaism has been widely accepted, not all scholars make that assumption.

It must be kept in mind that a whole complex of dichotomies existed, such as the Tobiad and Oniad families, though just to complicate matters these were actually related through intermarriage. There were the promoters of Hellenization in contrast to the rest of the people. These dichotomies also do not line up neatly, but rather intertwine in a complicated fashion; e.g., there were pro-Ptolemaic Tobiads and pro-Seleucid Tobiads. As for the pro- vs. anti-Hellenists, this was only a relative matter, since all Judaism by this time was as Hellenized as the rest of the ancient Near East (*HJJSTP 2*: 125–65). Some of the major theories have been summarized in a convenient fashion, most thoroughly by Bernhardt (2017: 485–514; see also Honigman 2014: 11–32; Gruen 1993: 250–64; Bickerman 1937a: 36–49//1979: 24–31; Tcherikover 1959: 175–85; Bringmann 1983: 99–111).

11.1. *Ancient Views*

E. J. Bickerman (1937a) *Gott der Makkabäer*, 17–35//(1979) *God of the Maccabees*, 9–23.

In 1 Maccabees Jewish persecution is taken for granted. It is just assumed that 'wicked' individuals, whether 'heathen' or Jewish 'apostates', will do such things without any particular motivation. A good deal of emphasis seems to be placed on the 'arrogance' of Gentiles (e.g., 1 Macc. 1.21).

2 Maccabees sees the major cause of the religious suppression in the sins of Israel itself. The Gentiles are only a scourge in the hand of God to punish for such wrongs as the removal and murder of Onias III and the neglect of the temple by the priests (2 Macc. 5.17-20; 6.12-16). It is presumed that the Gentiles will of course eventually be punished for their arrogance, but the emphasis falls on the 'apostate' Jews.

Our earliest source, the historian Polybius, seems to explain it as due to Antiochus's character. He describes Antiochus's activities in a way which suggests that at least some of them would have appeared peculiar to his subjects (Polybius 26.1; cf. §4.10). He also cites the pun by which Antiochus was called *Epimanes* ('mad') instead of Epiphanes ('[God] manifest') (Polybius 26.1a). While such an explanation can never be ruled out, it is not very useful because it ultimately admits there is no logical explanation. That is, the final answer is put down simply to the caprice of an unbalanced – or at least unpredictable – individual. On the other hand, there is evidence that Antiochus was a very able ruler, on the whole, and that a number of his actions are explained by his long sojourn in Rome. Some of his actions which would have seemed strange to the Syrians were those which were normal among the Romans (Goldstein 1976: 104–5). Further, Polybius's assessment of Antiochus is by no means wholly negative but has a positive side as well. He calls him 'active' or 'effective' (πραγματικός), 'harbouring great designs' (μεγαλεπίβολος) and 'worthy of the royal dignity' (τῆς βασιλείας προσχήματος ἄξιος) (28.18). In his study of Antiochus, Mørkholm has spent a good deal of space on the question (especially 1966: 181–91) and summarizes the situation (1966: 187; quoted in §14.2 below). A similar assessment is given by Habicht (1989: 341–43).

The Roman historian Tacitus presents a view which has also been popular in modern times in a slightly modified form: Antiochus was desirous of converting the Jews from their barbaric ways and exclusive religion to more enlightened and liberal views (*Hist.* 5.8).

11.2. *Hellenization of Antiochus's Empire*

K. J. Rigsby (1980) 'Seleucid Notes', *TAPA* 110: 233–54.

This explanation was a favourite one among 19th-century scholars and still seems to be the explanation advanced in the standard handbook of SCHÜRER (1:147–48). The problem with this is that there is no evidence that Antiochus IV was a greater Hellenizer than his predecessors or that he actively promoted Hellenization for idealistic reasons. The main evidence for his policy was the number of Greek foundations (i.e., native cities allowed to organize themselves as *poleis* 'Greek cities') that occurred during his reign. This has been reckoned as high as fifteen or so, but the actual number may have been rather fewer (Mørkholm 1966: 115–18). In any case, they were fewer than under his predecessors Seleucus I and Antiochus I. After a hiatus of many decades, in which few Greek cities were founded, his father Antiochus III began the practice again, though in a number of cases with both Antiochus III and Antiochus IV, it was a case of *re*foundation rather than a new one. More importantly, the initiative always came from the natives themselves. Far from being forced to adopt a Greek constitution, this was considered an important privilege for which they paid well into the king's coffers. Any encouragement of Hellenization by Antiochus IV was clearly for *political*, not cultural or religious reasons, in each case.

Jerusalem was a *polis* for a number of years from 175 BCE with no religious implications. Even if Antiochus had been pushing a policy of

Hellenization, it would clearly have made no sense to force new religious measures on the Jews. To have done so with the aim of leading Jerusalem to become a *polis* would also have been unusual, since the native cults of other sacred Oriental cities were not disturbed when allowed to be incorporated (Bickerman 1937a: 90–92//1979: 61–62; Tcherikover 1959: 471 n. 9).

Antiochus no doubt wanted his empire unified, and the Greek incorporation of native cities would help with this, but there is no evidence that he forced 'Hellenization' or suppressed native customs. On the contrary, to have done so would not create unity but discontent and strife; it would have been a 'suicide' policy, as Bringmann (1983: 103, 146) notes. Appeal is often made to the statement of 1 Macc. 1.41-43 that Antiochus sent a decree to all his subjects to abandon their native customs. Yet this statement is incredible for two reasons: (1) there is no corroborating evidence that such a decree was issued by Antiochus; (2) there is no reason to think that the various peoples in the Seleucid empire would abandon their local customs more easily than the Jews. Why should the ancient nation of the Phoenicians give up their long-established customs, their gods, their culture more readily than their Jewish neighbours? On the contrary, it is clear that even when the native peoples became 'Hellenized', they continued to preserve their old culture alongside the Greek (Bickerman 1937a: 90–104//1979: 61–68). Furthermore, there were many Jews in the Seleucid empire outside Palestine, yet it is not clear that they suffered religious infringement or persecution (Bickerman 1937a: 120–24//1979: 79–80).

11.3. *Antiochus's Promotion of the Cult of Zeus*

In some ways, this section could be placed within the one on 'Hellenization' above, but there are certain further twists to the thesis that make it best to enter it separately. This is the argument often advanced that Antiochus promoted the cult of Zeus Olympius and deified himself in the image of Zeus, which was seen as significant in his measures later taken toward Jerusalem. This is originally an older argument that has tended to be discounted by most recent interpreters. However, its revival in the recent monograph by Bernhardt (2017: 166–274) means that it requires an extensive consideration. Briefly, Bernhardt argues that Antiochus promoted the cult of Zeus, combining it with his personal ruler cult, as a way of legitimating his claim to the Seleucid throne. Later, when Judah was seen as revolting against his rule, he imposed the ruler cult on the Jerusalem temple as a means of the Jews affirming their loyalty to him.

This is an important position and needs to be considered in some detail. Bernhardt uses several arguments to establish his position, which are laid out in more detail in another chapter (§15.2.2). The main problem is that not everyone agrees that there is evidence for a special promotion of the Zeus cult by Antiochus. Furthermore, if Antiochus did indeed favour the Zeus cult, it is far from clear what significance this would have.

11.4. Thesis of E. J. Bickerman

One of the most important theories was developed by E. J. Bickerman in 1937 in his *Gott der Makkabäer* (English translation 1979). He broke ranks with many of the writers on the Maccabaean revolt and the general consensus of the time. This puts the blame solidly on the 'extreme Hellenists', i.e., Menelaus and the Tobiads (though at times he also refers to Jason in a way that suggests he was to be included with Menelaus). The 'Hellenists' were attempting to create an enlightened Yahwism in which the degenerate and anachronistic accretions (i.e., circumcision, food taboos, purity regulations) were removed and the pristine original could once more shine forth (cf. Strabo 16.2.35-37). The barriers which had separated Jews from the surrounding world would then be removed. The reformed religion thus emerging was in many ways parallel with the Reform Judaism which arose in the 19th century (cf. Bickerman 1937a: 132//1979: 86–87; Bringmann 1983: 110–11). Several statements in the primary sources are important for this argument: Dan. 11.30, 32 refer to the concourse of Antiochus with those Jews who 'forsake the covenant', a statement paralleled in 1 Macc. 1.11. According to Josephus it was Menelaus who 'had compelled his nation to violate their own laws' (*Ant.* 12.9.7 §385). 2 Maccabees 13.3-8 also has Menelaus more or less putting Antiochus up to what was done.

This theory has great ingenuity and has been accepted by Hengel (1974: 1:287–303), yet it has also suffered extensive criticism from other eminent specialists (a fact to which Hengel gives far too little attention), especially by Heinemann (1938), Tcherikover (1959: 183–85) and Bringmann (1983: 103–11); cf. also Goldstein (1983a: 99–103). Tcherikover asks why Menelaus should be made into the fanatical ideologue that Antiochus was not. Menelaus was interested in power, not an idealized syncretistic religion. He was not a sophisticated philosopher or historian of religion. While the account which associates him with temple robbery (2 Macc. 4.39-42) may contain an element of slander, it certainly suggests an individual more concerned with personal gain and advancement than the ideals of religious innovation. Also, while Menelaus is said to have led

Israel to sin, and while the Jews themselves are blamed for the Hellenistic reform, only Antiochus's name is associated with the persecution, and no religious slogans are connected with the reform. Hengel, in his defence of Bickerman, also seems to rely too much on the statements of hostile sources about the actual motives of the 'renegades' instead of recognizing that we have inherited a very tendentious interpretation.

11.5. *Thesis of V. A. Tcherikover*

As well as criticizing the theories of Bickerman and others, Tcherikover (1959: 186–203) advances his own explanation. He argues that resistance to Hellenization had already developed in Jerusalem, led by the Hasidim. When Jason attempted to retake the city during Antiochus's second invasion of Egypt, Menelaus fled to the Akra; it was the Hasidic-led faction of the people who drove Jason out of the city and attempted to restore the status quo which had prevailed under Onias III. This revolt caused Antiochus to take and sack Jerusalem on his way back from Egypt, but the revolt must have flared up again after he left, and it was necessary to send Apollonius with troops to Jerusalem to install a military colony or *cleruchy*. These troops, probably of Syrian origin, were also citizens of the *polis* of Jerusalem. They wanted to carry on worshipping their own native deities but also had no desire to offend the local god. Thus, they set up their own worship in the Jerusalem temple. Menelaus could hardly refuse this since it was part of the inherent logic of abolishing the old constitution, but in the eyes of pious Jews the temple was desecrated and they ceased to worship there.

Many Jewish inhabitants of Jerusalem had already fled, either because of having their property confiscated or as a form of passive resistance. Desecration of the temple caused further Jewish resistance. Antiochus saw that religion was the basis of the new revolt. The Torah had become the watchword of Jewish resistance and had to be extirpated, so he issued decrees prohibiting the practice of Judaism in Palestine. (Tcherikover seems uncertain as to whether Jews outside Palestine were affected; while not arguing that they were, he appears to allow that they might have been.) Thus, the revolt was not a response to the persecution, but persecution the response to the revolt.

Hengel's criticism of Tcherikover is valid but hardly does justice to the full range of the argument (Hengel 1974: 1:287; cf. also Goldstein 1983a: 98–99). One point is the emphasis which Tcherikover places on the role of the Hasidim. He himself reconstructs the Hasidim according to the model of the rabbinic sage (cf. Tcherikover 1959: 125–26, 196–97), but this is unjustified (§6.1). Another problem is the assumption that the only Hellenizers were the upper class while the common people were basically anti-Hellenistic; in fact Tcherikover's description of the aims of Menelaus and the Tobiads (Tcherikover 1959: 201–3) seems to come close to representing them as the ideologues, something that he denies to Bickerman. Finally, Tcherikover's assumption that the occupying force in Jerusalem was a cleruchy of native Syrian soldiers now seems unlikely (Bar-Kochva 1989: 92–105, 438–44).

11.6. *Thesis of J. A. Goldstein*

In a lengthy section of his introduction, Goldstein (1976: 104–60) attempts to tackle the problem in a different way. He points out how various foreign cults were frequently suppressed in Rome during the republican period. This was especially true of the Dionysus (Bacchus) cult. During the time that he was a hostage in Rome, Antiochus would have seen several expulsions of foreign cults. Thus, when Antiochus became involved with the Jews, he identified their cult with that of Dionysus, something which was frequently done by outsiders. Seeing that their religion seemed to be the basis of their revolts against him, he simply followed the Roman model and attempted to suppress the religion which he saw as the basis of the 'Jewish problem'. On the other hand, he also attempted to impose a religious reform, a 'return' to what he thought was the older and more pure form of Judaism without its ritualistic accretions. Menelaus is to some extent exonerated in that he was not in agreement with the imposed cult and 'dragged his feet' in implementing it until Antiochus sent other officials to do the job.

Goldstein's thesis attempts to resolve the major problem: why would religious suppression accompany a rebellion which was a political matter. Already Tcherikover (1959: 199) had pointed out that cults could be suppressed if they seemed to be the basis of revolution, so Goldstein's idea is not *prima facie* improbable. On the other hand, it makes Antiochus into an ideologue, which has already been shown above to be problematic. A number of the criticisms levelled at Bickerman would also apply here. Further, his discussion is filled with the language of conjecture: 'we may suppose...'; 'Did Antiochus...?'; 'Could the Jews have...?; 'If this reconstruction is correct...' One of his points was that Antiochus attempted to regulate the Dionysus cult, yet his sole argument was a tenuous interpretation of something to do with the Babylonian Nergal cult (Goldstein 1976: 128–29). His interpretation of Daniel often depends on an emended reading. Much of the support for his thesis – ingenious and learned as it is – is of a similar insubstantial nature. This hardly gives confidence that there is a solid basis for it, especially when the data are lacking at crucial points.

In a refreshingly self-critical section of his second volume, Goldstein (1983a: 98–112) considered problems with and criticisms of his original reconstruction. His final thesis there has much in common with Bickerman's. That is, the imposed religion was a 'heterodox Judaism', by which he means a type of polytheistic Judaism practiced in pre-exilic times, at Elephantine, and otherwise known of from hints in the sources. Parallel to Tcherikover, he suggests that this religion was most probably introduced by the garrison placed in the Akra (the 'fortifiers of strongholds' in his interpretation of Dan. 11.39), which he argues was made up of Jewish soldiers (perhaps from Egypt) who practiced this sort of Judaism. This included the use of cult stones and pillars (*maṣṣēvôt*) in worship. These Jews were among those who advised Antiochus on his attempt to reform the Jerusalem cult. As will be obvious, a number of the criticisms of Bickerman and Tcherikover also apply to Goldstein's thesis.

11.7. *Thesis of K. Bringmann*

One can characterize Bringmann's thesis (1983: especially 120–40) as by and large a combination of the best insights of Bickerman and Tcherikover, but the resulting synthesis includes Bringmann's own original contributions and thus represents a new thesis. Some of the main elements seem to be the following:

- Antiochus was no crusading ideologue but a practical politician who needed money. He allowed the 'Hellenistic reform' of Jason because it brought money and because it seemed a way of resolving the intra-Jewish conflict between Onias III and Simon the Tobiad.
- Jason's reform did not in any way affect the traditional Jewish worship. On the contrary, Jason and the priesthood had a major interest in maintaining the purity and sanctity of the temple since this was the main source of revenue for the priests (including Jason himself [Bringmann 1983: 74–82]).
- When Menelaus displaced Jason, he had no reason to continue the Hellenistic reform since it was supported mainly by Jason's followers. Thus, far from taking Hellenization further Menelaus actually brought the condition of being a *polis* for Jerusalem to an end (Bringmann 1983: 93–94).

- Menelaus had promised Antiochus a good deal of money but was soon in difficulties regarding payment. A ready solution was to begin selling the temple vessels, but this brought a revolt of the people and the death of Lysimachus, Menelaus's brother. Menelaus had little support among the Jews but maintained his position with the help of Antiochus's troops.
- During Antiochus's second expedition to Egypt, when Jason attempted to take back the priesthood by force, Antiochus intervened to drive off Jason's forces and then proceeded to establish a military colony in Jerusalem.
- The military settlers may have been Syrian, though they could also have come from Asia Minor. They naturally brought their native worship of Baal Shamem ('Lord of heaven') with them. The Jerusalem sanctuary was dedicated to Zeus, but this was no doubt simply the Greek term for Baal Shamem, who could also be identified with Yahweh. The presence of the troops and their cult made the sanctuary 'unclean' in the eyes of most Jews.
- Menelaus was not an ideologue (contra Bickerman), but determined to maintain power at all costs. One way of doing this was to institute a new cult in the Jerusalem temple, which would break the tie with the old covenant as well as the constraints imposed by the hereditary priesthood. The peculiar measures in the new religion forced on Judaea was created by Menelaus himself. He chose the Syrian cult for pragmatic reasons, but there were important differences, since the Syrians also practised circumcision and avoided pork. In certain ways, the new measures were standing Judaism on its head (e.g., sacrificing pigs which had previously been forbidden). Antiochus accepted Menelaus's proposals, partly because he had no choice but to support Menelaus and partly because he was unaware of the likely repercussions. He probably did not have advisors knowledgeable in Jewish matters other than Menelaus himself.

Thus, the religious measures owed something to the Syrian military cleruchy as proposed by Tcherikover (since the basis of the cult was Syrian) and were mainly instigated by Menelaus (as Bickerman argued). Yet the official decrees came from Antiochus, since he was the one issuing them (on Menelaus's advice), but his main concern was to stabilize the province and bring it to heel under the high priest officially designated by him.

Several objections can be brought against Bringmann's thesis. One such objection could be raised by asking, Why would Menelaus have created a religion which forced on the Jews practices which contravened such deeply ingrained elements of Judaism as circumcision and abstinence from pork? If his aim was simply to maintain power, this seems a strange way of going about it. To his credit, Bringmann has partially dealt with the question but not completely satisfactorily. Another problem is the proposed military colony in Jerusalem and the Akra, which is so important to his thesis. As with Tcherikover, none of the sources mention the role of a military colony. Furthermore, Bar-Kochva (1989: 92–105, 438–44) has also argued against a military colony composed of Syrian troops, which undermines one aspect of Bringmann's thesis. It also now seems unlikely that the cult in the temple was a native one (§15.2.3).

11.8. *Thesis of Erich Gruen*

Erich Gruen focuses on the unrest in Jerusalem, downplaying Hellenization. He also dispenses with a folk uprising. The 'Day of Eleusis' was a bitter blow for Antiochus; therefore, when Jason effected his coup, Antiochus launched an attack to put down the unrest. He also established the Akra with a military garrison, all as a way of restoring justice and order in the kingdom. Thus, his actions with regard to Jerusalem and the temple were a way of displaying power and also showing greater strength than ever. Gruen's thesis is taken over by Doran, and Seeman develops certain points (2013: 89–93). Several questions arise. The 'Day of Eleusis' was no doubt seen as humiliating by some outsiders, but was it for Antiochus? As suggested elsewhere it may actually have got him out of a serious dilemma (§15.1). It is clear, as Gruen shows, that it was important to Antiochus to demonstrate his power and authority. But why do so by attacking the religious institutions? As Seeman also acknowledges (2013: 92), an attack on religion was not likely to be effective in demonstrating his power. Finally, the measures taken seem to show an intimate knowledge of Jewish religion, yet Judah was not that important for the Seleucid empire.

11.9. *Thesis of Anathea Portier-Young*

Anathea Portier-Young bases her thesis on postcolonial theory, primarily the concept of 'state terror'. The Seleucid conquest of the Levant led to community tensions in Judah, including the establishment of a garrison and a high tribute burden. In the 170s Seleucid control of the holy places in Coele-Syria and Phoenicia let to increased conflict with various Jewish groups (Portier-Young 2011: 79–91). Portier-Young gives greater weight to Hellenization than Gruen. Establishment of the gymnasium and the ephebate did not mean Jews' giving up their own identity but did open the door to the total opposite: Greek culture (Portier-Young 2013: 91–114). The 'Day of Eleusis' was not such a catastrophe, but it did lead to a people's revolt, which required Antiochus to demonstrate his might over his kingdom. The attack on religion and the persecution to replace Jewish identity, history, and social memory was a means of making a new world order. But if securing Coele-Syria and Phoenicia was his main goal, why is the supposed people's revolt (rejected by Gruen and others) a welcome excuse for demonstrating his power? Especially problematic is the concept of 'state terrorism', which seems to come from modern situations such as Argentina in the 1970s. The concept contradicts the actual observed focus on acceptance and promotion of local traditions made by the Seleucids (Ma 1999). The same applies to reading Daniel and Enoch as 'resistance literature'. Some aspects of this thesis look too much linked to modern terrorism and colonization rather than the situation in antiquity.

11.10. *Thesis of Steven Weitzman and Sylvie Honigman*

We begin with the thesis of S. Weitzman on which Honigman partially depends by her own acknowledgment. Weitzman appealed to Hayden White on the question of the relationship of fiction to historical narrative. He related the pre-Hasmonaean narrative to a set of Babylonian texts which have a similar narration of temple plundering, abolition of festivals and rededication of temples by kings. The purpose of the persecution narrative was to legitimate the Hasmonaeans and their taking over of the high priesthood. A similar aim underlies the establishment of the Hanukka festival. The religious persecution of Antiochus IV is largely a literary creation. On the other hand, Weitzman does not deny that decisive events took place in Jerusalem under Antiochus IV. The question of the relationship of fact and fiction is left open. He also acknowledges that it is unclear how the Babylonian material reached and was taken up by the Maccabaean writers.

In her 2014 study S. Honigman took the thesis of S. Weizman further. She began with an argument about the aims of 2 Maccabees, with the thesis that it was dynastic history; also, it was not written by a Jew from the diaspora but one living in Jerusalem. Then she moved on to economic matters, pointing out that a financial reform had apparently already begun under Seleucus IV but continued to be developed under Antiochus IV (Honigman 2014: 316–61). It was Seleucus's reforms to regulate the temples and taxes more closely in Coele-Syria and Phoenicia that led to the confrontation between Heliodorus and the Jerusalem high priest Onias III (2 Macc. 3). Heliodorus had been somehow thwarted in his attempt to take Hyrcanus's money, and Antiochus wished to have Onias removed from office. Having his brother Jason displace him was a way of solving the difficulty. The extra tribute payment was part of Antiochus's new tax regime, not something that Jason offered freely. Honigman also argues that no religious suppression took place. This was a literary construct created by the writers of 1 and 2 Maccabees. Antiochus's measures were political, not religious. She accepts that the temple was polluted by alien sacrifices and an alien cult, but these were instituted for political reasons. Antiochus had to establish his authority in the face of the Judaean rebellion against his rule.

Honigman's far-reaching reconstruction requires a detailed response. Attempts to give one are presented at various points in the final chapters (§14.4.1; §14.4.4; §15.2.2).

11.11. *Socio-Economic Causes*

The main discussion here is whether the Maccabean resistance was a class war or 'peasant's revolt'. See above at §5.1 for a discussion of this and other related questions.

11.12. *Conclusions*

No theory has so far been able to command a consensus of scholars, despite the ingenuity of some hypotheses. Some suggestions can be ruled out in the present stage of study, however, and some clearly have more merit than others. Both the theories of the two giants – Bickerman and Tcherikover – have a great deal to commend them, yet occasion some profound disagreements as well. Also, Goldstein's thesis may have an important contribution to make even though the theory as such seems improbable. The various explanations are not necessarily mutually exclusive, which points us toward some sort of synthesis. Bringmann has indeed come up with an important synthesis.

Recent discussions, however, have tended to focus on particular points. Honigman, Gruen and Portier-Young in particular have emphasized Antiochus's need to prove his authority. He had to be seen to take effective action, especially after the 'Day of Eleucis' when many thought he had lost face. Although all the theories have loose ends (which theory does not?), they seem to get us closer to an answer. But what none of the theses establishes is why Antiochus would have attempted to suppress the practice of Judaism. It was not uncommon in antiquity to loot or even destroy temples. The statues of the gods might be taken away or even melted down, but no attempt was ever made to force the native peoples to change their worship or give up their local customs. In the absence of a consensus at the present time, the following points seem fairly solid:

- The Jews were already a part of Hellenistic world and no different from other *ethnoi* of the ancient Near East in the general process of Hellenization which had begun with Alexander.
- Antiochus did have an initial problem with legitimation. He enacted several measures that aided this, including marrying Seleucid IV's widow and adopting his nephew (Seleucid's son) as his son. This may also have been why he promoted the cult of Zeus Olympius, although his immediate Seleucid predecessors had favoured Dionysus as the dynastic deity. As suggested by Bunge (1973), both Seleucus's son and the Ptolemaic king Ptolemy VI were seen as the legitimate successors of Seleucus IV by many, and they promoted the traditional cult of Dionysus. Yet Antiochus IV, although celebrating Zeus Olympius on some of his coins, did so only on the ones minted at Antioch and Ake-Ptolemais. The coins from these two mints were the main ones servicing his army, but Antiochus's other coins tended to have Dionysus. Thus, Zeus was pictured on these to promote loyalty to Antiochus. Yet Antiochus's dealings with the Jews, as with other peoples, was on a political level with political aims, not religious or ideological.
- The initial Hellenistic reform of Jason was met with enthusiasm by a significant (if minority) section of the population and was certainly not actively opposed by the rest.
- Judaism as a religion was not impaired under Jason. While in the eyes of some very conservative individuals Jason's actions may have looked impious, we have to keep in mind that 2 Maccabees was written in the aftermath of the religious persecutions and the Hasmonaean successes. When the rhetoric is ignored and only the actual data examined, it is clear that the basic Jewish observances in and out of the temple continued. There was no devotion to pagan deities nor any sort of blatant breach of Jewish law.

- The argument that there was no persecution is not in and of itself impossible. Some of the persecution and martyrdom examples in 1 and 2 Maccabees seem to be inventions. Yet a full consideration of all the sources suggests that there was some individual persecutions, in addition to the pollution of the temple and the suppression of the cult, which were also a type of persecution (see further at §15.2.2).
- Menelaus was a different sort of person and brought a significant twist to matters. There is evidence that his actions eventually met with resistance, both from the ruling council of the *polis* and the ordinary people who rioted and killed his brother Lysimachus.
- Whatever the exact reason for Antiochus's anti-Judaism decrees, some Jews seem to have been involved in some way with the anti-Judaism decrees. Antiochus was concerned with politics, and religious matters were only incidental to his main goals which were those of most politicians: money and power.
- What is not explained is why a religious persecution; it was something new in history. We are all familiar with religious persecution, but this by and large comes from later times and tends to be carried out by monotheistic religions. For an ancient polytheist to engage in religious persecution appears to be unprecedented.

Chapter 12

RELIGION: TEMPLE, SCRIPTURE, BELIEF AND PRACTICE

This chapter endeavours to summarize religion and religious beliefs during the period from about 175 to 4 BCE. It continues earlier descriptions found in *HJJSTP 1* (209–61) and *HJJSTP 2* (225–65). Nothing new can be said on some of the earlier topics, in which case they are omitted here, though they may appear again in the forthcoming *HJJSTP 4*. For example, much of the description of the temple and its cult does not seem to have changed in this period and need not be repeated. In other cases, beliefs and practices continued to develop in a way attested in sources for this period.

12.1. *The Temple and Synagogues*

The temple continued to be the centre of the Jewish religion and even the culture of Judaea. Its importance became abundantly clear when it, first, became the subject of strife over who would be high priest, and then, secondly, when it was polluted following the decrees of Antiochus IV. This is discussed in Chapter 14 in detail and need not be repeated here. Once the temple was purified and the cult restored, the temple was clearly of major concern to the people and the subsequent Hasmonaean rulers. 2 Maccabees shows the centrality of the temple to Jewish worship (§3.1). Also, the high priest became the leader of the people and, once independence was declared, the ruler of the nation. According to Josephus (*War* 1.3.1 §70; *Ant.* 13.11.1 §301), Aristobulus I was the first one to adopt the title of 'king', though some have speculated that John Hyrcanus might have used it. As far as we know, however, the basic temple hierarchy and organization and operation of the cult continued as in previous centuries. Although in the time of Herod a major project of rebuilding, expansion and beautification of the temple took place, the basic operation of temple and cult appears to have continued as before (§18.4.2). For the cult set up in Jerusalem when the temple was polluted, see §15.2.3; for the Leontopolis temple, see §10.2.1.3.

Synagogues were originally a diaspora institution. We find them attested already in the 3rd century BCE in Egypt (*HJJSTP 2*: 234–38). There is no evidence of them in Judaea, however, until much later. We have references to them in sources in the 1st century CE (see *HJJSTP 4*), and the Theodotus inscription suggests that a synagogue existed in Jerusalem in the 1st century BCE (*HJJSTP 4*; though this dating has been contested, it seems the most likely one). It is hardly surprising that the need for a meeting place, either for study or communal worship would have first been felt in the diaspora. Although regular attendance at the temple was possible only for those Jews living in the vicinity of Jerusalem, Jews further afield in Palestine could still have attended at one or more of the annual festivals. Thus, the picture given in Lk. 2.41 of Jesus's parents going to Jerusalem every year for Passover seems a feasible one. But the synagogue does not seem to have been a central religious institution in Judaea until near the end of the Second Temple period.

12.2. Development of the Biblical Texts

D. Barthélemy (1963) *Les devanciers d'Aquila*; **S. P. Brock** (1996) *The Recensions of the Septuagint Version of I Samuel*; **D. J. A. Clines** (1984) *The Esther Scroll: The Story of the Story*; **J. Cook** (1997) *The Septuagint of Proverbs: Jewish and/or Hellenistic Proverbs?*; **F. M. Cross** (1964) 'The History of the Biblical Text in the Light of Discoveries in the Judaean Desert', *HTR* 57: 281–99; **idem** (1966) 'The Contribution of the Qumran Discoveries to the Study of the Biblical Text', *IEJ* 16: 81–95; **idem** (1975) 'The Evolution of a Theory of Local Texts', in F. M. Cross and S. Talmon (eds), *Qumran and the History of the Biblical Text*, 306–20; **F. M. Cross and S. Talmon (eds)** (1975) *Qumran and the History of the Biblical Text*; **K. De Troyer** (2000) *The End of the Alpha Text of Esther: Translation and Narrative Technique in MT 8:1-17, LXX 8:1-17, and AT 7:14-41*; **C. V. Dorothy** (1997) *The Books of Esther: Structure, Genre and Textual Integrity*; **L. L. Grabbe** (1977) *Comparative Philology and the Text of Job: A Study in Methodology*; **idem** (1998) *Ezra and Nehemiah*; **idem** (2006) 'The Law, the Prophets, and the Rest: The State of the Bible in Pre-Maccabean Times', *DSD* 13: 319–38; **idem** (2009) 'Jubilees and the Samaritan Tradition', in G. Boccaccini and G. Ibba (eds), *Enoch and the Mosaic Torah: The Evidence of Jubilees*, 145–59; **S. P. Jeansonne** (1988) *The Old Greek Translation of Daniel 7–12*; **S. Jellicoe** (1968) *The Septuagint and Modern Study*; **K. H. Jobes** (1996) *The Alpha-Text of Esther: Its Character and Relationship to the Masoretic Text*; **A. Lacocque** (1999) 'The Different

Versions of Esther', *Biblical Interpretation* 7: 301–22; **T. McLay** (1996) *The OG and Th Versions of Daniel*; **T. J. Meadowcroft** (1995) *Aramaic Daniel and Greek Daniel: A Literary Comparison*; **J. Sanderson** (1986) *An Exodus Scroll from Qumran: 4QpaleoExod^m and the Samaritan Tradition*; **S. Schorch (ed.)** (2018) *The Samaritan Pentateuch: A Critical Editio Maior: III Leviticus*; **S. Talmon** (1970) 'The Old Testament Text', in P. R. Ackroyd and C. F. Evans (eds), *Cambridge History of the Bible: Volume 1*, 159–99; **idem** (1975) 'The Textual Study of the Bible – A New Outlook', in F. M. Cross and S. Talmon (eds), *Qumran and the History of the Biblical Text*, 321–400; **E. Tov** (2011) *Textual Criticism of the Hebrew Bible*; **E. C. Ulrich** (1978) *The Qumran Text of Samuel and Josephus*; **idem** (1999) *The Dead Sea Scrolls and the Origins of the Bible*; **B. K. Waltke** (1965) *Prolegomena to the Samaritan Pentateuch*; **idem** (1970) 'The Samaritan Pentateuch and the Text of the Old Testament', in J. B. Payne (ed.), *New Perspectives on the Old Testament*, 212–39.

The understanding of the text's development has become transformed for this period because of the Dead Sea Scrolls, even though there are still many questions unanswered. The biblical manuscripts, with at least fragments of every book in the Hebrew canon except perhaps Esther, originated almost entirely in the period between 175 BCE and 68 CE, though with some going back to 200 BCE or so in some cases (according to some palaeographers). An overview of textual development was given in *HJJSTP 2* (247–53). Here the focus will be on the text as it was found in the Hasmonaean and Herodian periods, as far as it is represented by textual discoveries.

Before we start with the details of the text, the issue of the Hebrew Bible canon needs a comment. As was noted in *HJJSTP 2* (245–47), Ben Sira had indicated that many of the books that make up the present Hebrew Bible were considered authoritative by about 200 BCE. We have no comparable list for our period, but the contents of the Qumran scrolls indicate that at least for that community there was no definitive list of authoritative books. If there was such a circumscribed collection, we have no indication of it. Judging from the number of copies of some writings, such as *1 Enoch*, the authoritative writings for the community included books that are not part of the later Hebrew canon. If some Jewish communities had a prescriptive list of writings at this time, we have no evidence of it. In other words, we are back to Ben Sira's account (in 44–49) for a possible list of 'scriptural' writings in temple circles in this period.

What we need to keep in mind is the importance of this period for the development of the text. It seems that perhaps beginning in the 3rd century major textual evolution took place in many of the books that became the Hebrew Bible. The Qumran scrolls, as well as some other textual witnesses, give us data to understand this. For example, representatives of all three of the main text-types previously known in Jewish history – the Masoretic text (MT), the LXX and the Samaritan Pentateuch (SP) – were in use by those producing the Scrolls, yet with many Scrolls showing textual readings not found in these three basic types. We also find developments relating to biblical translations, especially the Greek.

It is not always easy to delineate a particular text-type, but it could be misleading to assume that all the various biblical manuscripts found at Qumran could be shoehorned into one of the three main text-types previously known. This has been attempted (e.g., Cross in Cross and Talmon 1975: 177–95, 278–92, 306–20), but there are good arguments to accept that there is greater diversity than this among the Qumran manuscripts (cf. Tov 2011). We cannot put this great diversity at Qumran down to the unofficial eccentricities of a breakaway sect. On the contrary, it is clear that a priestly writer such as Josephus was quite willing to use the LXX text (sometimes in its Lucianic version) as the basis of his history even when it differs considerably from the MT. For example, his Esther story is based on the LXX version with its variations and extra content, and his story of the initial return after the exile is based on 1 Esdras (cf. Grabbe 1998: 81–86).

Good examples of the Masoretic-type of consonantal text (the indication of vowels and accents by written points is medieval) established that that tradition was not a late invention by the Masoretes as some had argued. In a number of cases, even the main textual divisions were shown to have a history going back at least a millennium before the earliest dated MT manuscripts (see the survey of studies in Grabbe 1977: 179–97). Even the famous long Isaiah scroll from Cave 1 (1QIs^a) is basically a MT text-type, despite the impression sometimes given in early studies, while its fellow Isaiah scroll (1QIs^b) is even closer to the known MT.

We also find the SP – or better, the 'proto-Samaritan' Pentateuch – among the Qumran scrolls (4Q22 = 4QpaleoExod^m; Sanderson 1986). These are often referred to as 'proto-Samaritan' because they are not specifically Samaritan; i.e., the unique sectarian readings (e.g., the extra addition to the Decalogue referring to Mt Gerizim) are not present (where these passages survive), suggesting that we have a stage of the SP before it was taken over and adapted by the Samaritan community. This leads to the conclusion that most of the peculiarities of the SP were not developed by the Samaritans themselves but had already originated in another (Jewish?) context and were then taken over by the Samaritan community for whatever reason. It is now agreed that the SP has a long history, going back to Second Temple times. More difficult is its relationship to the MT and the LXX. Its oft agreement with the LXX has led some to suggest that it was the original on which the LXX was based, but this is a superficial judgment since the SP is actually closer to the MT than the LXX in its primary readings (Waltke 1965, 1970). Many SP passages indicate expansion from other sections of the text, which gives it greater bulk without increasing the amount of primary material (e.g., Exod. 32.10-11, expanded by an addition from Deut. 9.20). This secondary expansion is a natural process attested in most texts that have been copied over centuries, biblical and otherwise. The SP resemblance to the LXX is primarily caused by the secondary expansions that they share. One of the main areas where the SP, the LXX and the MT (and even *Jubilees*!) disagree is over the genealogies in Genesis 5 (Grabbe 2009).

There are a few fragments of the LXX in Greek at Qumran (4Q119-122 = 4QLXXLev[a,b], 4QLXXNum, 4QDeut). Yet the LXX text-type in Hebrew is also represented at Qumran. That is, other manuscripts, although in Hebrew, show a text in line with that known from the LXX. One of the main examples comes from the book of Jeremiah. The different order and text of the LXX Jeremiah, for example, are attested in 4QJer[a] (4Q70). In other cases, readings known from the LXX have been found in texts that otherwise belong to another text-type. Thus, the Scrolls have well established that readings unique to the LXX are in many cases due to the use of a different underlying Hebrew reading and not the product of the translator. In most books of the Bible the differences between the LXX and the MT affect mainly individual words or phrases; however, in some books the LXX can be said to represent not just a different text-type but almost a different version of the book. For example, the LXX text is one-eighth shorter in Job and one-sixth shorter in Jeremiah, while the LXX in Proverbs is often different from the MT (cf. Cook 1997).

It appears that with time, attempts were made to revise the LXX text, apparently to bring it more in line with the developing Hebrew text. This led first of all to more than one version of the LXX itself. One revision which was probably pre-70 is the so-called 'Lucian revision', named for the patristic figure around AD 400 once thought to have created the revision. However, the basic Lucian revision is attested in texts from Jewish circles long before the historical Lucian: for example, it seems clear that Josephus used the Lucianic text in Greek as the basis of his account paralleling Samuel and Kings (Ulrich 1978; Brock 1996). This suggests that the patristic figure may have had something to do with the final revision but did not initiate the first revision, which was probably Jewish in origin.

There is also evidence of another revision now called the *kaige* version of the text (Barthélemy 1963), named from the Greek particle used to translate the Hebrew particle *wĕgam* 'and also', which is one of the characteristics of this version. It was a more literal representation of the Hebrew text. The *kaige* version used to be associated with the patristic writer Theodotion of the 2nd century CE; however, it is clear that the basic 'Theodotion' text was in existence long before the historical figure. Again, modern scholarship is more or less unanimous that the *kaige* represents a Jewish revision of the LXX to bring it more into line with the Hebrew text. This text may later have been revised by the historical Theodotion to improve the Greek (Brock 1996).

Rather than simply the existence of several textual variations among the Qumran scrolls, we may actually be observing a text still growing organically. The fluidity of the text, at least for certain books, is well illustrated from some recent studies. This is exemplified in the book of 1 Samuel, for which three versions seem to be attested: 4QSam[a] showing the fullest text, followed by the LXX and finally the MT as the shortest. The Greek Daniel is known in two versions, the older LXX version preserved in only a few manuscripts, and the later 'Theodotion' version which is found in most manuscripts. Although the differences are often explained on the basis of a differing Hebrew or Aramaic text (e.g., Jeansonne 1988; contrast McLay 1996), others have argued that there is at least a strong theological basis for the differences in many passages (Meadowcroft 1996). Another example is Esther, which also has two Greek versions, the LXX and the alpha-text (sometimes known as the L- or Lucianic text), which has been explained on the basis of differing Hebrew texts (Clines 1984; Jobes 1996; Dorothy 1997). De Troyer, however, has argued that the alpha-text is a revision to interpret the book in the light of events in the time of Agrippa I (De Troyer 1997; also Lacocque 1999).

The rabbinic Targums will be discussed in *HJJSTP 4*. Yet the practice of translating some portion of biblical books into Aramaic is clearly attested already for our period. We know this because remains have been found at Qumran (4QtgJob = 4Q157; 4QtgLev = 4Q156; 11QtgJob = 11Q10), but since the finds are so far limited to Leviticus and Job, this does not suggest that a targum of the whole Bible had been made. The targumic material from Qumran represents a fairly literal translation and gives no support for the idea that a paraphrastic, midrashic targum analogous to *Targum Pseudo-Jonathan* (and to a lesser extent to *Neofiti*) was in circulation. Part of the argument about the targums has to do with their supposed origin in the synagogue services. This is a complicated question, but the Aramaic translations from Qumran look like learned translations, the product of a scribe or an academy of some sort, not the mere collection of a popular oral tradition.

The points made in this section can be summarized as follows:

- We have no information on a 'canon' of Hebrew Bible books at this time. The implied list in Ben Sira 44–49 probably prevailed in some circles (such as among temple personnel?), but the variety of writings at Qumran does not suggest a fixed collection, at least not one corresponding to our present Hebrew Bible.
- The existence and use of a number of text-types among the Jews at least until the 1st century CE is clearly demonstrated.
- There is a still a question of how many text-types there were. The argument that all the variants can be reduced to three is not convincing.
- It is clear that some biblical books circulated in more than one version which differed in more than just the normal variants associated with textual development. This includes Samuel, Jeremiah, Daniel and Esther.
- We have no evidence supporting a preference for the MT text-type or any other text-type in areas outside Qumran at this time.

12.3. *Beliefs and Practice*

Just as most of the religious beliefs (from our point of view, since they may not have thought of them as a separate 'religion', different from 'ancestral traditions') associated with the Jews continued from the Persian period into the time of Greek rule, so the beliefs of the early Hellenistic period generally continued into the later Hellenistic period and to the time of Roman rule. We see a gradual evolution of 'Judaism', i.e., some beliefs remained much the same while others developed slowly. There were not a lot of major innovations, but there were some important new emphases, if not innovations as such. For some topics (e.g., 'the Deity') see the discussions in *HJJSTP 1* and *2*.

12.3.1. *Circumcision*

S. J. D. Cohen (1999) *The Beginnings of Jewishness*; **B. Eckhardt** (2012) '"An Idumean, That Is, a Half-Jew" Hasmoneans and Herodians between Ancestry and Merit', in B. Eckhardt (ed.), *Jewish Identity and Politics between the Maccabees and Bar Kokhba*, 91–115; **idem** (2013) *Ethnos und Herrschaft*.

Circumcision has a long history in Israel and Judaism. It was probably the common practice of a number of Semitic peoples in the region for thousands of years and is of course mentioned in various passages in the Hebrew Bible. Thus, circumcision was by no means unique to Israel nor to Jewish identity. Several biblical passages do in fact put a good deal of weight on circumcision (e.g., the circumcision of Abraham and his household in Gen. 17 and the Shechemites in Gen. 37). Yet circumcision is surprisingly absent from whole stretches of the Hebrew Bible. Even Ezra and Nehemiah do not mention it.

It becomes a major indication of Jewish identity only in this period of the 2nd century BCE, however, at least as far as the extant texts indicate. Circumcision among the Jews is seldom if ever mentioned in references to the Jews in Near Eastern, Greek, or Roman writings before this period. Suddenly, it bursts forth in the books of Maccabees as a *sine qua non* of the 'proper' Jew. It is first mentioned in 1 Macc. 1.48 when the king's decree supposedly forbids circumcision, and in 1.60-62 where women are put to death for circumcising their sons. Then in 1 Macc. 2.46 one of the first acts of Mattathias and his followers is to go through Judah circumcising all the uncircumcised boys that they find. The culmination of this practice comes when various groups living in the borders of the expanding Hasmonaean kingdom are required to convert to Jewish practices, which includes circumcision. This is the case with the Idumaeans under John Hyrcanus (§9.1) and the Ituraeans under Aristobulus I (§9.2). Circumcision appears at this point as one of the major identifying signs of being Jewish and of course continues until modern times.

12.3.2. *Ritual Purity and Mikva'ot*

> **A. M. Berlin** (2005) 'Jewish Life before the Revolt: The Archaeological Evidence', *JSJ* 36: 417–70; **P. F. Craffert** (2000) 'Digging up *Common Judaism* in Galilee: *Miqva'ot* at Sepphoris as a Test Case', *Neotestamentica* 34: 39–55; **E. Netzer** (1962) 'Ancient Ritual Baths (*Miqvaot*) in Jericho', *Jerusalem Cathedra* 2: 106–19; **E. Netzer (ed.)** (2001) *Hasmonean and Herodian Palaces at Jericho: Final Reports of the 1973–1987 Excavations, Volume I: Stratigraphy and Architecture*; **E. Regev** (2000) 'Pure Individualism: The Idea of Non-Priestly Purity in Ancient Judaism', *JSJ* 31: 176–202; **idem** (2013) *The Hasmoneans: Ideology, Archaeology, Identity*.

Ritual purity was important from the beginning for cultic worship in Israel. The basic regulations for ritual purity are laid down in the book of Leviticus. Yet Israelites were not required to be in a state of purity all the time; indeed, it was not possible. But it was essential to be ritually pure when entering the temple and participating in the cult. Thus, purity was not a new concept in the Hasmonaean period, not by any means. What was new, however, was the *miqveh* (מקוה) or ritual bath, at least according to most archaeologists. In the Hebrew Bible it is 'living water' that purifies, sometimes accompanied by a specific period of time before the person becomes pure (e.g., 'until sunset'). The idea of a ritual bath is a new concept in this period, as far as we know at the present.

The idea that these pools are ritual baths has been challenged, however (cf. the summary and other arguments in Craffert 2000). A. M. Berlin (2005: 451–53) has noted that even among the large majority who accept the concept, there is a 'maximalist position' (the presence of the *miqveh* meant broad acceptance of the purity rules known from rabbinic texts) and a 'minimalist position' (heightened but extra-legal concerns about personal purity by the local residents). The argument is that archaeology has turned up what seem to be the first *miqva'ot* at the Hasmonaean palaces at Jericho and Cypros, the earliest dated perhaps to about the beginning of the 1st century BCE (Netzer 1962; Netzer [ed.] 2001; cf. Regev 2013: 253–55; Berlin 2005: 451–53). According to the excavator, this includes 'treasuries' or pools connected with a conduit to the *miqva'ot* to supply pure water to them. The identification of these pools as *miqva'ot* is accepted here for the present, while it remains to be seen whether the challenges persist.

12.3.3. *Angelic Beings*

> **M. J. Davidson** (1992) *Angels at Qumran: A Comparative Study of 1 Enoch 1–36, 72–108 and Sectarian Writngs from Qumran*; *DDD²*; **L. L. Grabbe** (1987) 'The Scapegoat Ritual: A Study in Early Jewish Interpretation', *JSJ* 18: 152–67; **T. Guerra** (forthcoming) *Encountering Evil: Apotropaic Magic in the Dead Sea Scrolls*; **P. J. Kobelski** (1981) *Melchizedek and Melchireša'*; **M. Mach** (1992) *Entwicklungsstadien des jüdischen Engelglaubens in vorrabbinischer Zeit*.

The question of heavenly beings other than God in the early Hellenistic period was discussed in *HJJSTP 2* (256–58). Here the focus will be on the texts from the later Hellenistic and early Roman period. Although the angelology of *1 Enoch* was touched on, this book is a collection of material that covers from the Ptolemaic to the Roman period and well illustrates the complex Jewish view of the angelic (and demonic) world during this time. The book of *1 Enoch* is one of the richest sources for views about the deity and the spirit world, though it must be kept in mind that the different sections do not necessarily reflect the same set of beliefs or constituency or time period. The *Book of Watchers* (1–36) picture was discussed in *HJJSTP 2* (256–57). The rest of the Enoch tradition, especially the *Similitudes of Enoch*, is similar in theme, if not always in detail. This will be discussed in *HJJSTP 4*.

The late book of Daniel not surprisingly shows a considerable development in its angelology. Two major angelic figures in the book are Michael (Dan. 10.13, 21; 12.1) and Gabriel (Dan. 8.16; 9.21), though it is implied that other angelic beings exist. Demonic figures also seem to occur: Gabriel mentions being opposed by the 'prince of Persia' (Dan. 10.13, 20-21) who was evidently an angelic figure with responsibility for or control over that nation. The picture is not entirely clear, but it appears that each nation has its own angelic guide, with Gabriel and Michael both assigned to the Jews. One might assume that the angels over the other nations are all a part of the heavenly court, but it looks more as if these are now being regarded in some sense as opponents of God.

The texts from Qumran, as might be expected, contain many references to angelic figures (see the survey in Guerra forthcoming). The *Damascus Covenant* has several passages about the main demonic personage Beliel, the first being the 'three nets of Beliel' passage (CD 4.12-21); this Beliel is an opponent of the 'Prince of Lights' (CD 5.17-19). The fallen angels myth known from *1 Enoch* is also alluded to (CD 2.18-21). The 'two spirits' section of the *Community Rule* (1QS 3.13–4.26) speaks of the 'Prince of Lights' who is opposed by the 'Angel of Darkness'; both vie for the control of humanity. The wicked will be punished by 'angels of destruction' (1QS 4.12). The *War Scroll* (1QM; 1Q33; 4Q491-496 = 4QM1-6) envisages an eschatological battle in which the forces of Beliel (the 'sons of darkness') are confronted by the 'sons of light' (see especially 1QM 1), but the angels also participate in the battle (1QM 1.10-11). 4QVisions of Amram[b] (4Q544) has a dispute between angels for control over him. The *Melchizedek Scroll* (11Q13) has a heavenly figure Melchizedek ('king of righteousness'), identified with Michael, who is opposed by a Melchireša' ('king of wickedness'), if the reconstruction is correct (see Kobelsky 1981). Finally, the *Songs of the Sabbath Sacrifice* (4QShirShab = 4Q400-407; 11QShirShab = 11Q17; MasShirShabb) show the praise given to God by the heavenly 'priests'. Interestingly, the name Satan does not occur among the Qumran scrolls.

Demonic figures, including the classic image of the devil, are also found in other texts from this period. *Jubilees* (5.1-11) also mentions the fallen angels myth, so well known from the *Book of Watchers*. It has Noah utter a prayer against demons (*Jub*. 10.1-14). The name Mastema is used for the wicked angelic leader several times (17.15-18; 48.9-19). *Vita Adae et Euae* has a reference to Satan's fall from heaven (12–16). The lost ending of the *Testament of Moses* apparently had a dispute between Michael and Satan, judging from the comments in the New Testament (Jude 9).

12.3.4. *Eschatology and Ideas of Salvation*

> **H. C. C. Cavallin** (1974) *Life after Death: Paul's Argument for the Resurrection of the Dead in 1 Cor 15, Part I: An Enquiry into the Jewish Background*; **P. R. Davies** (1985) 'Eschatology at Qumran', *JBL* 104: 39–55; **U. Fischer** (1978) *Eschatologie und Jenseitserwartung im hellenistischen Diasporajudentum*; **L. L. Grabbe** (1999) 'Eschatology in Philo and Josephus', in A. Avery-Peck and J. Neusner (eds), *Judaism in Late Antiquity, Volume 4: Special Topics: (1) Death and the Afterlife*, 35-62; **M. Kolarcik** (1991) *The Ambiguity of Death in the Book of Wisdom 1–6: A Study of Literary Structure and Interpretation*; **G. W. E. Nickelsburg** (1972) *Resurrection, Immortality, and Eternal Life in Intertestamental Judaism*; **E. Puech** (1993) *La croyance des Esséniens en la vie future: Immortalité, résurrection, vie éternelle? Histoire d'une croyance dans le Judaïsme Ancien*, Volume I: *La résurrection des morts et le contexte scripturaire*; Volume II: *Le données qumraniennes et classiques*; **L. V. Rutgers** (1998b) 'Jewish Ideas about Death and Afterlife: The Inscriptional Evidence', in *The Hidden Heritage of Diaspora Judaism*, 157–68.

By the late Hellenistic period, a number of ideas about eschatology and the afterlife had developed. The old idea, dominating the Hebrew Bible, that there was no afterlife, was still around and supposedly embraced by such groups as the Sadducees (§6.2). Yet the two main beliefs that envisaged an afterlife were very much in evidence:

- The idea of an immortal soul
- The concept of a resurrection

As has been noted, the idea of a resurrection of the dead seems to be envisaged already in the late 'Isaiah apocalypse' (Isa. 24–27), which is probably the earliest reference to the resurrection, though the dating of this passage is controversial. Here the resurrection of the dead into their previous bodily form seems to be in the mind of the author (26.19-21). Other passages of the Old Testament have been interpreted as references to the resurrection but probably did not have that original meaning.

The book of Daniel is especially important for developments in the concept of afterlife. Although Daniel 7–12 may not contain the earliest reference to a resurrection, it is the earliest datable text (ca. 166–165 BCE) which clearly speaks of one (12.2-3). The wording of the passage suggests that not all the dead will be resurrected, only 'some' for reward and 'some' for punishment. Since the specific context is the period of the Maccabaean revolt, those resurrected may simply be the martyrs whose life had been cut short and the exceptionally wicked who were not punished in this life. On this view, the rest of the dead had their reward or punishment in this life and would not be resurrected; however, the book does not spell out the precise connotation. The 'wise' or 'knowledgeable' (משכילים *maśkîlîm*) are conceived of as attaining 'astral immortality' by becoming like the stars of heaven. A number of passages in Daniel imply a cosmic eschatology, including the vision of the image (Dan. 2.44), the vision of the four beasts (Dan. 7.23-27) and the wars between the King of the North and the King of the South (Dan. 11.40–12.3). God would establish his rule over all the kingdoms, with his people as the head of the nations.

The term 'resurrection' is often assumed to be or to include resurrection of the body, and this is true in many cases. For example, 2 Maccabees (e.g., 7.9, 11, 14, 23; 14.46) has several passages that suggest an afterlife, and these mostly relate to a resurrection of the body. It may be that only the pious dead can expect a resurrection (2 Macc. 12.43-45). The *Psalms of Solomon* apparently continue the view of death found in much of the Old Testament. The wicked are destroyed forever (*Pss. Sol.* 3.10-12; 13.11; 15.12-13) and inherit Sheol and darkness (*Pss. Sol.* 14.6-9); contrary to most of the Old Testament, however, the righteous have a chance to live forever (*Pss. Sol.* 13.11; 14.1-5), perhaps through a resurrection (*Pss. Sol.* 3.10-12), though nothing is said about a resurrection of the body. A day of judgment is mentioned but no specifics are given (*Pss. Sol.* 15.12-13). However, in Jubilees we appear to have resurrection of the spirit only (*Jub.* 23.22-31): 'And their bones shall rest in the earth, and their spirits shall have much joy; and they shall know that the Lord is one who executes judgement' (*Jub.* 23.20-22). The book also mentions a new creation when heaven and earth will be renewed (*Jub.* 1.29).

The concept of a soul that survives death and serves as a basis for a future life occurs early among the Jews and is (in spite of occasional assertions to the contrary) as characteristic of Judaism as is the resurrection. The earliest concept in Judaism seems to be attested in *1 Enoch*. The *Book of the Watchers*, probably from Ptolemaic times, describes a tour of the underworld in which Enoch sees four 'beautiful places' or chambers into which the souls or spirits of the dead are gathered until the day of judgment (*1 En.* 22). The souls of the dead are already experiencing reward and punishment in their intermediate state. In this case, the existence of the soul after death seems to be combined with the idea of a final judgment. This may imply a general resurrection, though this is not stated explicitly. *1 Enoch* 10.6 mentions a final judgment when the fate of the fallen angel Asael would be announced (even though he has been bound for the present). The *Epistle of Enoch* assumes the spirits of the righteous will be rewarded at death and the spirits of the wicked punished in Sheol (*1 En.* 102.3–104.6); a final judgment is also mentioned (*1 En.* 104.5), with astral immortality for the righteous (*1 En.* 104.2). In some sections of *1 Enoch*, a resurrection is also alluded to, such as the *Dream Visions* and the *Epistle of Enoch* (*1 En.* 90.33; 91.10; 92.3-4). The *Similitudes of Enoch*, probably dating from a little after our period, in the 1st century CE, also mention a resurrection (*1 En.* 46.6; 51.1; 61.5).

The writer of the Wisdom of Solomon has two aims: negatively, to refute the false notion of death held by the wicked and, positively, to persuade the reader to love justice and God (Kolarcik 1991: 160). Wisdom of Solomon 1.13-15 states that God did not create death and does not delight in it; on the contrary, he created life, and righteousness is itself immortal. The goal of life is immortality, and the soul at least has the potential for immortality in it (Wis. 2.23; 3.4). Less clear is whether the soul is naturally immortal. The text seems to suggest that immortality is a gift to the righteous, not an inherent condition of the soul itself (Wis. 3.4; 4.1; 8.13, 17; 15.3). Death is used in three different senses in the book: (a) mortality, (b) physical death as punishment and (c) ultimate death, defined as separation from God and the cosmos (Kolarcik 1991: 156–58, 170). One passage could imply *metempsychosis* or the transmigration of souls: 'a good soul fell to my ["Solomon's"] lot' (Wis. 8.19-20; also said to be a belief of the Pharisees by Josephus [§6.3.1]). It would assume that 'Solomon's' soul was good because of effort in a previous life. However, this is not explicitly stated, and it may just be that his soul was created by God to enter the body being prepared for him at the time of birth. This raises all sorts of questions about why he inherited a good soul, how he was chosen for the privilege, whether souls were predestined to be good or bad and so on. Unfortunately, the author does not answer many of the questions he raises.

When we come to Qumran, however, the view found in the 'sectarian' scrolls is not easy to interpret, nor can we be sure that there was a uniform belief. This group of the Scrolls seems to be shot through with the view that they were living in the end time (e.g., CD 1.11-12; 1QS[a] 1.1), and their eschatological beliefs are determined by this context. There are passages that have been interpreted to refer to a resurrection (e.g., 1QH 14.29, 34; 19.12 [older 6.29, 34; 11.12]); unfortunately, these are not clear cut. Puech (1993) argues for the concept of a resurrection but bases this only on two passages (4Q521 and 4Q385). Other passages, however, clearly envisage the community members as already dwelling with the angels and somehow partaking of eternal life even in this life (1QH 11.19-22; 19.3-14 [older 3.19-22; 11.3-14]). What exactly this intends is by no means clear, but it suggests that death is not a major break in the existence of the righteous. This can be taken to mean that the community of the Scrolls believed in a soul that continued to exist after the body died (cf. the beliefs alleged for the Essenes [§6.5.1]; Nickelsburg 1972: 166–69). The fate of the wicked is described in various passages. 1QH 11.27-36 (older 3.27-36) describes fiery 'streams of Belial' that rise up and overflow even into Abaddon. Angels of destruction torment them in the fire of the dark regions (1QS 4.11-14).

A cosmic eschatology is found in a few passages from this period, though the main writings for this concept come from the 1st century CE. A number of Hebrew Bible texts had indicated a developing concept of the 'day of Yhwh' (sometimes just referred to as 'that day'), a day of judgment on Israel and/or the nations (see further *HJJSTP 1*: 249–50). In the Second Temple period this concept eventually came to form a full-blown belief in a cosmic judgment and a catastrophic climax of history. This cosmic eschaton is often preceded by an oppressive world empire, with God intervening to destroy it. In Daniel this is Antiochus Epiphanes's Seleucid empire (7.19-27; 8.23-25; 11); other oracles against the Greeks are found in the *Sibylline Oracles* (e.g., 3.520-72). A number of passages in Daniel imply a cosmic eschatology, including the vision of the image (Dan. 2.44), the vision of the four beasts (Dan. 7.23-27) and the wars between the King of the North and the King of the South (Dan. 11.40–12.3). God would establish his rule over all the kingdoms, with his people as the head of the nations. As we shall see in *HJJSTP 4*, the later writings generally see this empire as Rome.

12.3.5. *Messiah*

> **K. Atkinson** (1998b) 'On the Herodian Origin of Militant Davidic Messianism at Qumran: New Light from *Psalm of Solomon* 17', *JBL* 118: 435–60; **G. J. Brooke** (1998) 'Kingship and Messianism in the Dead Sea Scrolls', in J. Day (ed.), *King and Messiah in Israel and the Ancient Near East*, 434–55; **J. H. Charlesworth** (1992) *The Messiah. Developments in Earliest Judaism and Christianity*; **J. H. Charlesworth, H. Lichtenberger and G. S. Oegema (eds)** (1998) *Qumran-Messianism: Studies on the*

Messianic Expections in the Dead Sea Scrolls; **J. J. Collins** (1994) 'The Works of the Messiah', *DSD* 1: 98–112; **idem** (1995) *The Scepter and the Star: The Messiahs of the Dead Sea Scrolls and Other Ancient Literature*; **L. L. Grabbe** (1999) 'Eschatology in Philo and Josephus', in A. Avery-Peck and J. Neusner (eds), *Judaism in Late Antiquity, Volume 4: Special Topics: (1) Death and the Afterlife*, 35–62; **M. A. Knibb** (1995) 'Messianism in the Pseudepigrapha in the Light of the Scrolls', *DSD* 2: 165–84; **A. Laato** (1997) *A Star Is Rising: The Historical Development of the Old Testament Royal Ideology and the Rise of the Jewish Messianic Expectations*; **J. Neusner, W. S. Green and E. S. Frerichs (eds)** (1987) *Judaisms and Their Messiahs at the Turn of the Christian Era*; **G. S. Oegema** (1998) *The Anointed and his People: Messianic Expectations from the Maccabees to Bar Kochba*; **J. C. O'Neill** (1991) 'The Man from Heaven: SibOr 5.256-259', *JSP* 9: 87–102; **E. Puech** (1999) 'Le "Fils de Dieu" en 4Q246', *Eretz-Israel* 26: 143*–52*; **J. Starcky** (1963) 'Les quatres étapes du messianisme à Qumrân', *RevB* 70: 481–505; **J. D. Tabor and M. O. Wise** (1994) '4Q521 "On Resurrection" and the Synoptic Gospel Tradition: A Preliminary Study', *JSP* 10: 149–62; **J. Zimmerman** (1998) *Messianische Texte aus Qumran: Königliche, priesterliche und prophetische Messiasvorstellungen in den Schriftfunden von Qumran.*

Several recent studies have attempted to survey the general question of messiahs and messianic figures during the Second Temple period (Oegema 1998; Collins 1995; Charlesworth 1992; Neusner, Green and Frerichs 1987). Other specialized studies have focused on particular texts or figures (Zimmerman 1998; Charlesworth, Lichtenberger and Oegema 1998; Grabbe 1999). This is of course but a sample of the many studies that have appeared on the question and various aspects of it. The aim here is to focus on the last two centuries BCE. The concept of messiah continued to develop, and the subsequent evolution will be surveyed in *HJJSTP 4*.

The concept of a messianic figure is well attested for this period. To what extent it was entertained in Hasmonaean circles is an interesting question, not least the issue of what sort of messiah would have been envisaged by them. We have several texts from this time, not to mention the important texts from Qumran. These sources attest to different concepts of a messiah, however, and it would be wrong to speak of 'the' messianic expectation at this time, since there was a variety.

We can begin with the *Psalms of Solomon* (from about 40 BCE), one of the earliest datable texts to discuss the question of a messiah, especially in *Psalms of Solomon* 7–18. The messianic figure is a king in the image of David (*Pss. Sol.* 17.21), righteous and holy (*Pss. Sol.* 17.35). He will smash the gentile oppressors of Jerusalem with a rod of iron (*Pss. Sol.*

17.22-25). There is nothing about this figure that indicates a heavenly origin, however; he appears to be a human being with perhaps some larger than life characteristics. Nothing is said about how long he would reign, whether he would have successors, and the like; in short he is very much in the image of various Hebrew Bible passages that give a similar picture.

Qumran is the most extensive and also the most complicated source on the matter. A variety of eschatological figures occurs in those Qumran texts that seem to be related to one another; however, the messianic expectations at Qumran appear not to have been a major part of their eschatological view. At least, the texts do not refer to them often, though they are there in the background. It has also been argued – not unreasonably – that their views developed and changed over time, perhaps from the expectation of only one messianic figure to a situation with several. For example, the *War Scroll* (1QM) describes a series of eschatological battles between the Sons of Light and the Sons of Darkness, yet this writing says nothing about a messianic figure. The *Damascus Document* speaks of 'the anointed of Aaron and Israel' (CD 12.23–13.1). Is this meant to be one messiah or two? CD 19.10-11 seems to have one figure in mind when it refers to 'the messiah of Aaron and Israel'. On the other hand, the *Community Rule* speaks of 'the prophet and the messiahs of Aaron and Israel' (1QS 9.11). In none of these passages is the function of the messiah described. The passages which refer explicitly to a messiah or messiahs are few and somewhat unspecific. Another important passage is found in the text sometimes referred to as the *Messianic Rule* (1QS^a 2.11). Here a messiah of Aaron (priestly messiah) and a messiah of Israel seem to be distinctly envisaged.

Qumran also has the concept of a heavenly messiah, which seems to be a later development in Judaism. One of the earliest texts with the idea is 11QMelchizedek (perhaps from the 1st century BCE). In this text, the Melchizedek of Gen. 14.18-20 (cf. Ps. 110.4 and Heb. 5 and 7) is a heavenly figure (identical with the archangel Michael) who opposes Satan. At one point we have the following statement about an 'anointed one' (messiah): 'it is the time for the "year of grace" of Melchizedek, and of [his] arm[ies, the nat]ion of the holy ones of God, of the rule of judgement, as is written... Its interpretation: The mountains [are] the prophet[s]... And the messenger i[s] the anointed one of the spir[it] as Dan[iel] said [about him. (*Dan 9.25*]' (2.9, 17-18). The fragmentary nature of the text makes it difficult to interpret, but the deliverance comes at the end of ten jubilees (490 years), just as with Daniel 9. Indeed, Dan. 9.25 seems to be cited, though whether 'the anointed one' is identical with Melchizedek or is a separate figure is not clear.

Other texts from Qumran have messianic overtones, or at least have been so interpreted. One of the main ones is the *Messianic Apocalypse* (4Q521) which describes the various marvellous things that 'the Lord' will do, along with mention of 'his messiah'. In language borrowed from Isa. 61.1, it is stated that the captives will be released, the blind given sight, the wounded healed and the dead brought to life (4Q521 2.II.7-8, 12-13). This has been compared with a passage in the gospels (Mt. 11.2-5//Lk. 7.19-22; Tabor and Wise 1994), though the text as read by most scholars seems to describe what 'the Lord' does, and is not ascribing these actions to the messiah (cf. Collins 1995: 121; Zimmermann 1998: 347). Precisely what form of a messiah is being spoken of here is difficult to say, though possibly he is an eschatological prophet on the model of Elijah (Collins 1995: 120–22).

The interpretation of some other texts is rather controversial. For example, in the *Son of God* text (4Q246) the term 'messiah' is not used in the extant remains; however, the description of what the 'son of God' does matches descriptions of messianic activities elsewhere. A variety of explanations has been given for this text (Brooke 1998: 445–49), but the messianic interpretation has been argued at some length by Collins (1995: 154–72). One of the main problems is whether it is describing the activities of a historical figure or an eschatological one. To take another example, some have seen 4Q541 as messianic. The text refers to the succession of high priests, including possibly the last one, but it does not clearly refer to an eschatological messiah (Brooke 1998: 449; Collins 1995: 124–26; contrast Zimmermann 1998: 275–77).

Finally, we come to perhaps the most controversial text: 4Q285. Eisenman and Wise (1992) proposed that a slain messiah was depicted in the text. Because the idea of a suffering messiah seems to be post-Christian and not in any early texts, this interpretation could have been sensational, since many Christian scholars had long sought a Jewish predecessor to the image of Jesus as a suffering messiah. This interpretation, which depends on the interpretation of a rather fragmentary text, has been met with almost universal rejection (Collins 1995: 58–60; Zimmermann 1998: 86–87). (The 'Messiah ben Joseph', a Jewish martyr figure, has been seen as early by some; this figure will be discussed in *HJJSTP 4*.)

The Qumran messianic picture is not a simple one, therefore; quite some time ago Starcky (1963) had argued for a four-stage historical development of beliefs on the question. Although this is overly schematic, a chronological development is still probably a factor in the variety of messianic figures (Brooke 1998: 450–52). The Qumran texts in general tend to put the emphasis on the priestly and prophetic elements of leadership rather than the princely, which may explain why so little is said about the messiah from Judah.

The *Sibylline Oracles* contain material covering a period of about 300 years, but *Sibylline Oracle* 3 seems to relate to our period. *Sibylline Oracle* 3.489-829 has various eschatological passages. There are references to the 'king from the sun' (*Sib. Or.* 3.652) who is also said to be the 'seventh' (*Sib. Or.* 3.193, 3.318, 3.608). It is generally agreed that the reference is to one of the Ptolemaic rulers, perhaps the most likely being Ptolemy VI Philometor who had good relations with the Jews. *Sibylline Oracle* 3.702-31 describes the 'sons of the great God' living in peace around the temple, while *Sib. Or.* 3.741-95 pictures a renewed form of life on earth, a type of golden age or millennium. A messianic figure in the form of the Egyptian king and a messianic age were thus expected in the 2nd century BCE. Some later passages seem to relate to Cleopatra VII and perhaps an expectation that she would fill the role of messiah. A reference to a 'mistress' (*despoina*) seems to have her in mind and to predict the subjugation of Rome to Asia (*Sib. Or.* 3.350-80). Several other prophecies relating to the end time (*Sib. Or.* 3.46-63; 3.75-92) indicate a period after the disappointment of Actium when hope in Cleopatra had failed.

Belief in a messiah was not uniform nor was there a unilinear development of beliefs, though the main source of such beliefs in all their variety appears to have been the anointed ruler and the anointed priest of pre-exilic times. The main 'anointed' figure (Hebrew *māšîăḥ*; Aramaic *měšîḥā'*) was the king (e.g., 1 Sam. 10.1; 16.1, 13; 24.7; Ps. 2; Laato 1999). The term could be used not only of a native king but also of a foreign king such as Cyrus who was seen as a deliverer (Isa. 45.1-6). However, the high priest was also anointed and could be called by that title (Lev. 7–8; 10.7; Ps. 133.2). These two concepts appear to inform and channel all the speculations on the subject in the Second Temple period. The messianic concept in the texts from the last two centuries BCE can be summarized as follows:

- The main messianic figure is a future earthly king. This also has its biblical roots since a number of passages refer to David *redivivus*, an ideal king on the model of David who would rule a restored Israel (e.g., Jer. 23.5; 30.9). It is the picture that probably appealed to many Jews through the Second Temple period, though the actual attestation in extant texts is somewhat skimpy; however, it seems to be quite clear in *Psalms of Solomon* 17–18.

- Various hints in Josephus about different revolutionary movements suggest that some were messianic in nature (see further in *HJJSTP 4*).
- The concept of a priestly figure appears in Qumran with 'messiah of Aaron' concept.
- The idea of the messiah as a heavenly figure seems to be a late development, but we already find it at Qumran. A number of passages picture a heavenly messiah, including 11QMelchizedek.
- No messianic figure is evident is several texts, such as the Wisdom of Solomon.

12.3.6. *Martyrdom*

J. W. van Henten (1997) *The Maccabean Martyrs as Saviours of the Jewish People: A Study of 2 and 4 Maccabees*; **J. W. van Henten (ed.)** (1989) *Die Entstehung der jüdischen Martyrologie*.

Although martyrdom does not have the prominent place in Judaism that it does in Christianity, we have a number of Jewish writings about persecutions (e.g., 2 Macc. 7; *3 Maccabees*). It appears that about this time an incorporation of martyrs and martyrdom into the religious picture took place. Some writings project this to an even earlier period, but at least from Maccabaean times martyrdom becomes the focus of certain passages or whole writings (Henten [ed.] 1989; Henten 1997). These writings often end with the vindication of the innocent sufferers. However, the first time Jews were executed for their religious practices appears to be at the time of the Antiochene persecutions about 168 BCE, at least as claimed by 1 and 2 Maccabees. Opposition to foreign rule or persecution did not necessarily take the form of violent action or outright rebellion. There were those who believed that they also serve who only stand and wait. In many apocalyptic and related writings, the emphasis is not on what people do but what God does. They describe a history which is more or less foreordained. Israel may do certain things, and the Gentiles may do certain things, but none of their actions ultimately affect the divine plan. Exactly how that plan unfolded varied from writer to writer.

For many, all history would be leading to a period of troubles and even cosmic cataclysm that would immediately precede the intervention of God and the creation of 'new heavens and a new earth'. Others saw a more gradual and less tumultuous ushering in of God's kingdom, without the cosmic upheaval found in many apocalypses. But in all these scenarios, it is God who takes the action, not the people. Their duty is to obey, whatever the cost. In a book such as Daniel (11.33-35) and the *Testament of Moses* (9), the righteous do their bit by giving themselves up to martyrdom, but they do not take up arms against the oppressor. The fact that apparently righteous individuals died for their beliefs (rather than being delivered by God) may have led to the doctrine of the resurrection (cf. Dan. 12.2). The later accounts in 2 and 4 Maccabees describe the deaths of a number of individuals from a martyr perspective, with their blood seen as a factor in defeating the Seleucids and cleansing the land. Similarly, the willing deaths of Taxo and his seven sons in *Testament of Moses* 9 will cause God to avenge their blood.

12.4. *Apocalyptic and Prophecy*

D. E. Aune (1983) *Prophecy in Early Christianity and the Ancient Mediterranean World*; **J. J. Collins** (1998) *The Apocalyptic Imagination: An Introduction to Jewish Apocalyptic Literature*; **L. L. Grabbe** (1995) *Priests, Prophets, Diviners, Sages: A Socio-historical Study of Religious Specialists in Ancient Israel*; idem (2003a) 'Prophetic and Apocalyptic: Time for New Definitions – and New Thinking', in L. L. Grabbe and R. D. Haak (eds), *Knowing the End from the Beginning*, 107–33; idem (2003b) 'Poets, Scribes, or Preachers? The Reality of Prophecy in the Second Temple Period', in L. L. Grabbe and R. D. Haak (eds), *Knowing the End from the Beginning*, 192–215; idem (2011) 'Daniel: Sage, Seer…and *Prophet*?' in L. L. Grabbe and M. Nissinen (eds), *Constructs of Prophecy in the Former and Latter Prophets and Daniel*, 87–94; **R. Gray** (1993) *Prophetic Figures in Late Second Temple Jewish Palestine: The Evidence from Josephus*; **R. A. Horsley** (1999) '"Like One of the Prophets of Old": Two Types of Popular Prophets at the Time of Jesus', *CBQ* 47: 435–63; idem (1986) 'Popular Prophetic Movements at the Time of Jesus: Their Principal Features and Social Origins', *JSNT* 26: 3–27; **R. A. Horsley and J. S. Hanson** (1985) *Bandits, Prophets, and Messiahs*; **A. P. Jassen** (2019) 'Prophecy and Priests in the Second Temple Period', in L.-S. Tiemeyer (ed.), *Prophecy and its Cultic Dimensions*, 63–88; **J. R. Levison** (1994) 'Two Types of Ecstatic Prophecy according to Philo', *SPA* 6: 83–89; idem (1995) 'Inspiration and the Divine Spirit in the Writings of Philo Judaeus', *JSJ* 26: 271–323; **W. A. Meeks** (1967) *The Prophet-King: Moses Traditions and the Johannine Christology*; **B. D. Sommer** (1996) 'Did Prophecy Cease? Evaluating a Reevaluation', *JBL* 115: 31–47; **H. M. Teeple** (1957) *The Mosaic Eschatological Prophet*; **S. White Crawford and C. Wassén (eds)** (2018) *Apocalyptic Thinking in Early Judaism: Engaging with John Collins'* The Apocalyptic Imagination; **D. Winston** (1989) 'Two Types of Mosaic Prophecy according to Philo', *JSP* 2: 49–67.

As argued in the past, it seems that from the point of view of a formal definition, prophecy is a form of divination. Likewise, apocalyptic is a sub-division of prophecy (Grabbe 1995: 139–41). This does not mean that each has precisely the same origin or social location. This is not the place to discuss this point in detail, but some brief remarks are in order.

One of the main differences between many prophets and apocalypticists is that the prophet is usually in some way a public figure who delivers divine messages often in a public way, though this could be in a variety of contexts: speeches, sermons or pronouncements in a public place; more privately to specific individuals, such as officials, elders and even leaders and rulers; or in a cultic place. Less frequently might be to commit the prophecy to writing. Apocalypticists are not usually public figures, as far as we know, since they usually hide their identity behind an ancient patriarchal figure. They might be recording actual visionary experiences, but they usually communicate them in writing (at least, we do not usually hear of them making public pronouncements).

Once the utterance of a prophet has been reduced to writing (the only way it reaches us), however, it does not differ in any significant way from a prophecy or apocalypse created by a scribe. It is not always possible to distinguish prophecy from apocalyptic by formal characteristics; however, even when it is, the impact on the reader and its general credibility may not be any different. The fact that one takes a form already known from the biblical prophetic corpus while another belongs to the genre apocalypse or a related form may be a point of indifference to the reader who sees both as revelation from God, giving his will and perhaps hinting at what would come to pass hereafter. Therefore, the debate over the alleged differences is not particularly relevant at this point. They both function in society in much the same way.

Were apocalypticists not mere scribes toiling at their desks but rather individuals who had visions or mantic experiences which was the source of the information in their writings? There seems to be no way to confirm this, but it is equally foolish to deny it, at least as a possibility. Thus, both prophetic and apocalyptic writings point to two potential social origins: first are the 'inspired' individuals who receive messages in one form or another and proceed to teach or write their message for posterity; secondly, there are scribal individuals who compose prophetic or apocalyptic writings with the aim of influencing their co-religionists (or even the Graeco-Romans in a few cases, such as perhaps the *Sibylline Oracles*).

Prophecy and apocalyptic have already been discussed extensively in *HJJSTP 1* (250–52) and *HJJSTP 2* (260–62; cf. 306–11). One question of relevance here, however, is this: Did prophecy cease in the Second

Temple period? The question of whether prophecy ceased sometime in the early post-exilic period has often been answered in the affirmative, yet seldom has the question been investigated seriously. This was done in an article (Grabbe 1998e) which should be consulted for the full study and more details; only an abbreviated version is given here.

12.4.1. *Did Prophecy Cease in the Second Temple Period?*

Although Ben Sira is often seen as an opponent of special revelations and all the various practices relating to the future, he accepts the concept of prophecy, at least with regard to the classical prophets. In describing the ideal sage he notes that this individual seeks out the wisdom and prophecies of the ancients (Ben Sira 39.1-3). Continuing in the same vein he calls on God to fulfil his prophecies and for the prophets to be found trustworthy (Ben Sira 36.20-21). Isaiah is said to have seen the future, revealed what was to occur to the end of time and predict the hidden things before they happened (Ben Sira 48.24-25). Joshua was considered the successor of Moses in the prophetic office (Ben Sira 46.1). Thus, whether Ben Sira thought that prophecy continued in his own time or not, he at least recognized that true prophecies had taken place in the past.

One of the main sources for the view that prophecy had ceased is 1 Maccabees. First was the matter of the stones from the polluted altar which were stored away until a prophet should come to reveal what to do with them (1 Macc. 4.44-46). The context does not suggest that prophets were only a phenomenon of the distant past; on the contrary, although there was no prophet currently available, it was still possible for one to come along in the future. The passage does not really argue for the cessation of prophecy but only that acceptable prophets were not necessarily common. A similar idea occurs a bit later in the book (1 Macc. 14.41). The passage most explicitly stating the view that prophecy had ceased is 1 Macc. 9.27: 'So there was great tribulation in Israel, such as had not been since the days that prophets ceased to appear among them'. According to this, prophets ceased sometime in the past and are no longer extant; however, it agrees with other passages in not ruling out a future prophet.

Some of the Qumran texts express belief in the appearance of a future prophet who seems to be separate from the Messiah(s) of Aaron and Israel (1QS 9.9-11). A good case can be made that the Teacher of Righteousness was seen by many as this eschatological prophet. For the people of the Scrolls, Daniel was also a prophet: '[a]s is written in the book of Daniel the prophet [הנביא]' (4QFlor frag. 1, II, 3, 24, 5.3). The Scrolls also indicate an attitude toward the interpretation of prophetic literature which differs significantly from what we think of as biblical interpretation. With regard to one passage, the *Habakkuk Commentary* states, 'Its interpretation concerns the Teacher of Righteousness to whom God has made known all the mysteries of the words of his servants, the prophets' (1QpHab 7.3-5). The Teacher was inspired to interpret prophecies of Habakkuk even though the original prophet himself did not understand them. The implication is that interpretation was not just a matter of interpretative rules or techniques; on the contrary, interpretation was a matter of inspiration by the same spirit which had inspired the original prophetic writer.

Philo of Alexandria is an important witness to Jewish views about the concept of prophecy at the turn of the era. He discusses the subject at some length, especially in *De Vita Mosis*. The first passage is *Mos.* 1.263-99 which recounts the story of Balaam. Philo makes the distinction between augury (which Balaam formerly practised) and prophecy (*Mos.* 1.264-68). But then Balaam became possessed, and the true prophetic spirit fell upon him and banished his mantic art. The oracles he spoke were the repetition of words which another had put into his mouth. For Philo Moses is the prophet *par excellence* (*Mos.* 2.187), and he distinguishes several sorts of prophecy (*Mos.* 2.188-91, translation from LCL):

> Of the divine utterances, some are spoken by God in His own Person with His prophet for interpreter, in some the revelation comes through question and answer, and others are spoken by Moses in his own person, when possessed by God and carried away out of himself...

The inspiration of prophets in general is described as a sort of possession in which God speaks through his mouth, using him simply as a channel (*Her.* 259-66; *Spec.* 1.65). Philo is quite important for another idea already noted at Qumran, the concept of inspired interpretation (*Mos.* 2.264-65, 268-69). Interestingly, Philo sees himself as understanding scripture by means of inspiration (*Cher.* 27; see also *Migr.* 34-35; *Somn.* 2.164-65).

Josephus speaks of prophecy as foreknowledge from God about what to guard against (*Ant.* 8.15.6 §418), indicating his view that prophecy includes knowledge about the future. He is not afraid to use 'prophecy' and 'prophet' for figures other than the Old Testament prophets; for example, Daniel is called a prophet (*Ant.* 10.11.4 §§245-49; 10.11.7 §§267-69, 280; 11.7.6 §322), as is Joshua (*Ant.* 4.7.2 §165), and John Hyrcanus had the gift of prophecy (*War* 1.2.8 §§68-69; *Ant.* 13.10.7 §299). Josephus refers to a number of individuals as 'false prophets', indicating that they had the persona of a prophet (*War* 2.13.5 §§261-63; 6.5.2 §§285-87; 7.11.1-3 §§437-50; *Ant.* 20.5.1 §97; 20.8.6 §169; 20.8.10 §188; *Life* 76 §§424-25). He also refers to the use of the ephod by the high priests to determine the future as prophecy or prophesying (*Ant.* 6.6.3 §115; 6.12.4-5 §§254, 257; 6.5.6 §359; 7.4.1 §76). Prophecy is also associated with the interpretation of Scripture. For example, the Essenes have those who foretell the future because they are educated in the holy books and the sayings of the prophets from an early age (*War* 2.8.12 §159). Josephus also associates interpretation of the biblical books with prophecy and connects this with dream interpretation – and he claims these skills for himself (*War* 3.8.3 §§351-53).

A question of particular concern is how Josephus regarded himself, since he claims to be able to foretell the future and predicted to Vespasian that he will become emperor. So why does he not refer to himself as a prophet? There are probably two reasons for this. The lesser is that he identifies himself as a priest and claims to obtain at least part of his skill through this fact. The other is more subtle but also more likely: a blatant claim to be a prophet might cause a reaction. Some people were suspicious of prophets, and it was also preferable that others acclaim him than that he do it himself. In this case he probably thought that 'the wise would understand', and those who did not were probably not important, anyway.

The *Liber Antiquitatum Biblicarum* (or Pseudo-Philo) agrees with Philo in envisaging prophecy as the result of the spirit taking possession of the prophet and describing the future. It tells the story of a judge named Cenaz (not in the Bible, unless he is to be identified with Othniel's father). The holy spirit came upon him, taking away his senses, and he began to prophesy; upon finishing, he woke up but did not know what he had spoken (*LAB* 28.6-10).

The writings of the New Testament and other early Christian literature give a number of examples of prophetic activity by living prophets or in some way presuppose that such existed. These are collected in Grabbe (2003b).

12.4.2. *Conclusions about Prophecy and Apocalyptic*

What can we conclude about the question? Here are some points that seem relevant:

- We seem to have two separate evaluations of the social situation. Passages such as 1 Macc. 9.27 appear to say that the prophets are in some sense in the past, yet other passages speak of 'prophets' who are contemporary with the writer. Josephus exemplifies both attitudes. He mentions the gift of prophecy and the existence of prophets (or alleged prophets) long after the biblical period, yet he also states that the 'exact succession of the prophets' had ceased

after the time of Artaxerxes (*Ag. Ap.* 1.8 §§40-41). Josephus's concern in this passage is to explain the status of certain writings when there was no further 'exact succession', and sacred scripture was no longer written, however; he nowhere suggests that prophecy as such had completely ceased.
- The model of the prophet which emerges from the Second Temple literature includes a number of characteristics. As in the Hebrew Bible, the prophet is someone who claims to have a message from God. He is likewise someone who gives information about the future, which is also the case with many biblical prophets. This foreknowledge of the future is an important aspect of being a prophet according to a number of sources.
- We find three different sources for prophecy during the Second Temple period. First, prophets deliver oracles received from the deity in a variety of ways, including visions and dreams; secondly, prophetic material is written by scribes or sages who may or may not be in a state of 'inspiration'; thirdly, prophetic and other material is interpreted via a special sort of inspiration which goes beyond mere intellect or training.
- There is the question of sociological versus literary analysis of the data. Horsley (1986: 25 n. 15, in criticism of Aune 1983: 121–29) has pointed out that literary descriptions of prophets (the 'prophet like Moses', etc.) should not be lumped in with the social phenomena. Although the attempt at a sociological analysis is commendable, it must not be forgotten that we do not have sociological field data. All we have are descriptions in ancient literature, and our sociological analyses represent an attempt to extract sociological data from literature. This suggests some methodological points that must be considered:
  (1) The descriptions themselves may be influenced to a lesser or greater extent by literary-theological models.
  (2) The social phenomena may have been influenced by, or even inspired by, the literary-theological models extant at the time.
  (3) A further problem is that the data in the ancient sources are far from complete. The fact that certain elements are lacking in the description (e.g., religious motives or messianic expectations) does not mean that they were not present in the actual historical situation. Of course, one has no right to read them into the description without evidence, but it certainly complicates any task of classification and makes one cautious about accepting any system which is overly schematic.

12.5. Revelation from Textual Interpretation

The use of texts was known to Graeco-Romans as well as Jews if we think of such writings as the *Sibylline Oracles*, but the repository of religion primarily in a book was a special feature of Judaism. As noted in the previous section (§12.4.1), Josephus stated that he himself used the Jewish sacred writings as a basis for predictions, though he does not give specific examples. Perhaps the clearest examples are found in the Qumran texts, especially the *pesharim*, where the recent history of the sect is found in minute detail in the first two chapters of Habakkuk. To be able to find information about the future in the pages of Holy Writ must have given special piquancy to the knowledge that one was one of the Chosen and that one's group was so plainly designated by God. Even the prophets themselves had not understood what they were writing, but God had revealed it to the Teacher of Righteousness (4QpHab 7.1-6).

12.6. Chronography

L. L. Grabbe (1979) 'Chronography in Hellenistic Jewish Historiography', *Society of Biblical Literature 1979 Seminar Papers*, 2:43–68; **idem** (1981) 'Chronography in 4 Ezra and 2 Baruch', *Society of Biblical Literature 1981 Seminar Papers*, 49–63; **idem** (1982) 'The End of the World in Early Jewish and Christian Calculations', *RevQ* 41: 107–8; **idem** (1997b) 'The 70-Weeks Prophecy (Daniel 9:24-27) in Early Jewish Interpretation', in C. A. Evans and S. Talmon (eds), *The Quest for Context and Meaning: Studies in Biblical Intertextuality in Honor of James A. Sanders*, 595–611; **A. Laato** (1998) 'The Apocalypse of the Syriac Baruch and the Date of the End', *JSP* 18: 39–46; **N. Roddy** (1996) '"Two Parts: Weeks of Seven Weeks": The End of the Age as *Terminus ad Quem* for *2 Baruch*', *JSP* 14: 3–14; **M. O. Wise** (1997) 'To Know the Times and the Seasons: A Study of the Aramaic Chronograph 4Q559', *JSP* 15: 3–51.

Another mode of trying to work out the future was to use a combination of methods to try to calculate the age of the world. It was also taken for granted that certain patterns had been put into history by God himself and needed only to be calculated by the one to whom God's spirit had revealed such things. Two examples will illustrate this, one involving the supposed age of the world and the other 70 weeks of Daniel 9.

The Age of the World. Based on Ps. 90.4 the view developed that human history followed the plan of a thousand-year week. That is, all human history would be packed into 6,000 years, followed by a millennial sabbath. Exactly how early this developed is not clear. One of the earliest plain references to it is from about 150 CE in the early Christian writing

Epistle of Barnabas (15.4). However, the same idea seems to lie behind 2 Pet. 3.8 and especially Rev. 20.4. This model for human history then became quite widespread in early Christian writers, though in time there was a reaction against what was seen as too much emphasis on the physical 'indulgences' expected during the Millennium. The question is how early the concept arose in Judaism. *Jubilees* 4.30 has a statement similar to Ps. 90.4 but does not go further. From the 1st century the *Testament of Abraham* seems to presuppose a 7,000-year programme of human history, though one version (*T. Abr.* B 7.15-16) is clearer than the other (*T. Abr.* A 19.7, but one manuscript has '6,000 years' instead of 'seven thousand ages'). Josephus mentions that the earth was about 5,000 years old in his own time (*Ant.* Proem. 3 §13; *Ag. Ap.* 1.1 §1).

4 Ezra has the puzzling figure of 5,042 years to the time of Ezra (*4 Ezra* 14.48 Syriac version). Although this has never been satisfactorily explained before, one could argue that it is to be tied in with the Messianic Age of 400 years in *4 Ezra* 7.28 (Grabbe 1981). If we assume that the 5,042 years is meant to refer to the biblical Ezra, this would make the writing of the book (ca. 100 CE) close to the year 5600. If we add the 400 years of the Messiah, this gives an age of the world of 6,000 years before God then brings about the cosmic regeneration. If so, then the writer seems to have believed that he was living near the time of the coming of the Messiah. A number of Christian writers put the birth of Jesus in the year 5500 from the creation of the world, which also seems to fit in with the idea that human history would run for 6,000 years before 'God's time' would be introduced (cf. Grabbe 1982).

The 70 Weeks Prophecy. As discussed in more detail in Grabbe (1997b), Daniel 9 has one of the most startling prophecies with a specific time frame. This passage explicitly asks about the prophecy of 70 years mentioned by Jeremiah (25.11-12; 29.10). It then goes on to reinterpret Jeremiah's prophecy as a reference to 70 *weeks of years* (Dan. 9.24-27). What is surprising is that more explicit reference is not made to Daniel 9, especially to speculate on its meaning. It is normally taken to refer to the death of the high priest Onias III about 170 BCE just before the Maccabaean revolt (2 Macc. 4.32-34), but it becomes important in later Christian writings as a way of calculating the coming of the messiah. There is also some evidence that speculation about it occurred among Jewish interpreters, but the evidence is more circumstantial.

Perhaps one of the clearer and more interesting examples is found in the Qumran scrolls. The Damascus Document 1.5-11 speaks of a figure of 390 years. This of course corresponds with the period of Israel's punishment as stipulated in the book of Ezekiel (Ezek. 4.4-5), but this would not prevent the writer from also thinking of Daniel 9. The 390 years in the Damascus Document is followed by the figure of 20 years of groping until the Teacher of Righteousness comes. There are statements to the effect that a period of 40 years would elapse between the death of the Teacher until the end of the age (CD 20.14-15; 4QpPs^a 2.6-8). If one allows another figure of 40 years (= one generation) for the life of the Teacher, we come to 490 years. The two figures of 40 years are stereotyped, but stereotyping is typical of this sort of chronographical speculation.

Two further interpretations may have the 70 weeks of Daniel as their base. In his description of the siege of Jerusalem, Josephus (*War* 6.5.4 §311) refers to an oracle that the city and temple would be taken when the latter was made four-square, which he alleges happened when the Antonia was demolished. He also mentions a second oracle in the same context (*War* 6.5.4 §§312-13). He claims an ambiguous oracle found in the 'scriptures' that one of their own countrymen would become the ruler of the world. He of course states that they misunderstood it, and it really referred to Vespasian. Josephus is unclear as to which biblical passages both these oracles are supposed to have been taken from. It is difficult to find one which seems to fit better than Daniel 9, however, which is why many scholars have connected one or both these with the 70-weeks prophecy. This suggests that it was used as a means of trying to work out the end of the age in some circles, though the failure of such prophecies may have been the reason that clearer examples have not survived (see Grabbe 1997b for a further discussion and examples).

12.7. *Conclusions*

Some studies (especially those relating to the New Testament) emphasize the importance of eschatology in early Judaism. The eschatological interest can be exaggerated, especially since it is clear that many Jews had little concern for such views. What emerges from a study of the extant texts is the variety of views about what happened to the individual at death and eventually to the cosmos. To state that certain views were 'characteristic' of Judaism (e.g., the resurrection of the body) is to mislead in most cases. Since the survey of the texts yields such a mixture of concepts, this section will give a more systematic picture of the different views that can be extracted from the sources.

Most of the books of the Hebrew Bible do not seem to envisage life after death as such. Life in its proper sense ends at death, even if there is some shadowy vestige which continues to exist in Sheol (it has many parallels with the realm of Hades as pictured in the Homeric poems). This also seems to be the view in Ben Sira, and the Sadducees are supposed to have maintained this belief if we can believe our sources. When belief in some form of afterlife began to enter Israelite thinking is not known. Recent study on the cult of the dead suggests that the idea that the dead could communicate with and influence the living may have been around in some parts of Israelite society from an early time (Grabbe 1995: 141–45). What is clear is that at least as early as sometime in the Persian or early Greek period, ideas about an afterlife had entered Jewish thinking.

The frequent assertion that the resurrection of the body was the characteristic Jewish belief is not borne out by the data. Resurrection is apparently found in Isa. 27.19 and certainly in Dan. 12.1-3, but there is little reason to think that it was earlier or more characteristic of Jewish thinking than the immortality of the soul or resurrection of the spirit. And it is clear that some Jews still maintained the older belief in no afterlife. Therefore, it would be quite wrong to refer to any of these beliefs as 'characteristically' Jewish or *the* Jewish belief on the subject.

After the book of Daniel, the resurrection appears regularly – though not universally – in Jewish writings, including 2 Maccabees, the later sections of *1 Enoch* and apparently the *Psalms of Solomon*. (It is of course found in later writings, such as the *Apocalypse of Moses*, *Pseudo-Philo*, *4 Ezra* and *2 Baruch*). The exact form of the resurrection is not always specified. 2 Maccabees 7 seems to expect the resurrection of the body, because the parts cut off in torture would be restored. However, we should not expect it always to entail resurrection of the body: sometimes only the resurrection of the spirit seems to be in mind, as in *Jub.* 23.20-22.

Belief in the immortality of the soul is known at least as early as the beginning of the Greek period, as witnessed by the *Book of Watchers* (*1 En.* 1–36; see especially 22). Other sources indicate belief that death is the separation of body and soul (a widespread definition of death in the Hellenistic period) and give no indication of a resurrection at all. Several of these are from Alexandria (or likely to be) such as Philo and the Wisdom of Solomon, but not all are.

There was a widespread view that the age of the world was finite and that history was played out according to a predetermined divine plan (see further at §12.6 above). This is indicated by the 'review of history' found in many of the apocalypses and related writings. Reviews of history – *vaticinia ex eventu* (prophecies after the event) – are found in Daniel 11, the *Animal Apocalypse* (*1 En.* 85–90) and the *Apocalypse of Weeks* (*1 En.* 93.2-9 + 91.12-17) (and such later writings as the *Testament of Moses* and *2 Bar.* 53–74). One of the most characteristic elements of apocalyptic and related literature is the view that the eschaton has come, either for the individual or for the whole human race, in which case the world itself was in its last days.

There was also belief in a cosmic eschatology by some in this period. The cosmic eschaton is often preceded by an oppressive world empire, with God intervening to destroy it. In Daniel this is Antiochus IV Epiphanes's Seleucid empire (Dan. 7.19-27; 8.23-25; 11); other oracles against the Greeks are found in the *Sibylline Oracles* (e.g., 3.520-72). In most of the writings, however, the empire is Rome. Most of these are later writings (e.g., the eagle vision of *4 Ezra* 11–12; Rev. 13; 17; *Sib. Or.* 4.130-48; 5.162-78), but see *Sib. Or.* 3.350-64. Some writings of this period also include 'tours' of the heavens and the nether world, but this topic and the developments in literature of the 1st century CE and later will be covered in *HJJSTP 4*.

Part IV

HISTORICAL SYNTHESIS

Chapter 13

Background: The Ptolemies, the Seleucids and the Romans

From the coming of the Greeks and the death of Alexander in the late 4th century BCE Judah was under one or the other of the Greek kingdoms: after a rather chaotic period in the struggles between the Diadochi the province was, first, under the Ptolemies (from 301 to 200 BCE), then under the Seleucids (from 200 BCE). With Antigonids in charge of the Greek mainland, and the Levant (including Judah) caught between the Ptolemies and Seleucids, the eastern Mediterranean was dominated by Greek kingdoms that descended from Alexander's realm. These kingdoms continued to determine the world that the Judaean homeland inhabited during the 2nd century BCE and into the 1st. Yet there was a new ingredient in the mixture: the Romans. The interplay of these powers determined to a significant degree the course of events in Judah.

This and the next five chapters seek to synthesize the data we have and interpret it to give – as far as we are able – a narrative history of the Jews and Judaism during the Hasmonaean and Herodian domination. As always, the emphasis will be given to the primary sources (archaeology and inscriptions; Jewish, Greek and Roman historians), but these sources have to be interpreted. Putting the data of the sources together from a critical perspective is the principal aim. But a simply narrative description is not always possible: a critical discussion of the sources, especially when they contradict each other, will often be required.

Because the first Ptolemies and the Seleucids have already been discussed in the previous volume (*HJJSTP 2*), the survey here begins about 200 BCE, with Ptolemy V and Seleucus IV. It is thus not meant to be a free-standing summary of the two dynasties, only those rulers in the 2nd and 1st centuries BCE.

13.1. The Ptolemaic Realm

G. Hölbl (2001) *A History of the Ptolemaic Empire*, 192–94; **W. Huß** (2001) *Ägypten in hellenistischer Zeit: 332-30 v. Chr.*

The Ptolemaic kingdom had many advantages. It had been created by Alexander's general Ptolemy I who harnessed the old Egyptian realm for his new fiefdom. It was more unified than the Seleucid empire which encompassed many different peoples and countries, and the Ptolemaic rulers quickly drew on Pharaonic tradition to interpret and support their rule. This does not mean that the Ptolemies were not interested in extending the Egyptian empire. Already in 301, in spite of an agreement that Coele-Syria should be part of the domain of Seleucus I, Ptolemy seized it and refused to give it up (*HJJSTP 2*: 280–81). Four 'Syrian wars' were fought in the 3rd century in which the Seleucids unsuccessfully tried to gain Syria-Palestine. But then in the Fifth Syrian War Antiochus III succeeded in taking Coele-Syria, which the Seleucids always regarded as rightfully theirs.

This did not end the matter, and another four Syrian wars were fought before the Ptolemaic and Seleucid empires ceased to exist, though Syro-Palestine did not change hands again. The Syrian territory was not the only territory that the Egyptians were able to claim for a time. Cyprus was often under rule from Alexandria during the Ptolemaic period. Occasionally, certain colonies were established in Asia Minor, at least, on a temporary basis. However, the Ptolemaic kingdom was itself threatened with possible foreign rule in the 'Sixth Syrian War', where we take up the story (§15.1). Ptolemaic rule is an important backdrop to some of the events in Palestine at this time.

Outline of Ptolemaic History

NB: dates of rulers are based on Huß 2001. However, his numbering of the Ptolemies differ from that often used, but the conventional numbering is followed here.

Ptolemy V Theos Epiphanes (204–180 BCE) was a minor for the first fifteen years of his reign, and Egypt suffered considerably during this time, including the loss of most territories in the Aegean and Asia Minor. The main event was the loss of Palestine and southern Syria to Antiochus III in 200 BCE. An agreement was finally sealed with a marriage to Cleopatra I, a daughter of Antiochus. His coronation is the event described on the Rosetta Stone. He had not given up his claim to the Syrian possessions, however, but was assassinated before he could do anything about it.

Ptolemy VI Philometor (180–145 BCE) was only a young boy when he came to the throne, but his regents planned an invasion of Antiochus IV's realm which they launched about 170. Antiochus was victorious and made Ptolemy his ward; the regents then put his brother **Ptolemy VIII Euergetes II** (Physcon) (145–116 BCE) on the throne where he ruled jointly with Ptolemy VI and the latter's sister-wife Cleopatra II for several years. This cooperation led to another invasion by Antiochus in 168, but this time the Romans warned the Seleucid king off. Ptolemy VI then ruled alone, though his younger brother was given Cyrenaica. After Philometor's death, Euergetes took the throne, becoming guardian to Philometor's son **Ptolemy VII Neos Philopator** but soon had him executed. His two wives, Cleopatra II and Cleopatra III (mother and daughter), became rivals. Cleopatra II drove him out of Egypt for a number of years, during which time she reigned in his stead, but he soon returned and established an uneasy truce with his wives.

After Ptolemy VIII's death the two Cleopatras again became rivals, each apparently championing one of the two sons, though Cleopatra III became the main player and reigned jointly with each son in turn. The elder son **Ptolemy IX Soter II** (Lathyrus) (116–107, 88–80 BCE) ruled first but was displaced by his younger brother **Ptolemy X Alexander I** (107–88) and set up his own rule in Cyprus. In the meantime, an illegitimate son of Ptolemy VIII named Ptolemy Apion took up rule in Cyrenaica. At his death in 96, his will left the region to Rome. Ptolemy X also decided to leave Egypt to Rome in his will; however, he was driven from Egypt by a revolt (dying soon afterward), and Ptolemy IX returned to take up his second period of rulership. An embassy from Rome came in 86 and was well received, but the Romans were impressed only by Egypt's apparent wealth.

When Ptolemy IX died, the Romans now began the first of a series of increasing interventions in Egypt. Ptolemy IX's half-sister Berenice took the throne, but the Romans sent as king a son of Ptolemy X (and step-son of Berenice), **Ptolemy XI Alexander II**, who murdered Berenice. However, the Alexandrians in turn quickly assassinated him. A son of Ptolemy IX, **Ptolemy XII Neo Dionysus** (Auletes) (80–58, 55–51 BCE) took over rule, apparently without Roman intervention, but Rome was an ever-present power to be reckoned with. Pompey did not interfere in his activities in the east in 65–63; nevertheless, he took control of territory right up to Egypt's border. When Rome took over Cyprus, Ptolemy XII was driven out by his own people and his daughter Berenice ruled in his place. He sought Roman help and retook his throne, after which he had his daughter killed. (The one who brought him back to Egypt was

Gabinius, who was accompanied by Antipater the father of Herod the Great.)

When he died, he left instructions that his daughter **Cleopatra VII** (51–30 BCE) should marry her younger brother **Ptolemy XIII** (51–47). Cleopatra worked hard to strengthen her relations within her own country and became the only Ptolemy to speak the Egyptian language; however, she was only seventeen and was opposed by powerful functionaries. She fled to Syria, and the Romans became involved in her attempt to regain her throne. Ptolemy XIII was killed in the fighting, and she ruled jointly with her younger brother **Ptolemy XIV** (47–44) until she had him assassinated. Her involvement with Caesar and later Mark Antony demonstrated her skill in manipulating circumstances to gain the best deal for Egypt in a difficult period. This included regaining Cyprus for Egypt. She was also a major thorn in the side of Herod and would probably have had him deposed if he had not been so useful to Mark Antony. Nevertheless, the Romans as a whole opposed her, so when Mark Antony was defeated at Actium in 31, she had nowhere else to turn and committed suicide. She had associated her son **Ptolemy XV Caesar** (Caesarion) (36–30) with her on the throne, claiming that Julius Caesar was his father. He was executed on Octavian's orders.

13.2. *The Seleucid Empire*

B. Chrubasik (2016) *Kings and Usurpers in the Seleukid Empire: The Men Who Would be King*; **K. Ehling** (2008) *Untersuchungen zur Geschichte der späten Seleukiden (164–63 v. Chr.): Vom Tode des Antiochos IV. bis zur Einrichtung der Provinz Syria unter Pompeius*; **E. S. Gruen** (1984) *The Hellenistic World and the Rise of Rome*; **M. Sartre** (2001) *D'Alexandre à Zénobie: Histoire du Levant antique, IVe siècle avant J.-C., IIIe siècle aprè J.-C.*; **S. Sherwin-White and A. Kuhrt** (1993) *From Samarkhand to Sardis: A New Approach to the Seleucid Empire*.

There have been two predominant views of the Seleucid empire (Sherwin-White and Kuhrt 1993: 7–8). A 'weak view' has often prevailed, in which the Seleucid empire was characterized 'as a mere patchwork of separate "nations" or countries without cohesive structure and therefore easily fragmented – in fact in slow decline right from the death of its founder, Seleucus I' (ibid.). The 'strong view', which seems more likely the correct one, recognizes that the Seleucid empire lasted for the best part of two-and-a-half centuries. It was the successor of the Achaemenid empire, which itself was still strong and unified when attacked by Alexander. Granted, there were usurpers to Seleucid rule already from the 3rd century, and much depended on the competence and reputation of the Seleucid king (Chrubasik 2016: 2–10). This 'fragility' of the Seleucid ruler existed from the beginning, but it is clear that usurpers did not really have their way until the 2nd century BCE. In that sense, Chrubasik's observation (2016: 10), that the model of a strong Seleucid empire has been called into question, is exaggerated. But he has made a valuable point about the importance of considering not just the Seleucid kings but also the Seleucid usurpers.

All empires eventually fall, but Seleucid rule maintained itself robustly over a vast territory and multiple peoples for a good century and a half. Two main factors led to the decline of the Seleucid empire (Sherwin-White and Kuhrt 1993: 217–23): one was the advance of the Parthians who eventually took over Babylonia and the eastern part of the Seleucid realm (§9.4); the other was the rise of internal rival dynasties for the Seleucid throne. Accompanying this latter difficulty was the intervention of Rome. As will be noted at various points, Roman intervention in the east has often been exaggerated, especially for an early time, and the attempt to see Roman manipulation of Seleucid rivals for the throne is probably misguided for the 2nd century (Gruen 1984: 481–528). As Sherwin-White and Kuhrt point out (1993: 218), the Roman-centric interpretation is not helpful: 'The dates of 188 (Peace of Apamea), 168 (Battle of Pydna) and 146 (sack of Corinth) mark significant phases in Rome's eastward expansion, but are of relatively slight significance for understanding the end of Seleucid rule'. Yet in the end Roman intervention eventually became important and a significant factor in the collapse of Seleucid rule.

From the middle of the 2nd century the eastern part of the Seleucid empire was lost to the Parthians, Rome continued to move slowly but inexorably eastward and the rival Seleucid pretenders fractured administration and loyalty and exhausted resources. But during the 2nd century the Seleucid empire was the main background for what was happening in Judah, eventually to be replaced in the 1st century with Roman domination.

Outline of Seleucid History

NB: dates of Seleucid rulers are not always certain; for them Ehling 2008 and Sartre 2001 are drawn on.

Antiochus III (223–187 BCE) had extended his rule well into the 2nd century, but he was already discussed in *HJJSTP 2*: 317–18. Because the Jews were allowed to continue living as they had done, there is no indication of immediate change in the general circumstances of life in Judaea. Antiochus III was, however, occupied with persistent attempts to expand his empire into Asia Minor, which brought him into conflict with the Romans. He did not long outlive his defeat at Magnesia in 191 and was succeeded by his son **Seleucus IV Philopator** (187–175 BCE). Although Seleucus's rule seems to have been a rather quiet one, this may be due to administrative skills rather than lack of ability or motivation. He also evidently maintained good relations with Jerusalem (2 Macc. 3.2-3), with the exception of the alleged incident involving his minister Heliodorus (2 Macc. 3.4-40). Beyond this we hear nothing relating to Judaea until the reign of Antiochus IV, though it is proposed that he attempted to overhaul the tax system (§5.1). Seleucus's reign came to an end in 175 when he was murdered by Heliodorus, the minister mentioned in 2 Maccabees. A sketch of **Antiochus IV Epiphanes** (175–164 BCE) is given at §14.2.

Antiochus V Eupator (164–162 BCE) was unfortunate in being the son of Antiochus IV. Under other circumstances, it might have been a tremendous advantage; however, his father died when he was still quite young, which meant that he was under the 'guidance' (dictatorship, in reality) of regents. The main regent was Lysias, who had been a companion of Antiochus IV. He had been made vice-regent and guardian of the king's son, who seems to have been only about seven or eight, in 166 BCE before Antiochus IV marched east. The rule of Antiochus V is thus more or less based on the actions of Lysias. Several times 1 Maccabees (e.g., 6.28, 57, 60) refers to the king as reacting to events, evidently forgetting that the king was a minor. Lysias interacted with Judas (§15.4.4). When Judas began to besiege the Seleucid garrison in Jerusalem, Lysias defeated Judas's forces decisively and besieged the Jews in Jerusalem itself (1 Macc. 6.18-63; 2 Macc. 13). But then Lysias broke off the engagement and made an offer to the Jews, lifting the siege and allowing the inhabitants to leave unmolested. The reason that Lysias wanted to come to terms with the defenders was that Philip, another regent, had returned from Persia with the intent of taking over (1 Macc. 6.63). Lysias needed to confront him, which he did, and defeated him. But his control of Seleucid affairs did not last much longer, for about this time Demetrius the son of Seleucus IV escaped from Rome and made his claim for the Seleucid throne as Demetrius I. In late 162 he defeated Lysias and executed him, along with the young Antiochus V.

Demetrius I Soter (162–150 BCE) was the son of Seleucus IV. He was a hostage in Rome, but despite repeated requests to the Senate, had not been allowed to return to Syria. In 162 BCE, he slipped secretly away to take Antioch and execute the boy ruler Antiochus V. In Judah, the Jewish high priest Alcimus had been recognized by the Seleucids and also accepted by the majority of the Jews. He went to Demetrius to ask for help against the rebels led by Judas Maccabaeus (1 Macc. 10.37). Judas was killed shortly afterward, and Jonathan Maccabee took his place as leader of those Jews (a minority) who refused to make their peace with the Seleucids. At this time, rivalry for the Seleucid throne began, which created a wonderful opportunity for the Maccabees who could now play one side against the other.

The first rival was **Alexander I Balas** (150–145 BCE). Alexander claimed to be the son of Antiochus IV (and was so accepted by many in antiquity, though scholars generally doubt it today) and thus rightful heir to the throne. Because of Demetrius's bad relations with Rome the Senate decided to back Alexander (Polybius 33.18). As soon as Alexander came on the scene, Demetrius sent an offer of peace with a number of concessions to Jonathan Maccabee, knowing that he needed all the allies he could get (1 Macc. 10.1-6). Alexander made a counter-offer, including the high priesthood, which Jonathan accepted. Demetrius came back with another offer, but Jonathan did not trust him and favoured Alexander (1 Macc. 10.22-47). Jonathan proved to have made the right move when Alexander defeated and killed Demetrius in battle about the year 151 BCE.

Demetrius II Theos Nicator Philadelphus (145–140, 129–126 BCE) was the son of Demetrius I. In 147 Demetrius II moved against Alexander Balas to take back his father's kingdom. Jonathan Maccabee took advantage of the situation to lay siege to the Jerusalem citadel which was still in Syrian hands. When Demetrius demanded an accounting, Jonathan went boldly to him and came away with some important concessions. Demetrius was soon glad of Jonathan as an ally, for he helped Demetrius put down a revolt in Antioch; however, Demetrius then reneged on his promises. Shortly afterward Diodotus Tryphon, a general of Alexander Balas, crowned Alexander's son and proclaimed him king **Antiochus VI Dionysus Epiphanes** (ca. 145–140 BCE). Demetrius was defeated in the subsequent battle and fled, leaving the throne open to Antiochus VI. But although Demetrius II had been defeated by Tryphon, he was still alive and had not conceded the throne. Tryphon granted some honours to Jonathan Maccabee, but subsequently captured him by trickery and executed him. Not long afterward he did away with Antiochus VI and took the throne for himself as **Diodotus Tryphon** (ca. 142–138 BCE). Simon Maccabee negotiated with Demetrius who made some far-reaching concessions. Demetrius II then marched east in hopes of gaining further assistance against Tryphon, but was taken prisoner by the Parthians.

His brother Antiochus had come of age and was in Rhodes when news arrived of Demetrius's captivity. He obtained support from sufficient cities in Syria to be declared king, as **Antiochus VII Euergetes** (139–129 BCE), also called **Sidetes** because of growing up in the city Side. He married Demetrius's wife Cleopatra Thea and met the challenge of ousting

Tryphon. Antiochus had called on Simon Maccabee for help in the siege of Tryphon, but when he was out of the way, Antiochus made demands of Simon. When Simon tried to negotiate, Antiochus sent an army against Judah. When it was defeated, Antiochus himself took command about 134 BCE, by which time Simon was dead and his son John Hyrcanus led Judah. Antiochus besieged Hyrcanus in Jerusalem. Agreement was finally reached between Antiochus and Hyrcanus. In 130 BCE Antiochus led a campaign against Parthia to restore the eastern part of the Seleucid empire. John Hyrcanus accompanied him with a band of Jewish soldiers. At first, Antiochus made good progress, but the Parthians came back with new resources, and Antiochus died. Fortunately, John Hyrcanus had apparently returned to Judah.

When Demetrius II had returned from Parthian captivity and reclaimed his throne for his second period of rule (129–126 BCE), Ptolemy VIII put up a rival called **Alexander II Zabinas** (129–123 BCE). In a decisive battle, Demetrius was defeated and then shut out of Ptolemaus (where he had sought refuge) by his own wife Cleopatra Thea, before being assassinated in Tyre. Thea associated their second son with her on the throne, as **Antiochus VIII Epiphanes Philometor Kallinikos** (125–96 BCE), with the nickname of **Grypus** because of his hooked nose. He ruled in name for four years, though 'all the power of the throne rested with his mother' (Justin 39.1.9). But then when his mother supposedly tried to poison him, he turned the tables on her and now reigned in his own right. When Alexander Zabinas began to show signs of becoming independent, Ptolemy VIII abandoned him and put the resources of Egypt behind Grypus. The latter successfully defeated Alexander and had him executed. Although Alexander had been supported by the Jews (*Ant.* 13.9.3 §269), Antiochus did not take any action against them.

But then Grypus's half-brother Antiochus became his rival. **Antiochus IX Philopator** (113–95 BCE) was nicknamed **Cyzicenus** from the town Cyzicus where he was educated. He was son of Antiochus VII; however, his mother Cleopatra Thea had been successively the wife of Demetrius II (from whom she bore the future Antiochus VIII) and Antiochus VII, father of Antiochus IX. After a supposed attempt of Antiochus VIII to poison him, Antiochus IX began to seek the throne actively about 116 BCE. About this time Cleopatra IV was made to leave her husband in Egypt by her mother-in-law. She chose to go into exile in Syria, bringing with her the garrison of Cyprus. When she married Cyzicenus, this gave him the forces he needed to gain the upper hand against his half-brother, driving him into Asia Minor. But after a time Grypus was able to return to control northern Syria, though Cyzicenus remained in the south. When

Grypus took Antioch, Cleopatra IV was made a prisoner. Grypus's wife Tryphaena was her half-sister; nevertheless, Tryphaena insisted on her execution, in spite of Grypus's objections. A short time later, Tryphaena was herself captured by Cyzicenus who took his revenge on her. When hostilities between Antiochus VIII and XI resumed, Antiochus VIII did not live long but was assassinated. Cyzicenus then had a short reign of being the sole king, but he outlived his half-brother by only a year.

Antiochus VIII Grypus had five sons. At his death, the eldest became King **Seleucus VI Epiphanes Nicator** (96–95 BCE). He was the one who defeated and killed Antiochus IX Cyzicenus. Cyzicenus was succeeded by his son who became **Antiochus X Eusebes** ('Pious') **Philopator** (ca. 95–94). He married his father's wife Selene and took over his father's territory. He had a large task before him, however, because the five sons of Grypus were all arrayed against him. He quickly defeated Seleucus VI (who withdrew to Mopsuestia in Cilicia but upset the local people, who rebelled and brought an end to his rule). Eusebes could not rest for long, however, because two other sons of Grypus came up against him. These were **Philip I** and Antiochus XI Epiphanes. We know little about **Antiochus XI Epiphanes Philadelphus** (ca. 95 BCE). Antiochus XI took on himself the role of avenger for the death of his brother Seleucus VI. He first attacked and burned Mopsuestia, to punish those who had killed his brother, and then went against Eusebes. This may have been in concert with his brother Philip I, but this is not certain. Regardless of this, Antiochus XI perished, along with his army, when he fought against Eusebes. Philip picked up the mantle dropped by his brother, though without any real success.

Demetrius III Theos Philopator Soter Eucaerus (ca. 95–87), another son of Grypus, was one of four claimants to the Seleucid throne about 90 BCE. By this time the Seleucid dynasty was in rapid decline. In the Jewish kingdom, Alexander Jannaeus ruled (103–76 BCE; Josephus, *War* 1.4.1-8 §§85-106). Major opposition against him from his own people had developed. They called in Demetrius III against Jannaeus. The Syrian army won the initial clash of arms, but then the Jews who had called on Demetrius abandoned him, to join Jannaeus. Demetrius now feared defeat and retreated. Shortly afterward, Demetrius fought with Philip but was taken captive by Philip's Parthian ally. During this time the Armenian king Tigranes II had been expanding his control in Mesopotamia since he took the throne about 100 BCE; then in 83 BCE he occupied Syria. According to Appian, Antiochus succumbed to him at this time (*Syr.* 48; 69). We hear nothing more of Philip after this, suggesting that Tigranes brought an end to his reign about this time as well.

We know of Antiochus XII primarily from Josephus who claims – wrongly – that he was the last of the Seleucid rulers (*War* 1.4.7 §§99-102; *Ant.* 13.15.1 §§387-391). About 87 BCE **Antiochus XII Dionysus** (ca. 87–84 BCE), another son of Antiochus VIII, took over Damascus and proclaimed himself king. He soon marched against the Nabataeans, but while he was away his brother Philip was allowed into the city by Antiochus's garrison commander; however, he lost it shortly afterward when Antiochus's commander shut him out. Antiochus quickly returned to establish his authority in Damascus, but then led a second expedition against the Nabataeans. This time he elected to go via Judah with his army. Apparently, his aim was only to march through, but Alexander Jannaeus hastily constructed a defensive ditch and wooden wall to stop him. Antiochus had no difficulty pushing though it (and might have returned later to punish Jannaeus for this act), but was defeated and killed by Aretas III.

The last Seleucid king was **Antiochus XIII Philadelphus Asiaticus** (ca. 83?–64), though it is possible that he came to the throne after it had been vacant for some few years. According to Appian (*Syr.* 70), he was the son of Eusebes and Selene, but Justin (40.2.2) makes him the son of Cyzicenus. For a period of time (83–69 BCE) Tigranes II of Armenia took over Syria. Most of the Seleucid realm, such as it was by this time, fell into his hands (except for certain cities such as Seleucia-in-Pieria). Antiochus X Eusebes had two sons, who came to Rome and asked to be declared king, but there is little evidence that they actually occupied the Seleucid throne in any active way. When the Romans attacked Tigranes, while in pursuit of Mithridates who had sought refuge in his territory, Antiochus took his chance to assume the throne secretly, but Lucullus the Roman commander in the region did not object when he learned of it (Appian, *Syr.* 49; Justin says that Lucullus actually put him on the throne [40.2.2]). But when Pompey replaced Lucullus, he removed Asiaticus from the throne, with the sarcastic comment that he had not taken away a throne that was his, nor would he give to him a throne which he could not defend but had given up to Tigranes. Asiaticus was the last ruler over the Seleucid kingdom, which now came to an end, though it had been an empire in name only for many years.

13.3. *The Rise of Rome*

E. J. Bickerman (1980) *Chronology of the Ancient World*; **A. M. Eckstein** (2006) *Mediterranean Anarchy, Interstate War, and the Rise of Rome*; **idem** (2008) *Rome Enters the Greek East: From Anarchy to Hierarchy in the Hellenistic Mediterranean, 230–170 BC*; **E. S. Gruen** (1984) *The*

Hellenistic World and the Rise of Rome; **W. V. Harris** (1991) *War and Imperialism in Republican Rome*; **idem** (2016) *Roman Power*; **N. Rosenstein** (2012) *Rome and the Mediterranean 290 to 146 BC*; **H. H. Scullard** (1982) *From the Gracchi to Nero*; **C. Seeman** (2013) *Rome and Judea in Transition*; **C. Steel** (2013) *The End of the Roman Republic 146 to 44 BC*; **C. R. Whittaker** (1978) 'Carthaginian Imperialism in the Fifth and Fourth Centuries', in P. D. A. Garnsey and C. R. Whittaker (eds), *Imperialism in the Ancient World*, 59–90.

The Roman presence might have appeared on the horizon originally as a cloud no bigger than a man's hand. It is hard to know how the Romans were regarded in that part of the Greek world in the 3rd century BCE. But by 200, it had become apparent that this was a power that could not be ignored – perhaps it was even recognized as a serious cause for concern much earlier. When we scan the history of Rome it is clear that it was becoming a regional power before Alexander and a Mediterranean power in the century afterward. However the Greek world thought of the Romans, their existence had made itself felt in unmistakable terms by the time Judah came under Seleucid rule.

What became the Roman empire had begun as a small nation or community centred on the Roman hills and under a king, alongside other ethnic groups in Italy, such as the Etruscans. The Romans were one of the Latin tribes, but they began to go their own way when they got rid of their king and exchanged monarchy for a republican form of government in the late 6th century BCE. Over the next two centuries the area of Rome gradually expanded to include control of all Italy (by about 275 BCE). This represented a period of almost continual fighting, since hardly a year went by without a significant military encounter with neighbours (in the period 327–241 BCE, there were only four years without a military campaign [Harris 2016: 21]). Eventually this expansion led to conflict with nations external to Italy. Although they continued to have regular conflicts with the Gallic tribes to the north of Italy, the Romans now developed hostilities concerning Illyria in the east and, especially, with the Carthaginians.

We should be clear about the Carthaginians: they were not just a peaceable trading nation or empire whom Rome attacked because she wanted to take over her commercial routes. On the contrary, Carthaginian history shows her as belligerent as the Romans (cf. Whittaker 1978). Carthage often attacked rivals; nevertheless, by this point Roman–Carthaginian relations had been developing for some time and were not necessarily hostile. Yet the First Punic War (as the Romans called it; we do not know how the Carthaginians designated it), which began about 264 BCE, started almost by accident. Up until shortly before this time, Rome had not had a navy, but in 260 BCE they built a fleet with ships based on Carthaginian designs. In spite of her seafaring prowess, the Carthaginian navy was destroyed by the Romans at Mylae off the Sicilian coast. Carthage lost the war by 241 and, in addition to paying a large amount of silver in war reparations, they conceded Sicily and Sardinia to Roman control.

Nevertheless, a Second Punic war broke out about 218 BCE over Hannibal's siege of the Spanish city Saguntum which was a Roman ally. Although Hannibal had given the Romans serious difficulties with his unpredicted invasion of Italy by coming with his army through the Alps, his own government undermined his efforts by failing to support him with the necessary money and manpower. In the end, the Romans were victorious in 202 BCE; as a footnote, Hannibal fled to Antiochus III for refuge yet the Greek king had no alternative but to give in to the Romans when they demanded that Hannibal be turned over to them. When Hannibal saw the Roman soldiers coming for him, he committed suicide in 182 BCE. But for our purposes this is a side issue.

Two events took place about the same time, with far-reaching consequences. First, defeating Carthage in the Second Punic War was a major step forward for Rome, eroding Carthage's ability to compete commercially with Rome. The other important matter – the one of primary concern for the history of Judaea – was what happened in Rome in 201 BCE. In 201 BCE the Second Punic War was coming to an end. At this point, Rome made a fateful decision that might well not have been expected. To explain that decision, we need to consider two major approaches to the rise of Rome among recent modern historians. Many have followed W. V. Harris (1991, 2016), who argued that Rome from at least the 4th century BCE was uniquely aggressive and militaristic, with 'a deep devotion to merciless war, spread all across Roman society' (2016: 66). Another approach was taken by E. S. Gruen (1984) and especially by A. M. Eckstein (2006, 2008; cf. also Seeman 2013: especially Chapters 4–5). Eckstein did not deny the militarism and rapaciousness of Rome; he simply argued that most other Mediterranean states were the same, not only the large and middle-sized political entities but even many small ones:

> ...the desire to dominate, to exert as much control over one's environment as possible, and the habit of command – like the engagement in constant warfare – does not differentiate the Roman Republic from any other Classical or Hellenistic state. (2008: 247)

Those who favour the second position – which appears to be the most plausible one – point to the continual vacillation about embassies from eastern rulers and countries and the constant position to 'watch and wait' when some crisis seems to have arisen outside Italy. This was in part a matter of pragmatism, since the constant wars that Rome did fight (often closer to home) were a continual drain on resources, which meant that they had to be careful about overextending themselves and running out of military manpower. C. Seeman (2013: 131–32) summarizes succinctly the position taken by the Senators when dealing with the Greek East: he notes a two-fold predisposition on their part: (1) a tendency to acquiesce in the presence of distant events, and (2) a clear preference for making strong pronouncements rather than taking concrete action.

With this background, we can now look at the important event in the Senate in 201 BCE (Eckstein 2006: 257–92; 2008: 230–70). In that year four major embassies from the east came with the same message: Philip V of Macedonia and the Seleucid king Antiochus III had become a major threat to the other countries and kings of the region. The reason is that the Ptolemaic power had collapsed significantly. Therefore, the three-fold balance of power between Macedonia, Egypt and Syria no longer prevailed, and Syria and Macedonia now were in a position to dominate the region. They drew the Senate's attention to this threat and requested Rome to intervene. There were major objections from the Roman side. The exhausting war with Carthage was only just finished, and the Roman people were drained. Yet the Senate ultimately decided to intervene. The result was that the Mediterranean system, formerly divided between the regional subsystems of east and west, now became one state system. This of course had the side effect of facilitating the rise of Roman domination of the Mediterranean world.

According to one view (not that of Harris) Rome – like Britain allegedly did – came to acquire an empire in the East almost by accident. She realized that she had interests in that area, of course, and had already intervened at various times (e.g., against Antiochus III) to see that the balance of power was maintained, but this was not the same as acquiring possessions or taking over. As already noted, for a century she was occupied in her fight to the death with Carthage in the three Punic Wars, ending finally in 146 with the fall of Carthage and the conquest of Greece. The imperialistic stage began in 133 when Rome was willed the kingdom of Pergamum on the death of its king Attalus III. This was not an unmixed blessing since it would require resources to defend. It was the time of social reforms under the Gracchi brothers, however, and the question became mixed up in the heated controversies between opposing social factions within Rome itself. Eventually, the bequest was accepted and made into the Roman province of Asia, though portions of the original kingdom of Pergamum were given to other kingdoms or made independent.

After the transfer of Pergamum, Cilicia had become a stronghold of pirates, and the praetor Antonius was sent to rid the area of the problem. Part of his solution was to make Cilicia into a province in 102 BCE. As had already been recognized, such outposts were not necessarily easy to defend, especially with the troubles which affected Rome itself during this period. Mithridates VI, king of Pontus (120–63 BCE), had already expanded his territory to the east and up the coast of the Black Sea. In 93 he attempted to move south into Cappadocia, and in 90, west into Bithynia but was stopped by Rome each time. The Italian War (91–87) provided the opportunity for Mithridates to try again. He took Bithynia and then Asia where he was welcomed as a liberator. He even sent an army into Greece and, with the help of the Athenians, occupied most of the country. This began the First Mithridatic War (88–85). Despite his own troubles at home, the Roman general Sulla set out against Mithridates in 86, drove him out of the lands he had taken, and forced him to return to Pontus and pay a large indemnity for the trouble he had caused.

Mithridates was not beaten, however, and he had little trouble with the Roman commander during the so-called Second Mithridatic War (83–81 BCE). It was also during this time that Tigranes I of Armenia (ca. 100–56 BCE) began expanding, taking over the remaining Seleucid kingdom. The Third Mithridatic War (74–63 BCE) was the decisive one. It was initiated by the Roman annexation of Bithynia, which had been willed to Rome on the death of its ruler. Mithridates captured Bithynia in the initial stages but was worsted by the Roman consul Lucullus who drove him into Armenia. Tigranes was continuing his drive down the Syrian coast and posing a major threat to Judaea under the rule of Alexandra Salome. However, Tigranes turned back to Armenia when he heard of Mithridates's presence in his country. With Tigranes's help, Mithridates raised another army. Lucullus retaliated by taking Syria away from Tigranes and placing a Seleucid on the throne once again (the Antiochus XIII Asiaticus mentioned above, §13.2). After Mithridates retook Pontus in 67, the new Roman commander sent to oppose him was the able and respected Pompey, who soon demonstrated why he bore the epithet 'the Great'.

Pompey was already in the eastern Mediterranean where he had been commissioned in 67 to clear the area of pirates who had grown up again in the 40 years since Antonius's campaign. Pompey took only about a year to defeat Mithridates decisively in 66. After fleeing to Colchis, the latter eventually committed suicide when he was unable to gain support even from his own son for a further army. With this menace out of the way, Pompey proceeded to use the wide-ranging powers given him by the Senate and annex Asia Minor and Syria as far as the Euphrates. Among the casualties was Antiochus XIII who, having been installed by the Romans, was now removed by them. One of the few areas to escape was Armenia since Tigranes had the good sense to respect the Roman military power. However, Pompey was drawn into the internecine fighting of the Hasmonaean rivals Hyrcanus II and Aristobulus II and put an end to the independence of that state (§17.2).

It was conventional in Roman documents to record years by the names of consuls who were in office at that time. For a list of the Roman consuls year by year, see Bickerman 1980: 140–62.

Chapter 14

EVENTS PRECEDING THE MACCABAEAN REVOLT
(175–168 BCE): A NEW CONSTITUTION FOR
JERUSALEM

J. C. Bernhardt (2017) *Die jüdische Revolution: Untersuchungen zu Ursachen, Verlauf und Folgen der hasmonäischen Erhebung*; **E. J. Bickerman** (1937a) *Der Gott der Makkabäer: Untersuchungen über Sinn und Ursprung der makkabäischen Erhebung* // **idem** (1979) *The God of the Maccabees: Studies on the Meaning and Origin of the Maccabean Revolt*; **K. Bringmann** (1983) *Hellenistische Reform und Religionsverfolgung in Judäa: Eine Untersuchung zur jüdisch-hellenistischen Geschichte (175–163 v. Chr.)*; **J. K. Davies** (1984) 'Cultural, Social and Economic Features of the Hellenistic World', in F. W. Walbank et al. (eds), *The Cambridge Ancient History, Volume 7, Part 1: The Hellenistic World*, 257–320; **J. A. Goldstein** (1976) *I Maccabees: A New Translation with Introduction and Commentary*; **idem** (1983a) *II Maccabees: A New Translation with Introduction and Commentary*; **C. Habicht** (1989) 'The Seleucids and their Rivals', *CAH²* 8:324–87; **M. Hengel** (1974) *Judaism and Hellenism*; **S. Honigman** (2014) *Tales of High Priests and Taxes: The Books of the Maccabees and the Judean Rebellion against Antiochos IV*; **M. G. Morgan** (1990) 'The Perils of Schematism: Polybius, Antiochus Epiphanes and the "Day of Eleusis"', *Historia* 39: 37–76; **M. Rostovtzeff** (1941) *The Social and Economic History of the Hellenistic World*; **J. Sievers** (1990) *The Hasmoneans and their Supporters: From Mattathias to the Death of John Hyrcanus I*; **V. A. Tcherikover** (1959) *Hellenistic Civilization and the Jews*; **S. Tedesche and S. Zeitlin (eds.)** (1950) *The First Book of Maccabees*.

The present chapter begins with the accession of Antiochus IV to the Seleucid throne in 175 BCE and covers the sequence of events that led to the suppression of Judah and the subsequent revolt of the Judaeans against the Seleucids. As we shall see in this chapter, there are many puzzling statements in the sources; also, much recent study modifies or even contradicts ideas and interpretations found in older secondary literature. Make no mistake: there are few easy answers for this period. All we can do is be as careful, thorough and honest with the sources as we can and argue our case for how we think they should be interpreted.

As noted in the previous chapter (Chapter 13), the historical background of the Hellenistic empires and the advance of Rome are important factors in understanding what happened in the small area of Palestine, and this background will be drawn on here. An important actor in events during this period was also the Seleucid king Antiochus IV Epiphanes. This is why a section is devoted to him, to give readers background on events about to take place or already taking place. But we also have the problem of the literary sources describing events in Judaea (including the Greek and Roman historians), and a word needs be said about them in the present context, even though they were discussed in Chapters 3–4 of this book. In the end, much of this chapter is devoted to *reconstructing* what we think happened, because there is no one source that we can read off as giving a reasonable narrative for the sequence of events.

14.1. *The First 25 Years of Seleucid Rule*

As outlined in the previous volume (*HJJSTP 2*: 322–27) Seleucid rule seemed to begin well. Antiochus III had ended a century of Ptolemaic rule by taking back Coele-Syria in the Fifth Syrian War (202–199 BCE). The province of Judaea and many of the Jews outside it in Syria were now under Seleucid rule. Yet Antiochus III began his lordship over Jerusalem with a decree that recognized traditional Jewish rights and religious requirements and, especially, the temple in Jerusalem (*Ant.* 12.3.3-4 §§129-46). The majority of the Jews appeared to approve of Antiochus III's rule, his decree on behalf of Jerusalem and the Jews was positive, and despite some war damage the economy of Jerusalem was prospering. Nevertheless, there were some ominous clouds on the horizon: Seleucid expansion brought the Seleucid empire into conflict with the Romans, who were also extending their influence eastward (§13.3).

The Romans had conducted a war with Philip V of Macedonia, the so-called Second Macedonian War (200–196 BCE). Now Antiochus foolishly toppled into a war with the Romans, which was both unnecessary and also disastrous for him. After a defeat at Magnesia in 191 BCE, the treaty of Apamea in 188 placed heavy restrictions on Antiochus, including a war indemnity and the requirement for a son to be sent to Rome as a hostage. Thus, the future Antiochus IV was sent to Rome about 188 BCE and remained there until about 176. Antiochus III himself died in

187 BCE and was succeeded by his son Seleucus IV (187–175 BCE). Seleucus reigned quietly for the most part and did not engage in military ventures. He paid off much of the war indemnity but fell behind in payments toward the end of his reign, which left his successor to finish the final instalments. Seleucus IV apparently had a financial quarrel with Judah, as reflected in the tale of Heliodorus and the temple treasure (2 Macc. 3), even if the precise situation is not clear (*HJJSTP 2*: 327–28). Seleucus himself ended his life prematurely when he was assassinated, allegedly by this same Heliodorus, which left a power vacuum. This proved a stroke of luck for his younger brother Antiochus who had been released from his term as hostage in Rome and was in Athens.

Normally, the son of the ruler would take over on the death of the father, but his older son Demetrius had just settled in Rome as a hostage for the Seleucids' keeping the peace (in place of his uncle Antiochus IV). Seleucus's other son, Antiochus, was only about 4-5 years old. His mother (Seleucus's wife) Laodice became regent. But Seleucus's brother Antiochus was in Athens, apparently on his way back home. For whatever reason, Eumenes II king of Pergamum encouraged him psychologically but also with material assistance to take the throne. Antiochus quickly sailed from Athens to Antioch, supported by soldiers provided by Eumenes, and took the Seleucid throne as Antiochus IV Epiphanes. He apparently married Seleucus's widow Laodice and adopted the young Antiochus as his son (Mørkholm 1966: 49–50). Both this marriage and the adoption look to be steps toward securing and legitimating his own rule, even if for the moment he ruled jointly with the younger Antiochus. There is no doubt that Antiochus IV looms large in our sources and was a significant player in the events described here. It is also true that recent studies have argued that Antiochus has been wrongly evaluated by some past historians of this period. This is why we shall begin with an overview of his reign, which comes in the next section (§14.2).

14.2. *Antiochus IV (175–164 BCE)*

F. Altheim and R. Stiehl (1970) 'Antiochos IV. Epiphanes und der Osten', *Geschichte Mittelasiens im Altertum*, 553–71; **A. Aymard** (1953–54) 'Autour de l'avènement d'Antiochos IV', *Historia* 2: 49–73; **J. G. Bunge** (1974a) 'Münzen als Mittel politischer Propaganda: Antiochos IV. Epiphanes von Syrien', *Studii Clasice* 16: 43–52; **idem** (1974b) '"Theos Epiphanes": Zu den ersten fünf Regierungsjahren Antiochos' IV. Epiphanes', *Historia* 23: 57–85; **idem** (1975) '"Antiochos-Helios": Methoden und Ergebnisse der Reichspolitik Antiochos' IV. Epiphanes von Syrien im Spiegel seiner Münzen', *Historia* 24: 164–88; **P. F. Mittag** (2006) *Antiochus IV. Epiphanes*; **O. Mørkholm** (1966) *Antiochus IV of Syria*.

We know of Antiochus IV not only from Jewish sources but also the Greek historians, especially Polybius though also others, including Diodorus, Appian, and Pompeius Trogus (in Justinus's epitome), and the Roman historian Livy. Diodorus, Appian, Pompeius, and Livy are at least in part dependent on Polybius, which makes him an important original source. On the other hand, Polybius had a certain prejudice against Antiochus, and tends to counter any positive comments with accompanying negative statements, to give a more negative portrait than is perhaps justified (Mittag 2006: 19–21). The two main recent biographies of Antiochus (Mørkholm 1966 and Mittag 2006) show a much more positive and able character than emerges from Polybius and other ancient authors and, especially, many modern treatments. Another reason for the negative portrait so often painted is the image of a heavily maligned figure that comes from the Jewish sources, especially 1 and 2 Maccabees and Josephus.

Antiochus had been sent as a hostage to Rome about 188 BCE against Antiochus III's good behaviour, as the Romans saw it. In addition to a heavy war indemnity, the Peace of Apameia required the Seleucids to provide a member of the royal family as a hostage in Rome. Antiochus thus had a considerable part of his education in Rome and knew many of the upper-class Romans at the time. In 176 BCE he was replaced as hostage by Seleucus IV's eldest son (later to become Demetrius I) and was on his way back to Syria when he heard of his brother's death. This gave him the opportunity to make his bid for the throne, with the encouragement and active help of Eumenes II of Pergamum. He had little difficulty in taking the throne from his nephew (who may have already been proclaimed king), though they apparently ruled as supposed joint rulers for a few years (before the younger Antiochus was evidently executed by his uncle). Thus began the reign of one of the most promising and possibly one of the most able of the Seleucid rulers; however, like his father he had history against him. Holding on to the ambitions of a proper Seleucid empire, Antiochus spent the first five years of his reign accumulating the necessary resources to bring this about. It was during this time that he was quite happy to receive a large sum of money from Jason to become high priest in place of his brother and to turn Jerusalem into a Greek foundation.

It is alleged that Antiochus intended to gain control of Egypt: by becoming king according to some, or as the power behind the throne according to others. The trouble was that the Ptolemies were also plotting to take back Coele-Syria and Phoenicia that they had lost to Antiochus III. Who started the Sixth Syrian War is to some extent a fruitless debate, since they were both preparing for war. For example, both had sent recent delegations to Rome, though Antiochus thought he had right on his side and probably saw himself able to wield a relatively free hand with regard to Egypt (Polybius 28.1). According to Polybius (28.20-21; also Diodorus 30.15-16) Ptolemy VI took the initiative by advancing into Syrian territory in late 170 or early 169 BCE. Although others (Livy 42.29.5-6; Appian, *Syr.* 66; Justin 34.2.7; the Jewish sources) blame Antiochus, this seems the natural reaction; Polybius – in bucking the natural surmise – is more likely to be right. Antiochus responded with a counter-attack which soon turned into an invasion of Egypt itself. Having defeated the Egyptians and succeeded in becoming the protector of his nephew Ptolemy VI, Antiochus returned in triumph about September 169.

This was followed by another invasion in 168 which seems to have been successful initially (it has even been argued that Antiochus was declared king of Egypt at one point in the campaign: cf. Will 1982: 319), but then the Romans intervened. A Roman mission confronted Antiochus and gave him the ultimatum of withdrawing from Egypt or being an enemy of Rome. This was the infamous 'Day of Eleusis', and Antiochus had no choice but to withdraw in the face of their ultimatum (though he may have welcomed their intervention: see §15.1). It was at this point that he heard about the fighting in Jerusalem and sent a military unit to intervene in what he interpreted (perhaps correctly) as a revolt. The problems in Judaea were undoubtedly important but they were hardly the major ones on his mind. More important was the securing of funds for the depleted treasury after his war expenses, as well as seeing to the rest of his empire. A year or two after the second invasion of Egypt, probably in the summer of 166, he organized an enormous celebration and military display at Daphne. Shortly after this, probably in the autumn of the same year, he began a series of campaigns toward the east. Antiochus appears concerned in the main to consolidate and expand his empire in an area where there were no constraints from the Romans, though he also took the occasion to replenish his coffers when he had a chance. It was on this campaign that he died in late 164 BCE.

We can assess Antiochus's character at this point. As noted, Polybius is one of our main sources about him, but he is biased against Antiochus and is mostly negative. Yet it is also true that his assessment of Antiochus occasionally has a positive side as well (e.g., Polybius 28.18). There is evidence that Antiochus was a very able ruler, on the whole, and that a number of his actions are possibly explained by his long sojourn in Rome. At least some of his actions which would have seemed strange to the Syrians were those which were normal among the Romans (Goldstein 1976: 104–5). In his study of Antiochus, Mørkholm (1964: especially 181–91) has spent a good deal of space on the question and summarizes the situation as follows:

> The result of these considerations must be that Antiochus IV, in spite of some miscalculations, was actually a shrewd politician who may even deserve to be called a statesman. His campaigns in Egypt and Armenia show him to have been an able general too. If we review the Seleucid king list we may safely rate Antiochus IV well above average. (Mørkholm 1964: 187)

A similar assessment is given by Habicht (1989: 341–43). As far as we can see, Antiochus was driven by political needs and pragmatism, not ideology.

14.3. *The Problem of Sources: Different Accounts of How the Revolt Began*

We have several accounts of the beginning and initial phases of the Jewish revolt against Seleucid rule, not only Jewish but also Greek and Roman. This poses a problem because

- The early Graeco-Roman sources (such as Polybius) do not mention the situation in Judah, which means that we are almost entirely reliant on Jewish accounts for the start of the Maccabaean period.
- The Jewish sources differ among themselves, except where one account depends heavily on another (e.g., Josephus's *Antiquities* which depends greatly on 1 Maccabees).
- The only detailed account of the events leading up to the revolt is the one in 2 Maccabees 4. This means that even if we critique it, doubt it or reject it, it is ultimately the only information we have, and everything not from it becomes surmise or even speculation.

Almost universally, modern historians have reconstructed their accounts of what happened in the years 175–168 BCE from 2 Maccabees, with perhaps a detail or two from 1 Maccabees, but ignored the version in Josephus's *War* and the Greek and Roman ones. There are good reasons for this choice, but has sufficient attention been devoted to the other accounts before rejecting them? Here the accounts will be analyzed before an attempt is made to reconstruct the events of the first few years of the revolt.

We have four main sources that tell us about the beginning of the Maccabaean revolt and Hasmonaean rule. Although there are certain agreements, all four differ in certain ways from one another. Normally, the two sources with the closest agreements are 1 and 2 Maccabees, but 1 Maccabees has almost nothing on the events preceding Antiochus's invasion of Egypt, whereas 2 Maccabees gives the most detailed account of what happened. Josephus has two versions, one in the *War of the Jews* and the other in the *Antiquities of the Jews*. They agree in part but also have some differences. The account in *War* is mostly ignored by reconstructions of the history of this time.

According to the *War* (1.1.1-4 §§31-39) the situation began at the time Antiochus IV was opposing Ptolemy VI: a dispute grew among Jewish dignitaries, and 'one of the high priests' Onias expelled the Tobiads from Jerusalem (on the Tobiads, see *HJJSTP 2*: 75–78, 293–97). With great indignity they went to Antiochus and offered to act as guides for his army to capture Jerusalem. Antiochus was already desirous of taking Jerusalem and accepted their offer, took an army to Jerusalem, besieged and conquered it and plundered the city. He robbed the temple and stopped the sacrifices for three and a half years. The high priest Onias fled to Heliopolis in Egypt and founded a temple on the same plan as the one in Jerusalem. This summarizes the account in the *War*. Whereas Josephus clearly used 1 Maccabees as his main source in the *Antiquities*, his source for the *War* is not immediately clear. Since his main source for the Hasmonaeans was Nicolaus of Damascus (§4.6), however, it is likely that Nicolaus is also his source here.

The *Antiquities* (12.5.1 §§37-41) says that the high priest Onias died, and the priesthood was given to his brother Jesus. Antiochus became angry with him, however, and gave the priesthood to his younger brother, also named Onias. Of the three sons of Simon, Jesus was also called Jason, and Onias, Menelaus. Jesus-Jason revolted against Onias-Menelaus, and the people were divided, with Tobias supporting Onias-Menelaus but most of the people supporting Jesus-Jason. Menelaus and the Tobiads went to Antiochus and said they wanted to abandon their national laws and follow the king's laws and the Greek way of life. They petitioned him to let them build a gymnasium, and they masked their circumcision and adopted foreign practices.

The various accounts can be laid out as follows (1 Maccabees says little on events before Antiochus's invasion of Egypt and is therefore omitted here):

14. *Events Preceding the Maccabaean Revolt (175–168 BCE)*

2 Maccabees 4.7-34	Josephus, *War* 1.1.1–4 §§31-39	Josephus, *Ant.* 12.5.1 §§237-41
Onias (III) was in Antioch.	Onias 'one of the high priests'.	Onias (III) died.
His brother Jason paid Antiochus IV to take high priesthood. He also paid to build a gymnasium.		Jesus-Jason given high priesthood by Antiochus IV. Onias-Menelaus and Tobiads gained permission to build gymnasium.
Menelaus promised payment to Antiochus and took high priesthood from Jason.		Antiochus angry with Jesus-Jason and gave the high priesthood to Onias-Menelaus. The people supported Jason, but Tobiads, Menelaus.
	Onias expelled Tobiads from Jerusalem. They went to Antiochus and offered to be guides if he invaded Jerusalem. Antiochus invades Judaea, takes Jerusalem, and plunders the temple, stopping the sacrifices for 3 1/2 years. Onias flees to Ptolemy in Egypt and builds temple at Heliopolis.	Forced out of Jerusalem by Jason, Menelaus and Tobiads asked Antiochus to leave Jewish law and adopt Greek customs.

The two accounts of Josephus are quite different, except for his making the Tobiads an essential part of each account. The *War* makes no mention of a transfer of the high priesthood. The *Antiquities* makes Simon have two sons named Onias, and this Onias-Menelaus is a son of Simon instead of a brother of Simon from another priestly family; Onias (III) died before Jason received the high priesthood; Antiochus makes an unprovoked attack on Jerusalem. However, the *Antiquities* have some agreement with 2 Maccabees: the priesthood transferred from Jason to Menelaus; and the building of a gymnasium (though the *Antiquities* ascribes it to Menelaus, but 2 Maccabees to Jason).

Josephus's main source in the *Antiquities* in general was 1 Maccabees, but most of his two accounts here have little in common with 1 Maccabees. It also seems clear from his accounts overall that he did not know 2 Maccabees. Thus, his sources for the beginning of the revolt was evidently independent of both 1 and 2 Maccabees. On the other hand, it seems unlikely that the same source lay behind both of Josephus's accounts, since they are so different. Because his accounts seem muddled in both cases, there are reasons to be sceptical of Josephus's versions of the beginning of the revolt. This is why most modern scholars have simply ignored his versions. 1 and 2 Maccabees were much closer to the actual events and probably give us the basic outline of events, even though their picture is certainly coloured by biases of the authors. Thus, like so many others the account here will basically ignore Josephus for the beginning of the revolt, though later on he apparently has some helpful material.

It may be that Josephus has some useful data, but it is very difficult to separate the worthless from the historical. One possible datum that might be helpful concerns the participation of the Tobiads in the events. As discussed in the previous volume (*HJJSTP 2*: 293–97), the Tobiad family was one of the dominant powers in Judaea in the 3rd century BCE, and this apparently continued into the first part of the 2nd century (cf. 2 Macc. 3.11). It would hardly be surprising if they continued to try to influence events to their advantage. Since the Tobiads disappear from Jewish history about this time, this may be have been their final hurrah, perhaps because their attempt to direct events was unsuccessful. The fact that 1 and 2 Maccabees do not mention the Tobiads in this context might be because their actions backfired. If Josephus's accounts have any merit, it is probably in bringing the actions of the Tobiads to our attention, but it is not clear that the Tobiad activity ended up being very significant.

14.4. *A New Constitution for Jerusalem*

B. Bar-Kochva (1976a) *The Seleucid Army: Organization and Tactics in the Great Campaigns*; **R. Doran** (1989) 'The Non-Dating of Jubilees: Jub 34–38; 23:14-32 in Narrative Context', *JSJ* 20: 1–11; **idem** (1990) 'Jason's Gymnasium', in H. W. Attridge, J. J. Collins and T. H. Tobin (eds), *Of Scribes and Scrolls: Studies on the Hebrew Bible, Intertestamental Judaism, and Christian Origins Presented to John Strugnell on the Occasion of his Sixtieth Birthday*, 99–109; **L. L. Grabbe** (2001) 'A Dan(iel) for All Seasons: For Whom Was Daniel Important?', in J. J. Collins and P. W. Flint (eds), *The Book of Daniel: Composition and Reception*, 1:229–46; **idem** (2008b) 'Sanhedrin, Sanhedriyyot, or Mere Invention?" *JSJ* 39: 1–19; **G. T. Griffith** (1935) *The Mercenaries of the*

Hellenistic World; **R. G. Hall** (1989) 'Epispasm and the Dating of Ancient Jewish Writings', *JSP* 4: 71–86; **L. Jonnes and M. Ricl** (1997) 'A New Royal Inscription from Phrygia Paroreios: Eumenes II Grants Tyriaion the Status of a *Polis*', *Epigraphica Anatolica* 29: 1–30; **O. W. Reinmuth** (1948) 'The Ephebate and Citizenship in Attica', *TAPA* 79: 211–31; **S. Yalichev** (1997) *Mercenaries of the Ancient World*.

14.4.1. *Jason Displaces Onias as High Priest*

Sources: 1 Macc. 1.10-15; 2 Macc. 3–4;
War 1.1.1-4 §§31-39; *Ant.* 12.5.1 §§237-41.

Twenty-five years of Seleucid rule went by fairly smoothly but not without some upsetting events (primarily the Heliodorus episode [*HJJSTP 2*: 327–29]); however, Seleucid rule was ostensibly no more oppressive than that of the previous imperial rule that Jews had endured for centuries under the Neo-Babylonians, Persians and Ptolemies. Yet things changed almost immediately when Antiochus IV came to the throne in 175 BCE, though the reasons are complex.

Antiochus IV began his reign in September 175 BCE (§1.3.2). What actions did he take with regard to the Jews? If we follow 1 and 2 Maccabees, the answer is surprising: *he did nothing*! From the main Jewish sources of 1 and 2 Maccabees we have no indication that Antiochus had any particular interest in the Jews. True, the first encounter with the Jews does seem to have come about fairly soon after he began his reign, but it was not initiated by him, at least according to 2 Macc. 4.7-10. On the contrary, Jason (brother of the Jerusalem high priest Onias III) approached Antiochus with a very attractive proposition: he offered to pay 360 talents of silver, plus another 80 from another source, a total of 440 talents of silver (2 Macc. 4.8). For this he requested to be given the high priesthood in place of his brother. He also offered another 150 talents to be able to build a gymnasium in Jerusalem, giving 590 talents in all. Several issues seem to be hidden in this straightforward statement of 2 Maccabees:

- According to 2 Maccabees the initiative came from the Jewish side: no suggestion is made that Antiochus approached the Jewish leadership or attempted in any way to interfere with Judah at this point.
- The payment offered seems to have been an increase on the annual tribute already being paid to the Seleucids by the high priest on behalf of the province. Thus, the amount promised was not made

just once but was an annual enhanced contribution to the Seleucid overlord. (The 150 talents to build the gymnasium, however, might have been a one-off payment rather than an annual one.)
- Although not stated explicitly, the request to build a gymnasium and draw up an ephebate list seems clearly part of an initiative to have Jerusalem made into a *polis*, i.e., a city organized in the Greek manner. In such a system, some of the population (though by no means all) would be citizens, with particular privileges. Their children would become 'ephebates' or candidates for citizenship, which they would gain formally at a certain age. The concept of the ephebate probably goes back at least to the 5th century BCE. The fact remains, however, that our clear documentation of it is no earlier than about 335 BCE (Reinmuth 1948). Preparation for citizenship included attendance at an educational institute called the 'gymnasium'. This was not just a place for exercise, though physical training was an important part of the education. In its origins, the gymnasium prepared young men for war, so that physical exercises and other military training was a key part of the curriculum. With time, however, the military training became less accentuated and, although physical exercises were still important, a good deal of emphasis was placed on the intellectual requirements of citizenship, especially use of the (Greek) language in both writing and speech; rhetoric, since citizens might be required to speak in public; and Greek literature (with an emphasis on Homer).

The focus of rulers has always been on power: to establish their power; to consolidate their power; to expand their power. Anything supporting these aims would be welcome, but many of the mechanisms to support power required finance. As an astute ruler, Antiochus had grand plans for his empire, but funds would be required to realize these. Many royal ventures would require troops, and troops cost money. You have to feed and pay troops, even if they are conscripts, though Hellenistic rulers also made a good deal of use of mercenary troops (cf. Griffith 1935; Bar-Kochva 1976a; Yalichev 1997). Hiring mercenary troops could be like taking a viper into your bosom. To keep such troops on side, the ruler needed to pay more than they could get from his enemies; otherwise, he could suddenly find himself with an opposing army in his very heartland, since it was common for the victorious general to enlist the opponent's troops in his own army. (It was unusual for the troops to refuse, though this sometimes happened, e.g., with Antiochus VII's troops when the Parthians tried to use them; cf. Yalichev 1997: 198.)

Thus, any proposal to Antiochus that seemed likely to bring revenue into his coffers would probably meet with his approval. This does not mean that he was short of funds (cf. Bernhardt 2017: 118 n. 210; 181), but any extra income would still be welcome. In this case, there were many positive features to Jason's offer: it made no difference to Antiochus who was high priest in Jerusalem; in any event, the office was still in the family; and Jason had at least showed some sign of having a bit of gumption and might turn out to be useful in other ways; above all, he seems to have paid cash on the barrel head (at least, we hear of no reports that he reneged on his promise). Finally, Antiochus appears to have encouraged a number of the native cities in his empire to become *poleis*.

This interpretation follows the scenario in 2 Maccabees that Jason initiated the offer to Antiochus. Recently, however, Sylvie Honigman has argued that the initiative came from Antiochus who was finishing tax reform measures that had begun with Seleucus IV (Honigman 2014: 316–61). According to her reconstruction, 1 Maccabees 3 and the episode with Heliordorus was a fictionalized account of Seleucus's attempt to regulate the temples and taxes more closely in Coele-Syria and Phoenicia. Simon's dispute with Onias III (2 Macc. 3.2-6) was over Simon's response to an imperial request for a report that may have included the money in the temple deposited there by Hyrcanus Tobiad. In Honigman's view, Antiochus IV was continuing this dispute (since Heliodorus had been somehow thwarted in his attempt to take Hyrcanus's money) and wished to have Onias removed from office. Having his brother Jason displace him was the simplest way of dealing with the problem. The extra tribute payment was not something that Jason offered freely but was part of Antiochs's new tax regime.

Honigman's thesis has much to commend it, though the interpretation of events given here is somewhat closer to the text of 1 and 2 Maccabees – though drawing on Honigman's insights, especially about the tax situation (see §5.1, §14.5, and above). Yet one must ask why 1 Maccabees would have presented it as a proposal by Jason to Antiochus, when it was actually Antiochus making demands on Onias. It could be argued that this was a means of discrediting Jason, but the author of 2 Maccabees has much more serious charges to bring against Jason. He is also very opposed to Antiochus IV and would have little reason to water down a demand by the Seleucid king. Thus, there seems no good reason why 2 Maccabees' version should be rejected at this point.

Another scenario, differing from Honigman's, may be presented here. It recognizes the literary nature – and biases – of 1 and 2 Maccabees but is perhaps less sceptical of their data. Antiochus had only begun his reign when the encounter with Jason took place; it is unlikely that he had put a particular economic programme to increase taxes in place this early. On the other hand, Jason may have seen the wind blowing in a particular direction and took his chance to gain the priesthood but also to establish Jerusalem as a *polis* (probably for several reasons). Jason's petition fell right into Antiochus's long-term plans and needs. (What happened with Jason might have been the model for what Antiochus did in Mesopotamia.) In any case, once Jason was put in office, he seems to have been paying his taxes, so why replace him with an unknown figure like Menelaus? Also, Antiochus and his tax collectors knew what the province could deliver and were unlikely to have made the mistake of over-taxing the inhabitants. On the other hand, if Menelaus came to Antiochus with promises of greater contributions to the royal coffers, Antiochus would have shrugged and accepted his offer. After all, although he was not desperate for money, as all indications suggest, additional funds were always welcome. The story in 2 Maccabees of Menelaus's approach to Antiochus is thus credible.

Yet whether you accept the traditional reading of 2 Macc. 4.7-10 (that Jason initiated the approach to Antiochus) or Honigman's thesis (that Antiochus made a proposal to Jason to replace Onias as high priest), the net result is much the same: Jason became high priest but the annual tribute became substantially more. Yet Jason had more in mind than just the office held by his brother, and he was willing to pay even more than the enhanced level of tribute demanded by Antiochus. It seems evident from Jason's actions that he also had visions of making Jerusalem a city to be reckoned with in the Hellenistic world. For some reason, the author of 2 Maccabees is not completely explicit about what Jason was asking for, but the reason is probably that to the ancient reader, as well as to the modern reader knowledgeable in Hellenistic culture, it would have been clear what was happening. Jason was bidding for the right to make Jerusalem into a *polis*, a city modelled on the cities in Greece proper but also the many Greek foundations that followed in the wake of Alexander's conquests.

The basic government of the ancient Greek mainland was the city-state: a main city with a small citizen population and a large slave population, a territory with land owned by the citizens, and a certain number of non-citizens ('metics'), foreigners and others. The government of the city-state varied considerably, especially in the Hellenistic Near East, but the citizens often had a hand in making the laws and governing their state. As Alexander conquered his way across the ancient Near East, he periodically set up cities modelled on the Greek city-state. The citizens were his Macedonian veterans and their families. A city was built, with a gymnasium, and land was confiscated and assigned to the veterans; however, it was not farmed directly by them but by slaves or, as was often the case in Asia, by serfs who were bound to the land.

As time went on, however, a number of native cities requested to become *poleis* and were granted that privilege, especially under the Seleucids. Yet these native cities often adapted the *polis* model to their own pre-existing internal structure and conventions. Their 'constitution' and governing structures often differed in certain ways from the standard Macedonian model (see Honigman 2014: 361–77). This also apparently included Jerusalem, which seems to have exercised conventions and practices that differed from the traditional Greek ones, especially in areas relating to the divinity and to Jewish law. As we shall see, a close examination of the text suggests that some of the traditional Greek practices that most Jews would have found objectionable seem to have been dropped in Jason's version of the *polis*.

Recently an inscription was published that relates to a request from a native city for the status of a *polis* (Jonnes and Ricl 1997). The inscription contains the letters from Eumenes II responding to the request by the people of Tyriaion. The most important passage outlines the privileges granted by the king:

> [26] …I grant both you and those living with you [27] in fortified places to organize yourselves into one citizen body and [28] to use your own laws: if you yourselves are satisfied with some of these, [29] submit them to us so that we inspect them for [30] anything contrary to your interests. If not, let us know [31] and we shall send you the men capable of appointing both the council and the magistrates, [32] of distributing the people and assigning them to tribes, [33] and of building a gymnasium and providing oil for the youths. [Jonnes and Ricl 1997: 4]

The parallel to what happened in Jerusalem is obvious:

- The initiative to become a *polis* came from the native city.
- The grant allowed organizing into a body of citizens.
- They were permitted to use their own laws, though these were to be inspected and 'approved' by the king.
- The king would assist them by helping them to appoint a council or *boulē* and magistrates, and divide them into tribes (which was the standard organization of a city).
- The king would assist them in building a gymnasium.

In the case of Jerusalem, the initiative came from the Jewish side. Jason drew up a list of citizens and built the gymnasium. A council (called a *gerousia* in most of our sources but sometimes a *boulē*) already existed, and the high priest had apparently already appointed magistrates. It seems evident that their native laws continued to be followed, and we have no evidence that Antiochus asked for them to be drawn up and approved by him. While the Tyriaion decree is very similar to what happened in Jerusalem, it seems that Jason was more independent and personally responsible for the course of events in the establishment of his city.

The emphasis on the gymnasium in 2 Maccabees 4 is clearly for a reason. It shows why, in addition to the 440 talents of silver already offered, Jason added another 150 into the bargain to 'permit by his own authority to set up a gymnasium and organize a system of youth training, and to enrol the citizens of Jerusalem as Antiochenes' (2 Macc. 4.9). The gymnasium was in many ways the centre of the city. As noted above, a gymnasium was not just a place of exercise, as in the modern world, but served as both the educational and the cultural centre of the Greek city: it was 'architecturally and culturally the defining institution of Greek urban civilization, recognized as such alike by those who wished to exploit its opportunities and by those who saw in it a symbol of alien influence' (Davies 1984: 308; see also Rostovtzeff 1941: 1058–61; Doran 1990: 100). It also served as an important focus for social activities in the city.

14.4.2. *Who Were the 'Hellenizers'?*

The term 'Hellenizer' or 'Hellenist' is often bandied about in modern studies in a rather undifferentiated way. This is hardly surprising, since such explicit or implied usage is already found in the books of Maccabees. To the authors of these histories, the adjective 'Hellenistic' or 'Greek' was a catchword to condemn those people or things so labelled, and such usage is not lacking in some modern writings. Yet careful consideration shows that a number of rather different phenomena have been lumped together in the terms 'Hellenizer/Hellenistic/Greek'. The broader question of Hellenization and the Jews is dealt with in *HJJSTP 2* (Chapter 6). The discussion here will focus on the identity of the so-called 'Hellenists' in the context of the Hellenistic reform and the subsequent revolt.

One of the first problems we have is that of the sources. No surviving source speaks for any of the 'Hellenizers'; all our main sources are hostile and were simply not interested in giving a fair or complete account. We do not know directly the objectives or aspirations of individuals such as Jason and Menelaus, nor do we know how they justified these to themselves or others. Any conclusion about these is inferential at best.

We can perhaps engage in reasonable speculation about the aims of Jason (cf. Hengel 1974: 1:277-78) but we can hardly hope to do them justice. For example, Menelaus seems much more difficult to sympathize with, but many writers are content with simply repeating the accusations of the enemies of both groups without bothering to weigh the evidence. What does emerge from careful study of the literary sources is that there were clear differences between the activities of Jason and those of Menelaus, and the reaction of the common people to each was not identical. It would be useful to look briefly at each in turn.

Jason plainly had a program which he wished to carry out, namely, to make Jerusalem into a Greek *polis*, though we can only speculate about his motives. While deposing his brother and taking the high priesthood was opportunistic, it seems difficult to believe he was merely an opportunist. Possibly he was an idealist who believed in some sort of *rapprochement* between the Jews and their neighbours (cf. Bringmann 1983: 67). It has been suggested that he had economic motives (Tcherikover 1959: 168-69, opposed by Bringmann 1983: 74). But whatever his reasons for the Hellenistic reform, it was a cultural/political matter rather than a religious one. We see no evidence that Jason had any desire to change the traditional cult or worship.

It is always risky to attempt to psychoanalyze historical figures, but it seems to me that Jason had some sort of vision for the future of Judah. One can easily argue that he saw the promotion of Jerusalem to become a Greek city as a wise move toward greater economic benefits. But there is also the strong impression that Jason admired Greek culture, which was why he was happy to adopt certain aspects of it for his city of Jerusalem. This would not be unusual, since the Jews had been a part of the Hellenistic world for nearly a century and a half by this time. Many aspects of Greek culture had been adopted, consciously or perhaps more readily in the urban areas but to some extent by all. This has been discussed at length in a previous volume (*HJJSTP 2*: Chapter 6), and only a brief summary is given here.

From the time of Alexander, Greek culture became a new element within the ancient Near East. It did not replace the native cultures; on the contrary, the Greeks were not interested in cultural imperialism. They regarded themselves as superior and looked down on the natives. It was the natives, especially those of the upper classes, who saw that it could be useful to learn Greek, gain a Greek education, and adopt some of the Greek ways of doing things. It was also natural that Greek influence of some sort permeated the entire society, especially as time went on. The entity created by this mixing of the Greek and the native was a new creation, Hellenization. The Hellenistic world owed as much to the old Near Eastern cultures as it did to the Greek; it was not Greek but *sui generis*. The Greek and the native formed a new synthesis; however, it was not a melting together of the different cultures (*Verschmelzung* in German) but more like a suspension, with elements of both cultures existing side by side.

The Jews were a part of this Hellenistic world, just like all the other native peoples. We have no evidence that they reacted to Hellenization any differently from other Near Eastern peoples. Greek influence made inroads but the old way of life also continued much as it had for most people. There were new overlords to take taxes and to impose their will, and they spoke a different language. But to the peasant man following his ox down the furrow or the peasant woman grinding grain or drawing water, life continued much as it had for thousands of years. To those with education, however, Greek culture no doubt had its attractions. The upper classes, many of them priests, and the inhabitants of Jerusalem would have come into greater direct contact with the Greek administration, the Greek language and Greek customs.

After almost a century and a half of Greek rule, it would be hardly surprising if there were not those who thought that it could be good for the Jews as a whole if Jerusalem became a *polis*. This did not have to involve a change in the Jewish religion. We know of many 'Hellenized' Jews who lived in Greek cities, spoke Greek, and participated in various aspects of Greek culture without compromising their religion. A good example is Philo of Alexandria whose first language – and possibly only language – was Greek (he seems to have known little or no Hebrew), who was indeed an Alexandrian citizen – which most Jews of the city were not – and yet who defends all aspects of the traditional Jewish law in his many biblical commentaries. (Philo will be discussed in *HJJSTP 4*.)

We must also not forget the indication of Hellenistic influence in the books of Maccabees themselves. First of all, they are written in Greek. 1 Maccabees was initially written in Hebrew, but this has not survived. In any case, it was soon translated into Greek which became the main version. 2 Maccabees was written in a good Greek style from the start. An important leader and diplomat in Maccabean circles was Eupolemus. His father John had negotiated the continuation of traditional Jewish customs with Antiochus III, yet Eupolemus is a Greek name, he wrote in Greek and was no doubt chosen for his diplomatic roles because of his knowledge of the Greek language. He is generally identified with the Eupolemus who wrote a history of Israelite kings in Greek, now preserved only in fragments (see *HJJSTP 2*: 86–89; Grabbe 2001: 243–44).

Similarly, the Samaritan temple at Shechem was dedicated to Zeus Xeniou ('Zeus, hospitable' or 'Zeus, friend of strangers'), yet there is no indication that a change of cult or religion took place. Rather, the Samaritans apparently continued to operate a cult which was very similar to that which had been banned in Jerusalem, yet under a Greek label. Similarly, statements about 'changing to Greek ways' (2 Macc. 6.8; 11.24) actually have to do with leaving Judaism rather than adopting specifically Greek customs. Thus, 'Hellenistic/Greek/ Hellenize' is sometimes used in our sources simply to mean 'non-Jewish' (Bringmann 1983: 141–45; cf. also Honigman 2014: 197–228).

Jason's aims in his Hellenistic reform seem to have been those that, in another context, many would applaud. Evidently, he wished to open up Judah in general and Jerusalem in particular to all the advantages that might accrue from having their capital city as a Greek *polis*. This no doubt included the benefits of trade and commerce which would come from throwing open Jerusalem to the outside world in a much more conducive way. The more cultural aspects of the change may not have represented immediate financial gains, but these clearly had an intellectual and recreational appeal to many of the inhabitants of Jerusalem.

There may have been a variety of reactions on the part of the Jewish people to Jason's constitutional changes, but we are not told this by any of the extant sources. We can infer that many of those in Jerusalem welcomed the *polis* because they participated in it. We also know that the Jews would not tolerate a violation of the law or a defilement of the temple or cult. (We know this because when it was rumoured that Menelaus had sold some of the temple vessels, the population rioted and the council of elders – the council set up by Jason – sent an embassy to Antiochus to accuse Menelaus.) The Jews were not indifferent to their religion, and they were not afraid to defend it when necessary. Anticipating some of the events that will only be described later in this and the following chapters, we can suggest the following scheme for the so-called 'Hellenizers':

- There was a segment of the population, probably many of them living in the country and making their living from agriculture, whose contact with Greek culture and the Greek world was minimal and who took a quite conservative approach. This does not mean they should be called 'the pious' or 'the orthodox'. The practice of Judaism among the culturally conservative and the people on the land may nevertheless have varied considerably. In any case, it is taking sides religiously – and being unhistorical – to use such terms as 'pious' and 'orthodox' for such people.

- Another group, which evidently included the high priest Jason, was open to Hellenistic culture but religiously conservative and upheld the continuation of the temple and its cult as previously. This included members of the *gerousia* of the Hellenistic city of Jerusalem who opposed Menelaus and his brother Lysimachus (2 Macc. 4.43-44). It included the inhabitants and citizens of Jerusalem who attacked Lysimachus's troops and ended up killing Lysimachus himself for allegedly selling off temple vessels (2 Macc. 4.39-42).
- A further group were those who supported the Seleucid government and continued to do so even during the Maccabaean revolt. This evidently included the high priest Menelaus. Although often labelled an 'extreme Hellenist', his precise views on Hellenistic cultures are not clear, but his support of the Seleucid government – even at times against his own people – is clear. This group includes those who manned the Seleucid fortresses, including the Jerusalem Akra, alongside the troops of the Seleucid government. At various points in the books of Maccabees disparaging references are made about such individuals (e.g., 1 Macc. 3.15; 6.21; 7.5; 9.23, 25, 58, 69, 73; 10.61; 11.25). We must keep in mind, though, that the Maccabaean authors were happy to label even the 'moderate Hellenizers' in this way. In any case, the precise proportion of the population who fell into this grouping is very difficult to determine; however, the bulk of the population does not seem to be in this category.
- Although this broad three-fold grouping seems to have included most Judaeans, there might have been some in-between groupings, but a further refinement would be difficult from the presently extant sources. For example, from all we can determine the Hasmonaean family, when it comes on the scene, appears to have fallen broadly into the middle category, along with Jason and the Hellenistic Jerusalem *gerousia*.

14.4.3. *Jason and His Hellenistic Jerusalem in Perspective*

R. Doran (1989) 'The Non-Dating of Jubilees: Jub 34–38; 23:14-32 in Narrative Context', *JSJ* 20: 1–11; **L. L. Grabbe** (2002a) 'The Hellenistic City of Jerusalem', in John R. Bartlett (ed.), *Jews in the Hellenistic and Roman Cities*, 6–21; **J. W. van Henten** (1997) *The Maccabean Martyrs as Saviours of the Jewish People: A Study of 2 and 4 Maccabees*; **M. A. Knibb** (1989) *Jubilees and the Origins of the Qumran Community*; **D. S. Russell**

14. Events Preceding the Maccabaean Revolt (175–168 BCE)

(1960) *Between the Testaments*; **idem** (1967) *The Jews from Alexander to Herod*; **S. Talmon** (1958) 'The Calendar Reckoning of the Sect from the Judaean Desert', in C. Rabin and Y. Yadin (eds), *Aspects of the Dead Sea Scrolls*, 162–99; **R. Warner (trans.)** (1954) *Thucydides, History of the Peloponnesian War*; **H. G. M. Williamson** (1979) 'The Origins of the Twenty-Four Priestly Courses: A Study of 1 Chronicles xxiii–xxvii', in *Studies in the Historical Books of the Old Testament*, 251–68.

Sources: 2 Maccabees 4.

In this section, we come back to the question, did Jason and his supporters also have a vision of a different future for the *Jewish religion* from the one suggested by its past? This has often been assumed, but there are a number of issues to consider. Judging from the names in the books of Maccabees, many of the leading figures in Judaea at this time were thoroughly Hellenized, with Greek names (alongside their native ones). Such individuals would have supported Jason's move and may even have encouraged him in his enterprise. As educated and status-bearing individuals, the priests would have been at the forefront of this acculturation process.

Jason's vision for Jerusalem, at least, was to adopt the trappings of the old Greek city-state, in which the inhabitants would become citizens. This was a new concept. Up until this time the Jews identified themselves as members of an *ethnos*, a people. The idea of being a citizen of a city was something introduced into Judah for the first time. To be a citizen of a Greek city carried privileges and was jealously guarded. As noted above, many of those who lived in a *polis* were not actually citizens. We are not given details of who became citizens of the new *polis* of Jerusalem, but we can be sure that the wealthy and the aristocracy were among the first on the list. Jason himself had the task of drawing up the list of citizens; one would not be surprised if he charged for the privilege; in any case, he probably built up political credit with those of power and influence.

What is the pronouncement of the books of Maccabees on Jason's enterprise? In a word, they were opposed to it. The story is told in detail in 2 Maccabees 4: Jason 'set aside the customs valid for the Jews by royal philanthropy, negotiated through John the father of Eupolemus' (2 Macc. 4.11). This refers back to the initial conquest of Palestine by Antiochus III who confirmed the traditional Jewish observances (see the discussion in *HJJSTP 2*: 324–26). Evidently John had been crucial in negotiating with Antiochus that the Jews' traditional religious and political rights continued unhindered. 2 Maccabees then goes on to give its verdict on Jason's enterprise:

> ¹⁰...he [Jason] immediately transformed his fellow countrymen over to the Greek life-style. ¹¹He set aside the customs valid for the Jews by royal philanthropy, negotiated through John the father of Eupolemus (the one who was made the official journey for friendship and alliance with the Romans); abolishing the laws of the citizens, he introduced lawless customs. ¹²For eagerly he founded a gymnasium by the acropolis itself and induced the noblest of the trainee citizens to wear the traditional Greek hat. ¹³It was thus a peak of Hellenism and an explosion in the adoption of foreign customs through the excessive wickedness of the impious Jason – who was no high priest. ¹⁴The priests were no longer devoted to the service of the altar, but treating the temple with contempt and neglecting the sacrifices, they hastened to participate in the lawless public spectacles in the arena after the summons to the event. ¹⁵They set at nothing the ancestral honours but regarded the Hellenic status symbols as the best... (2 Macc. 4.10-15)

It is clear that 2 Maccabees thinks Jason was acting contrary to the law. The question is whether this was correct: what exactly did Jason do that was wrong? What *specific act* of breaking the law does the text of 2 Macc. 4.10-15 name? The author of this passage throws lots of adjectives and adverbs around: 'wicked', 'unlawful', 'ungodly' – yet a close look shows that he does not at any point tell us anything concrete.

It would probably be agreed, at least by most readers, that Jason should not have taken the high priesthood from his brother Onias. If there is a sin or crime or wrongful act, this would have been it. But beyond that, 2 Maccabees gives no specific examples of anything unlawful. The most he can say is that the priests were not as intent on their service at the altar as they should have been, but even this may be a matter of interpretation. We know the daily *tamid* offering did not cease because when it was stopped a few years later, it was an extremely traumatic experience (see further at §15.2.3). Were the people who brought their various sacrifices not being attended to? Were there long queues of tired people dragging along thirsty sheep and goats bleating away, because the priests were not doing their job?

No indication of any such thing occurs in the sources.

As far as we can tell, the cult continued as normal. What is alleged is that priests left the altar at a certain time of day to attend the sports in the wrestling arena. Priests were not required to be on duty twenty-four hours a day. There were more priests than were needed to take care of the sacrificial system, and eventually a system developed in which they were divided into twenty-four courses (Talmon 1958; Williamson 1979). They were on duty for a week twice a year and, in addition, all were on

14. *Events Preceding the Maccabaean Revolt (175–168 BCE)* 331

duty at the festivals. So who were the priests who went to the wrestling arena? Were they priests on duty? If so, no specific law would have been broken, though there was a greater danger that a priest might become ritually polluted if away from the temple. Or were they priests who were not on duty and were looking for things to occupy their time? Or has the writer simply created a caricature? No details are given, so it is hard to evaluate, but the fact is that *all* the writer can say is that the priests were not as diligent as they should be. Considering the author's earnest desire to attack Jason, his descent into mere rhetoric, without specific examples, speaks loudly that Jason upheld the law and the correct temple procedure.

This is probably why the charges of lawbreaking by 1 and 2 Maccabees are generally so unspecific. The laws were not broken at the time. But writing many years later, in the aftermath of Antiochus's suppression of Judaism, the authors of the two books naturally saw Jason's reform as the start of the problem. He was wicked in their eyes, so they asserted this. But since they had no evidence to go on, they talked generally or used stereotyped language much as Job's friends had. The sin is not described so much as implied. Just as Job 'must have' done some dastardly things to suffer as he did, so Jason 'must have' done wicked things which brought God's wrath on the city and people.

In this whole chapter, only one possible example of a breach of the law is in 2 Maccabees, which states:

> [18]When they held the quinquennial athletic games in Tyre, with the king present, [19]the vile [in case you might have forgotten!] Jason sent Antiochene envoys from Jerusalem carrying 300 silver drachmas for the sacrifice of Hercules, which the messengers thought improper to be used for sacrifice because it was unseemly; instead, they applied the expense to something else. [20]Although this sum was designated for the sacrifice to Hercules by him who sent it, because of the messengers it was instead spent for the equipment of warships. (2 Macc. 4.18-20)

If this is accepted at face value, as it usually is, then Jason violated the law, though it would have been a violation outside the territory of Judah. However, one should look at this account carefully. First, if Jason planned to send 300 silver drachmas to Tyre, he would pick his couriers very carefully – men he could trust. There was a plethora of distractions between Jerusalem and Tyre: taverns, brothels, markets, traders and so on. But if he chose trustworthy men, they would also be people who would not take the money for one purpose and then use it for something else when they got there. Secondly, it is easy to allege that it was intended for another purpose, but where is the evidence? The money was not in fact used for a pagan sacrifice but for warships. This all suggests that Jason really originally sent the 300 drachmas as a gift with the intent that the silver be used to buy warships. Someone, however – perhaps even the author of 2 Maccabees – simply put the worst possible interpretation on the act. Certainty is not possible, but the account as it stands is problematic and clearly meant as detrimental to Jason.

One other allegation is – surprisingly – not found in 2 Maccabees. Rather, it is 1 Macc. 1.14-15 that states that those who built the gymnasium 'removed the marks of circumcision' (ἐποίησαν ἑαυτοῖς ἀκροβυστίας). It is not easy to evaluate whether this is anything more than a wild allegation because it is mentioned by no independent sources (such as 2 Maccabees). However, even if we take it at face value and put the worst interpretation on it, there are still two points to be kept in mind. The first point concerns the operation itself. There is a description of 'uncircumcision' in an ancient medical text:

> And, if the glans is bare and the man wishes for the look of the thing to have it covered, that can be done; but more easily in a boy than in a man; in one in whom the defect is natural, than in one who after the custom of certain races has been circumcised... Now the treatment for those in whom the defect is natural is as follows... But in one who has been circumcised the prepuce is to be raised from the underlying penis around the circumference of the glans by means of a scalpel. This is not so very painful [!], for once the margin has been freed it can be stripped up by hand as far back as the pubes, nor in so doing is there any bleeding. The prepuce thus freed is again stretched forwards beyond the glans; next cold water affusions are freely used, and a plaster is applied... And for the following days the patient is to fast until nearly overcome by hunger lest satiety excite that part. (Celsus 7.25.1, translation LCL)

One can say without fear of contradiction that it would have required a certain amount of motivation to undergo such an operation in a time before anaesthetics were available! We can be confident they were not queuing up at the surgeon's door.

If some did go through with this, it would most likely have been to compete in athletic contests in other cities. It must be pointed out – contrary to common assumption – that there is no evidence that exercises were done in the nude in the Jerusalem gymnasium, even if this was common in a Greek context. 2 Maccabees does not suggest that they were, and Thucydides (1.6.5-6) shows that it was not necessarily always the custom:

> They [the Spartans], too, were the first to play games naked, to take off their clothes openly, and to rub themselves down with olive oil after their exercise. In ancient times even at the Olympic Games the athletes used to wear coverings for their loins, and indeed this practice was still in existence not very many years ago. Even today *many foreigners, especially in Asia*, wear these loincloths for boxing matches and wrestling bouts. (translation of Rex Warner 1954: 38, italics mine)

They could, therefore, have done their exercises in loincloths (cf. Goldstein 1983: 229–30). Some have seen a condemnation of nudity in the Jerusalem gymnasium in *Jubilees*, which states:

> But from all the beasts and all the cattle he granted to Adam alone that he might cover his shame. Therefore it is commanded in the heavenly tablets to all who will know the judgment of the Law that they should cover their shame and they should not be uncovered as the gentiles are uncovered. (*Jub.* 3.30-31, from Knibb 1989: 16–17)

This does not strike one as a polemic against fellow Jews, but as a general comment on the practices of the Gentiles and an admonition not to imitate them (cf. Doran 1989). It is not even clearly a reference to exercises in the arena. It is further sometimes pointed out that it was also normal for the Greek gymnasia to be dedicated to Hermes. But we have no hint that this was the case in Jerusalem. We have to keep in mind that the author of 2 Maccabees is looking for any possible indication of scandal, and he is able to give none. His silence about both concerns is a strong indication that there was neither nude exercise nor any pagan ceremonies connected with Jason's gymnasium.

The second point is that there is no reason to think that if some young men did remove the signs of circumcision, Jason was responsible. Youth are known in every age for kicking over the traces. All we can say is that it may well have happened, though one suspects it was only a few cases – but all the author of 1 Maccabees needed was one example, or even a rumour. There is also no evidence that it was a deliberate policy on the part of Jason.

We now come to the all important question: what was the reaction of the people to all this activity in association with Jerusalem's becoming a *polis*? In handbooks one often reads statements along the lines that 'the orthodox Jews in Jerusalem were incensed at these things' (e.g., Russell 1960: 27; 1967: 37). There are two problems with such statements. First, the question of who is 'orthodox' is begged. Who determines who is orthodox; who are we to say who was considered pious at the time and who was not – and by whom? The second problem is closely related: it concerns the reaction of the people. And what was their reaction? The answer is, *there was no negative reaction*. None of the sources say anything of a reaction against these initiatives. We can assume, probably with some confidence, that there was a variety of reactions. Some of those living in the country were no doubt displeased with what was happening, or at least sceptical about it. This is the natural reaction of country people to the wicked 'big city'. But this is speculation because we do not know for sure.

What we *do* know is that many people embraced this new Hellenistic city, because they became a part of it. It may have been called Antioch, or perhaps Antioch-at-Jerusalem, since the citizens were called 'Antiochenes' (Ἀντιοχεῖς: 2 Macc. 4.9, 19; cf. Tcherikover 1959: 161, 404–9). It is clear from both books of Maccabees that there were no riots and demonstrations against Jason's plan. Indeed, the people of Jerusalem even welcomed Antiochus in magnificent fashion when he visited Jerusalem a couple or so years before his first invasion of Egypt (2 Macc. 4.21-22). Apart from Jason's act of taking the high priesthood itself, there is little evidence of a breach of the Torah. As it was, Jason's power base continued to be that traditional to the high priest: the temple and cult and the leadership opportunities which this gave in the absence of a formal native political office (Bringmann 1983: 72–84). There seems little reason to suggest that Jason did not think of himself as anything but a loyal and law-abiding Jew and a credit to the office he held.

14.4.4. *Menelaus Takes the Office of High Priest*

Jason's Hellenistic office lasted only about three years before he was displaced by Menelaus (2 Macc. 4.23-26). Who was this Menelaus? According to Josephus, who has an account independent of the books of Maccabees (*Ant.* 12.5.1 §§237-40), he was the brother of Onias and Jason and was actually named Onias as well – Onias-Menelaus. Most scholars have rejected this account, and no doubt rightly. According to 2 Maccabees, Menelaus was one of three brothers. Simon was an officer of the temple (*protastēs*), mentioned in 2 Macc. 3.4-6, who had had a disagreement with Onias over the running of the city market. A third brother was Lysimachus, who features in the account below. It has often been asserted that these brothers were simply lay Jews, which would mean that Menelaus would have been become high priest without being even a Levite, much less an Aaronite. This conclusion is based on the statement in 2 Macc. 3.4 that Simon was 'of the tribe of Benjamin'. This wording is indeed to be found in the majority of Greek manuscripts, but it is scarcely credible. Simon was captain of the temple, a priestly office (2 Macc. 3.4). When Menelaus became high priest, there is no evidence of opposition from the people, which there surely would have been if he had not been of priestly descent (as subsequent events show).

Instead of 'tribe of Benjamin', the Old Latin and Armenian versions have 'tribe of Balgea', which was evidently a priestly family known as Bilgah in Neh. 12.5, 18 (see the data in Hanhart 1976: 55). This seems to be the simplest and, therefore, the most likely explanation; however, others are possible. For example, J. W. van Henten (1997: 32 n. 44) suggests that Simon was indeed from the tribe of Benjamin but that he was not really the brother of Menelaus; rather, the writer made the connection to suggest Menelaus's illegitimacy. In either case, Menelaus could still be from the priestly tribe of Bilgah. This might make the family of Bilgah another 'mafiosa' family, along with the Tobiads and Oniads (as discussed in *HJJSTP 2*: 77, 222–23, 294–95; on this family, see further Bernhardt 2017: 110–29). As will be discussed in the next chapter (Chapter 15), another family should be included among the 'mafiosa', as well: the Hasmonaean family, who also had political ambitions in relationship to Judah.

Since Jason had in essence double-crossed his brother, there is no reason why others could not play that game. According to 2 Maccabees this Menelaus did precisely what Jason had done: he went to Antiochus and offered him even more money to hold the office of high priest. Honigman has suggested that Antiochus, having replaced Onias III with Jason, took the initiative and now replaced Jason with Menelaus (2014: 269–81). This argument is difficult to follow. Jason was evidently compliant with Antiochus's demands, and he was also apparently paying up the tribute due. Why would Antiochus decide to replace him? It makes no sense. On the other hand, if Menelaus came to him and offered a further increase in tribute, one could easily see that Antiochus would be interested. Menelaus is said to have added a further 300 talents to the amount being paid by Jason. This was a large sum by any standards, and if it was meant to be an annual contribution as seems likely, it was an impossible sum of 890 talents (or at least 740 talents, if the 150 talents for the gymnasium was a one-off payment). We know it was impossible because Menelaus did not pay it! By long experience the bureaucracies of kingdoms and empires knew what could be extracted from their subjects without damaging their ability to pay – without killing the cash cow, as it were. It is likely that Antiochus himself or his treasury officials would have calculated that

Judah was paying sufficient tribute under Jason, which is why I do not think the idea of practically doubling it was his (contra Honigman 2014: 354–61). But if Menelaus *offered* to double the tribute, Antiochus would have accepted it, whatever reservations he might have had about the province's being able to bear it.

Therefore, what we see is another example of the struggle over the priesthood, which seems to have a long history. Most of this is probably lost to us, but there are hints in the Hebrew Bible which in various passages has Levitical priests, Aaronite priests, Zadokite priests and even a Moses priest according to Judg. 17.30. So although even the author of 2 Maccabees sees Menelaus's crime as worse than Jason's (2 Macc. 4.25), since Jason was at least from the traditional high priestly family, Menelaus was still probably a priest. Later on, we shall see another priestly family – the Hasmonaeans – assert itself to strive for leadership. Nor was this the end of the struggle for the high priesthood, for other families achieved this high office under Herod (§18.4) and under the Romans (see *HJJSTP 4*).

Menelaus soon got into trouble because he was not paying the money he had promised to Antiochus (2 Macc. 4.27-34). He was summoned to appear before the king, but when he arrived, the king was away dealing with a revolt. Menelaus had to appear before another high minister named Andronicus who was temporarily in charge of the running of the kingdom. Here was a chance to gain time, so Menelaus – according to 2 Maccabees – stole some of the golden temple vessels, giving some to Andronicus and selling others in the area of Tyre. If 2 Maccabees is to be believed, he in this way not only gained a breathing space with regard to his debt but also bribed Andronicus into murdering Onias (Onias III, the original high priest). Onias had taken refuge in a temple near Antioch – a pagan temple no less – but it did not save him. How much of this is true and how much is only an attempt to blacken Menelaus's name is hard to say. But some people evidently believed the rumours about the temple vessels.

For back in Jerusalem rumours had begun to spread about the stolen temple vessels, which gives us a crucial piece of historical data (2 Macc. 4.39-42). What was the people's reaction to the (supposed) theft of the temple vessels? *They rioted in the streets*. Lysimachus, who was governing while Menelaus was away, came out with a large band of armed soldiers to attack the crowd. But this was no ordinary mob. They were out in such numbers and so agitated by the rumours of the temple desecration that they drove off the soldiers and even killed Lysimachus. This account puts a number of the previous events in perspective. The people of Jerusalem – many of them citizens of the 'Hellenistic *polis*' – were not indifferent to matters of religion. They had the same regard for the temple and its cult as their ancestors had. It was a most sacred place and not to be treated lightly. Selling off temple vessels was a breach of its holiness and a serious affront to the religious susceptibilities of the people.

This is why the silences of 2 Maccabees need to be regarded. If the people react so strongly to rumours of selling off the temple vessels, they would have reacted equally strongly to a breach of the law on the part of Jason. His Hellenistic reform clearly did not affect Jewish worship; it only concerned matters in what we today would call the 'secular realm'. The ancients did not make the same distinction between 'religious' and 'secular' as we do but, on the other hand, they had no trouble distinguishing that which had to do with the temple and the deity from what was confined to ordinary profane life. They would normally have had no trouble deciding whether something was a violation of traditional religious law or not. It also indicates that Menelaus must have been of a priestly family because his occupying the high priestly office would not have been tolerated otherwise. It must be emphasized again that those who rioted were the citizens of Jerusalem, the 'Antiochenes', not some 'pious' gathering from the countryside. In fact, they seem to have been Jason's people, as is indicated by the immediately following event.

As soon as the riot had ceased, the *gerousia* sent a delegation to complain to the king. The *gerousia* is mentioned a number of times in the books of Maccabees and other writings from about this time (Grabbe 2008b). The name implies a 'council of elders' (from *gerōn* 'elder, old man') just as does 'senate' (from Latin *senex*), and seems to be part of the tradition about an advisory council to the high priest (often referred to as 'the Sanhedrin'). The indications are that this traditional feature of the Jerusalem temple government had been incorporated into the city government set up by Jason. Furthermore, it was made up of those who went along with Jason's reforms. Yet they were the leaders in fighting a threat to the temple and the law. This is why talk of 'Hellenists' versus 'the pious' is absurd: the so-called Hellenists were a part of the pious.

Things do seem to have been different once Menelaus took over. The distinction in approach and attitude between Menelaus and Jason has often been overlooked. Even the seminal work by E. J. Bickerman (1937//1979) lumps Jason and Menelaus together as 'Hellenizers', just as 1 and 2 Maccabees do. Perhaps the bias of our sources is such that possibly no study has done justice to Menelaus up to the present time. But in trying to read carefully the sources in the light of their prejudices, there appears to be a clear difference between Jason and Menelaus. The interpretation of the data suggests that Jason was an ideologue, perhaps to some extent a dreamer, who admired Greek culture and who saw the adoption of some aspects of it as beneficial to his people. But Menelaus looks more like an opportunist, whose actions are those of a man out to gain whatever he can for himself without regard for the consequences to the Jewish people.

This description is probably too simplistic, since here and there are examples suggesting there was more to Menelaus than just this picture of a selfish narcissist. For example, some years later Menelaus evidently told Antiochus V that the people of Judah wanted to follow their own customs rather than the dictates of the king (2 Macc. 11.29-32). But after becoming high priest Menelaus very quickly attracted not just passive opposition but riots in the streets by the citizens of Jerusalem, evidently the very people who had welcomed the Hellenistic reforms of Jason. Their motivation in resisting Menelaus was purely religious, from all we can tell. The so-called 'Hellenizers' of the Jason faction took the temple, the cult and the Jewish religion very seriously, and they were willing to put their lives on the line to defend it.

It is often stated that Menelaus was an 'extreme Hellenizer' (cf. Tcherikover 1959: 170–71); however, this designation does not appear very appropriate. First, none of Menelaus's actions have anything particularly Hellenistic about them. Apart from his Greek name we would not know that he differed from previous high priests who fought over the office; on the contrary, all that he did suggests a concern for power only. Secondly, it has even been argued that Jason's 'Hellenistic reform' came to an end as such (Bringmann 1983: 93–94). This is probably not the case, especially since there is nothing in the text to indicate changes in Jerusalem in this regard. However, it is true that Jason's supporters were unlikely to have welcomed Menelaus. Indeed, when opposition to Menelaus came to the surface, prominent in it were members of the *gerousia* who had been Jason's supporters.

14.5. *Conclusions*

Much ground has been covered; here is a summary of what was said or implied about the Hellenistic reform:

- Jason was an idealist in some sense, with a vision of how Judah should go forward. To make Jerusalem into a Greek *polis* would, in his opinion, be beneficial for the inhabitants of Jerusalem and the Jews as a whole. His precise reasons are not given, though one expects economics to be a part of them. Yet it is also probably true that Jason found many aspects of Greek culture attractive and felt that the Jews were being left behind.

14. Events Preceding the Maccabaean Revolt (175–168 BCE)

- Jason's reform was a cultural and political one. On the religious side, he considered himself a loyal Jew and made no significant alterations to the practice of the Jewish religion or the operation of the temple cult. This comes through, despite the bias of our major sources.
- Menelaus seems to have been a rather different character. He strikes one as an opportunist and as one without much of a wider vision beyond self-interest. This picture may simply be due to the bias of the sources, but even the prejudiced sources we possess suggest a clear differentiation between Menelaus and Jason.
- Yet Menelaus seems to have been from a priestly family (in spite of the 'tribe of Benjamin' found in many manuscripts), probably the family of Bilgah. The fact that he is nowhere criticized as a non-priest or as unworthy of the office because of his descent is a good indication that he was a legitimate priest. His faults lay elsewhere.
- The books of Maccabees are valuable sources. Without them we would know little about the Maccabaean revolt or what led up to the Hasmonaean state. In the past, 2 Maccabees was sometimes slighted because it is more blatantly theological and pietistic. Yet for the crucial events preceding the attempt to suppress Judaism, it is 2 Maccabees which gives the most details, showing that 2 Maccabees can also be an extremely important source. If we had to rely on the other accounts available to us, even 1 Maccabees, we would have only a bare outline of what happened and none of the vital detail. In this case, the account in 1 Maccabees 1, in contrast to some other episodes, strikes one as stereotyped, propagandistic and indifferent to careful recitation of the events. Despite its bias, 2 Maccabees 4 seems concerned to lay out events with some care and attention to detail.
- Despite their importance – or *because* of their importance – we have to approach these two books critically, noting their biases, their confusions, their omissions, their deafening silences. It is this failure to read the books – and to read them critically – which has led to a superficial interpretation which in fact overlooks much that is in the text itself. We must read them for what they say and also for what they do not say.

Chapter 15

The Maccabaean Revolt to the Death of Judas (170–161 BCE)

B. Bar-Kochva (1976) *The Seleucid Army: Organization and Tactics in the Great Campaigns*; **idem** (1989) *Judas Maccabaeus: The Jewish Struggle against the Seleucids*; **M. Becker** (2016) *Porphyrios,* Contra Christianos: *Neue Sammlung der Fragmente, Testimonien und Dubia mit Einleitung, Übersetzung und Anmerkungen*; **J. C. Bernhardt** (2017) *Die jüdische Revolution: Untersuchungen zu Ursachen, Verlauf und Folgen der hasmonäischen Erhebung*; **E. J. Bickerman** (1937a) *Der Gott der Makkabäer: Untersuchungen über Sinn und Ursprung der makkabäischen Erhebung* // **idem** (1979) *The God of the Maccabees: Studies on the Meaning and Origin of the Maccabean Revolt*; **K. Bringmann** (1983) *Hellenistische Reform und Religionsverfolgung in Judäa: Eine Untersuchung zur jüdisch-hellenistischen Geschichte (175–163 v. Chr.)*; **J. J. Collins** (1993) *A Commentary on the Book of Daniel*; **R. Doran** (2012) *2 Maccabees: A Critical Commentary*; **K. Ehling** (2008) *Untersuchungen zur Geschichte der späten Seleukiden (164–63 v. Chr.): Vom Tode des Antiochos IV. bis zur Einrichtung der Provinz Syria unter Pompeius*; **D. Gera** (1998) *Judaea and Mediterranean Politics*; **J. A. Goldstein** (1976) *I Maccabees*; **idem** (1983a) *II Maccabees*; **E. S. Gruen** (1984) *The Hellenistic World and the Coming of Rome*; **idem** (1993) 'Hellenism and Persecution: Antiochus IV and the Jews', in P. Green (ed.), *Hellenistic History and Culture*, 238–74; **M. Hengel** (1974) *Judaism and Hellenism*; **S. Honigman** (2014) *Tales of High Priests and Taxes: The Books of the Maccabees and the Judean Rebellion against Antiochos IV*; **W. Huβ** (2001) *Ägypten in hellenistischer Zeit*; **P. F. Mittag** (2006) *Antiochos IV. Epiphanes*; **M. G. Morgan** (1990) 'The Perils of Schematism: Polybius, Antiochus Epiphanes and the "Day of Eleusis"', *Historia* 39: 37–76; **O. Mørkholm** (1966) *Antiochus IV of Syria*; **M. Sartre** (2001) *D'Alexandre à Zénobie*; **D. R. Schwartz** (2008) *2 Maccabees*; **I. Shatzman** (1991) *The Armies of the Hasmonaeans and Herod: From Hellenistic to Roman Frameworks*; **J. Sievers** (1990) *The Hasmoneans and their Supporters: From Mattathias to the Death of John Hyrcanus I*; **V. A. Tcherikover** (1959)

Hellenistic Civilization and the Jews; **S. Weitzman** (2004) 'Plotting Antiochus's Persecution', *JBL* 123: 219–34; **S. Tedesche and S. Zeitlin (eds)** (1950) *The First Book of Maccabees*.

The previous chapter described the important sequence of events that preceded the Maccabaean revolt. This chapter describes the crucial Sixth Syria War and the subsequent events in Judah that quickly escalated into a revolt, the pollution of the temple and the military response that was ultimately led by Judas the Maccabee. Though there is still much not known about the details, the sources will be critically examined – and sometimes found wanting – and a number of theories will be noted about particular events. Yet in spite of uncertainty about certain details, the overall course of events seems clear.

15.1. *The Sixth Syrian War*

H. Braunert (1964) 'Hegemoniale Bestrebungen der hellenistischen Großmächte in Politik und Wirtschaft', *Historia* 13: 80–104; **J. D. Grainger** (2010) *The Syrian Wars*; **J. D. Ray** (1976) *The Archive of Hor*; **F. W. Walbank** (1979) *Polybius III*; **E. Will** (1982) *Histoire Politique du Monde Hellénistique II*.

As described in a previous volume (*HJJSTP* 2:280–81), Coele-Syria and Phoenicia were assigned to Seleucus I in 301 BCE by the coalition that had just defeated Antigonus. Although Ptolemy I had not taken part in the fighting, he moved quickly into the territory and took it over for Egypt. Because Seleucus owed Ptolemy for helping him to take Babylonia in the first place, he did not press him to relinquish the territory. But the Seleucid rulers did not give up their claim and continued to press their right of possession through a series of 'Syrian Wars' throughout the 3rd century BCE. Finally, in the Fifth Syrian War Antiochus III took back Syro-Palestine and Phoenicia for the Seleucid realm from Ptolemy V in 200 BCE. Now it was the Ptolemies who claimed that the territory belonged to them and intended to recover it, though Ptolemy V was assassinated before he had a chance to do anything about it.

Therefore, in 175 BCE, when Antiochus IV took the Seleucid throne, both he and the Egyptian rulership were aware that war was likely to come again over ownership of Syro-Palestine. Ptolemy VI (180–145 BCE) was only a minor, controlled by regents. According to Polybius (28.1), it was these regents (named as Eulaeus and Lenaeus) who were allegedly set on taking back Syro-Palestine by force, though it was always a long-term Ptolemaic goal (cf. Diodorus 30.2). The move toward war became especially evident by about 173 BCE. The Ptolemies sent an embassy to Rome to renew the Egyptian friendship, but Antiochus did the same, to assure the Romans and the world that the Seleucids were not initiating war (Polybius 28.1). As usual, the Senate heard both embassies and renewed their friendship with Egypt, but otherwise they did nothing. Since they were at this time engaged in the Third Macedonian War with Perseus (171–168 BCE), they might not have been too bothered if the Ptolemies and Seleucids ended up fighting each other.

Although he probably did not attack first, Antiochus was clearly prepared for war. This may be why he visited Jerusalem about 172 BCE (2 Macc. 4.21-22), where he was enthusiastically welcomed by Jason and the citizens of Jerusalem (though it did not prevent Jason being displaced by Menelaus shortly afterward). Jerusalem was close enough to the Egyptian border to be part of an inspection tour and also a stage for a show of Seleucid force from the army accompanying Antiochus.

In the year 170 BCE, events involving Jerusalem were overtaken by events in the wider world. It is clear that tensions had been mounting, and both sides seemed to expect a war to break out. Antiochus was apparently attacked by Ptolemy VI, in late 170 or early 169 BCE, though parts of the data are disputed. The exact time is debated, though Walbank (3:321–24) gives good reasons why it was likely about February 169 rather than earlier, but there are still arguments for about November 170 BCE (e.g., Gera 1998: 124–31). It also seems evident that the Egyptians attacked first (Polybius 28.20-21; also Diodorus 30.15-16), even though both Jewish and Roman tradition seem to blame Antiochus (Walbank 1979: 3:325). Antiochus was well prepared to meet the attack and quickly defeated the Egyptians, advancing decisively toward Alexandria. Ptolemy VI replaced his advisors who had counselled for war, and sent a mission of third-party ambassadors to Antiochus to sue for peace. Antiochus received them graciously, explained why his claims to Coele-Syria were legitimate, and agreed terms for the cessation of fighting (Polybius 28.20).

Antiochus was successful, arranging the Ptolemaic government in a way that would favour him and the Seleucid administration in general. He returned with his army, but possibly not with much spoil (cf. Morgan 1990: 58), in later 169 BCE. On his way back, at this time he apparently visited Jerusalem. The qualification 'apparently' is important, because the account in 2 Maccabees (5.1, 15-21) associates it with the second invasion of Antiochus in 168. However, 1 Maccabees also mentions what seems to be the same event but describes it as taking place after the first invasion (1 Macc. 1.16-24). It makes most sense that this visit to Jerusalem took place after the first invasion because Antiochus came to Jerusalem peacefully, which was not the case after the second invasion. Antiochus was taken on a tour of the temple by Menelaus (2 Macc. 5.15-16) – a clear breach of the law – and then appropriated much of the temple treasury before going on his way back to Antioch. It was probably the case that Antiochus justified this seizure of temple treasure as payment for the back tribute still owed by Menelaus.

Antiochus's arrangements in Egypt did not last: almost immediately Ptolemy VI associated his brother (Ptolemy VIII) and sister (Cleopatra II) on the throne with himself, clearly contrary to Antiochus's own interests. Antiochus felt he had no choice but to invade Egypt again, which he did only a year later in the spring of 168. It has even been argued that he was declared king of Egypt at this time (cf. Braunert 1964: 96–98; Will 1982: 319), though this seems doubtful. It appears that Antiochus had no plans to incorporate Egypt into the Seleucid empire; he simply wanted to dictate peaceful coexistence between Egypt and Syria (Huβ 2001: 547; Mørkholm 1966: 81–83). Nevertheless, this time the Romans intervened. The story as told by Polybius is an interesting one (29.27). The Senate had passed a motion requiring Antiochus to withdraw, but it was to be delivered only if the Romans won the battle of Pydna. When the Roman commander Popilius Laenas approached Antiochus – they both knew each other – he greeted him from a distance but refused to shake hands. Instead he handed him the *senatus consultum*. After reading it, Antiochus said he would need to consult with his advisers. Popilius took the staff he was carrying and drew a circle around Antiochus. He then said the Seleucid king had to make his decision before stepping outside the circle. Antiochus, after a few minutes' hesitation, agreed to the Senate's demands, at which point Popilius shook his hand warmly.

It is generally assumed that was a rather humiliating experience for Antiochus, and perhaps it was at the personal level. However, there are several things to contemplate. First, he was in no position to oppose Rome. Even if he had been so inclined, the recent Roman defeat of Perseus would have been a shrill warning. But he knew the Romans and Roman power, and resistance was unlikely even to cross his mind. He had no choice but to withdraw from Egypt even though he probably could have taken it. He was in something of a bind. The Egyptians had not surrendered, in spite of a clear defeat. If they refused to capitulate, what would Antiochus do? Alexandria would have been difficult to conquer, but otherwise he had most of Egypt under his control and could make Egypt a part of his empire. But this could have many repercussions whose ends were hard to predict. He would apparently have been happy controlling Egypt through a puppet government, but direct rule could be problematic.

M. G. Morgan (1990: 53–72) has made the important point that Antiochus may have actually welcomed Roman intervention (cf. also J. Grainger 2010: 307–8):

> Antiochus could well have moved on Alexandria in June deliberately, to precipitate Roman intervention: whatever the risks to himself, that intervention would solve once for all the problem of Ptolemaic threats to Coele-Syria, since the Romans tended to think that territory part of the Seleucid realm, while the Lagids would not be able to ignore Rome's emissaries the way they had ignored Antiochus. (Morgan 1990: 67)

Thus, there is good reason to think, as Morgan and Grainger suggest, that the Roman ultimatum alleviated Antiochus from the problem of what long-term arrangements to make with regard to Egypt. To take Alexandria would have required a large outlay in money and manpower. He could not have abandoned the siege without losing face, but no one could blame him for bowing to the Roman threat. Most important of all, his goal – to remove the continuing Ptolemaic threat to try to retake Coele-Syria – was accomplished, because now the Ptolemies were forced by the Romans themselves to give up their goal of retaking the region. From Antiochus's perspective, no better outcome could have been hoped for. Antiochus was able to return to Antioch with much Egyptian spoil and his territory now secure by Roman guarantee. Yet to many observers on the Mediterranean scene, it would have looked like a humiliation. Was it necessary, as many think, for Antiochus to do something to put this right?

From the Egyptian scriber Hor, we know that Antiochus and his army left Egypt at the end of July 168 BCE (Ray 1976: 14–20, 124–30). The only blot on the landscape was what Antiochus interpreted as a rebellion in Judaea – indeed, there may have been an actual revolt. In any case, things flared up substantially in Jerusalem at this time. The reason according to 2 Macc. 5.5 is that a false rumour had reached Jason in Transjordan (where he had taken refuge) that Antiochus had been killed. Evidently, Jason interpreted this as a heaven-sent opportunity to try to take back the high priesthood which he thought was rightfully his. His calculation was partially right in that Jason's troops quickly retook Jerusalem, but Menelaus holed up in the Akra and could not be dislodged. In the meantime, the reports that had reached Antiochus make him think – rightly or wrongly – that a revolt was underway (see next section, §15.2).

Antiochus immediately sent an army to put down the assumed rebellion (it is not clear whether he led it himself). What happened next remains obscure in both 1 and 2 Maccabees. In the six months between when Antiochus withdrew from Egypt in July 168 and the cessation of the temple cult in December 168, our sources relate a number of puzzling events which allegedly led up to the suppression of Judaism.

15.2. *The Judaean 'Revolt' and Its Consequences*

Sources: 1 Macc. 1.16-63; 2 Macc. 5–7; *War* 1.1.2 §§34-35; *Ant.* 12.5.2-4 §§242-56; Tacitus, *Hist.* 5.8.2.

15.2.1. *Critical Analysis of the Reports on the Revolt*

We now come to the crucial period. Trying to sort out the precise sequence of events which led to the prohibition of Judaism and the Maccabaean revolt is a difficult one. This is due not only to differences between the sources but also to complications within them pointing to intrigues and intricate manoeuvrings on the part of various interests and factions. Let's first rehearse each account separately, then try to construct a critical synthesis from them:

2 Maccabees 5–7 is our main source, since the others are generally quite skimpy on the events immediately preceding the suppression of Judaism, but this means that many of its points cannot be cross-checked. According to 2 Macc. 5.1-26, Antiochus made a second expedition against Egypt at this time (with an omen of soldiers fighting appearing in the sky over Jerusalem!). Only 2 Maccabees mentions two expeditions of Antiochus, not 1 Maccabees (though it seems to assign some events to the second that actually belong to the first). While he was fighting there, a rumour arose that he had been killed. Jason took the opportunity to invade Jerusalem with a large force in an attempt to regain the office of high priest. He was initially successful in entering the city, but Menelaus took refuge in the Akra. Eventually, Jason himself was forced to flee. Antiochus in the meantime had heard that Jerusalem was in revolt and brought his army against the city, killing 40,000 inhabitants and enslaving another 40,000. Antiochus himself entered the temple, with Menelaus, and took away a good deal of the gold. He left a viceroy (*epistatēs*) named Philip to keep the people in line (also, a similar officer in charge of Samaria). Later he sent Apollonius, commander of the Mysians, who took Jerusalem with violence, killing and enslaving a large number of people (his orders were to kill all the adult men and sell all the women and children into slavery). Finally, according to 2 Macc. 6.1-2, some time after this Geron the Athenian was sent to compel the Jews to leave their ancestral laws. The rest of 2 Maccabees 6 goes on to relate examples of the persecution, especially focusing on the martyrdom of the scribe Eleazar, while 2 Maccabees 7 is about the martyrdom of a mother and seven sons.

1 Maccabees 1.16-63 states only that Antiochus invaded Egypt and conquered it. On his way back he took Jerusalem and despoiled the temple, stealing the incense altar, the *menorah*, the showbread table and other golden objects within the temple (this part is similar to 2 Maccabees, except that it appears to be related to his first invasion of Egypt, not his second as in 2 Maccabees). Then two years later he sent an officer of the Mysians (the text is problematic, but if correctly reconstructed, this was apparently the same as Apollonius of 2 Maccabees) to take Jerusalem, kill many people and plunder it; they then fortified the city of David to make it into a fortress, the Akra, garrisoned by 'renegades' (1 Macc. 1.34: παρανόμους) who were apparently Jews. After this Antiochus issued a decree that all his subjects were to abandon their native laws and become one people. The 'Gentiles' (1 Macc. 1.43: τὰ ἔθνη) and 'even many from Israel' obeyed this decree. Those obeying the true religion were persecuted, sometimes even to death, all over the country. It was at this point that the abomination of desolation was set up in the temple and the revolt subsequently began.

Josephus's two accounts differ in a number of ways (on these, see further at §14.3). The *War* (1.1.1-2 §§31-35) briefly states that when Antiochus was disputing with Ptolemy VI over Syria, rivalry arose among the Jews. Some of these went to Antiochus and guided him and his army to Jerusalem, which he had long wanted to take. He captured and pillaged the city, killed many followers of Ptolemy, and desecrated the temple, causing the sacrifices to cease for 3 years and 6 months. The high priest Onias fled to Egypt, and Antiochus forced the Jews to violate their laws. A garrison commanded by Bacchides enforced Antiochus's degrees against Judaism. According to Josephus's second account (*Ant*. 12.5.2 §§242-56), Antiochus marched into Egypt and defeated Ptolemy VI, but the Romans intervened and forced him to abandon any designs on Egypt. On his way home he marched up to Jerusalem, and the gates were opened to him; nevertheless, he took a large spoil after killing those who opposed him. Then two years later he took the city again, despoiled the temple, killed some, took some captive with their wives and children and stopped the temple sacrifices. At this point, he built the Akra and put a Macedonian garrison in it, along with some 'impious' (ἀσεβεῖς καὶ πονηροί) of the people, meaning Jews.

It is important to be aware of the separate accounts and note the differences because many modern reconstructions ignore them, especially the rather different data of Josephus. Certainly, there is a similarity in overall outline and even in many of the details, but the differences may be the key to a proper understanding of what actually took place. Each source is written from its own (biased) perspective, with some unique data, and thus gives only part of the picture or even a false one.

None of our sources gives a coherent portrayal of the events leading up to the suppression of Jewish worship (the chronological scheme followed here is my own reconstruction). As already noted above, we know that Antiochus invaded Egypt twice (§15.1). The first time was probably early 169 (though possibly as early as November 170) when he successfully defeated Ptolemy VI and then forced an alliance by marrying his daughter off to him (cf. Dan. 11.28; 1 Macc. 1.16-24). It was while on his way back in September 169 that he probably entered the Jerusalem temple and looted its treasures. Some think that he attacked the city at this time, but there is no reason why he should have engaged in any fighting. There is no evidence that any resistance was offered to his initial entry when he took the temple money, nor does he seem to have interfered with the temple cult or taken actual objects from the temple. Indeed, the seizing of temple funds was probably a compensation for the arrears of tribute that Menelaus had not paid (cf. 2 Macc. 4.27-28). It is true that Menelaus is alleged to have stolen some temple vessels, but the incense altar, *menorah* and showbread table were used on a daily basis and are not likely to have been touched by him, even if the allegations were correct. Thus, no violence appears to have taken place at this time (cf. Dan. 11.28). In the spring of 168 he invaded once again, but this time things were different (Dan. 11.29-30; 2 Macc. 5.1-17). Although he was victorious over the Egyptians, the Romans intervened and forced him to withdraw (July 168: see §1.3.4).

Now, it is necessary to consider possibilities not in the text. According to the text, it was most likely at this point that news of Jason's assault on Menelaus came to Antiochus's attention. However, Tcherikover (1959) posited that there had already developed a much more extensive revolt, led by the Hasidim. This thesis was widely rejected at the time, but now a number of scholars have argued that this was not just an exaggerated report but that an actual revolt was indeed underway in Jerusalem (D. R. Schwartz 2008: 250–55; Honigman 2014: especially 378–97). Although no such revolt is explicitly described in either 1 or 2 Maccabees, there are several hints within the text, suggesting that fighting extended more widely than simply Jason against Menelaus:

- When Antiochus's army approached Jerusalem, a normal response would be for the city to open its gates. The fact that Antiochus's troops attacked the city would suggest that there were defenders on the walls who shut the gates of the city against the Seleucid force.
- The ferocity of the attack by Antiochus's forces suggests there was something more than a local civil war going on in Jerusalem.

- Antiochus's placing an overseer not only in Jerusalem but also in Gerizim suggests a revolt wider than just in Jerusalem.
- The author of 2 Maccabees is incensed about those killed by Jason, even though he was implacably opposed by Menelaus. This suggests that those killed by Jason were not Menelaus's followers but another group – a rebellion of 'traditionalists' or 'nationalists', according to Schwartz (2008: 255). Contrary to Tcherikover, however, there is no reason to posit the Hasidim as the leaders of this revolt (on the Hasidim, see §6.1).

The accounts at this point leave some major difficulties. For example, 2 Maccabees mentions only the second invasion of Egypt (in 168 BCE), but 1 Maccabees, while mentioning only the one invasion of Egypt (in 170/169), seems to bring in events relating to the second invasion (cf. Bickerman 1937a: 18, 69–70//1979: 10, 45–46). Similarly, Josephus in *War* only mentions one attack on Jerusalem, with which he associates all events, while *Antiquities* (12.5.2-3 §§242-46) erroneously associates the Roman intervention with the first invasion of Egypt instead of the second. But he does seem to make a distinction between Antiochus's actions in Jerusalem in 169 BCE and those in 168. Nevertheless, having sorted out the general chain of events, we are still left with multiple questions:

- If Antiochus's army took the city and put down the revolt, why was there need to send Apollonius the Mysiarch (i.e., in charge of a contingent of Mysian soldiers) to take the city by subterfuge sometime later (2 Macc. 5.23-26; 1 Macc. 1.29-36)?
- Moreover, Apollonius is ordered to kill all the men and to enslave the women and children (2 Macc. 5.24), a strange move after Antiochus's army had already slain or enslaved practically all of them!
- And why did Antiochus feel it necessary even after that to send Geron the Athenian to set up pagan worship in the temple (2 Macc. 6.1-11) when the supposed revolt of the Jews had long since been dealt with?

We are simply not given sufficient data and can only make informed guesses at best.

There is no clear evidence that Antiochus himself took part in capturing the city after his second invasion (Bringmann 1983: 38; SCHÜRER 1:152 n. 37; contra Tcherikover 1959: 186). Rather, the actions ascribed to him are probably those of Apollonius; that is, Apollonius was sent to put down a rebellion, which would suggest duplicate events in 2 Macc. 5.11-14 and 5.23-26. The fight between Jason and Menelaus had given the impression of a revolt, or perhaps showed the continuation of one. When Apollonius got there, the city was already peaceful (apparently because Jason had already left the scene), but he took it by a ruse and carried out Antiochus's orders. After this, Philip the *epistatēs* was sent. It is often thought that his task was to settle a colony of soldiers in Jerusalem, that is, to establish a military cleruchy to be ready for any further trouble (Tcherikover 1959: 194–95; Bringmann 1983: 87–89, 127); however, as Bar-Kochva (1989: 438–44) has argued no colony was founded, only a garrison. Nowhere in the sources is a military colony suggested. Indeed, it would not have made sense to try to establish one in hostile territory, since the soldiers were supported from their land which was farmed by serfs. But this would be difficult to maintain if surrounded by enemies. But the important thing here is that a Syrian military detachment was installed in Jerusalem (probably in the Akra). Philip remained there, with Menelaus continuing as high priest, until the actual Maccabaean revolt began (cf. 2 Macc. 6.11; 8.8).

The real puzzle is why a little later Antiochus sent Geron to crush the Jewish religion. A number of suggestions have been made over the years, some of them to be rejected outright with others rather better but none wholly satisfactory (Chapter 11). If religious suppression took place, it would have been unique in antiquity. Religious intolerance has historically been a practice of monotheistic religions. While Judaism itself was often seen by the Greeks and Romans as intolerant, polytheism is usually tolerant by its nature. Antiochus was no religious zealot. He had no occasion to suppress Judaism for ideological reasons, while Jews outside Palestine itself and even in the very capital of Antioch evidently carried on with their worship without hindrance (Bickerman 1937a: 120–22//1979: 79–80; Bringmann 1983: 102 n. 8).

15.2.2. *Two Recent Theories to Explain Antiochus's Actions*

A number of proposals have been made to explain what happened at this point and why it generated a revolt in Judah. A number of these explanations have been explored in Chapter 11, and only some relevant material will be repeated here. However, two recent theories deserve more attention. They were summarized briefly in Chapter 11 but are treated more fully here.

First, S. Honigman (2014, building on S. Weitzman 2004) has explained the situation by arguing that no religious suppression took place – that this was a scenario created by the writers of 1 and 2 Maccabees, a literary construct that can be dismissed. Antiochus's measures were political, not religious. Yes, the temple was polluted by alien sacrifices and an alien cult, but these were instituted for political reasons, primarily to establish his authority in the face of the Judaean rebellion against his rule. J. C. Bernhardt (2017: 255–64) presents a similar case. Weitzman, Honigman and Bernhardt have argued their case well, and there are many aspects of the argument that are convincing or at least possible. Nevertheless, on their overall thesis that there was no religious persecution, a diversity of independent sources seems to suggest the opposite, which creates a problem for their conclusion. Note the following points:

- We can all agree that the harrowing martyrdom account in 2 Maccabees 7 is a literary fiction. A blatant misalignment with historical reality is the presence of Antiochus at the alleged torture and death of the mother and the seven sons.
- Daniel is another independent witness. A number of passages in Daniel relate to pollution of the temple, which Weitzman, Honigman and Bernhardt accept. Daniel 11.33, however, seems to speak of individuals killed for their religious beliefs or deeds, though the type of persecution on individuals is not clearly described because the coded language is not always easy to interpret (Dan. 7.21, 25; 8.10, 24).
- Porphyry, though writing in the 3rd century CE and mediated through Jerome's Daniel commentary, nevertheless seems to have had reasonably good sources for this period of Jewish history. However, his testimony is problematic for two reasons: first, he makes reference to the books of Maccabees in his comments (e.g., on Dan. 11.34-35: Becker 2016: 249), and he also knew Josephus (e.g., the prologue to Daniel: Becker 2016: 220–22); secondly, several of his statements are absent from Becker (2016) and may not be authentic. For example, the comment on Dan. 8.9 and 11–12 that the Jews were forced to worship idols is absent, as is the comment on Dan. 11.33 about the Jews suffering from fire and sword, slavery, rape and death (listed among the 'Dubia' in Becker 2016: 508). But in his comment on Dan. 11.37-39, he states that the Jews had to worship an alien god, which was probably Jupiter (= Zeus) (Becker 2016: 261–63). His comment about the saints being tested and made white is in the context of referring to the books of Maccabees (Becker 2016: 249–51).

15. *The Maccabaean Revolt to the Death of Judas (170–161 BCE)* 351

These points either support the arguments of Weitzman, Honigman and Bernhardt, or at least do not clearly contradict their thesis. But notice the following additional points:

- Harder to dismiss is the death of Eleazer (2 Macc. 6.18-31), though the details may be the contribution of the author; likewise, the accounts of the women executed for having their sons circumcised (2 Macc. 6.10; cf. a similar account in 1 Macc. 1.60-61) and those killed while keeping the sabbath in caves outside the city (2 Macc. 6.11). We need to keep in mind that 1 Maccabees and 2 Maccabees may be independent witnesses here. Yet the paucity of examples might lead one to conclude that these incidents were due only to the excesses of over-zealous local officials.
- The *Testament of Moses* 8 speaks of a persecution. Circumcision is specifically singled out as a factor (*T. Mos.* 8.1, 3). This looks like a reference to the Maccabaean crisis.
- Diodorus 34-35.1.3-4 states that Antiochus wanted to counter Jewish hatred against the rest of mankind. As a result, he sacrificed a great sow on the altar and then sprinkled their holy books with the meat juices; further, he compelled the high priest and the other Jews to eat of the meat.
- Tacitus, *Hist.* 5.8.2, speaks of Antiochus trying to get rid of Jewish superstition (*superstitionem*).
- The letter of Antiochus IV making concessions to the Judaeans (2 Macc. 11.27-38) mentions that the Jews wanted to use their own foods and follow their own laws. This indicates that these practices had been officially suppressed for a time. See also the letter of Antiochus V (2 Macc. 11.23-26).

These sources show how complicated the matter is. The pollution of the temple and altar (from the Jewish point of view) is confirmed, but this was not doubted. Also, as they argue, it is clear that some of the accounts of persecution – and certainly many of the details – are fictional. Yet the latter examples look more credible, such as those relating to punishment of families for circumcising their boys. Some of the later accounts, such as the *Testament of Moses*, are harder to evaluate. Are they relying on the books of Maccabees or do they have independent sources? The latter is possible. But crucial it seems are the 'pagan' accounts (Diodorus and Tacitus), which accept the picture of religious suppression (and may even approve of it). The matter is difficult because we do not know their sources, but although we do not know the sources used by Diodorus and Tacitus, there is no reason to assume they were Jewish. More likely is that they were Greek or even Roman. If so, this would reinforce the view that Antiochus indeed attempted in some way to suppress Judaism in Judaea.

But the statements in the Seleucid letters seem decisive: there were decrees affecting Jewish foods and other religious laws. Thus, along with pollution of the temple and pagan sacrifices, which all accept, there were also attempts to suppress the Jewish religion, though some of these could have been only local persecution. The list of specific examples of atrocities in 1 Macc. 1.56-58, 60-61 and 2 Macc. 6.10-11 suggests that the persecution was more limited than the exaggerated claims of later accounts, yet an actual attempt at weaning the people of Judaea away from Judaism and toward pagan worship appears to have taken place. But considering the strong blame laid on Antiochus by some of the sources, it seems to have been an imperial decree, not just a local matter. Granted, the statement in 1 Macc. 1.41-51 that implies an empire-wide prohibition of Judaism is to be rejected (cf., e.g., Bernhardt 2017: 255–56). And some of the examples of atrocities against individual Jews, if true, could be due to the excessive zeal of local Seleucid officials. Yet such passage as 2 Macc. 11.24-25 and 11.27-38 seem difficult to interpret as anything but a decree or decrees issuing from the highest levels of Seleucid administration.

To summarize, there seems no doubt that those (Weitzman 2004; Honigman 2014; Bernhardt 2017) who have recently argued that Antiochus's measures – whatever they were precisely – were to establish his authority are correct. Judaea had rebelled in his eyes (and perhaps in actuality), and he needed to make an example of it. Yet the suppression of Jewish worship would also no doubt have been a watershed, not only in Jewish history but in the history of antiquity, because it was not the custom to forbid local religious expression. *Make no mistake: there was religious persecution.* From the Jewish point of view no greater attack on their religion could be made than expunging the *tamid* offering or polluting the altar with pagan sacrifices.

All seem to accept that the temple was polluted and a foreign cult introduced and – as quite rightly pointed out – for political rather than ideological reasons. But when it comes to enforced 'idol worship', is there really a major difference between the political measures and outright religious suppression? What about the forbidding of circumcision? When it comes to compelling Jews to eat unclean foods, surely we have crossed into religious matters. To repeat, the suppression of the *tamid* offering – which Antiochus undoubtedly saw as political – was perceived as profound religious suppression by Jews. The point is that it is hard to draw a line, and by any reckoning Antiochus's measures amounted to religious suppression from the Jewish point of view, however he regarded them.

The other recent study proposing a far-reaching thesis about the possible religious suppression and the subsequent uprising is originally an older argument that has tended to be discounted by most recent interpreters. However, its revival in the recent monograph by Bernhardt (2017: 166–274) means that it requires an extensive consideration. This is the argument that Antiochus promoted the cult of Zeus Olympius and deified himself in the image of Zeus, which was seen as significant in his measures later taken toward Jerusalem. Briefly, Bernhardt argues that Antiochus promoted the cult of Zeus, combining it with his personal ruler cult, as a way of legitimating his claim to the Seleucid throne. Later, when Judah was seen as revolting against his rule, he imposed the ruler cult on the Jerusalem temple as a means of making the Jews affirm their loyalty to him. This is an important position and needs to be considered in some detail. Bernhardt uses several arguments to establish his position:

- *Antiochus promoted the cult of Zeus Olympius.* This appears to be true up to a point, but there are examples of Antiochus's honouring other gods (e.g., Polybius 30.25.13). The question is the significance of the specific examples with a focus on Zeus (Mittag 2006: 139–43). For example, some of his ancestors – especially on his mother's side – already supported Zeus; also, he did not abandon the support of Apollo that had been traditional in the Seleucid dynasty up to his time (Mittag 2006: 140). It is also interesting that the coins with Zeus are all from Ake-Ptolemais and Antioch, while other mints seem to promote Apollo, the argument being that the coins from the former mints were used to pay soldiers who would approve the image of the conquering Zeus.
- *He gifted a considerable amount to Athens to finish their building of the temple to Zeus.* Although the temple was not completed before Antiochus's untimely death, his contribution to its completion was significant (Mittag 2006: 143). Yet his choice of this project in Athens is hardly a pointer to a particular devotion to Zeus, since there is no other project that was likely to be so prestigious for the city at that time. One can easily make the case that the dedication of the temple to Zeus was coincidental to Antiochus's choosing this building project to bestow honours on Athens.

- *Antiochus had a great statue of Zeus placed in the Apollo temple at Daphne, along with a statue of himself.* This appears to be mistaken. The evidence is a statement in Ammianus Marcellinus (22.13.1). Mittag (2006: 144–45) argues that the statement must be understood in the light of Libanius (*Or.* 60.12), that the statue was one of Apollo, not Zeus.
- *A statue of Zeus was placed in the Jerusalem temple, probably alongside one of Antiochus himself.* It is indeed true that Jerome stated that a statue of Zeus Olympius was placed in the Jewish temple (Jerome, *Comm. in Danielem* on Dan. 8.9 and 11.31). Although this might have happened, it seems doubtful, for three reasons. One reason is that neither 1 nor 2 Maccabees mention a single word about a cult statue of any sort; on the contrary, they only talk of polluting sacrifices and debauched activities taking place within the temple (1 Macc. 1.54, 59; 2 Macc. 6.1-4). Neither does the book of Daniel mention any cult image, as far as we can tell from the cryptic language used by the writer to describe contemporary activities (cf. Dan. 11.31). A second point is that according to the latest collection of Porphyry's fragments, this statement about a statue of Zeus in the Holy of Holies was not from Porphyry (Becker 2016). Finally, it seems that the allegations in Jerome were not taken from Polybius (as Bernhardt [2017: 224–28] argues) but were only his own (plausible) inference from the situation.

We must also keep in mind Antiochus's general outlook: we have the statements of Polybius (26.1.10-11) and Livy (6.147) that Antiochus was especially pious toward the gods in general, not just Zeus. Mørkholm's assessment is important (1966: 186):

> Antiochus IV was not a zealous Hellenizer, nor a religious innovator who tried to identify himself with Zeus Olympius. His persecution of the Jews had no religious basis, but must be regarded as [a] purely political measure.

Bernhardt of course argues that is was political, not religious, but did it involve a special focus on Zeus? The problem is that the original sources do not suggest any religious measures taken by Antiochus that arise from a devotion to Zeus. All we have are that the temple at Jerusalem was dedicated to Zeus Olympius, and the one on Gerizim, to Zeus Xenius. But these temples had to be dedicated to a deity or deities. The question is, where in our sources is any statement connecting

Antiochus's alleged religious devotion to Zeus to his political actions as king, whether against the Jews or otherwise? It seems that Bernhardt's efforts are expended on making a circumstantial case, but this is because he cannot make one from direct statements in the sources.

If a religious suppression in some form is a historical fact, as still seems the most likely case, who gave the order and why? Some have seen Menelaus as the instigator. Indeed, 2 Macc. 13.3-8 seems to blame Menelaus for the situation. Josephus, who does not appear to know 2 Maccabees, nevertheless states that Menelaus 'had compelled the Jews to violate their ancestral religion' (*Ant.* 12.9.7 §385). The problem is that Menelaus was also apparently no ideologue but purely a powerseeker. It seems reasonable to assume that he was in some way involved in the prohibition, either as an active agent or simply as one who acquiesced to Antiochus's requirements. He did, for example, conduct Antiochus into the temple, perhaps even the Holy of Holies, according to 2 Maccabees (5.15), though Jason on a similar visit of Antiochus did not carry out such a sacrilegious act (2 Macc. 4.31-22). While Bickerman's thesis of Menelaus as the creator of an 'enlightened religion' does not stand up, Bringmann (1983: 129–40) has argued that the imposed cult was the product of Menelaus himself as part of a power play.

A number of sources blame Antiochus. This is not surprising, because the order would ultimately have had to come from him. But why would he do such a thing? The old idea of his being a religious zealot or a promoter of Hellenization has long been disproved. As a number of scholars have pointed out (e.g., Bernhardt, Honigman, Gruen, Portier-Young – see Chapter 11), Antiochus's measure were political, not ideological ones: 'decision making was the outcome of pragmatic negotiations framed by local custom between the central (imperial) power and the local elites' (Honigman 2014: 25). He was no ideologue: any measures he took would almost certainly have been (in his eyes) for pragmatic reasons. Was this where Menelaus came in, perhaps advising the king that their religion was what caused the Jews to act in certain ways? This seems certainly a possibility. In any case, the order was an unusual – unprecedented – one and had consequences that Antiochus probably could not have begun to predict. If he had had any inkling of what would be the results, it is very doubtful that he would have given the order.

Finally, when did the pollution of the temple and the cessation of the daily (*tamid*) offering take place? 1 Maccabees 1.54 puts the date as Kislev, 145 SE. As argued in §1.3.4, this date would be calculated from a Jewish Seleucid date reckoning from Nisan 312 BCE, making the date November–December 168 BCE. It has become conventional since Bickerman's arguments (1937a: 155–68//1979: 101–11) to give this date as 167 BCE; however, in recent years a number of researchers have argued for 168 BCE (Bernhardt 2017: 222, 540; Bringmann 1983: 15–28; Grabbe 1991). A further consideration, often overlooked, is that the cleansing of the temple took place *before* Antiochus's death, which we know was in November–December 164 BCE (see further at §15.4.3).

15.2.3. *The 'Alien Cult' Set up in the Temple*

> **E. J. Bickerman** (1951) 'Les Maccabées de Malalas', *Byzantion* 21: 63–83; **E. Nestle** (1884) 'Der Greuel der Verwüstung', *ZAW* 4: 248; **R. A. Oden** (1977) 'Ba'al Sāmēm and 'El', *CBQ* 39: 457–73; **K. J. Rigsby** (1980) 'Seleucid Notes', *TAPA* 110: 233–54; **J. C. VanderKam** (1981b) '2 Maccabees 6, 7A and Calendrical Change in Jerusalem', *JSJ* 12: 52–74.

The book of Daniel talks about an 'abomination of desolation' (שקוץ שמם *šiqqûṣ šōmēm*: Dan. 11.31; 12.11), but the precise significance of this is not immediately obvious. What exactly happened with regard to the Jerusalem temple and pagan worship? Our sources are almost entirely 1 and 2 Maccabees, though the book of Daniel gives one or two important pieces of data. Yet the cult imposed on the Jerusalem temple is not clear from the sources. The following points emerge from 1 and 2 Maccabees:

- The temple was dedicated to Zeus Olympius (2 Macc. 6.2).
- The primary cause of pollution and sacrilege was something erected on the altar of burnt offering (1 Macc. 1.54; 4.43-47). This included a pagan altar (*bōmos*) on top of the original altar in the temple courtyard (1 Macc. 1.59). According to other sources (e.g., Diodorus 34–35.1.3-4) swine were offered on this altar, though why 1 and 2 Maccabees would have omitted this fact is a major question (cf. Bernhardt 2017: 254).
- There was a monthly celebration of the king's birthday (2 Macc. 6.7).
- Worship of Dionysus took place on the king's feast day, with processions in his honour (2 Macc. 6.7).

The first point to note is that there is no indication that an idol of any sort was placed in the temple, as would be expected with a Greek cult (contra Bernhardt 2017: 224–25). It is almost inconceivable that the presence of such would have been ignored by Daniel or 1 and 2 Maccabees. The cessation of the *tamid* offering was seen as shaking the cosmos to its foundations: how much more the statue of a pagan god set up in the Holy of Holies! Granted, there is a very late statement that a statue of Zeus Olympius was erected in the temple. This is by the church father Jerome (*Comm. in Dan.* to 8.9 and 11.31), allegedly quoting Porphyry; however, this may have been Jerome's own deduction, since these passages are omitted from the latest edition of Porphyry (Becker 2016). J. C. Bernhardt (2017: 226–29) argues that the information is from Polybius, but this seems doubtful. In any case, the silence of Daniel and 1 and 2 Maccabees seems a strong argument against any such statue. (Bickerman suggests this is only a reference to votive gifts, not a cult image [1937a: 102–4//1979: 67–68].)

Although the temple is said to have been dedicated to Zeus Olympius (2 Macc. 6.2), this does not necessarily imply a change to a Greek form of worship. The Samaritan temple was also dedicated to Zeus, apparently without any change of cult. Despite the view that he was a particular devotee of Zeus Olympius, Antiochus IV made no attempt to impose the cult elsewhere (cf. Rigsby 1980: 233–38). It was E. Nestle (1884) a century ago who first pointed out that the epithet 'abomination of desolation' was most likely a Hebrew play on the name Baal Shamem ('the lord of heaven'; cf. Oden 1977), a traditional god in Phoenicia and the region. It had become common to give Greek names to native deities, and Baal Shamem of the Phoenicians and others was frequently designated 'Zeus' in Greek writings (Bickerman 1937a: 92–96//1979: 62–65; Oden 1977: 466–67). Bickerman himself argued that the cult was Syro-Canaanite, and this has been widely accepted (Tcherikover 1959: 194–95; Goldstein 1976: 142–57, though cf. his reservations about Nestle's thesis). Part of the reason is that the imposed cult focused on the altar, and one of the characteristics of Syrian religions was the practice of imageless, altar-based cults.

The celebration of the king's birthday was a customary matter in the Seleucid empire and easily explained. More of a problem is the Dionysus worship (2 Macc. 6.7). D. R. Schwartz (2008: 274, 541–43) has argued that this is characteristic of the Ptolemaic realm rather than the Seleucid and was thus a literary creation of the author of 2 Maccabees. Drawing on an article of J. C. VanderKam (1981b), R. Doran (2012: 137–38) rejects this and argues that 2 Macc. 6.7 is historical. Yet it should be noted that Schwartz had taken note of VanderKam's article and opposed it. The matter is difficult, but it seems that Schwartz's cautions should be heeded. Was this a Greek cult? In view of the 'Zeus' worship, it seems possible that 'Dionysus' in this case is simply the Greek name for a Syro-Canaanite deity (cf. Bickerman 1937a: 113–14; 1979: 74; Goldstein 1976: 153–55).

Whether a goddess was also associated with the worship (Bickerman 1937a: 113; 1979: 73–74; Goldstein 1976: 152–53) is perhaps debatable, since the only evidence is late (cf. Bickerman 1951).

The argument so far seems to be pushing for a Near Eastern cult rather than a Greek; however, Bringmann (1983: 109–20, 130–32, 141) has noted that there is more to be considered than just the imposition of a native Syrian cult. Elements of the forced new worship go contrary to local Canaanite religion, in particular the sacrifice of swine (rejected by some) and the prohibition of circumcision. Thus, he argues that it was 'neither a Greek nor a pure Syrian cult' (*weder einen griechischen noch einen rein syrischen Kult* [Bringmann 1983: 109]). This is one of the arguments used to support his view that the cult was Menelaus's own creation. Yet J. C. Bernhardt (2017: 217–74) has made a strong case that the cult must have been a Greek one. Although certain aspects of his thesis have been questioned above (§15.2.2), he provides a good deal of convincing material on this question. After all, a cult imposed by Antiochus was bound to be a Greek one. This does not nullify Nestle's important observations, since it was common for native peoples to assimilate Greek and Roman deities to their more familiar ones. The writer of Daniel could well have referred to Zeus Olympius as Baal Shamem when speaking Hebrew, and then made a cutting pun on the name for his own purposes.

15.3. *The Beginnings of the Revolt*

15.3.1. *The Initial Resistance*

Sources: 1 Macc. 2.1-3.9; 2 Macc. 8.1-7;
War. 1.1.3-6 §§36-47; *Ant*. 12.5.5–6.3 §§257-84.

According to 1 Maccabees 2, the fight-back against Seleucid religious suppression began with Mattathias, the father of the Maccabaean brothers. There are a number of reasons to doubt this (see especially the next section, §15.3.2). A further complication is that resistance seems to have got underway before the Maccabees came on the scene (Sievers 1990: 34). For example, we later read of Hasidim who are clearly a resistance group not initially affiliated with the Maccabaean circle (1 Macc. 2.42). 2 Maccabees 5.27 states that Judas and ten associates fled into the countryside when the persecution started in Jerusalem. There they lived like animals for a period of time. This suggests little support or organization for the initial resistance of the Hasmonaean family. Rather than others joining them (as 1 Macc. 2.42-43 alleges), it may be that it was they who joined others (cf. Sievers 1990: 34).

Although we can only speculate, it is likely that several anti-Seleucid groups arose in Judah in reaction to Antiochus's measures, and it was only with time that the Maccabees came to dominate. If we go by historical analogy, these groups probably competed with one another – perhaps even with violence on occasion – until they were all either wiped out, disbanded or brought under the Maccabaean umbrella. We need to keep in mind that the single-minded focus on the Maccabees by the text was likely a later idealization and sanitizing of the early history of the revolt. Studies of such resistance movements in history leaves this strong message.

15.3.2. *The Question of Mattathias*

Because of the persecution many people fled from Jerusalem into the countryside. Armed resistance allegedly began with the Hasmonaean family. According to 1 Maccabees 2, this was initially led by Mattathias accompanied by his five sons: John, Simon, Judas (Maccabaeus), Eleazar and Jonathan. He and his sons had left Jerusalem to live in Modein which was probably the ancestral home of the family. The story given is that there soldiers of the king attempted to force a public pagan sacrifice. This would fit with the description of the persecution as affecting not just the temple worship but also involving pagan sacrifices at various locations. According to the legend, Mattathias killed both an apostate Jew who acceded to the order for sacrifice and the commander of the soldiers, then fled with other Jews into the wilderness. He lived only about a year after this and, while on his death bed, turned the military leadership over to Judas who seems not to have been the eldest of the sons.

Although Bar-Kochva (1989: 194–99) defends this scenario, most recent research has been sceptical of it (cf. Sievers 1990: 29–36; Bernhardt 2017: 275–85). There are a number of reasons:

- Mattathias is completely ignored by 2 Maccabees, who focuses on Judas. (Bar-Kochva [1989: 197–99] thinks there are hints that Mattathias was known to the author, but he also assumes – contrary to many other scholars – that 1 Maccabees was a source for 2 Maccabees.)
- A number of issues that are associated with Mattathis actually seem to have come up later in Hasmonaean history, such as the question of fighting on the sabbath, which perhaps came up about 161 BCE (cf. 1 Macc. 9.43-49; Sievers 1990: 32–34).

- Mattathias and his deeds are nowhere else referred to in 1 Maccabees after chap. 2, especially in the summary of Maccabaean deeds in 1 Macc. 14.27-45. Even though the actions of those other than Simon are downplayed and Simon's doings emphasized, other Maccabaean activity is mentioned. Yet although Mattathias is mentioned as the father of Simon (1 Macc. 14.29-30), nothing is said about his part in initiating the revolt, this despite mention of Simon's brothers' fighting.
- In spite of supposed activities on the part of Mattathias as early as 168 BCE, the actual report of actions on the Jewish side does not really begin until a couple of years later, in 166 BCE (Bernhardt 2017: 276).
- Josephus (*War* 1.1.3 §36-37) has a story about Mattathias, but it differs considerably from the one in 1 Maccabees 2.
- As will be clear from some of the points noted below, the Mattathias account serves very well for Hasmonaean propaganda and legitimation.

The primary reason for rejecting the story of 1 Maccabees 2 is that Mattathias is not mentioned later in the account, especially at 1 Maccabees 14, where we would certainly expect his name to occur. There are also questions about 1 Macc. 2.65-66 and the statements about the brothers there. Was Simon really the eldest? Did Mattathias entrust military leadership to Judas but urge Simon to be the overall leader and advisor? The subsequent account says little about Simon and certainly does not make him the one looked up to by the brothers. Judas is clearly the leader until his death.

15.4. *Judas Maccabaeus*

Whatever the initial stages of the revolt, the Hasmonaean family eventually established leadership over the movement. But there is also the question of leadership within the Hasmonaean family. While it is possible that leadership did not go to the eldest son, chances are that it did, so was Judas likely only the third son? Josephus (*War* 1.1.3 §37) states that Judas was the eldest of the sons, but whether he got this from a source or only makes his own deduction is questionable. Arguments since Wellhausen have pointed out that 1 Maccabees seems to give most prominence to Simon, suggesting that we may see an attempt here to downplay Judas's initiative to some extent (cf. Tcherikover 1959: 205, 384). Certainly, the story as it stands has elements suggestive of romantic colouration (e.g., the Phineas-like act of Mattathias).

Whatever its precise origins, the Jewish resistance under Judas and his brothers took some time to get underway. The first actions seem to have been against 'apostate' Jews (1 Macc. 2.44-48; 3.8). The village of Modein served as the natural centre of operations (Bar-Kochva 1989: 194–99). It was the home village of the Hasmonaean family. Although itself close to the Seleucid garrisons at Jerusalem and Gezer and easily approachable by a hostile force, it was right next to the Gophna Hills to which the Jewish fighters could easily retire if threatened. The resistance was conducted by guerrilla tactics initially and probably did not worry the Seleucid central government at first; however, the local administration saw the need to do something about the harassment.

15.4.1. *Judas Maccabee's Initial Campaigns*

The details of Judas's campaigns have not been studied extensively in recent times by military historians, the main examination being those of B. Bar-Kochva (1976, 1989), though I. Shatzman (1991) has written generally on the military aspects of the Hasmonaeans and Herod. Several general points need to be made, before going on to a more detailed analysis:

- The main source is 1 Maccabees, followed by Josephus. Although Josephus is mainly paraphrasing 1 Maccabees in the *Antiquities*, which is the main source (*War* has few helpful details except in the battle for Beth Zecharias), he does have some understanding of battle conditions and occasionally has sources other than 1 Maccabees.
- According to Bar-Kochva (1989: 153–55, 158), 1 Maccabees is remarkably accurate for the most part, being written by a participant or someone who had interviewed eye witnesses for many of the battles. There are some occasions where 1 Maccabees does not have such direct information, as will be noted below. This accuracy does not generally extend to troop demographics, especially with regard to the Seleucid side, where 2 Maccabees generally has a better understanding. Thus, 1 Maccabees is usually more reliable about details relating to the Jewish side of things, and 2 Maccabees is evidently more knowledgeable about the Seleucid military and administrative structure and hierarchy.
- Bar-Kochva (1989: 171) also argues that the author of 2 Maccabees is often ignorant of the geography and topography of Palestine and is thus not normally a reliable source for details of the battles.

- It is generally agreed that the troop numbers given for the Seleucid armies are usually grossly exaggerated, probably in order to make Jewish victories seem more spectacular (Bar-Kochva 1989: 29–67; Shatzman 1991: 25–35). The numbers for forces on the Jewish side are generally more realistic, if sometimes discounted to make their victories more surprising.

In spite of the fine words about the Maccabaean fight for the law against the heathen, Judas's first excursions were against his fellow Jews, those they considered as collaborators – labelled the 'ungodly' (τοὺς παρανομήσαντας: 1 Macc. 2.44; *Ant.* 12.6.4 §286). As so often in such situations, the community was divided, and former neighbours and even kin were at each other's throats. Fellow Jews also made an easier target than Seleucid troops. But those who went along with the Seleucid demands were seen as part of the enemy and thus fair game for reprisals. Judas also raised his army from among his kin and fellow countrymen (2 Macc. 8.1).

Defeat of Apollonius and Seron

B. Bar-Kochva (1976b) 'Sēron and Cestius Gallus at Beith Horon', *PEQ* 108: 13–21; **idem** (1989) *Judas Maccabaeus*, 194–218.

Sources: 1 Macc. 3.1-37; 2 Macc. 8.1-7; *Ant.* 12.6.4-7.2 §§285-97.

Judas was probably not initially perceived as a major threat by the Seleucids; however, he made enough of a nuisance of himself that they decided to intervene. This seems to have been a decision at local level and did not involve the higher echelons of government. According to 1 Macc. 3.10-12 the first attempt to crush the revolt came from Apollonius, who led a force from Samaria. This clash of arms is only vaguely described in 1 Maccabees, suggesting the author knew little about it, and it is not even mentioned in 2 Maccabees: we do not even know when or where it was supposed to have occurred. Apollonius was probably a garrison commander, possibly the same individual as the commander of the Mysians mentioned earlier (1 Macc. 1.29; 2 Macc. 5.24). Josephus (*Ant.* 12.7.1 §287) makes him governor (*meridarchēs*) of Samaria, identifying him with the individual mentioned in the letter of the Sidonian colony (cf. *Ant.* 12.5.5 §261). The two possibilities are not mutually exclusive, since the commander of the Mysians could have been posted on to Samaria, but it is also true that 'Apollonius' was a fairly common name at the time: we cannot be sure that he is to be identified with either of these other individuals. No real details are given except that Apollonius was himself killed (with Judas taking his sword and fighting with it for the rest of his life).

Next was Seron who advanced via Beth Horon (1 Macc. 3.13-26). Unfortunately, this battle is also described in rather vague, often biblical, language, again suggesting that the author had little actual knowledge of the engagement (2 Maccabees also omits this episode). Seron is said to be 'general' (*archōn*) of the Syrian army (1 Macc. 3.13) or even governor (*stratēgos*) of all Coele-Syria (*Ant.* 12.7.1 §288). Both these are unlikely: the commander of the Syrian or Seleucid army was the king, while the *stratēgos* of Coele-Syria and Phoenicia at the time was Ptolemy son of Dorymenes (1 Macc. 3.38; 2 Macc. 4.45; 8.8). This Seron was not a high-ranking officer, and all 'the considerations and data noted above tend to show that Seron was no more than one of the commanders of the mercenary garrisons in the region' (Bar-Kochva 1989: 133). Interestingly, it is alleged that 'renegade' Jews were part of Seron's force (1 Macc. 3.15; *Ant.* 12.7.1 §289). Seron seems to have overstepped his authority and also his capability: 'I shall make a name for myself and win honour in the kingdom' (1 Macc. 3.14). This was evidently a defeat for the Seleucid forces, but despite the rather pious language, this was no 'miraculous' win for the Jews. Seron's troops were defeated at the ascent of Beth Horon, a favourite spot for ambush (as the Romans found out almost 250 years later [*War* 2.19.8 §§546-50]). Also, 2 Macc. 8.1 suggests that Judas had a force of about 6,000 at this time, rather than the gross underestimation so frequently found in the books of Maccabees.

Despite the impression given by 1 Maccabees, both these were local attempts with small contingents of Seleucid soldiers (Bar-Kochva 1989: 199–218). As noted, both the named leaders were probably in command of local garrisons. Thus, the statement that these defeats were enough to begin to make Judas's name known to the surrounding nations (1 Macc. 3.25-26) is clearly an exaggeration (Bar-Kochva 1989: 218).

Battle of Emmaus and Further Conflicts at Local Level

B. Bar-Kochva (1989) *Judas Maccabaeus*, 219–74.

Sources: 1 Macc. 3.27–4.25; 2 Macc. 8.8-36; *Ant.* 12.7.2-4 §§293-312.

1 Maccabees 3.27-37 (cf. *Ant.* 12.7.2 §§293-94) now suggests that Antiochus's entire attention was focused on Judah and the rebellion under Judas, and he paid his army a year's wages and planned to send

his entire force against Judah. This is wishful thinking on the part of the author: contrary to this picture, Antiochus had far more important things demanding his attention. The effect of the Maccabaean revolt on the Seleucid empire at this early stage was like the bites of a gnat on an elephant. It is doubtful that news of the Jewish defeat of Apollonius and Seron had even come to Antiochus's ears, but if it had, it was not likely to have seemed very significant to him. After a very effective demonstration of his military power and glory at Daphne in 166 BCE (the standard date, contra Bar-Kochva 1989: 466–73), he embarked on a campaign to the Upper Satrapies, i.e., the eastern part of his empire whose response to Seleucid rule was often lukewarm. In late 166 or early 165 BCE Antiochus put his chief minister Lysias in charge of the western part of the empire as vice-regent, made him guardian of his son (later to became Antiochus V) who was only seven or eight years of age, and took the greater part of his army across the Euphrates to the eastern provinces (Mittag 2006: 296–97; Mørkholm 1964: 166–67).

1 Maccabees 3.37-40 (cf. 2 Macc. 8.9) gives the impression that half the Seleucid army was now concentrated on defeating Judas. Far from it: the numbers of Seleucid soldiers, as usual, are greatly exaggerated. However, Judas's gang was causing problems at the local level and was brought to the administration's attention by Philip, the local governor in Jerusalem (cf. 2 Macc. 5.22), who realized he needed help to gain the initiative against the resistance (2 Macc. 8.8-9). By this time, Antiochus was well away in the east, and the response to Philip's appeal came from Ptolemy son of Dorymenes, the military commander (*stratēgos*) of Coele-Syria and Phoenicia. Nicanor son of Patroclus was in charge overall, though the general Gorgias was sent to assist him. Although its precise size is uncertain, the Seleucid force probably outnumbered the Jewish fighters. But the total number was not the crucial factor because of the tactics Judas was able to use.

Bar-Kochva (1989: 220, 238) argues that the writer was an eyewitness to – even a participant in – the battle; however, he argues that 1 Macc. 3.57 and 4.3-4 are corrupt, with 4.3-4 reading, 'And Judas heard, and he and the valorous advanced to smite the king's army at Emmaus, as the army was scattered outside the camp <and they camped south of Emmaus>' (angles in the original). In any case, one can see an example of Judas's tactical skill in this case. He evidently had good intelligence (cf. 1 Macc. 4.3) and was aware that Gorgias planned to attack the Jewish camp near Mizpah (which was 23 km or about 14 miles from Emmaus). Judas took a mobile force by night to Emmaus and attacked the Seleucid camp at day break. The Seleucid soldiers left to defend their camp were evidently careless in assuming that Gorgias would destroy the Jewish camp and were taken by surprise by Judas's force. It was probably also the case that the Jewish unit was similar in size to the Seleucid opponents at this point. The Syrian soldiers were quickly defeated and fled. Judas had the camp set on fire, no doubt to intimidate the troops returning from Gorgias's thwarted raid. The returning Syrians were sufficiently demoralized that they too were quickly put to flight by Judas's men.

It is important to assess the military situation, since the narratives in 1 Macc. 4.1-24 and 2 Macc. 8.8-36 emphasize a miraculous victory through divine aid. Even though Judas had only about 6,000 men (2 Macc. 8.16, 22), his force was probably about the same strength as the Syrian unit – 1 Macc. 4.1-2 admits it was a separate unit of only about 5,000 men – which he first attacked. This resulted not only in an enormous boost to Jewish morale and reputation but also in the capture of considerable funds, weapons and other goods important to keep the resistance going. Included in this was a large sum of money left by slave dealers, who had accompanied the Seleucid army in hopes of great profits from selling captured Jews as slaves. Nicanor, however, managed to escape the battlefield and make his way to Antioch (2 Macc. 8.34-36). Thus, in one of those unusual happenings which history occasionally throws up, a spectacular victory was won contrary to normal expectations.

In a peculiar passage, 2 Macc. 8.30-36 goes on without a break to assert that Judas defeated Timothy and Bacchides, killing 20,000 and capturing high fortresses. They killed Timothy's commander (apparently Timothy was not present) and they captured much spoil, whose division included those who had been tortured, the widows and the orphans (just as related a few verses earlier in 2 Macc. 8.28). This repetition is strange and suggests an insertion of the passage 2 Macc. 8.30-33 into the narrative at a later stage. It then says the rest of the spoil was taken to Jerusalem. At this point, 'they burnt the ones who set on fire the sacred gates and Callisthenes' (2 Macc. 8.33). What exactly this incident was and why they carried out such a cruel reprisal at this time is not explained. It appears to provide a certain parallel with 1 Macc. 5.6-7 and especially 2 Macc. 12.2, 17-25 (Bar-Kochva 1989: 510–15). See further below, §15.4.4.

Stand-off and Truce with Lysias

B. Bar-Kochva (1989) *Judas Maccabaeus*, 275–90.

Sources: 1 Macc. 4.26-35; 2 Macc. 10.10–11.38; *Ant.* 12.7.5 §§313-15.

Judas's revolt now seems to have been perceived seriously enough to engage the attention of the Seleucid vice-regent Lysias, left in charge of

Antioch when Antiochus took his army to the east. However, 1 Maccabees (followed by Josephus in *Antiquities*) is only interested in recording a victory by Judas and then immediately pushing on to the retaking of the temple. As in the previous section, 1 Maccabees is dominated by pious considerations, but whereas in the earlier section the comments relating to religion expanded a small description of military activity, here the battle and its circumstances are described only briefly. In fact, the situation as given more fully in 2 Maccabees was rather different from the one presented to us by 1 Maccabees (and the *Antiquities* parallel).

Although the story is given more detail in 2 Maccabees, it seems to misplace certain events, especially putting the cleansing of the temple before Judas's battle with Lysias. The battle with Lysias was probably the prelude to the retaking of the temple, as 1 Maccabees (followed by *Antiquities*) makes it. According to 1 Macc. 4.28 it was 'the next year' (ἐν τῷ ἐρχομένῳ ἐνιαυτῷ: probably the summer of 165 BCE) that Lysias himself led an invasion force, this time coming from the south up through Idumaea to Beth-Zur (1 Macc. 4.28-35; 2 Macc. 11.1-21). The number given for the Syrian force is the usual exaggeration, but interestingly the Jews are credited with 10,000 men. Although 1 and 2 Maccabees make this another Jewish victory, this seems doubtful (Bar-Kochva 1989: 134–35, 275–90). Lysias had superior numbers, and a major defeat as described would have led to a panic-stricken rout, yet Lysias is described as conducting an orderly retreat. But if he was not defeated, why did he withdraw to Antioch? Both 1 and 2 Maccabees ascribe it simply to divine favour and Jewish bravery. The actual reason is probably more prosaic and realistic, as the next section (§15.4.2) discusses.

15.4.2. *Concessions by the Seleucids to the Jews*

At this point we find a series of four letters in 2 Maccabees that seem to give us important information about diplomatic moves on the part of both the Jews and the Seleucids at this time. The events here in 2 Maccabees are probably out of order at this point, including the arrangement of the letters. But the important thing is that these seem to be original documents that give us valuable information about events around this time. The order and dating of the letters is discussed above (§3.2.4). As suggested there, the earliest letter is probably that of Antiochus IV to the Jews, which reads as follows (Letter #3: 2 Macc. 11.27-33):

> [27]The letter of the king to the nation was as follows:
>
> 'King Antiochus to the council of elders of the Jews and to the other Jews, greetings. [28]If you are well, this is as it ought to be, which is what we wish;

15. *The Maccabaean Revolt to the Death of Judas (170–161 BCE)* 367

we are also in health. ²⁹Menelaus has informed us that you want to return home to take care of your own affairs. ³⁰To those returning by the 30th of Xanthikos [February–March] the right hand is given without fear, ³¹allowing the Jews to use their own foods and laws just as formerly, and to let no one bother them in any manner concerning things done in ignorance. ³²I have also sent Menelaus to comfort you. ³³Be in health. *Year 148 [of the Seleucid era], 15th Xanthikos.*

The main problem is the date (in italics in 2 Macc. 11.33). The date in the middle of the document (2 Macc. 11.30) gives a deadline for taking advantage of an offer of amnesty, yet the date of the letter is only a couple of weeks before this deadline. The situation makes no sense: there would have been no time to post the letter's contents publicly before the deadline had passed, much less give people time to respond. There would not have been time for a letter dated to Xanthikos 15 to come from the eastern provinces, be distributed to the Jews and have them return home all in two weeks. Not even a letter sent from Antioch on Xanthikos 15 would benefit those Jews who wanted to return home by the 30th. It is almost universally agreed that the date of the letter in 2 Macc. 11.33 is the result of an editor's or copyist's error. The date in 2 Macc. 11.30 is more likely to be correct, since colophons are more likely to get changed or substituted than an essential part of the internal text. This would make the deadline for the amnesty about March 164 BCE, with the letter itself having been written some months before, perhaps the autumn of 165 BCE (cf. Bernhardt 2017: 546, 554). The date of this letter may have been copied accidentally from the Roman letter that follows it in the text of 2 Maccabees.

There are several interesting points in this letter. First, it was instigated by Menelaus who had evidently travelled to the east to consult Antiochus who was on campaign. However, it is possible that the letter was even issued before Antiochus embarked on his campaign to the Upper Satrapies (Doran 2012: 229). In any case, Menelaus had argued that it would be in the king's best interests to cancel the repressive measures that had elicited a general rebellion in Judah. Whatever his faults, Menelaus had come to realize that the cultic and other measures taken by the Seleucids in Judah were a mistake – perhaps he even empathized with the sufferings of the many Jews who saw him as their opponent.

Another point of interest is that it seems to withdraw the primary causes for Jewish agitation (although the wording of the decree is perhaps not as generous as the later one by Antiochus V below). Furthermore, the letter was evidently not addressed to Judas and his group, or at least not primarily to them, but to the governing *gerousia* of Jerusalem and to 'other' Jews. What seems to be the case, though, is that Judas and his followers ignored this amnesty. This is strongly suggested by the fact that through this period Judas conducted raids and brought on attacks by the local commanders, Apollonius and Seron (§15.4.1).

However, we have another letter (#1), this time from the vice-regent Lysias. Again, the date is a problem, but it appears to be a response to a Jewish delegation – evidently not from Judas but other Jews. Whether it was before or after the stand-off at Beth-Zur (§15.4.1) is unclear. But it fits with Lysias's evident desire for negotiations with Judas (though it should be noted that he does not address Judas specifically). Apparently the original letter had the initial request attached, though this has unfortunately not been preserved in 2 Maccabees (Letter #1: 2 Macc. 11.17-21):

> [17]'Lysias to the Jewish community, greetings. John and Absalom, who were sent from you, furnished me with the administrative document copied below [but now lost] and made a request concerning its contents. [18]Whatever then it was necessary to present orally to the king, I stated plainly; and whatever was feasible, he has granted. [19]If then you will preserve good will toward the government, in the future I shall attempt to be responsible jointly for good things. [20]But concerning the details I commend them for discussion with you by your representatives and mine. [21]Farewell. *Year 148 of the Seleucid era, month Dios Korinthos 24th.*'

This letter seems to show that Lysias withdrew at this time because of attempts at negotiations. Also, we must not forget that Menelaus was still high priest, and the letter of Antiochus IV above indicates that he still had a conscience and was concerned about the welfare of his people. Antiochus apparently supported representatives from some of the Jews (Judas and his associates or some other faction?) when they approached Lysias to ask for terms (or perhaps independently made recommendations). Why would the Jews have asked for a truce if Lysias had been trounced in battle as 1 and 2 Maccabees claim? This provides good grounds for judging that the battle between Lysias and Judas was at least a standoff and more likely a defeat for the Jews.

Again, there is a problem with the date, since no month Dios Korionthos is known for the Seleucid or Macedonian calendar. There are several possibilities (discussed in §3.2.4), but the most likely situation is that Lysias's letter was written about the same time as the Roman letter and as the expiration of the original amnesty granted by Antiochus IV (cf. Bernhardt 2017: 550–54). Lysias's letter may have been copied to a Roman delegation in the region or perhaps they got to hear of it another way. For a Roman delegation in the region sent the following letter (Letter #4: 2 Macc. 11.34-38):

15. *The Maccabaean Revolt to the Death of Judas (170–161 BCE)* 369

³⁴Also the Romans sent a letter to them having (the contents) thus:

> 'Quintus Memmius, Titus Manius, ambassadors of the Romans, to the people of the Jews, greetings. ³⁵Lysias the relative of the king has conceded rights to you, and we consent. ³⁶But whatever he determined to bring to the attention of the king, you give it thought and then send someone immediately concerning your views, in order that we might make suggestions to you, as is appropriate. For we are approaching Antioch. ³⁷Therefore, hurry and send someone, that we might also know of your decision. ³⁸Be in health. Seleucid year 148, Xanthikos 15.'

The Roman letter was evidently a response to Lysias's (and perhaps also Antiochus's) concessions, which means that they must have heard or received his letter (whether officially or unofficially) in time to write their own by Xanthikos 15. Roman involvement is interesting, showing that they were still closely monitoring Antiochus's activities. (They probably received his letter officially, since Antiochus would have wanted to keep the Romans satisfied that he was maintaining his side of the bargain.)

Finally, we have a letter that is clearly from Antiochus V (because he refers to the death of his father) that would have come about the spring or summer of 163 BCE, after the death of Antiochus IV (Letter #2: 2 Macc. 11.23-26):

> ²³King Antiochus to his brother Lysias, greetings. After our father joined the gods, the ones who desired to be calm went to the king about their own business, ²⁴We heard, however, that the Jews had not consented to the conversion to Hellenistic ways by our father, but chose their own way of life and pleaded to be permitted to have their own law. ²⁵Since this nation has chosen to be free from disquiet, we have decided to restore to them their temple and to let them conduct their life according to the customs of their forefathers. ²⁶It is well, then, that you send a message and give your right hand, so that seeing our policy, they might be reassured and live cheerfully, achieving their own goals.

This letter is a culmination of a series of proclamations and negotiations. What they show in their totality is that the situation had reverted to the *status quo ante* with regard to the temple and the practice of Judaism (although the earlier letter of Antiochus IV seems to have already conceded this). Of course, the 'restoration' of the Jerusalem temple to the Jews (in Antiochus V's letter) was in some sense a matter of indifference, since the Jews had already retaken it and reinstated the cult there. But now what they were doing was official and could not be interfered with by the garrison in the Akra (as the next section [§15.4.3] will show). These documents create some problems about order and precise references, but they confirm and expand the narratives found in 1 and 2 Maccabees and elsewhere and qualify as original sources for this period.

15.4.3. *Temple Retaken and Returned to Service*

Sources: 1 Macc. 4.36-59; 2 Macc. 10.1-9; *Ant.* 12.7.6-7 §§316-25.

We now come to the climax of Hasmonaean revolt: the retaking and restoration of the temple. There are many questions, especially about the chronology but also about the aims and intent of the revolt: was it to restore religious rites and rights or was it to gain independence from Seleucid rule? This section will focus on the first question, but the second will be addressed later on in the chapter (§§15.4.6; 15.4.7).

Because of Lysias's withdrawal and the general military situation, Judas felt sufficiently encouraged to march on Jerusalem and retake the temple area. There was apparently no resistance, but Judas appointed a guard to keep the Syrians holed up in the Akra while the temple was cleansed and rededicated. Although Judas and his brothers were members of a priestly family, the cleansing of the temple was delegated to other priests who evidently maintained a certain independence *vis-à-vis* him (1 Macc. 4.42-58; cf. Sievers 1990: 47–48).

The description of the temple site in 1 Macc. 4.38 ('weeds growing up in the courts as in a forest') indicates no activity had been going on there for some time. This raises a question about the original desecration of the temple. If the Seleucid military garrison in the Akra had instituted their own (pagan) worship in the temple, there is no reason why they should have then abandoned it. The description in 1 Maccabees makes it appear as if the desecration was a deliberate attempt to pollute the temple as punishment for the Jewish revolt, not to introduce another continuing Greek or local cult.

According to 1 Macc. 4.52-59 and 2 Macc. 10.5 this rededication was accomplished on 25 Kislev. 1 Maccabees states this was precisely three years after it was first polluted, though 2 Macc. 10.3 gives the figure of 'two years' (μετὰ διετῆ χρόνον). One suspects that since they were near the third anniversary of the pollution, Judas specifically planned the rededication to fall on that exact day of the month. Or they simply put it about that it was rededicated exactly three years after the Abomination of Desolation was set up, regardless of the exact real date. On the other hand, there would have been too many witnesses to displace it very much. It was a memorable event of Jewish history, still commemorated in Judaism today by Hanukkah or the Festival of Lights. 2 Maccabees

10.6-8 indicates that an eight-day festival was instituted at that time, to be celebrated each year. The letter of 2 Maccabees 1, perhaps to be dated to about 125 BCE, also refers to celebration of Hanukkah (2 Macc. 1.9); however, neither passage uses the name Hanukkah, which seems to be a later coining.

The date given (1 Macc. 4.52) is year 148 SE. By the reckoning argued for in Chapter 1 (§1.3.3), this would be November–December 165 BCE. As already noted, the suggested date for the pollution of the temple in November–December 168 BCE was not popular for many years, but a number of specialists have now accepted this date (Bringmann 1983: 15–28; Bernhardt 2017: 222, 540). A further indication is that this cleansing of the temple took place *before* the death of Antiochus. This is the order of events in 1 Maccabees, whose order of events is usually preferred (§3.1). Bringmann also accepts 165 for the cleansing of the temple, but Bernhardt (2017: 555–61) argues for mid-summer 164. He apparently bases this primarily on the figures of 3 1/2 years for the cessation of the daily sacrifice found in Daniel (Dan. 7.25; 12.7). The 3 1/2 years look like a stereotyped number, half of the important symbolic number of seven, well known in an apocalyptic context (cf. also Schwartz 2008: 373 n. 1). Granted, one could argue that three can also be a stereotyped number in some contexts, but this seems less likely here than 3 1/2. The 'two years' of 2 Macc. 10.3 would be a further reason for not extending the time to more than three years; although incorrect it is easy to see this as a mistaken counting of three (or perhaps even another example of inclusive reckoning) but not of half of seven.

15.4.4. *Final Military Activities of Judas*

Just as there were perhaps four important initial military campaigns of Judas against the Seleucids, before the retaking of the temple, so there were four further battles after the retaking of the temple and the death of Antiochus IV.

Events from the First Siege of Lysias to his Second

> **B. Bar-Kochva** (1976a) *The Seleucid Army: Organization and Tactics in the Great Campaigns*, 174–83; **idem** (1989) *Judas Maccabaeus*, 291–346; **D. Gera and W. Horowitz** (1997) 'Antiochus IV in Life and Death: Evidence from the Babylonian Astronomical Diaries', *JAOS* 117: 240–52.

> Sources: 1 Macc. 4.60–6.63; 2 Macc. 9.1-29; 10.10–12.45; *Ant.* 12.7.5 §§313-15; 12.8.1–9.7 §§327-88.

For the next year Judas seems to have been able to operate free from bother by the Syrians; instead he turned his attention to the local neighbours in Idumaea, Galilee and Transjordan. There are some textual considerations here, which different commentators have handled differently. 1 Maccabees 5 appears to be parallel to both 2 Macc. 10.14-38 and 2 Macc. 12.10-45. The question is how to explain this. R. Doran is somewhat non-committal but thinks the author of 2 Maccabees at least sees two different individuals named Timothy: the Timothy of 2 Macc. 8.32-33 and 10.24-38 being different from the Timothy of 2 Maccabees 12 (2012: 10–11, 179). J. R. Schwartz (2008: 27–31, 417–20) explains it as duplicate passages (as well as displacement of text needing rearrangement). He argues that 2 Macc. 12.10-45 depends on Jason of Cyrene, while 2 Macc. 10.14-38 depends on a secondary source. Although the present study does not generally follow Schwartz's rearrangement of 1 Maccabees material, his argument for duplicate passages is convincing: thus, there is only one Timothy.

Part of the campaign during these months was rescue operations to help Jews being attacked in areas outside Judaea itself. Many Jews were brought back as refuges from Galilee, the Golan and Transjordan. As usual the blame for starting the troubles is put on 'the Gentiles', though at least in some cases Judas's group seems to have taken the initiative. In any event, there seems to have been no official state persecution of Jews (Sievers 1990: 57). This includes a rescue mission north into the Galilee by Simon, pursuit of Timothy into the Transjordanian area by Judas and Jonathan, a rescue mission into the Golan by Judas and Jonathan, an abortive attack by the Jewish commanders Joseph son of Zecharias and Azariah against Gorgias, and a campaign by Judas and his brothers against Idumaea (though Gorgias is said to have escaped).

We also have the curious letter, allegedly from Antiochus IV on his deathbed, in 2 Macc. 9.9-27. There are some problems with it, as pointed out elsewhere (§3.2.4); therefore, it may not be authentic. Yet the wording of the contents differs from the surrounding narrative (for example, it is not a 'letter of entreaty' as the writer of 2 Maccabees introduces it), suggesting a king who recognizes his mortality but is not repenting of his past actions against the Jews. If authentic in the main, it is an interesting letter:

> [19]To the worthy Jewish citizens: many greetings and health and prosperity, from the king and governor Antiochus. [[20]If you are in good health, and your children and affairs are prospering for you, I give thanks to God with great joy, having hope in heaven: [21]and I became ill, remembering affectionately your honour and good will.] [22]After returning from the region of Persia

and falling ill, which created a grievous situation, I regard it as necessary to think of the common safety of all people. ²³Although not abandoning my situation as hopeless but rather having much hope to recover from the illness, I also considered that my father (on the occasions that he fought in the upper regions) appointed a successor regent. ²⁴That was if anything should happen contrary to expectation or even there was unwelcome news difficult to bear, those in the countryside would see the one left behind to look after the administration and would not be deprived of peace of mind. ²⁵Moreover, observing the neighbouring dynasties and those adjacent to the kingdom, who wait for the propitious moment and look forward with anticipation to what might happen, I appoint my son Antiochus king. When hastening into the upper satrapies many times, I entrusted and commended him to most of you. I have written to him these orders. ²⁶I call on you, then, and request each – remembering the benefits public and private – to be faithful toward me and my son. ²⁷For I firmly believe he will follow closely behind me with kindness and philanthropy with the intention to accommodate himself to you.

One phrase that some have latched onto to show inauthenticity is the expression of thanks 'to God with great joy, having hope in heaven' (9.20); however, as the brackets around the sentence indicate, the editor of the text (Hahnhart 1976) thinks that this sentence is perhaps a later insertion. The letter looks like a responsible monarch making provision for the succession in case of his death, and writing to one of his subject peoples. Of course, if such a message had been dictated by the king, multiple copies of it would have been written, each addressed to a different people within his empire. Thus, the idea of Antiochus sending such a message is not unlikely in itself, and also defies the pious fraud of 2 Maccabees that he ascribed his illness to his persecution of the Jews.

The placing of Antiochus's last days and death in the narrative of 1 Maccabees is important (1 Macc. 6.1-16). Most important, it follows the cleansing of the temple, for some of the news he receives is that 'they had removed the abomination that he had built upon the altar in Jerusalem' (1 Macc. 6.7). He heard this news while very much alive. Since we know from a cuneiform text that Antiochus died in November–December 164 BCE, this puts the dating of the cleansing of the sanctuary earlier than this. Bar-Kochva (1989: 277–78), who usually accepts the 1 Maccabees version, attempts to argue the event is misplaced in this case, but the only reason is that the temple must have been renewed in 164 BCE – a good case of circular reasoning! The placing of Antiochus's death fits well the dating of the renewal of the Jerusalem temple cult to about December 165 BCE.

As indicated by 1 Macc. 6.18-27, Judas was also busy in Jerusalem itself. He had not only retaken the temple area but was now besieging the Seleucid garrison in the Akra; he had to be dealt with. Thus, shortly after Antiochus IV's death, Lysias found it necessary to embark on a second expedition (summer 163). According to 2 Macc. 13.1-26, the king Antiochus V led the attack, but that seems unlikely because he was still only about ten years old; we know Lysias was present, and he was probably the one leading the Seleucid army. Nevertheless, minor kings might accompany an army to gain experience, even though command lay with a senior experienced officer (Bar-Kochva 1989: 304). The course of the march was once again from the south through Idumaea to Beth-Zur, which Lysias besieged. Judas left off the siege of the Akra to come to meet the Syrians and was defeated in a battle near Beth-Zechariah (2 Macc. 13.19-23 makes it victory for Judas!). Lysias then took Beth-Zur, with the defenders agreeing to surrender the fortress for a promise of safe conduct.

Precisely what Judas did at this point is uncertain. According to 1 Maccabees (followed by *Antiquities*) Judas took refuge in the temple where he was besieged by Lysias (1 Macc. 6.48-54; cf. 2 Macc. 13.22-24); however, Josephus says that he fled to Gophna which probably means the area of Modein, his original country of refuge (*War* 1.1.5 §45). Most likely while some of his men were defending the attack on the temple, Judas himself slipped off to his old base in the hills (Bar-Kochva 1989: 337–38; cf. 2 Macc. 13.14). An important point made by 1 Macc. 6.48-54 is that this was a sabbatical year, which made it even more difficult for the Jewish defenders because of a lack of food.

Lysias did not press his siege of the temple but came to terms with the defenders so that he could return to the capital. Evidently, the reason Lysias had to return to Antioch was that Philip, Antiochus's vice-regent, had returned from the east with Antiochus IV's body but was now set on taking over rulership of the kingdom (1 Macc. 6.55-63; 2 Macc. 13.23-24). We know after the king died in November–December 164 BCE that Philip had set out to bring his body back to Antioch. The Babylonian Astronomical Diaries suggest that he had reached Babylon with Antiochus's body by 16 January 163 BCE (Gera and Horowitz 1997: 250). There was still a long way to go to get to Antioch, but he was probably there by the spring or early summer of 163, perhaps after Lysias and Antiochus V had already departed for Judah. In any case, once they were absent Philip was ready to make his move. In the end, he was not successful. Lysias and the king returned and quickly defeated and killed Philip.

Lysias's basic concession was to confirm the freedom of the Jews to practice their traditional religion. Although this had already been done earlier, it was important to provide further guarantees. Also, they had it in writing from the Seleucids that the temple was lawfully in their hands and not just being occupied by them against Seleucid will. The letter from Antiochus V makes this clear (Letter #2: 2 Macc. 11.22-26, quote above §15.4.2). At this time, probably on his way back from Judaea, Lysias had Menelaus executed. The exact reason is not made clear, but it was likely due to the realization that no peace with the Jews would be possible as long as Menelaus continued to hold the office of high priest (*Ant.* 12.9.7 §§383-85). After the execution, Alcimus was appointed to take Menelaus's place (cf. 1 Macc. 7.5; 2 Macc. 14.3-13).

We are now in a position to summarize the course of events but making use of the additional information from original Seleucid documents, the letters of 2 Maccabees 11. These are very important for a reconstruction of what happened, but the dating of them is a problem (cf. §3.2.4). The order of events seems to be that:

- Lysias defeated Judas in battle, and a Jewish delegation – probably from another group, but possibly including some of Judas's own men – went to Lysias to bargain for terms.
- About the same time, Menelaus realized the situation (on his own, or perhaps in support of the other Jewish delegation) and went to Antiochus IV, asking for an end to the religious measures.
- Antiochus conceded, on grounds that hostilities by the Jews also cease (Letter #3, Antiochus IV to the Jews: 2 Macc. 11.27-33).
- As a result Lysias broke off his first engagement so that the Jews would have time to cease from hostilities and accept the new grant of religious freedom (Letter #1: 2 Macc. 11.16-21). The Romans, being apprised of this, also indicated their own opinion by a letter to the Jews (Letter #4: 2 Macc. 11.34-38).
- Judas did not actually cease hostilities but marched on Jerusalem and proceeded to retake and purify the temple (late 165 BCE).
- Antiochus IV died (late 164 BCE).

For over a year (autumn 165 to spring 163) the Syrians left Judaea alone. Yet Judas's group had refused to cooperate, not only retaking the temple area but also besieging the Seleucid garrison in the Akra. Since the hostilities had not come to an end, Lysias found it necessary to invade once more (spring 163) and inflict a decisive defeat on Judas. But events in Antioch prevented his following up that victory, and he negotiated with those besieged in the temple. Finally, once Antiochus V was securely on the throne (but under Lysias's guardianship), he wrote confirming the concessions, including their control of the temple (Letter #2, Antiochus V to Lysias: 11.22-26).

Skirmishes with Nicanor

> **B. Bar-Kochva** (1976a) *The Seleucid Army: Organization and Tactics in the Great Campaigns*; **idem** (1989) *Judas Maccabaeus*, 347–58;
>
> Sources: 1 Macc. 7.26-32; 2 Macc. 14.15-25.

This Nicanor (whether the same as the one at 2 Macc. 12.2 or not) had been commander of the Seleucid elephant corps; he was now made governor (*stratēgos*) of Judaea (2 Macc. 14.12). At this point, 1 Macc. 7.27-32 and 2 Macc. 14.15-25 give somewhat different stories. 2 Maccabees claims that Nicanor's and Judas's armies clashed at Dessau, with Simon getting into trouble, but Nicanor broke off the fight and attempted to negotiate. 1 Maccabees has Nicanor approaching Judas peaceably and offering to negotiate, while actually trying to carry out a plan to kidnap Judas. 2 Maccabees 14.15-25 is more generous toward Nicanor, who is initially said to have followed a policy of attempting to come to terms with Judas rather than meet him in battle (though there may have been some skirmishes between the two sides as well). It is alleged that this policy was pursued with such patience that Judas even went so far as to marry and settle down for a period of time at Nicanor's recommendation (2 Macc. 14.25). Bar-Kochva (1989: 354–56) claims this is only a literary invention, but it seems strange that the author of 2 Maccabees would have invented such a scenario. There are at least suggestions that a truce was in place for some time, despite the attempt of 1 Macc. 7.29-30 to play it down. Nicanor lived in Jerusalem for a time, as would befit the governor of the province. It is clear, in any case, that whatever truce was in place broke down and hostilities resumed. They fought at Kafar Salama, which seems to have been near to Gibeon (Bar-Kochva 1989: 356–58). Nicanor's forces were defeated and fled to Jerusalem, about 8 km or 5 miles away.

Battle of Adasa; Nicanor Day Proclaimed

> **B. Bar-Kochva** (1989) *Judas Maccabaeus*, 359–75.
>
> Sources: 1 Macc. 7.39-50; 2 Macc. 14.26–15.36.

In Jerusalem Nicanor is alleged to have pronounced an oath against the temple if Judas was not handed over to him (1 Macc. 7.33-38; 2 Macc. 14.31-36). The fiercely negative response of the priests is interesting because Alcimus was in charge of the temple and supposedly on Nicanor's side (1 Macc. 7.36-38; 2 Macc. 14.34-36). Nicanor apparently also sent for reinforcements, since further troops came to meet him near Beth Horon (1 Macc. 7.39). Judas was encamped not far away in Adasa (ca. 6 km or 3 or 4 miles from Beth Horon). They joined battle on 13 Adar 161 BCE. The description of the battle suggests that Judas actually had numerical superiority (Bar-Kochva 1989: 360), and Nicanor was defeated and killed. According to 2 Macc. 15.30-35 Judas had his head (and also the arm that he supposedly stretched out in a threat against the temple) displayed in Jerusalem as a grisly token of victory. Although this might have been contrary to the *halakha* (Bar-Kochva 1989: 371–72), the account should not be rejected on these grounds: we do not know necessarily how the Maccabees viewed the matter, especially in time of war. Judas declared 13 Adar a public holiday known as Nicanor's Day. This is a day before Purim and did not become a traditional Jewish holiday, perhaps becoming assimilated to Purim.

Bacchides's Second Expedition and Battle of Elasa

B. Bar-Kochva (1976a) *The Seleucid Army*, 184–200; **idem** (1989) *Judas Maccabaeus*, 376–402.

Sources: 1 Macc. 9.1-22.

In the wake of Nicanor's defeat Demetrius I (on his appearance, see §15.4.6 below) sent Bacchides (along with the high priest Alcimus) for the second time to invade Judaea and fight against Judas's army. Since Nicanor had fallen in Adar (the last month of the year), probably in 161 BCE, the new army must have marched into Judaea almost immediately. The time of the battle is said to the first month of year 152 SE. This seems to be a Jewish date (§1.3.3) and thus counted from spring 312, to give Nisan 161. The intervening time would have been short, even if there had been an intercalary Adar (i.e., two months of Adar, which happened every two or three years, to bring the lunar calendar in line with the solar). If Bar-Kochva (1989: 377) is correct, the battle account in 1 Maccabees is very accurate (2 Maccabees had come to an end before this battle, so that his hero was still alive). The two armies met at Elasa, perhaps about 15 km (10 miles) north of Jerusalem. Judas was killed in this encounter. His death marks the beginning of a hiatus of several years when we hear little or nothing further about his followers. The Maccabees were still a long way from gaining control of Judaea and even further from independence from Syrian rule.

15.4.5. *The Embassy to Rome*

> **V. Babota** (2014) *The Institution of the Hasmonean High Priesthood*, 106–9; **E. J. Bickerman** [Bikermann] (1930) 'Makkabäerbucher', *PW* 14:779–800; **T. Fischer** (1974) 'Zu den Beziehungen zwischen Rom and den Juden im 2. Jahrhundert v. Chr.', *ZAW* 86: 90–93; **C. Seeman** (2013) *Rome and Judea in Transition*, 113–36; **D. Timpe** (1974) 'Der römische Vertrag mit den Juden von 161 v. Chr.', *Chiron* 4: 133–52; **W. Wirgin** (1969) 'Judah Maccabee's Embassy to Rome and the Jewish-Roman Treaty', *PEQ* 101: 15–20; **L. Zollschan** (2008) '*Justinus* 36.3.9 and Roman-Judaean Diplomatic Relations in 161 BCE', *Athenaeum* 96: 153–71; **idem** (2012) 'A Bronze Tablet from the Church of San Basilio in Rome', *Classica et Mediaevalia* 63: 217–45; **idem** (2016) *Rome and Judaea: International Law Relations, 162–100 BCE*.

According to 1 Macc. 8.1-32 Judas sent ambassadors to Rome, including Eupolemus son of John and Jason son of Eleazar. The embassy that Judas sent evidently had two aims (1 Macc. 8.17-18): to establish a treaty of friendship and alliance (φιλίαν καὶ συμμαχίαν) and to remove the yoke that the Seleucids had put on them (τοῦ ἆραι τὸν ζυγὸν ἀπ' αὐτῶν). Yet the ironic situation was that they gave the impression of having become free and independent of the Seleucids (Seeman 2013: 122–27). It was not true, of course, and 1 Maccabees does not mention any such thing at this point. Yet Justin (36.3.9) states that the Jews were 'the first of all eastern peoples to receive freedom' (*primi omnium ex orientalibus libertatem acceperunt*) so that the Romans were happy to make an alliance with them (cf. also Diodorus 40.2).

Did Judas expect Rome to provide military support to his revolt? Why would Rome have responded positively to the embassy? 1 Maccabees 7.50–8.1 places the embassy directly after the defeat of Nicanor, when 'the land of Judah had rest for a few days'. This recent Jewish victory over Nicanor could be taken as evidence of their freedom. It is doubtful that the Romans would have made an alliance with a people ostensibly still a part of the Seleucid empire. But the time between that battle and Judas's death was probably only a short time. If so, the embassy could not have relied on that victory alone to clinch an alliance; in any case, such a mission took years, not days. Since the mission apparently reported back to Judas before his death, it must have been dispatched long before the victory over

Nicanor; it seems doubtful that the author of 1 Maccabees had a clear idea of when the embassy was sent to Rome. But the relations between Rome and the Seleucids was a bit tense at this time, since Demetrius had left Rome without Senate approval and then taken the Seleucid throne (below §15.4.6). Thus, from both the Maccabaean and the Roman perspective, this was probably a good time to be sending an embassy to Rome.

Although the historicity of this mission and treaty has often been doubted, the present consensus is in favour of its authenticity (Bernhardt 2017: 364–69; Seeman 2013: 114–27). The question of authenticity partly arises out of a widespread modern distinction often made between the *foedus aequum* (a treaty between equals) and a *foedus iniquum* (an unequal treaty). The trouble is that no such technical terms occur in the sources, and no such distinction appears to have been made by the ancient Romans (Gruen 1984: 14–15, 26–27, 40–46). From the 2nd century BCE, especially after Pydna in 168 BCE, the Romans often made treaties with small kingdoms. But the purpose of these treaties was symbolic, and it seems to be a mistake to start investigating these from a legalistic point of view. Thus, when L. T. Zollschan (2016) argues that the treaty between Judas and Rome in 161 BCE was not a *foedus* but a treaty of friendship (*amicitia*) and thus had different obligations and a different relationship between parties, she seems to have missed the point. This discussion must leave it to specialists in Roman law to argue the issue, but an attempt to understand matters from a legal point of view seems to be misplaced. The Romans did not intervene on behalf of the Jews because of the type of treaty but because inaction was their normal *modus operandi*. It seems that the many examples cited by Gruen demand this conclusion.

If Judas had expected military assistance, he was in for a heavy dose of reality: the Romans were not in the business of giving military support unless it directly affected their own needs. The Senate was happy to make treaties and even to make promises, but the conditions of the treaty recorded in 1 Macc. 8.23-30 show no promise of military muscle. Instead, the clauses of alliance (1 Macc. 8.26, 28) say that each will not aid the enemy of the other – nothing more. The Romans were not going to send troops to fight on Judas's side. They did allegedly write a letter to Demetrius I (1 Macc. 8.31-32), yet not long afterward they received Demetrius in a friendly fashion (Polybius 31.33.1-5; 32.2.1-3; 33.3.13). The letter to Demetrius itself (and there is some question as to whether the harsh phrasing in the present version was really in the original) does not refer to 'removing' a Seleucid yoke from the Jews but only to 'lightening' it.

This treaty would no doubt have been a useful boost to the morale of Judas's party and further assist the establishment of his rule over Judaea, but it seems to have provided little practical help for the Jews against the Syrians – the Romans were always happy to make such agreements, as long as there was no practical obligation on them to do anything. As Seeman notes, 'Judas' embassy did not materially affect Judea's relations with its Seleucid overlord' (2013: 125), and 'it is difficult to escape the conclusion that…Rome was simultaneously [tacitly] conceding their subject status vis-à-vis Demetrius' (2013: 119). E. Gruen (1984: 45–46) well summarizes the situation as follows:

> As so often, one must be wary of interpreting events as if Rome seized the initiative and actively implemented an eastern policy. In fact, the evidence, taken as a whole, reveals a remarkable passivity on the part of the senate… [After the death of Judas at Seleucid hands the] Romans played no role, indeed offered no protest… Nothing here suggests a patterned policy designed to weaken the Syrian kingdom… For the Maccabees some international recognition might be a valuable element in their struggle. To the senate, the alliance carried no concrete implications… An unmistakable pattern recurs: strong senatorial statements without a trace of implementation.

The main benefit of Judas's treaty with Rome was a propaganda victory over the domestic enemies. With the widespread acceptance of Alcimus's legitimacy, Judas had to do something to bolster his own reputation as an alternative leader. This treaty with Rome would go a long way toward doing that.

15.4.6. *The Death of Judas*

B. Bar-Kochva (1989) *Judas Maccabaeus*, 194–218; **S. Schwartz** (1991) 'Israel and the Nations Roundabout: 1 Maccabees and the Hasmonean Expansion', *JJS* 42: 16–38.

Sources: 1 Macc. 7–9; 2 Macc. 14–15; *Ant.* 12.10.1-11.2 §§389-434.

The military campaigns were described above for the sake of completeness. These ended in Judas's death. Now, however, we need to retrace our steps to pick up some of the other events in which Judas was involved before his death, beginning with the coming of Demetrius I as a rival claimant to the Seleucid throne.

About 162 BCE Demetrius the son of Seleucus IV escaped from Rome. He had been sent as a hostage to replace his uncle Antiochus IV in 176. Despite two personal appearances before the Senate he had not been allowed to return to Antioch. He now did so with the connivance of some of his Roman friends and made his claim for the Seleucid throne as Demetrius I. The Romans evidently tolerated his actions, though scholars remain divided on whether Rome eventually recognized him as king (see Ehling 2008: 140 for discussion and references). In late 162 or early 161, shortly after making a truce with Judas, Lysias and the young Antiochus V were defeated and executed by Demetrius. Alcimus went to Demetrius for confirmation of his high priestly office and, at the same time, asked for help against Judas's group (1 Macc. 7.5-7; 2 Macc. 14.3-13). The latter was still offering military opposition to Alcimus and the new Seleucid administration, despite the declaration of religious freedom (1 Macc. 10.37). Demetrius dispatched an army under his deputy Bacchides to install Alcimus in Jerusalem and to deal with the problem of Judas.

This incident well illustrates the complexity of views and divisions among the Jews at this time. 1 Maccabees 7.14 notes only that Alcimus was of the line of Aaron, suggesting that he was not of the traditional high priestly line (to which Onias and Jason had belonged); however, a more careful look gives some reason to think that Alcimus was actually an Oniad (cf. Sievers 1990: 63 n. 66). Regardless of whether or not this was so, the important issue is that many Jews were willing to accept him, including those who had opposed Menelaus. For example, the important (if enigmatic) group known as the Hasidim (§6.1) gave up their part in the Jewish resistance and made peace with the Seleucids (1 Macc. 7.12-14). Despite the impression given by the partisan account of 1 Maccabees, it is clear that for many Jews the issue was simply one of religious freedom. These people were not interested in the broader nationalistic goals of Judas and his followers, which is why they took the opportunity to make peace when they were guaranteed freedom of worship under an acceptable high priest. The leadership of the Maccabean resistance by no means embodied the aspirations of the nation as a whole. Of course, it is difficult to determine the size of the support for Judas since the sources try to give the impression that most of the Jews were united under him. From the number of soldiers in his army it seems likely that throughout most of the revolt, he had considerable backing (Bar-Kochva 1989: 47–63, but note the criticisms of Schwartz 1991: 16 n. 2). However, there are also a number of hints that this was not always the case. One of these is the action of the Hasidim; others will be noted in the appropriate places below.

The author of 1 Maccabees ignores the implications of the move by the Hasidim to make peace; instead he is quick to point out that they suffered for this: 60 of them were supposedly arrested and executed in one day by Bacchides (1 Macc. 7.12-18). Because of the clear bias of our source at this point, it is difficult to evaluate precisely what happened and why. If such happened as alleged, it would no doubt have driven them back into the arms of Judas. But for this exact reason it was hardly in Bacchides's self-interest to provoke a section of the population which was willing to accept his orders; furthermore, we do not have any indication that the Hasidim as a group returned to Judas's camp. However, the text of 1 Maccabees ascribes the deception and then the sudden slaughter of the Hasidim to Alcimus. It may be that he was settling old scores at this point, regardless of the potential consequences for Seleucid overtures to the Jews.

In any case, it appears that the Jews as a whole were willing to recognize Alcimus as high priest and accept Syrian domination in return for freedom of worship (1 Macc. 7.20-21). Note that even though Alcimus supposedly had trouble maintaining his high priesthood, 1 Macc. 7.21-22 admits that Alcimus 'gained mastery of the land' (κατεκράτησαν γῆν). Judas in turn reverted to his old practice of attacking fellow Jews who opposed or were a problem for him (1 Macc. 7.23-24), indicating that he had lost control of the Judaean population as a whole. Nevertheless, Judas continued his fight against all opponents, eventually making things so difficult that Alcimus once more had to appeal to Demetrius for help. This time Nicanor, the commander of the elephant corps, was made governor over Judaea (2 Macc. 14.12) and sent to deal with the situation. The interaction and final battle with Nicanor has already been described (§15.4.4 above).

2 Maccabees breaks off at this point, seeing the defeat of Nicanor as the climax to Judas's career (and no doubt to avoid the ignominy of having to deal with Judas's death). But this was hardly the end of the story, which did not finish so gloriously. To summarize the account above (§15.4.4), in the spring of 161 BCE, Bacchides invaded once more to avenge the humiliation of Nicanor's army. This time the battle went against the Jews; Judas was slain and his soldiers routed. Judas's body was buried in Modein (1 Macc. 9.19). There was, of course, no assistance from the Romans. The Maccabaeans' apparent desire to take on the Seleucid empire was ill conceived. By appropriate tactics, adequate resources and sheer good luck Judas and his band – now an army – had done well, but there had been no miracles. Judas's luck had now run out, and so had apparently the fortunes of the Maccabees. They would now be on the run for many years.

15.4.7. Achievements of Judas Maccabaeus

The successes achieved by Judas's force were extremely important for the course of Jewish history. There seems no doubt about the considerable tactical skill of its leaders and the fighting ability of the soldiers. The Maccabaean resistance also deservedly goes down in history for one or two exceptional victories; nevertheless, most of its success is fully explicable by normal military factors:

First, we must not forget that many of Judas's actions were against fellow Jews. These are usually alleged to be apostates, but this is doubtful in many cases. It is likely that they were simply fellow countrymen who chose not to follow the path of the Maccabees. Whether or not they actively collaborated with the Seleucid government is probably irrelevant, because they would probably be targeted regardless. It seems unlikely that most Jews actively collaborated unless forced to do so.

Secondly, the actual numbers of Seleucid troops is usually grossly exaggerated by the Jewish sources while the Jewish numbers are often far too low (Bar-Kochva 1989: 29–68; 1976a: 7–19). For example, the expedition led by Nicanor is said to have included 40,000 foot soldiers and 7,000 cavalry (1 Macc. 3.39), but even the lesser figure of 20,000 (2 Macc. 8.9) is too large. The number of soldiers employed on each side in even major military campaigns was only about 50,000. For example, at the important battle of Raphia in which he was confronting the entire Ptolemaic force (*HJJSTP 2*: 298–301), Antiochus III had 35,000 heavy infantry, 21,000 light and 6,000 cavalry (Polybius 5.79; Bar-Kochva 1989: 33; 1976a: 132). On the other hand, after retaking the temple, it appears that Judas could assemble a force of 20,000 at short notice (Bar-Kochva 1989: 49–51; 1976a: 185–87).

Thirdly, Judas's force was regarded only as a nuisance at the beginning (which is another reason why the initial forces sent against him would have been small). Despite the attempt by the Jewish sources to make the defeat of Jewish resistance the number-one priority of Antiochus, he in fact had much larger things on his mind and left the quashing of this minor irritation to subordinates. Indeed, as already noted, the initial campaigns were conducted locally, and the central government became involved only in response to a request for help from the governor of the Palestinian area (2 Macc. 8.8).

Fourthly, luck seems to have played an important part, as it has in many famous victories and defeats. No matter how carefully and brilliantly the strategy is planned, all military historians are aware of how much can go wrong in the actual battle. For example, it was more or less by chance that only a part of Nicanor's force at Emmaus first encountered Judah and thus was opposed by an enemy much more equal in strength than if the full Syrian army had been there (1 Macc. 4.1-15; 2 Macc. 8.16). The resulting defeat was sufficient to demoralize the rest of the Syrian forces and make possible a final Jewish victory against larger odds. Thus, while giving full credit to the Jews for their unusual successes, one should be careful not to regard them as unique in the annals of military history.

Finally, the Jewish sources sometimes ignore defeats or even make defeats appear as victories for the Jews. For example, although 2 Maccabees assures us that the Seleucid army was defeated in Lysias's second invasion (2 Macc. 13.22), the rest of the data shows that Judas had to go into hiding afterward. As the parallel account in 1 Macc. 6.47-54 frankly admits, it was a Jewish defeat (as Josephus also confirms: *War* 1.1.5 §§41-46; cf. *Ant.* 12.9.4-5 §§367-78).

As Bar-Kochva notes, Judas's contribution lay not in miraculous victories against overwhelming odds but in a much more practical sphere: developing a regular army:

> The greatness of Judas Maccabaeus, however, lies not in local military-tactical achievements, but mainly in the construction and development of a great and powerful army which could not be destroyed by isolated failures. Even the defeats suffered by the Jewish commanders brought the independence they aspired to closer: to the enemy, unable to leave a large garrison in the country, they underlined the vast potential in the Jewish army, and the need to compromise with it... [T]he efforts of Judas Maccabaeus to modify his operational methods to conform to the new circumstances after the purification of the Temple and organize his army accordingly, building an up-to-date large army, were much more demanding than the initial guerrilla war. (Bar-Kochva 1989: 407–9)

Judas's accomplishments were not only on the military side of endeavours. One of his main achievements was retaking the temple and putting it back into operation. Ultimately, this is what the revolt was about, and it was probably Judas's initial goal. But having accomplished that, he seems to have set his sights higher: to the independence of Judaea as a Jewish state once more. This was not the aim of most of his fellow countrymen, and his support seems to have fallen off drastically once peace and their religious rights were restored. This is probably why he died in his last battle – his fellow Judaeans did not see the need to continue risking their lives in needless (as they saw it) battles against the Seleucids. As the next chapter will show, this independence did come about, but it was because of circumstances beyond the fighting abilities and resources of the Jews of Judaea.

15.5. Conclusions

The previous chapter (Chapter 14) outlined the events leading up to the Sixth Syrian War and the Maccabaean revolt. This chapter began with the Sixth Syria War out of which sprang many of the events that took place subsequently in Judaea, including one of the most traumatic events in Jewish history, Antiochus's measures with regard to the temple and the practice of Judaism. In late 170 or early 169 BCE the Ptolemaic realm invaded Coele-Syria of which Judaea was a part. Antiochus IV was ready, however, and quickly pushed the Egyptian army back to Alexandria. He placed Ptolemy VI (his nephew) on the throne as his protectorate and returned to Syria in triumph, with much spoil. However, his arrangements quickly unravelled, and he marched into Egypt a second time in early 168 BCE. This time, however, he was met by a Roman delegation who ordered him to leave Egypt. This is often depicted (in ancient times as well as today) as a major humiliation for Antiochus, but some have recently argued that the Roman ultimatum actually got him out of a bind and was a relief. In any case, he returned with great spoils and also a Roman guarantee that Egypt would not try to take Coele-Syria again.

It was at this time that Antiochus thought Judaea had revolted against his rule. His conclusion has usually been portrayed as a misreading of the situation in Jerusalem, in which the former high priest Jason attempted to retake his office from the current incumbent Menelaus. But even though there is no source describing an actual widespread revolt (instead of a more minor civil dispute), some recent scholarship has argued for an actual serious revolt, not only in Judaea but possibly further afield. No king can allow a revolt to succeed but must regain authority as quickly as possible. Antiochus did this by taking Jerusalem, suppressing the fighting and establishing a Seleucid garrison in the Akra there. This was not all, however: he also caused the daily continual (*tamid*) offering to cease and polluted the temple with a foreign cult. The ancient sources also claim that he went so far as to attempt to suppress the practice of Judaism in Judaea. This claim has recently been dismissed as a literary and ideological construct. No doubt some of the stories about persecution and martyrdom (e.g., 2 Macc. 7) are literary inventions. Yet the pollution of the temple and the alien cult were real, and some reports of punishing Jews for practising circumcision or avoiding unclean meats seem to be credible, especially in the light of later letters from Antiochus IV and Antiochus V. The persecution may have been exaggerated, but religious suppression and even persecution seem to have been real.

After centuries of accepting submission peacefully, some Jews fought back. It might have been several different groups initially, but eventually they coalesced around the Maccabaean family. According to 1 Maccabees 2, the fight-back began with the father Mattathias, yet his alleged exploits are nowhere else referred to in 1 Maccabees, and he is not even mentioned in 2 Maccabees, which has made specialists doubt his supposed role. Both 1 Maccabees and especially 2 Maccabees give a prominent place to Judas Maccabaeus. He and his band of guerrilla fighters began by attacking other Jews whom they perceived as being unfaithful to their religion or of supporting the Seleucids. Their first encounters with Seleucid troops seem to have involved small numbers, led by local Syrian commanders without the necessary military skill or resources, and were beaten back. But with time Judas's actions began to be taken more seriously, and his band developed into a full-fledged Jewish army. In spite of biased Jewish sources, Judas was not always successful, but he finally prevailed sufficiently – sometimes surprisingly – to take back the temple, have it cleansed by the priests and the proper temple cult restored, and maintain it against Seleucid threats.

For almost a century the date of the temple's pollution and the establishment of the 'abomination of desolation' (Daniel's term for what was apparently a Greek cult) was given as 167 BCE, with its restoration in 164 BCE. But in line with some recent studies, the present volume argues for November–December 168 BCE, with the restoration three years later to the month in 165 BCE. This makes a number of conventional dates for some events in the Maccabaean revolt (not all) a year later than those argued for here.

For a number of reasons, the Seleucids not only sought to sort matters out by military means but also attempted to negotiate with Judas and other Jewish leaders. (Judas himself evidently sent an embassy to Rome and made a treaty of friendship with the Senate; however, it is doubtful that this affected matters in Judaea one way or the other.) With the temple once more in Jewish hands, Antiochus IV himself accepted advice that the Jews wanted to live by their own laws and allowed it. The high priest Menelaus was executed by the Seleucids, and a new high priest Alcimus appointed. It appears that most of the Jews were happy to accept the amnesty concession and the opportunity to return to their normal lives and temple worship as offered by the Seleucids. They also seemed content with the new high priest. But Judas and his following, having achieved the reinstatement of their traditional religion, appear to have had other goals, primarily a desire for the full independence of Judaea from Seleucid rule.

They continued to fight until Judah was killed (evidently in early 161 BCE), after which the Maccabees had only a handful of followers and were on the run from the Seleucid forces. But that was not the end of the story, as the next chapter shows.

Chapter 16

The Hasmonaean Kingdom:
From Jonathan to Alexandra Salome
(161 to 67 BCE)

V. **Babota** (2014) *The Institute of the Hasmonean High Priesthood*;
J. R. **Bartlett** (1973) *The First and Second Books of the Maccabees*; J. C.
Bernhardt (2017) *Die jüdische Revolution: Untersuchungen zu Ursachen, Verlauf und Folgen der hasmonäischen Erhebung*; K. **Ehling** (2008) *Untersuchungen zur Geschichte der späten Seleukiden*; J. **Goldstein** (1976) *1 Maccabees*; J. **Grainger** (2010) *The Syrian Wars*; G. **Hölbl** (2001) *A History of the Ptolemaic Empire*; W. **Huß** (2001) *Ägypten in hellenistischer Zeit: 332–30 v. Chr.*; C. **Seeman** (2013) *Rome and Judea in Transition*;
J. **Sievers** (1990) *The Hasmoneans and their Supporters: From Mattathias to the Death of John Hyrcanus I*.

In spite of the death of Judas Maccabee, the Maccabaean revolt had not really come to an end, at least as far as the Maccabaean brothers were concerned. Yet a major milestone had been passed: a significant juncture had already taken place with the cleansing of the temple and Antiochus IV's lifting of the sanctions on the practice of Judaism. But the death of Judas created a crossroads for the rebel movement: would Judah continue in revolt against the Seleucid empire or was its primary goal – the renewal of the temple cult – accomplished and a return to the *status quo ante* the logical conclusion? For the vast majority of the Jews, the latter seemed the logical choice. But not for the Maccabees: they would continue to fight and would eventually win the status of a (relatively) independent state for the greater part of a century. Yet this achievement did not take place in a vacuum; far from it. The Hasmonaean state struggled for and maintained its status against the backdrop of Seleucid decline and fall and the relentless advance of Rome eastward. The shifting fortunes of these three players are described in this chapter.

16.1. Jonathan Maccabee (161–143 BCE)

B. Bar-Kochva (1975) 'Hellenistic Warfare in Jonathan's Campaign near Azotos', *Scripta Classica Israelica* 2: 83–96; **E. J. Bickerman** (1938) *Institutions des Séleucides*; **H. Burgmann** (1980) 'Das umstrittene Intersacerdotium in Jerusalem 159-152 v. Chr.', *JSJ* 11: 135–76; **L. Capdetrey** (2007) *Le pouvoir séleucide: Territoire, administration, finances d'un royaume hellénistique (312–129 avant J.-C.)*; **J.-D. Gauger** (1977) *Beiträge zur jüdischen Apologetik: Untersuchungen zur Authentizität von Urkunden bei Flavius Josephus und im I. Makkabäerbuch*; **D. Gera** (1985) 'Tryphon's Sling Bullet from Dor', *IEJ* 35: 153–63; **J. Murphy-O'Connor** (1976) 'Demetrius I and the Teacher of Righteousness (I Macc., x, 25-45)', *RB* 83: 400–420; **M. O. Wise** (1989–90) 'The Teacher of Righteousness and the High Priest of the Intersacerdotium: Two Approaches', *RevQ* 14: 587–613.

Sources: 1 Macc. 9.23–12.53; *War.* 1.2.1 §§48-49;
Ant. 13.1.1–6.6 §§1-212

16.1.1. Jonathan Takes Over But Is on the Run

With the death of Judas Maccabee there is a good deal of uncertainty about the immediate events in the Maccabaean camp. This is partly because our sources are not very enlightening. According to 1 Macc. 9.23-31 the 'lawless' (ἄνομοι) appeared everywhere in Israel, and Bacchides put 'impious' (ἀσεβεῖς) men in charge, who harassed the followers of Judas and brought 'great tribulation' (θλῖψις μεγάλη). Nevertheless, the 'friends' (φίλοι) of Judas chose his brother Jonathan to succeed him. Taking account of the bias of the sources, the situation appears to be the following:

The Jews as a whole seem to have accepted the continuance of Seleucid rule now that they had an acceptable high priest in Alcimus and freedom to practise traditional Judaism. To what extent they continued to follow Judas is a question. Judas still had a (small) army and still engaged in fighting the Seleucids, but his support among the populace may have declined considerably. Once Judas was removed from the scene, the followers of the Maccabees seems to have been few, while the Seleucids were able to take back any administrative control they had lost and to place Jews loyal to themselves in positions of leadership. Also, there was evidently a severe famine (1 Macc. 9.24), which would have focused the people's attention on their own situation and the need for the able bodied to produce food rather than fighting the regime.

Jonathan's military force now appears to have been quite small, too small to tackle the Syrian army, and he and his band were very much on the run. For the Syrians were not content to let things stand as they were, and Bacchides pursued Jonathan. He probably recognized that this group would continue to be a thorn in the side unless destroyed once and for all. Jonathan's group fled into the wilderness near Tekoa (1 Macc. 9.33). A little later Jonathan is said to fortify Bethbassi (1 Macc. 9.62), which has been identified as Khirbet Beth-bassa about 5 km (3 miles) from Tekoa. That appears to have been their general area of refuge for the time being (though they did not always stay there; see below). Jonathan maintained a connection with the Nabataeans and attempted to send his brother John to deposit their baggage with them, but John was killed by a local family (called Jambri) near Medaba in Transjordan. Jonathan took revenge by ambushing a Jambri wedding party.

At this time Jonathan and his brother Simon reportedly took refuge in a marshy area near the Jordan, because Bacchides pursued them there (1 Macc. 9.34, 42-49), but Jonathan managed to escape (the alleged killing of 1,000 of Bacchides's men seems a gross exaggeration). Bacchides supposedly launched his attack on the sabbath, but the Maccabees had long before decided to defend themselves in such circumstances. Unsuccessful in taking Jonathan's group, Bacchides had to content himself with fortifying various sites with garrisons (Jericho, Emmaus, Beth Horon, Bethel, Timnath, Pharathon, Tephon, Beth-Zur, Gazara and the Jerusalem Akra) and taking hostages from the leading Jews and placing them in the Akra (1 Macc. 9.50-53).

It was apparently early in 160 BCE that the high priest Alcimus suddenly died. Because this happened during alterations to an inner wall of the temple, some Jews saw this as divine punishment (cf. 1 Macc. 9.54-56). However, there is no evidence of violation of the law, and the judgment probably only reflects different sectarian opinions about the arrangement of the temple courts (Goldstein 1976: 391–92). His death was the occasion for Bacchides to return to Antioch, which allowed a period of calm for Jonathan.

Then, allegedly at the instigation of 'lawless' (*anomoi*) Jews, the fight was renewed after two years (1 Macc. 9.57-73). These Jews loyal to the Seleucid regime attempted to capture Jonathan, but were unsuccessful: indeed, Jonathan turned the tables and assassinated a number of them. This was followed by an attack by Bacchides on Jonathan's stronghold at Bethbasi near Tekoa. Leaving Simon in charge, Jonathan slipped away into the countryside. Here the text is ambiguous, seeming to say that Jonathan 'attacked' (ἐπάταξεν) Odomera and his relatives, as well as the sons of Phasiron 'in their tents' (1 Macc. 9.66). But there are good reasons to emend the text to 'summon, command' (ἐπέταξεν), so that Jonathan was not attacking them but calling on them for help as allies in his fight with

Bacchides (cf. Goldstein 1976: 395). In spite of an intense siege, Simon's men managed to hold out until Jonathan returned with reinforcements, at which point they trapped Bacchides between the two Jewish forces and obliged him to withdraw. Bacchides was apparently angry at the Jews who had brought him in and executed some of them. On hearing of this Jonathan took the opportunity to negotiate with the Syrian general, which led to a truce and the release of hostages, and Bacchides left the land.

16.1.2. Gains Made by Jonathan

Jonathan's exploits were a significant development for the Maccabaean movement, for several reasons:

- Jonathan was no longer being harassed by Syrian troops. This opportunity for a period to rest and recuperate would have been greatly welcomed by Jonathan's followers who had been fighting for nearly a decade.
- The agreement with Bacchides no doubt included nominal submission to the Seleucid administration of Judah. Bacchides was unlikely to be so naive as to assume that Jonathan had accepted defeat, but a temporary peace left him free to return home and pursue other projects. The chances were that any further unrest in Judah would have to be dealt with by someone else.
- 1 Macc. 9.54 mentions the 2nd month of year 153 SE (spring 160 BCE), followed by a reference to 'two years' of peace for the land (1 Macc. 9.57) before Bacchides's invasion (1 Macc. 9.58). Since the next date given is 160 SE (1 Macc. 10.1, ca. 153–152 BCE), this indicates that the period of calm and recovery lasted for perhaps five years, which would have been a boon to Jonathan and his following. It would have allowed a major opportunity for Jonathan to consolidate his power and spread his influence
- Jonathan was not yet strong enough to set up his headquarters in Jerusalem, still dominated by the Seleucid Akra and its garrison, which is why he settled in Michmash. Part of his agreement with Bacchides may have been to stay out of Jerusalem (Babota 2014: 121).
- Yet there was now a hiatus in leadership of the province: no new high priest had been appointed, some hostages had been repatriated, while those Jews supporting the Seleucids had been to some extent discredited by Bacchides himself. This put Jonathan in a good position to begin trying to establish his dominance, as well as to get back at his Jewish opponents.

- Jonathan had been able to recruit sufficient supporters to defeat Bacchides in battle. This shows that although there is no indication that the bulk of the population wished to pursue the Maccabaean goals, especially those that involved continuing to fight the Seleucid army, there was evidently a great deal of good will toward the Hasmonaean family. After all, they had been the ones to lead the nation in the return to religious freedom. This would have been especially true in the rural areas away from Jerusalem and perhaps a few of the major towns. Many would have looked up to Jonathan as their natural leader, as long as they could get on with their lives. This suggests that he was viewed as the leader for many in Judah. This is likely the meaning of 1 Macc. 9.73 that he 'began to judge [κρίνειν] the people' during this period (though the biblical language should not be overlooked).

The question is whether there was an actual cessation of hostilities as the text seems to say ('and the sword rested from Israel' – 1 Macc. 9.73). It is important to notice that there is a gap of about five years or so until the next major event in the year 160 SE (= 153–152 BCE: 1 Macc. 10.1). During that time Jonathan 'did away with the impious from Israel' (1 Macc. 10.73), which suggests some violent actions on his part. It also emphasizes the extent of the internal opposition to the Maccabaean movement at this time. In any case, this is an intriguing gap that our extant sources have not filled. Bernhardt (2017: 378–82) suggests that a relative of Alcimus might have been appointed high priest during this period.

16.1.3. *Appointed High Priest by the Seleucids*

That no new high priest had been appointed in Alcimus's place is the impression left by our sources (though it is possible that a relative of his was appointed). It is true that Josephus states in *Antiquities* (12.10.6 §§414, 419; 12.11.2 §434) that Judas was high priest for three years, although elsewhere (*Ant.* 20.10.3 §237) he seems to accept that the office was vacant for seven years after the death of Alcimus. It has been proposed (e.g., by Murphy-O'Connor 1976) that there was indeed another high priest during this time, one deliberately excised from the records by the pro-Hasmonaean historians, who became the leader of the Qumran group called the Teacher of Righteousness after he was ousted from his office. While this is an ingenious proposal, it has little support from the preserved sources: neither the books of Maccabees nor Josephus suggest it, nor do the Qumran texts (though admittedly the Qumran documents are, as usual, couched in allusive language). There is no reason to assume that a hiatus in the high priesthood would not have been allowed. The temple could function routinely on the cultic level without a serving high priest. The one problem would be the ceremonies on the Day of Atonement (Lev. 16). (For a further critique of the thesis, see Burgmann 1980; Wise 1989–90; Babota 2014: 131–39.) *Antiquities* 13.2.3 §46 states that Jonathan succeeded to the post four years after Judas's death, but this is blatantly wrong (see further below).

The real opportunity for the Maccabees came some years later in 153–152 BCE when Alexander I Balas became the rival of Demetrius I for the Seleucid throne (1 Macc. 10.1-14; Polybius 33.15.1-2; 33.18.6-14; Justin 35.1.6–2.4). Alexander claimed to be the son of Antiochus IV (and was apparently so accepted by many in antiquity, though many ancient writers, as well as scholars today, generally doubt it [cf. Polybius 33.18.6-13; Diodorus 31.32a; Justin 35.1.6-8; Appian, *Syr.* 11.67]) and thus rightful heir to the throne. Unlike Demetrius I who left Rome without permission, Alexander first sought formal permission from the Senate, then set out to try to take the Seleucid crown. Demetrius, knowing that he needed all the allies he could get, sent an offer of peace to Jonathan. The letter has had a mixed reception (Murphy-O'Connor 1976; Babota 2014: 430–31; Bernhardt 2017: 348–51).

The letter gives Jonathan the authority to assemble an army and to be given the Jewish hostages in the Akra (1 Macc. 10.25-45; Jonathan's negotiations for the release of hostages already some years before did not include those in the Akra [1 Macc. 9.70]). Jonathan had had his headquarters at Michmash (1 Macc. 9.73), but now he moved to Jerusalem and began fortifying it. To what extent Jonathan had become recognized as a leader by the inhabitants of Judah as a whole by this time is difficult to say. 1 Maccabees had taken his authority for granted (e.g., 9.73); however, it may be that over the several years of peace he had managed to become de facto leader in the eyes of many Jews. In any case, once he had established his headquarters in Jerusalem with Seleucid authority, those who opposed him (whether Jews or others) were left with little support and evacuated the strongholds erected by Bacchides: only in the Akra in Jerusalem and in Beth-Zur did opposition continue (1 Macc. 10.7, 14).

Having heard of the concessions made by Demetrius, Alexander Balas now made his own promises to Jonathan in a letter, which included making him high priest and also included the title of Friend (*philos*), which was a significant honour for a Seleucid king to bestow on anyone. The king's 'Friends' were the inner circle of counsellors and associates (Bickerman 1938: 40–46; Capdetrey 2007: 278–80), though, as we shall see, there were various grades of 'friendship' (cf. 1 Macc. 10.20, 65, 89).

Alexander's letter (1 Macc. 10.18-20) has been labelled a forgery because of the address to Jonathan as 'brother' (e.g., Gauger 1977: 117–18), since 'brother' was usually used only of higher 'friends' of the king. Yet Ehling (2008: 149–50 n. 328) has argued that this is rather a mark of authenticity, since the office of high priest would have put him on a par with Alexander and justified the title of 'brother' to the king. Being a Friend was probably the most significant honour from the Seleucid point of view, but as far as the people were concerned the most prestigious title given to Jonathan by Alexander was no doubt that of high priest. These new titles allowed Jonathan to wear both a purple robe and a golden crown (which Alexander had sent him as a gift).

Jonathan therefore donned these at the Feast of Tabernacles (apparently in 153 BCE), thus formally beginning the tradition of the Hasmonaean high priesthood. As noted above, the office of high priest had probably been vacant since the death of Alcimus about seven years before (cf. *Ant.* 13.2.3 §46; 20.10.3 §237). Vying with Demetrius to gain Jonathan's favour was not necessarily the first thing on Alexander's mind; on the contrary, as Joseph Sievers (1990: 84) has noted,

> Presumably something was done to bring Jonathan's achievements to Alexander's attention and to suggest the advantages of an alliance, as well as the appropriate price. Since Jonathan benefited considerably from the arrangement we may reasonably conjecture that he instigated it, and, through his friends in Alexander's circle asked for the office, in return for loyalty to Alexander and perhaps other inducements.

Jonathan seems to have approached Alexander and then negotiated with him for the items seemingly granted unconditionally in the letter. If so, this emphasizes that while Jonathan was able to gain by playing off the two Seleucid rival claimants to the throne, much depended on his own skill in negotiating and defending his corner in Judaea. There is also the place of his own family in his success. Sievers (1990: 84) points out that, according to Josephus (*Ant.* 20.10.3 §238), it was members of the 'descendants of the Hasmonaeans' (i.e., his own family) who appointed him high priest. It should also be noted that Jonathan was apparently assisted – and constrained – by a council of elders which was evidently a continuation of the old *gerousia* (1 Macc. 12.6, 35; cf. *HJJSTP 2*: 229–34). His remarkable achievements had assistance from many others.

Demetrius I made further offers in a long letter 'to the Jewish nation' (τῷ ἔθνει τῶν Ἰουδαίων): release from various taxes, the transfer of various sources of income to the temple, control of the Akra in Jerusalem, the transfer of three districts from Samaria to Judah, the grant of the city of

Ptolemais and the enrolment of Jews in the Seleucid army (1 Macc. 10.25-45). Although most of these privileges eventually came to the Jews, it is doubtful that Demetrius would have made such sweeping promises, which he could not keep, suggesting that the letter is a Jewish forgery (Ehling 2008: 150); however, Demetrius might have offered concessions in his desperate situation that he had no intention of honouring. In any case, Jonathan and his advisers evidently did not believe Demetrius's promises and continued to favour Alexander; indeed, the addressees of the letter might imply Jonathan's leadership as not being recognized by Demetrius. The wisdom of such a choice was demonstrated soon afterward when Alexander defeated and killed Demetrius in battle about 150 BCE (exact year unknown; cf. *Ant.* 13.2.4 §§58-61; Justin 35.1.9) and commenced his rule (150–145 BCE).

In the same year, when Alexander married Ptolemy VI Philometor's daughter (Cleopatra Thea), he invited Jonathan to Ptolemais and publicly honoured him by enrolling him 'among his First Friends' (τῶν πρώτων φίλων), and making him general and governor (μεριδάρχην, of the province of Judaea?) (1 Macc. 10.65-66). As this shows, despite the honours and concessions, Judaea was still a province overseen from Antioch and the Akra was still in the hands of a Syrian garrison. A delegation from the opposition to Jonathan's rule attempted to see Alexander but was refused a hearing. Judaea was by no means united behind Jonathan even yet. However, it must also be noted that at this time Alexander – and presumably Judah – looks to have been very much under the thumb of Ptolemy VI, for the coins celebrating the marriage of Alexander and Cleopatra Thea seem to give her greater prominence (Ehling 2008: 155–56).

16.1.4. *Seventh Syria War (147–145 BCE)*

> **K. Ehling** (2008) *Untersuchungen zur Geschichte der späten Seleukiden*, 159–64; **J. Grainger** (2010) *The Syrian Wars*, 337–50; **G. Hölbl** (2001) *A History of the Ptolemaic Empire*, 192–94; **W. Huβ** (2001) *Ägypten in hellenistischer Zeit: 332–30 v. Chr.*, 582–96.

In 147 BCE the son of Demetrius I, later to become Demetrius II (145–140, 129–126 BCE), sailed from Crete to attempt to take back his father's kingdom from Alexander Balas (1 Macc. 10.67-89; Justin 35.2.1–4; Diodorus 32.9c-d; 33.3-4; Appian 11.67; Livy, *Periochae* 52). According to 1 Macc. 10.69 his appointment of a governor of Coele-Syria named Apollonius was among his first actions. Josephus (*Ant.* 13.4.3 §§87-88) states that Alexander appointed Apollonius to this office, which sounds unlikely on the surface; however, it may be that it was Alexander who originally appointed him, but he went over to Demetrius when the latter landed (cf. Ehling 2008: 159). Apollonius camped with a military force near Yavneh (Jamnia) and sent a letter, challenging Jonathan to fight him. Since Alexander was busy making secure his position in Antioch, Jonathan could not count on his help. Also, Apollonius was superior in cavalry forces which he could use against Jonathan in the Shephelah region. Nevertheless, Jonathan at first ignored Apollonius but joined with Simon and besieged Joppa, which opened its gates to him. Only then did Jonathan and Simon follow Apollonius's forces to Azotus (Ashdod), but the governor attempted to ambush them with cavalry; however, Jonathan won a major victory and burned the temple of Dagon in Ashdod where many of Apollonius's soldiers had taken refuge. Ashkelon submitted without a fight, and in gratitude Alexander also gave Akkaron (Ekron) and its territories to Jonathan. He had now gained control over much of the old area of Philistia.

At first Ptolemy VI Philometor supported his son-in-law Alexander, but then he turned against him and sided with Demetrius II (1 Macc. 11.1-12; Diodorus 32.9c-d, 10.1). The reason according to Josephus is that Alexander plotted against Ptolemy (*Ant.* 13.4.6 §106-8; cf. 1 Macc. 11.10). But to complicate matters further, it seems that Ptolemy was hoping to bring Coele-Syria back under Ptolemaic rule (cf. 1 Macc. 11.13), which had been lost half a century before in 200 BCE (see *HJJSTP 2*: 319–22). This is why it was another 'Syrian War' in the long line of attempts by Egypt to regain Coele-Syria. Ptolemy VI's support of Demetrius would potentially have had far-reaching outcomes for the region. But then Ptolemy VI got cold feet, perhaps thinking that taking over this territory would bring Roman wrath down on him (*Ant.* 13.4.7 §§113-14). Consequently, he acted only in the name of Demetrius and provided forces that helped Demetrius to defeat Alexander and establish his rulership in the year 145 BCE (1 Macc. 11.13-19; Justin 35.2.1-4). Ptolemy VI himself died shortly after Alexander's defeat and death, leaving the field clear for Demetrius II.

16.1.5. *Jonathan Makes Further Gains for Judah*

Taking advantage of the struggle over the Seleucid throne, Jonathan laid siege to the Akra, which was still in Syrian hands now two decades after the rededication of the temple. When some Jews from the Akra reported the siege to Demetrius, he demanded an accounting from Jonathan. The latter not only had his troops continue the siege but went boldly to Demetrius, though with substantial gifts (and also accompanied by 'elders and priests'), and came away with major concessions from the king, despite a delegation of 'lawless' Jews with accusations against him (1 Macc. 11.23-37).

He was named a 'First Friend' of Demetrius, had his high priesthood confirmed, and was allowed to govern Judaea and the three provinces acquired from Samaria 'free of tribute' (ἀφορολόγητον [1 Macc. 11.28]). This last concession may be less generous than it seems because Jonathan actually promised 300 talents to the king for it. The reason was probably the usual one: Demetrius's imperial coffers were low, and a single payment on the spot was more attractive than the uncertain promise of future tribute (cf. Goldstein 1976: 430–31). However, the Akra was evidently able to hold out against Jonathan's force.

Demetrius II was soon glad of Jonathan as an ally, for troubles developed between him and his army, apparently over pay, and also with the citizens of Antioch (1 Macc. 11.38-53; cf. *Ant.* 13.4.9 §§129-30; Diodorus 33.4.1-4). Jonathan requested that Demetrius turn the still unconquered Akra over to him and remove the troops in the other citadels in Judah (primarily Beth-Zur and Gazara [cf. 1 Macc. 9.52]). The Syrian ruler was glad to make any promises necessary to gain loyal troops. Apparently in the summer of 145 BCE a force of 3,000 Jewish soldiers was dispatched to Antioch and arrived in time to help Demetrius put down a revolt of his own citizens in the city. Following this victory, Demetrius evidently reneged on any implied concessions and even demanded back taxes (cf. *Ant.* 13.5.3 §143), but the situation was quickly overtaken by events, for there was suddenly another pretender to the Seleucid throne. Diodotus Tryphon, who had been a general of both Demetrius I and Alexander Balas, took advantage of the unrest against Demetrius. At this time, Alexander's young son Antiochus was in the care of the Arab king named either Imalkoue (1 Macc. 11.39) or Malchos (*Ant.* 13.5.1 §131). Tryphon, as he is usually known, became the *epitropos* or 'tutor' of the young Antiochus and proclaimed him king as a rival to Demetrius II, leading a revolt against him (1 Macc. 11.54-59; Diodorus 33.3-4a; Appian, *Syr.* 68). In the resulting engagement (probably in the summer of 145 or 144 BCE) Demetrius II was defeated but fled, and the new king, with the name of Antiochus VI Epiphanes Dionysus, wrote to Jonathan to confirm him in his offices, including that of high priest, and to add one further district to his territory, perhaps Ekron (the exact identification of this is not given in any of the sources, but cf. 1 Macc. 10.89). According to 1 Macc. 11.57 he was also designated a 'Friend' of the king, but the gifts mentioned in the text suggest that he had a higher rank, that of 'Relative' (*suggeneis*: Ehling 2008: 170–71). Simon Maccabee was appointed general over the armies from the region of Tyre to the borders of Egypt (cf. *Ant.* 13.5.4 §146). Jonathan was probably commander over the whole of Coele-Syria (cf. 1 Macc. 11.60).

Despite his initial defeat, Demetrius II was still alive and had not conceded the throne – a long civil war continued between him and Tryphon/Antiochus VI. Therefore, it fell to Jonathan to make his area secure for Antiochus VI (1 Macc. 11.60-74; *Ant.* 13.5.5-7 §§148-62). As he marched through Philistia (145 BCE?), Ashkelon welcomed him but Gaza submitted only after a siege. Jonathan left Simon to take care of Judah while he marched north to engage some of the generals loyal to Demetrius in Galilee and later in the area of Hazor, near Kadesh. Simon laid siege to Beth-Zur and eventually expelled its Syrian garrison and replaced it with a Jewish one. 1 Maccabees 12.24-32 seems to describe a continuation of Jonathan's conflict with Demetrius II. It was probably the next year (144 BCE?) that he marched to meet an invading force in northern Syria south of Amathitis (Hamath), but it withdrew back north without a fight. Jonathan took the opportunity to attack the Zabadaean Arabs (Josephus makes them Nabataeans [*Ant.* 13.5.10 §174], probably an error), even though they were still north of Damascus and well outside Judaean territory. Zabdiel the Arab who executed Alexander Balas was apparently in this area (1 Macc. 11.16-17), but the motive might have been persecution of Jews in Beth-Zabdai (cf. *Megillah Taanith*; referred to by Bartlett 1973: 171).

In the meantime, Simon was busy on the eastern border of Judah (1 Macc. 12.33-38). He marched toward Ashkelon but then turned aside and took Joppa, which was about to go over to Demetrius. When Jonathan returned from northern Syria, he consulted with the elders and then set in motion a programme that looked very much like a movement to secure independence. With the military situation in hand, Jonathan's next move was to make Judah more secure by building additional strongholds. Included in this were plans to strengthen the defences of Jerusalem by repairing and raising its walls and pressing a more determined assault on the Akra, by building a wall to isolate it from the city. Simon had the responsibility of building and fortifying Adida (Hebrew Hadid) in the Shephelah.

16.1.6. *The Embassies Allegedly to Rome and Sparta*

O. Amitay (2013) 'The Correspondence on 1 Maccabees and the Possible Origins of the Judeo-Spartan Connection', *SCI* 32: 79–105; **E. J. Bickerman [Bikermann]** (1930) 'Makkabäerbucher', *PW* 14: 779–800; **B. Cardauns** (1967) 'Juden und Spartaner: Zur hellenistisch-jüdischen Literatur', *Hermes* 95: 317–24; **L. Feldman** (1984) *Josephus and Modern Scholarship*; **E. S. Gruen** (1996) 'The Purported Jewish-Spartan Affiliation', in R. W. Wallace and E. M. Harris (eds), *Transitions to Empire*, 254–69; **idem** (1998)

Heritage and Hellenism, 246–91; **C. P. Jones** (1999) *Kinship Diplomacy in the Ancient World*; **R. Katzoff** (1985) 'Jonathan and Late Sparta', *AJP* 106: 485–89; **S. Schuller** (1956) 'Some Problems Connected with the Supposed Common Ancestry of Jews and Spartans and their Relations during the Last Three Centuries B.C.', *JSS* 1: 257–68; **C. Seeman** (2013) *Rome and Judea in Transition*, 113–36, 143–49; **J. VanderKam** (2004) *From Joshua to Caiaphas*, 124–37; **W. Wirgin** (1969) 'Judah Maccabee's Embassy to Rome and the Jewish-Roman Treaty', *PEQ* 101: 15–20.

It was also about this time (perhaps 145–144 BCE) that Jonathan was alleged to have renewed the treaty with Rome and to have written a letter to the Spartans about the common kinship between them and the Jews (1 Macc. 12.1-23). Already in the time of Onias I or II (according to Josephus: *Ant.* 12.4.10 §§225-27) there was a letter from one of the Spartan kings, claiming kinship with the Jews through a common descent from Abraham. This information was supposedly found by the Lacedaemonians in their archives. A very similar story occurs in 1 Macc. 12.7-23, except that in this story Jonathan Maccabee takes the initiative to write to the Spartans of their kinship, and a reply from Areus the king [*sic*] confirms this information (the alleged texts of both letters quoted in 1 Macc. 12.6-12). Of the Spartan dual kings this could only be Areus I in 309–265 BCE (Seeman 2014: 146). Nevertheless, three questions are raised by this information: (a) What is the relationship between the two accounts in Josephus and 1 Maccabees? (b) Was there actually correspondence to this effect between the Jews and Spartans? (c) What was the basis for this assumption of kinship?

On the first question, there does seem to be a definite close relationship between the texts of the letters in 1 Maccabees and Josephus; a comparison strongly suggests that 1 Maccabees is the source of the latter, even though Josephus has 'corrected' the text in the light of his knowledge of Hellenistic usage. On the question of whether there was actual correspondence, this is a moot point. Certainly, it is more likely that the Jews wrote to the Spartans than the other way around. Many writers consider the letter from Areus to Onias an old piece of Jewish propaganda, though Jonathan may well have considered it genuine (e.g., Bickerman 1930: 786). Several writers have suggested that the Spartans did have such a tradition, perhaps taken from Hecataeus of Abdera's treatise *On Abraham* (Wirgin 1969: 15–17; Feldman 1984: 218–19; Goldstein 1976: 455–62). Feldman himself suggests that the idea of kinship arose from the legend about Cadmus (a Phoenician) who sowed dragon's teeth from which armed men (*spartoi* 'sown men') sprang up; the term for 'sown man' (*spartos*) is very similar to 'Sparta' (*Spartē*).

Although there have been quite a few who defended the historicity of the Sparta correspondence (including recently Amitay 2013), most recent discussion has rejected it (Bernhardt 2017: 147–53; Seeman 2013: 143–49; Gruen 1996; 1998: 246–91). An Aramaic substratum seems to underlie its linguistic wording (Goldstein 1976: 453–62), which would suggest composition in Judaea rather than Sparta. This sort of argument from kinship, by appeal to standard classical mythology, was widespread in the Hellenistic period (Gruen 1998: 246–91). It was quite common in developing diplomatic or political ties with another people to find some distant relationship via mythical ancestors (C. P. Jones 1999; Gruen 1996). But for Spartans to approach the Jews on the basis of kinship through Abraham owes nothing to Spartan literary or cultural background but everything to Jewish traditional knowledge.

As noted above (§15.4.5), it was claimed that Judas had already sent a mission to the Roman senate a decade or so earlier, an assertion that is widely accepted. Nevertheless, the report of Jonathan's embassy to the Romans remains even more credible, partly because of the circumstances surrounding it, both with regard to Roman history and the situation of the Hasmonaeans up to this point. Justin (36.3.9) also states that Judah sought friendship with Rome under Demetrius II's rule.

We need to keep in mind the history of Rome during these years. The Third Macedonian War (171–168 BCE) had ended with the battle of Pydna, in which the Roman army had trounced the army of Perseus. The mission led by Popillius Laenus had then required Antiochus IV to cease his advance into Egypt (§15.1). For the next two decades Rome had been primarily concerned with matters in the west. They had then fought the Third Punic War (149–146 BCE), which they had largely provoked, destroying Carthage in the year 146 BCE. At the same time, they had confronted a new threat in Greece, which had ended with the sack of Corinth (also in 146 BCE). This left Rome as the unchallenged master of most of the Mediterranean world. As discussed earlier (§15.4.5), the general procedure of the Senate was to make agreements, write letters and otherwise use fine words – while doing little or nothing. Rome had little interest in or commitment to military action unless their own interests and sovereignty were directly threatened.

Thus, Rome was not about to go to war on behalf of Judah, especially in an area where it had no troops. Yet it would hardly have been surprising for Judah to consider it useful to make an alliance with this new power that had extended its tentacles toward the borders of Coele-Syria. Jonathan's activities all suggest that he was working hard toward a situation in which Judaea could act as an independent state. But it would also serve to legitimate Jonathan's claim internally to leadership of Judaea (Seeman 2013: 149–50). That Roman good will would be very useful goes without saying, but the letter to Sparta was also important. The Spartans seem to have had Roman favour at this time, partly because of a claim to kinship with them (Goldstein 1976: 447–48). A Jewish claim to common ancestry with the Spartans would perhaps not go amiss in the political manoeuvrings. But regardless of whether the alleged Spartan correspondence is authentic, the renewal of the treaty with Rome seems to have taken place under Jonathan.

16.1.7. *Death of Jonathan*

But Jonathan's plans were cut short by Tryphon (1 Macc. 12.39-53). The latter first marched to Beth-Shean in Judaea where he was met by Jonathan (autumn 144 BCE?). He honoured Jonathan and gave him gifts, with a display of entirely peaceful intentions. Tryphon then suggested that Jonathan dismiss the Jewish army who had come with him and come to Ptolemais for a formal relinquishing of Syrian control over Judaea. Jonathan accepted his word and came with only a bodyguard. Once in the city the Jewish bodyguard was slaughtered and Jonathan taken captive. Tryphon also sent troops to Galilee and the Valley of Jezreel to wipe out Jonathan's soldiers. These heard of what had happened to Jonathan, however, and they prepared for battle. The Syrian troops realized they had lost the advantage of surprise and returned home.

Nevertheless, Tryphon thought he had an advantage and set out to put pressure on Judah (1 Macc. 13.1-30). It now fell to Simon to oppose Tryphon's attack, which quickly followed. When Simon met the Syrian army at Adida, Tryphon attempted to negotiate by claiming that Jonathan was only a hostage for money owed to the Seleucid government. Simon paid the ransom (100 silver talents) and sent Jonathan's sons as hostages, as Tryphon had demanded. But it was all to no avail, for Tryphon only pressed the attack without releasing Jonathan. Simon's army moved parallel to the Syrians without engaging them but forcing them to take an indirect route to avoid areas under Jewish control. It was apparently Tryphon's intent to relieve the garrison in the Akra, but he was prevented from doing this by a heavy snowfall. Instead, he retreated into Gilead and executed Jonathan at a place called Baskama. Why he gave up his plan to rescue the Akra garrison is not stated, though it might be because of some threat or other elsewhere in his area of rule, perhaps from Demetrius II (so Ehling 2008: 176). Simon buried Jonathan in Modein and also erected monuments to him, their parents and the four dead brothers.

Jonathan's period of rule had been an important and successful one in the long term. He had gone from a period of little power and a handful of followers to high priest and formal leader of the nation. He had had to fight many battles to do this, and was evidently not inferior to Judas as a military leader. Yet he had made the real gains by political moves, primarily exploiting the rivalry over the Seleucid throne. Except for misjudging Tryphon, which cost him his life, he might have continued to lead the emerging nation. Judah was not yet independent of Seleucid control, but large steps had been taken in this direction. For this, Jonathan deserves much credit. It has been proposed that there was a major rivalry between him and Simon for leadership. This will be discussed at greater length in the next section (§16.2.1).

16.2. Simon (143–135 BCE)

K. Atkinson (2016) *A History of the Hasmonean State*, 32–46; **V. Babota** (2014) *The Institution of the Hasmonean High Priesthood*, 225–67; **C. Seeman** (2013) *Rome and Judea in Transition*, 150–72; **J. Sievers** (1990) *The Hasmoneans and their Supporters*, 105–34.

Sources: 1 Macc. 13.1–16.17; *War* 1.2.3 §§50-54; *Ant.* 13.6.7-7.4 §§213-28.

16.2.1. Initial Actions

Simon was now the last of the Maccabean brothers and the third to become leader of the Hasmonaean movement. From an overall point of view, he continued on the same basic road as Judas and Jonathan, evidently aiming at an independent Jewish state. However, we have to keep in mind that our main source remains 1 Maccabees, which is very pro-Simon. It is interesting that Josephus ceases to use 1 Maccabees as his main source once Simon became the leader, and his account (*Ant.* 13.6.7-7.4 §§215-29) tends to be shorter and more neutral in its description of his term of office. J. C. Bernhardt (2017: 358–59) suggests that this is because Josephus's family preserved a tradition that Simon was in some ways involved in the elimination of Jonathan's line from the leadership. Bernhardt has proposed that Simon was actually in rivalry with Jonathan and staged a takeover of the high priestly office. Jonathan's capture by Tryphon was his opportunity. He not only got himself declared leader (including high priest: 1 Macc. 13.1-9), but by delivering Jonathan's sons to Tryphon Simon had ensured that there would be no rivals to his taking Jonathan's place (because Tryphon would execute them, which he seems to have done).

Whatever the exact relations between Jonathan and Simon, the majority of the Palestinian Jews seem by this point to have accepted the Hasmonaeans as leaders. With this popular backing and a temporary calm, Simon was in a position to continue the efforts of his brothers to effect the independence of the state by building fortresses and preparing stores of food in case of protracted war (1 Macc. 13.33). Tryphon had shown his true colours as far as the Jews were concerned, and Simon took the logical step of negotiating with Demetrius II. Tryphon had taken control of Antioch and northern Syria and Cilicia, but Demetrius evidently still ruled the coastal cities, including Tyre and Sidon and other parts of Coele-Syria (Ehling 2008: 168–70; Atkinson 2016: 43–44). Antiochus VI continued as the nominal king only a short time longer before Tryphon took the throne. According to 1 Macc. 13.31 and all other ancient sources (Diodorus 33.28; Appian, *Syr.* 68; Justin 36.1.7), Tryphon was responsible for the death of the young Antiochus; some (e.g., *Ant.* 13.7.1 §218; Livy, *Per.* 55) say he died under the surgeon's knife, but still blame Tryphon. In any case, this seems to have been in 141 BCE, because of coins and other evidence (Ehling 2008: 178–79). Tryphon naturally wanted to ingratiate himself with Rome and sent a golden crown to the Senate (Diodorus 33.28a). They accepted it but in the name of the late Antiochus VI!

16.2.2. *Independence for Judah and Praise of Simon*

> **V. Babota** (2014) *The Institution of the Hasmonean High Priesthood*, 225–45; **J. W. van Henten** (2001) 'The Honorary Decree for Simon the Maccabee (1 Macc 14:25-49) in its Hellenistic Context', in J. J. Collins and G. Sterling (eds), *Hellenism in the Land of Israel*, 116–45; **C. Seeman** (2013) *Rome and Judea in Transition*, 151–61; **J. Sievers** (1990) *The Hasmoneans and their Supporters*, 119–27.

In the meantime, Demetrius II once again made a variety of far-reaching concessions in a letter to Simon, even including permission to mint his own coinage (though no such coins have turned up so far – §2.3). This time Demetrius was not in a position to withdraw his offer, and the writer of 1 Maccabees could write that in the 1st year of Simon – the 170th year of the Seleucid era (143–142 BCE) – 'the yoke of the Gentiles was lifted from Israel' (ἤρθη ὁ ζυγὸς τῶν ἐθνῶν ἀπὸ τοῦ Ισραελ: 1 Macc. 13.41-42).

There is no doubt that this was a significant date and event since Judah had been a vassal state of one sort or another for about 600 years – since the time of Tiglath-pileser III (about 736 BCE). Subsequent events were to show that this state of 'liberation' was short-lived – the Seleucids still claimed the territory and at times still imposed their rule – and Simon himself died violently as had all his brothers. Judaea was now an independent state in name, as proclaimed internally, but the reality was somewhat different. Nevertheless, as a psychological high point the formal proclamation of liberty should be given its due: it formally marked a new phase in Judaean history.

Indeed, for a time the Judaeans evidently dated their contracts and legal documents from Simon's first year (though nothing with such dating has survived). His reign is summarized in language influenced by the biblical description of Solomon's reign (1 Macc. 14.4-15):

> The land was quiet all the days of Simon, and he sought good for his people. His power and honour were pleasing to them all his days... They worked their ground in peace, and it gave its yield and the trees of the plain their fruit. The elders sat in the streets, all talking together about good things... He maintained peace in the land, and Israel rejoiced with great joy. Each person sat under his own vine and fig tree, and there was no one making them afraid.

In Simon's 3rd year a stela was erected, which recounted his and his brothers' deeds and confirmed him in the office of high priest (1 Macc. 14.27-47). This stela is probably genuine, since 1 Maccabees was written not long after it would have been erected so that its existence would have been plain to any Jerusalem readers. Yet the stela itself had an interesting message when read carefully (Sievers 1990: 119–27; Seeman 2013: 151–60; Bernhardt 2017: 384–94). J. W. van Henten (2001) argues that the decree is something new, an innovation in Hellenistic Judaism. It is a means of legitimating Simon's office and position, based on his accomplishments and those of his brothers.

In spite of the adulatory language of the decree, it is plain that Simon's powers – as high priest, leader and military commander – are being granted by a coalition of 'priests and people and rulers of the nation and the elders of the country' in a public assembly (1 Macc. 14.28: ἱερέων καὶ λαοῦ καὶ ἀρχόντων ἔθνους καὶ τῶν πρεσβυτέρων τῆς χώρας). Finally, the decree is ratified by 'all the people' (1 Macc. 14.46: πᾶς ὁ λαός). The fact that his powers had to be officially granted, including his high priestly authority, indicates many still needed convincing to accept these as yet (cf. Sievers 1990: 120–24; Seeman 2013: 155). Also, they were apparently negotiated with various power groups, which is why they were declared only in his 3rd year. It is further interesting that Demetrius's letter that began it all is addressed to Simon the high priest 'and to the elders and nation of the Jews' (1 Macc. 13.36: καὶ πρεσβυτέροις καὶ ἔθνει Ἰουδαίων). Sievers (1990: 122) cites the interesting analogy of Vespasian, whose proclamation as emperor by the legions was then ratified formally by the Senate, followed by a popular assembly. Those who have undoubted actual power do not need such assurances.

16.2.3. *Treaty with Rome*

>**J. C. Bernhardt** (2017) *Die jüdische Revolution*, 369–71; **A. Giovannini and H. Müller** (1971) 'Die Beziehungen zwischen Rom und den Juden im 2. Jh v. Chr.', *Museum Helveticum* 28: 156–71; **E. S. Gruen** (1984) *The Hellenistic World and the Coming of Rome*, 42–46, 748–51; **C. Seeman** (2013) *Rome and Judea in Transition*, 162–71; **J. Sievers** (1990) *The Hasmoneans and their Supporters*, 116–19.

Simon is also said to have renewed the treaties with Rome and Sparta (1 Macc. 14.16-24; 15.15-24). The initial statement in 1 Macc. 14.16-18 that Rome and others took the initiative to renew the alliance can be immediately discounted: Rome did not do this. Rather, it was most likely Simon who sent an embassy to Rome under Numenius, with the gift of a large golden shield weighing about a thousand minas (about 565 kg or 1250 pounds) (1 Macc. 14.24). The Roman reply is given in the name of a certain Lucius who is labelled ὕπατος, often understood to be 'consul'. The letter is addressed to King Ptolemy (VIII) of Egypt but also evidently to various rulers and countries of the region, notifying them that the Romans were renewing their treaty of friendship and alliance with Simon and the Jewish people (1 Macc. 15.15-21). Reference is made to Simon and the gift of a golden shield, and calls on the kings and peoples of the region not to harm the Jewish people and to send any plotters against Simon in bonds to Jerusalem (the so-called 'extradition clause').

When this alleged *senatus consultum* (senatorial document) in the name of Lucius is looked at more closely, however, many problems emerge: (1) the name 'Lucius' with no other qualifications is not standard and could refer to a great many different persons; (2) the 'extradition clause' is unparalleled in documents of this sort; (3) the list of peoples and kingdoms to whom the letter is addressed is very strange; there is no particular order, some of those on the list are very unlikely to have contact with Judah, much less reason to molest it; (4) the one real enemy of Judah at this time, Tryphon, is not mentioned. This is why a number of researchers think it is inauthentic or at least have doubts about it (A. Giovannini and H. Müller 1971; Sievers 1990: 117–18; cf. Gruen 1984: 749–50).

To complicate matters, Josephus (*Ant.* 14.8.5 §§144-48) gives a senatorial decree, which he claims was a memorial to Hyrcanus II set up in the Roman Capitol. However, this decree (allegedly by Julius Caesar), given in the name of the *stratēgos* Lucius Valerius, does not fit the context or activities of Hyrcanus II. Reference is made to the gift of a golden shield worth 50,000 gold pieces (1,000 minas equals 50,000 drachmas) and to a Jewish embassy led by Alexander son of Jason, Numenius son of Antiochus and Alexander son of Dorotheus. The subject is the renewal of the previous relationship of goodwill and friendship. No mention is made of either Hyrcanus or of Simon, but the decrees of the Senate in both 1 Maccabees 15 and in Josephus look too similar to be coincidental: they must surely refer to the same embassy. The question is, whose embassy?

If we follow 1 Maccabees 15, it would be Simon's embassy. The context of 1 Maccabees 14–15 is the memorial to Simon by the 'people', with a long recounting of his good deeds (see further at §16.2.2). In 1 Macc. 14.40 a favourable response of Rome to a Jewish embassy is connected with Demetrius II's recognition of Simon's office of high priest. This suggests that the embassy must have been no earlier than 143–142 BCE when Demetrius II declared Simon as high priest (1 Macc. 13.35-41; 14.38-39). A number of researchers reject this as too early in Simon's reign; however, Bernhardt (2017: 373–74) has argued that Simon sent an embassy to Rome when Tryphon took Jonathan captive, before he executed him. He sees this as fitting in with his thesis that Simon effected a coup against the rule of his brother Jonathan (discussed above). Gruen (1984: 749–50) also sees an embassy about 143–142 as being the most likely.

If there was an embassy to Rome early in Simon's reign, was it the one associated with the 'golden shield' or was that another embassy? C. Seeman (2013: 189–94) accepts that an embassy took place in the time of Simon; however, he wishes to assign the 'golden shield' embassy to the reign of John Hyrcanus. The reason for the dating is the reference to L. Valerius in the decree quoted by Josephus (*Ant.* 14.8.5 §§144-48). This term *stratēgos* is often a reference to a praetor, but sometimes it can mean consul. Seeman takes it to mean 'praetor'; since a L. Valerius Flaccus was consul in 131, he would most likely have been praetor by about 134 BCE. That would put the mission at the beginning of John Hyrcanus's reign. This position is well argued but not at all certain. While L. Valerius Flaccus might have been praetor in 134, he could have held that office some years earlier. There was sometimes a long hiatus between holding the office of praetor and becoming consul. There is also the fact that our list of praetors in this period is very incomplete, and an unknown L. Valerius could be the person in the epistle in Josephus (Sievers 1990: 117).

Granted that Josephus's decree is misplaced, should we assume that the one in 1 Maccabees 15 is also misplaced – two misplaced documents in two separate writings about the same embassy, as Seeman thinks? Finally, Seeman (2013: 193–94) has assigned three separate embassies to Rome under John Hyrcanus. Is that very likely, especially considering one is put in 134 BCE and the next only a few years later in 129 BCE? Would it not be more logical all round to assign the 'golden shield' decree to Simon as the author of 1 Maccabees does? It seems that those who assign the 'golden shield' embassy to the reign of Simon are more probably right (Sievers 1990: 116–19; Gruen 1984: 749–50; Babota 2014: 248; Bernhardt 2017: 373–74).

What did this alliance with Rome accomplish? Simon thought it worth a half-tonne golden shield. 1 Maccabees 14.40 itself suggests that Demetrius recognized Simon because of hearing about the positive response of the Romans to his mission. This is most unlikely (cf. Seeman 2013: 158). The embassy to Rome would not have reported back to Simon before his possession of the high priesthood was recognized by Demetrius (1 Macc. 13.35-40). Also, there is no indication that the Romans did anything about Tryphon, not even so much as writing a letter of warning to him. They were following their normal practice at this time of issuing warm words but without any deeds to accompany them. Nevertheless, Simon could use it internally to his advantage to strengthen his position.

As for the supposed letter from the Spartans in 1 Macc. 14.20-23, it looks like a reply to Jonathan's alleged letter to them (§16.1.6). It also looks very much like something that has been copied and cobbled together from the correspondence in 1 Macc. 12.6-23.

16.2.4. *Main Accomplishments of Simon*

A. J. Sachs and H. Hunger (eds) (1996) *Astronomical Diaries and Related Texts from Babylonia, III: Diaries from 164 B.C. to 61 B.C.*

A variety of accomplishments is credited to Simon. He first took Gezer (Gazara, following Josephus [*Ant*. 13.6.7 §215] and 1 Macc. 13.53, rather than the 'Gaza' of 1 Macc. 13.43). He also made Joppa into a Jewish port (1 Macc. 12.33-34; 14.5, 34). However, probably the most important accomplishment was at last taking the Akra and expelling the Syrian garrison from it in about May 142 BCE ([171 SE, 2nd mo, 23 day), since this removed the last formal symbol of Seleucid rule over the country (1 Macc. 13.49-52). The day was declared a holiday (1 Macc. 13.52; *Megillat Ta'anit*).

According to Josephus's account Simon also decided to level the citadel hill to prevent it from overlooking the temple area as it had up to this time (*Ant.* 13.6.7 §§215-17; *War* 1.2.2 §50). This is contradicted by 1 Macc. 13.52, which states that he strengthened the Akra, and 1 Macc. 14.37 (cf. *War* 5.4.1 §139), however, which states, 'He settled Jewish men in it [the Akra] and fortified it for the security of the land and the city, and he built high the walls of Jerusalem'. Also taking account of the archaeology, it seems unlikely that such a reduction in height ever took place (§2.1.1.25).

After Demetrius II had made concessions to Simon to enlist his friendship, he was too busy to be concerned with Judaea. Early in 139 he marched east against the Parthians (the date is uncertain but probably this year rather than earlier [Ehling 2008: 182; contrast Atkinson 2016: 41-42; 1 Macc. 14.1 gives it as 172 SE or 141–140 BCE). The Parthians had become a major threat to the Seleucid empire by this time. 1 Maccabees (14.1) and Josephus (*Ant.* 13.5.11 §186) state that his eastern campaign was to gain assistance against Tryphon, but Demetrius seems to have had a genuine concern for the whole of the Seleucid empire: the coins suggest the Parthian expedition had been planned before Tryphon became a threat (cf. Ehling 2008: 183–84). In any case, after some initial successes in the Upper Satrapies, Demetrius was taken captive by the Parthian leader Mithradates I (or perhaps his successor Phraates II [138–127 BCE]) about 138 BCE (Justin 36.1.1-6; 38.9.1-3; Appian, *Syr.* 11.67; on the date Sachs and Hunger 1996: 161). Demetrius's wife Cleopatra sent for his brother Antiochus to marry her and take the throne as Antiochus VII Sidetes (138–129 BCE). Antiochus attacked Tryphon about 138 BCE and besieged him in Dor. He applied to Simon for aid and no doubt received it (1 Macc. 15.10-14, 25-26; *Ant.* 13.7.2 §§223-24; the statement of 1 Macc. 15.27 that Antiochus then refused it is not credible). Tryphon managed to escape from Dor but was tracked to Apamea and met his death there in 137 BCE (*Ant.* 13.7.2 §223; Appian, *Syr.* 11.68; Strabo 14.5.2; Syncellus 351.13).

With Tryphon out of the way, however, Antiochus turned on Simon with demands which showed that he considered Judaea still a Seleucid vassal (1 Macc. 15.27-36): he sent one of his Friends Athenobius and demanded that Simon's conquests of Joppa and Gazara outside Judaea proper be given up (as well as the Jerusalem Akra) and back-tribute and damages to the tune of 1,000 silver talents be paid. Simon's counteroffer of 100 talents was considered only an insult and an excuse to declare war on him. The reason is not hard to guess: Antiochus sorely needed funds for his fight against Tryphon, and Simon had taken two important cities

(Joppa and Gazara) that Antiochus believed were Seleucid possessions; he wanted them back, with compensation for the lost tribute. Antiochus made his Friend Cendebaeus commander-in-chief for the region (ἐπιστράτηγον τῆς παραλίας) and sent him with an army against Judah (1 Macc. 15.38–16.10). Simon was now too aged to take to the field (so 1 Macc. 16.2-3, though Josephus has him lead the army, or a section of it [*War* 1.2.2 §§52-53; *Ant.* 13.7.3 §§226-27]), but his sons John and Judah assumed command and were able to defeat Cendebaeus's force near Kedron (modern Qatra) and Azotus (Ashdod).

16.2.5. *Death of Simon*

After a rule of eight years, Simon was invited to a banquet near Jericho by his son-in-law, Ptolemy son of Abubus, the Jewish governor (*stratēgos*) over the plain of Jericho (1 Macc. 16.11-17). Ptolemy used the occasion to assassinate Simon and imprison Simon's wife and two other sons, but the third son John Hyrcanus was forewarned and managed to escape. This came about in the year 177 SE, 11th month (Shevat), or about February 135 BCE (1 Macc. 16.14). Simon had reigned over seven years. Thus, the last of the Maccabaean brothers met his end by violence, demonstrating that the promised peace of Simon's rule was more apparent than real. Nevertheless, Simon's achievement was considerable and his reign an important watershed in Jewish history. Perhaps the symbolism was more important than the reality – the Seleucids had by no means abandoned their claim to Judaea as one of their provinces – but the image of Israel being free from the 'yoke of the Gentiles' in the 170th Seleucid year (= 143–142 BCE) was a powerful one. Although Simon's battles and other accomplishments were less than those of Jonathan, his achievements were important and a continuing ascension of Hasmonaean control over the area of Palestine.

16.3. *John Hyrcanus I (135–104 BCE)*

K. Atkinson (2016) *A History of the Hasmonean State*, 47–79; **E. Dąbrowa** (2010) *The Hasmoneans and their State*, 67–83; **T. Rajak** (1981) 'Roman Intervention in a Seleucid Siege of Jerusalem?' *GRBS* 22: 65–81; **J. Sievers** (1990) *The Hasmoneans and their Supporters*, 135–56.

Sources: 1 Macc. 16.18-24; *War* 1.2.3-8 §§54-69;
Ant. 13.7.4-10.7 §§228-300.

16.3.1. *Beginning of Hyrcanus's Reign*

After his escape from Ptolemy's murderous plot, Hyrcanus fled to Jerusalem, where the people refused entry to Ptolemy. Hyrcanus acceded to the office of high priest: so states Josephus (*War* 1.2.3 §56; *Ant.* 13.8.1 §230) without any discussion or qualification. Yet the matter could not have been straightforward since Hyrcanus had not been designated officially as Simon's successor (cf. 1 Macc. 14, which says nothing about a successor). It seems likely that in this time of crisis Hyrcanus was able to rally support and take charge by means of his military resources. With his forces mobilized, he immediately turned the attack on Ptolemy who washed up in a fortress above Jericho called Dagon (according to Josephus, though more properly Doq), but besieged him without success. Ptolemy held out until the *shmittah* (sabbatical) year (Tishri 135–Tishri 134 BCE), when Hyrcanus terminated the siege. Ptolemy then murdered Hyrcanus's mother and two brothers before escaping to Philadelphia. Why he terminated the siege is unclear: Josephus says it is because no work was done in the sabbatical year, which is patently untrue (cf. Lev. 25.1-7). Some see the sabbatical year as a problem because of their dating of the Jewish Seleucid year; assuming Hyrcanus took over from Simon in February 134 BCE. But with the chronology followed in this book, Hyrcanus took over about February 135 BCE, and the sabbatical year began in the autumn of 135 (§1.3.6).

Soon afterward, Hyrcanus himself was besieged in Jerusalem by Antiochus VII, the cause apparently being the cities such as Joppa that Simon had taken from the Syrians. Antiochus showed his generosity – at least, in religious matters – by allowing a truce during the Feast of Tabernacles and even sending in sacrifices to be offered on his behalf at the temple (cf. Diodorus 34/35.1.1-2, 4-5). Agreement was finally reached between Antiochus and Hyrcanus that tribute would be paid for Joppa and the other cities on Judaea's border (cf. also Diodorus 34/35.1.1-5; [Pseudo-]Plutarch, *Moralia* 184E-F). It has been argued that it was more than just Hyrcanus's skill as a negotiator which ended the fighting (Rajak 1981); rather, the Romans intervened to provide the practical aid which they had agreed in theory in a treaty with Simon. As argued above (§15.4.5), however, it seems doubtful that the possibility of Roman intervention was taken seriously by the Seleucids (cf. also Sievers 1990: 138–39, and §16.3.4 below). In any case, in addition to receiving payment for the cities Antiochus also tore down the defensive walls of Jerusalem. He wanted a Syrian garrison in the city, as well, but Hyrcanus managed to substitute hostages (including his own brother) and a further payment of silver instead.

In order to obtain the necessary cash, Josephus states that Hyrcanus opened David's tomb and took out a large amount of silver (*War* 1.2.5 §61; *Ant.* 13.8.4 §249). The statement is made without any qualification or explanation, but it raises many questions, not least whether an ancestral tomb could have existed unmolested for centuries even though supposedly containing a huge amount of wealth. A more likely explanation is that Hyrcanus was drawing on a large treasury inherited from Simon (cf. 1 Macc. 15.32-36; Dąbrowa 2010: 81–82). The suggestion that the money came from David's tomb may have just been a cover story to divert questions about why the Hasmonaeans were accumulating such wealth. It is also alleged that Hyrcanus used some of this money to hire mercenaries, the first Jewish leader to do so. Again, why he needed mercenaries is not stated, though they would have been handy to protect his interests in Judaea when he was away with Antiochus VII fighting the Parthians.

The agreement between Hyrcanus and Antiochus VII put them on good terms. Thus, when Antiochus marched east against the Parthians about 130 BCE, Hyrcanus accompanied him with a contingent of Jewish troops. Nicolaus of Damascus mentioned that allowance was made for Jewish religious observances (*Ant.* 13.8.4 §§251-52). Antiochus engaged the Parthians, led by Phraates II, where he was killed in the fighting (ca. 129 BCE). Antiochus was succeeded by his brother Demetrius II, whom the Parthians released from his captivity and allowed to become king again. Nothing is said about Hyrcanus at this point. He apparently returned to Judaea, though whether it was before the battle with the Parthians or afterward is not clear (cf. Sievers 1990: 140; Pucci 1983 who thinks he made a deal with the Parthians, a most unlikely interpretation). In either case, he seems to have got off lightly in the Parthian campaign, with his troops mainly intact, judging by the military expeditions he undertook after Antiochus VII's death.

16.3.2. *Eighth Syrian War (ca. 128–122 BCE)*

J. Grainger (2010) *The Syrian Wars*, 369–85; **G. Hölbl** (2001) *A History of the Ptolemaic Empire*, 197–201; **W. Huβ** (2001) *Ägypten in hellenistischer Zeit: 332–30 v. Chr.*, 608–18.

Sources: *Ant.* 13.9.3-10.1 §§267-74; Justin 38.9.1; 39.1.1-2.

The 'Syrian Wars' were generally named for attempts by the Seleucids to take back Coele-Syria from the Ptolemies, or after 200 BCE for the Ptolemies to try to take it back from the Seleucids. The 'Eighth Syria War' was a bit different, however, since it did not involve Coele-Syria, though it did affect the Egyptian throne. The rulership of both the Ptolemaic and the Seleucid realms was rather complicated at this time. Demetrius II had been married to Cleopatra Thea when he was captured by the Parthians in 139 BCE and kept in confinement in the east. Antiochus VII took his brother's place on the Seleucid throne but also married Cleopatra Thea. As already noted, Antiochus marched against the Parthians (taking a contingent of Jewish troops under John Hyrcanus's command) and was killed in the fighting in 129 BCE. Shortly afterward, the Parthians released Demetrius II from his confinement, and he returned to take back his throne and his wife, Cleopatra Thea.

At this time, the Egyptian throne was being disputed between Ptolemy VIII Euergetes and his mother, Cleopatra II. Ptolemy had gradually taken over much of Egypt, and Cleopatra was confined to Alexandria, though it was a formidable fortified city and would not be easy to take. She appealed to Demetrius II for assistance, promising him the Egyptian throne. The Parthian pressure was temporarily relieved at this time (because the Sakas from even further east had attacked the Parthians), enabling Demetrius to take his army to Egypt in 128 BCE. When he got to Pelusion, the fortress guarding the entry to Egypt, he was stopped. At this point, his wife Cleopatra Thea rebelled and apparently declared their own son as Antiochus VIII Epiphanes (based on coins). Demetrius had no choice but to return to Antioch to secure his own throne.

This left Ptolemy VIII with the continuing problem of how to take Alexandria, especially if Demetrius were to return to Egypt. Therefore, he set up an alleged son of Alexander Balas as a rival, in the person of Alexander II Zabinas (ca. 128–122 BCE). This left a three-way contest for the Seleucid throne: Alexander Zabinas, Cleopatra Thea and Antiochus VIII, and Demetrius II. When Alexander and Demetrius met in battle in 127 or 126 BCE, Demetrius was defeated. He fled from the battle, but Cleopatra Thea refused to let him take refuge in Ptolemais-Ake. He moved on to Tyre, where he was killed. Cleopatra Thea took the throne but then shared it with Antiochus VIII.

In the meantime, Cleopatra II fled from Alexandria with the state treasury and took refuge with Cleopatra Thea and Antiochus VIII. Ptolemy VIII had taken Alexandria, but his mother was still active. Over a number of years they became reconciled. By 124 BCE Ptolemy VIII was ready to abandon Alexander Zabinas and support Antiochus VIII. In a battle in 123 or 122 BCE, Alexander Zabinas came off second best and was eventually captured and given over to Antiochus, who had him executed.

16.3.3. Territorial Expansion and Conquests

For most of the rest of his reign Hyrcanus was free to conduct his own affairs with little interference from the Syrians, the reason being the rivalry between the two lines of contenders for the throne. This preoccupation of the Syrian rulers with securing their own throne against rivals allowed Hyrcanus the freedom he needed. He gave no further tribute or help to them after the death of Antiochus VII (129 BCE [*Ant.* 13.10.1 §273]); instead, he took the opportunity to expand his territory, which he did with considerable success. As soon as Antiochus VII died fighting the Parthians, Josephus suggests that Hyrcanus 'immediately' (εὐθύς) set out on a campaign against various cities of Syria (*Ant.* 13.9.1 §254). There is a discrepancy at this point, for the taking of the major centres of Samaria and Gerizim seems to be no earlier than about 112 BCE. This means a gap of at least a decade and a half between 129 BCE and the taking of Gerizim. What was Hyrcanus doing during this time? It may be that he was occupied with the internal revolt against his rule at this time, about which we know little (§16.3.5).

The first he is alleged to have attacked were Medaba and Sarnoga in Transjordan. This seems unlikely: the distance was great, while the tendency would be to engage initially with nearby opponents. Also, Medaba was apparently taken by Alexander Jannaeus (*Ant.* 13.15.4 §397). The towns, whose names may have become corrupted in the manuscript tradition, were probably not far from Shechem (cf. *Ant.* 13.9.1 §255). One of his most significant acts was the siege and capture of Shechem and Mt Gerizim, at which time he allegedly destroyed the Samaritan temple, which the archaeology seems to confirm (§2.1.1.9). Why Hyrcanus took the Samaritan temple is an interesting question on which the sources throw no light. Although there had been friction between the Samaritans and Jerusalem, there had also clearly been a lot of social and cultural interchange. The Samaritans apparently distanced themselves from the Jews in the time of Antiochus IV (§8.2.3), which might have created long-term resentment if there were other such acts not recorded in the extant sources (on the Samaritans, see further Chapter 8). There is also the question of when he carried out this siege. Coins found at the site suggest it was probably about 112/111 BCE.

He next took some of the major cities of Idumaea, extended his rule over the entire country, and is said to have forcibly converted the inhabitants to Judaism. Exactly how this is to be interpreted is difficult. Forced conversion is generally not very successful, yet Josephus states that the Idumaeans continued to be Jews (*Ant.* 13.9.1 §258). See further at §9.1.

The next area to fall was the city of Samaria itself. Hyrcanus may have begun the attack (*Ant.* 13.10.2 §§275-76), but at some point he turned it over to his sons Aristobulus and Antigonus. After a lengthy siege, the citizens called on either Antiochus VIII (*War* 1.2.7 §65) or IX (*Ant.* 13.10.2 §§276-78) for help which was readily given; however, Aristobulus's forces defeated Antiochus's troops and resumed the siege. After a second request by the Samaritans, Antiochus sent a body of soldiers to invade Hyrcanus's territory and conduct guerrilla action without directly confronting the Jewish army. This included a contingent supplied by Ptolemy VIII. This also did not work, and Samaria fell after a year (ca. 108 BCE is the date often given, but it could have been a year or two earlier).

Why he attacked Samaria is obscure. Josephus states it was because the people of Samaria had attacked the Idumaean city of Marisa at the instigation of the Syrians (*Ant.* 13.10.2 §275). But because of distance and location, the people of Samaria were unlikely to be engaging with the people of Marisa (Sievers 1990: 144–45). It may be that the 'Marisa' is a corruption of 'Garizim' or something similar, and Hyrcanus (although having conquered Shechem and Gerizim) was actually defending the Samaritans from the Macedonian colonists at Samaria. More likely, however, is that Hyrcanus took the city for strategic reasons, since it seems to have been an important stronghold from which Antiochus IX could dominate this part of his territory (Dąbrowa 2010: 73–74). When it fell, Hyrcanus was able to take control of the whole region. They then moved on to Scythopolis (Beth-Shean) and took the territory between it and Mt Carmel (the Seleucid commander Callimandrus is said to have betrayed Scythopolis: *Ant.* 13.10.3 §280).

16.3.4. *Contacts with Rome*

> **E. Baltrusch** (2002) *Die Juden und das Römische Reich: Geschichte einer konfliktreichen Beziehung*, 106–10; **J. C. Bernhardt** (2017) *Die jüdische Revolution*, 474, 478, 479; **T. C. Brennan** (2000) *The Praetorship in the Roman Republic*; **C. Seeman** (2013) *Rome and Judea in Transition*, 184–202.

It is apparent from the text of Josephus that Hyrcanus sent at least two embassies to Rome. The first was evidently early in his reign, under Simon son of Dositheus, Apollonius son of Alexander and Diodorus son of Jason (*Ant.* 13.9.2 §§259-66). A *senatus consultum* of friendship and alliance was issued in the name of Fannius son of Marcus (στρατηγός). The document refers to the Judaean request that various cities taken from Judah by Antiochus VII be restored, that Seleucid troops not be allowed to march through Judah and that Antiochus's laws contrary to the Senate be annulled (what these last were is not clear). The Senate was happy to renew the treaty of friendship and alliance but stated that the matters relating to Antiochus would have to be considered at a later time when the Senate had more 'leisure' (εὐσχολησῃ). This demonstrates once again that the Romans were hesitant to get involved in affairs not their own.

A major question is when this embassy was sent. Fannius being called by the Greek term *stratēgos* could indicate that he was either praetor or consul. The term more often means praetor, but Josephus certainly used it for the office of consul. We know that Fannius was consul in 122 BCE, which is when T. C. Brennan (2000: 119) thinks he most likely authorized this document. If it was when he was praetor, however, it would have been a few years earlier. Since Hyrcanus came to an agreement with Antiochus VII about 132 BCE, it is unlikely he would have sent such an embassy between that time and Antiochus's death in 129 BCE (Seeman 2013: 187–88). This would seem to favour the year when Fannius was consul – 122 BCE – but a few years earlier when he was apparently praetor is also a possibility.

Josephus also quotes a decree from Pergamum during the time of Hyrcanus II (*Ant.* 14.10.22 §§247-55). It mentions a decree of the Roman Senate, in response to an embassy from Hyrcanus the high priest, that 'Antiochus, son of Antiochus' should not harm the Jews and that he should restore the territory and cities that he had seized. As with another document discussed earlier (§16.2.3), this makes no sense in the time of Hyrcanus II when Seleucid rule had come to an end. This looks rather like a misplaced decree from the time of John Hyrcanus. During Hyrcanus I's period of rule, the only 'Antiochus, son of Antiochus' was Antiochus IX Cyzicenus (113–95 BCE). If so, the embassy could have come anytime during the last part of Hyrcanus I's reign. Seeman (2013: 196–97) argues cogently that it refers to an otherwise-unknown occupation of Judaean territory by Antiochus IX about 113/112 BCE.

In addition to these two embassies, Seeman (2013: 189–94) has argued that a third embassy – indeed, the first one, by his reckoning – took place in 134 BCE. It was argued above that this embassy that Seeman assigns to John Hyrcanus should actually be dated to about 143–142 BCE and placed in the reign of Simon (see the discussion in §16.2.3).

16.3.5. *The Rest of John Hyrcanus's Reign*

The Jews in Palestine were apparently thriving at this time. Hyrcanus I seems to be the first to mint coins, which may have helped boost the economy. But the Jews of Egypt and Cyprus were also flourishing (*Ant.* 13.10.4 §§284-87). Two of the sons of the Onias who built the temple at Leontopolis (§10.2.1.3) were generals in the army of Cleopatra III (fl. 140–100 BCE), Chelkias and Ananias. The unnamed general of Cleopatra III who was executed by her (Justin 39.4) might be one of them; however, the Jewish sources give no hint of any friction between the queen and her Jewish generals.

Nevertheless, opposition developed and Hyrcanus had to spend some time putting down rebels. Exactly what form this rebellion took or when is unclear, though it might have been in the hiatus between 129 and about 112 BCE. In the *War* Josephus refers simply to some of Hyrcanus's 'countrymen' (τῶν ἐπιχωρίων: *War* 1.2.8 §67). In the *Antiquities* he makes the Pharisees his opponents, relating an anecdote about Hyrcanus and the Pharisees. According to Josephus, Hyrcanus had himself been a Pharisee but, after falling out with them, he became a Sadducee (*Ant.* 13.10.5-7 §§288-99). In any event, he soon reduced the opposition and spent the rest of his reign peacefully, dying a natural death after a rule of 31 years. So much for the internal opposition. As Sievers notes, 'contradictions and the omission of the Pharisees in *J[ewish] W[ar]* make us doubt Josephus' statements about their importance at the time of Hyrcanus and about Hyrcanus' Pharisees' (1990: 149).

Josephus notes in passing that Hyrcanus had three of the best qualities: rule of the nation, office of high priest and prophetic ability, which allowed him to foretell the future (*War* 1.2.8 §68; *Ant.* 13.10.7 §299). Two examples of the last are his foreseeing his sons' defeat of Antiochus (*Ant.* 13.10.3 §§282-83) and his prediction that his two eldest sons would not be leaders of the nation (*War* 1.2.8 §69; *Ant.* 13.10.7 §300). There is more to this latter prediction: God is said to have appeared to Hyrcanus in his sleep, at which point he asked which of his sons would rule. He was disappointed that Alexander Jannaeus appeared, because he loved his two eldest sons best (*Ant.* 13.12.1 §§321-22). This goes against the common assumption that prophecy had ceased by this time (see further §12.4.1).

We also apparently have some evidence that a memorial to John Hyrcanus was preserved in Athens. Josephus (*Ant.* 14.8.5 §§148-55) quotes this, though, assigning it to Hyrcanus II; however, its content does not fit the context or activities of Hyrcanus II but more likely those of John Hyrcanus. The decree (allegedly by Julius Caesar) is said to be in the ninth year of Hyrcanus, which is commonly emended to '29th' and assigned to Hyrcanus I, because the decree refers to the archonship of Agathocles (106–105 BCE). It mentions 'Hyrcanus son of Alexander', but the reference to Alexander was probably added by Josephus since he was trying to identify the decree with Hyrcanus II. It refers to the goodwill that Hyrcanus has shown toward Athens and the individual Athenian citizens, and says he will be honoured with a golden crown and also a bronze statue to be set up in the temple of Demos and the Graces. Sadly, no such statue has so far been found by archaeologists.

16.4. *Judah Aristobulus I (104–103 BCE)*

K. Atkinson (2016) *A History of the Hasmonean State*, 47–79; **E. Dąbrowa** (2010) *The Hasmoneans and their State*, 84–85.

Sources: *War* 1.3.1-6 §§70-84; *Ant.* 13.11.1-3 §§301-19.

We have the peculiar statement of Josephus that John Hyrcanus had left his wife in charge of the kingdom. It is only made in passing, without any details, but it suggests that he did not have confidence in any of his sons to take over the office from him. Her eldest son disputed the matter with her, because she apparently would not give up her position easily. In any case, it is clear that Aristobulus soon gathered the reins of government into his own hands, imprisoning his own mother and even starving her to death. He also imprisoned his brothers, apart from Antigonus.

Whereas Josephus's accounts of the previous Hasmonaean rulers had a much shorter version in the *War*, for Aristobulus they are very much parallel and sometimes even in the same words. This suggests that Josephus is using the same source in both cases. It is only at the very end of the account that his later work has some additional information (*Ant.* 13.11.3 §§318-19). Was this source the account given by Nicolaus of Damascus? If so, why is the version in the *War* so like the one in the *Antiquities*, when normally the latter work represents a considerable elaboration? Even though Aristobulus reigned for only one year, most of Josephus's description is taken up with how he was tricked into having his brother Antigonus killed, along with an anecdote about the remarkable prognostications of Judah the Essene.

Aristobulus was apparently close to his brother Antigonus. But 'the queen and the men plotting with her' (ἡ βασιλίσσα καὶ οἱ συνεπιβουλεύοντες αὐτῇ: *Ant.* 13.11.2 §308) convinced him that Antigonus, who was evidently a formidable military leader, was planning to take over the rulership. They got Aristobulus to send for him with instructions to come unarmed; instead, the queen and her conspirators saw to it that the message received by Antigonus was to come armed and equipped to show his brother. In an underground passage on his way to see his brother, Antigonus was waylaid and killed. The deed is said to have troubled Aristobulus so much, it led to his early death. Although this is an anecdote, it has several points that require closer scrutiny.

First, the queen – Aristobulus's wife – is the leader of the conspiracy against Antigonus. Second, the tenor of the story is that Antigonus was wrongly suspected and was completely innocent – but can we be sure of that? Perhaps the queen knew something that Aristobulus did not see, and perhaps did not wish to see: that his favourite brother was actually planning a *coup d'état*. When they managed to convince Aristobulus and to have Antigonus killed, they were only protecting Aristobulus himself. Political manoeuvrings were nothing new in court life, and the Hasmonaean court had its share. Furthermore, 'the queen' may well have been the woman who was later to become the Hasmonaean ruler Alexandra Salome (see §16.5 for a discussion).

The little that we learn about Aristobulus's reign can be summarized in a few brief points:

- He was supposedly the first to actually take the diadem and title of king, previous Hasmonaean high priests having acted as rulers but not having used the actual title. This is a bit uncertain because Strabo (16.2.40) states that it was his brother and successor Alexander Jannaeus who took the title of king. This is slightly supported by the fact that Aristobulus I's coins do not contain the title 'king' on them (§2.3).
- He had the title *Philhellene*, which suggests that he contributed to certain building projects in Greek cities. There is no confirmation that he was a Philhellene, either from the *War* or other historians, though one wonders why anyone would have invented the datum if untrue.
- He took the area of Ituraea (in southern Lebanon) and required the inhabitants to adopt circumcision and live according to Jewish law. This suggests that he continued with Hyrcanus's policy of expanding the borders of Judah but also of forceable circumcision for those living in the boundaries of Judaea (§9.3).
- He minted coins, though they were very similar to his father's, and none had the title of 'king'.

This all suggests that Aristobulus's reign was significant in various ways despite its brevity. His personal character is pictured as cruel in that he supposedly starved his mother to death. Yet this picture is contradicted by Josephus's own statement that the king was of a 'kindly nature' and 'wholly given to modesty', a statement then backed up with a quotation from Strabo (*Ant.* 13.11.3 §319). Clearly, being 'kindly' is in the eye of the beholder.

16.5. *Alexander Jannaeus (103–76 BCE)*

K. Atkinson (2016) *A History of the Hasmonean State*, 47–79; **D. B. Barag** (2012) 'Alexander Jannaeus—Priest and King', in Aren M. Maeir, Jodi Magness, and Lawrence H. Schiffman (eds), *'Go Out and Study the Land' (Judges 18:2): Archaeological, Historical and Textual Studies in Honor of Hanan Eshel*, 1–5; **E. Dąbrowa** (2010) *The Hasmoneans and their State*, 85–93; **A. Fantalkin and O. Tal** (2003) 'The "Yannai Line" (*BJ* I, 99–100; *AJ* XIII, 390–91): Reality or Fiction?' *PEQ* 135: 108–23; **L. L. Grabbe** (1997a) 'The Current State of the Dead Sea Scrolls: Are There More Answers than Questions?' in S. E. Porter and C. A. Evans (eds), *The Scrolls and the Scriptures: Qumran Fifty Years After*, 54–67; **C. Rabin** (1956) 'Alexander Jannaeus and the Pharisees', *JJS* 7: 3–11; **A. Schalit** (1967–69) 'Die Eroberungen des Alexander Jannäus in Moab', *Theokratia* 1: 3–50; **M. Stern** (1981) 'Judaea and her Neighbors in the Days of Alexander Jannaeus', *The Jerusalem Cathedra* 1: 22–46; **E. Van 't Dack et al.** (1989) *The Judean-Syrian-Egyptian Conflict of 103–101 B.C.: A Multilingual Dossier concerning a 'War of Sceptres'*.

Sources: *War* 1.4.1-8 §§85-106; *Ant.* 13.12.1-16.1 §§320-406.

Josephus gives more detail about Alexander Jannaeus than any other Hasmonaean ruler. Although the *Antiquities* contains more information than the *War*, the overall picture is essentially the same, with one exception: the significance of the Pharisees (who are absent from the *War*). Most of what we learn about Alexander's reign is devoted to two issues: further expansion of territory and the internal Jewish opposition to his rule.

At Aristobulus's death his widow Alexandra Salina or Salome released the brothers from prison but appointed Alexander Jannaeus ruler. Once again this shows her political clout, which could not be overlooked. Jannaeus put to death one remaining brother, but another one was allowed to live a private life. An immediate question is whether Queen Alexandra became Jannaeus's wife. Although Josephus does not say so explicitly, he certainly implies it. K. Atkinson (2016: 85–86) has recently argued, however, that Aristobulus's widow and Jannaeus's wife were two separate individuals. He gives a number of reasons that are well taken, and of course certainty is impossible, but in the end the evidence tips the balance toward Aristobulus's widow becoming Jannaeus's wife and, later, a Hasmonaean ruler in her own right.

Atkinson is right that there is no evidence of a levirate marriage, but there is no reason why a widow could not marry a brother-in-law without its being a levirate marriage. It is true that Lev. 21.10-15 presupposes that the high priest will marry a virgin, but this was a new situation: surely the widow of a high priest could become the wife of another high priest! The main argument for identity is the name: both Salina and Salomē might be attempts to render into Greek the queen's Hebrew name, which seems to have been *Šĕlamṣiyon* (4Q331, frg. 1, col. 2, line 7; 4Q332 frg. 2, line 4; cf. *Ant.* 18.5.4 §130). Finally, Alexandra Salome seems the same type of person who would engage in radical political moves such as having Antigonus murdered and Jannaeus put on the throne.

At the beginning of his rule, Alexander Jannaeus continued the territorial expansion initiated by his father Hyrcanus I. He first besieged the city of Ptolemais on the coast. This got him involved in what has been called the 'War of the Scepters' (Van 't Dack et al. 1989). At this time, Antiochus VIII and Antiochus IX were fully engaged in a struggle over the Seleucid throne. The local ruler of Straton's Tower and Dora and perhaps also Gaza, named Zoilus, attempted to help, but more promising was Ptolemy IX Soter II (Lathyrus) (116–96 BCE) who controlled Cyprus at this time (in opposition to his mother Cleopatra III Berenice who controlled Egypt). When Ptolemy IX arrived, the people of Ptolemais had changed their mind and did not admit him and his soldiers. By his time, however, Jannaeus was apparently also attacking Gaza, and Zoilus asked Ptolemy for help. Jannaeus's response was to raise the siege of the cities and send his armies home, but at the same time to make an alliance with Ptolemy IX (with the promised payment of 400 talents). Ptolemy turned against Zoilus but then learned that Jannaeus had sent for his (Ptolemy's) mother Cleopatra III to oppose him. Ptolemy invested Ptolemais but took most of his army against Jannaeus. He captured Asochis in Galilee, though failing to take Sepphoris. Ptolemy and Jannaeus joined battle near Asophon, and the Judaean army was defeated. Ptolemy went on to ravage further Judaean territory and also to take Ptolemais.

At this point Cleopatra III intervened, concerned at the nearness of Ptolemy to Egypt, by sending a fleet and a land army under her Jewish generals Chelkias and Ananias. Ptolemy attempted to seize Egypt behind the backs of the army but failed. Apparently, the general Chelkias died in the fighting at this time. Cleopatra drove Ptolemy out of Egypt, and eventually he returned to Cyprus. Jannaeus approached Cleopatra with gifts, and her Jewish general Ananias also spoke on his behalf, so that she made an alliance with Jannaeus.

Jannaeus lost no time in continuing with his territorial conquests. His first target was Gadara, followed by Amathus. That latter – perhaps both – belonged to Theodorus son of Zenon who was a strongman in the Transjordanian area. This was followed by Raphia and Anthedon. By this time, Gaza was no longer occupied by either Cleopatra or Ptolemy. Jannaeus attacked it and took it after bitter fighting (the Gazaeans had hoped the Nabataean king Aretas would come to their aid). The exact date is uncertain, but the city probably fell about 100 BCE after a long siege.

The strife between the two Seleucid rivals to the throne came to an end in 96 BCE with the death of Antiochus VIII Gryphus at the hands of one of his ministers. Antiochus's son Seleucus VI Epiphanes Nicator succeeded him and continued the fight with Antiochus IX Cyzicenus, eventually defeating and killing him. Cyzicenus's son succeeded him as Antiochus X Eusebes Philopater, marching to Aradus where he engaged with Selecudus VI. Seleucus was defeated and fled to Mopsuestia where he died at the hands of the local people. Antiochus X now ruled over the whole of Syria. Seleucus's brother succeeded him as Antiochus XI Epiphanes Philadelphia. He attacked Antiochus X but perished with his army, and his brother Philip I Epiphanes Philadelphus succeeded him. At this point, the Ptolemies decided to add to the confusion: Ptolemy IX Soter II (called Lathyrus by Josephus) took a fourth brother and made him king in Damascus as Demetrius III Theos Philopator Soter. Antiochus X Eusebes fought both Philip and Demetrius, but then he died fighting the Parthians, and Syria was divided between Philip I and Demetrius III.

At this point in Alexander Jannaeus's reign a revolt developed. It began at the Feast of Tabernacles when he was pelted with citrons while sacrificing in his capacity as high priest. The exact reasons for this opposition are not clear. Josephus gives only the trivial charge that his mother had been a captive and, therefore, he was unfit to hold the office (since she would most likely have been raped at the time). This sounds more like a pretext than the true reason. Some have cited anecdotes from rabbinic literature (*m. Sukkah* 4.9; *b. Yoma* 26b; *b. Sukkah* 48b) that a certain high priest – who disagreed with the Pharisaic popular custom of pouring out water at Sukkot – deliberately spilled his container of water and was pelted with citrons (the people paraded with citrons during the Feast of Tabernacles). The rabbinic story from centuries later is not relevant, however, being simply an anachronistic attempt to assert rabbinic dominance over temple ritual at an early time. This was not a sectarian dispute but a serious rebellion. According to Josephus, Jannaeus contained the revolt, killing 6,000 of his opponents. Even if exaggerated, a large number of dead like this suggests an even larger number of opponents. Apparently, a major revolt against Jannaeus's rule had developed.

Having quelled the revolt, at least temporarily, Jannaeus continued with his wars of conquest. This time he moved east, taking Moab and

Galaaditis (Gilead). He also attacked the Arab king Obodas I but was decisively beaten and himself almost killed. The defeat by the Arabs seems to have encouraged his opponents, since he now had a civil war on his hands which took up the next six years. He is alleged to have killed 50,000 of his own countrymen during this time. Mercenaries were evidently important to Jannaeus for his conquests, and, perhaps even more importantly, for his suppression of the revolt. (During this time, the territory just taken in Moab and Galaaditis was lost.)

The climax came when his opponents called in Demetrius III from Damascus about 90/88 BCE (the exact date is uncertain [Ehling 2008: 244 n. 1080]). Demetrius and Jannaeus met near Shechem, with large numbers of Jews fighting on both sides, though Jannaeus's mercenaries also took part. Demetrius seems to have got the better of the contest, and Jannaeus fled. However, according to Josephus, those Judaeans who had asked Demetrius's aid now abandoned him, and many Jews rallied to Alexander. If so, the new balance of manpower meant that Demetrius had little choice but to retire from the country. There may have been another, perhaps more important, reason: Philip I was now threatening Damascus, and Demetrius needed to protect his capital. The two causes are not mutually exclusive, since it may be that Demetrius planned to move on to Jerusalem, which would have been anathema even to Jannaeus's opponents and caused them to change sides at this point.

Demetrius III besieged his brother Philip in Beroea (Aleppo), but Philip called in allies. Demetrius was defeated and captured and sent to Mithradates II (ca. 123–87 BCE), king of the Parthians, where he lived the rest of his life as an honoured captive. He never again threatened Judaea. Philip went on to take Antioch and become king of Syria, but he had a rival in his brother Antiochus XII Dionysus Epiphanes Philopator Callinicus, who took Damascus and the title of king. When Antiochus launched a campaign against the Nabataeans, however, Philip took the opportunity to come against Damascus, which was delivered up to him by the governor of the city. But he failed to reward those who delivered the city to him and was soon shut outside the walls by them. When Antiochus returned from Arabia, Damascus remained under his control.

After Demetrius III had left Judaea, the revolt against Jannaeus continued, but he brought it to a close by driving many of his opponents into the city Bemeselis and taking it. He then had 800 of the captured men crucified and their families slaughtered before their eyes, while he and his concubines feasted and watched the spectacle. The unprecedented action made a great impact on his opponents, and 8,000 of them fled the country as long as Jannaeus was alive. The incident also seems to be referred to in the Qumran commentary on Nah. 2.12 (4QpNah 1.6-7):

> Interpreted, this concerns the furious young lion [who executes revenge] on those who seek smooth things and hangs men alive, [a thing never done] formerly in Israel.

This gained him the sobriquet of 'Thracian' (because the Thracians had a reputation for cruelty).

It is important to note at this point that many writers state wrongly that Jannaeus's opponents were Pharisees. Josephus is not afraid to refer to the Pharisees, but in neither of his accounts does he suggest that Jannaeus's opponents were Pharisees or that those crucified were Pharisees. The expression 'seekers after smooth things' is often said to refer to Pharisees. This may indeed *sometimes* be the case, but there is no clear evidence that the term always has Pharisees in mind (cf. Grabbe 1997a). No doubt Pharisees were among Jannaeus's opponents and probably also made up some of those crucified, but there is simply no evidence that all those revolting against Jannaeus were Pharisees; on the contrary, the numbers alleged would suggest they encompassed a great many groups in Judaean society.

Soon after the internal revolt was put down, Judah was invaded by the army of Antiochus XII (ca. 86 BCE), whose aim seems to have been only to march through to fight against Arabia. According to Josephus (*War* 1.4.7 §§99-102; *Ant.* 13.15.1 §§389-91), Jannaeus hastily constructed a defensive ditch and wooden wall from Antipatris to Joppa, which Antiochus had no difficulty pushing through. Some remnants of this 'Jannaeus line' (or 'Yannai line') were allegedly found archaeologically (*NEAEHL* 4:1455); however, a more recent study has called this into question (Fantalkin and Tal 2003). At the moment, it looks as if no remains have been found so far by archaeologists. What Antiochus would have done to Judah had his campaign been successful is not clear, but in the event he was defeated by the Arabs and killed. Shortly afterward Aretas III the Nabataean king invaded Judah, but Jannaeus was able to come to terms with him.

With his enemies now out of the way, Jannaeus was left to get on with his external military activities for the rest of his reign. He soon developed quartan fever but nevertheless kept to the field until his death. His activities were mainly in the northeast area, near the Sea of Galilee, where he took several cities, including Pella or Dion (Dium), Gerasa (emended from Essa), Gaulana, Seleucia, 'Valley of Antiochus' and Gamala. According to Josephus (*Ant.* 13.15.4 §§395-97), at the end of Jannaeus's reign Judah's territory included cities of Syria, Idumaea and Phoenicia: on the coast, Straton's Tower, Apollonia, Joppa, Jamneia, Azotus, Gaza, Anthedon, Raphia and Rhinocorura; in the interior, Adora,

Marisa, the whole of Idumaea, Samaria, Mount Carmel, Mount Tabor, Scythopolis and Gadara; in Gaulanitis, Seleucia and Gamala; in Moab: Essebon (Heshbon), Medaba, Lemba, Oronaim, Agalain, Thoma, Zoara, the Valley of the Cilicians and Pella. If this is correct, Jannaeus's territory was the largest extent of Israel since the time of the monarchy. While besieging the fortress of Ragaba in Transjordan, Alexander Jannaeus died at the age of 49, after reigning 27 years.

At this point in the narrative, there is a significant difference between Josephus's two accounts. The *Antiquities* claims that before his death, Jannaeus advised his wife Alexandra Salome to make peace with the Pharisees, grant them a certain amount of power and pretend to have disapproved of her husband's activities. The result was that they gave the king a magnificent funeral with many eulogies. This is another incident that has led some scholars to infer that most of the opponents of Alexander were Pharisees. Against this are several considerations: (1) this is simply an anecdote of doubtful historicity; it does not sound very likely, whether for Jannaeus, his wife, or the Pharisees; one suspects that the death-bed scene was recounted (or even invented?) by Josephus to explain the influence of the Pharisees over Alexandra Salome during her rule; (2) the *War* not only makes no mention of this death-bed incident but makes no mention of the Pharisees at all during Alexander's reign; (3) the *Antiquities* mention the Pharisees only at this point in the narrative of Jannaeus; despite this conclusion to his account in the *Antiquities*, Josephus himself does not otherwise refer to the Pharisees during Alexander's reign; on the contrary, he at no point suggests that those who opposed, fought and were killed by Alexander were specifically Pharisees (cf. also Rabin 1956). Therefore, one can only conclude that Pharisaic opponents – which most probably existed – were only a part of the opposition against him.

16.6. *Alexandra Salome (76–67 BCE)*

K. Atkinson (2016) *A History of the Hasmonean State*, 134–45; **E. Baltrusch** (2001) 'Königin Salome Alexandra (76–67 v. Chr.) und die Verfassung des Hasmonäischen Staates', *Historia* 50: 163–79; **E. Dąbrowa** (2010) *The Hasmoneans and their State*, 93–97.

Sources: *War* 1.5.1-4 §§107-19; *Ant.* 13.16.1-6 §§407-32.

The one feature which stands out in both of Josephus's accounts is the extent to which the Pharisees dominated the reign of Alexandra. In much later rabbinic literature there were still preserved traditions of the reign of Alexandra as a golden age (e.g., *b. Taan.* 23a). Although the *Antiquities* says that Alexandra 'restored' (ἀποκατέστησεν) the Pharisaic regulations which John Hyrcanus had abolished (*Ant.* 13.16.2 §408), the *War* knows nothing of this. As already noted (§16.5), there is good reason to question the extent of Pharisaic influence in Alexander Jannaeus's time, and the ability of the Pharisees to impose their own regulations as law probably originated under Alexandra, as Josephus's earlier account seems to indicate (*War* 1.5.2 §110). Under Alexandra, the Pharisees clearly possessed considerable political clout, including the ability to get rid of a number of their enemies. It finally reached the stage that some eminent citizens (δυνατοί) appealed directly to Alexandra (with the aid of her son Aristobulus) for a guarantee of safety. A long section in *Antiquities*, full of pathos, looks like a rhetorical expansion of a shorter statement in *War*. But the Pharisaic attempt to get rid of some of Jannaeus's ministers seems real enough. To appease those loyal to Jannaeus and also herself, she allowed some of the importunates to guard certain of her fortresses (except Hyrcania, Alexandrium and Machaerus).

Alexandra herself was evidently a good administrator, apart from the question of the Pharisees. She doubled the size of the Jewish military forces, in addition to keeping a large mercenary contingent, and as a result was able to maintain peaceful relations with the surrounding rulers. She also concluded terms with Tigranes of Armenia when he was besieging Cleopatra Selene in Ptolemais: evidently, Alexandra supposed that Judaea might be his next target. The treaty was never tested, though, since Tigranes had to return quickly to Armenia when Mithradates VI Eupator (ca. 115–63 BCE) of Pontus retreated there after being defeated by the Romans under Lucius Licinius Lucullus.

The one thorn in Alexandra's side was her son Aristobulus. The elder son Hyrcanus had been appointed high priest on Alexander Jannaeus's death and would have been the natural heir to his mother. Yet Aristobulus seems to have been the more dynamic of the two, and there were doubts about Hyrcanus's ability and even desire to rule. When Alexandra became ill, Aristobulus took his chance. He occupied 22 fortresses in which a number of his supporters had been made guards, hired a mercenary army and proclaimed himself king. He apparently used the pretext that if he did not, the Pharisees would seize power on his mother's death. Alexandra quickly responded to this by imprisoning Aristobulus's wife and children, but her illness prevented her from taking further action. As Aristobulus was amassing a large army, she died at the age of 73 after a reign of 9 years.

The few evaluative statements made by Josephus up to this point indicate that Alexandra was a good administrator but was dominated by the Pharisees. At the end of the account in the *Antiquities*, however, he gives a lengthy assessment, mainly centring on the despotism of her rule and the lack of inhibitions normally associated with a woman. Exactly what he has in mind is not clear, though he does refer to her siding with those 'hostile to her family'. Are these the Pharisees? Is his concluding verdict mainly hostility to her as a female ruler? Is he using a different source here? It is difficult to know, but it seems somewhat at odds with the account of her reign he had given in the *War* and up to this point in *Antiquities*.

16.7. Conclusions

This chapter has covered a fair stretch of Hasmonaean history. Some of the main points are the following;

- The death of Judas was a major blow to the Maccabaean cause. It appears, however, that the people of Judaea had got mainly what they wanted: a restoration of all customary rights (religious and otherwise), a restoration of the temple and cult and an acceptable Aaronic high priest. There was little appetite at this time to continue the conflict with the Seleucid empire.
- Jonathan, who was Judas's successor, was on the run with his brothers and a small band of followers for many years. Yet he proved himself to be a shrewd and far-sighted leader. With time he succeeded in winning a few battles against Seleucid troops and securing a truce which allowed a period of years to recuperate. During that time he seems to have advanced his claim to leadership among the Judaean population more widely. But his real chance came when a rival claimant to the Seleucid crown arrived. By playing one off against the other, he gained the high priesthood and a significant leadership position vis-à-vis the Seleucids, as well over his own people. He managed to take over a number of Seleucid fortresses, but his main accomplishment was that he was well on his way to achieving the apparent Hasmonaean aim of Judaean independence, when an exceptional miscalculation on his part ended his career and life.
- Simon had gained a good deal of experience and prestige as Jonathan's lieutenant. One researcher has recently argued that Simon was planning a coup against Jonathan all along. If so, Jonathan's capture and death delivered the opportunity he wanted, because Jonathan's sons were given over to Tryphon in an attempt

to free Jonathan, but to no avail (apparently the sons were also executed). Whether planned or not, Simon was now able to finish what Jonathan seems to have been on the way to accomplishing: the formal independence of Judaea. This happened shortly after Simon took over, in the 170th year SE, when Judah was declared independent and Simon and his family were acclaimed by the population as their saviours and leaders. The reality was different: the Jews were hardly independent of Seleucid rule, and continued to pay tribute or at least to have Seleucid demands for tribute and military support for many years. But the symbolic value was great and put a new vision of leadership in place, one based on deeds rather than heredity. Simon also managed finally to take back the Akra into the hands of his followers.

- It was under John Hyrcanus rather than Simon that the Seleucid yoke was finally thrown off. It took time, but he reached that goal. Although Jonathan and Simon had begun to expand Judaean territory, John Hyrcanus moved systematically north into Samaria and the Galilee, south into Idumaea and perhaps into Transjordan. Whether he forcibly converted the Idumaeans is doubtful, but whatever attempts he made to join them to the Jewish people seems to have worked. He was also the first to mint his own coins. The Hasmonaeans had always had Jewish opponents, but most of these had been swept away with military success. But significant opposition now developed among the people, though we are not given much in the way of detail. In any case, Hyrcanus seems to have been able to check it.
- Hyrcanus's son Aristobulus I reigned only a year. He supposedly brought the Ituraeans into the fold of Judaism by forceable conversion, but neither the archaeology nor other literary sources support this. He did take the title king, according to Josephus, though his coins do not indicate this.
- Aristobulus's brother Alexander Jannaeus took the throne after him. He went on a campaign of territorial expansion and extended the limits of Jewish rule the widest since the time of the monarchy. But he had considerable opposition both internally and externally, and spent most of his adult life in military campaigning. The opposition from his own people was considerable, and he killed many fellow Jews over the years of his reign. Among his opponents were apparently the Pharisees, though they constituted only a part of the opposition. But it put them in a position of strength by the end of Jannaeus's rule.

- Although not certain, it looks as if Alexandra Salome was successively the wife and queen of Aristobulus I, Alexander Jannaeus, and then ruler in her own right. She was a good administrator and generally a successful ruler, but it is alleged – evidently correctly – that she was dominated by the Pharisees. Her reign, however, was also blighted by the conflict between her two sons, the younger and most ambitious of whom wanted to be high priest and ruler. This would have far-reaching consequences after Alexandra's death.
- A feature of Hasmonaean rule was the missions to Rome, seeking a treaty of alliance and friendship. Although once doubted, this now appears to have begun with Judas himself. Jonathan renewed it, and Simon apparently sent more than one mission. John Hyrcanus also renewed the treaty, but then subsequent rulers do not appear to have made the effort. It has sometimes been suggested that various things happened to Hasmonaean advantage because of the threat of Roman intervention on their side. But this is not the way the Senate acted through several centuries of the Republic. They were quite willing to issue words of encouragement and support, and occasionally even to write letters, but they took action only when there was a strong reason because of the needs or advantage of Rome herself. The eastern kings knew this, and it is doubtful if the Jewish treaties with Rome ever served as a deterrent against planned action by them against Judaea; however, the treaties were very useful internally, which is why the first Hasmonaeans pursued them.

Chapter 17

END OF THE HASMONAEAN KINGDOM
AND THE BEGINNING OF ROMAN DOMINATION
(67–40 BCE)

N. Sharon (2017) *Judea under Roman Domination: The First Generation of Statelessness and its Legacy*.

The death of Alexandra Salome marked a watershed in Hasmonaean rule. The accession of her two sons was the beginning of the end: their rivalry rapidly led to Roman domination of the region. It was probably inevitable that Rome would conquer the region about this time, but there seems no doubt that Aristobulus II and Hyrcanus II hastened the process in their struggle for the leadership of Judah.

17.1. *The Roman Republic in the First Century BCE to the Roman Civil War (100–49 BCE)*

E. Baltrusch (2011) *Caesar und Pompeius*; *CAH*[1], vol. 10 (1934) *The Augustan Empire, 44 B.C.–A.D. 70*; *CAH*[2], vol. 9 (1994) *The Last Age of the Roman Republic, 146–43 B.C.*; **M. Cary and H. H. Scullard** (1975) *A History of Rome*; **M. H. Crawford** (1978) *The Roman Republic*; **M. Gelzer** (1968) *Caesar: Politician and Statesman*; **idem** (2005) *Pompeius: Lebensbild eines Römers*; **T. Holland** (2003) *Rubicon: The Triumph and Tragedy of the Roman Republic*; **C. Meier** (1995) *Caesar*; **N. Rosenstein** (2012) *Rome and the Mediterranean 290 to 146 BC*; **H. H. Scullard** (1982) *From the Gracchi to Nero*; **R. Seager** (2002) *Pompey the Great: A Political Biography*; **C. Steel** (2013) *The End of the Roman Republic 146 to 44 BC*; **H. Swain and M. E. Davies** (2010) *Aspects of Roman History, 82 BC–AD 14*; **E. Will** (1982) *Histoire politique du monde hellénistique (323–30 av. J.-C.): Tome II*.

Some of the earlier history of Rome, especially in the East, was surveyed in §13.3. The weaknesses of the Roman Republican system of government had already begun to show up soon after the Third Punic War, even though Rome continued to triumph abroad through its military might and other facilities. There were the attempted reforms of the Gracchi brothers in 130s and 120s and their subsequent murder by members of wealthy conservative Senatorial families. But this social class was showing itself unable to resolve the problems that were coming to face the Roman Republic, both within and without. One of these problems was the Social War (91–89 BCE) with the Italian allies. A promising young politician, C. Marius, was voted into the office of consul multiple times, in hopes of solving some of the difficulties. When Sulla was appointed by the Senate to campaign in the east against Mithradates, an armed conflict broke out between his faction and that of Marius. Sulla eventually won, became dictator in 81 BCE, and took revenge on his opponents. Shortly afterward he retired and died, and many of his reforms were reversed.

But the social tensions continued, by which time the main actors of the Roman Civil War were on the scene, including Pompey, Crassus, Cicero, and Julius Caesar. Because piracy had become a real headache for the entire Mediterranean area, the Senate finally decided to do something and commissioned Pompey to deal with it. When this was accomplished, he was then sent against Mithradates in 66 BCE, which led to confrontation with the situation in Judaea. Not long after Pompey's conquest of the East, the widening cracks in Roman society and politics led finally to collapse and confrontation with his rival Caesar. The Roman Civil War, often dated from 49 BCE, continued more or less until 31 BCE, i.e., from the breakout of open war between Julius Caesar and Pompey to the triumph of Octavian over Mark Antony. Yet this was only the last episode in what had been almost a century of civil unrest in Rome.

While Pompey was fighting in the Greek areas, the political scene in Rome was dominated by such individuals as Julius Caesar, Crassus and Cicero. A major issue was the bad feelings between the Knights (*equites*) and the Senate, which Cicero was trying to mediate. Pompey's return to Rome from the East was followed shortly afterward in 60 with the formation of what is often called the First Triumvirate between Pompey, Crassus and Caesar (thought by Cicero and others to be the main cause of the Civil War a decade later). Caesar was elected consul for the first time in 59 BCE and secured command of all Gaul and Illyricum. After he took up his post, political infighting seemed to be presaging a major breach between the triumvirs; however, the triumvirate was renewed in a conference at Luca in 55.

The First Triumvirate broke up in 54 when Crassus was killed in a foolish attack on Parthian territory. Also, the personal bond between Caesar and Pompey was severed when Pompey's wife (Caesar's daughter) died. The stage was now set for confrontation between the two. Caesar's war in Gaul had been a resounding victory. Now, with his many military successes, it became clear that Caesar's imminent return to Rome could provoke physical conflict with Pompey. Thus, a motion was passed by the Senate in late 50 that both individuals should give up their military commands. When extremists among the conservatives refused to accept this, Pompey was called on to come to the rescue of the Republic. Not surprisingly, Caesar was not ready to accept Pompey as the dominant politician and tried to negotiate a more satisfactory solution. Finally, the Senate issued an ultimatum to Caesar: his response was the famous crossing of the Rubicon river which initiated the Civil War in early 49 BCE.

17.2. *Aristobulus II and Hyrcanus II (67–63 BCE)*

K. Atkinson (2016) *A History of the Hasmonean State*, 146–57; **E. Dąbrowa** (2010) *The Hasmoneans and their State*, 96–102.

Sources: *War* 1.6.1-7.7 §§120-58; *Ant.* 14.1.1-4.5 §§1-79.

According to *Ant.* 14.1.2 §4 (cf. *War* 1.6.1 §120) Hyrcanus II took the throne in the 177 Olympiad when Q. Hortensias and Q. Metellus Creticus were Roman consuls. That would be 70–69 BCE, two or three years before Alexandra died. In spite of this, Aristobulus II was not ready to accept Hyrcanus as king and declared war on his brother as soon as their mother was in her grave. They met in battle near Jericho, and Aristobulus quickly attacked and defeated Hyrcanus, who took refuge in the Akra. Using Aristobulus's family as a bargaining chip, he arranged a deal in which he was permitted to live unharmed as a private citizen while the rulership went to his brother. Although such is not made explicit at this point in the narrative, statements elsewhere indicate that Aristobulus also obtained the office of high priest, which had previously been given to Hyrcanus II (*Ant.* 14.6.1 §97; 20.10.4 §§243-44).

At this juncture Josephus introduces a character by the name of Antipater whom he identifies as an Idumaean (but see §17.9.1), whose father Antipas had been appointed governor of Idumaea by Alexander Jannaeus. Antipater stirred up the leading Jews against Aristobulus. After a time, he also persuaded Hyrcanus that he had made a mistake in giving up the kingship and indeed was in danger of being executed by Aristobulus.

Receiving a guarantee of safety from the Nabataean ruler Aretas III in Petra, Hyrcanus fled to the Arab. Hyrcanus promised to return to Aretas twelve cities that Jannaeus had supposedly taken from Nabataea. He thus managed to obtain the aid of an army (allegedly of 50,000) under Aretas, and attacked Aristobulus, defeated him and besieged him in Jerusalem to which he had fled. This was apparently at Passover time (*Ant.* 14.2.1-2 §§21, 25). The outcome of the siege was still in the balance when the Romans intervened.

The Roman general Pompey had been fighting against the Armenians. The Armenian king Tigranes surrendered in 66 BCE. Pompey then sent his lieutenant Scaurus to Syria. As soon as he arrived in Damascus, Scaurus heard of the Jewish civil war and marched south. Delegates from both the sons of Alexandra met him with bribes, but Scaurus sided with Aristobulus (who supposedly gave the larger bribe) and forced Aretas to raise the siege of Jerusalem. Scaurus returned to Damascus, but shortly afterward Aristobulus defeated Hyrcanus in battle at a place called Papyron (Antipater's brother fell in the battle). This was the way things stood until Pompey himself arrived in Syria where he was entreated by both sides. Also appearing was a delegation from 'the Jewish nation' (τῶν Ἰουδαίων...τὸ ἔθνος) [*Ant.* 14.3.2 §41]; Diodorus [40.2] says this was more than 200 of the leading men), asking that Judaea be allowed to continue as a theocracy without the high priest also acting as a king. After hearing the different sides, Pompey delayed a decision, saying he first needed to deal with the Nabataeans. This was too much for Aristobulus (who had presented a large bribe to Pompey), and he set off for Judaea. Taking this as an insult, Pompey followed after him with a large force and caught up with him at the fortress of Alexandrium (Alexandreion). At first the two leaders negotiated, then Pompey ordered Aristobulus to give up his fortresses. Aristobulus reluctantly sent instructions to the various commanders as required by Pompey but then himself withdrew to Jerusalem and prepared for war.

Pompey marched after him immediately, before he had time for much preparation. Aristobulus realized the folly of resistance and met Pompey on the last leg of his march, between Jericho and Jerusalem, promising money as well as entry into Jerusalem. Aristobulus's followers had a different idea, however, and shut the city against the Romans. The people of the city were divided between the supporters of Aristobulus and those of Hyrcanus. The former withdrew into the temple, cutting the bridge to the upper city, while the latter opened the gates to Pompey. The siege of the temple lasted three months, apparently until about mid-summer (on details of the fall of Jerusalem, see §1.3.5.1). The Romans were assisted by Hyrcanus and his followers. The Roman army also took advantage of the sabbath to advance their siege works, since the Jews would not fight if not directly attacked. During this time and even in the final assault when many were being killed, the priests continued their sacrificial duties. When the Romans finally broke through, many of the defenders were slaughtered by their fellow Jews who were adherents of Hyrcanus. Supposedly, 12,000 Jews died. Pompey and others of the Romans entered the temple area and even went inside the Holy of Holies. This may have been partly out of curiosity but also to demonstrate that the Romans were now in charge; however, the temple itself was respected: neither the vessels nor the temple treasure was touched, and the temple was cleansed and the cult resumed the next day at Pompey's command.

Thus, Judaea as an independent kingdom came to an end. N. Sharon (2017) has made the point that Pompey's conquest of Judaea in 63 BCE should be viewed as a watershed no less significant than the fall of Jerusalem in 70 CE. The impact of the loss of sovereignty and the beginning of Roman domination meant that the roots of the 66–70 CE revolt lay already in this period. Although Judaea was to be a 'friendly kingdom' (essentially a vassal kingdom – §18.4.1) of Rome for many years under Herod the Great and Agrippa I, it was not again to be a sovereign nation for another two millennia. The territory gained by successive Hasmonaean rulers was taken away to leave only the area which roughly made up the province of Judah under the Babylonians and Persians. Although Hyrcanus was restored to the high priesthood, he did not have the title of king, and a heavy tribute was imposed on the country. In short, despite the positive evaluation of Rome in 1 Maccabees, by this time the Judaeans as a whole had come to hate the Romans. Little good came from Rome to Jerusalem in the next century to make them change that attitude.

17.3. Pompey's Settlement in Judaea and the Region

D. C. Braund (1983) 'Gabinius, Caesar, and the *publicani* of Judaea', *Klio* 65: 241–44; **A. H. M. Jones** (1971) *The Cities of the Eastern Roman Provinces*; **B. Kanael** (1956) 'The Partition of Judea by Gabinius', *IEJ* 6: 98–106; **D. Magie** (1950) *Roman Rule in Asia Minor, to the End of the Third Century after Christ*; **A. Momigliano** (1934b) 'Richerche sull' organizzazione della Giudea sotto il dominio romano (63 a. C.–70 d. C.)', *Annali della Scuola Normale Superiore di Pisa*, Classe di Lettere 3, 183–221, 347–96; **A. N. Sherwin-White** (1984) *Roman Foreign Policy in* the East, 168 B.C. to A.D. 1, 226–34; **E. M. Smallwood** (1967) 'Gabinius' Organisation of Palestine', *JJS* 18: 89–92; **R. S. Williams** (1978) 'The Role of Amicitia in the Career of A. Gabinius (Cos. 58)', *Phoenix* 32: 195–210.

From its position as an independent state, with considerable territory, resources and even prestige, Judaea had an ignominious fall. After his conquest, Pompey went about reorganizing the administration of the various areas in what is known as his notorious 'settlement of the East' (Magie 1950: 1:268–78). Of the conquered territories, most lost out in some way, but none more so than Judaea. Once more a province, Judaea was not attached to Syria as might have been the case, but was allowed to maintain a separate identity with her own rule. Also, Hyrcanus retained the office of high priest which included some civil authority, but the country itself was reduced essentially to the old boundaries of Judah as they had been in Persian times, and a Roman governor was appointed (cf. Jones 1971: 256–59). On the other hand, the conquered Hellenistic cities gained: they were restored to their old constitutions for the most part, though for many of them this came about in practical terms only later under Gabinius: on the coast: Dora, Straton's Tower, Apollonia, Joppa, Azotus, Anthedon, Gaza, Raphia, Ascalon; in the interior and Transjordan: Marisa (in Idumaea), Samaria, Scythopolis, Arethusa, Jamnia, Abila, Hippus, Gadara, Pella and Dium. A number of these cities in the interior were grouped together with others which had not been under Jewish rule to form the league known as the Decapolis.

Pompey's settlement may have seemed very unfortunate from the Jewish point of view at the time, but it was mild compared to the drastic further reorganization which came about under Gabinius. The significance of this further division is not explained by Josephus (*War.* 1.8.5 §170; *Ant.* 14.5.4 §91), but it has usually been interpreted as a way of bringing the potentially rebellious province to heel by a process of divide and conquer (Schalit 1969: 30–33; *WHJP* 7:39–43). The continual rebellions led by Aristobulus and his sons (§17.4; §17.6) clearly had a good deal of popular support. Instead of quietly shouldering the yoke of Roman rule, Judaea looked to be a continuing problem. Something had to be done, and the solution was that which had already worked in Macedonia. From the conqueror's point of view it was effective, though its consequences for the conquered could eventually be disastrous, bringing economic ruin by commercial isolation of the various parts of the country.

Gabinius's solution was to divide the country into five administrative councils (*sunodoi, sunedria*), with centres at Jerusalem, Jericho, Amathus in Transjordan, Sepphoris in Galilee and 'Gadara'. The identification of the last-named city is disputed: Kanael argues that it should logically be a city of Idumaea, perhaps a corruption of Adora (1956: 102–4), though this assumes that Idumaea was included in the territory left to Judaea, which some scholars do not accept. Others would read 'Gazara' or Gezer (cf. SCHÜRER 1:268 n. 5). As for the makeup of these councils, Josephus does not discuss them in detail, though he states that the country was once more an 'aristocracy' (*Ant.* 11.4.8 §111, probably meaning a theocracy, i.e., a political entity governed by the priesthood), which pleased many Jews. Thus, the membership of the councils was presumably made up of individuals (many of priestly origin) willing to cooperate with Roman rule.

B. Kanael has argued against the explanation that it was a case of 'divide and rule'. Far from being an attempt to cow the Jews, it was meant as a way of unifying them behind Hyrcanus. Gabinius was planning to invade Parthia and needed a united Judaea. The five-fold division was a means of providing administrative centres because of the growing opposition to Hyrcanus and support for the sons of Aristobulus. One argument in support of Kanael's thesis is that the divisions of Gabinius seem to correspond basically to those under Herod's later rule. However, regardless of whose explanation is correct, Gabinius left his arrangements in effect for only a few years, perhaps because they were not succeeding. After a further revolt in 55 BCE, he more or less turned the administration over to Antipater: 'having gone to Jerusalem, Gabinius reorganized the government (πολιτείον) according to Antipater's wishes' (*War.* 1.8.7 §178; cf. *Ant.* 14.6.4 §103).

Judaea continued to pay tribute (§5.2). It has often been argued (following Momigliano 1934: 187–89) that Gabinius took the process of tax collection out of the hands of the Roman tax farmers (*publicani*) and made them the responsibility of the Jews themselves. However, it now seems likely that the *publicani* were not removed until later, probably by a decree of Caesar about 47 BCE (Braund 1983). In any case, Gabinius seems to have shown a certain restraint in his administration and not to have robbed the province, for Josephus commends him: 'Gabinius had accomplished great and splendid works during his governorship' (*Ant.* 14.6.4 §104). This is a rather odd conclusion in light of the fact that when he returned to Rome, Gabinius was charged with extorting 100 million drachmas from Syria! (Dio 39.55; see next section [§17.4]).

17.4. *Jews under Roman Administration: Scaurus, Gabinius, Crassus and Cassius*

Sources: *War* 1.8.1-9 §§159-82; *Ant.* 14.5.1-7.3 §§80-122.

With his reorganization Pompey felt his work here was done. He turned the whole region over to Scaurus and made his way back to Rome, taking Aristobulus and his sons with him as captives (though one son Alexander escaped on the way). Pompey had been planning to inspect the Nabataean situation when interrupted by the events in Judaea. Now, Scaurus picked up the military moves that Pompey had not managed to complete. The main one of these was to get control of the Nabataeans. When he marched against Petra, however, his men lacked sufficient food. Antipater and Hyrcanus stepped in and provided grain and other provisions from Judaea. Scaurus then sent Antipater to negotiate with King Aretas (III?), persuading him to pay 300 talents as tribute so that the Romans would leave him alone. (These are only two of the far-sighted actions that Antipater took, but it was characteristic of him that he benefitted so often from such opportunities.) In the meantime, Aristobulus's son Alexander had raised a small army and was threatening Hyrcanus by making raids on Judaea. Scaurus's term of office came to an end in ca. 61 BCE. We know that two further governors came and went (though Josephus omits the information): Marcius Philippus (61–60 BCE) and Lentulus Marcellinus (59–58 BCE) (Appian, *Syr.* 8.51; Cicero, *Pro Sestio* 43).

Next, Gabinius, a former consul, was appointed governor (στρατηγός) of the region (57–54 BCE). In contrast with Antipater's perspicuity, the shortsightedness of the Hasmonaeans was soon demonstrated in several attempts by Aristobulus and his son Alexander (and later Alexander's brother Antigonus) to lead revolts and re-establish their rule. By this time Alexander was trying to rebuild the wall in Jerusalem and refortify the city. When the Romans put a stop to this, Alexander raised a larger force (said to have been 10,000 heavy infantry and 1,500 cavalry) and set up fortifications at Alexandrium, Machaerus and Hyrcania. Gabinias defeated them, not only with Roman troops (partly led by Mark Antony), but also a Jewish force (including Antipater's picked troops) commanded by Malichus and Peitholaus. Alexander fled to Alexandriun, where he was besieged and eventually surrendered, including all the fortresses. Hyrcanus could now take up his place as high priest in the temple. Garbinius rebuilt or repaired many cities damaged in the fighting, including Scythopolis, Samaria, Anthedon, Apollonia, Jamnia, Raphia, Marisa, 'Gamala' (probably Gezer), Azotus, Adora and Gaza.

The next year (56 BCE?) Aristobulus himself, along with his son Antigonus, escaped from Rome and led a new rebellion. As a former priest-king he had no trouble in gaining a large following. Indeed, Peitholaus the 'legate' (*hupostratēgos*) of Jerusalem, who had earlier led Antipater's picked troops against Alexander (above), deserted to him with a thousand men. Aristobulus intended to refortify Alexandrium, but Gabinius's army (under Sisenna, Antony and Servilius) came against him too quickly. Aristobulus dismissed all his following who did not have the proper equipment but still alleged to have had 8,000 armed troops to take a stand against the Romans, indicating the large following collected together in this short time. Unfortunately, the outcome was completely predictable, and Aristobulus retreated to Machaerus where he and Antigonus were taken prisoner and returned to Rome. The two sons (Alexander and Antigonus) were released by the Senate to return to Judaea, however, because Gabinius had promised this to their mother when negotiating to have the fortresses surrendered.

This soon proved to be a mistake, because Alexander revolted a second time. The context of this revolt was an incident that landed Gabinius in trouble back in Rome (Dio 39.55; Josephus, *War* 1.8.7 §§175-77). Ptolemy XII had been deposed by his daughter Berenice IV and wanted the throne back. The Roman Senate opposed this and was apparently backed by a Sibylline oracle. When Ptolemy promised a large sum of money to Gabinius, however, the latter decided to intervene in defiance of the Senate. He took an army to Egypt (55 BCE), with the assistance of Hyrcanus and Antipater, and restored Ptolemy XII to the rule Egypt (who promptly executed his daughter). While Gabinius was thus engaged in Egypt, Alexander took the opportunity to instigate another revolt. Antipater once again acted as mediator and managed to persuade many Jews to abandon their following of Alexander; nevertheless, the latter was still left with a large army (said to be 30,000, no doubt grossly exaggerated) with which he met the Romans near Mt Tabor, but again it was to no avail.

Gabinius then proceeded to Jerusalem, organized the government according to Antipater's desires and marched against the Nabataeans, defeating them. His governorship was now at an end, and he returned to Rome. Here, according to Cassius Dio (39.55) he was charged with the extortion of 100 million drachmas from Syria but was acquitted, allegedly through bribery and influence. Lesser charges were brought, however, and he was found guilty and exiled (though only for a short time, again because of friends in high places).

The next governor of Judaea was Crassus (54–53 BCE), the triumvir, noted by Josephus only for robbing the temple of its gold (though curiously he says nothing about Gabinius's alleged extortions, noted above). Unlike Pompey who had not touched the temple treasure or precious vessels, Crassus made off with 2,000 talents in money as well as the rest of the gold in the sanctuary. The purpose of this appropriation was to help pay for Crassus's ill-conceived expedition against Parthia where he met his death (53 BCE). He was succeeded by his quaester Cassius (53–51 BCE), who had survived the expedition against the Parthians. Cassius's main concern was to hold back the Parthians who were now pushing west as a result of their victory over Crassus. Josephus relates two things about Cassius: he took the city of Tarichaeae in Galilee and enslaved 30,000 Jews, and he executed the turncoat Peitholaus at the instigation of Antipater. The exact reason for the first action is not given, though one wonders whether it might not be related to the second, for Peitholaus's supposed crime was that he was trying to continue the revolt of Aristobulus by inciting his followers. Was the taking of Tarichaeae a part of the suppression of this revolt?

17.5. *First Phase of the Roman Civil War to the Death of Caesar (49–44 BCE)*

[For bibliography, see §17.1.]

With the Senate behind him and control of Italy and most of the Empire, Pompey may have seemed in a strong position. Caesar had only one legion and control of Gaul. However, Pompey was hampered by having only two legions in Italy, and they were legions which Caesar had loaned to him initially and thus of doubtful loyalty. Caesar quickly added further troops when he defeated the governor of Transalpine Gaul. Attempts at negotiation failed, and Pompey retreated to Greece, which left Caesar in control of Italy. Caesar's first task was to take Spain, which he did quickly, though in the meantime the task force sent to Africa by him was soundly defeated. Caesar returned to Rome, where he was given a dictatorship which enabled him to enact certain necessary measures, but he then gave it up after holding it only 11 days.

When Caesar crossed to Greece early in 48, Pompey had assembled a large force of both troops and ships. The first engagements were indecisive, partly because Pompey could be resupplied by ships whereas Caesar had to find provisions by land. The decisive battle was at Pharsalus. Pompey was defeated but escaped to Egypt with a small company; however, he was killed as soon as he landed by the men of Ptolemy XII. Caesar followed and spent the winter in Alexandria where Cleopatra VII, the sister of Ptolemy and joint ruler, became his mistress. At first Ptolemy supported Caesar, but then turned against him. In the spring of 47 enough troops had joined Caesar to enable him to defeat Ptolemy and replace him with his younger brother Ptolemy XIII who now reigned jointly with Cleopatra. After a brief campaign in Asia Minor, Caesar returned to

Rome in mid-47. (For events in Judah during the fight between Caesar and Pompey, see §17.6 below.)

Caesar, now dictator a second time, still had Pompeian forces in Africa to deal with. The campaign against them was conducted in the winter and spring of 46, followed by one against Pompey's sons in Spain toward the end of the year. Caesar's return to Rome was his final one. After being elected consul (for the fifth time), along with Antony for the year 44, he was appointed dictator for life. A month later he was killed in a conspiracy which aimed for the restoration of the Republic, an impossible ideal.

17.6. *Judah during the First Phase of the Roman Civil War: Julius Caesar (49–44 BCE)*

[For bibliography, see §17.1.]

Sources: *War* 1.9.1-10.4 §§183-203; *Ant.* 14.7.4-9.1 §§123-57.

When the Roman Civil War began in 49 BCE, with Julius Caesar's crossing of the Rubicon and Caesar's and Pompey's opposing each other, Caesar released Aristobulus from prison with the intention of putting him at the head of two legions; the plan was thwarted, however, when adherents of Pompey poisoned him before he even left Rome. Likewise, his son Alexander was executed in Antioch by the proconsul of Syria Q. Metellius Scipio (49–48 BCE) at Pompey's orders, but Antigonus and his two sisters were taken under the protection of Ptolemy, king of Calchis (*Ant.*14.7.4 §§126; *War* 1.9.2 §§185-86). Josephus says nothing about the activities of Antipater and Hyrcanus at this time; perhaps they wisely bided their time to see which way the war went. After Pompey's death in 48, though, Antipater quite decisively took the side of Caesar and distinguished himself in aiding Mithridates of Pergamum, the leader of the Roman forces, to capture Egypt. This was done by diplomacy in securing Arab and Syrian aid, and in persuading the Jews in the district of Onias to support Caesar and allow his army through, as well as by military prowess in which Antipater showed both outstanding personal bravery and strategic ability in battle. According to Josephus, Mithridates and Antipater commanded different wings of the army when they met the enemy at the 'Camp of the Jews' ('Ιουδαίων στρατόπεδον: *War* 1.9.4 §§191-92; *Ant.* 14.8.2 §§133-36), and Mithridates even credited Antipater with winning the battle when reporting to Caesar (although Josephus no doubt exaggerates here, Antipater's military skill and personal courage certainly came to Roman attention). Apparently at this time, or probably earlier, Antipater was appointed governor (ἐπιμελητής) of the Jews (*Ant.* 14.8.1 §127).

Caesar rewarded Antipater and Hyrcanus for their usefulness. Hyrcanus was confirmed in the priesthood and Antipater given Roman citizenship and exemption from taxation. These honours were increased when Antigonus, Aristobulus's son, foolishly accused Antipater and Hyrcanus before Caesar: Antipater was made 'procurator' (ἐπίτροπος) of Judaea. Although only mentioned in a decree, Hyrcanus was apparently also raised to ethnarch of Judah by Caesar (*Ant.* 14.10.2 §190, but he seems to have been called 'king' by the Jews themselves [*War* 1.10.4 §§202-3; 1.10.9 §214; *Ant.* 14.8.5 §§148, 151; 14.9.1 §157; 14.9.3 §165; 14.9.4 §§168, 172]). Permission was also given to rebuild the walls of Jerusalem, which had been in ruins since Pompey's siege. Caesar supposedly commanded that these honours were to be recorded in the Roman Capitol, according to Josephus, yet the decree that he quotes was apparently one relating to Hyrcanus's grandfather John Hyrcanus (*Ant.* 14.8.5 §§144-48; see further at §16.3.5).

17.7. Next Phase of the Roman Civil War: Octavian and Antony (44–40 BCE)

R. Alston (2015) *Rome's Revolution: Death of the Republic and Birth of the Empire*; **J. Bleicken** (2015) *Augustus: The Biography*; **W. Eck** (2007) *The Age of Augustus*; **A. Goldsworthy** (2014) *Augustus: From Revolutionary to Emperor*; **M. Goodman** (1997) *The Roman World 44 BC–AD 180*; **B. Levick** (2010) *Augustus: Image and Substance*; **F. Millar and E. Segal (eds)** (1984) *Caesar Augustus: Seven Aspects*; **J. S. Richardson** (2012) *Augustan Rome 44 BC to AD 14*.

After the assassination of Julius Caesar, Antony as consul led the opposition to the conspirators. They had sufficient support to prevent any immediate retribution, but Antony skilfully manipulated public opinion against them by publishing Caesar's will and by his funeral oration. Thus, two of the most important conspirators Brutus and Cassius were forced to quit Rome, leaving Antony basically in charge. He had been joined by the young Octavian, Caesar's grand-nephew, but Antony was bitter because Caesar's will had named Octavian his heir rather than Antony. This led Cicero and some others to look to Octavian as a possible champion. One of the parties to the conspiracy had been the governor of Cisalpine Gaul by the name of Decimus Brutus. When he refused to relinquish his territory to Antony, the latter besieged him. This gave Cicero the chance to persuade the Senate to send an army against Antony, with Octavian as one of the commanders.

Antony was defeated, but the Senate then made the mistake of snubbing Octavian. When he was refused a consulship, he marched on Rome to take the office by force. In the meantime Antony was joined by the former consul Lepidus, and the two of them took Cisalpine Gaul from Decimus Brutus. Things now rapidly turned against the Republicans. The amnesty against the murderers of Caesar was revoked. Octavian met with Antony and Lepidus in November 43 to form the Second Triumvirate, essentially a dictatorship of the three men. Death sentences were passed on several hundred Senators, including Cicero, and a large number of Knights. Brutus and Cassius had been awarded command of Asia Minor and Syria respectively before their amnesty had been revoked. Cassius had taken advantage of his position to collect tribute in Judaea to support the war effort (cf. §17.9.3). Now he and Brutus joined forces and crossed to Greece where Octavian and Antony met them at Philippi. Defeated in two separate battles, both Cassius and Brutus committed suicide.

The Empire was now essentially divided between Octavian and Antony, though Lepidus was to have Africa if it was thought appropriate later. But there was friction between the two major leaders from the beginning. Antony went to the East to raise funds and organize the region, but when he returned to Italy in 40 BCE, he was refused admission, for which he blamed Octavian. Whatever the reason for the misunderstanding, what seemed like imminent war was averted with some difficulty. Instead, in October 40 Octavian and Antony agreed to the Treaty of Brundisium, which gave Italy and the West to Octavian, with Antony having the East, and Lepidus Africa. It was just at this time that the Parthians overran Palestine and put Antigonus on the throne.

17.8. *Relationship of Antipater and Hyrcanus*

R. Laqueur (1920) *Der jüdische Historiker Flavius Josephus*; **A. Schalit** (1969) *König Herodes: Der Mann und sein Werk*.

Hyrcanus is often pictured as the tool of Antipater who was alleged to be the real head of state. For example, after Julius Caesar left Palestine, Antipater went around the country counselling support of Hyrcanus and making threats against any who might be thinking of revolution (*War* 1.10.4 §§201-3; *Ant.* 14.9.1 §§156-57). In this way, he restored order by his own initiative and authority, even if it was in the name of Hyrcanus. R. Laqueur (1920) argued that Josephus gives two different pictures, with the *War* making Hyrcanus simply a titular head whereas the *Antiquities* showed him to be the one in charge, with Antipater only doing his bidding (because Josephus was more anti-Herodian in the latter work). This thesis was very much opposed by Marcus, who combated it in regular footnotes in his LCL translation of *Antiquities* 14 (pp. 500–501, 514, 531, 600–601). Nevertheless, although there are passages which do not support Laqueur's thesis (e.g., *War* 1.10.5 §207 and *Ant*. 14.9.2 §162 emphasize Antipater's continuing loyalty to, and even friendship for, Hyrcanus; also *Ant*. 14.6.3 §101; 14.11.4 §283), there are certainly others which seem to agree with his conclusions (*War* 1.10.6 §§208-9; also *War* 1.8.7 §175 // *Ant*. 14.6.2 §99; *Ant*. 14.8.1 §127 // *War* 1.9.3 §§187-88; *Ant*. 14.8.1 §§131-32 // *War* 1.9.4 §190; cf. *Ant*. 14.8.5 §144 // *War* 1.10.3 §199). Laqueur may thus have a point about a certain difference of approach in the two works, though he probably overpresses the evidence.

Laqueur argued that Hyrcanus was rather different from the description given by Josephus, viz., that Hyrcanus was a retiring individual who preferred a quiet life (*War* 1.5.1 §109; *Ant*. 13.16.1 §407); rather, Laqueur argued that he was much stronger and more ambitious than assumed (1920: 134–36). Schalit also disagrees in so far as Hyrcanus's actions are very much those of an ambitious individual, but evaluates his leadership capacity much as Josephus did (Schalit 1969: 15–17; *WHJP* 7:37–38). One can easily agree that Hyrcanus was ambitious, but more difficult is the question whether he was as ineffectual as presented (*War* 1.5.1 §109; 1.10.4 §203; *Ant*. 13.16.1 §407; 14.9.2 §158) and whether Antipater was the real boss. Are we too much at the mercy of Josephus's own personal evaluation (which may ultimately come from Nicolaus of Damascus, anyway)? Yet whatever Hyrcanus's abilities, it seems he was no match for Antipater and especially Herod, but one must also admit that Herod was an exceptional individual.

17.9. *Early Career of Herod*

Sources: *War* 1.10.4–12.7 §§203-47; *Ant*. 14.9.2–13.2 §§158-329.

17.9.1. *Ancestry of Herod*

A. Schalit (1962) 'Die frühchristliche Überlieferung über die Herkunft der Familie des Herodes', *ASTI* 1: 109–60; **idem** (1969) *König Herodes: Der Mann und sein Werk*.

Josephus, the main source for the life of Herod, states that Herod's father Antipater was an Idumaean (*War* 1.6.2 §123; *Ant*. 14.1.3 §8). Thus, it is commonplace to state that Herod was only partially Jewish, or even that he was a foreigner ruling over Judaea (cf. *Ant.* 14.15.2 §403). Several points should be made about this:

- Other traditions give a different ancestry for Herod, such as the Christian tradition that Antipater was from Ascalon (Justin Martyr, *Dial. Trypho* 52; Julius Africanus, *apud* Eusebius, *Hist. eccl.* 1.7.11). Granted, most scholars who deal with the subject consider this tradition as unlikely (Schalit 1962; 1969: 677), and Julius Africanus's statement that Antipater was a slave in Apollo's temple indeed looks like slander. On the other hand, Josephus writes that Nicolaus of Damascus, who wanted to please Herod, said that his family came from among the leading Jewish families who migrated to Judaea from Babylon (*Ant.* 14.1.3 §9). Josephus's argument that Nicolaus said this only out of a desire to flatter Herod is a two-edged sword, since his own version could arise from a desire to *slander* the Herodian family. Also, it is difficult to see why Herod would be pleased to be linked with Babylonian Jews if this were not true. Most important, why should Herod feel ashamed of Idumaean ancestry?
- According to the account of Josephus, the Idumaean area was forceably converted to Judaism by John Hyrcanus (*Ant.* 13.9.1 §§257-58). Matters were probably not that simple, as discussed (§9.1). But the Idumaeans did enter into the Jewish community and remained within it at least well into the 1st century CE. It may have been that Herod's family were Jews who simply lived in the Idumaean area. But even if they were originally of completely Idumaean ancestry, the indication is that they were Jewish converts.
- Herod appears to have lived as a Jew (§18.4.7). Any conclusion about his ethnicity cannot ignore this point. If he was not originally of Jewish descent, his family had adopted Judaism.
- Antipater is said to have married an 'Arabian' woman named Cypros (*War* 1.8.9 §181), though she was allegedly taken 'from among' (παρά) the Idumaeans (*Ant.*14.7.3 §121). Whether she was Jewish by religion is not stated.
- *Testament of Moses* 6.2-6, a passage normally interpreted as referring to Herod, accuses him among other things of being a non-priest. On the other hand, nothing is said about his being a foreigner or non-Jew.

It seems that the arguments for Herod as a Jew are not negligible. But the many incidental details that tie him to Idumaea cannot be ignored, either. What is clear is that like a lot of Idumaeans, Herod lived as a Jew.

If his family had been originally Jewish, they were still possibly converts. Whatever else his identity might have included, he was certainly Jewish.

17.9.2. *Governor of Galilee*

A. Gilboa (1979–80) 'The Intervention of Sextus Julius Caesar, Governor of Syria, in the Affair of Herod's Trial', *Scripta Classica Israelica* 5: 185–94.

Sources: *War* 1.10.4-14.4 §§203-85; *Ant.* 14.9.2-14.4 §§158-385.

Josephus explicitly states that Hyrcanus was indolent, which he says required Antipater to take charge of organizing the province (*War* 1.10.4 §203; *Ant.* 14.9.2 §158). This led Antipater to appoint Herod governor (στρατηγός) of Galilee while his older brother Phasael was placed over Jerusalem (ca. 47 BCE). Herod was quite young (probably about 25, though an implausible 15 according to *Ant.* 14.9.2 §158). Herod's energy and leadership ability were quickly demonstrated by one of his first acts, which was to catch and execute Ezekias (Hezekiah), a bandit leader, along with many of his men. This earned him the favour of the Syrians in this area, because Ezekias had been a serious threat to them, and brought him to the attention of the Syrian governor Sextus Caesar. In attempting to emulate his younger brother by sound rule, Phasael gained the good will of the people of Jerusalem. Because of his own actions and those of his sons, Antipater himself was respected by the nation and allowed to exercise the authority which in name belonged to Hyrcanus (§17.8).

Not surprisingly, opposition soon developed to the growing power of Antipater's family. Herod was singled out as a special target for attack. Although Hyrcanus's exact attitude at first was unclear, the constant criticism and lobbying by some of the leading Jews eventually goaded him into calling Herod to account before the Sanhedrin. The pretext was his execution of Ezekias without benefit of a trial first before the Sanhedrin. Herod's response was a model of sagacity: he complied but came with a bodyguard large enough to show that he was not intimidated but not so large as to imply a threat to Hyrcanus. The precise course of the trial is unclear because Josephus gives contradictory accounts which could be interpreted in three or four different ways. What does seem clear is that Sextus Caesar sided with Herod, sending instructions to Hyrcanus for the charges to be dropped, and that Herod decided to consult Sextus in Damascus. One reason for Sextus's intervention is probably that as a Roman citizen Herod did not have to stand trial before a local court (Gilboa 1979–80). In any case, Sextus gave greater authority to Herod, making him governor of Coele-Syria and Samaria as well. Whether Herod was ordered to appear before the Sanhedrin a second time as Josephus states is problematic because of his other statements; however, it may be that Herod was intent on attacking Jerusalem with an army in revenge for his treatment; if so, he was dissuaded by the wiser counsel of Antipater and Phasael.

17.9.3. *Death of Antipater*

In 46 a supporter of Pompey named Caecilius Bassus assassinated Sextus Caesar and took control of the area. When Julius Caesar's forces arrived, Antipater and his sons aided them against Bassus in the siege of Apamea. Caesar sent Lucius Staius Murcus to replace C. Antistius Vetus (Dio 47.27) and lead the fight. After Julius's assassination in 44 BCE, Cassius came to take over the Roman forces in the area. The war with Bassus still continued. Cassius ended the struggle between Bassus and Murcus and enlisted the two generals and their forces behind himself. His next step was to impose tribute on the whole of Syria to raise funds for the coming war, including 700 talents of silver from Judaea, with responsibility for collecting from the different regions apportioned to various individuals. Herod was the first to produce his quota from Galilee (100 talents), winning Cassius's favour by this and other acts of friendship. Another Jewish leader Malichus gained his disfavour, however, and would have been executed had not Antipater intervened with a large gift to Cassius (alleged to be from Hyrcanus).

In 43 BCE Malichus rewarded Antipater by plotting against him. The exact reason is unclear: on one occasion (*War* 1.11.3 §223) Josephus implies that it was to make way for his own ambition, while in his other account (*Ant.* 14.11.3 §277) it is stated that Malichus wanted to secure Hyrcanus's rule. Malichus is said to have used Hyrcanus as a tool on several occasions and could have supported Hyrcanus with the ultimate intent of using him as a puppet (*War* 1.11.7 §232; *Ant.* 14.11.6 §290), in which case he may simply have wanted to do what Antipater had been doing for years. Why he should be so ungrateful to Antipater is also not explained, though one must always be aware that Antipater's solicitude may have been greatly exaggerated in Josephus's source. It could be a straightforward case of ambition as Josephus implies. Such a charge is easy to make and hard to refute because it is plausible, but one wonders whether there is more to the incident than we are being told.

In 43 BCE Cassius and Murcus raised an army in Syria to support the side of Cassius and Brutus against Octavian and Antony. They saw Herod as a valuable tool in their enterprise and made him governor (στρατηγός) of Syria. There is a bit of a problem because no other source mentions it, whereas Appian (*Bell. Civ.* 4.63) states that Cassius's nephew (unnamed) was over Syria. But Herod's exact position is somewhat vague (*War* 1.11.4 §225 has 'procurator' [ἐπιμελητής] which is probably an exaggeration in any case, though the word has more than one translation), and he might not have been at the top of the hierarchy over the province. In any case, they apparently promised him that he would be king of Judaea after the war. Herod's older brother Phasael is not mentioned in this episode: Herod was clearly seen as the rising star.

Whatever the cause of Malichus's opposition to Antipater, one of his multiple plots eventually bore fruit, and he succeeded in poisoning him (apparently in 43 BCE), possibly out of alarm at Herod's rapid rise. Herod was persuaded by Phasael's argument that they should bide their time about taking revenge, lest a direct attack with soldiers be seen as starting a revolt. On the other hand, when Herod had to intervene in Samaria, to put down a sedition and civic quarrels, he returned with his troops at the time of a festival. But when Malichus tried to keep him and his troops out of Jerusalem, Herod simply ignored the message which came through Hyrcanus. He then wrote to Cassius for permission to get rid of Malichus, which Cassius was happy to give. Herod got his revenge when Malichus was in Tyre (after Cassius took Laodicea in 43 BCE) and had him executed for planning to return to Jerusalem and raise a revolt against the Romans while Cassius was preoccupied with his war against Anthony. It is interesting that Hyrcanus was present as a bystander and asked who gave the order; when told it was Cassius, he commended the execution of Malichus!

There were others with plans, as well. The international situation was such that several revolts broke out together. As soon as Cassius left Syria in 42 BCE, a Jewish general Helix attacked Phasael. Herod was in Damascus with the governor Fabius but was unable to help because of an illness; however, Phasael managed without his brother. Hyrcanus is said to have sided with Helix and to have turned a number of fortresses over to Malichus's brother, including Masada; these Herod retook as soon as he had recovered. Antigonus, the son of Aristobulus II, had been allowed to return to the area and was aided by Marion the ruler of Tyre. Herod led the campaign against them with considerable success: he not only defeated Antigonus but also Marion who had invaded Galilee. It was after this success that Herod was publicly betrothed to Hyrcanus's granddaughter Mariamme. She would become his second wife, he having already married a Jewish woman named Doris.

Herod and Hyrcanus do not seem to have been particularly affected by their support of Cassius in the fight against Antony and Octavian. After Cassius's defeat and death, Antony came to take over rulership of the East (42 BCE). An embassy of leading Jews met him and accused Herod and Phasael of governing the country with Hyrcanus as a mere puppet. Antony ruled in favour of the two brothers, not only because of his personal regard for Herod but also allegedly because of a large bribe. The opposition did not cease, however, and two more delegations came before Antony with accusations. When the second of three made their charges, Antony asked Hyrcanus who were the better rulers of the nation, and the latter indicated Herod and Phasael (presumably, the choice was between the two brothers and the 'leading Jews' who made up the delegation). The result was that Antony made Herod and his brother tetrarchs while imprisoning a handful of their opponents. The last delegation was much larger, a thousand men, but now Antony was losing patience. Herod and Hyrcanus met the delegation and urged them to back down, for the sake of national peace and also their own safety, but they refused. Antony had had enough and sent troops who killed a large number of them. It must be recognized, however, that the size of the group and its attitude indicated the beginnings of a revolt.

17.10. *Conclusions*

With Pompey's capture of Jerusalem in 63 BCE, it was a cruel blow to many Jews for their country to be returned to her previous borders and once again subordinate to another power. Yet it was more or less inevitable. In all its history, Israel had been able to thrive and maintain independence only when the imperial powers centred in Mesopotamia, Egypt and later to the west were in decline. Solomon's rule – such as it was – flourished because it fell at a time when both Assyria and Egypt were in a trough. Israel's geographical position was such that it did not have the resources to build and maintain an empire but would always be squeezed between the great powers to the north and south. The independence achieved under the Hasmonaeans, while certainly an extraordinary accomplishment, could only be temporary. Josephus blames Hyrcanus and Aristobulus for the end of the Hasmonaean state because of their internecine warfare (*Ant.* 14.4.5 §77), but if it had not been that, it would have been something else: it was only a matter of time until the country came under Roman domination. Those with vision would have seen this and made the best of the situation. The Hasmonaeans did not have this vision – the family of Antipater did. Hyrcanus prospered as long as he allowed Antipater to take the lead; Aristobulus and his family butted against the Roman wall until it broke them.

The government of Judaea was restored to its position as a theocracy (rule by priests) in place of the monarchy which it had become under the

Hasmonaeans. The country was again under foreign rule, with important social and economic consequences. The next 30 years were primarily shaped by the collapse of the Roman Republic and its civil wars, events in which Judaea and its leaders were heavily involved. Although Hyrcanus was the high priest (and later ethnarch) initially, it was Antipater and his offspring who dominated the next 70 years and more of Jewish history. Antipater's son Herod, outstanding for both his military and political skills, later rose to become the most important member of a remarkable family. The first years of Roman rule saw a series of governors (Scaurus, Gabinius, Crassus) until the defeat of the Pompeian forces by Julius Caesar in 48. At that time Antipater and Hyrcanus were rewarded by Caesar for their support. Cassius was in command of the region after Caesar's assassination until defeated and killed by the forces of Antony and Octavian in 42. Mark Antony now took charge of the region and controlled it for more than a decade until his own defeat by his erstwhile ally Octavian, as will be related in the next chapter.

Chapter 18

THE REIGN OF HEROD THE GREAT (40–4 BCE)

E. Baltrusch (2012) *Herodes: König im Heiligen Land – Eine Biographie*;
K. Fittschen and G. Foerster (eds) (1996) *Judaea and the Greco-Roman World in the Time of Herod in the Light of Archaeological Evidence*;
L.-M. Günther (ed.) (2009) *Herodes und Jerusalem*; D. M. Jacobson and N. Kokkinos (eds) (2009) *Herod and Augustus*; A. Kasher (1988) *Jews, Idumaeans, and Ancient Arabs*; idem (2007) *King Herod: A Persecuted Persecutor*; N. Kokkinos (1998) *The Herodian Dynasty: Origins, Role in Society and Eclipse*; T. Landau (2006) *Out-Heroding Herod: Josephus, Rhetoric, and the Herod Narratives*; P. Richardson (1996) *Herod: King of the Jews and Friend of the Romans*; S. Rocca (2008a) *Herod's Judaea: A Mediterranean State in the Classical World*; A. Schalit (1969) *König Herodes: Der Mann und sein Werk*; G. Vermes (2014) *The True Herod*.

Although the previous chapter began to recount Herod's early career, it is the present chapter that gives the main part of his life and the most substantial of his achievements. Herod was a notable participant in a significant period of Roman history and came into contact with some of the most important Romans of this period. It is vital to understand his actions in the context of the history of late Republican Rome and the beginning of the Roman Imperial period.

The basic chronology of Herod's reign is clear, with some of the major dates (mostly) undisputed (§1.3.5): declared king of Judaea by the Romans (40 BCE), Jerusalem retaken (summer 37 BCE), battle of Actium (September 31 BCE), death (4 BCE). A number of the major events are not clearly dated by Josephus, however, either because no exact date is given or because more than one date is given for the same event. In such cases, a best estimate is made, using the data in Josephus and the views of Roman historians. Normally, only a year or two separates different estimates for the dating of most events.

18.1. Last Phase of the Roman Civil War: Octavian and Antony (40–31 BCE)

R. Alston (2015) *Rome's Revolution: Death of the Republic and Birth of the Empire*; **J. Bleicken** (2015) *Augustus: The Biography*; **W. Eck** (2007) *The Age of Augustus*; **M. Goodman** (1997) *The Roman World 44 BC–AD 180*; **A. Goldsworthy** (2010) *Antony and Cleopatra*; **idem** (2014) *Augustus: From Revolutionary to Emperor*; **B. Levick** (2010) *Augustus: Image and Substance*; **F. Millar and E. Segal (eds)** (1984) *Caesar Augustus: Seven Aspects*; **J. S. Richardson** (2012) *Augustan Rome 44 BC to AD 14*.

Now that his differences with Antony were temporarily sorted out by the treaty of Brundisium (about September 40 BCE), Octavian could turn to dealing with the pockets of Pompeian supporters still resisting the new regime. Pompey's son Sextus Pompeius had built up a power base in Sicily and Sardinia. Octavian asked for help from Antony, but this was not immediately forthcoming, so Octavian turned to his equestrian ally Marcus Agrippa. Nevertheless, the triumvirate of Octavian, Antony and Lepidus was renewed in 37 for another four years. Sextus Pompeius was defeated in 36 by the combined forces of Octavian and Lepidus, but when Lepidus claimed Sicily for himself, Octavian removed him from the office of triumvir. Octavian and Antony had been the main rivals for some time, but Lepidus's removal made this all the more plain.

Antony's major task was to deal with the Parthians who had overrun Syria in 40 BCE. In 39 Antony pushed the Parthians back beyond the Euphrates. By this time he had become involved with Cleopatra, who had done away with her brother Ptolemy XIV to reign as sole ruler. In 37 he sent his wife Octavia (Octavian's sister) back to Italy, though not divorcing her, and openly acknowledged his children by Cleopatra. With her financial support he invaded Parthia in 36 in a disastrous campaign which cost him a third of his force. His successful invasion and capture of Armenia in 34 hardly made up for this.

Antony's involvement with Cleopatra was becoming a propaganda weapon for Octavian, who was also strengthening his position by espousing traditional Italian values and customs. When Antony proclaimed Cleopatra's son Caesarion as Caesar's legitimate son and King of Kings, ruling jointly over Egypt with Cleopatra as Queen of Kings, it was an additional factor to make the powers in Rome question Antony's judgment. When the official triumviral powers lapsed in 33 BCE, Octavian laid aside his title, although Antony did not. In the developing crisis, Octavian largely had the support of Italy and the western provinces. A proclamation was issued removing Antony's powers and declaring war on Cleopatra.

The decisive battle was that at Actium in September 31 BCE. Although Antony seemed to have a strong fleet, the battle was quickly given up. Antony and Cleopatra sailed back to Alexandria with a few ships while most of the fleet came into Octavian's hands. It was another year before Octavian pursued Antony to Egypt, since he had to deal with his veterans. At that time Antony, deserted by his troops, committed suicide. Cleopatra was taken prisoner but also committed suicide in captivity. After a century of continual civil war, Rome was finally at peace again.

18.2. *First Phase of Herod's Reign (40–30 BCE)*

Sources: *War* 1.15.1-20.3 §§286-393; *Ant.* 14.14.5 §386–15.6.7 §195.

18.2.1. *The Parthians Take Palestine*

In the spring of 40 BCE Pacorus, son of King Orodes II of Parthia, and the Parthian satrap Barzaphranes, led a Parthian invasion of Syria and Palestine. They were aided by the Roman turncoat Quintus Labienus Parthicus, who had been a supporter of Pompey. This invasion was the opportunity for the opponents of Herod. Antigonus, son of Aristobulus II, once more planned to take over Judah, this time with Parthian aid. He apparently promised a thousand talents and 500 women to the Parthians to depose Hyrcanus and make him king, as well as to get rid of Herod and his entourage. Many Jews flocked to his banner. After a brief skirmish near Carmel, Antigonus was soon besieging some opponents in the palace in Jerusalem. Evidently, Phasael was not in Jerusalem at the time because he and Herod came to intervene in the siege. Large numbers on both sides were fighting in Jerusalem. It was basically a standoff until Pentecost (Feast of Weeks), when many from the countryside came to Jerusalem for the festival. Quite a few of these seem to have joined Antigonus at this time, though Herod beat off another concerted attack. This time the Parthians intervened in the person of Pacorus, a Parthian general (not the Parthian king's son), who claimed to be coming to Jerusalem to help settle the fight. Phasael received him cordially and even agreed that he and Hyrcanus should go to discuss matters with the Parthian satrap Barzaphranes near Tyre, against the advice of Herod who remained in Jerusalem.

Herod's suspicions proved right, for Phasael and Hyrcanus were taken prisoner by the Parthians. The plan was to capture Herod as well, but already wary he received advance news of what had happened to Phasael and avoided the trap. Instead, he collected his family and followers and fled Jerusalem in the middle of the night to Idumaea. He had to fight off not only his Parthian pursuers but also attacks from Jewish groups. At the site where he engaged one group of Jewish opponents, he later founded a city called Herodium (not the fortress). He left his immediate family with a guard in Masada and scattered the rest around the country, because of the number of refugees with him (about 9,000, according to Josephus). He made his way to Petra with the thought of raising ransom money for his brother from King Malchus, but Malchus refused and ordered him out of his territory. Herod then pushed toward Egypt. It was on the way there that he received word of what had happened: the Parthians had given the throne to Aristobulus who had mutilated Hyrcanus's ears so he could no longer be high priest. Phasael had bravely committed suicide.

Herod hurried on to Alexandria and took a ship for Rome even though it was now the winter sailing season and thus a dangerous time to be on the seas. At Rome he was well received by Antony and Octavian, who were currently cooperating because of the recent treaty of Brundisium. They determined that the best way to oppose Antigonus and the Parthians was to make Herod king. According to Josephus (*Ant.* 14.14.5 §§386-87) Herod was not expecting to be given the kingship but was planning to propose it for a grandson of Hyrcanus. So it was apparently in late 40 that Octavian and Antony presented Herod to the Senate, and he was declared king of Judaea.

18.2.2. *Retaking of Jerusalem*

After being declared king by the Senate, Herod had immediately returned to the east (about December 40 or January 39 BCE) and gathered an army to fight against Antigonus. In the meantime, his brother Joseph had been able to hold Masada against the enemy, partly because unexpected rain had provided them with needed water. Ventidius the Roman general in the area was supposed to be giving aid to Joseph but did nothing because of alleged bribery by Antigonus; instead, he left his subordinate Pupedius Silo with a body of troops encamped near Jerusalem, while he went off to chase the Parthians. Antigonus was able to suborn Silo as he had Ventidius.

By now it was well into 39 BCE. Galilee as a whole went over to Herod. Ostensibly, Ventidius and Silo had been ordered to aid him, but Ventidius was occupied with local revolts caused by the Parthian invasion, and Silo had to be rescued by Herod from attacks by Jews. Before he could relieve Masada, however, he had to take Joppa, which had turned against him. He then headed for Masada, where many local people supported him, and rescued his relatives. He also took the fortress of Oresa (or Rhesa). After securing Idumaea and sending his relatives to Samaria, he finally came against Jerusalem. Herod offered an amnesty to the defenders, but Antigonus rejected it. An attempt was made to thwart the siege by Silo, who claimed that his men did not have enough food, but Herod quickly remedied the situation and, to insure secure supplies in the future, took Jericho and garrisoned it. Galilee, Idumaea and Samaria were now firmly in Herod's hand, and he was able to winter his troops in these districts. Although it is difficult to assess Antigonus's strength, he evidently had areas of support in Palestine as well as a line of influence still to Silo. Herod did not rest even in the winter: he sent his brother Joseph with troops to occupy Idumaea. Herod himself took Sepphoris, which had been in Antigonus's hands, and then used the opportunity to go against certain 'brigands' (λῃστάς) living in caves in the area near Arbela. Exactly who these were is not stated, though they seem to have had considerable strength and required a good deal of force and ingenuity to dislodge. Some of them may have been ordinary bandits, but others were probably opposition groups to Roman and Herodian rule (cf. *Ant.* 14.15.6 §§432-33). In fact, as soon as he had left, some Galileans revolted and killed the commander Herod had left in charge (see below). Although the context is not clear, it may have been some of the 'bandits' who promoted the revolt.

Herod now had Galilee under control and could pay his men and send them to their winter quarters. At this point, Silo's underhand dealings with Antigonus came back to haunt him. He had allowed Antigonus to winter some of his troops near Lydda, in exchange for the latter's provisioning of Silo's own soldiers. Antigonus did supply them for a month but then suddenly stopped, instructing the local inhabitants to gather up all available provisions and take refuge in the hills, leaving the Roman soldiers to starve. Silo had no choice but to come cap in hand to Herod. The latter tasked his younger brother Pheroras with provisioning Silo's troops, which he did in abundance. Pheroras was also given the job of repairing and garrisoning the fortress at Alexandrium.

About this time (autumn 39 BCE) Antony went to Athens, which he made his home for a couple of years. In the meantime, Ventidius was fighting the Parthians in Syria. He called for Silo and Herod to assist him as soon as things in Judaea were sorted out. Herod was glad to let Silo go to Ventidius immediately, while he attended to matters in his own kingdom. He first removed the brigands remaining in the caves. After putting his general Ptolemy in charge of the region, he went off to fight Antigonus. But opposition remained and succeeded in doing away with Ptolemy. Herod hastily returned, killing many of the rebels and ending the revolt. He fined the cities in the region a hundred talents for supporting the rebels.

The Parthians were defeated in the summer of 38 BCE. Antony had Ventidius send his commander Machaeras with two legions to help Herod; however, he only blundered and at one point even killed many of Herod's supporters. Herod was determined to go to Antony who was besieging Samosata on the Euphrates and complain. Machaeras managed to talk him out of the complaint, but Herod made his journey anyway, to give help to Antony, leaving his brother Joseph in charge. With the siege won, Antony dispatched Gaius Sosius, his governor of Syria, with several legions, to Herod's aid. As he was on his way back, however, Herod learned that his brother Joseph had foolishly taken to the field against some of Antigonus's forces, and his inexperienced troops had been massacred and himself killed. Immediately following this, Galilee and apparently Idumaea (the reading 'Judaea' in *Ant.* 14.15.10 §450 seems to be an error) had revolted.

Herod had his revenge. He made a forced march through Mount Lebanon to Ptolemais, gaining reinforcements on the way. He first attacked in Galilee where he met considerable resistance, but when another Roman legion joined his forces, the enemy abandoned their position. Herod then moved on to Jericho. During this time the Roman commander Machaerus was fortifying a place called Gittha in southern Judaea, where Antigonus was fighting against him. Antigonus sent his own general Pappus against Herod. Herod engaged Pappus near the village of Isana (Jeshanah), north of Jerusalem. In the battle Herod was himself wounded by a javelin, but his forces were victorious. He cut off Pappus's head in revenge, because the latter had killed and beheaded his brother Joseph.

Herod now invested Jerusalem where Antigonus had holed up. After setting up the siege, Herod showed his contempt of Antigonus's military prowess by going off to Samaria to marry Mariamme. There were in effect two generals: Herod at the head of his own army and Sosius who had been sent by Antony in command of the Roman force. With the size of the besieging army (30,000 according to *Ant.* 14.16.1 §468), the outcome was quite predictable; nevertheless, the defenders fought ferociously. Yet when the Lower City and the outer portions of the temple had fallen to the Romans and Herod, the defenders asked for sacrificial animals to be brought to them, and Herod agreed, thinking it might make them more likely to surrender. But since they fought even more strongly, he pressed the attack. When the attackers finally broke through, none of the defenders was spared; indeed, the Jews of Herod's army were as determined to leave no living opponents as the Romans. Antigonus surrendered to Sosius, however, and was taken prisoner. Herod had two concerns: one was to keep his non-Jewish troops from violating the temple; the other was to prevent wholesale looting of the city and slaughter of the population. He managed the latter only by promising generous gifts to all the officers and men from his own purse, a promise which he was quick to fulfil. Before quitting Jerusalem, Sosius dedicated a crown of gold to God.

The exact length of the siege of Jerusalem and the time of its fall are uncertain. The siege had probably begun sometime in the spring of 37 BCE: this fits nicely with the defeat of the Parthians and Herod's return with Sosius's troops. According to *War* 1.18.2 §351 the city fell only in the fifth month of the siege; according to *Ant.* 14.16.4 §487, in the third. The statement that the city was conquered on the 'day of the fast' (Day of Atonement) exactly 27 years after its fall to Pompey seems stylized and rather suspicious; more likely, it was sometime in the summer (θέρος: *Ant.* 14.16.2 §473) of 37 BCE (§1.3.5.3). In the *Antiquities* (14.16.4 §§489-90) Josephus claimed that Herod was afraid that if Antigonus was taken to Rome, he might plead his case before the Senate and end up displacing Herod as king. So he bribed Antony to do away with Antigonus in Antioch. This might be true, but it is unlikely that the Senate would have accepted such a rebel as Antigonus in place of a friend such as Herod. This looks like another one of Josephus's anti-Herod comments (*Ant.* 15.1.2 §§5-9 seems to support this interpretation). Antigonus was executed by Antony in Antioch by beheading (so also Strabo, as quoted in *Ant.* 15.1.2 §§8-10; Plutarch, *Antony* 36; Dio 49.22 says he was crucified and flogged, though then beheaded), thus bringing the Hasmonaean kingly rule to an end. That Antigonus can be considered the last of the Hasmonaean kings is indicated by his many coins, which give his title in Hebrew as 'Mattathias the high priest and the *hever* of the Jews' (מתתיה הכהן הגדל וחבר היהודים *mttyh hkhn hgdl wḥbr hyhwdym*) but in Greek as 'King Anti(gonus)' (βασιλεως αντι [cf. §2.3]).

18.2.3. *Troubles with Cleopatra*

Up to this point, Josephus's two accounts have been very much parallel, with differences for the most part only slight ones of detail. Now, however, the *War* skips over the next six years very hastily to get to the battle of Actium. The *Antiquities* gives quite a detailed account but one permeated with anti-Herodian statement and innuendo, giving reason at times to suspect a source different from Nicolaus of Damascus in this section. Herod had a number of troubles caused by Cleopatra who not only wanted to take over control of Palestine but also seemed to have disliked Herod personally. Fortunately, Antony was well disposed toward Herod despite his infatuation with Cleopatra; this, along with skilful diplomacy on Herod's part, managed to keep his throne and kingdom for him even though certain territories were taken away.

The Parthians had allowed Hyrcanus to settle among the Jews in Babylon where he was greatly honoured. He wanted to return to Palestine, however, and Herod invited him to come home, sending an envoy with gifts to the Parthian king Phraates asking for his return. (It is hard to see how this could show anything but positive feelings for Hyrcanus on Herod's part, but Josephus manages to see this as a nefarious plot on Herod's part against Hyrcanus.) The Parthians let him go, and Herod received him with a splendid homecoming.

Cleopatra's designs were allegedly not just on Judaea but on Arabia and other territories as well. She was given an area in Coele-Syria by Antony when she first pressed him (*Ant.* 15.3.8 §79). Later, he added certain territories in Arabia and Jericho, which Herod leased back from her, along with a large section of the coast of Palestine and Phoenicia (*Ant.* 15.4.1-2 §§94-96). Cleopatra apparently even visited Jerusalem (or at least Judaea) on one occasion (*War* 1.18.5 §§361-62; *Ant.* 15.4.2 §§96-103). When Antony set out on his ill-fated campaign against the Parthians in 34 BCE, she escorted him as far as the Euphrates before returning through Judaea. It was on this occasion that Herod leased back (for 200 talents) his territories given to her by Antony, evidently part of an attempt by Herod to appease her. Complicating matters was Herod's own domestic situation. Hyrcanus could not be high priest now because of his mutilation, and Herod appointed Ananel (Hananel) from a priestly family in Babylon.

This angered Hyrcanus's daughter Alexandra who thought that her own son Jonathan Aristobulus should have been given the office. She appealed to Cleopatra to use her influence on Antony. Antony's friend (and lover?) Quintus Delius visited Herod and was impressed with the boy's charm and beauty. He suggested to Antony to send for the boy (as a possible paramour?). But by this time, Herod decided the best course of action was to accede on this, make an excuse as to why the boy could not leave Judaea and appoint him (who was only 17) as high priest. When the lad presided at the altar during the Feast of Tabernacles (ca. 35 BCE), he was acclaimed enthusiastically by the people there, which was a danger sign that there might be threats to Herod's kingship. Thus, when a year later Aristobulus was drowned while swimming at the palace in Jericho, Alexandra blamed Herod and wrote to Cleopatra with an accusation of murder against him. Cleopatra persuaded Antony to summon Herod to answer the charges, but Herod was cleared by Antony. This did not stop the allegations that Herod was responsible for his death.

But did Herod have the youth assassinated as Josephus alleges? Most modern writers on Herod have accepted the verdict of Josephus – and Alexandra – as reliable, in spite of the evident bias of both individuals.

E. Baltrusch (2012: 186–88), however, argues that this scenario is less than credible because Aristobulus's death created great problems for Herod. First, to assassinate him in his own palace was bound to bring questions and accusations down on his head. Secondly, he was already under scrutiny from Cleopatra, who had Antony's ear. If she decided to accuse him to Antony (as she did), the outcome was unpredictable: Herod could well have lost his throne. Finally, he needed to get the people on his side, and getting rid of a popular, young, handsome high priest was the last thing he needed to do. Herod was a shrewd calculator throughout his career, as we have already seen demonstrated, and if he had contemplated removing Aristobulus, he would have realized this was a poor way to go about it. Aristobulus's death at this time and in this manner brought him nothing but grief.

Although Antony was under Cleopatra's thumb, he was clearly reluctant to condemn one whom he had made king not that many years before. There was also Herod's charm, rhetorical ability in defending himself and the fact that he was very useful to Antony. The result was that he even accompanied Antony part of the way on his Parthian venture. Nevertheless, there were repercussions for Herod's household, though Josephus gives more than one version. The most believable story (in *Ant.* 15.3.5-9 §§65-87) is that Herod had left his brother-in-law Joseph (probably not his 'uncle' θεῖον, despite *Ant.* 15.3.5 §65) in charge, with instructions to put Mariamme to death if anything happened to him when he went to Antony. Unfortunately, Joseph told Mariamme and her mother about these orders. When Herod returned, Joseph's wife Salome made Herod jealous by charges that Joseph was frequently with Mariamme. The latter defended herself so well that Herod apologized, but then she accused Herod of wanting her dead. This convinced him that Mariamme would have learned of this from Joseph only if he was intimate with her, and he had him executed. But there are other versions of this story that need to be considered (discussed below, §18.4.5).

18.2.4. *Actium: On the Losing Side*

The year 31 BCE saw the final showdown between Antony and Octavian. Herod's rule and situation in Judaea were in good shape, he having captured the fortress Hyrcania, which was still being held by Antigonus's sister. According to Josephus, Herod was ready to aid Antony in any way possible but, fortunately for Herod, Antony did not feel he needed him at the battle of Actium. Instead, he sent him to fight the Nabataeans who were refusing to pay the tribute owed. (Josephus says that this was at Cleopatra's instigation, since she thought she would gain, whether Herod or Malichus I, king of the Arabs, lost [*Ant.* 15.5.1 §110].) However, even though this scenario is widely accepted (e.g., Schalit 1969: 122), there is reason to be sceptical (Kasher 1988: 135-49). It seems very unlikely that Antony would have refused help if it had come. The fight with the Arabs (despite some difficulties) was rather convenient when we look at subsequent events: it made sure that Herod was otherwise engaged when the time came for the battle between Antony/Cleopatra and Octavian. A politician as astute as Herod could no doubt see what was coming, with the odds very much against Antony's succeeding. He also knew that if Antony was successful, Cleopatra's full fury might well have been unleashed on him. There are signs that already a year or two before Actium, he was preparing to take any steps needed to survive in the new order.

The armies of Herod and Malichus met at Diospolis (Dion?). Initially, Herod was successful until Athenion, one of Cleopatra's generals, unexpectedly intervened on the side of the Arabs and helped them to defeat the Jews at a place called Canatha (or Cana). Herod was able to carry on the fight only by guerrilla tactics for a time. But a large earthquake struck Judah and did considerable damage in the spring of 31 BCE. About 30,000 people supposedly died in their houses, along with a good proportion of the livestock. The Arabs thought they could conquer the ruined and demoralized country. As it happened, the Judaean army had not been very much injured by the earthquake so that Herod was able to inflict a decisive defeat on the Arabs near Philadelphia.

Antony's defeat at Actium in September 31 BCE left Herod on the losing side. He also had enemies or potential enemies in his own court. Especially problematic was Hyrcanus and those of his family who were hostile to Herod. Hyrcanus's daughter Alexandra (also Herod's mother-in-law) urged her father to escape Herod's sphere by appealing to Malichus the Nabataean king. Although Hyrcanus apparently rejected this advice at first, he was eventually persuaded to write to Malichus, appealing for refuge. But the relative to whom they entrusted the letters to Malichus betrayed them to Herod. Herod allowed the letters to go to Malichus, who replied that he would give asylum to Hyrcanus and his family and also to any other Jews who sought it. Herod went to the Sanhedrin with these letters and had Hyrcanus condemned to death. After Hyrcanus's execution, Herod placed his mother, sister and children in Masada, Mariamme and Alexandra in Alexandrium and put his younger brother Pheraras in charge. One other move apparently made was to send a force to support the Roman commander Quintus Didius who was confronting a band of gladiators who were going to Antony's aid after Actium.

Herod was now ready to make his move in the changed circumstances in which the Actium defeat had left him. The question was what action he should take. Typically, he made a bold stroke: sometime in the spring of 30 BCE he sailed to meet Octavian at Rhodes. Herod appeared before the Roman victor without his crown and dressed as a commoner but otherwise with regal demeanour. Josephus gives two different speeches of Herod before Octavian (*War* 1.20.1 §§388-90; *Ant.* 15.6.6 §§189-93). Neither is likely to be what Herod actually said, but they might suggest his approach and some of his arguments: he candidly stated that he had supported Antony as a faithful ally and would have been at Actium if Antony had not given orders to the contrary. He had been a fast friend and adviser of Antony, even after the latter's defeat at Actium. Now, he placed his crown before Caesar but would serve him just as staunchly as he had Antony if allowed to. Octavian urged him to be his friend now, as he had been to Antony, and restored his diadem. There were probably a number of reasons why Octavian was happy to restore Herod's crown and confirm his rule, not least his past record and his administrative ability. Also, it was Octavian's policy to leave Antony's client rulers in power once they had acknowledged his sovereignty. Nevertheless, one suspects – as Josephus himself suggests – that Octavian admired in Herod's actions the same courage and sheer guts that he himself possessed. Whatever one might think of Herod in other respects, he had what it took to be leader in a crisis.

18.3. *Reign of Augustus (31 BCE–14 CE)*

[For bibliography, see §18.1.]

The genius of Augustus's reign was that he acted as a constitutional monarch while maintaining the outward trappings of the Republic. Further, the machinery of government was so well designed that it was not only passed on in a smooth transition at his death but continued to work and keep the peace at home – for the most part – for another two centuries. He worked with the Senate and was careful to treat it with respect, but he also created it in his own image by taking the opportunity to weed out potential opposition in reducing the numbers and replacing vacancies with his supporters. He worked through the offices and powers voted to him by the Senate and even declined certain honours on occasion. Nevertheless, there was no question in all this that he was the head of government whose source of power was ultimately the legions under his command.

The first desire of the people was for peace, and the veterans wanted their rewards of discharge and land. So after taking Egypt in 30 BCE, Octavian did not attempt to invade Parthia as many undoubtedly expected. Instead, he returned to Rome and began the task of building a stable government in a welcome respite from fighting. His military career was by no means at an end, and he spent many of the next four decades of rule away from Rome in different areas of the empire. But his greatest achievements were civil, governmental and domestic, with most of the fighting on the frontiers being conducted by subordinates. He reduced the number of legions from 60 to 28, a number more or less retained under later rulers.

On his return to Rome in 29 BCE, he celebrated his triumph and began a programme of public building. The treasury captured from Egypt was very helpful in financing all this, which was also useful in maintaining his popular support. He closed the temple of Janus, which signified the return of peace. Now was the time for reform of the government, which he began immediately, though it was to continue and develop throughout the rest of his life.

Things were sufficiently in progress that he was able to make a bold but calculated move in early 27 BCE to renounce all his powers and offices before the Senate. The result was that the Senators would not hear of it. Finally, after a show of reluctance he accepted authority over the provinces of Spain, Gaul and Syria, as well as remaining consul as he had each year up to then. Accepting administration over these provinces may have seemed rather less than the rule one associates with an emperor; however, most of the legions were stationed in these areas, and their commanders were Octavian's men. Thus, his carefully planned move was such that he could keep the forms of the Republic while maintaining his actual power of supreme ruler. An additional bonus was that he was voted the name Augustus, declared *princeps* or first citizen, and the sixth month of the Roman calendar (which at that time began in the spring) was named August in his honour. This is referred to as the First Settlement.

Shortly after the First Settlement he left Rome for three years to conduct campaigns and other activities in Gaul and Spain. A conspiracy discovered shortly after his return showed that there were still those ready to challenge or oppose his authority, but he weathered these successfully. Then he became deathly ill and, since he thought he might not survive, made provision for his life-long friend and brilliant military commander Marcus Agrippa to succeed him. Fortunately, he recovered and had the chance to carry out his developments in full, but he decided to resign his consulship as another tactical move. This made way for others to hold the office and reduce the occasion for resentment at his being continually consul. Therefore, the Senate voted two new powers: his *imperium* would not cease to operate within the city boundary, and he was voted the *maius imperium proconsulare*, which gave him authority even over the governors of senatorial provinces. These powers meant that he could give command to any administrator or military official anywhere in the empire and expect to be obeyed. Further, he was voted a tribunate without some of the restrictions normally inherent in the office. This so-called Second Settlement had thus conferred civil, provincial, and military authority practically without limit, which continued to be the basis of the rule of the emperors who succeeded him. Of course, the secret of his smooth governance lay in the tact and restraint with which he used these almost unlimited powers.

Marcus Agrippa was sent to the East in 23 BCE where he began a friendship with Herod. Despite famine in Rome, which he dealt with without accepting a dictatorship, Augustus himself visited the East for three years (22–19 BCE). Augustus's organization and solidification of government was such that a celebration could be made in 17 BCE proclaiming the new age which Augustus had founded. Agrippa was again in the East in 14 BCE, not long before his early death, where his friendship with Herod became a close one. Throughout most of his reign, Herod kept in close touch with Augustus and was able to maintain a good relationship with the emperor himself as well as other members of the family.

18.4. *The Rest of Herod's Reign (30–4 BCE)*

Sources: *War* 1.20.3–33.9 §§393-673; *Ant.* 15.6.7 §195 – 17.8.3 §199.

18.4.1. *Administration under Herod*

M. Avi-Yonah (1966) *The Holy Land from the Persian to the Arab Conquests*, 86–101; **idem** (1974b) 'Historical Geography of Palestine', in S. Safrai and Menahem Stern (eds), *The Jewish People in the First Century*, 1:91–113; **D. Braund** (1984) *Rome and the Friendly King: The Character of Client Kingship*.

Octavian came through Palestine some months after confirming Herod in his kingship on his way to retaking Egypt (30 BCE). Herod not only entertained him and his troops lavishly but also made available ample provisions (especially water) for the march across the desert; he was similarly unsparing in expense on Augustus's return from Egypt. His personal accommodation for Octavian was not only most splendid, but was accompanied by a gift of 800 talents. The effect (no doubt intended by

Herod) was for Augustus to conclude that he was being generous beyond the means of his small kingdom and to reward him with additional territories. Throughout most of his reign Herod enjoyed the close friendship and confidence of Augustus and was honoured with titles and other accoutrements of status as well as further grants of territory. One immediate gift to Herod was Cleopatra's bodyguard of 400 Gauls.

The widening of Herod's kingdom took place over a decade or so (*War* 1.20.3-4 §§396-400; *Ant.* 15.7.3 §217; 15.10.1 §343; 15.10.3 §360). Initially in 30 BCE, Herod received back the territories taken away by Cleopatra, plus land southeast of the Sea of Galilee (Gadara, Hippus) and certain coastal cities (Gaza, Anthedon, Straton's Tower [later Caesarea]), though Ashkelon was kept back by Octavian. (He is also said to have received Samaria and Joppa at this time, but the former was probably already restored by Antony [Appian, *Bell. Civ.* 5.75.319] and the latter by Julius Caesar [*Ant.* 14.10.6 §202].) Some years later (ca. 23 BCE) he was awarded territories northeast of the Sea of Galilee (Trachonitis, Batanaea, Auranitis), and finally (ca. 20 BCE) land north of the Sea of Galilee, connecting the Galilee with Trachonitis (including modern Huleh and Paneas [Caesarea-Philippi]; cf. Dio 54.9).

These gifts do not just represent Roman greatness of heart toward Herod. Judaea was a frontier kingdom, and it was known that Herod would take great care for its security, thus also keeping a vital link in the Roman boundary safe from barbaric encroachment. For example, the territories of Trachonitis, Batanaea and Auranitis (roughly equivalent to the areas of Bashan and Gilead often mentioned in the Hebrew Bible) had a problem with brigands who hung out in the mountainous and wilderness areas. A local ruler named Zenodorus was in league with some of the robber bands who especially preyed on the people of Damascus. Since the region had come under Roman rule, the local people appealed to the governor Varro who reported the matter to Caesar. This was one of the reasons Augustus assigned the territories to Herod, because he expected him to take care of the problem – which he did. Zenodorus went to Rome to complain against Herod but without success.

Herod ruled as a client king (or friendly king) of Rome. There were a number of these during the late Republic and early Empire, especially as long as the boundaries of the Empire continued to be expanded (Braund 1984). Client kingship was useful to the Romans because the client kingdom served as a buffer to the areas not under Roman control and could be called upon to render military aid when needed. On the other hand, Rome did not have to expend valuable resources in administration and the posting of legions on a permanent basis, for the client kingdom took care of its own administration and defence of its borders under normal circumstances.

Thus, by the end of his reign Herod controlled a state reaching from southern Lebanon to the Negev and from the Mediterranean to the Transjordan. It was an area basically as large as that under Alexander Jannaeus and probably as large as, perhaps larger than, anything under the Israelite monarchy. The population was not homogenous but composed of Jews, Samaritans, Greeks, Syrians and Arabs. The administration varied from area to area because of historical factors as well as pragmatic ones. The various sorts of administration are as follows:

1. *Greek cities*. These were supervised by a commissioner known as the *stratēgos* (*Ant*. 15.7.9 §254). Attached to Gaba, Heshbon and perhaps Azotus were military colonies (cleruchies) administered much as they had been under Ptolemaic and Seleucid rule.
2. *Jewish section of the kingdom*. The old Hasmonaean division into provinces (*meris*), subdivided into toparchies, with these in turn further subdivided into villages, was apparently maintained. All administrative officials were appointed directly by the king.
3. *Jerusalem held a unique position*. A Sanhedrin still existed in name, apparently, but we have no record of decisions made by it once Herod became king. When the king was himself not there, a *stratēgos* was responsible for affairs of state (*War* 1.33.3 §652; 2.1.3 §8; *Ant*. 17.6.3 §156; 17.9.1-2 §§209-10).

Herod himself ruled as a typical Hellenistic monarch under Roman domination. He was the quintessential client king who was often in the company of the emperor, the emperor's family and high Roman officials, whether in his own kingdom or in Rome or elsewhere. He travelled to Rome and other parts of the Eastern empire periodically. His children were educated in Rome. In addition to his own enormous internal building program, he also provided for a number of projects in various parts of the old Greek areas (in the next section, §18.4.2). One area where he tried to make a difference was in the realm of law and justice (*Ant*. 16.1.1 §§1-5). One law caused much controversy, however: he decreed that burglars (τοιχωρύχους) should be sold into slavery abroad. It was pointed out to him that this violated traditional Jewish law. Herod changed the penalty to repayment of 400 percent; if the criminal could not make the payment, he would be sold but not abroad and would be released after six years. Some still saw this as too harsh a penalty.

18.4.2. Magnificent Buildings

S. Applebaum (1989b) 'The Beginnings of the Limes Palaestinae', *Judaea in Hellenistic and Roman Times*, 132–42; M. Ben-Dor (1986) 'Herod's Mighty Temple Mount', *BAR* 12, no. 6 (Nov.–Dec.): 40–49; H. Geva (1981) 'The "Tower of David" – Phasael or Hippicus?' *IEJ* 31: 57–65; M. Gichon (1967) 'Idumea and the Herodian Limes', *IEJ* 17: 27–42; R. P. Goldschmidt-Lehmann (1981) 'The Second (Herodian) Temple: Selected Bibliography', *Jerusalem Cathedra* 1: 336–59; A. Kasher (1988) *Jews, Idumaeans, and Ancient Arabs*; L. I. Levine (1975) *Roman Caesarea*; A. Lichtenberger (1999) *Die Baupolitik Herodes des Großen*; B. Mazar (1978) 'Herodian Jerusalem in the Light of the Excavations South and South-West of the Temple Mount', *IEJ* 28: 230–37; E. Netzer (1975) 'The Hasmonean and Herodian Winter Palaces at Jericho', *IEJ* 25: 89–100; idem (1977) 'The Winter Palaces of the Judean Kings at Jericho at the End of the Second Temple Period', *BASOR* 228: 1–13; idem (1981) *Greater Herodium*; idem (1999) *Die Paläste der Hasmonäer und Herodes' des Großen*; idem (2008) *The Architecture of Herod the Great Builder*; E. Netzer et al. (1981) 'Symposium: Herod's Building Projects', *Jerusalem Cathedra* 1: 48–80; A. Raban (ed.) (1989) *The Harbours of Caesarea Maritima, Volume I: The Site and the Excavations*; P. Richardson (1985) 'Religion and Architecture: A Study in Herod's Piety, Power, Pomp and Pleasure', *Bulletin of the Canadian Society of Biblical Studies* 45: 3–29; idem (1986) 'Law and Piety in Herod's Architecture', *SR* 15: 347–60; idem (2004) *Building Jewish in the Roman East*; S. Rocca (2008b) *The Forts of Judaea 168 BC–AD 73: From the Maccabees to the Fall of Masada*; D. W. Roller (1998) *The Building Program of Herod the Great*; Y. Tsafrir (1982) 'The Desert Fortresses of Judaea in the Second Temple Period', *Jerusalem Cathedra* 2: 120–45; J. Wilkinson (1975) 'The Streets of Jerusalem', *Levant* 7: 118–36; Y. Yadin (ed.) (1975) *Jerusalem Revealed*.

One of the major achievements of Herod's rule was his building program, which was spectacular even by Roman standards. There were two aspects to it, the civic/personal and the military/defensive, though some works had elements of both connected with them. The dating of these is not easy, partly because Josephus lists them all together in the *War* without any chronological framework. A rough chronological framework is given in the *Antiquities*, but the precise dates are not always clear even here. A further problem is that sometimes more than one date is given for the same project. A number of these buildings are discussed in Chapter 2 on archaeology.

18. *The Reign of Herod the Great (40–4 BCE)*

Herod's first project (though the *War* states that it was only in the 192nd Olympiad, ca. 10–9 BCE) was the inauguration of tetrennial games in honour of Augustus, for which he built a theatre and a large amphitheatre (*Ant.* 15.8.1-2 §§267-79; *War* 1.21.8 §415) in Jerusalem. There was also a hippodrome (*Ant.* 17.10.2 §255), though this was perhaps identical with the amphitheatre. Of particular interest is the story that the decoration of the theatre caused a disturbance among certain Jews who thought they included human images (*Ant.* 15.8.1-3 §§276-81). He had a number of 'trophies' scattered around the theatre that commemorated his success in war. But some were convinced that these had human images at their heart. When Herod learned of this, he called some prominent leaders of the group to see for themselves. They immediately cried out that these were human images. But when he had the ornaments that decorated the outside of the particular trophy removed, they could see for themselves that no image lay at the core. Most only laughed and accepted that they had been mistaken; unfortunately, a few refused to change their opinion that Herod was introducing unlawful ways.

The fortifications of the realm were naturally very important. His palace in the upper city of Jerusalem was comprised of two buildings called Caesareum and Agrippeum after Augustus and Agrippa (*War* 1.21.1 §402; *Ant.* 15.9.3 §318), while one of the protective towers was called Phasael after his brother who had been killed by the Parthians (*War* 1.21.9 §418; *Ant.* 16.5.2 §144). To protect the temple he built the fortress called Antonia, after Mark Antony (*War* 1.21.1 §401; *Ant.* 15.8.5 §292). South of Jerusalem he created the fortress of Herodium (named for himself) by artificially raising a hill to an even greater height (*War* 1.21.10 §§419-21; *Ant.* 15.9.4 §§323-25). Near Jericho he constructed a fortress named Cypros after his mother (*War* 1.21.9 §417; *Ant.* 16.5.2 §143). These all formed part of a fortification system on the border with Arabia which prefigured the *limes Palaestina* (Roman frontier defence system) of later centuries (Kasher 1988: 152–56; Applebaum 1989; Gichon 1967; cf. Tsafrir 1982). Included in this were the pre-existing fortresses of Masada, Macherus and Alexandrium which Herod also strengthened and improved (*War* 7.8.3-4 §§280-303; 7.6.2 §§171-77; *Ant.* 16.2.1 §13). Exactly why this was thought necessary, since the Nabataeans were nominally Roman allies, is a question.

Next, probably about 27–25 BCE, he rebuilt Samaria, renaming it Sebaste, the Greek equivalent of 'Augustus' (*War* 1.21.2 §403; *Ant.* 15.8.5 §§292-93, 296-98). Only a day's journey from Jerusalem, it could also serve as a fortress to control the entire country if necessary. Because it was dedicated to the emperor, it had a magnificent temple at its centre. About 6,000 of Herod's veteran allies were settled in and around it and were offered equitable laws (εὐνομίαν).

On the coast the old city of Straton's Tower was rebuilt with a magnificent man-made harbour and called Caesarea, again after Augustus (*War* 1.21.5-7 §§408-14; *Ant.* 15.8.5 §293; 15.9.6 §§331-41). The work on this finished in Herod's 28th year (ca. 10–9 BCE), though it is said to have taken 10 years (*Ant.* 16.5.1 §136) or 12 (*Ant.* 15.9.6 §341). It was later to be the seat of the Roman government of Palestine. In addition to these works, which also served as a part of the system of fortifications, Herod built a number of other sites which he named after Roman friends or family members. The village of Anthedon which had been destroyed in warfare was rebuilt under the name Agrippium (*War* 1.21.8 §416) or Agrippias (*Ant.* 13.13.3 §357). North of Jericho, probably in last years of his reign, he built a city named Phasaelis after his brother (*War* 1.21.9 §418; *Ant.* 16.5.2. §145). In the Plain of Sharon north of Joppa, a new town was founded with the name Antipatris after his father Antipater (*War* 1.21.9 §417; *Ant.* 16.5.2 §§142-43).

The crowning achievement of his building projects, and one which would have done most to endear him to the Jewish people, was the restoration and rebuilding of the temple at Jerusalem (*War* 1.21.1 §401; *Ant.* 15.9.1-7 §§380-425), probably beginning about 19 BCE. The care with which this was carried out and the enormous cost involved (apparently paid for by Herod himself – *Ant.* 15.11.1 §380) suggests that its alleged fame throughout the Roman empire was not exaggerated. He doubled its area. The work of building could be done only by priests and had to be carried out in such a way as to maintain the dignity of the house and not disrupt the regular cultic services. He assured the people that he would tear none of it down until the building materials for the reconstruction were all assembled. The main work was completed in a year and a half, though work continued for more than eighty years until not long before it was destroyed by the Romans (*Ant.* 20.9.7 §§219-20; cf. Jn 2.20).

Herod also made a name for himself for his generosity in funding building projects in the Greek and Roman worlds (*War* 1.21.11-12 §§422-28; *Ant.* 15.9.5 §§326-30). This included gymnasia, market places, theatres, aqueducts and even temples for cities in Phoenicia and Syria, but also Asia Minor, Rhodes and even Greece itself. He endowed the Olympian games (which seemed to be declining) and was made president of the celebrations. He was careful, however, not to erect temples, statues or other pagan religious buildings in Judaean territory.

18.4.3. *From Actium to the Death of Agrippa (30–14 BCE)*

Much of Herod's attention during this period was taken up by his many building projects. But about 25 BCE, the country was hit by a major drought for at least two years. Malnutrition led to disease. Herod's treasury was low because of his building projects, though in any case neighbouring regions were also suffering drought and famine and not able to sell food to Judaea. As was typical for him, he took bold action: he stripped his palace of gold and silver, including artistic ornaments, and turned it into money. He then applied to his friend Petronius who was prefect of Egypt (24–21 BCE) to buy grain from there. Egypt was the bread basket of Rome, and its grain was normally restricted to official Roman use. Petronius made an exception in Herod's case, however, and supplied him with much of what was needed. Herod also gave aid to cities in the region and helped out as far away as Syria. He even took care to supply clothing, since many flocks had had to be eaten, which had caused a shortage of wool. When the drought turned, he resourced fifty thousand men to bring in the harvest. All in all he supplied 80,000 cors of wheat to Judaea and another 10,000 to the wider region. His solicitude and generosity toward his people went a long way to changing attitudes toward his rule.

It was about this time that Augustus sent Aelius Gallus on a campaign against the Sabaeans of Arabia (Strabo 16.4.23; Dio 53.29; Pliny 60.28.160). The expedition accomplished nothing, but Herod supplied 500 men from his own bodyguard to accompany Gallus. It was also about this time that Herod fell for another Mariamme, the daughter of the Alexandrian priest Simon, son of Boethus. Herod removed the current high priest, Jesus son of Phiabi, from office and made Simon high priest instead, after which he married the daughter.

Marcus Vipsanius Agrippa, Caesar's son-in-law, trusted friend and general, came to the east for the first time about 23–22 BCE. While he wintered on the island of Lesbos at Mitylene, Herod who was a close friend visited him. Shortly afterward, some of the men of Gadara (a city given to Herod by Augustus) complained of Herod to Agrippa, who simply turned them over to the king (however, Herod released them without punishment). Zenodorus now stirred up trouble by selling Auranitis to the Arabs. Thus, the Arabs disputed ownership of the territory with Herod, attempting to use both legal proceedings and force. Surprisingly, Herod tried to placate them rather than meet force with force. Then about 20 BCE (Herod's 17th year) Augustus came to visit Syria (cf. Dio 54.7). Urged on by Zenodorus, the Gadarenes accused Herod before Caesar.

When they saw that Augustus and his councillors were friendly toward Herod, however, they did not pursue their complaint, and a number committed suicide. Zenodorus also died shortly afterward.

It was on this occasion that Augustus gave Zenodorus's territory (lying between Trachonitis and Galilee and containing Ulatha and Paneas) to Herod. Caesar also instructed the procurators of Syria to gain Herod's consent, presumably with regard to matters affecting his kingdom rather than on all that they undertook. *War* (1.20.4 §399) says he was made procurator (ἐπίτροπος) of all Syria at this time, but this seems unlikely, though requiring his approval for matters affecting his kingdom from the established procurators seems more likely. Herod asked Augustus for his brother Pheroras to have a tetrarchy. Apparently, Peraea (Transjordan) was assigned to him (*War* 1.24.5 §483), as well as an income of 100 talents per year. After Augustus left the area, Herod built a magnificent temple to the emperor near Paneas, which later became Caesarea-Philippi.

Shortly afterward Herod reduced the taxes for the people of his kingdom by a third. The reason given seems to be to allow them to recover from drought, though Josephus alleges it was really to placate his people because they were unhappy with his departure from normal Jewish customs. Perhaps it was for both reasons. When he says the citizens were not allowed to assemble, were spied on and were sometimes secretly detained, imprisoned and even killed, he is probably correct, but this seems to have been normal in empires and monarchies of the time – as documented in more recent centuries. He required an oath of loyalty from all his subjects, punishing those who objected. Yet he also exempted Pollion the Pharisee and Samaias and their disciples, as well as the Essenes. In both cases it was because of their support or alleged predictions of his success at crucial points in his career.

It was about 19 BCE (the 18th year of his reign [*Ant.* 15.11.1 §380], though the *War* [1.21.1 S401] has the 15th year) that he began perhaps his most important project: refurbishment of the temple (see further at §18.4.2).

Marcus Agrippa was again sent to Asia Minor in 14 BCE to place a king friendly to the Romans on the throne of Cappadocia. Herod went to meet him and invited him to Judaea. There he gave Agrippa a magnificent welcome in the autumn of that year, showing him the new cities of Sebaste and Caesarea and the fortresses of Alexandrium, Herodium and Hyrcania. He ended the tour in Jerusalem, where people welcomed him with great acclaim. Agrippa had to sail before winter, but the next spring Herod engaged in a protracted sea voyage (because of unfavourable winds) to catch up with him in Pontus, and Agrippa was delighted to see him. They returned overland, making their way by a lengthy route. Herod demonstrated his generosity to many of the peoples and cities en route. He also supported petitions or made recommendations on behalf of some who approached Agrippa with requests for favours. It was on this occasion that the Jews of Ionia petitioned Agrippa because they were being mistreated, especially in not being able to observe their own laws (e.g., they were being required to appear in court on Jewish holy days, undertake military and civic duties from which they had been exempted, and not being allowed to send the temple tax to Jerusalem). Herod spoke up for them and even got his friend the historian and rhetorician Nicolaus of Damascus to deliver a speech in their defence before Agrippa. The result was that Agrippa granted their petition and confirmed their traditional religious rights. After Agrippa sailed away (apparently taking Herod's son Antipater with him to Rome [§18.4.4]), Herod remitted a quarter of the taxes for one year in honour of his friendship with him and the accomplishments of the visit. Unfortunately, Agrippa himself died only a year later in 12 BCE.

After more than a decade of building, the completion of Caesarea came in 10–9 BCE (Herod's 38th year, the 192nd Olympiad). Herod held an extravagant dedication ceremony, having 500 talents to spend because both Augustus and his wife Livia made donations toward the festivities. He arranged for a continuation of the celebration at four-year intervals. All of his building projects cost money, and an anecdote says Herod opened David's tomb, as John Hyrcanus allegedly had done. He found no money, however, but only some gold ornaments. But when two of those opening the tomb were killed by a flame, he built a costly entrance of white marble to it. Like the story of Hyrcanus and David's tomb, this story has a suspiciously stereotyped format.

18.4.4. *Conflicts with the Arabs*

Shortly after Herod returned from Rome with his sons, after accusing Mariamme's boys before Caesar (§18.4.5), a conflict with the Arabs occurred. This was in 10–9 BCE (*Ant.* 16.9.1-4 §§271-99; 16.10.8-9 §§335-55; only the last part is in *War* 1.29.3 §§574-77). A group of men from Trachonitis had traditionally supplemented their living by brigandage. When Herod took over rule, he put a stop to this so that they had to earn their living only by farming (§18.4.1). This caused problems because the soil was poor and probably also because it went against their traditional way of life. While Herod was in Rome, a revolt developed which was quickly put down, but about forty of the leaders fled to Arabia. Although the Arab king was Obodas II, the real power behind the throne was Syllaeus (*Ant.* 16.7.6 §220-25; 17.1.1 §10), who gave refuge to the brigands and allowed them to raid Judaea and Coele-Syria from a secure base in Arabian territory. Herod killed many of their relatives in Trachonitis, but they continued to attack his territory. To add insult to injury, Syllaeus reneged on repayment of a loan from Herod (said to be 60 talents in *Ant.* 16.9.1 §279 but 500 in *Ant.* 16.10.8 §343, possibly two separate loans). Part of the problem may have been personal since Syllaeus had once been betrothed to Herod's sister Salome, but the marriage had been prevented by Herod's insistence that Syllaeus adopt Jewish practices (§18.4.5).

Herod was unable to stop the raiders by normal methods and finally lost patience. He consulted with the Roman governors of Syria, Saturninus and Volumnius. They produced an agreement that each party – Herod and Syllaeus – would return the other's subjects who had taken refuge in his territory; also Syllaeus would repay the debt to Herod in thirty days. The result was that many of the brigands were found to be in Arab territory (in spite of Syllaeus's denials). But then Syllaeus went away to Rome without meeting his responsibilities according to the agreement. The Roman officials gave Herod permission to take unilateral action. They supported him by agreeing that he would be justified in taking his army into Arabia. Herod was wholly successful, destroying the brigand stronghold at Rhaepta (unknown) and capturing the defenders; however, he was then attacked by an Arab force and killed its commander in defending himself. To prevent future recurrences of brigand activity, Herod settled a cleruchy of 3,000 Idumaeans in Trachonitis. He reported what he had done to the Roman authorities in Phoenicia, and they judged that he had acted reasonably.

Yet Herod was on thin ice here. A friendly king of Rome, such as he was, had pretty much a free hand in his own kingdom and could do more or less what he wanted. But it was a quite different matter when it came to external matters, such as acting against a fellow client king, and in spite of getting local Roman approval Herod had overstepped his authority – an exceptional misjudgment on his part. Furthermore, on the diplomatic front he was outwitted by Syllaeus who was in Rome during Herod's military actions. Putting his case before Augustus, Syllaeus was able to convince him against Herod to the extent that the emperor wrote him a harsh letter and would not even receive a delegation to give his side of the event. This was serious for Herod, who had enjoyed Augustus's support and friendship up to this point.

18. The Reign of Herod the Great (40–4 BCE)

Syllaeus wrote back to Arabia and told them not to hand over the brigands, so they continued their plundering of Herod's territory. They even attacked the military colony of Idumaeans that he had settled in the area. Herod could do nothing but endure the raids and the general humiliation for a period of time. Then, Obodas died and Aretas IV (§9.2) took the throne. This action irritated Augustus whose permission should normally have been sought; on the other hand, it meant that the Arabian camp was now divided. Aretas sent a golden crown and many gifts to Caesar, but he also wrote a letter with a number of accusations against Syllaeus; however, Augustus ignored the accusations and returned the gifts. Now, however, Herod tried once more to present his case to Caesar by sending his assistant Nicolaus of Damascus. This time Augustus heard Herod's case and was persuaded by Nicolaus who not only was an effective orator but also had the support of Aretas's faction in his charges against Syllaeus (e.g., some incriminating letters). Augustus was sorry for the breach that had been created with Herod and became reconciled with him. Syllaeus, on the other hand, he condemned to death. Augustus was apparently even of a mind to add Arabia to Herod's domain but decided against it because of Herod's age and family troubles. So he confirmed Aretas on the Arabian throne, though rebuking him for his boldness in taking the kingship without first receiving Roman confirmation. (We have Nicolaus's own account of this episode preserved in a fragment of his *Life*; see *GLAJJ* 1:250–60.)

At some point Herod sought to give the people some protection from the brigands in Trachonitis by creating a buffer zone in Batanaea (*War* 2.17.4 §421; *Ant.* 17.2.1-3 §§23-32; *Life* 11 §§46-61). He heard that a group of Jews under a certain Zamaris had come to Antioch from Babylonia with up to 600 men. Herod offered Zamaris land, fortresses and a village free of taxes and tribute by the name of Bathyra. This colony would also help to protect pilgrims journeying from Babylonia to Jerusalem. Over several generations the people of this settlement not only fulfilled their original function but also served as a royal bodyguard, up to the time of Agrippa II.

In spite of Augustus's death sentence on Syllaeus, he seems to have had freedom of movement (*War* 1.29.3 §§574-77; *Ant.* 17.3.2 §§52-57). He had returned home to the kingdom of Aretas and had apparently been involved in the assassination of several prominent Nabataeans, but had not paid his debt to Herod as directed by Augustus. He returned to Rome at the same time as Antipater was there (ca. 6 BCE). Antipater brought charges against him, including a plot to have Herod killed by an Arab servant of his named Corinthus. Herod arrested Corinthus and two other Arabs in his household, who confirmed the plot. Saturninus, the governor of Syria, sent them to Rome for trial. Josephus says nothing further about Syllaeus or his fate. Our only information comes from the historian and geographer Strabo (16.4.24) who says that Syllaeus was responsible for the failure of the expedition of Aelius Gallus against south Arabia (*Arabia Felix*), as well as other offences (not named but no doubt including the attempt to poison Herod) and as a result he was beheaded in Rome.

18.4.5. *Family Quarrels and Problems*

Most of the rest of Josephus's narrative about Herod (in both the *War* and the *Antiquities*) is taken up with the rather unedifying spectacle of family jealousies, hates, intrigues and executions. The problem for the historian is how to evaluate this information. It is not the stuff of history but of soap opera. This does not mean that many of the events described did not take place, or even did not occur much as recounted, but woven into the narrative is continual moral evaluation, assigning of motives, descriptions of states of mind and general pseudo-psychoanalysis. To take this at face value – as many writers unfortunately have done – is to treat the stuff of romance as if it were straightforward history. Most of the data can be summarized fairly briefly, and lose nothing by conciseness. In some cases there is good reason to question the accounts because Josephus contradicts himself, but even where he does not, one can only point out what is said without necessarily supposing that it represents a high degree of accuracy.

The first episode in this business was the execution of his wife Mariamme, the granddaughter of Hyrcanus. Two separate scenarios are given, dated several years apart, so that determining which (if either) is correct is not easy. According to the *War* (1.22.2-4 §§436-44), the other women of the household (on Herod's side of the family) began intriguing against Mariamme, accusing her of adultery. Then, when Herod was away in 30 BCE, he entrusted her to his brother-in-law Joseph, leaving instructions that he was to slay her if he was sentenced to death since he could not bear the thought of her marrying another man. But Joseph told her of these instructions, and on Herod's return Mariamme confronted him with this information. He assumed that she could have gained access to it only if intimate with Joseph; therefore, he had them *both* executed. A similar episode is found in the *Antiquities* (15.3.5-9 §§62-87 – and summarized above [§18.2.3]), except that it is dated to Herod's trial before Antony because of Cleopatra's accusations (ca. 34 BCE), and only Joseph was executed, not Mariamme.

But a little later (*Ant.* 15.6.5 §§183-86; 15.7.1-4 §§202-34) a further similar incident is narrated. It could almost be the same as the story of Joseph and Mariamme, with just the names changed. The occasion was when Herod went to meet Octavian after the battle of Actium (30 BCE). Left to protect and guard Mariamme was Soemus, Herod's faithful Ituraean servant. Through kindness and manipulation, Mariamme learned from Soemus that Herod had given instructions to kill her if something happened to him when he met Octavian – precisely the scenario with Herod's brother-in-law Joseph when Herod went to defend himself before Antony. When Mariamme eventually accused Herod of not loving her and revealed that she knew of his instructions, he had Soemus executed. However, he put Mariamme formally on trial, with charges including administering love potions and drugs to him secretly. She was found guilty, and even her own mother Alexandra repudiated her (no doubt in an attempt to protect herself).

Because of the great similarity, it seems likely that one of the accounts in the *Antiquities* is the doublet of the other, perhaps because Josephus had two versions of the same event. One might draw some significance from the fact that the time of Mariamme's execution is the same in both accounts even though the co-accused is different; however, it is not clear that Josephus is all that reliable on chronological matters when he departs from the framework of Nicolaus of Damascus, which he seems to be doing more in the *Antiquities* than in the *War*. Yet if we trust Josephus's rather overheated narratives, Herod seems to have been very much in love with Mariamme – or at least obsessed with her. If she had been more astute, she undoubtedly could have manipulated him and got him to do whatever she wanted. Instead, she played on her 'royal' Hasmonaean connections and openly showed her contempt for and hatred of her husband. He would get angry but would then cool off and seek reconciliation, but she apparently refused to bend.

Perhaps more fatefully her contempt also extended to the females in Herod's family, his mother Cypros and his sister Salome. Mariamme's attitude toward them was eventually one of the significant causes of her downfall, because they worked on Herod to make him jealous and suspicious until he finally took action against Mariamme in spite of his feelings for her. But once she had been executed, Herod seems to have had a mental breakdown. At times he seemed to think she was still alive; he went off by himself in the wilderness under the pretext of hunting. This evident mental distress led after a time to his contracting a serious illness and seeming to be on his deathbed. Mariamme's mother Alexandra, not for the first time scheming against Herod, tried to get control of two key fortresses in Jerusalem, one protecting the city (the Akra?) and one protecting the temple. She used the excuse that they should be surrendered to her and Herod's son (by Mariamme?), in case a usurper should try to take them if Herod died. But those in charge of the fortresses were loyal friends of Herod and informed the convalescing king of her scheme, and he had her put to death. Much of these narratives in Josephus are naturally interpretations, most probably Josephus's own, but possibly those of his source (perhaps a combination of the two). Can we trust their psychoanalyzing of Herod? They seem to make sense up to a point, and Herod's actions after Mariamme's execution seem to bear out strong feelings for her.

Another relative who tried to betray Herod was the high-ranking Idumaean Costobarus. He had been married to Herod's sister Salome (after her former husband Joseph was executed) and made governor of Idumaea and Gaza. This was at a time when Antony was still in control (ca. 35–34 BCE), and Costobarus decided to hedge his bets by writing secretly to Cleopatra that she should try to gain possession of Idumaea. She asked Antony for Idumaea (among other territories), but he did not grant her wish. Herod, however, got to hear of Costobarus's treachery, and would have executed him but for the intercession of his mother and sister. But later Salome fell out with Costobarus and divorced him. She also claimed to have learned that Costobarus, along with Antipater (otherwise unknown), Lysimachus (otherwise unknown) and Dositheus (a friend of Hyrcanus [*Ant.* 15.6.2 §168]), were planning a revolt (this was about 25 BCE). She presented as evidence the 'Sons of Baba'. This was an influential group or family who opposed Herod's rule and supported the Hasmonaeans. After Herod retook Jerusalem in 37 BCE, Costobarus helped the Sons of Baba to escape the city secretly and hid them on his estate for 12 years, in spite of attempts by Herod to find them. After Salome's accusations, Herod sent his men who discovered the Sons of Baba as claimed and killed them. Costobarus and the other alleged conspirators also met their end at this time.

Intrigues among Herod's relatives also eventually led to the execution of Alexander and Aristobulus, Mariamme's two sons by Herod (*War* 1.23.1-27.6 §§445-551; *Ant.* 16.1.2 §§6-11) – he had three sons by her but one died as a youth. They received their education at Rome, staying in the house of Pollio (presumably C. Asinius Pollio). They were likely heirs to Herod's kingdom at this time. Herod sailed to Rome in about 18 BCE to meet Augustus and to bring the lads home. But having returned to Judah, they seem to have been very resentful over the treatment of their mother, though Josephus also claims they had a 'desire to get control/have power' (τοῦ κρατεῖν ἐπιθυμίᾳ). The accounts in Josephus generally take the view that they were just rather bitter young men, who spoke up when it would have been wiser to keep their mouths shut, rather than guilty of actual plots against Herod's life. Josephus also alleged that Salome and others slandered the young men to Herod. There was even a report that they planned to use Alexander's father-in-law Archelaus of Cappadocia as a way to bring a charge against Herod to Augustus.

A further complication was the question of their half-brother Antipater, son of Herod's first wife Doris. When Herod married Mariamme, he divorced Doris and exiled her son Antipater from Jerusalem (*War* 1.22.1 §§432-33). The indiscretions and outspokenness of Alexander and Aristobulus resulted in Herod's recalling Antipater from exile and showing him various favours. Once Antipater was present in court, rivalry was inevitable between the potential heirs, especially since Antipater was the firstborn even though not considered heir after Herod married Mariamme. According to Josephus, who is probably following Nicolaus's own bias here, Antipater was the main instigator of charges, rumours and lies against the sons of Mariamme. He was now declared Herod's successor, both publicly and in Herod's will. In 13 BCE Herod entrusted Antipater to Agrippa who was returning to Rome (*Ant.* 16.3.3 §86), with the apparent aim of advancing the lad by exposure to the culture and elite of the capital of the Empire.

Events first came to a head about 12 BCE when Herod finally took Alexander (so *War* 1.23.3 §452; *Ant.* 16.4.1 §90 also includes Aristobulus) to be accused before Augustus in Rome. The outcome of this was a reconciliation of Herod and his son(s) through the good offices of Augustus. Herod made a present of 300 talents to Augustus, and the latter presented Herod with management of the Cyprus copper mines and half their revenue. On his way back to Judaea he visited Archelaus of Cappadocia, who was pleased to hear of the reconciliation. The accused sons and Antipater returned with him to Jerusalem, where all three were declared joint heirs.

The reports of plottings against Herod did not cease, however. Josephus ascribes much of this to Antipater, who was allegedly skilful in manipulating matters to implicate Alexander and Aristobulus, though Salome is also implicated. At the same time, Antipater was supposedly ingratiating himself with Herod in various ways. To make matters worse, the actions of Alexander's wife Glaphyra (daughter of Archelaus of Cappadocia) also aroused the resentment of Herod's sister Salome, partly because of her disdain toward Aristobulus's wife Berenice (Salome's daughter). Pheroras, Herod's brother, also became involved. Herod had betrothed him to his own daughter by Mariamme, Salampsio, but Pheroras had fallen for a female slave. Finally, Herod married Salampsio to his nephew Phasael (son of his brother Phasael). Herod then offered another daughter by Mariamme, Cypros, to Pheroras. At first, he claimed to have renounced the slave but he in fact did not do so. Then Pheroras approached Alexander and claimed that Herod was enamoured of his wife Glaphyra. Alexander confronted Herod who became furious with Pheroras who in turn blamed Salome!

At one point Pheroras was accused of planning to flee to Parthia with his slave mistress. In her turn Salome was accused by him of planning to marry Syllaeus, the administrator of the realm of the Arab king Obodas. This last accusation was true, though the *War* and the *Antiquities* give different perspectives. According to *War* (1.24.6 §487) Herod learned of this when Pheroras accused Salome – as if it was a conspiracy. But according to *Antiquities* (16.7.6 §§220-28), when Syllaeus visited Herod's court, the feelings between him and Salome were reported to the king, who had Pheroras observe their behaviour. Pheroras confirmed their relationship, but not long afterward Syllaeus came to Herod with a marriage proposal. When Herod consulted Salome, she agreed. Herod then required that Syllaeus adopt Jewish customs (τῶν Ἰουδαίων ἔθεσι), which he refused to do, and the marriage was off. Only then did Pheroras make scandalous accusations against Salome.

Josephus goes on at great length about the accusations and Herod's morbid fears that put him in a state of mental torture. He then has Herod on a campaign of suspicion and torture against all, even his long-term and intimate friends. How much of this we can believe is a question. One of the main reasons for being cautious is that Herod's other actions and decisions during this time seem rational and reasonable.

Continuing the saga, as Josephus recounts it: at one point three of Herod's personal servants who were eunuchs admitted to relations with Alexander. Only under torture did they reveal supposed intimate talk which suggested that he would be ruling instead of Herod before long. After further inquiries, Herod had Alexander imprisoned. This time his father-in-law Archelaus, king of Cappadocia, managed to reconcile him with Herod. He also reconciled Herod with his brother Pheroras. In a turnabout, though, Herod was able to reconcile Archelaus with Marcus Titius, governor of Syria, who had been in dispute with him. Nevertheless, several more years of continual suspicions, charges and reports followed. One cause of friction was a visit to court by the Spartan C. Julius Eurycles (mentioned by Pausanias 2.3.5). He was a friend of Antipater but pretended to befriend Alexander and Aristobulus, yet all the while reporting back to Antipater. Eventually, a letter of Alexander's was found (though he claimed it was a forgery) in which he planned to assassinate Herod and flee to the fortress Alexandrium. Herod imprisoned Alexander and Aristobulus and wrote to Augustus for his permission to punish them.

This was at the time when Augustus had been angry with Herod over the affair of Syllaeus and Arabia. The letter reached the emperor, however, after Nicolaus had succeeded in changing Caesar's view (§18.4.4) toward the king. Augustus gave Herod permission to deal with his sons according to the nature of their crimes, but advised him to examine them before a council. Herod assembled such a council of governors, officials and appropriate family members – 150 in all. Although several argued for a more lenient punishment, the council as a whole voted for the death penalty. It was now about 6 BCE. Herod met Nicolaus, who was returning from Rome, at Tyre. Nicolaus told him that his friends at Rome thought the young men should be imprisoned but not executed. Notwithstanding this opinion, Herod had his sons put to death by strangling at Sebaste and then buried in Alexandrium (with their maternal grandfather Alexander). Yet he was concerned to take care of the widows and orphans. He sent Glaphyra back to her father but also gave her back her dowry. He then arranged marriages for Aristobulus's widow Bernice and for a number of the children of Alexander and Aristobulus.

Antipater is alleged by Josephus, probably following Nicolaus, to be not only the chief plotter against the two sons of Mariamme but also against Herod himself. Because of Nicolaus's anti-Antipater bias, it is difficult to know whether to give credence to this charge even though it is not by any means implausible. In any event, the family intrigues were supposed to have continued even after the executions of Mariamme's sons. Herod seems to have turned management of his court over to Antipater because of confidence in him. Pheroras found it useful to pay homage to Antipater, but he was undone by his devotion to his wife. She, with her mother and some other women, were alleged to have formed a cabal against Herod. They insulted two of Herod's daughters and aroused the animosity of Herod's sister Salome.

One of the incidents that aroused suspicions with regard to Pheroras's wife concerned the Pharisees. Herod required an oath of loyalty to Caesar and also to himself (§18.4.3). The 6,000 Pharisees refused to swear this oath, and Herod punished them with a fine. Pheroras's wife paid the fine on their behalf, however, after which some of them predicted that the throne would be taken from Herod and come to her and her husband. This by itself was bad enough, but Herod found that Pharisees had made inroads into his court and corrupted certain individuals. Apparently promises of offspring and rulership were made to a certain eunuch (cf. Isa. 56.3-5). Herod put him and some other courtiers to death but also some of the Pharisees.

Finally, Herod convened an assembly of friends and accused Pheroras's wife before them. Pheroras was called on to divorce her but refused. Eventually, Herod banished both Pheroras and his wife. Pheroras went back to his tetrarchy in Transjordan where he became ill and died. But some of his men claimed that he had been poisoned by his wife. Inquiry confirmed this to Herod who confronted her. She tried to commit suicide, failed and revealed all under the promise of immunity. She admitted the poisoning, but her testimony and that of various servants also implicated Antipater, his mother Doris and also Mariamme the daughter of the high priest (and Herod's wife). Herod stripped Doris of her finery and banished her. He removed Mariamme's father Simon from the high priesthood, replacing him with Matthias son of Theophilus from Jerusalem. He also divorced Mariamme and cut her son Herod out of his will.

The question was what to do about Antipater who had now been accused from a variety of quarters. In spite of his previous confidence in Antipater, Herod now believed the various charges against him. Antipater had travelled to Rome a while before to meet Augustus and also to take Herod's will, which designated him as Herod's successor. He had made himself useful in prosecuting Syllaeus at this time (§18.4.4) but had also been instrumental in getting letters sent to Herod that accused Archelaus and Philip (sons of Herod who were being educated in Rome at this time) of plotting against him. Antipater did not suspect anything, having heard nothing of the accusations against him, but returned home after seven months in Rome. Herod assembled a council of friends and relatives, including those of Antipater, at the centre of which was the legate of Syria, Quintilius Varus, who was to be the chief judge. Nicolaus of Damascus had the main task of prosecution. Although Antipater defended himself, Herod had him bound and imprisoned, and both he and Varus wrote to Caesar. Shortly afterward, letters as if from Salome were found to have been forged by Acme, a servant of the empress Livia, at Antipater's instigation, a further charge against him. Herod altered his will making Herod Antipas his heir (and passing over both Archelaus and Philip).

18.4.6. *Death of Herod*

D. J. Ladouceur (1981) 'The Death of Herod the Great', *Classical Philology* 76: 25–34.

By this time it was late 5 or early 4 BCE. Herod became seriously ill and steadily got worse. From the sequence of events in Josephus, it appears that the illness lasted only a few months, though the precise progress of the disease is unclear. The description of it is horrendous but part or even much of this could be a literary concoction; certainly one should be careful in taking the description at face value to the point of trying to determine the precise affliction as has sometimes been done (cf. Ladouceur 1981). Herod's attempts to find a cure or even relief from the pain were unsuccessful.

On one occasion rumour had it that Herod was dead. There were two religious teachers by the name of Matthias son of Sepphoraeus and Judas son of Margalus or Margalothus. These two men are called 'sophists' or 'teachers' (σοφισταί) by Josephus and are said to have a reputation of being experts in the ancestral laws and their interpretation. They are often identified as Pharisees, but knowledge of and expertise in the laws was hardly limited to Pharisees, and Josephus has no hesitation in identifying people as Pharisees. The fact that he does not do so here is a good indication that they were *not* Pharisees. No images had been allowed in the refurbished temple; however, over the main gate of the temple Herod had had a golden eagle erected as a votive offering (but perhaps also in homage to Augustus specifically or the Romans generally). Matthias and Judas instigated their disciples to tear it down. An officer of the king (and of the temple?) brought a large force and arrested about forty of those who did not flee, fearing that more extensive riot or even revolt was in the making (which was probably the case according to *War* 2.1.2 §5). When brought before the king, they defended themselves with the statement that they were serving God, and death would be only a passage to a greater reward. Herod had them taken to the amphitheatre in Jericho and charged them with sacrilege (ἱεροσύλων). He had the teachers and the chief culprits burned alive and the rest executed. Josephus claims an eclipse of the moon took place on the day of the executions, which was probably seen as a divine sign by some (perhaps even Josephus himself; cf. Plutarch, *Aemilius Paullus* 17.7-10).

Herod's health continued to deteriorate. He went to the warm baths at Callirrhoe near Jericho but this did not help. Josephus claims he gathered notable Jews from all over his kingdom into the hippodrome. He is then alleged to have instructed Salome and her husband Alexas to have them shot down by the soldiers when he died, that the nation would mourn at his death – even if not for him! This is another damning anecdote whose credibility is often taken at face value in spite of serious doubts about its truth. First of all, no such slaughter in fact took place, which immediately casts doubt on Herod's supposed intent. Secondly, E. Baltrusch (2012: 216–17) has argued that as a precaution against a revolt against his successor, Herod assembled the elite among the Judaeans in Jericho as hostages, though no harm came to them nor was meant to. After his death an anti-Herodian tradition developed that he was planning to kill them.

More credible is the statement that letters arrived from Caesar, giving Herod the authority to banish or execute Antipater. The sentence was not carried out immediately. Then Herod tried to kill himself with a paring knife but was prevented; however, a rumour went around the palace that he was dead. Antipater heard this and tried to bribe his jailor to release him. When this was reported to the king, he had Antipater summarily executed and buried in the Hyrcania fortress. Herod then changed his will one last time, giving kingship of Judaea to Archelaus (son of his wife Malthace), a tetrarchy of Galilee and Peraea to Antipas (also son of Malthace) and a tetrarchy of Trachonitis, Batanaea and Paneas to Philip (son of his wife Cleopatra). Five days after Antipater's execution Herod died. This was shortly before Passover, in late March or early April 4 BCE. He had reigned 37 years since he was made king in 40 BCE, 34 years since the execution of Antigonus in 37 BCE.

Archelaus laid on a magnificent funeral, followed by a mourning period of seven days. Some of the people made demands on Archelaus, mostly about taxes, on which he yielded. When they called for punishment on some with regard to the eagle incident, though, he was reluctant to accede. When they refused to hear his messengers and occupied a section of the temple, Archelaus sent in a cohort of soldiers which was repulsed, with many apparently killed. This time he sent in the army, which reportedly killed 3,000 while the rest fled into the hills. Archelaus now headed for Rome, though he met with Sabinus, Caesar's procurator (ἐπίτροπος), in Syria, who was planning to take charge of Herod's property, including his fortresses and treasuries. But Varus, Sabinus's superior, forbade him from doing this. Sabinus complied but moved on to Jerusalem where he occupied Herod's palace.

Others also went to Rome, including Salome and Antipas; only Philip evidently remained at home to look after the country. A number of the party were opposed to Archelaus and wrote allegations against him to Caesar. Many favoured Antipas. Augustus convened a council of leading Romans and listened to the case of each side. He then made no decision but decided to think the matter over. But while he was doing so, a letter from Varus arrived, reporting a revolt in Judaea. Varus had anticipated unrest after Archelaus left and had gone to Jerusalem, quieted it down and left a legion to keep order. Sabinus who remained in Jerusalem ended up stirring up the populous by resuming his plan to take over the various fortresses under his control and seek for Herod's treasures (evidently for the purpose of personal gain!). When Pentecost came, many from Galilee, Idumaea and Transjordan joined Judaeans with the intent of confronting Sabinus. He realized he was in trouble and wrote to Varus, while taking refuge in the fortress of Phasael. He sent soldiers to attack the Jews, and the fight encompassed portions of the temple. Since many Jewish fighters mounted the porticoes on the outer portions of the temple, giving them a height advantage, the Romans set fire to the porticoes. In addition to getting rid of many of the enemy, it allowed the Romans to get access to the temple treasury and loot it; Sabinus is said to have taken 400 talents for himself.

The rebels were not defeated, however, and now besieged Sabinus. Most of the royal troops had joined the rebels, but an elite group of 3,000 Sebastenians (i.e., from Samaria) remained loyal. In Idumaea about 2,000 of Herod's veterans also rebelled, and rebel leaders arose in several different places. In a number of cases these were evidently messianic pretenders, claiming royalty and a divine mission. Judas, the son of the brigand chief Ezechias (executed by Herod), organized a group in Galilee and aimed for royalty. A slave of the king Simon took the crown and made raids in the countryside in Peraea, though his group was stopped by the Sebastenians, and he was killed. A shepherd named Athrogaeus also took on the persona of a king, and with his four brothers led effective raids against not only Romans and those loyal to the king but apparently all fellow Jews as well.

When Varus got Sabinus's letter he set out with two legions and collected additional auxiliaries on the way, including Arab troops from Aretas of Petra. He sent part of his army into Galilee, which captured Sepphoris and routed the opposition. Varus himself marched to Samaria but spared the city because it had not joined the rebels. Several villages were burnt, including Emmaus. By the time Varus reached Jerusalem the besieging rebels had fled, while the remaining Jews in the city asserted to him that they were innocent bystanders, caught up in the fighting. Sabinus, meanwhile, had slipped off to the coast, apparently not wanting to be confronted by Varus about his thoroughly botched military operation. The Romans went through the countryside, hunting out rebels. Two thousand were said to have been crucified. Aretas's soldiers had been undisciplined and hard to control, however, and were sent home. A contingent of 10,000 Jews in Idumaea surrendered to Herod's cousin Achiab before Varus could attack them. Varus was willing to pardon most of the rebels but sent the leaders to Rome, where Augustus in turn pardoned many of them but not those of Herod's relatives, who had joined the rebels. Varus left a legion in Jerusalem and returned to Antioch.

Philip was now also in Rome, sent there on the advice of Varus. Also arriving to present a case before Augustus was a delegation of fifty Jews that Varus had allowed to travel with a claim to represent the people. Supported by a large number of local Jews from Rome itself (allegedly 8,000), they were allowed to petition against Herod's rule and Archelaus as his successor, asking for Judaea to be joined to Syria and no longer have a king – in other words, to revert to being part of a Roman province. Nicolaus of Damascus replied to their accusations, defending Herod and Archelaus. August deliberated for several days, then essentially followed Herod's final will: Archelaus to have half the territory (including Judaea, Samaria, and Idumaea); Antipas, the tetrarchy of Galilee and Peraea; and Philip, the tetrarchy of Trachonitis, Batanaea, Auranitis and part of the old domain of Zenodorus (§18.4.1). A number of the Greek cities were put under Syria, including Gaza, Gadara and Hippus. Salome received a large cash payment, an annual stipend and Jamneia, Azotus, Phasaelis and the palace of Ascalon. Caesar also rejected the 1,500 talents left to him by Herod and had it distributed among the king's offspring, keeping only a few inexpensive ornaments as mementos of the king. Archelaus was ethnarch, not king, though the possibility of the title in future was dangled before him by the emperor.

18.4.7. *Assessment of Herod's Reign*

> **M. J. S. Chiat** (1981) 'First-Century Synagogue Architecture: Methodological Problems', in L. I. Levine (ed.) *Ancient Synagogues Revealed*, 49–60; **S. J. D. Cohen** (1985) 'The Origins of the Matrilineal Principle in Rabbinic Law', *AJS Review* 10: 19–53; **W. D. Davies and D. C. Allison** (1988) *The Gospel According to Saint Matthew, volume 1*; **L. H. Feldman** (1984) *Josephus and Modern Scholarship (1937–1980)*; **R. T. France** (1979) 'Herod and the Children of Bethlehem', *NovT* 21: 98–120; **P. Richardson** (1986) 'Law and Piety in Herod's Architecture', *SR* 15: 347–60; **A. Schalit** (1969) 'A Clash of Ideologies: Palestine under the Seleucids and Romans', in A. Toynbee (ed.), *The Crucible of Christianity*, 47–76.

Herod has been such a notorious and controversial figure that any evaluation of him is very difficult. In assessing his reign, one must ask, Against what standard? Other Graeco-Roman despots? The Hasmonaean rulers? Some golden ideal of kingship? Ancient views of Herod were generally negative and have gone a long way to shape the modern ones. Perhaps one of the views which has had most influence in later Christian history is the labelling of Herod as 'slaughterer of the innocents'.

According to Mt. 2.16-18, Herod asked the Magi to tell him where the baby born king of the Jews was located. When they disregarded this, he is alleged to have slain all males of two years old and under in Bethlehem. Some histories and commentaries still take this at face value, but it is clearly a piece of legend, probably Christian, though whether it was meant consciously to be anti-Herodian or only to demonstrate opposition to the Christ child seems uncertain. The legendary nature of the story is indicated by (a) the whole context of men from the east following a star; (b) the idea that Herod would have taken such a mission to find a newborn 'king of the Jews' seriously; (c) the fact that Josephus, who has many distinctly anti-Herodian passages and even outright slander, says nothing about such a thing (e.g, the criticisms of Herod by a Jewish delegation before Augustus do not use such an example even though it would have been an unparalleled example of cruelty and despotic rule – *War* 2.6.2 §§84-86; *Ant.* 17.11.2 §§304-10); (d) the fact that no other writer mentions what would surely be a point of interest to any Roman reader about this Jewish king; (e) the common motifs found in a variety of accounts of the birth of important religious figures. It has been argued that the origin of many of the motifs of this section of Matthew lie in the Moses haggadic traditions (Davies and Alison 1998: 192–94, 264–66; contra France 1979).

Modern scholarship has presented a mixed picture of Herod. To its credit there are those who have attempted to provide a positive side of the man, but probably the majority of accounts that one reads tend to take much of Josephus's assessment at face value (cf. the summary in Feldman 1984: 278–87). Such views can be summed up by the title of S. Sandmel's book, *Herod: Profile of a Tyrant* (1967). The autocratic and even tyrannical aspect of Herod's rule can be taken for granted, but such is the nature of one-ruler states throughout history. The question is to what extent his rule should be characterized by the negative aspects and to what extent these are countered by other, more positive features. Schalit's study (1969) attempted a revision of the negative view, as have several more recent works (e.g., Richardson 1996; Baltrusch 2012). The studies would hardly be classified as a whitewash, but they do go a long way toward pointing out the positive features of Herod's rule, which not only helped the Jews in many ways during his lifetime but paved the way for his descendants (such as Agrippa I and Agrippa II) to act as advocates for the Jewish people on a number of occasions.

One thing to keep in mind in any discussion is that the bulk of the accounts which have come down to us are either hostile or neutral; favourable portraits of Herod such as that by Nicolaus of Damascus have not survived intact. Jewish legend and tradition have been much along the lines of the rather biased picture of Josephus. In a tragic stereotype which probably owes much to Nicolaus, Josephus presents Herod as a man who had extraordinary good fortune in his rise to the throne and in his rule; countering this, as if a divine law, were the misfortunes which arose from his own family. There is undoubtedly truth in this binary opposition, but one must keep in mind that Josephus/Nicolaus is following a literary device which may have forced conformity of some of the data to the scheme. Herod's problems within his own family occasioned the anecdote which ascribed to Augustus the observation, 'I would rather be Herod's pig (Greek *hus*) than his son (Greek *huios*)' (Macrobius, *Saturnalia* 2.4.11). The ascription does not have to be correct to illustrate the tradition about Herod preserved in the non-Jewish world. But even if Augustus said such a thing, it could hardly have escaped his notice that he experienced similar troubles within his own family during his long reign. Thus, Herod was not the only capable ruler whose competence changed remarkably as he passed from the throne room into the living quarters.

As a Hellenistic monarch and a client-king under Rome, Herod was probably exceptional in his accomplishments and his generosity toward the general Hellenistic culture. His exercise of power was not particularly arbitrary by the standards of the time, nor were his exactions from his own people more burdensome than in other kingdoms. On the other hand, he respected the religious feelings in the Jewish areas of his territory. When once confronted by a delegation which accused him of putting pagan images in the Jerusalem theatre, he showed that this was a simple misunderstanding. His coinage was aniconic. He rebuilt the Jerusalem temple into one of the outstanding edifices of the Roman world. The only significant religious violation which some could point to was the golden eagle over the temple entrance, but even that was meant to be a votive offering.

Indeed, the point must be made that Herod considered himself a Jew, by all indications. It is common to label him a 'foreigner' because sources such as Josephus identify him as an Idumaean: 'a half-Jew' (*Ant.* 14.15.2 §403). But apart from the question of descent, which is not an easy one (§17.9.1), he regarded himself – and was regarded by the Romans, if the anecdotes are true – as a Jew. Notice the following considerations:

- His respect for Jewish customs: There are no examples of blatant disregard for them. Even in the midst of a tirade about the introduction of 'foreign' and 'unlawful' customs by Herod, Josephus has then to admit that this did not really involve a breach of Jewish law, as Herod himself demonstrated to his critics (*Ant.* 15.8.1-2 §§267-79).
- His coins with no human portraits on them (cf. §2.3).
- His requirement that a Nabataean convert to Jewish practices before he would marry his sister Salome to him (*Ant.* 16.7.6 §§221-25).
- The amount of money and interest he put into the Jerusalem temple.
- His fortress at Herodium, considered by many to have had a synagogue in it (though this identification is not accepted by everyone [Chiat 1981]). Even his most private quarters at Masada used no offensive motifs in the skilful decorations (cf. Richardson 1986).
- His speech about building the temple which refers to the ancient Israelites as '*our* fathers' (*Ant.* 15.11.1 §385).

No one of these by itself is decisive; each one individually could be explained differently, but there is a cumulative effect. Unfortunately, the tendency is to judge Herod by an artificial standard because of prejudice against him. For example, no one seems to question the Jewish identity of Agrippa I, yet all his coins outside Judea have human portraits on them, whereas his grandfather Herod did not use human images on any of his coins. Why should the one be ignored for his benefit, while the positive side of the other is dismissed as mere politics? It has sometimes been alleged that Herod would not have been considered Jewish because his mother was not Jewish; however, this appears to be anachronistic since the matrilineal descent of Jewishness is a later development. In Herod's own time Jews seem to have regarded the ethnicity of the father the important factor (Cohen 1985).

On the economic side, it is often stated that he burdened his subjects with taxes. All rulers taxed their subjects, and this would always weigh more heavily on the poor and politically impotent, but there is no indication that Herod's taxes were greater than those of previous or later rulers (§5.3). On the contrary, his rule probably relieved some of the burden since the indication is that the taxes placed by the Romans in the period between 63 and 40 was crushing, partly because of war expenses and partly because a good deal of territory was taken away from Jewish control. Under Herod most of this was regained; in addition, he opened up new land to cultivation in certain desolate regions. Also, it now seems clear that Herod did not pay regular tribute to the Romans (despite the assertion in many standard works that he did).

Further on the financial side, he was able to diffuse criticism at various times by acts of generosity to his own people: He prevented the soldiers from looting Jerusalem when it fell in 37 BCE by rewarding them from his own pocket (§18.2.2). He relieved a famine at considerable expense to himself, which silenced his critics and established general good will even among many who were formerly hostile (§18.4.3 [*Ant.* 15.9.1-2 §§299-316]). In honour of his meeting with Agrippa he rescinded a quarter of the taxes for the year 12 BCE, which is said to have won over his immediate audience of a large assembly consisting of the people of Jerusalem and many from the country (*Ant.* 16.2.5 §§64-65). The enormous expenses of the temple building supposedly came from his own coffers (*Ant.* 15.11.1 §380). Much of the cost of his other building projects may have come from the half-shekel tax on Jews, including those in the diaspora.

Yet one would hardly call him a benevolent monarch. He governed as absolute ruler and could be completely ruthless in suppressing opposition (*Ant.* 15.10.4 §§365-72). At the beginning of his rule he made the Sanhedrin completely impotent – as far as any check on his activities is concerned – by executing a number of its members and cowing the rest (*Ant.* 14.9.4 §175). Although it was subordinate to the Hasmonaean rulers, it does seem to have functioned as a form of restraint on them, whereas it ceased to have any political function under Herod, as far as can be determined. But was he worse than other monarchs of the time – whether local potentates, monarchs of sizable kingdoms or even the Roman emperor himself? Indeed, was he really any different from the Hasmonaean rulers before him? Remember the concerted opposition to Alexander Jannaeus – but also to John Hyrcanus and others.

It is very difficult to judge public opinion in the days before scientific polls (and perhaps even since!). There were certainly those who detested him and his rule, but to extrapolate beyond that to say that he was unpopular with the Jews – as is so often done – is simply to go beyond our knowledge. We do not know that he was any more unpopular than, for example, Alexander Jannaeus. Some who were critical changed their minds, at least temporarily, according to statements in Josephus. Certain groups and individuals evidently benefited from his rule, not least the temple priests and personnel. Much of his contribution to building projects elsewhere in the Hellenistic world could have been primarily egocentric but would still help the reputation of the Jews, who were often being criticized for their unusual customs at this time. And he was able to intercede on behalf of certain Jewish communities with the Roman authorities on occasion (e.g., *Ant.* 16.2.3-5 §§27-65). In fact, he seems to have had a special concern for Jews in the diaspora, as has been pointed out (§10.2.2). Any judgment on Herod must consider the positive as well as the negative. There lies the final question: Whatever his faults, was Herod's rule not preferable to that of direct Roman rule? Some thought not at the time of his death, but what about in the decades after 6 CE when Judaea was once again a Roman province? The Jewish delegation that asked Augustus for direct Roman rule may have rued their words when Judaea did actually revert to being a Roman province once again.

18.5. *Conclusions*

Under Antony and Octavian, Herod proved to be an extremely useful ally of the Romans and was declared king after the Parthian take-over of Palestine in 40 BCE. Only a few years after he had retaken Jerusalem and established his rule, the battle of Actium in 31 found Herod on the losing side. Nevertheless, he was confirmed in his kingship by Octavian and became close friends with the emperor and his family. Much of positive value can be seen in Herod's rule, when all considerations are taken into account, though the last part of his reign was clouded by sordid events within his family and his own reactions to them.

Judah's destiny was now inexorably tied up with Rome, and Herod's personal relationship with leading Romans was extremely important for what happened not only to the people of Judaea but also to Jews over the Mediterranean world. The Jews were very much caught up in the Roman civil war. Even from his first public responsibility as governor of Galilee, Herod himself was a cog in this destructive Roman conflict. The conflict also served as a vehicle for inter-Jewish rivalries and enmities, but could also be a useful means of protecting one's back. Herod made use of the Roman governor of the region to defend him against a charge before the Sanhedrin that seems mainly politically motivated, but his father Antipater lost his life in the greater Roman struggle (though by a Jewish rival). Herod also gained Roman help in defeating his Hasmonaean enemy Antigonus, who had been supported by the Parthians. He was able to establish his kingship with Roman support (from 40 BCE), then had Antony on his side for almost a decade, though Antony's paramour Cleopatra was a definite thorn in his side for much of this time.

Although seemingly having Antony's support, Herod's position and power were under continual threat from his Jewish opponents, who in turn received aid from Cleopatra. From his point of view, the battle of Actium in 31 BCE could not have come at a more opportune time. Yet it left him on the losing side, because he had been a friend and ally of Antony. This time he seemed threatened by the power of Rome. But he went boldly to Octavian, frankly admitted his friendship and alliance with Antony, and offered the same now to the winner. Octavian welcomed him as a friend and ally, and he remained this for most of the rest of his reign (except for one small period when he got on Octavian's wrong side). This friendship with the emperor's family was to stand him in good stead, but not only him: it benefitted the Jews enormously, both in Judaea itself but also throughout the Roman empire.

In the western part of the Roman empire events tended to be determined by Rome's interactions with those on its borders as it expanded further to the west and north. The main area of conflict came in the east. First, there was the uneasy truce, the 'cold war', between Octavian and Mark Antony, which was fought for many years with the tools of propaganda – rumour, innuendo, allegation, pamphleteering – until it finally ended in Actium. After a year or so in charge of Syria and Palestine following their conquest in 40 BCE, the Parthians were defeated by the Romans and withdrew. But this was not the end of Parthian and Roman conflict. The new emperor Augustus negotiated peace with Parthia, but clashes continued intermittently for the next several centuries. But Herod's troubles with Parthia were at an end, and once he had defeated Antigonus, his rulership was established. After Actium it was undisputed.

Herod ruled an area about as large as Judaea was ever to control. He was a 'friendly king' (sometimes called a 'client-king') with Rome and had mostly autonomy within his own realm. Herod collected taxes from Judaeans, but there were no separate taxes imposed by Rome – friendly kingdoms were not generally taxed by Rome, though the kings often made generous gifts to the emperor or Rome by other means, and Herod was no exception. From all the actual data extant, Herod's taxation was not a major burden, and the people prospered. They did not have the freedom exercised by those in a modern democracy, but by the standards of government of the time, Judaeans had little reason to complain. The administration monitored political activity carefully (i.e., the citizens were spied upon in various ways), and potential revolts were quickly pounced on. But this was essentially the situation throughout rule in the Mediterranean world over the centuries before and after this time.

Herod's building programme seems to have benefitted the country, not only in prestige and in gaining Roman good will but also in providing work for many artisans and ordinary workmen. The refurbishment of the Jerusalem temple was one of Herod's major achievements and one that benefitted Jews both in Judaea and those visiting from the diaspora. Another major project, of commercial value and profit to the kingdom, was the port of Caesarea. Herod's outreach to Jews outside of Judaea was also an innovation under him. Some of the Hasmonaean rulers had shown some concern for Jews in Egypt, for example, but Herod was really the first one to attempt to defend and champion communities outside the homeland, especially when their rights were threatened by the actions of local officials.

Herod himself lived as a Jew (whatever his ancestry, which is not as clear cut as often presented), and established a Jewish dynasty that in many ways continued that of the Hasmonaeans. As will be seen in the next volume (*HJJSTP 4*), direct Herodian rule was not always in place, mostly because of the failings of Herod's heirs themselves. But Herodian descendants remained on the scene and influential for most of the century after Herod's death. His family troubles dominated the last years of his rule and were a concern not only of himself but also the wider population of the country and even of the Roman government. It was family conflicts that also led to the breakup of his kingdom after his death.

Yet for all his faults, Herod was clearly a remarkable individual whose positive achievements must be recognized and weighed against his failings. His long reign gained many benefits for his people and achieved a level of peace and prosperity in society that was seldom matched during this period. Some still wanted a return of Palestine to Roman rule after his death. When they got their wish about a decade later, there is no doubt that they quickly had reason to regret it.

Part V

CONCLUSIONS

Chapter 19

Judaism from Onias III to Herod the Great:
A Holistic Perspective

For centuries the Jews of Palestine had lived under imperial rule of one empire after another – Assyrian, Egyptian, Babylonian, Persian, Greek. They seem to have adapted to it, survived and sometimes even prospered, but they did so by living peacefully and not challenging the overlord. Things changed in the middle of the 2nd century BCE. After a long period of fighting – which continued throughout this time – Judah actually became an independent state for the first time since probably the 8th century BCE. It did not last long, but it was an important symbolic victory and became a part of the collective memory until today.

Jewish history was thoroughly bound up with the prevailing empires under whose rule they lived. When the Jews came under Seleucid rule in 200 BCE, things seemed to go along much as normal. The Seleucid empire was at its height and continued to exercise great power and organization for at least the next century. It was not a ramshackle, failing entity as so often pictured, at least not until the 1st century BCE. It was a powerful opponent to take on, and Judah succeeded only because of special circumstances. But rising on the western horizon was Rome, whose presence had hardly made itself felt in the East until the time of Antiochus III. The Jews saw good reason to make a treaty of friendship with the Roman Senate and saw it as a champion that they should court. The irony is that a century later they would view Rome as a hated enemy, as just another imperial power set on enslaving them – and they would rebel multiple times.

The Judaeans had begun to prosper economically by the early 2nd century. All indications are that Jerusalem was becoming an important centre in the region for trade and culture. It was hardly unexpected, therefore, when at the beginning of Antiochus IV's reign (about 175 BCE) the Jews approached him to request that Jerusalem become organized as a Greek city, a *polis*. This was not forced on the Jews by the Seleucids; on the contrary, it was a privilege that required the king's approval, though he seems to have been glad to give it. From all we can see in our sources, the Jews in general welcomed it, at least those in Jerusalem (many of whom would have become citizens of the *polis*). If this was all there was, it would probably have remained a footnote in Jewish history. Unfortunately, the request was bound up with some other less creditable activities.

According to 2 Maccabees 4, the brother of the high priest Onias III approached Antiochus and offered him money to be given the office of high priest. The brother's Greek name was Jason, and he offered a total of 440 silver talents to take the high priesthood. This looks like a raising of the annual tribute from about 300 talents to a much larger sum. In addition, Jason paid 150 talents to make Jerusalem into a *polis*, though this might have been a one-off payment. The version of 2 Maccabees has mostly been accepted by scholars, though it has recently been suggested that the initiative came from Antiochus, who was reforming the tax system (begun by his predecessor Seleucus IV), which included raising the tax assessment. Because Onias III was refusing to cooperate, Antiochus was looking for someone more amenable to his requirements.

Whatever the case, Onias was deposed and Jason took his place as high priest. But Jason also asked for Jerusalem to be made into a *polis*, which included the building of a gymnasium and establishing the ephebate or list of young men who were being trained for citizenship. What was the reaction of the community to this? No reaction is recorded, except that the people of Jerusalem seem to have welcomed the new Hellenistic city. The author of 2 Maccabees, writing after the revolt and the destruction of the temple cult, claims that Jason breached the law – but he can put his finger on no specific violation! This is clear from his rhetoric, which says a lot of nasty things about Jason but nothing concrete. The only possible example is the claim that Jason sent money for a pagan sacrifice in Tyre; however, those carrying the gift instead gave it over to help pay for building warships. This looks very suspect: Jason would have sent trusted couriers. If the money was used for warships, that was no doubt what Jason originally intended!

The point is that Jason was a promoter of Hellenistic culture; nevertheless, his power base was the temple, and he held his office to care for the temple cult. The daily *tamid* offering continued, people still brought their personal sacrifices to the altar, the temple still functioned. Greek culture may not have been to everyone's taste – though it evidently was to many in Jerusalem, at least – but there was no reason why it should have interfered with the traditional Jewish worship. More could be said here, but the charges of 2 Maccabees 4 against Jason are carefully analyzed in the appropriate place (§14.4.3).

The problem was that if Jason could take the office of high priest with the king's approval, others could play the same game. This time it was a member of another family of priests, Menelaus who offered Antiochus even more money for the office (it has been suggested that the initiative to remove Jason came from Antiochus, but there seems little reason why, since Jason was apparently paying the required tribute). So, after three years Jason lost the high priesthood to the rival Menelaus and fled Jerusalem. The problem for Menelaus is that he had promised too much and could not meet the payments he himself seems to have proposed. It was rumoured that he had even sold some of the temple vessels to raise money.

Selling temple vessels was too much for the populace of Jerusalem (who evidently believed the rumours, whatever the evidence). Menelaus was away in Antioch, but he had left his brother Lysimachus in charge. The citizens rioted, confronted Menelaus's soldiers in such numbers that they repulsed them and killed Lysimachus by mob violence. Note that those rioting and even murdering one of the supposed miscreants were not religiously conservative peasants from the countryside or members of some pietistic sect. They were members of the Hellenistic city established by Jason. This is very clear, because after the riot the ruling council of the city sent a delegation to Antiochus to bring charges against Menelaus. Jason's citizens were clearly very protective of the temple and its service.

Shortly after these events, the Sixth Syrian War between Antiochus and Egypt began (late 170 or possible early in 169 BCE). Some ancient sources blame Antiochus, but the balance of the evidence is that Egypt invaded Coele-Syria. Antiochus was ready, however, and quickly marched into Egypt and defeated her army. He returned later in 169 with great spoils, after establishing a form of government in Egypt that he thought was advantageous to keeping the peace and favourable to him. As soon as his troops had marched back into Syro-Palestine, however, these arrangements quickly broke down, and Antiochus felt compelled to initiate a new campaign in the spring of 168 BCE. Again, he was successful in the early part of his march into Egypt, but as he approached Alexandria it became clear that he was going to have a difficult fight on his hands. Antiochus was in a dilemma: he would lose face if he backed down, but it would take great resources of blood and treasure to really conquer Egypt. The matter was taken out of his hands, however, by the intervention of the Romans. They had recently won the Second Macedonian War at the battle of Pydna and were in a position of power. A Roman mission in the region met Antiochus and demanded that he pull out of Egypt. He had no choice and did what was demanded (an Egyptian document shows that he left Egypt in late July 168 BCE).

This Roman intervention, referred to as the 'Day of Eleusis', has been widely interpreted as a humiliation for Antiochus. It seems to have been so interpreted by some of the other Mediterranean powers at the time but, as already noted, it actually got Antiochus off the horns of a dilemma. He secretly may have welcomed it, especially since he knew that fellow kings would not blame him for acceding to Roman power. In any case, he returned from Egypt with enormous spoils, and his goal of holding Coele-Syria without continual threats from Egypt was fulfilled, since the Romans were now guarantors that Egypt would give up the goal of retaking the territory.

Yet Antiochus returned to find Judaea – or at least Jerusalem – in uproar. According to 2 Maccabees 5, a false rumour had circulated that Antiochus had met his end in Egypt. Jason had thought this was a good chance to retake the office of high priest (which he had stolen from his brother fair and square!). He had attacked Menelaus's faction with a large force and compelled the latter to seek refuge in the Akra, where he besieged them. Antiochus interpreted this as revolt, and immediately sent a military contingent to put it down. Some modern scholars argue that this was not just a bit of internecine fighting but was indeed a widespread revolt of Judaea and perhaps even some of the neighbouring areas, and Antiochus's intervention was completely necessary. In any case, the subsequent actions are somewhat hard to interpret because they do not always make sense against the historical background of the time, which may mean that things were going on about which we are left in the dark by our sources.

First, Antiochus is said to have come with his army against Jerusalem. According to 2 Macc. 5.7 Jason had already given up the fight and fled the scene. Yet the Seleucid army is said to have killed 40,000 people and sold another 40,000 into slavery. Was this because factions within the walls were still fighting, or did he attack a peaceful city? Apart from the fact that no such numbers of people lived in Jerusalem at the time, it makes nonsense of subsequent events. It is also stated that Menelaus gave Antiochus a tour of the temple's inner sanctum, and that Antiochus helped himself to 1,800 talents from the temple treasury. There is some question about these events. It is not certain that Antiochus himself led the army that came against Jerusalem, and his robbing of the temple looks more like an event following the first invasion of Egypt in 169 BCE. In any case, Philip was left as governor. Yet not long afterward, Apollonius, the commander of a force of Mysian soldiers, came to the city, found it at peace and proceeded to attack it on the sabbath and kill many – a strange spectacle since the populace had already been killed or sold into slavery not long before (perhaps this is only a doublet of the alleged attack by Antiochus's forces). Next came Geron the Athenian who is said to have had the task of forcing the people to give up their religion (2 Macc. 6.1-11). In recent years, this passage has occasioned a good deal of controversy.

What is clear is that the 'abomination of desolation' was set up in the temple from 15 Kislev 145 SE (1 Macc. 1.54-61), which is reckoned here as November/December 168 BCE. A few days later the daily (*tamid*) offering was stopped. As far as many Jews were concerned – such as the author of Daniel – the cosmos was shaken to its foundations (cf. Dan. 8.25; 11.36). On the 25 Kislev a pagan altar was built on the altar in the temple and sacrifices made on it. This appears to be the 'abomination of desolation' in the coded language of Daniel. This pollution of the temple has often been regarded as the first act in a province-wide or even empire-wide persecution of the Jews. Yet it seems as if Jews outside Judaea were not affected by whatever royal decrees were promulgated. Recognizing that the pollution of the temple and the cancellation of the daily offering were very much an act of religious persecution against Judaeans, was there an additional decree banning the practice of Judaism?

1 and 2 Maccabees leave no doubt this was the case (1 Macc. 1.41-61; 2 Macc. 6.1-11), nor do those that follow them, such as Josephus. The problem is that the accounts of the persecution tend to follow the pattern of what has been called the 'foundation myth' of the Hasmonaeans. Yet a number of sources (e.g., Daniel), while fully endorsing the sacrileges committed against the temple, do not mention any persecution of individuals for practising Judaism, such as circumcising male babies, keeping the sabbath or avoiding unclean meats. Also, a number of the accounts of martyrdom (e.g., the mother and seven sons of 2 Macc. 7) can be dismissed as unhistorical legendary propaganda. This has led several recent researchers to argue there was no religious persecutions of individuals. The trouble is that there may be a residue of data that suggests some sort of decree against the Jewish religion and a subsequent persecution of some individuals, perhaps only a very few, which might even be just overzealous local officials. It is hard to erase all the reports in the various sources, especially those of Antiochus IV and Antiochus V that allude to such repressive measures.

The turning of the temple and its cult into the worship of Zeus Olympius was certainly religious persecution as far most Jews were concerned, whether or not this was combined with the ruler cult of Antiochus or with Dionysus worship or other pagan religious activities (as 2 Macc. 6.7 alleges). The result was the rise of resistance movements. There seems to have been more than one of these, and that of the Maccabees might have developed only a bit later. The story in 1 Maccabees 2 that Mattathias, the father of the Maccabaean brothers, began the flight, is not otherwise known later in the book of 1 Maccabees nor in any other original source. What seems to have happened is that Judas and his brothers fled Jerusalem but later joined up with other groups and gradually took over the leadership.

The Maccabaean battles are sometimes presented as miraculous victories, one reason being that this is how they are sometimes presented in the books of Maccabees, especially 2 Maccabees. But although the Maccabees were able to obtain some surprising wins, considering the strength of the Seleucid empire, they are all explained by normal military means: often the numbers of soldiers on each side was roughly the same (the numbers given in the books of Maccabees cannot be trusted, often exaggerating Seleucid numbers and under-estimating Jewish numbers), the Seleucid generals were often local leaders who did not have the expertise to lead well, the guerrilla tactics sometimes used by the Maccabees worked well in circumstances in which they could use their local knowledge to an advantage, Judas was able to raise a considerable levy of soldiers from Judaea, and sometimes the local people helped to harass a retreating enemy. At first the Seleucids did not take the Judaean threat seriously. When they did do so and sent in the regular Syrian army, the Jews were often defeated (though 2 Maccabees especially describes defeats as victories!). Such an opposition by a superior, well-generalled Seleucid force led to Judas's death, after which the Maccabees were chased from pillar to post for many years.

The most remarkable achievement under Judas's leadership was the retaking and rededication of the temple. This was supposedly exactly three years after its pollution. Although the dating may to some extent have been engineered or even invented, the period of approximately three years seems correct (against the 3 1/2 years of Daniel, which has been followed by one modern researcher). Thus, the temple was cleansed and the *tamid* offering renewed on 25 Kislev 142 SE, or December 165 BCE. This was an outstanding accomplishment and was considered by many Jews the goal of their revolt against Antiochus and the Seleucids. The event was soon followed by concessions by Antiochus IV and later his son Antiochus V, allowing the Jews their freedom of worship and to follow their traditional customs. Most Jews appear to have been happy with this state of affairs, and the Maccabaean following evidently melted away. When Alcimus was chosen as high priest to replace Menelaus (who had been executed by the Seleucids), even the Hasidim were willing to accept him as a valid high priest.

Another of Judas's accomplishments was making a treaty of alliance and friendship with Rome. In one sense, it was no big deal – though some researchers have treated it as such – because Rome was quite promiscuous about making agreements with eastern kingdoms. But while these treaties might have promised much, they delivered nothing, unless Rome's direct interests were involved. Thus, Judas received not one soldier to assist him or one threat against his opponents. The Romans were happy to offer warm words, but action was taken by the Senate only when they were alarmed by what might seem to be a threat to Rome herself, or at least against Roman interests. Yet this treaty with Rome was probably useful for internal consumption: it raised Judas's prestige among his fellow countrymen. This is why it was renewed under several successive Hasmonaean rulers.

Only the Maccabees and their (now small) band of followers remained aloof from this settlement. The Jerusalem Akra was still in Seleucid hands, which could be a threat to the temple and the population of the city. But the main goal of the Maccabees was now – or perhaps always had been – the independence of Judaea from Seleucid rule. As some have indicated, this meant that from the beginning they had felt the need to take over the high priesthood if they were to accomplish their goal. That is, the eventual possession of the high priestly office by the Hasmonaeans was not an accident of history but a planned event by the Maccabees as a means of achieving their goal of national independence.

With Judas dead, Maccabaean leadership fell on Jonathan, but he and his now small band of followers were being pursued by the Seleucids. For a number of years they managed to survive periodic skirmishes and elude capture. But with the death of Alcimus in 159/158 BCE, Bacchides withdrew from Judaea for a couple of years, giving relief to Jonathan's weary band. Now, pro-Seleucid Jews apparently requested the return of Bacchides. Jonathan fortified Bethbasi, and withstood a siege of Bacchides. Eventually, a truce was negotiated according to which Bacchides withdrew to Antioch and Jonathan settled in Michmash. This allowed a period of several years in which Jonathan could build his strength. He was apparently also able to gain a greater recognition of his leadership with the population during this time.

Jonathan's real chance came, however, with the arrival of Alexander I Balas (claiming to be the son of Antiochus IV), who secured the recognition of the Romans and set up a rival dynasty against Demetrius I. Demetrius wrote a letter to Jonathan, allowing him to recruit troops. It was now possible for him to move to Jerusalem and set up his base there. Alexander then wrote a letter to Jonathan with further concessions, including the office of high priest. Jonathan put on the purple robe and crown gifted by Alexander at the Feast of Booths in 153 BCE. Jonathan had achieved one of the major Maccabaean goals that had eluded Judas: the Hasmonaean family now possessed the high priesthood and official leadership of Judaea. They had got there not by their military prowess but by diplomacy and pitting one rival Seleucid dynasty against another.

Over the next decade Jonathan managed to gain control of most of the cities and fortresses of Judaea. After the death of Demetrius I at the hands of Alexander, Demetrius II took his place, and Jonathan had to fight his army. Ptolemy VI turned against Alexander and attempted to gain control of Coele-Syria. When Alexander was killed in battle and Ptolemy VI died soon afterward, Jonathan managed to make peace with Demetrius II and gained three districts that had been part of the province of Samaria. He also sent troops to aid Demetrius in his troubles with the population of Antioch, but then Demetrius went back on promises made to Jonathan. It was about this time that Jonathan sent a mission to Rome to renew the treaty of friendship. Tryphon now set up Alexander's son Antiochus VI as a rival to Demetrius. He then negotiated with Jonathan but suddenly seized him by trickery.

Simon took over leadership of the Judaeans and tried to negotiate Jonathan's release, including payment of a ransom and sending Jonathan's two sons to Tryphon as hostages. Instead, Tryphon killed Jonathan (as well as apparently his sons: they are not referred to again). It has been proposed that Simon deliberately aimed at replacing Jonathan and his family as Hasmonaean leaders with his own family. If so, the situation with Tryphon fell right into his hands, with the elimination of Jonathan and his heirs in one fell swoop. Whether this was deliberate or not on Simon's part, the result was a change of Hasmonaean leadership to Simon and his family, where it remained for the rest of the Hasmonaean kingdom.

At this point, we might pause to consider the Hasmonaean achievement in the light of events of the 3rd and early 2nd centuries BCE (as described in *HJJSTP 2*). It was noted that in some ways control of Judah was contested by various prominent Jewish families, in a sort of mafiosa-style contest. There were the Tobiads who gained notable success until thwarted by the Seleucid takeover of Coele-Syria. They were in some sense opposed by the high priestly family of the Oniads, though the two families were actually intermarried. The Tobiads and Oniads continued to struggle for power under Seleucid rule, but a third family enters here, the priestly family of Bilgah. It succeeded in gaining the high priesthood with Menelaus, though this might have been in alliance with the Tobiads. But the repression of Antiochus IV again thwarted the ambitions of all these families, whose efforts were annulled by those of a fourth family, the Hasmonaeans. By time and chance, but also ambition and political skill, the Hasmonaeans won, but their ambitions and tactics were no less mafia-like than those of the Tobiads, Oniads and Bilgans.

Simon was able to avoid the traps set by Tryphon (who tried to take the throne by assassinating the young Antiochus VI) and to become reconciled with Demetrius II. Demetrius granted him exemption from payment of tribute and command of the fortresses in Judaea. Simon next took the Akra in Jerusalem. Judaea was now firmly under his control, and the people (no doubt under Simon's 'guidance') declared the independence of the kingdom of Judaea in the year 170 SE, or 143/142 BCE, Simon's first year. He then engineered an assembly of the people and priests in his third year, in 141–40 BCE, who set up a memorial declaring Simon's perpetual priesthood and leadership (though it does not mention his descendants). Judaea was now independent in name, though the reality was to be different for many more years.

Demetrius II's son Antiochus VII now wrote to confirm the concessions to Simon. Simon sent troops to aid Antiochus VII in his siege of Tryphon in Dor. Antiochus, however, reneged on his concessions and demanded compensation for the cities taken and the 'damage' done to the Seleucid interests. As far as the Seleucid king was concerned, Judaea was still a Seleucid possession. Simon's sons defeated the Seleucid army sent against them. But then Simon and two of his sons were assassinated by his son-in-law near Jericho in February–March of the year 135 BCE. But the third son, John Hyrcanus, was not there and escaped to take control of the leadership.

John Hyrcanus had a long and important reign (135–104 BCE). He besieged his brother-in-law, the assassin of his father, in Jerusalem for almost a year, but the latter escaped. John was then himself besieged by Antiochus VII. They eventually came to an agreement that John would give compensation and also aid Antiochus in his march to the east against the Parthians. John indeed took an army with Antiochus against the Parthians, but he somehow managed to avoid the disaster when Antiochus's forces were defeated by the Parthians and Antiochus himself killed (perhaps Simon had already returned to Jerusalem).

This was now about the year 129 BCE. At some point, Simon embarked on a campaign of conquest against various groups on the border of Judaea. Josephus gives the impression it was immediate, but some of the major conquests were 15 or 20 years later. At some point, though, John conquered Idumaea and required the Idumaeans to adopt Jewish customs and circumcision. This allegation is somewhat puzzling, because we know that the Idumaeans retained their Jewish identity and loyalty at least until the 66–70 CE war against Rome, when they fought on the Jewish side. Also, Strabo suggests that the adoption of Judaism was voluntary. Perhaps many of the Idumaeans were already circumcised and following Jewish customs, perhaps many Jews already lived in that region, perhaps the majority voluntarily adopted Jewish customs and only a minority were compelled. But whatever the precise process, most (though not all) Idumaeans took on Judaism.

Hyrcanus also conquered Samaria and Shechem and Mt Gerizim about 110 BCE. The latter brought him into conflict with the Samaritan sect. The population of the region of Samaria included a variety of ethnic groups. One important group who had built a temple on Mt Gerizim were the Samaritans, who claimed to be descendants of ancient Israel and who had a religion similar to the Jews in many ways, because they used a version of the Pentateuch and followed the instructions in it. There had been friction between the Samaritans and the Jews, going back at least to the time of Nehemiah, but there was also clearly communication between them and sometimes even friendly relations. Some scholars think that Hyrcanus's destruction of the Gerizim temple put an end to mutual communication and interchange between the two communities, but others have argued that an almost complete breach came later. (This and many other questions about the Samaritans are discussed in Chapter 8.)

John Hyrcanus was succeeded by his son Aristobulus, who reigned only a year (104–103 BCE). He imprisoned his mother and his brothers, except Antigonus. The latter had a considerable reputation as a warrior but Aristobulus had him assassinated, allegedly through trickery of his wife and advisers. He is said to have been a 'phil-Hellene', though exactly how he acquired that reputation is not clear. He is also supposed to have conquered the Arab tribe of Ituraeans north of the Galilee and forcibly converted them to Judaism, but the archaeology suggests otherwise. Possibly it was only a group within Galilee. Above all, he is said to have taken the title king, though this title does not appear on his coins. It is not surprising that this title was finally adopted, since the earlier Hasmonaean rulers had long acted like monarchs, but neither Aristobulus nor any of the succeeding Hasmonaean rulers renewed their treaty with Rome. Possibly the title of king had something to do with it.

At Aristobulus's death his wife Alexandra released his brothers from prison, arranged for Alexander Jannaeus to be acclaimed high priest and ruler and married him. Alexander had a long but troubled reign (104–76 BCE). He continued the conquests of Aristobulus and especially Hyrcanus into the Galilee and Transjordan to make the territory of Judaea possibly the largest it had ever been, certainly since the Israelite and Judahite monarchy. But considerable internal opposition developed. This had already begun under John Hyrcanus, but that ruler had squelched it. Jannaeus was less successful in putting down the revolt. Some of his opponents even managed to get the Seleucid ruler Demetrius III to invade.

According to Josephus, Jannaeus was defeated but then some of his Jewish opponents switched sides so that Demetrius no longer held the upper hand and withdrew. However, it may also be that the threat of his brother Philip in Damascus was a factor, requiring him to return to his capital. Alexander fought his opponents, capturing some. He crucified 800 and slaughtered their families in front of them, an act of cruelty that is even mentioned in the Qumran scrolls. It is often alleged that these were Pharisees, but while Pharisees were among his opponents, there is no evidence that Pharisees in particular were pursued by him. Josephus, for example, does not single out Pharisees as either his opponents or those slaughtered by him. Judaea was also invaded by the Antiochus XII, though he seems to have been mainly passing through to fight the Arabs, yet Jannaeus tried to prevent his passage. Since he was killed by the Arabs, his possible return to take revenge on Jannaeus did not happen.

When Jannaeus was on his deathbed, he allegedly advised his wife to court the Pharisees. Whether or not this is true, Alexandra Salome succeeded him as queen (76–67 BCE), but her rule is said to have been dominated by the Pharisees. They were able to eliminate some of their opponents and to have their own laws passed (though exactly what these were is not clarified). But apart from the dictates of the Pharisees, she had considerable trouble from her sons, Hyrcanus II and Aristobulus II. She appointed the elder Hyrcanus to the office of high priest, but Aristobulus is said to have been the more dynamic of the two. Some of the ruling class came to him for help against some of the excesses of the Pharisees. He is even said to have rebelled while she was still reigning. But on the whole her reign was a peaceful one, though she made use of mercenaries, and she seems to have been a good administrator.

As soon as Alexandra died, a fight for the throne developed between Hyrcanus II and Aristobulus II. Hyrcanus was defeated and agreed to become a private citizen, and leave the kingship and high priesthood to his brother. At this point, an individual named Antipater come on the scene. He had been governor of Idumaea under Alexander Jannaeus and was evidently a prominent individual in Judaean society. He convinced Hyrcanus that he should not give up the throne and got him to flee to the Nabataean Aretas III for support (Antipater had good relations with Aretas). With Nabataean and Antipater's support Hyrcanus was now a formidable opponent, and the country was divided between the two claimants to the Hasmonaean throne. It was about this time that Pompey appeared in the region, with the aim of attacking the Parthians. Now, in 63 BCE the two Judaean brothers appealed first to his subordinate Gabinius and then to Pompey himself (naturally, including bribes). When Pompey delayed a decision, Aristobulus impatiently marched off toward Jerusalem. Pompey took this as a hostile act and pursued after him.

Aristobulus relented and surrendered to Pompey, but some of his followers closed the gates of Jerusalem on the Roman army. Hyrcanus's followers opened the gates, but Aristobulus's group took refuge in the temple. Pompey besieged the temple for three months before it fell. Priests were slaughtered as they offered up sacrifices, ignoring the attacking soldiers. Pompey himself went into the Holy of Holies but found it empty. The next day he ordered the priests to cleanse the temple and resume the sacrificial service. Judaea was once more under the rule of a foreign power. The Hasmonaean kingdom had come to an end. Rome was now in charge.

The Maccabees and later the Hasmonaeans seemed to have steered a course between ideology and pragmatism. To take on the might of the Seleucid empire was not done for ideological reasons. Once the temple was retaken and the cult restored, there was no reason for the Maccabees to continue fighting, as most Judaeans realized. Nevertheless, the Maccabaean family continued on what looked like a suicide mission, motivated – one can only assume – by ideology. Yet they had the incredible luck that a rival Seleucid dynasty rose to claim the throne, which they could harness for the ends of Jewish independence. Here the pragmatic side prevailed.

The Hasmonaeans maintained an outward show that conformed fully with their Hellenistic neighbours: the use of the Greek language (both 1 and 2 Maccabees were preserved in Greek), various Greek ways of doing things (the military, architecture, trade), ostentatious building projects such as royal palaces, and so on. Yet internally a different mode of life seems to have prevailed. The ostentatious palaces, with gardens, banqueting halls and guest quarters, were non-luxurious and plain inside at the level of the regular inhabitants. This 'plainness' is evident in the material culture, especially of the central hill country. There is an emphasis on using local pottery and other products, a falling off of imported luxuries and a keen attention to matters of ritual purity. This last was evidenced in the rise and extension of *mikva'ot* across Judaea and the widespread use of limestone pots, cups and tableware, which was not subject to ritual purity in the way that ordinary pottery was. The material culture suggests that this began in the old centre of Judaea but then spread out to the more peripheral areas, including those more recently conquered.

In their move to expand their territory, they acted like any Hellenistic kingdom of the time. Some have suggested that the Hasmonaean territorial conquests were done in pursuit of restoring some idealistic 'Greater Israel'. There is no evidence for this, and they seem to have conquered for economic and power reasons, just as the other Mediterranean states and kingdoms did. On the other hand, to forcibly convert subject populations by requiring circumcision and the adoption of Jewish customs suggests an ideological drive, though the pragmatic was also there in that such converts were more likely to be friendly toward their conquerors. These wars of conquest might not be the entire reason that anti-Jewish attitudes developed in the Graeco-Roman world, but they no doubt played their part. As will be seen, the subsequent aid that Judaea offered to the Romans was also a factor.

After Aristobulus's following was defeated by the Romans, Aristobulus himself was taken captive to Rome. His sons, however, were freed and allowed to remain in Judaea. This was probably a mistake, but the question of Judaean governance became complicated by the Roman civil war. Hyrcanus now had the high priesthood. Over the next several years Aristobulus's sons Alexander and Antigonus, and then Aristobulus himself, revolted and led forces to attempt to take back the office and rulership but without success. Some of the Roman governors also came to garner funds by taxation and appropriation for the Roman military, latterly to support fighting in the Roman civil war. Pompey and Julius Caesar came to warfare in 49 BCE. Caesar released Aristobulus from captivity in Rome and planned to put him in charge of military force, but he was poisoned by the Pompeians. At Pharsalus Caesar and Pompey confronted each other: Pompey was defeated and fled to Egypt where he met his end in 48 BCE. When Caesar came to invade Egypt, Antipater and Hyrcanus provided assistance. Hyrcanus was rewarded with the title of ethnarch of the Jews, and Antipater gained Roman citizenship. This did not endear the Jews to the Egyptians.

Through this period Antipater had enlisted his sons, Phasael and Herod, in the Judaean administration. Phasael was put over Jerusalem, and Herod over Galilee. Both proved themselves capable individuals, but Herod stood out for his bold leadership qualities. At one point, Herod fell foul of opponents when he cleansed his territory of 'bandits' who were troubling the population. He was accused of executing them without a proper trial and called before the Sanhedrin. Josephus gives two somewhat contradictory accounts, but according to each Herod was acquitted, possibly with Roman intervention. Later, when Cassius of the anti-Caesar party came to the region to raise funds for his side, Herod was the first to reach his appointed quota. When the pro-Caesar faction triumphed, it seems not to have caused any problems for Antipater and his sons; however, Antipater was assassinated by a Jewish opponent.

It was at this time, in 40 BCE, that the Parthians invaded Syria and Palestine and put Aristobulus's son Antigonus on the throne of Judaea. Phasael and Hyrcanus were captured by their Jewish opponents, with Parthian help. Phasael committed suicide, and Hyrcanus had his ears mutilated by Antigonus so that he could no longer serve as high priest. Herod, however, was circumspect and avoided capture. He fled first to Egypt, then sailed to Rome, arriving there in late 40 BCE. At this time, Mark Antony and Octavian were cooperating after the treaty of Brundisium, although their relations had at times been strained. They got the Senate to declare Herod king of Judaea and gave him their backing. Herod returned to Syro-Palestine and raised an army. With it and the assistance of the Romans, he besieged Jerusalem in early 37 BCE. The Parthians had withdrawn from the region by this time, and only Antigonus's forces opposed him. The city fell in late summer 37 BCE, Antigonus was taken captive, and was executed by Mark Antony who was in the region to campaign against the Parthians.

Octavian and Antony had divided up the empire between them, Antony taking the eastern part and Octavian the western. Antony had taken up with Cleopatra VII, queen of Egypt, and she became a thorn in the side of Herod. She was antagonistic to him and made several attempts to get Antony to oppose him. Antony evidently regarded Herod as a valuable ally and did not generally give in to Cleopatra's accusations, though he did give some of Herod's most profitable territories to her. During this time there was an intense propaganda war between Mark Antony and Octavian. It finally came to a head in 31 BCE when the two sides fought each other. At Actium in September 31 BCE Antony and Cleopatra were defeated and fled to Egypt. Subsequently, they both committed suicide, leaving Octavian as the victor and master of the Roman world.

This left Herod on the losing side. He had not fought at Actium because – whether through accident or possibly by design – he was fighting the Nabataeans at the time. But he had been a conspicuous friend of Antony. As was typical of him, Herod adopted an audacious strategy. He sailed to meet Octavian in Rhodes and appeared before him without his crown and dressed as a commoner but with a bold demeanour. He admitted that he had been a good friend to Antony, but that he would now be a good friend to Octavian and pursue the welfare of his cause. Perhaps Octavian recognized in Herod some of his own gumption, but he could also see that it would be advantageous to have Herod on his side. He restored Herod's crown to him and offered his friendship. The result was amicable and intimate relations for the rest of Herod's life, with one short exception.

As a 'friendly king' Herod was a valued colleague of the ruling family and enjoyed a close relationship with the imperial power in Rome. This could only be good for his Jewish subjects. This meant that Rome no longer collected taxes from Judaea. Although like his Hasmonaean predecessors, Herod taxed his subjects, the alleged bankruptcy of the country is a literary fiction. Studies have shown that Herod's taxes were very fair, by the standards of the time, and reasonable for the size of his realm and the number of people under his rulership. His magnificent building programme not only brought prestige to him and his kingdom – the refurbished Jerusalem temple was allegedly one of the most sublime buildings in the Graeco-Roman world – but in many cases benefitted trade and commerce (e.g., the new port facilities at Caesarea). An oft-forgotten fact is that they provided work for many local labourers and artisans.

Like all Hellenistic and Roman rulers, there were aspects of Herod's rule that would be abhorrent to us today, and were no doubt resented by many of his subjects. But in this he did not differ from other rulers, including the Hasmonaeans who preceded him and attempted to retake the throne from him. The family troubles occupying especially the last decades of his reign are a sorry spectacle, but they were hardly worse than those experienced by Augustus with his own family. Furthermore, they did not generally affect the populace at large, only those in Herod's more intimate circles. Thus, when a delegation from Judaea went to Augustus after Herod's death and asked to return to rule by Rome as a part of the province of Syria, they could hardly have known what they were asking. A decade later they got their wish – and they paid for it many times over (as will be shown in *HJJSTP 4*). Overall, Herod's rule was good for the Jews of Judaea: not only them but also for many of the Jews in the diaspora, since Herod began a process of reaching out to them in certain ways. When evaluated dispassionately Herod's kingship was on balance much more positive for the Jews than negative.

Herod was in many ways the last of the Hasmonaeans. He was not a Hasmonaean, nor could he be high priest (but neither could Alexandra Salome), but he worked closely with Hyrcanus II, his rule continued much of the Hasmonaean tradition and he clearly lived as a Jew. There is little to distinguish him from the Hasmonaean rulers except his mode of success. But the Roman conquest had dealt a severe blow to the hopes of many people in Judaea. They resented Roman rule, which was one of the reasons that many of them resented Herod's rule. The Roman conquest laid the seeds for later revolts over the next two centuries: the three major revolts in 66–70, 115–17, and 132–35 CE, but also many more minor insurrections by limited numbers of people. This seems to have included a plague of messianic pretenders.

Yet under the Hasmonaeans and then under Herod, the Jewish people as a whole multiplied and flourished, in spite of setbacks, both major (as in 63 BCE) and minor. The Roman conquest brought the Jews together under one Roman overlord, and the outreach from Judaea to those in the diaspora seems to have increased especially under Herod. With the right leadership things could have gone relatively well for the Jews. But with the death of Herod, the leadership deteriorated and things went awry. This will be an important theme in *HJJSTP 4*.

Bibliography

Abegg, Martin, Jr, Peter Flint, and Eugene Ulrich (eds). 1999. *The Dead Sea Scrolls Bible* (Edinburgh: T. & T. Clark).
Abel, F.-M. 1949. *Les libres des Maccabées*. Etudes bibliques; Paris: Lecoffre.
Adler, E. N., and M. Seligsohn. 1902a. 'Une nouvelle chronique samaritaine [1].' *REJ* 44: 188–222.
Adler, E. N., and M. Seligsohn. 1902b. 'Une nouvelle chronique samaritaine [2–3].' *REJ* 45: 70–98; 223–54.
Adler, E. N., and M. Seligsohn. 1903. 'Une nouvelle chronique samaritaine [4].' *REJ* 46: 123–46.
Adler, William. 1989. *Time Immemorial: Archaic History and its Sources in Christian Chronography from Julius Africanus to George Syncellus*. Washington, D.C.: Dumbarton Oaks Research Library and Collection.
Adler, William, and Paul Tuffin (ed. and trans.). 2002. *The Chronography of George Synkellos: A Byzantine Chronicle of Universal History from the Creation*. Oxford: Oxford University Press.
Ådna, Jostein. 1999. *Der Tempel und Tempelmarkt im 1. Jahrhundert n. Chr.* Abhandlungen des Deutschen Palästina-Vereins 25; Wiesbaden: Harrassowitz.
Aharoni, Yohanan (ed.). 1973. *Beer-Sheba I: Excavations at Tel Beer-Sheba 1969–1971 Seasons*. Publications of the Institute of Archaeology 2. Tel Aviv: Tel Aviv University Institute of Archaeology.
Albani, Matthias, Jörg Frey, and Armin Lange (eds). 1997. *Studies in the Book of Jubilees*. TSAJ 65. Tübingen: Mohr Siebeck.
Albright, William F., and James L. Kelso (eds). 1968. *The Excavation of Bethel (1934–1960)*. AASOR 39. Cambridge, MA: American Schools of Oriental Research.
Alon, G. 1977. 'The Origin of the Samaritans in the Halakhic Tradition.' In *Jews, Judaism and the Classical World: Studies in Jewish History in the Times of the Second Temple and Talmud*, 354–73. Jerusalem: Magnes.
Alston, Richard. 2014. *Aspects of Roman History, 31 BC–AD 117: A Source-Based Approach*. Aspects of Classical Civilisation. 2nd ed. Abingdon/New York: Routledge.
Alston, Richard. 2015. *Rome's Revolution: Death of the Republic and Birth of the Empire*. Ancient Warfare and Civilization. Oxford: Oxford University Press.
Altheim, F., and R. Stiehl. 1970. 'Antiochos IV. Epiphanes und der Osten.' *Geschichte Mittelasiens im Altertum*, 553–71. Berlin: de Gruyter.
Ameling, Walter (ed.). 2004. *Inscriptiones Judaicae Orientis, Volume II Kleinasien*. TSAJ 99. Tübingen: Mohr Siebeck.
Ameling, Walter, Hannah M. Cotton, Werner Eck et al. (eds). 2014. *Corpus Inscriptionum Iudaeae/Palaestinae, Volume III South Coast: 2161–2648*. Berlin: de Gruyter.

Ameling, Walter, Hannah M. Cotton, Werner Eck et al. (eds). 2018a. *Corpus Inscriptionum Iudaeae/Palaestinae, Volume IV: Iudaea/Idumaea, Part 1: 2649–3324*. Berlin: de Gruyter.

Ameling, Walter, Hannah M. Cotton, Werner Eck et al. (eds). 2018b. *Corpus Inscriptionum Iudaeae/Palaestinae, Volume IV: Iudaea/Idumaea, Part 2: 3325–3978*. Berlin: de Gruyter.

Amitay, Ory. 2013. 'The Correspondence on 1 Maccabees and the Possible Origins of the Judeo-Spartan Connection.' *SCI* 32: 79–105.

Applebaum, Shimon H. 1976. 'Economic Life in Palestine.' In *The Jewish People in the First Century: Historical Geography, Political History, Social, Cultural and Religious Life and Institutions*, ed. S. Safrai and Menahem Stern, 2:631–700. CRINT 1/2. Assen: Van Gorcum; Philadelphia: Fortress.

Applebaum, Shimon H. 1977. 'Judaea as a Roman Province: the Countryside as a Political and Economic Factor.' *ANRW II*: 8:355–96.

Applebaum, Shimon H. 1986. 'The Settlement Pattern of Western Samaria from Hellenistic to Byzantine Times: A Historical Commentary.' In *Landscape and Pattern: An Archaeological Survey of Samaria, 800 B.C.E.–636 C.E.*, ed. Shimon Dar, 257–69. Part i; BAR International Series 308[i]; Oxford: British Archaeological Reports, 1986.

Applebaum, Shimon H. 1989a. *Judea in Hellenistic and Roman Times: Historical and Archaeological Essays*. SJLA 40. Leiden: Brill.

Applebaum, Shimon H. 1989b. 'The Beginnings of the Limes Palaestinae.' In *Judaea in Hellenistic and Roman Times: Historical and Archaeological Essays*, 132–42. SJLA 40. Leiden: Brill.

Applebaum, Shimon H. 1989c. 'The Troopers of Zamaris.' In *Judaea in Hellenistic and Roman Times: Historical and Archaeological Essays*, 47–65. SJLA 40. Leiden: Brill.

Arav, Rami. 1989. *Hellenistic Palestine: Settlement Patterns and City Planning, 337–31 B.C.E.* British Archaeological Reports International Series 485. Oxford: BAR.

Archer, Gleason L. 1958. *Jerome's Commentary on Daniel*. Grand Rapids: Baker.

Ariel, Donald T. 2018. 'Coins from the Renewed Excavations at Qumran.' In *Back to Qumran: Final Report (1993–2004)*, ed. Yitzak Magen and Yuval Peleg, 403–29. JSP 18. Jerusalem: Israel Antiquities Authority.

Ariel, Donald T. (ed.). 1990. *Excavations at the City of David 1978–1985 Directed by Yigal Shiloh, Volume II: Imported Stamped Amphora Handles, Coins, Worked Bone and Ivory, and Glass*. Qedem 30. Jerusalem: Hebrew University.

Ariel, Donald T. (ed.). 2000a. *Excavations at the City of David 1978–1985 Directed by Yigal Shiloh, Volume V: Extramural Areas*. Qedem 40. Jerusalem: Hebrew University.

Ariel, Donald T. (ed.). 2000b. *Excavations at the City of David 1978–1985 Directed by Yigal Shiloh, Volume VI: Inscriptions*. Qedem 41. Jerusalem: Hebrew University.

Ariel, Donald T., and Alon De Groot (eds). 1996. *Excavations at the City of David 1978–1985 Directed by Yigal Shiloh, Volume IV: Various Reports*. Qedem 35. Jerusalem: Hebrew University.

Ariel, Donald T., and Gerald Finkielsztejn. 2003. 'Chapter 8: Amphora Stamps and Imported Amphoras.' In *Maresha Excavations Final Report I: Subterranean Complexes 21. 44. 70*, ed. A. Kloner, 137–51. IAA Reports 17. Jerusalem: Israel Archaeology Authority.

Ariel, Donald T., and Jean-Philippe Fontanille. 2012. *The Coins of Herod: A Modern Analysis and Die Classification*. AJEC 79. Leiden: Brill.

Ariel, Donald T., and Joseph Naveh. 2003. 'Selected Inscribed Sealings from Kedesh in the Upper Galilee.' *BASOR* 329: 61–80.

Ariel, Donald T., I. Sharon, J. Gunneweg, and I. Perlman. 1985. 'A Group of Stamped Hellenistic Storage-Jar Handles from Dor.' *IEJ* 35: 135–52.

Atkinson, Kenneth. 1998a. 'Towards a Redating of the Psalms of Solomon: Implications for Understanding the *Sitz im Leben* of an Unknown Jewish Sect.' *JSP* 17: 95–112.

Atkinson, Kenneth. 1998b. 'On the Herodian Origin of Militant Davidic Messianism at Qumran: New Light from *Psalm of Solomon* 17. *JBL* 118: 435–60.

Atkinson, Kenneth. 2004. *I Cried to the Lord: A Study of the Psalms of Solomon's Historical Background and Social Setting*. JSJSup 84. Leiden: Brill.

Atkinson, Kenneth. 2016. *A History of the Hasmonean State: Josephus and Beyond*. Jewish and Christian Texts in Contexts and Related Studies 23. London/New York: Bloomsbury T&T Clark.

Atkinson, Kenneth, and Jodi Magness. 2010. 'Josephus's Essenes and the Qumran Community. *JBL* 129: 317–42.

Aune, David E. 1983. *Prophecy in Early Christianity and the Ancient Mediterranean World*. Grand Rapids, MI: Eerdmans.

Austin, Michel M. 2006. *The Hellenistic World from Alexander to the Roman Conquest: A Selection of Ancient Sources in Translation*. 2nd ed. Cambridge: Cambridge University Press.

Avemarie, Friedrich, Predrag Bukovec, Stefan Krauter, and Michael Tilly (eds.). 2017. *Die Makkabäer*. WUNT 382. Tübingen: Mohr Siebeck.

Avigad, Nahman. 1975. 'A Bulla of Jonathan the High Priest.' *IEJ* 25: 8–12.

Avigad, Nahman. 1984. *Discovering Jerusalem*. Oxford: Blackwell.

Avigad, Nahman. 1985. 'The Upper City.' In *Biblical Archaeology Today: Proceedings of the International Congress on Biblical Archaeology, Jerusalem, April 1984*, ed. J. Amitai, 469–75. Jerusalem: Israel Exploration Society.

Avi-Yonah, M. 1966. *The Holy Land from the Persian to the Arab Conquests (536 B.C. to A.D. 640): A Historical Geography*. Grand Rapids: Baker.

Avi-Yonah, M. 1973. 'When Did Judea Become a Consular Province?' *IEJ* 23: 209–13.

Avi-Yonah, M. 1974a. 'Archaeological Sources.' In *The Jewish People in the First Century: Historical Geography, Political History, Social, Cultural and Religious Life and Institutions*, ed. S. Safrai and Menahem Stern, 1:46–62. CRINT 1/1. Assen: Van Gorcum; Philadelphia: Fortress.

Avi-Yonah, M. 1974b. 'Historical Geography of Palestine.' In *The Jewish People in the First Century: Historical Geography, Political History, Social, Cultural and Religious Life and Institutions*, ed. S. Safrai and Menahem Stern, 1:91–113. CRINT 1/1. Assen: Van Gorcum; Philadelphia: Fortress, 1974.

Aymard, A. 1953–54. 'Autour de l'avènement d'Antiochos IV.' *Historia* 2: 49–73.

Babota, Vasile. 2014. *The Institution of the Hasmonean High Priesthood*. JSJSup 165. Leiden: Brill.

Bagnall, Roger S., and Peter Derow (eds). 2004. *The Hellenistic Period: Historical Sources in Translation*. New ed. Blackwell Sourcebooks in Ancient History 1. Oxford: Blackwell.

Baltrusch, Ernst. 2001. 'Königin Salome Alexandra (76–67 v. Chr.) und die Verfassung des Hasmonäischen Staates.' *Historia* 50: 163–79.

Baltrusch, Ernst. 2002. *Die Juden und das Römische Reich: Geschichte einer konfliktreichen Beziehung*. Darmstadt: Wissenschaftliche Buchgesellschaft.

Baltrusch, Ernst. 2011. *Caesar und Pompeius*. 3rd ed. Geschichte kompakt. Darmstadt: WBG.

Baltrusch, Ernst. 2012. *Herodes: König im Heiligen Land—Eine Biographie*. Munich: C. H. Beck.
Baltrusch, Ernst, and Julia Wilker (eds). 2015. *Amici – socii – clientes? Abhängige Herrschaft im Imperium Romanum*. Berlin Studies of the Ancient World 31. Berlin: Edition Topoi.
Bammel, Ernst. 1959. 'Die Neuordnung des Pompeius und das römisch-jüdische Bundnis.' *ZDPV* 75: 76–82.
Bar-Adon, P. 1977. 'Another Settlement of the Judean Desert Sect at 'En el-Ghuweir on the Shores of the Dead Sea.' *BASOR* 227: 1–25.
Barag, Dan. 1992–93. 'New Evidence on the Foreign Policy of John Hyrcanus I.' *INJ* 12: 1–12.
Barag, Dan. 2000–2002. 'The Mint of Antiochus IV in Jerusalem: Numismatic Evidence on the Prelude to the Maccabean Revolt.' *INJ* 14: 59–77.
Barag, D. B. 2012. 'Alexander Jannaeus—Priest and King'. In *'Go Out and Study the Land' (Judges 18:2): Archaeological, Historical and Textual Studies in Honor of Hanan Eshel*, ed. Aren M. Maeir, Jodi Magness, and Lawrence H. Schiffman, 1–5. Leiden: Brill.
Barclay, John M. G. 2007. *Flavius Josephus, Volume 10:* Against Apion: *Translation and Commentary*. Leiden: Brill.
Bar-Kochva, Bezalel. 1975. 'Hellenistic Warfare in Jonathan's Campaign near Azotos.' *Scripta Classica Israelica* 2: 83–96.
Bar-Kochva, Bezalel. 1976a. *The Seleucid Army: Organization and Tactics in the Great Campaigns*. Cambridge Classical Studies. Cambridge: Cambridge University Press.
Bar-Kochva, Bezalel. 1976b. 'Seron and Cestius Gallus at Beith Horon.' *PEQ* 108: 13–21.
Bar-Kochva, Bezalel. 1989. *Judas Maccabaeus: The Jewish Struggle Against the Seleucids.* Cambridge: Cambridge University Press.
Bar-Kochva, Bezalel. 1996. *Pseudo-Hecataeus,* On the Jews*: Legitimizing the Jewish Diaspora.* Hellenistic Culture and Society 21. Berkeley/Los Angeles: University of California Press.
Bar-Kochva, Bezalel. 2016. 'The Religious Persecutions of Antiochus Epiphanes as a Historical Reality.' *Tarbiz* 84: 295–344 (Heb.) (Eng. abstract).
Bar-Nathan, Rachel (ed.). 2002. *Hasmonean and Herodian Palaces at Jericho: Final Reports of the 1973–1987 Excavations, Vol. III: The Pottery*. Jerusalem: Israel Exploration Society.
Bar-Nathan, Rachel, and Judit Gärtner (eds) 2013. *Hasmonean and Herodian Palaces at Jericho: Final Reports of the 1973–1987 Excavations, Vol. V: The Finds from Jericho and Cypros*. Jerusalem: Israel Exploration Society.
Barnes, T. D. 1968. 'The Date of Herod's Death.' *JTS* 19: 204–9.
Barth, Frederik (ed.). 1969. *Ethnic Groups and Boundaries: The Social Organization of Culture Difference*. Boston: Little, Brown & Co.
Barthélemy, D. 1963. *Les devanciers d'Aquila*. VTSup 10. Leiden: Brill.
Bartlett, John R. 1973. *The First and Second Books of the Maccabees*. Cambridge Bible Commentary on the New English Bible. Cambridge: Cambridge University Press.
Baslez, Marie-François, and Olivier Munnich. 2014. *La mémoire des persécutions: Autour des livres des Maccabées*. Collection de la Revue des Études juives. Leuven: Peeters.
Baumgarten, Albert I. 1983. 'The Name of the Pharisees.' *JBL* 102: 411–28.
Baumgarten, Albert I. 1984. 'Josephus and Hippolytus on the Pharisees.' *HUCA* 55: 1–25.
Baumgarten, Albert I. 1984–85. '*Korban* and the Pharisaic *Paradosis.*' *JANES* 16–17: 5–17.

Baumgarten, Albert I. 1987. 'The Pharisaic *Paradosis.*' *HTR* 80: 63–77.
Baumgarten, Albert I. 1991. 'Rivkin and Neusner on the Pharisees.' In *Law in Religious Communities in the Roman Period: The Debate over* Torah *and* Nomos *in Post-Biblical Judaism and Early Christianity*, ed. Peter Richardson and Stephen Westerholm, 109–26. Studies in Christianity and Judaism 4. Waterloo, ON: Wilfrid Laurier University Press.
Baumgarten, Albert I. 1997. *The Flourishing of Jewish Sects in the Maccabean Era: An Interpretation.* JSJSup 55. Leiden: Brill.
Baumgarten, Joseph M., Esther G. Chazon, and Avital Pinnick (eds). 2000. *The Damascus Document: A Centennial of Discovery: Proceedings of the Third International Symposium of the Orion Center for the Study of the Dead Sea Scrolls and Associated Literature, 4–8 February, 1998.* STDJ 34. Leiden: Brill.
Becker, Matthias. 2016. *Porphyrios,* Contra Christianos: *Neue Sammlung der Fragmente, Testimonien und Dubia mit Einleitung, Übersetzung und Anmerkungen.* Texte und Kommentare 52. Berlin: de Gruyter.
Ben-Dor, Meir. 1986. 'Herod's Mighty Temple Mount.' *BAR* 12/6 (Nov.-Dec.): 40–49.
Ben-Eliyahu, Eyal, Yehudah Cohn and Fergus Millar. 2012. *Handbook of Jewish Literature from Late Antiquity, 135–700 CE.* Foreword by Philip Alexander. Published for the British Academy by Oxford University Press.
Ben-Hayyim, Zeev. 1942–43. ספר אסטיר. *Tarbiz* 14: 104–90.
Ben-Hayyim, Zeev. 1943–44. ספר אסטיר. *Tarbiz* 15: 71–87.
Ben-Hayyim, Zeev. 1957–77. *The Literary and Oral Tradition of Hebrew and Aramaic amongst the Samaritans, Vols I–V.* Jerusalem: Academy of the Hebrew Language (Heb.).
Ben-Hayyim, Zeev. 1971. Review of J. D. Purvis, *The Samaritan Pentateuch and the Origin of the Samaritan Sect. Biblica* 52: 253–55.
Benoit, P., J. T. Milik, and R. de Vaux (eds). 1961. *Discoveries in the Judaean Desert II: Les grottes de Murabba'ât.* 2 vols. Oxford: Clarendon.
Bergren, Theodore A. 1997. 'Nehemiah in 2 Maccabees 1:10–2:18.' *JSJ* 28: 249–70.
Berlin, Andrea M. 1997. 'Between Large Forces: Palestine in the Hellenistic Period.' *BA* 60: 2–51.
Berlin, Andrea M. 1999. 'The Archaeology of Ritual: The Sanctuary of Pan at Banias/Caesarea Philippi.' *BASOR* 315: 27–45.
Berlin, Andrea M. 2002. 'Power and its Afterlife: Tombs in Hellenistic Palestine.' *NEA* 65: 138–48.
Berlin, Andrea M. 2005. 'Jewish Life before the Revolt: The Archaeological Evidence.' *JSJ* 36: 417–70.
Berlin, Andrea M. 2006. *Gamla I: The Pottery of the Second Temple Period.* IAA Reports 29. Jerusalem: Israel Antiquities Authority.
Bernegger, P. M. 1983. 'Affirmation of Herod's Death in 4 B.C.' *JTS* 34: 526–31.
Bernhardt, Johannes Christian. 2017. *Die jüdische Revolution: Untersuchungen zu Ursachen, Verlauf und Folgen der hasmonäischen Erhebung.* Klio Beihefte, Neue Folge 22. Berlin/Boston: de Gruyter.
Bernstein, Moshe, Florentino García Martínez, and John Kampen (eds). 1997. *Legal Texts and Legal Issues: Proceedings of the Second Meeting of the International Organization for Qumran Studies, Cambridge 1995, Published in Honour of Joseph M. Baumgarten.* STDJ 23. Leiden: Brill.
Berthelot, Katell. 2017. *In Search of the Promised Land? The Hasmonean Dynasty Between Biblical Models and Hellenistic Diplomacy*, trans. Margaret Rigaud. JAJSup 24. Göttingen: Vandenhoeck & Ruprecht.

Berthelot, Katell, and Daniel Stökl Ben Ezra (eds). 2010. *Aramaica Qumranica: Proceedings of the Conference on the Aramaic Texts from Qumran in Aix-en-Provence, 30 June–2 July 2008.* STDJ 94. Leiden: Brill.
Bickerman, Elias J. 1930. 'Makkabäerbücher (I. und II.).' *PW* 14:779–800.
Bickerman, Elias J. 1933. 'Ein jüdischer Festbrief vom Jahre 124 v. Chr. (II Macc 11–9).' *ZNW* 32: 233–54; ET 'A Jewish Festal Letter of 124 B.C.E.' In idem, *Studies in Jewish and Christian History: A New Edition in English*, ed. Amram Tropper, 1:408–31. AJEC 68. 2 vols. Leiden: Brill, 2007.
Bickerman, Elias J. 1937a. *Der Gott der Makkabäer: Untersuchungen über Sinn und Ursprung der makkabäischen Erhebung.* Berlin: Schocken Verlag. [ET below 1979].
Bickerman, Elias J. 1937b. 'Un document relatif a la persécution d'Antiochos IV Epiphane.' *RHR* 115: 188–223; ET 'A Document Concerning the Persecution by Antiochos IV Epiphanes.' In *Studies in Jewish and Christian History: A New Edition in English*, ed. Amram Tropper, 1:376–407. AJEC 68. 2 vols. Leiden: Brill, 2007.
Bickerman, Elias J. 1938. *Institutions des Séleucides.* Paris: Geuthner.
Bickerman, Elias J. 1951. 'Les Maccabées de Malalas.' *Byzantion* 21: 63–83. ET 'The Maccabees of Malalas.' In *Studies in Jewish and Christian History: A New Edition in English*. ed. Amram Tropper, 1:465–82. AJEC 68. 2 vols. Leiden: Brill, 2007.
Bickerman, Elias J. 1955. 'Une question d'authenticité: Les privilèges juifs.' In *Annuaire de l'institut de philologie et d'histoire orientales et slaves, Univ. de Bruxelles* 13: 11–34. ET 'A Question of Authenticity: The Jewish Privileges.' In *Studies in Jewish and Christian History: A New Edition in English*, ed. Amram Tropper, 1:295–314. AJEC 68. 2 vols. Leiden: Brill, 2007.
Bickerman, Elias J. 1958. 'Altars of Gentiles: A Note on the Jewish *Ius Sacrum.*' *Revue internationale des droits de l'Antiquité* (3rd ser.) 5: 137–64. Reprinted in idem, *Studies in Jewish and Christian History: A New Edition in English*, ed. Amram Tropper, 2:596–617. AJEC 68. 2 vols. Leiden: Brill, 2007.
Bickerman, Elias J. 1979. *The God of the Maccabees: Studies on the Meaning and Origin of the Maccabean Revolt*, trans. Horst R. Moehring. SJLA 32. Leiden: Brill. [ET of 1937a]. Reprinted in *Studies in Jewish and Christian History: A New Edition in English*, ed. Amram Tropper, 1025–1149. AJEC 68. 2 vols. Leiden: Brill, 2007.
Bickerman, Elias J. 1980. *Chronology of the Ancient World.* Revised ed. Aspects of Greek and Roman Life. Ithaca, NY: Cornell; London: Thames & Hudson.
Bickerman, Elias J. 2007. *Studies in Jewish and Christian History: A New Edition in English*, ed. Amram Tropper. AJEC 68. 2 vols. Leiden: Brill.
Bieberstein, Klaus. 2017. *A Brief History of Jerusalem: From the Earliest Settlement to the Destruction of the City in AD 70.* ADPV 47. Wiesbaden: Harrassowitz.
Bijovsky, Gabriela. 1994–99. 'A Coin of Demetrius I from Akko-Ptolemais.' *INJ* 13: 39–45.
Biran, Avraham. 1994. *Biblical Dan.* Jerusalem: Israel Exploration Society.
Biran, Avraham (ed.). 1996. *Dan I: A Chronicle of the Excavations, the Pottery Neolithic, the Early Bronze Age and the Middle Bronze Age Tombs.* Jerusalem: Hebrew Union College.
Biran, Avraham (ed.). 2002. *Dan II: A Chronicle of the Excavations and the Late Bronze Age 'Mycenaean' Tomb.* Jerusalem: Hebrew Union College.
Bivar, A. D. H. 1983. 'The Political History of Iran under the Arsacids.' In *Cambridge History of Iran: vol. 3, parts 1: The Seleucid, Parthian, and Sasanian Periods*, ed. Ehsan Yarshater, 100–115. Cambridge: Cambridge University Press.

Bleicken, Jochen. 2015. *Augustus: The Biography*, trans. Anthea Bell; London: Allen Lane. ET of *Augustus: Eine Biographie*. Berlin: Alexander Fest Verlag, 2000.

Bloch-Smith, Elizabeth. 2003. 'Israelite Ethnicity in Iron I: Archaeology Preserves What Is Remembered and What Is Forgotten In Israel's History.' *JBL* 122: 401–25.

Blosser, D. 1981. 'The Sabbath Year Cycle in Josephus.' *HUCA* 52: 129–39.

Blum, Erhard. 1997. 'Der "Schiqquz Schomem" und die Jehud-Drachme BMC Palestine S. 181, Nr. 29.' *BN* 90: 13–27.

Boccaccini, Gabriele. 1998. *Beyond the Essene Hypothesis: The Parting of the Ways between Qumran and Enochic Judaism*. Grand Rapids, MI: Eerdmans.

Bohak, Gideon. 1995. 'CPJ III, 520: The Egyptian Reaction to Onias' Temple.' *JSJ* 26: 32–41.

Bohak, Gideon. 1996. *Joseph and Aseneth and the Jewish Temple in Heliopolis*. SBLEJL 10. Atlanta: Scholars Press.

Bohak, Gideon. 1997. 'Good Jews, Bad Jews, and Non-Jews in Greek Papyri and Inscriptions.' In *Akten des 21. Internationalen Papyrologenkongresses, Berlin, 13.–19.8.1995*. ed. Bärbel Kramer et al., 105–112. Archiv für Papyrusforschung Beiheft 3. Stuttgart/Leipzig: Teubner.

Bond, Helen K. 2012. 'Josephus on Herod's Domestic Intrigue in the *Jewish War*.' *JSJ* 43: 295–314.

Bons, Eberhard, and Patrick Pouchelle (eds). 2015. *The Psalms of Solomon: Language, History, Theology*. SBLEJL 40. Atlanta: SBL.

Borchardt, Francis. 2014. *The Torah in 1 Maccabees: A Literary Critical Approach to the Text*. Deuterocanonical and Cognate Literature Studies 19. Berlin: de Gruyter.

Bourgel, Jonathan. 2016. 'The Destruction of the Samaritan Temple by John Hyrcanus: A Reconsideration.' *JBL* 135: 499–517.

Bowersock, G. W. 1983. *Roman Arabia*. Cambridge, MA: Harvard University Press.

Bowman, John. 1954. *Transcript of the Original Text of the Samaritan Chronicle Tolidah*. University of Leeds.

Bowman, John. 1977. *Samaritan Documents Relating to their History, Religion and Life*. Pittsburgh Original Texts and Translations 2. Pittsburgh: Pickwick.

Braund, D. C. 1983. 'Gabinius, Caesar, and the *publicani* of Judaea.' *Klio* 65: 241–44.

Braund, D. C. 1984. *Rome and the Friendly King: The Character of Client Kingship*. London: Croom Helm; New York: St. Martin's.

Braunert, Horst. 1964. 'Hegemoniale Bestrebungen der hellenistischen Großmächte in Politik und Wirtschaft.' *Historia* 13: 80–104.

Braverman, J. 1978. *Jerome's Commentary on Daniel: A Study of Comparative Jewish and Christian Interpretations of the Hebrew Bible*. CBQMS 7. Washington, D.C.: Catholic Biblical Association.

Brennan, T. Cory. 2000. *The Praetorship in the Roman Republic*. 2 vols. Oxford: Oxford University Press.

Brenner, Athalya (ed.). 1995. *A Feminist Companion to Esther, Judith and Susanna*. The Feminist Companion to the Bible 7. Sheffield: Sheffield Academic Press.

Briscoe, J. 1973. *A Commentary on Livy, Books XXXI–XXXIII*. Oxford: Clarendon.

Brett, Mark G. (ed.). 1996. *Ethnicity and the Bible*. BIS 19. Leiden: Brill.

Breytenbach, Cilliers. 1997. 'Zeus und Jupiter auf dem Zion und dem Berg Garizim: Die Hellenisierung und Romanisierung der Kultstätten des Höchsten.' *JSJ* 28: 369–80.

Bringmann, Klaus. 1983. *Hellenistische Reform und Religionsverfolgung in Judäa: Eine Untersuchung zur jüdisch-hellenistischen Geschichte (175–163 v. Chr.)*. Abhandlungen der Akademie der Wissenschaften in Göttingen, Phil.-hist. Klasse, 3. Folge, Nr. 132. Göttingen: Vandenhoeck & Ruprecht.

Brock, Sebastian P. 1984. 'The Psalms of Solomon.' In *The Apocryphal Old Testament*, ed. H. F. D. Sparks, 649–82. Oxford: Clarendon.

Brock, Sebastian P. 1996. *The Recensions of the Septuagint Version of I Samuel*. With a foreword by Natalio Fernández Marcos. Quaderni di Henoch 9. Torino: Silvio Zamorani Editore.

Brodersen, Kai. 1989. *Appians Abriss der Seleukidengeschichte: (Syriake 45,232–70,369) Text und Kommentar*. Münchener Arbeiten zur Alten Geschichte 1. Munich: Editio Maris.

Brodersen, Kai, Wolfgang Günther, and Hatto H. Schmitt (eds). 1997. *Historische griechische Inschriften in Übersetzung: Band II, Spätklassik und früher Hellenismus (400–250 v. Chr.)*. Texte zur Forschung 68. Darmstadt: Wissenschaftliche Buchgesellaft.

Brodersen, Kai, Wolfgang Günther, and Hatto H. Schmitt (eds). 1999. *Historische griechische Inschriften in Übersetzung: Band III Der griechische Osten und Rom (250–1 v. Chr.)*. Texte zur Forschung 71. Darmstadt: Wissenschaftliche Buchgesellaft.

Brooke, George J. 1985. *Exegesis at Qumran: 4Q Florilegium in its Jewish Context*. JSOTSup 29. Sheffield: Sheffield Academic Press.

Brooke, George J. 1998. 'Kingship and Messianism in the Dead Sea Scrolls.' In *King and Messiah in Israel and the Ancient Near East: Proceedings of the Oxford Old Testament Seminar*, ed. John Day, 434–55. JSOTSup 270. Sheffield Sheffield Academic Press.

Brooke, George J. 2005. *The Dead Sea Scrolls and the New Testament: Essays in Mutual Illumination*. London: SPCK.

Brooke, George J. (ed.). 1989. *Temple Scroll Studies: Papers Presented at the International Symposium on the Temple Scroll, Manchester, December 1987*. JSPSup 7. Sheffield: JSOT.

Brooke, George J., with Florentino García Martínez (eds). 1994. *New Qumran Texts and Studies: Proceedings of the First Meeting of the International Organization for Qumran Studies, Paris 1992*. STDJ 15. Leiden: Brill.

Brooke, George J., and C. Hempel (eds). 2016. *T&T Clark Companion to the Dead Sea Scrolls*. London: Bloomsbury T&T Clark.

Broshi, Magen. 1987. 'The Role of the Temple in the Herodian Economy.' *JJS* 38: 31–37

Broshi, Magen. 1999. 'Was Qumran at Crossroads?' *RQum* 19: 273–76.

Broshi, Magen, and Esther Eshel. 1997. 'The Greek King Is Antiochus IV (4QHistorical Text=4Q248).' *JJS* 48: 120–29.

Brown, Truesdell S. 1973. *The Greek Historians*. Civilization and Society. Lexington, MA: D. C. Heath.

Brownlee, William H. 1962. 'Maccabees, Books of.' *IDB* 3.204.

Brownlee, William H. 1982–83. 'The Wicked Priest, the Man of Lies, and the Righteous Teacher—the Problem of Identity.' *JQR* 73: 1–37.

Bruggen, J. van. 1978. 'The Year of the Death of Herod the Great.' In *Miscellanea Neotestamentica*, ed. T. Baarda et al., 1–15. NovTSup 48. Leiden: Brill.

Bunge, J. G. 1973. 'Der "Gott der Festungen" und der "Liebling der Frauen": Zur Identifizierung der Götter in Dan. 11,36–39.' *JSJ* 4: 169–82.

Bunge, J. G. 1974a. 'Münzen als Mittel politischer Propaganda: Antiochos IV. Epiphanes von Syrien.' *Studii Clasice* 16: 43–52.

Bunge, J. G. 1974b. '"Theos Epiphanes": Zu den ersten fünf Regierungsjahren Antiochos' IV. Epiphanes.' *Historia* 23: 57–85.

Bunge, J. G. 1975. '"Antiochos-Helios": Methoden und Ergebnisse der Reichspolitik Antiochos' IV. Epiphanes von Syrien im Spiegel seiner Münzen.' *Historia* 24: 164–88.

Burgmann, H. 1980. 'Das umstrittene Intersacerdotium in Jerusalem 159–152 v. Chr.' *JSJ* 11: 135–76.

Burstein, Stanley Mayer. 1985. *The Hellenistic Age from the Battle of Ipsus to the Death of Kleopatra VII*. Translated Documents of Greece and Rome 3. Cambridge: Cambridge University Press.

Buttrick, George A. et al. (ed.). 1962. *Interpreter's Dictionary of the Bible*, vols 1–4. Nashville: Abingdon.

Buttrick, George A. et al. (ed.). 1976. *Supplementary Volume*. Nashville: Abingdon.

Calduch-Benages, N., and J. Vermeylen (eds). 1999. *Treasures of Wisdom: Studies in Ben Sira and the Book of Wisdom: Festschrift M. Gilbert*. BETL 143. Leuven: Peeters/ University Press.

Callaway, P. R. 1988. *The History of the Qumran Community*. JSPSup 3. Sheffield: JSOT.

Campbell, Edward F., Jr. 1991. *Shechem II: Portrait of a Hill Country Vale: The Shechem Regional Survey*. ASORAR 2. Atlanta: Scholars Press.

Campbell, Edward F., and G. R. H. Wright. 2002. *Shechem III: The Stratigraphy and Architecture of Shechem/Tell Balâṭah*. 2 vols. ASORAR 6. Boston, MA: American Schools of Oriental Research.

Cancik, Hubert, Helmuth Schneider et al. (eds). 1996–2003. *Der Neue Pauly: Enzyklopädie der Antike*, vols 1–16. Stuttgart: Metzler.

Capdetrey, Laurent. 2007. *Le pouvoir séleucide: Territoire, administration, finances d'un royaume hellénistique (312–129 avant J.-C.)*. Collection 'Histoire'. Rennes: Presses Universitaires de Rennes.

Cardauns, Burkhart. 1967. 'Juden und Spartaner: Zur hellenistisch-jüdischen Literatur.' *Hermes* 95: 317–24.

Cargill, R. R. 2009. *Qumran through [Real] Time, A Virtual Reconstruction of Qumran and the Dead Sea Scrolls*. Piscataway, NJ: Gorgias.

Cary, M. 1963. *A History of the Greek World 323 to 146 BC*. 2nd ed. London: Methuen, 1951. Reprinted with new bibliography, 1963.

Cary, M., and H. H. Scullard. 1975. *A History of Rome*. 3rd ed. London: Macmillan.

Cavallin, H. C. C. 1974. *Life after Death: Paul's Argument for the Resurrection of the Dead in I Cor 15, Part I: An Enquiry into the Jewish Background*. ConBNT 7/1. Lund: Gleerup.

Champion, Craige B. 2004. *Cultural Politics in Polybius's Histories*. Berkeley and Los Angeles: University of California Press.

Chancey, Mark A. 2002. *The Myth of a Gentile Galilee*. SNTSMS 118. Cambridge: Cambridge University Press.

Charles, R. H. 1902. *The Book of Jubilees or the Little Genesis*. Oxford: Clarendon.

Charles, R. H. 1929. *A Critical and Exegetical Commentary on the Book of Daniel*. Oxford: Clarendon.

Charlesworth, James H. (ed.). 1983–85 *Old Testament Pseudepigrapha*. 2 vols. Garden City, NY: Doubleday.

Charlesworth, James H. (ed.). 2006. *The Bible and the Dead Sea Scrolls, Volumes 1–3*. The Second Princeton Symposium on Judaism and Christian Origins. Waco, TX: Baylor University Press.

Charlesworth, James H. et al. (eds). 1994–. *The Dead Sea Scrolls: Hebrew, Aramaic, and Greek Texts with English Translations. I–*. The Princeton Theological Seminary Dead Sea Scrolls Project. Tübingen: Mohr Siebeck; Louisville, KY: Westminster John Knox.

Charlesworth, James H., Hermann Lichtenberger, and Gerbern S. Oegema (eds). 1998. *Qumran-Messianism: Studies on the Messianic Expectations in the Dead Sea Scrolls*. Tübingen: Mohr Siebeck.

Chazon, Esther G., and Michael E. Stone (eds), with the collaboration of Avital Pinnick. 1999. *Pseudepigraphic Perspectives: The Apocrypha and Pseudepigrapha in Light of the Dead Sea Scrolls: Proceedings of the International Symposium of the Orion Center for the Study of the Dead Sea Scrolls and Associated Literature, 12–14 January, 1997*. STDJ 31. Leiden: Brill.

Cheon, Samuel. 1997. *The Exodus Story in the Wisdom of Solomon: A Study in Biblical Interpretation*. JSPSup 23. Sheffield: Sheffield Academic Press.

Chiat, M. J. S. 1981. 'First-Century Synagogue Architecture: Methodological Problems.' In *Ancient Synagogues Revealed*, ed. L. I. Levine, 49–60. Jerusalem: Israel Exploration Society.

Chrubasik, Boris. 2016. *Kings and Usurpers in the Seleukid Empire: The Men Who Would be King*. Oxford Classical Monographs. Oxford: Oxford University Press.

Chyutin, Michael. 1997. *The New Jerusalem Scroll from Qumran: A Comprehensive Reconstruction*. JSPSup 25. Sheffield: Sheffield Academic Press.

Clarysse, Willy. 1994. 'Jews in Trikomia.' In *Proceedings of the 20th International Congress of Papyrologists, Copenhagen, 23–29 August, 1992*, ed. Adam Bülow-Jacobsen, 193–203. Copenhagen: Museum Tusculanum Press.

Clines, David J. A. 1984. *The Esther Scroll: The Story of the Story*. JSOTSup 30. Sheffield: Sheffield Academic Press.

Coggins, Richard J. 1975. *Samaritans and Jews: The Origins of Samaritanism Reconsidered*. Growing Points in Theology. Oxford: Blackwell; Atlanta: John Knox.

Coggins, Richard J. 1987. 'The Samaritans in Josephus.' In *Josephus, Judaism, and Christianity*, ed. Louis H. Feldman and G. Hata, 257–73. Leiden: Brill.

Cohen, Getzel M. 2005. *The Hellenistic Settlements in Syria, the Red Sea Basin, and North Africa*. Hellenistic Culture and Society 46. Berkeley/Los Angeles: University of California Press.

Cohen, Jeffrey M. 1981. *A Samaritan Chronicle: A Source-Critical Analysis of the Life and Times of the Great Samaritan Reformer, Baba Rabba*. SPB 30. Leiden: Brill.

Cohen, Shaye J. D. 1979. *Josephus in Galilee and Rome: His Vita and Development as a Historian*. CSCT 8. Leiden: Brill, 1979.

Cohen, Shaye J. D. 1983. 'Conversion to Judaism in Historical Perspective: From Biblical Israel to Postbiblical Judaism.' *Conservative Judaism* 36: 31–45.

Cohen, Shaye J. D. 1984. 'The Significance of Yavneh: Pharisees, Rabbis, and the End of Jewish Sectarianism.' *HUCA* 55: 27–53.

Cohen, Shaye J. D. 1985. 'The Origins of the Matrilineal Principle in Rabbinic Law.' *AJS Review* 10: 19–53.

Cohen, Shaye J. D. 1986a. 'The Political and Social History of the Jews in Greco-Roman Antiquity: The State of the Question.' In *Early Judaism and its Modern Interpreters*, ed. Robert A. Kraft and George W. E. Nickelsburg, 33–56. SBLBMI 2. Atlanta: Scholars; Philadelphia: Fortress.

Cohen, Shaye J. D. 1986b. 'Was Timothy Jewish (Acts 16:1–3)? Patristic Exegesis, Rabbinic Law, and Matrilineal Descent.' *JBL* 105: 251–68.

Cohen, Shaye J. D. 1999. *The Beginnings of Jewishness. Boundaries, Varieties, Uncertainties.* Hellenistic Culture and Society 31. Berkeley/Los Angeles: University of California.

Cohen, Shaye J. D. 2014. *From the Maccabees to the Mishnah.* 3rd ed. Louisville, KY: Westminster John Knox.

Colledge, Malcolm A. R. 1967. *The Parthians.* New York: Praeger.

Collins, Adela Yarbro. 2007. *Mark: A Commentary*, ed. Harold W. Attridge. Hermeneia. Minneapolis: Fortress.

Collins, John J. 1977. *The Apocalyptic Vision of the Book of Daniel.* HSM 16. Atlanta: Scholars Press.

Collins, John J. 1989. 'The Origin of the Qumran Community: A Review of the Evidence.' In *To Touch the Text: Biblical and Related Studies in Honor of Joseph A. Fitzmyer, S.J.* ed. M. P. Horgan and P. J. Kobelski, 159–78. New York: Crossroad.

Collins, John J. 1993. *A Commentary on the Book of Daniel.* Hermeneia. Minneapolis: Fortress.

Collins, John J. 1994. 'The Works of the Messiah.' *DSD* 1: 98–112.

Collins, John J. 1995. *The Scepter and the Star: The Messiahs of the Dead Sea Scrolls and Other Ancient Literature.* Anchor Bible Reference Library. New York: Doubleday.

Collins, John J. 1997. *Apocalypticism in the Dead Sea Scrolls.* Literature of the Dead Sea Scrolls. London-New York: Routledge.

Collins, John J. 1998. *The Apocalyptic Imagination: An Introduction to Jewish Apocalyptic Literature.* 2nd ed, Grand Rapids, MI: Eerdmans.

Collins, John J. 2000. *Between Athens and Jerusalem: Jewish Identity in the Hellenistic Diaspora.* 2nd ed. The Biblical Resource Series. Grand Rapids, MI: Eerdmans; Livonia, MI: Dove Booksellers.

Collins, John J. 2009. *Beyond the Qumran Community: The Sectarian Movement of the Dead Sea Scrolls.* Grand Rapids, MI: Eerdmans.

Collins, John J., and Peter W. Flint (eds). 2001. *The Book of Daniel: Composition and Reception.* The Formation and Interpretation of Old Testament Literature 2 = VTSup 83. Leiden: Brill.

Collins, John J., and Robert Kugler (eds). 2000. *Religion in the Dead Sea Scrolls.* Studies in the Dead Sea Scrolls and Related Literature. Grand Rapids, MI: Eerdmans.

Cook, Johann. 1997. *The Septuagint of Proverbs: Jewish and/or Hellenistic Proverbs? Concerning the Hellenistic Colouring of LXX Proverbs.* VTSup 69. Leiden: Brill.

Cook, Johann. 2000. *Religion in the Dead Sea Scrolls.* Grand Rapids, MI: Eerdmans.

Cook, M. J. 1978. *Mark's Treatment of the Jewish Leaders.* NovTSup 51. Leiden: Brill.

Cotton, Hannah M., Leah Di Segni, Werner Eck et al. (eds). 2011. *Corpus Inscriptionum Iudaeae/Palaestinae, Volume I Jerusalem, Part 1: 1–704.* Berlin: de Gruyter.

Cotton, Hannah M., Leah Di Segni, Werner Eck et al. (eds). 2012. *Corpus Inscriptionum Iudaeae/Palaestinae, Volume I Jerusalem, Part 2: 705–1120.* Berlin: de Gruyter.

Craffert, Pieter F. 2000. 'Digging up *Common Judaism* in Galilee: *Miqva'ot* at Sepphoris as a Test Case.' *Neotestamentica* 34: 39–55.

Crane, Oliver Turnbull. 1890. *The Samaritan Chronicle or the Book of Joshua, the Son of Nun.* New York: John B. Alden.

Craven, Toni. 1983. *Artistry and Faith in the Book of Judith.* SBLDS 70. Atlanta: Scholars, 1983.

Crawford, M. H. 1978. *The Roman Republic.* Hassocles, Sussex: Harvester.

Cross, Frank M. 1961. *The Ancient Library of Qumran.* 2nd ed. Garden City: Doubleday.

Cross, Frank M. 1964. 'The History of the Biblical Text in the Light of Discoveries in the Judaean Desert.' *HTR* 57: 281–99.

Cross, Frank M. 1966. 'The Contribution of the Qumran Discoveries to the Study of the Biblical Text.' *IEJ* 16: 81–95.

Cross, Frank M. 1975. 'The Evolution of a Theory of Local Texts.' In *Qumran and the History of the Biblical Text*, ed. F. M. Cross and S. Talmon, 306–20. Cambridge, MA: Harvard University Press.

Cross, Frank M., and Esther Eshel. 1997. 'Ostraca from Khirbet Qumran.' *IEJ* 47: 17–29.

Cross, Frank M., and Shemaryahu Talmon (eds). 1975. *Qumran and the History of the Biblical Text*. Cambridge, MA: Harvard University Press.

Crowfoot, J. W., Kathleen M. Kenyon, and E. L. Sukenik (eds). 1942. *The Buildings at Samaria*. Samaria-Sebaste: Reports of the Work of the Joint Expedition in 1931–1933 and of the British Expedition in 1935, no. 1. London: Palestine Exploration Fund.

Crowfoot, J. W., G. M. Crowfoot, and Kathleen M. Kenyon (eds). 1957. *The Objects from Samaria*. Samaria-Sebaste: Reports of the Work of the Joint Expedition in 1931–1933 and of the British Expedition in 1935, no. 3. London: Palestine Exploration Fund.

Crown, Alan D. 1966. 'A Critical Re-examination of the Samaritan Sepher Yehoshua.' PhD diss., University of Sydney.

Crown, Alan D. 1971–72. 'New Light on the Inter-relationships of Samaritan Chronicles from Some Manuscripts in the John Rylands Library [1].' *BJRL* 54: 282–313.

Crown, Alan D. 1972–73. 'New Light on the Inter-relationships of Samaritan Chronicles from Some Manuscripts in the John Rylands Library [2].' *BJRL* 55: 86–111.

Crown, Alan D. (ed.). 1989. *The Samaritans*. Tübingen: Mohr Siebeck.

Crown, Alan D., Reinhard Pummer, and Abraham Tal (eds). 1993. *A Companion to Samaritan Studies*. Tübingen: Mohr Siebeck.

Cryer, Fred H. 1997. 'The Qumran Conveyance: A Reply to F. M. Cross and E. Eshel.' *SJOT* 11: 232–40.

Cryer, Frederick H., and Thomas L. Thompson (eds). 1998. *Qumran Between the Old and New Testaments*. JSOTSup 290 = Copenhagen International Seminar 6. Sheffield: Sheffield Academic Press.

Curtis, John (ed.). 2000. *Mesopotamia and Iran in the Parthian and Sasanian Periods: Rejection and Revival, c.238 BC–AD 642*. London: British Museum Press.

Dąbrowa, Edward. 2010. *The Hasmoneans and their State: A Study in History, Ideology, and the Institutions*. Electrum 16. Kraków: Jagiellonian University Press.

Dagut, M. B. 1953. 'II Maccabees and the Death of Antiochus IV Epiphanes.' *JBL* 77: 149–57.

Dahmen, Ulrich, and Johannes Schnocks (eds). 2010. *Juda und Jerusalem in der Seleukidenzeit: Herrschaft-Widerstand-Identität: Festschrift für Heinz-Josef Fabry*. BBB 159. Göttingen: Vandenhoeck & Ruprecht.

Dalman, Gustaf. 1932. *Arbeit und Sitte in Palästina*, vols 1–7. Repr. Hildesheim: Olms, 1964.

Danby, Herbert. 1933. *The Mishnah*. Oxford: Clarendon.

Dancy, J. C. 1954. *A Commentary on First Maccabees*. Oxford: Blackwell.

Dar, Shimon. 1986. *Landscape and Pattern: An Archaeological Survey of Samaria, 800 B.C.E.–636 C.E.*, with a historical commentary by Shimon Applebaum. Part i; BAR International Series 308[i]. Oxford: British Archaeological Reports.

Davidson, Maxwell J. 1992. *Angels at Qumran: A Comparative Study of 1 Enoch 1–36, 72–108 and Sectarian Writings from Qumran*. JSPSup 11. Sheffield: Sheffield Academic Press.

Davies, J. K. 1984. 'Cultural, Social and Economic Features of the Hellenistic World.' In *The Cambridge Ancient History, Vol. 7, Part 1: The Hellenistic World*, ed. F. W. Walbank et al., 257–320. 2nd ed. Cambridge: Cambridge University Press.
Davies, Philip R. 1977a. *1QM, the War Scroll from Qumran: Its Structure and History*. BibOr 32. Rome: Biblical Institute.
Davies, Philip R. 1977b. '*Hasidim* in the Maccabean Period.' *JJS* 28: 127–40.
Davies, Philip R. 1982a. *Qumran*. Cities of the Biblical World. Guildford, Surrey: Lutterworth.
Davies, Philip R. 1982b. 'The Ideology of the Temple in the Damascus Document.' *JJS* 33: 287–301.
Davies, Philip R. 1983. *The Damascus Covenant: An Interpretation of the 'Damascus Document'*. JSOTSup 25. Sheffield: JSOT.
Davies, Philip R. 1985a. *Daniel*. OTG. Sheffield: Sheffield Academic Press.
Davies, Philip R. 1985b. 'Eschatology at Qumran.' *JBL* 104: 39–55.
Davies, Philip R. 1987. *Behind the Essenes: History and Ideology in the Dead Sea Scrolls*. BJS 94. Atlanta: Scholars Press.
Davies, Philip R. 1988. 'How Not To Do Archaeology: The Story of Qumran.' *BA* 51: 203–7.
Davies, Philip R. 1995. 'Was There Really a Qumran Community?' *CR: BS* 3: 9–36.
Davies, Philip R., George J. Brooke, and Philip R. Callaway. 2002. *The Complete World of the Dead Sea Scrolls*. London: Thames & Hudson.
Davies, W. D. 1974. *The Gospel and the Land: Early Christianity and Jewish Territorial Doctrine*. Berkeley/Los Angeles: University of California Press.
Davies, W. D. 1982. *The Territorial Dimensions of Judaism*. Berkeley/Los Angeles: University of California Press.
Davies, W. D., and D. C. Allison. 1988–2000. *The Gospel According to Saint Matthew*, vols. 1–3. ICC. Edinburgh: T. & T. Clark.
Davies, W. D., and Louis H. Finkelstein et al. (eds). 1984–2017. *Cambridge History of Judaism 1–8*. Cambridge: Cambridge University Press.
Davis, Norman, and Colin M. Kraay. 1973. *The Hellenistic Kingdoms: Portrait Coins and History*. London: Thames & Hudson.
De Groot, Alon, and Donald T. Ariel (eds). 1992. *Excavations at the City of David 1978–1985 Directed by Yigal Shiloh, Volume III: Stratigraphical, Environmental, and Other Reports*. Qedem 33. Jerusalem: Hebrew University.
De Troyer, Kristin. 2000. *The End of the Alpha Text of Esther: Translation and Narrative Technique in MT 8:1–17, LXX 8:1–17, and AT 7:14–41*. SBLSCS 48. Atlanta: Society of Biblical Literature. ET of *Het einde van de Alpha-tekst van Ester: Vertaal- en verhaaltechniek van MT 8,1–17, LXX 8,1–17 en AT 7,14–41*. Leuven: Peeters, 1997.
Deines, Roland. 1997. *Die Pharisäer: Ihr Verständnis im Spiegel der christlichen und jüdischen Forschung seit Wellhausen und Graetz*. WUNT 101. Tübingen: Mohr Siebeck.
Delcor, M. 1962. 'Vom Sichem der hellenistischen Epoche zum Sychar des Neuen Testamentes.' *ZDPV* 78: 34–48.
Delcor, M. 1968. 'Le temple d'Onias en Egypte.' *RB* 75: 188–205.
Dentzer, J. M., F. Villeneuve, and F. Larché. 1982. 'Iraq el Amir: Excavations at the Monumental Gateway.' *SHAJ* 1: 201–7.
Dequeker, Luc. 1985. 'The City of David and the Seleucid Acra in Jerusalem.' *Orientalia Lovaniensia Analecta* 19: 193–210.

Dequeker, Luc. 2016. *Studia Hierosolymitana*. Contributions to Biblical Exegesis and Theology 81. Leuven: Peeters.

Derow, Peter. 1979. 'Polybius, Rome, and the East.' *JRS* 69: 1–15. Reprinted in *Rome, Polybius, and the East*, ed. Andrew Erskine and Josephine Crawley Quinn, 125–49. Oxford: Oxford University Press.

Derow, Peter. 2015. *Rome, Polybius, and the East*, ed. Andrew Erskine and Josephine Crawley Quinn. Oxford: Oxford University Press.

Dever, William G. (ed.). 1974. *Gezer II: Report of the 1967–70 Seasons in Fields I and II*. Annual of the Hebrew Union College/Nelson Glueck School of Biblical Archaeology 2. Jerusalem: Hebrew Union College.

Dever, William G. et al. 1971. 'Further Excavations at Gezer, 1967–1971.' *BA* 34: 94–132.

Dever, William G., H. Darrell Lance, G. Ernest Wright. 1970. *Gezer I: Preliminary Report of the 1964–66 Seasons*. Annual of the Hebrew Union College Biblical and Archaeological School 1. Jerusalem: Hebrew Union College.

Dexinger, Ferdinand. 1977. *Henoche Zehnwochenapokalypse und offene Probleme der Apokalyptikforschung*. SPB 29. Leiden: Brill.

Di Segni, Leah. 1997. 'A Dated Inscription from Beth Shean and the Cult of Dionysos Ktistes in Roman Scythopolis.' *Scripta Classica Israelica* 16: 139–61.

Dimant, Devorah (ed.). 2012. *The Dead Sea Scrolls in Scholarly Perspective: A History of Research*. STDJ 99. Leiden: Brill; Atlanta: SBL.

Dimant, Devorah, and Uriel Rappaport (eds). 1992. *The Dead Sea Scrolls: Forty Years of Research*. STDJ 10. Jerusalem: Magnes.

Dittenberger, Wilhelm. 1903–5. *Orientis graeci inscriptiones selectee*. 2 vols. Leipzig: S. Hirzel. Reprinted Hildesheim: Olms, 1960.

Doran, Robert. 1981. *Temple Propaganda: The Purpose and Character of 2 Maccabees*. CBQMS 12. Washington, DC: Catholic Biblical Association.

Doran, Robert. 1983. '2 Maccabees 6:2 and the Samaritan Question," *HTR* 76: 481–85.

Doran, Robert. 1989. 'The Non-Dating of Jubilees: Jub 34–38; 23:14–32 in Narrative Context.' *JSJ* 20: 1–11.

Doran, Robert. 1990. 'Jason's gymnasium.' In *Of Scribes and Scrolls: Studies on the Hebrew Bible, Intertestamental Judaism, and Christian Origins Presented to John Strugnell on the Occasion of his Sixtieth Birthday*, ed. H. W. Attridge, J. J. Collins, and T. H. Tobin, 99–109. College Theology Society Resources in Religion 5. Lanham, MD: University Press of America.

Doran, Robert. 2012. *2 Maccabees: A Critical Commentary*, ed. Harold W. Attridge. Hermeneia. Minneapolis: Fortress.

Dorothy, Charles V. 1997. *The Books of Esther: Structure, Genre and Textual Integrity*. JSOTSup 187. Sheffield: Sheffield Academic Press.

Drews, Robert. 1963. 'Diodorus and his Sources.' *AJP* 83: 383–92.

Dreyer, Boris, and Peter Franz Mittag (eds.). 2011. *Lokale Eliten und hellenistische Könige zwischen Kooperation und Konfrontation*. Oikumene Studien zur antiken Weltgeschichte 8. Berlin: Antike.

Driver, G. R. 1965. *The Judaean Scrolls: The Problem and the Solution*. Oxford: Blackwell.

Easterling, P. E., B. M. W. Knox, E. J. Kennedy, and W. V. Clausen (eds). 1982. *Cambridge History of Classical Literature: II Latin Literature*. Cambridge: Cambridge University Press.

Easterling, P. E., B. M. W. Knox, E. J. Kennedy, and W. V. Clausen (eds). 1985. *Cambridge History of Classical Literature: I Greek Literature*. Cambridge: Cambridge University Press.

Eck, Werner. 2007. *The Age of Augustus*. 2nd ed. Blackwell Ancient Lives. Oxford: Blackwell.

Eckhardt, Benedikt. 2012. '"An Idumean, That Is, a Half-Jew" Hasmoneans and Herodians between Ancestry and Merit.' In *Jewish Identity and Politics between the Maccabees and Bar Kokhba: Groups, Normativity, and Rituals*, ed. Benedikt Eckhardt, 91–115. JSJSup 155. Brill: Leiden.

Eckhardt, Benedikt. 2013. *Ethnos und Herrschaft: Politische Figurationen judäischer Identität von Antiochos III. bis Herodes I.* Studia Judaica 72. Berlin/Boston: de Gruyter.

Eckhardt, Benedikt. 2016. 'The Seleucid Administration of Judea, the High Priesthood and the Rise of the Hasmoneans.' *Journal of Ancient History* 4: 57–87.

Eckhardt, Benedikt (ed.). 2012. *Jewish Identity and Politics between the Maccabees and Bar Kokhba: Groups, Normativity, and Rituals*. JSJSup 155. Brill: Leiden.

Eckstein, Arthur M. 1995. *Moral Vision in* The Histories *of Polybius*. Hellenistic Culture and Society 16. Berkeley/Los Angeles: University of California Press.

Eckstein, Arthur M. 2006. *Mediterranean Anarchy, Interstate War, and the Rise of Rome*. Hellenistic Culture and Society 48. Berkeley/Los Angeles: University of California Press.

Eckstein, Arthur M. 2008. *Rome Enters the Greek East: From Anarchy to Hierarchy in the Hellenistic Mediterranean, 230–170 BC*. Oxford: Blackwell.

Edelstein, L., and I. G. Kidd (eds). 1989. *Posidonius, Volume I: The Fragments*. 2nd ed. CCTC 13. Cambridge: Cambridge University Press.

Edmondson, Jonathan, Steve Mason, and James Rives (eds). 2005. *Flavius Josephus and Flavian Rome*. Oxford: Oxford University Press.

Edwards, Douglas R., and C. Thomas McCollough (eds). 1997. *Archaeology and the Galilee: Texts and Contexts in the Graeco-Roman and Byzantine Periods*. SFSHJ 143. Atlanta: Scholars Press.

Edwards, O. 1982. 'Herodian Chronology.' *PEQ* 114: 29–42.

Egger, Rita. 1986. *Josephus Flavius und die Samaritaner: Eine terminologische Untersuchung zur Identitätsklärung der Samaritaner*. NTOA 4. Freiburg, Schweiz: Universitätsverlag; Göttingen: Vandenhoeck & Ruprecht.

Ehling, Kay. 1998. 'Seleukidische Geschichte zwischen 130 und 121 v. Chr.' *Historia* 47: 141–51.

Ehling, Kay. 2003. 'Unruhen, Aufstände und Abfallbewegungen der Bevölkerung in Phönikien, Syrien und Kilikien unter den Seleukiden.' *Historia* 52: 300–336.

Ehling, Kay. 2008. *Untersuchungen zur Geschichte der späten Seleukiden (164–63 v. Chr.): Vom Tode des Antiochos IV. bis zur Einrichtung der Provinz Syria unter Pompeius*. Historia Einzelschriften 196. Stuttgart: Steiner Verlag.

Eidinow, Esther. 2007. *Oracles, Curses, and Risk among the Ancient Greeks*. Oxford: Oxford University Press.

Eisenman, Robert. 1983. *Maccabees, Zadokites, Christians and Qumran*. SPB 34. Leiden: Brill.

Elgavish, Joseph. 1976. 'Pottery from the Hellenistic Stratum at Shiqmona.' *IEJ* 26: 65–76.

Ellenson, D. 1975. 'Ellis Rivkin and the Problems of Pharisaic History: A Study in Historiography.' *JAAR* 43: 787–802.

Endres, J. C. 1987. *Biblical Interpretation in the Book of Jubilees.* CBQMS 18. Washington, DC: Catholic Biblical Association.

Engel, Helmut. 1998. *Das Buch der Weisheit.* Neuer Stuttgarter Kommentar: Altes Testament 16. Stuttgart: Katholisches Bibelwerk.

Engels, David. 2017. *Benefactors, Kings, Rulers: Studies on the Seleukid Empire Between East and West.* Studia Hellenistica 57. Leuven: Peeters.

Eph'al, I. 1982. *The Ancient Arabs: Nomads on the Borders of the Fertile Crescent, 9th–5th Centuries B.C.* Jerusalem: Magnes.

Erickson, Kyle, and Gillian Ramsey (eds.). 2011. *Seleucid Dissolution: The Sinking of the Anchor.* Philippika: Marburger altertumskundliche Abhandlungen 50. Wiesbaden: Harrassowitz.

Eshel, Hanan. 2008. *The Dead Sea Scrolls and the Hasmonean State.* Studies in the Dead Sea Scrolls and Related Literature. Grand Rapids, MI: Eerdmans; Jerusalem: Yad Ben-Zvi.

Eshel, Hanan. 2015. *Exploring the Dead Sea Scrolls: Archaeology and Literature of the Qumran Caves*, ed. Shani Tzoref and Barnea Levi Selavan. JAJSup 18. Göttingen: Vandenhoeck & Ruprecht.

Everitt, Anthony. 2001. *Cicero: The Life and Times of Rome's Greatest Politician.* New York: Random House.

Falk, Daniel K. 1998. *Daily, Sabbath, and Festival Prayers in the Dead Sea Scrolls.* STJD 27. Leiden: Brill.

Fantalkin, Alexander, and Oren Tal. 2003. 'The "Yannai Line" (*BJ* I, 99–100; *AJ* XIII, 390–91): Reality or Fiction?' *PEQ* 135: 108–123.

Feldman, Ariel, Maria Cioată, and Charlotte Hempel (eds). 2017. *Is There a Text in this Cave? Studies in the Textuality of the Dead Sea Scrolls in Honour of George J. Brooke.* STDJ 119. Leiden: Brill.

Feldman, Louis H. 1984. *Josephus and Modern Scholarship (1937–1980).* Berlin: de Gruyter.

Feyel, Christophe, and Laetitia Graslin-Thomé (eds.). 2014. *Le projet politique d'Antiochos IV: Journées d'études franco-allemandes, Nancy 17–19 juin 2013.* Études nancéenes d'histoire grecque. Nancy: Association pour la Diffusion de la Recherche sur l'Antiquité.

Fidanzio, Marcello (ed.). 2017. *The Caves of Qumran: Proceedings of the International Conference, Lugano 2014.* STDJ 118. Leiden: Brill.

Fiensy, David A., and James Riley Strange (eds). 2014. *Galilee in the Late Second Temple and Mishnaic Periods: Volume 1 Life, Culture, and Society.* Minneapolis: Fortress.

Fiensy, David A., and James Riley Strange (eds). 2015. *Galilee in the Late Second Temple and Mishnaic Periods, Volume 2: The Archaeological Record from Cities, Towns, and Villages.* Minneapolis: Fortress.

Filmer, W. E. 1966. 'The Chronology of the Reign of Herod the Great.' *JTS* 17: 283–98.

Finegan, Jack. 1998. *Handbook of Biblical Chronology: Principles of Time Reckoning in the Ancient World and Problems of Chronology in the Bible.* Peabody, MA: Hendrickson.

Finkelstein, Israel. 1988–89. 'The Land of Ephraim Survey 1980–1987: Preliminary Report.' *TA* 15–16: 117–83.

Finkelstein, Israel. 1997. 'Pots and People Revised: Ethnic Boundaries in the Iron Age I.' In *The Archaeology of Israel: Constructing the Past, Interpreting the Present*, ed. Neil A. Silberman and David B. Small, 216–37. JSOTSup 239. Sheffield: Sheffield Academic Press.

Finkelstein, Israel. 1997. 'Pots and People Revised: Ethnic Boundaries in the Iron Age I.' In *The Archaeology of Israel: Constructing the Past, Interpreting the Present*, ed. Neil A. Silberman and David B. Small, 216–37. JSOTSup 239. Sheffield: Sheffield Academic Press.

Finkelstein, Israel. 2010. 'The Territorial Extent and Demography of Yehud/Judea in the Persian and Early Hellenistic Periods.' *RevB* 117: 39–54.

Finkelstein, Israel, and Zvi Lederman (eds.). 1997. *Highlands of Many Cultures: The Southern Samaria Survey: The Sites*. 2 vols. Institute of Archaeology Monograph Series 14. Tel Aviv: Tel Aviv University.

Finkielsztejn, Gérald. 1998. 'More Evidence on John Hyrcanus I's Conquests: Lead Weights and Rhodian Amphora Stamps.' *Bulletin of the Anglo-Israel Archaeological Society* 16: 33–63.

Finkielsztejn, Gérald. 2007. 'Poids de plomb inscrits du Levant: une réforme d'Antiochos IV?' *Topoi* Supplement 8: 35–60.

Fischer, T. 1974. 'Zu den Beziehungen zwischen Rom und den Juden im 2. Jahrhundert v. Chr.' *ZAW* 86: 90–93.

Fischer, T. 1975. 'Johannes Hyrkan I. auf Tetradrachmen Antiochos' VII.?' *ZDPV* 91: 191–96.

Fischer, T. 1980. *Seleukiden und Makkabäer: Beiträge zur Seleukidengeschichte und zu den politischen Ereignissen in Judäa während der 1. Hälfte des 2. Jahrhundersts v. Chr.* Bochum: Brockmeyer.

Fisher, Greg (ed.). 2015. *Arabs and Empires before Islam*. Oxford: Oxford University Press.

Fittschen, Klaus, and Gideon Foerster (eds). 1996. *Judaea and the Greco-Roman World in the Time of Herod in the Light of Archaeological Evidence: Acts of a Symposium Organized by the Institute of Archaeology, the Hebrew University of Jerusalem and the Archaeological Institute, Georg-August-University of Göttingen at Jerusalem, November 3rd–4th 1988*. Abhandlungen der Akademie der Wissenschaften in Göttingen, Philologisch-Historische Klasse, 3te Folge, Nr 215. Göttingen: Vandenhoeck & Ruprecht.

Fitzmyer, Joseph A. 1981. *The Gospel according to Luke I–IX*. AB 28. Garden City: Doubleday.

Fitzmyer, Joseph A. 1985. *The Gospel according to Luke X–XXIV*. AB 28A; Garden City: Doubleday.

Fitzmyer, Joseph A. 1990. *The Dead Sea Scrolls: Major Publications and Tools for Study*. Rev. ed. SBLRBS 20. Atlanta: Scholars Press.

Fitzmyer, Joseph A. 1998. *The Acts of the Apostles: A New Translation with Introduction and Commentary*. The Anchor Bible. New York: Doubleday.

Fitzmyer, Joseph A., and Daniel J. Harrington. 1978. *A Manual of Palestinian Aramaic*. BibOr 34. Rome: Biblical Institute.

Flint, Peter W. and James C. VanderKam (eds), with assistance of Andrea E. Alvarez. 1998. *The Dead Sea Scrolls after Fifty Years: A Comprehensive Assessment, vol. 1*. Leiden: Brill.

Flint, Peter W. and James C. VanderKam (eds), with assistance of Andrea E. Alvarez. 1999. *The Dead Sea Scrolls after Fifty Years: A Comprehensive Assessment, vol. 2*. Leiden: Brill.

Florentin, Moshe. 1999. *The Tulida: A Samaritan Chronicle: Text, Translation Commentary*. Jerusalem: Yitzhak Ben Zvi.

Flower, Harriet I. (ed.). 2004. *The Cambridge Companion to the Roman Republic.* Cambridge: Cambridge University Press.
Focke, Friedrich. 1913. *Die Entstehung der Weisheit Salomos: Ein Beitrag zur Geschichte des jüdischen Hellenismus.* FRLANT 22. Göttingen: Vandenhoeck & Ruprecht.
France, R. T. 1979. 'Herod and the Children of Bethlehem.' *NovT* 21: 98–120.
Freedman, David Noel (ed.). 1992. *Anchor Bible Dictionary.* 6 vols. Garden City, NY: Doubleday.
Frey, Jörg, Daniel R. Schwartz, and Stephanie Gripentrog (eds). 2007. *Jewish Identity in the Greco-Roman World / Jüdische Identität in der griechisch-römischen Welt.* AJEC 71. Leiden: Brill.
Frisch, Alexandria. 2017. *The Danielic Discourse on Empire in Second Temple Literature.* JSJSup 176. Leiden: Brill.
Frye, Richard N. 1984. *History of Ancient Iran.* Handbuch der Altertumswssenschaft 3/7. Berlin/New York: de Gruyter.
Funk, Robert W. 1958. 'The 1957 Campaign at Beth-Zur.' *BASOR* 150: 8–20.
Furstenberg, Yair (ed.). 2016. *Jewish and Christian Communal Identities in the Roman World.* AJEC 94. Leiden: Brill.
Gabba, Emilio. 1990. 'The Finances of King Herod.' In *Greece and Rome in Eretz Israel: Collected Essays*, ed. A. Kasher, U. Rappaport, and G. Fuks, 160–68. Jerusalem: Yad Izhak Ben-Zvi and Israel Exploration Society.
Gadot, Yuval, and Yiftah Shalev. Forthcoming. 'New Evidence for Persian and Hellenistic Jerusalem and the Implications for the Location of the City.' In *The Period of the Middle Maccabees: From the Death of Judas through the Reign of John Hyrcanus (ca. 160–104 BCE)*, ed. Andrea M. Berlin. 9th Nangeroni Meeting in Gazzada, Italy.
Gafni, Isaiah M. 1997. *Land, Center and Diaspora: Jewish Constructs in Late Antiquity.* JSPSup 21. Sheffield: Sheffield Academic Press.
Galinsky, Karl (ed.). 2005. *The Cambridge Companion to the Age of Augustus.* Cambridge: Cambridge University Press.
Galor, Katharina, and Gideon Avni (eds.). 2011. *Unearthing Jerusalem: 150 Years of Archaeological Research in the Holy City.* Winona Lake, IN: Eisenbrauns.
Galor, Katharina, and Hanswulf Bloedhorn. 2013. *The Archaeology of Jerusalem: From the Origins to the Ottomans.* New Haven, CT: Yale University Press.
Galor, Katharina, Jean-Baptiste Humber, and Jürgen Zangenberg (eds). 2006. *Qumran— The Site of the Dead Sea Scrolls: Archaeological Interpretations and Debates: Proceedings of a Conference held at Brown University, November 17–19, 2002.* STDJ 57. Leiden: Brill.
García Martínez, Florentino. 1988. 'Qumran Origins and Early History: A Groningen Hypothesis.' *Folio Orientalia* 25: 113–36.
García Martínez, Florentino. 1992. *Qumran and Apocalyptic: Studies on the Aramaic Texts from Qumran.* STDJ 9. Leiden: Brill.
García Martínez, Florentino, and Eibert J. C. Tigchelaar (ed. and trans.). 1997–98. *The Dead Sea Scrolls Study Edition, Volume 1: 1Q1–4Q273; Volume 2: 4Q274–11Q31.* Leiden: Brill. Paperback corrected reprint. Leiden: Brill; Grand Rapids, MI: Eerdmans, 2000.
García Martínez, Florentino, and A. S. van der Woude. 1989–90. 'A "Groningen" Hypothesis of Qumran Origins and Early History.' *RQum* 14: 521–41.
Gardner, Gregg. 2007. 'Jewish Leadership and Hellenistic Civic Benefaction in the Second Century B.C.E.' *JBL* 126: 327–43.

Gaster, Moses. 1908. 'Das Buch Josua in hebräisch-samaritanischer Rezension, endeckt und zum ersten Male herausgegeben.' *ZDMG* 62: 209–79, 494–549.

Gaster, Moses. 1925–28. 'The Chain of Samaritan High Priests.' *Studies and Texts* (London: Maggs), 1:483–502 (English translation), 3:131–8 (text).

Gaster, Moses. 1927. *The Asatir: The Samaritan Book of the 'Secrets of Moses' together with the Pitron or Samaritan Commentary and the Samaritan Story of the Death of Moses.* London: Royal Asiatic Society.

Gauger, Jörg-Dieter. 1977. *Beiträge zur jüdischen Apologetik: Untersuchungen zur Authentizität von Urkunden bei Flavius Josephus und im I. Makkabäerbuch.* Bonner Biblische Beiträge 49. Cologne/Bonn: Peter Hanstein.

Geertz, Clifford. 1973. *The Interpretation of Cultures.* New York: Basic Books.

Gelzer, Matthias. 1968. *Caesar: Politician and Statesman*, trans. Peter Needham. Cambridge, MA: Harvard University Press. ET *Caesar: Der Politiker und Staatsmann.* Wiesbaden: Franz Steiner, 1959.

Gelzer, Matthias. 2005. *Pompeius: Lebensbild eines Römers.* With Forschungsüberblick von Elisabeth Herrmann-Otto. Wiesbaden: Franz Steiner.

Gelzer, Matthias. 2014. *Cicero: Ein biographischer Versuch*, ed. Werner Riess. 2nd exp. ed. Stuttgart: Franz Steiner.

Georgi, Dieter. 1980. *Weisheit Salomos.* Jüdische Schriften aus hellenistisch-römischer Zeit III/4. Gütersloh: Mohn.

Gera, Dov. 1985. 'Tryphon's Sling Bullet from Dor.' *IEJ* 35: 153–63.

Gera, Dov. 1998. *Judaea and Mediterranean Politics 219 to 161 B.C.E.* Brill's Series in Jewish Studies 8. Leiden: Brill.

Gera, Dov, and Wayne Horowitz. 1997. 'Antiochus IV in Life and Death: Evidence from the Babylonian Astronomical Diaries.' *JAOS* 117: 240–52.

Geva, Hillel. 1981. 'The "Tower of David"—Phasael or Hippicus?' *IEJ* 31: 57–65.

Geva, Hillel (ed.). 1994. *Ancient Jerusalem Revealed.* Jerusalem: Israel Exploration Society; Washington, DC: Biblical Archaeology Society.

Geva, Hillel (ed.). 2000. *Jewish Quarter Excavations in the Old City of Jerusalem Conducted by Nahman Avigad, 1969–1982, Volume 1: Architecture and Stratigraphy: Areas A, W and X–2 Final Report.* Jerusalem: Israel Exploration Society.

Geva, Hillel (ed.). 2003. *Jewish Quarter Excavations in the Old City of Jerusalem Conducted by Nahman Avigad, 1969–1982, Volume II: The Finds from Areas A, W and X–2 Final Report.* Jerusalem: Israel Exploration Society.

Gibson, Bruce, and Thomas Harrison (eds.). 2013. *Polybius and his World: Essays in Memory of F. W. Walbank.* Oxford: Oxford University Press.

Gibson, Shimon, and Dan Urman. 1990–91. 'Three Coins of Alexander Jannaeus from El 'Al in the Golan Heights.' *Bulletin of the Anglo-Israel Archaeological Society* 10: 67–72.

Gichon, M. 1967. 'Idumea and the Herodian Limes.' *IEJ* 17: 27–42.

Gilbert, M., S.J. 1973. *La critique des dieux dans le Livre de la Sagesse (Sg 13–15).* AnBib 53. Rome: Pontifical Biblical Institute.

Gilbert, M., S.J. 1986. 'Sagesse de Salomon (ou Livre de la Sagesse).' In *Supplément au Dictionnaire de la Bible*, ed. J. Briend and E. Cothenet, 11:58–119. Paris: Letouzey & Ané.

Gilboa, A. 1979–80. 'The Intervention of Sextus Julius Caesar, Governor of Syria, in the Affair of Herod's Trial.' *Scripta Classica Israelica* 5: 185–94.

Giovannini, Adalberto, and Helmut Müller. 1971. 'Die Beziehungen zwischen Rom und den Juden im 2. Jh v. Chr.' *Museum Helveticum* 28: 156–71.

Gitin, Seymour. 1990. *Gezer III: A Ceramic Typology of the Late Iron II, Persian and Hellenistic Periods at Tell Gezer*, vols 1–2. Annual of the Nelson Glueck School of Biblical Archaeology 3. Jerusalem: Hebrew Union College.

Golb, Norman. 1995. *Who Wrote the Dead Sea Scrolls?* New York/London: Scribner.

Goldingay, John E. 1989. *Daniel*. WBC 30. Dallas: Word.

Goldschmidt-Lehmann, R. P. 1981. 'The Second (Herodian) Temple: Selected Bibliography.' *Jerusalem Cathedra* 1: 336–59.

Goldstein, Jonathan A. 1976. *I Maccabees: A New Translation with Introduction and Commentary*. AB 41. Garden City: Doubleday.

Goldstein, Jonathan A. 1983a. *II Maccabees: A New Translation with Introduction and Commentary*. AB 41A. Garden City: Doubleday.

Goldstein, Jonathan A. 1983b. 'The Date of the Book of Jubilees.' *PAAJR* 50: 63–86.

Goldsworthy, Adrian. 2010. *Antony and Cleopatra*. London: Weidenfeld & Nicolson.

Goldsworthy, Adrian. 2014. *Augustus: From Revolutionary to Emperor*. London: Weidenfeld & Nicolson.

Goodblatt, David. 1987. 'Josephus on Parthian Babylonia (Antiquities XVIII, 310–379).' *JAOS* 107: 605–22.

Goodblatt, David. 2006. *Elements of Ancient Jewish Nationalism*. Cambridge: Cambridge University Press.

Goodblatt, David. 2012. 'Varieties of Identity in Late Second Temple Judah (200 BCE–135 CE).' In *Jewish Identity and Politics between the Maccabees and Bar Kokhba: Groups, Normativity, and Rituals*, ed. Benedikt Eckhardt, 11–27. JSJSup 155. Brill: Leiden.

Goodman, Martin. 1995. 'A Note on the Qumran Sectarians, the Essenes and Josephus.' *JJS* 46: 161–66.

Goodman, Martin. 1997. *The Roman World 44 BC–AD 180*. With the assistance of Jane Sherwood. Routledge History of the Ancient World. London and New York: Routledge.

Goodman, Martin. 1999. 'A Note on Josephus, the Pharisees and Ancestral Tradition.' *JJS* 50: 17–20.

Goodman, Martin. 2008. 'The Place of the Sadducees in First-Century Judaism.' In *Redefining First-Century Jewish and Christian Identities: Essays in Honor of Ed Parish Sanders*, ed. Fabian E. Udoh, 139–52. Christianity and Judaism in Antiquity Series 16. Notre Dame, IN: University of Notre Dame.

Grabbe, Lester L. 1977. *Comparative Philology and the Text of Job: A Study in Methodology*. SBLDS 34. Chico: Scholars Press.

Grabbe, Lester L. 1979. 'Chronography in Hellenistic Jewish Historiography.' In *Society of Biblical Literature 1979 Seminar Papers*, ed. P. J. Achtemeier, 2:43–68. SBLSPS 17. Missoula, MT: Scholars Press.

Grabbe, Lester L. 1981. 'Chronography in 4 Ezra and 2 Baruch.' *Society of Biblical Literature 1981 Seminar Papers*, 49–63. SBLSPS. Chico, CA: Scholars Press.

Grabbe, Lester L. 1982. 'The End of the World in Early Jewish and Christian Calculations.' *RevQ* 41: 107–8.

Grabbe, Lester L. 1987a. 'Josephus and the Reconstruction of the Judaean Restoration.' *JBL* 106: 231–46.

Grabbe, Lester L. 1987b. 'The Scapegoat Ritual: A Study in Early Jewish Interpretation.' *JSJ* 18: 152–67.

Grabbe, Lester L. 1989. 'The Social Setting of Early Jewish Apocalypticism.' *JSP* 4: 27–47.

Grabbe, Lester L. 1991. 'Maccabean Chronology: 167–164 or 168–165 BCE?' *JBL* 110: 59–74.
Grabbe, Lester L. 1992. *Judaism from Cyrus to Hadrian: Vol. I: Persian and Greek Periods; Vol. II: Roman Period*. Minneapolis: Fortress.
Grabbe, Lester L. 1995. *Priests, Prophets, Diviners, Sages: A Socio-historical Study of Religious Specialists in Ancient Israel*. Valley Forge, PA: Trinity Press International.
Grabbe, Lester L. 1997a. 'The Current State of the Dead Sea Scrolls: Are There More Answers than Questions?' In *The Scrolls and the Scriptures: Qumran Fifty Years After*, ed. Stanley E. Porter and C. A. Evans, 54–67. Roehampton Institute London Papers 3 = JSPSup 26. Sheffield: Sheffield Academic Press.
Grabbe, Lester L. 1997b. 'The 70-Weeks Prophecy (Daniel 9:24–27) in Early Jewish Interpretation", in *The Quest for Context and Meaning: Studies in Biblical Intertextuality in Honor of James A. Sanders*, ed. Craig A. Evans and Shemaryahu Talmon, 595–611. Biblical Interpretation Series 28. Leiden: Brill.
Grabbe, Lester L. 1997c. '4QMMT and Second Temple Jewish Society.' In *Legal Texts and Legal Issues: Proceedings of the Second Meeting of the International Organization for Qumran Studies, Cambridge 1995, Published in Honour of Joseph M. Baumgarten*, ed. M. Bernstein, F. García Martínez, and J. Kampen, 89–108. STDJ 23. Leiden: Brill.
Grabbe, Lester L. 1997d. Review of N. Golb, *Who Wrote the Dead Sea Scrolls? DSD* 4: 124–28.
Grabbe, Lester L. 1997e. *Wisdom of Solomon*. Guides to Apocrypha and Pseudepigrapha. Sheffield: Sheffield Academic Press.
Grabbe, Lester L. 1998. *Ezra and Nehemiah*. Readings. London: Routledge.
Grabbe, Lester L. 1999a. 'Eschatology in Philo and Josephus.' In *Judaism in Late Antiquity: Volume 4. Special Topics: (1) Death and the Afterlife*, ed. Alan Avery-Peck and Jacob Neusner, 35–62. Handbuch der Orientalistik: Erste Abteilung, Der Nahe und Mittlere Osten, Bd. 17. Leiden: Brill.
Grabbe, Lester L. 1999b. 'Sadducees and Pharisees.' In *Judaism in Late Antiquity: Part Three. Where We Stand: Issues and Debates in Ancient Judaism: Volume 1*, ed. Jacob Neusner and Alan J. Avery-Peck, 35–62. HdO: Erste Abteilung, der Nahe und Mittlere Osten 40. Leiden: Brill.
Grabbe, Lester L. 1999c. Review article: A. I. Baumgarten, *The Flourishing of Jewish Sects in the Maccabean Era. JSJ* 30: 89–94.
Grabbe, Lester L. 2000a. 'Hat die Bibel doch recht? A Review of T. L. Thompson's *The Bible in History*.' *SJOT* 14: 117–39.
Grabbe, Lester L. 2000b. 'Warfare.' In *Encyclopedia of the Dead Sea Scrolls*, ed. Lawrence H. Schiffman and James C. VanderKam, 961–65. Oxford: Oxford University Press.
Grabbe, Lester L. 2000c. 'The Pharisees—A Response to Steve Mason.' In *Judaism in Late Antiquity, Part Three: Where We Stand: Issues and Debates in Ancient Judaism, Volume 3*, ed. Alan J. Avery-Peck and Jacob Neusner, 35–47. Handbuch der Orientalistik: Erste Abteilung, Der Nahe und Mittlere Osten, Bd. 53. Leiden: Brill.
Grabbe, Lester L. 2001. 'A Dan(iel) for All Seasons: For Whom Was Daniel Important?' In *The Book of Daniel: Composition and Reception*, ed. John J. Collins and Peter W. Flint, 1:229–46. The Formation and Interpretation of Old Testament Literature 2 = VTSup 83. Leiden: Brill.
Grabbe, Lester L. 2002a. 'The Hellenistic City of Jerusalem.' In *Jews in the Hellenistic and Roman Cities*, ed. John R. Bartlett. London: Routledge.

Grabbe, Lester L. 2002b. 'Betwixt and Between: The Samaritans in the Hasmonean Period.' In *Second Temple Studies III: Studies in Politics, Class and Material Culture*, ed. Philip R. Davies and John M. Halligan, 202–17. JSOTSup 340. Sheffield Academic Press. Earlier version published in *Society of Biblical Literature 1993 Seminar Papers*, ed. E. H. Lovering, Jr., 334–47. SBLSPS 32. Atlanta, GA: Scholars Press, 1993.

Grabbe, Lester L. 2003a. 'Prophetic and Apocalyptic: Time for New Definitions—and New Thinking.' In *Knowing the End from the Beginning: The Prophetic, the Apocalyptic, and their Relationships*, ed. Lester L. Grabbe and Robert D. Haak, 107–33. Journal for the Study of the Pseudepigrapha Supplements 46. London/New York: T&T Clark International.

Grabbe, Lester L. 2003b. 'Poets, Scribes, or Preachers? The Reality of Prophecy in the Second Temple Period.' In *Knowing the End from the Beginning: The Prophetic, the Apocalyptic, and their Relationships*, ed. Lester L. Grabbe and Robert D. Haak, 192–215. Journal for the Study of the Pseudepigrapha Supplements 46. London/New York: T&T Clark International. Earlier version published in *Society of Biblical Literature 1998 Seminar Papers*, 2.524–45. SBLSPS 37. Atlanta, GA: Scholars Press, 1998.

Grabbe, Lester L. 2004. *A History of the Jews and Judaism in the Second Temple Period 1: Yehud: A History of the Persian Province of Judah*. LSTS 47. London/New York: T&T Clark International.

Grabbe, Lester L. 2006. 'The Law, the Prophets, and the Rest: The State of the Bible in Pre-Maccabean Times", *DSS* 13: 319–38.

Grabbe, Lester L. 2008a. *A History of the Jews and Judaism in the Second Temple Period 2: The Coming of the Greeks: The Early Hellenistic Period (335–175 BCE)*. LSTS 68. London/New York: T&T Clark International.

Grabbe, Lester L. 2008b. 'Sanhedrin, Sanhedriyyot, or Mere Invention?' *JSJ* 39: 1–19.

Grabbe, Lester L. 2009. 'Jubilees and the Samaritan Tradition.' In *Enoch and the Mosaic Torah: The Evidence of Jubilees*, ed. Gabriele Boccaccini and Giovanni Ibba, 145–59. Grand Rapids, MI: Eerdmans, 2009.

Grabbe, Lester L. 2011. 'Daniel: Sage, Seer…and Prophet?' In *Constructs of Prophecy in the Former and Latter Prophets and Other Texts*, ed. Lester L. Grabbe and Martti Nissinen, 87–94. Society of Biblical Literature Ancient Near East Monographs 4. Atlanta: Society of Biblical Literature.

Grabbe, Lester L. 2015. 'Penetrating the Legend: in Quest of the Historical Ezra.' In *Open-Mindedness in the Bible and Beyond: A Volume of Studies in Honour of Bob Becking*, ed. Marjo C. A. Korpel and Lester L. Grabbe, 97–110. LHBOTS 616. London and New York: Bloomsbury T&T Clark.

Grabbe, Lester L. 2018. 'What Did the Author of Acts Know about Pre–70 Judaism?' In *Wisdom Poured Out Like Water: Studies on Jewish and Christian Antiquity in Honor of Gabriele Boccaccini*, ed. J. Harold Ellens, Isaac W. Oliver, Jason von Ehrenkrook, James Waddell, and Jason M. Zurawski, 450–62. Deuterocanonical and Cognate Literature Studies 38. Berlin/New York: de Gruyter.

Grabbe, Lester L. (ed.). 1998. *Leading Captivity Captive: 'The Exile' as History and Ideology*. JSOTSup 278 = ESHM 2. Sheffield: Sheffield Academic Press.

Gradel, Ittai. 2002. *Emperor Worship and Roman Religion*. Oxford Classical Monographs. Oxford: Clarendon Press.

Grainger, John D. 2010. *The Syrian Wars*. MnemosyneSup 320. Leiden: Brill.

Grainger, John D. 2015. *The Fall of the Seleukid Empire 187–75 BC*. Barnsley: Pen & Sword Books.

Gray, Rebecca. 1993. *Prophetic Figures in Late Second Temple Jewish Palestine: The Evidence from Josephus*. Oxford: Clarendon.
Greenfield, Jonas C., and Michael E. Stone. 1979. 'Remarks on the Aramaic Testament of Levi from the Geniza.' *RB* 86: 214–30.
Griffith, G. T. 1935. *The Mercenaries of the Hellenistic World*. Cambridge: Cambridge University Press.
Gruen, Erich S. 1974. *The Last Generation of the Roman Republic*. Berkeley/Los Angeles: University of California Press.
Gruen, Erich S. 1984. *The Hellenistic World and the Coming of Rome*. 2 vols. Berkeley/Los Angeles: University of California Press.
Gruen, Erich S. 1993. 'Hellenism and Persecution: Antiochus IV and the Jews.' In *Hellenistic History and Culture*, ed. Peter Green, 238–74. Hellenistic Culture and Society 9. Berkeley: University of California Press.
Gruen, Erich S. 1996. 'The Purported Jewish-Spartan Affiliation.' In *Transitions to Empire: Essays in Greco-Roman History, 360–146 B.C., in Honor of E. Badian*, ed. Robert W. Wallace and Edward M. Harris, 254–69. Oklahoma Series in Classical Culture 21. Norman: University of Oklahoma Press.
Gruen, Erich S. 1997. 'The Origins and Objectives of Onias' Temple.' *Scripta Classica Israelica* 16: 47–70. Reprinted in *The Construct of Identity in Hellenistic Judaism: Essays on Early Jewish Literature and History*, 359–82. Deuterocanonical and Cognate Literature Studies 29. Berlin: de Gruyter.
Gruen, Erich S. 1998. *Heritage and Hellenism: The Reinvention of Jewish Tradition*. Hellenistic Culture and Society 30. Berkeley: University of California Press.
Gruen, Erich S. 2001. 'Jewish Perspectives on Greek Culture and Ethnicity.' In *Ancient Perceptions of Greek Ethnicity*, ed. Irad Malkin, 347–73. Center for Hellenic Studies. Cambridge, MA: Harvard University Press.
Gruen, Erich S. 2002. *Diaspora: Jews amidst Greeks and Romans*. Cambridge, MA: Harvard University.
Gruen, Erich S. 2018a. *The Construct of Identity in Hellenistic Judaism: Essays on Early Jewish Literature and History*. Deuterocanonical and Cognate Literature Studies 29. Berlin: de Gruyter.
Gruen, Erich S. 2018b. 'Kinship Relations and Jewish Identity.' In *The Construct of Identity in Hellenistic Judaism: Essays on Early Jewish Literature and History*, 95–111. Deuterocanonical and Cognate Literature Studies 29. Berlin: de Gruyter.
Guerra, Tupã. Forthcoming. *Encountering Evil: Apotropaic Magic in the Dead Sea Scrolls*. LSTS. London: Bloomsbury T&T Clark.
Günther, Linda-Marie (ed.). 2009. *Herodes und Jerusalem*. Stuttgart: Steiner.
Habicht, C. 1976a. *Jüdische Schriften aus hellenistisch-römischer Zeit: Band I Historische und legendarische Erzählungen: Lieferung II. Makkabäerbuch*. Gütersloh: Gütersloher Verlagshaus Gerd Mohn.
Habicht, C. 1976b. 'Royal Documents in Maccabees II.' *Harvard Studies in Classical Philology* 80: 1–18.
Habicht, C. 1989. 'The Seleucids and their Rivals.' *CAH*2 8:324–87.
Habicht, C. 1990. *Cicero the Politician*. Baltimore: Johns Hopkins University Press.
Hachlili, Rachel. 2005. *Jewish Funerary Customs, Practices and Rites in the Second Temple Period*. JSJSup 94. Leiden: Brill.
Hackl, Ursula, Hanna Jenni, and Christoph Schneider. 2003. *Quellen zur Geschichte der Nabatäer: Textsammlung mit Übersetzung und Kommentar*. NTOA 51. Freiburg, Schweiz: Universitätsverlag; Göttingen: Vandenhoeck & Ruprecht.

Hadas, Moses. 1951. *Aristeas to Philocrates*. Dropsie College Jewish Apocryphal Literature. New York: Harper. Reprinted New York: Ktav, 1973.
Haenchen, Ernst. 1971. *The Acts of the Apostles*. Oxford: Blackwell; Philadelphia: Westminster.
Hall, Jonathan M. 1997. *Ethnic Identity in Greek Antiquity*. Cambridge: Cambridge University Press.
Hall, R. G. 1989. 'Epispasm and the Dating of Ancient Jewish Writings.' *JSP* 4: 71–86.
Halpern-Amaru, Betsy. 1999. *The Empowerment of Women in the* Book of Jubilees. JSJSup 60. Leiden: Brill.
Halpern-Zylberstein, M.-C. 1989. 'The Archeology of Hellenistic Palestine.' *CHJ* 2: 1–34.
Hamidović, David. 2013. *Aux origines des messianismes juifs: Actes du colloque international tenu en Sorbonne, à Paris, les 8 et 9 juin 2010*. VTSup 158. Leiden: Brill.
Hanhardt, Robert. 1964. 'Zur Zeitrechnung des I und II Makkabäerbuches.' In *Untersuchungen zur israelitisch-jüdischen Chronologie*, A. Jepsen and R. Hanhardt, 53–96. BZAW 88. Berlin: Töpelmann.
Hanhardt, Robert (ed.). 1976. *Maccabaeorum liber II*. 2nd ed. Septuaginta Vetus Testamentum Graecum 9/2. Göttingen: Vandenhoeck & Ruprecht.
Hann, R. R. 1982. *The Manuscript History of the Psalms of Solomon*. SBLSCS 13. Chico, CA: Scholars Press.
Hann, R. R. 1988. 'The Community of the Pious: The Social Setting of the Psalms of Solomon.' *SR* 17: 169–89.
Hanson, R. S. 1974. 'Toward a Chronology of the Hasmonean Coins.' *BASOR* 216: 21–23.
Harlow, Daniel C., Karina Martin Hogan, Matthew Goff, and Joel S. Kaminsky (eds). 2011. *The 'Other' in Second Temple Judaism: Essays in Honor of John J. Collins*. Grand Rapids, MI: Eerdmans.
Harnack, Adolph von (ed.). 1916. *Porphyrius, "Gegen die Christen", 15 Bücher: Zeugnisse, Fragmente und Referate*. Abhandlungen der Königlich Preussischen Akademie der Wissenschaften. Philos.-histor. Klasse 1916,1. Berlin: Königl. Akademie der Wissenschaften.
Harrington, D. J. 1980. 'The Wisdom of the Scribe According to Ben Sira.' In *Ideal Figures in Ancient Judaism: Profiles and Paradigms*, ed. John J. Collins and George W. E. Nickelsburg, 181–88. SBLSCS 12. Atlanta: Scholars Press.
Harrington, D. J. 1997. *Wisdom Texts from Qumran*. Literature of the Dead Sea Scrolls. London-New York: Routledge.
Harrington, Hannah K. 1995. 'Did the Pharisees Eat Ordinary Food in a State of Ritual Purity?' *JSJ* 26: 42–54.
Harris, William V. 1991[1979] *War and Imperialism in Republican Rome 327–70 B.C.* With a new preface and additional bibliography. Oxford: Clarendon.
Harris, William V. 2016. *Roman Power: A Thousand Years of Empire*. Cambridge: Cambridge University Press.
Hartman, L. F., and A. A. Di Lella. 1978. *The Book of Daniel*. AB 23. Garden City: Doubleday.
Hausmann, Jutta. 1987. *Israels Rest: Studien zum Selbstverständnis der nachexilischen Gemeinde*. BWANT 124. Stuttgart: Kohlhammer.
Hayward, C. T. Robert. 1982. 'The Jewish Temple at Leontopolis: A Reconsideration.' *JJS* 33: 429–43.
Heichelheim, F. M. 1938. 'Roman Syria.' In *An Economic Survey of Ancient Rome*, ed. T. Frank, 4:121–257. Baltimore: Johns Hopkins University Press.

Heinemann, I. 1938. 'Wer veranlaßte den Glaubenszwang der Makkabäerzeit?' *MGWJ* 82: 145–72.
Hendin, David. 2010. *Guide to Biblical Coins*. New York: Amphora.
Hendin, David. 2013. 'Current Viewpoints on Ancient Jewish Coinage: A Bibliographic Essay.' *CBR* 11: 246–301.
Hengel, Martin. 1974. *Judaism and Hellenism*. 2 vols. London: SCM. Philadelphia: Fortress. ET of *Judentum und Hellenismus: Studien zu ihrer Begegnung unter besonderer Berücksichtigung Palästinas bis zur Mitte des 2 Jh.s v. Chr.* 2nd ed. WUNT 10. Tübingen: Mohr Siebeck, 1973.
Hengel, Martin, and Roland Deines. 1995. 'E. P. Sanders' "Common Judaism", Jesus, and the Pharisees.' *JTS* 46: 1–70.
Hensel, Benedikt. 2016. *Juda und Samaria: Zum Verhältnis zweier nach-exilischer Jahwismen*. FAT 110. Tübingen: Mohr Siebeck.
Henten, Jan Willem van. 1997. *The Maccabean Martyrs as Saviours of the Jewish People: A Study of 2 and 4 Maccabees*. JSJSup 57. Leiden: Brill.
Henten, Jan Willem van. 2001. 'The Honorary Decree for Simon the Maccabee (1 Macc 14:25–49) in its Hellenistic Context.' In *Hellenism in the Land of Israel*, ed. John J. Collins and Gregory Sterling, 116–45. Notre Dame: University of Notre Dame Press.
Henten, Jan Willem van. 2007. 'Royal Ideology: 1 and 2 Maccabees and Egypt.' In *Jewish Perspectives on Hellenistic Rulers*, Tessa Rajak, Sarah Pearce, James Aitken, and Jennifer Dines, 265–82. Hellenistic Cultural and Society 50. Berkeley: University of California Press.
Henten, Jan Willem van. 2014. *Flavius Josephus, Volume 7b:* Judean Antiquities *15: Translation and Commentary*.
Henten, Jan Willem van (ed.). 1989. *Die Entstehung der jüdischen Martyrologie*. SPB 38. Leiden: Brill.
Herbert, Sharon C. (ed.). 1994. *Tel Anafa I,i and ii: Final Report on Ten Years of Excavation at a Hellenistic and Roman Settlement in Northern Israel*. 2 vols. Journal of Roman Archaeology, Supplementary Series 10 Part I, i-ii. Ann Arbor, MI: Kelsey Museum.
Herbert, Sharon C. (ed.). 1997. *Tel Anafa II, i: The Hellenistic and Roman Pottery: The Plain Wares* (by Andrea Berlin) *and the Fine Wares*. By Katheleen Warner Slane. Journal of Roman Archaeology, Supplementary Series 10 Part II, i. Ann Arbor, MI: Kelsey Museum.
Herbert, Sharon C., and Andrea M. Berlin. 2003. 'A New Administrative Center for Persian and Hellenistic Galilee: Preliminary Report of the University of Michigan/University of Minnesota Excavations at Kedesh.' *BASOR* 329: 13–59.
Herzog, Ze'ev, George Rapp, Jr, and Ora Negbi (eds). 1989. *Excavations at Tel Michal, Israel*. Tel Aviv University Institute of Archaeology Publication 8. Tel Aviv: Tel Aviv University Press. Minneapolis: University of Minneapolis Press.
Heszer, Catherine (ed.). 2010. *The Oxford Handbook of Jewish Daily Life in Roman Palestine*. Oxford: Oxford University Press.
Hieronymus (Jerome). 1964. *S. Hieronymi Presbyteri Opera: Pars I, Opera Exegetica 5: Commentariorum in Danielem, Libri III (IV)*. Corpus Christianorum, Series Latina 75A. Turnholt: Brepols.
Hirschfeld, Yizhar. 2004. *Qumran in Context: Reassessing the Archaeological Evidence*. Peabody, MA: Hendrickson.
Hirschfeld, Yizhar (ed.). 1997. *The Roman Baths of Hammat Gader: Final Report* (Jerusalem: Israel Exploration Society).

Hoffmann, Adolf. 2001. 'Hellenistic Gadara.' *SHAJ* 7: 391–97.
Hogan, Karina Martin. 1999. 'The Exegetical Background of the "Ambiguity of Death" in the Wisdom of Solomon.' *JSJ* 30: 1–24.
Hölbl, Günther. 2001. *A History of the Ptolemaic Empire*, trans. Tina Saavedra. London: Routledge. ET of *Geschichte des Ptolemäerreiches: Politik, Ideologie und religiöse Kultur von Alexander dem Grossen bis zur römischen Eroberung*. Darmstadt: Wissenschaftliche Buchgesellschaft, 1994.
Hölkeskamp, Karl-J. 2010. *Reconstructing the Roman Republic: An Ancient Political Culture and Modern Research*, trans. Henry Heitmann-Gordon. Rev. ed. Princeton: Princeton University Press.
Holladay, Carl R. 1983. *Fragments from Hellenistic Jewish Authors, Volume I: Historians*. SBLTT 20. Pseudepigrapha Series 10. Atlanta: Scholars Press.
Holladay, Carl R. 1989. *Fragments from Hellenistic Jewish Authors, Volume II: Poets: The Epic Poets Theodotus and Philo and Ezekiel the Tragedian*. SBLTT 30. Pseudepigrapha Series 12. Atlanta: Scholars Press.
Holland, Tom. 2003. *Rubicon: The Triumph and Tragedy of the Roman Republic*. London: Little, Brown.
Honigman, Sylvie. 2014. *Tales of High Priests and Taxes: The Books of the Maccabees and the Judean Rebellion against Antiochos IV*. Oakland, CA: University of California Press.
Hoover, Oliver D. 2003. 'The Seleucid Coinage of John Hyrcanus I: The Transformation of a Dynastic Symbol in Hellenistic Judaea.' *AJN* 15: 29–39.
Hoover, Oliver D. 2007. 'A Revised Chronology for the Late Seleucids at Antioch (121/0–64 BC).' *Historia* 56: 280–301.
Horbury, William, and David Noy (eds). 1992. *Jewish Inscriptions of Graeco-Roman Egypt. With an Index of the Jewish Inscriptions of Egypt and Cyrenaica*. Cambridge: Cambridge University Press.
Horgan, M. P. 1979. *Pesharim: Qumran Interpretations of Biblical Books*. CBQMS 8. Washington, DC: Catholic Biblical Association.
Hornblower, Simon, and Anthony J. S. Spawforth. 2012. '*ephēboi*.' In *The Oxford Classical Dictionary*, ed. Simon Hornblower, Anthony J. S. Spawforth, and Esther Eidinow, 508. 4th ed. Oxford: Oxford University Press.
Hornblower, Simon, Anthony J. S. Spawforth, and Esther Eidinow (eds). 2012. *The Oxford Classical Dictionary*. 4th ed. Oxford University Press.
Horowitz, G. 1980. 'Town Planning of Hellenistic Marisa: A Reappraisal of the Excavations after Eighty Years.' *PEQ* 112: 93–111.
Horsley, Richard A. 1985. '"Like One of the Prophets of Old": Two Types of Popular Prophets at the Time of Jesus.' *CBQ* 47: 435–63.
Horsley, Richard A. 1986. 'Popular Prophetic Movements at the Time of Jesus: Their Principal Features and Social Origins.' *JSNT* 26: 3–27.
Horsley, Richard A., with John S. Hanson. 1999. *Bandits, Prophets, and Messiahs: Popular Movements at the Time of Jesus*. 1985 ed. with new preface; Harrisburg, PA: Trinity Press International.
Houghton, Arthur, Catharine Lorber, and Oliver Hoover (eds). 2008. *Seleucid Coins: A Comprehensive Catalogue, Part II: Seleucus IV through Antiochus XIII, Volumes I and II*. New York: American Numismatic Society.
Hübner, Hans. 1999. *Die Weisheit Salomons: Liber Sapientiae Salomonis*. ATD. Apokryphen Band 4. Göttingen: Vandenhoeck & Ruprecht.

Humbert, Jean-Baptiste (ed.). 2003. *Khirbet Qumran et 'Ain Feshkha /The Excavations of Khirbet Qumran and Ain Feshka II: Etudes d'anthropologie, de physique et de chimie / Studies of Anthropology, Physics and Chemistry*. NTOA, Series Archaelogica 3. Fribourg: Academic Press Fribourg; Göttingen: Vandenhoeck & Ruprecht.

Humphries, W. L. 1973. 'A Life-Style for Diaspora: A Study of the Tales of Esther and Daniel.' *JBL* 92: 211–23.

Huß, Werner. 2001. *Ägypten in hellenistischer Zeit: 332–30 v. Chr.* Munich: Beck.

Hutchinson, John, and Anthony D. Smith (eds). 1996. *Ethnicity*. Oxford Readers. Oxford: Oxford University Press.

Ilan, Tal. 1987. 'The Greek Names of the Hasmoneans.' *JQR* 78: 1–20.

Isaac, Benjamin. 1983. 'A Donation for Herod's Temple in Jerusalem.' *IEJ* 33: 86–92 (Heb. version in *EI* 18 [1985] 1–4).

Isaac, Benjamin. 1991. 'A Seleucid Inscription from Jamnia-on-the-Sea: Antiochus V Eupator and the Sidonians.' *IEJ* 41: 132–44.

Isser, S. J. 1976. *The Dositheans: A Samaritan Sect in Late Antiquity*. SJLA 17. Leiden: Brill.

Jacobson, David M. 2007. *The Hellenistic Paintings of Marisa* (including a facsimile reprint of *Painted Tombs in the Necropolis of Marissa [Marêshah]*. By John P. Peters and Hermann Thiersch, ed. Stanley A. Cook [1905]. Leeds: Maney.

Jacobson, David M. 2014. 'Herodian Bronze and Tyrian Silver Coinage.' *ZDPV* 130: 138–54.

Jacobson, David M., and Nikos Kokkinos (eds). 2009. *Herod and Augustus: Papers Presented at the IJS Conference, 21st–23rd June 2005*. IJS Studies in Judaica 6. Leiden: Brill.

Jacoby, Felix. 1926–58. *Die Fragmente der griechischen Historiker*. Parts 1–17. Berlin: Weidman.

Jacoby, Felix. 1926. '90. Nicolas von Damascus.' In *Die Fragmente der griechischen Historiker*. Part 2A. Berlin: Weidman.

Jassen, Alex P. 2019. 'Prophecy and Priests in the Second Temple Period.' In *Prophecy and its Cultic Dimensions*, ed. Lena-Sofia Tiemeyer, 63–88. JAJSup 31. Göttingen: Vandenhoeck & Ruprecht.

Jeansonne, S. P. 1988. *The Old Greek Translation of Daniel 7–12*. CBQMS 19. Washington, DC: Catholic Biblical Association.

Jellicoe, Sydney. 1968. *The Septuagint and Modern Study*. Oxford: Clarendon.

Jeremias, Joachim. 1969. *Jerusalem in the Time of Jesus: An Investigation into Economic and Social Conditions during the New Testament Period*. London: SCM.

Jeselsohn, D. 1974. 'A New Coin Type with Hebrew Inscription.' *IEJ* 24: 77–78.

Jeselsohn, D. 1980. 'Hever Yehudim—A New Jewish Coin.' *PEQ* 112: 11–17.

Ji, Chang-Ho C. 2001. '''Irāq al-'Amīr and the Hellenistic Settlements in Central and Northern Jordan.' *SHAJ* 7: 379–89.

Ji, Chang-Ho, and Jong Keun Lee. 2004. 'From the Tobiads to the Hasmoneans: The Hellenistic Pottery, Coins, and History in the Regions of 'Irāq al-Amīr and the Wādī Ḥisbān.' *SHAJ* 8: 177–88.

Jobes, Karen H. 1996. *The Alpha-Text of Esther. Its Character and Relationship to the Masoretic Text*. SBLDS 153. Atlanta: Scholars Press.

Johnson, Sara Raup. 2004. *Historical Fictions and Hellenistic Jewish Identity: Third Maccabees in its Cultural Context*. Hellenistic Culture and Society 43. Berkeley and Los Angeles: University of California Press.

Jones, A. H. M. 1971. *The Cities of the Eastern Roman Provinces*. 2nd ed. Oxford: Clarendon.

Jones, Christopher P. 1999. *Kinship Diplomacy in the Ancient World*. Revealing Antiquity. Cambridge, MA: Harvard University Press.

Jones, Christopher P. 2009. 'The Inscription from Tel Maresha for Olympiodoros.' *ZPE* 171: 100–104.

Jones, Kenneth R. 2011. *Jewish Reactions to the Destruction of Jerusalem in A.D.70: Apocalypses and Related Pseudepigrapha*. JSJSup 151. Leiden: Brill.

Jones, Siân. 1997. *The Archaeology of Ethnicity: Constructing Identities in the Past and Present*. London/New York: Routledge.

Jonnes, L., and M. Ricl. 1997. 'A New Royal Inscription from Phrygia Paroreios: Eumenes II Grants Tyriaion the Status of a *Polis*.' *Epigraphica Anatolica* 29: 1–30.

Joosten, Jan. 2014. 'The *Samareitikon* and the Samaritan Tradition.' In *Die Septuaginta— Text, Wirkung, Rezeption*, ed. W. Kraus and S. Kreuzer, 346–59. WUNT 325. Tübingen, Mohr-Siebeck.

Kabasele Mukenge, André. 1998. *L'unité littéraire du livre de Baruch*. Etudes bibliques, nouvelle série no. 38. Paris: Librairie Lecoffre, Gabalda.

Kamp, Kathryn A., and Norman Yoffee. 1980. 'Ethnicity in Ancient Western Asia During the Early Second Millennium B.C.: Archaeological Assessments and Ethnoarchaeological Prospectives.' *BASOR* 237: 85–104.

Kampen, John. 1986. 'A Reconsideration of the Name "Essene" in Greco-Jewish Literature in Light of Recent Perceptions of the Qumran Sect.' *HUCA* 57: 61–81.

Kampen, John. 1988. *The Hasideans and the Origins of Pharisaism: A Study in 1 and 2 Maccabees*. SBLSCS 24. Atlanta: Scholars Press.

Kanael, Baruch. 1956. 'The Partition of Judea by Gabinius.' *IEJ* 6: 98–106.

Kanael, Baruch. 1971. 'Notes on the Dates Used During the Bar Kokhba Revolt.' *IEJ* 21: 39–46.

Kapera, Zdzisław (ed.). 1996. *Mogilany 1993: Papers on the Dead Sea Scrolls Offered in Memory of Hans Burgmann*. Qumranica Mogilanesia 13. Cracow: Enigma Press.

Kapera, Zdzisław (ed.). 1998. *Mogilany 1995: Papers on the Dead Sea Scrolls Offered in Memory of Aleksy Klawek*. Qumranica Mogilanensia 15. Cracow: Enigma.

Kaplan, J. 1972. 'The Archaeology and History of Tel Aviv-Jaffa.' *BA* 35: 66–95.

Kartveit, Magnar. 2009. *The Origins of the Samaritans*. VTSup 128. Leiden: Brill.

Kasher, Aryeh. 1982. 'Gaza during the Greco-Roman Era.' *Jerusalem Cathedra* 2: 63–78.

Kasher, Aryeh. 1985. *The Jews in Hellenistic and Roman Egypt: The Struggle for Equal Rights*. TSAJ 7. Tübingen: Mohr Siebeck.

Kasher, Aryeh. 1988. *Jews, Idumaeans, and Ancient Arabs: Relations of the Jews in Eretz-Israel with the Nations of the Frontier and the Desert during the Hellenistic and Roman Era (332 BCE–70 CE)*. TSAJ 18. Tübingen: Mohr Siebeck.

Kasher, Aryeh. 2007. (in collaboration with Eliezer Witztum). *King Herod: A Persecuted Persecutor: A Case Study in Psychohistory and Psychobiography*, trans. Karen Gold. Studia Judaica 36. Berlin/New York: de Gruyter.

Kasher, A., U. Rappaport, and G. Fuks (eds). 1990. *Greece and Rome in Eretz Israel: Collected Essays*. Jerusalem: Yad Izhak Ben-Zvi and Israel Exploration Society.

Katzoff, R. 1985. 'Jonathan and Late Sparta.' *AJP* 106: 485–89.

Keaveney, Arthur. 1981. 'Roman Treaties with Parthia circa 95–circa 64 B.C.' *AJP* 102: 195–212.

Keitel, Elizabeth. 1978. 'The Role of Parthia and Armenia in Tacitus *Annals* 11 and 12.' *AJP* 99: 462–73.

Kennell, Nigel M. 2005. 'New Light on 2 Maccabees 4:7–15.' *JJS* 56: 10–24.
Keyes, Charles F. 1997. 'Ethnic Groups, Ethnicity.' In *The Dictionary of Anthropology*, ed. Thomas Barfield, 152–54. Oxford: Blackwell.
Kidd, I. G. 1988. *Posidonius, Volume 2: The Commentary, (i) Testimonia and Fragments 1–149*. CCTC 14A. Cambridge: Cambridge University Press.
Kidd, I. G. 1988. *Posidonius, Volume 2, The Commentary, (ii) Fragments 150–293*. CCTC 14B. Cambridge: Cambridge University Press.
Kidd, I. G. 1999. *Posidonius, Volume 3: The Translation of the Fragments*. CCTC 36. Cambridge: Cambridge University Press.
Killebrew, Ann E. 2005. *Biblical Peoples and Ethnicity: An Archaeological Study of Egyptians, Canaanites, Philistines, and Early Israel 1300–1000 B.C.E.* SBLABS 9. Atlanta: Society of Biblical Literature.
Kindler, A. 1954. 'The Jaffa Hoard of Alexander Jannaeus.' *IEJ* 4: 170–85.
Kindler, A. 1968. 'Addendum to the Dated Coins of Alexander Janneus.' *IEJ* 18: 188–91.
Kippenberg, Hans G. 1982. *Religion und Klassenbildung im antiken Judäa*. 2nd ed. SUNT 14. Göttingen: Vandenhoeck & Ruprecht.
Kittel, Gerhard, and G. Friedrich (eds). 1964–76. *Theological Dictionary of the New Testament*. 10 vols. Grand Rapids, MI: Eerdmans.
Klawans, Jonathan. 2012. *Josephus and the Theologies of Ancient Judaism*. Oxford: Oxford University Press.
Kletter, Raz. 2006. 'Can a Proto-Israelite Please Stand Up? Notes on the Ethnicity of Iron Age Israel and Judah.' In *'I Will Speak the Riddles of Ancient Times': Archaeological and Historical Studies in Honor of Amihai Mazar on the Occasion of his Sixtieth Birthday*, ed. Aren M. Maeir and Pierre de Miroschedji, 573–86. Winona Lake, IN: Eisenbrauns.
Kletter, Raz, Irit Ziffer, Wolfgang Zwickel (eds). 2010. *Yavneh 1: The Excavation of the 'Temple Hill' Repository Pit and the Cult Stands*. OBO 30. Fribourg: Academic Press; Göttingen: Vandenhoeck & Ruprecht.
Kloner, Amos. 1980. 'A Tomb of the Second Temple Period at French Hill, Jerusalem.' *IEJ* 30: 99–108.
Kloner, Amos (ed.). 2003. *Maresha Excavations Final Report I: Subterranean Complexes 21, 44, 70*. IAA Reports 17. Jerusalem: Israel Antiquities Authority.
Kloner, Amos, Esther Eshel, Hava B. Korzakova, and Gerald Finkielsztejn. 2010. *Maresha Excavations Final Report III: Epigraphic Finds from the 1989–2000 Seasons*. IAA Reports 45. Jerusalem: Israel Antiquities Authority.
Kloppenborg, John S. 2008. *Q, the Earliest Gospel: An Introduction to the Original Stories and Sayings of Jesus*. Louisville, KY: Westminster John Knox.
Knibb, Michael A. 1989. *Jubilees and the Origins of the Qumran Community*. Inaugural Lecture in the Department of Biblical Studies. London: King's College.
Knibb, Michael A. 1995. 'Messianism in the Pseudepigrapha in the Light of the Scrolls.' *DSD* 2: 165–84.
Kobelski, Paul J. 1981. *Melchizedek and Melchirešaʿ*. CBQMS 10. Washington, DC: Catholic Biblical Association.
Koch, Klaus. 1995. *Die Reiche der Welt und der kommende Menschensohn: Studien zum Danielbuch (Gesammelte Aufsätze 2)*, ed. Martin Rösel. Neukirchen-Vluyn: Neukirchener Verlag.

Koch, Klaus. 1997. *Europa, Rom und der Kaiser vor dem Hintergrund von zwei Jahrtausenden Rezeption des Buches Daniel*. Berichte aus den Sitzungen der Joachim Jungius-Gesellschafter der Wissenschaften E. V. Hamburg, Jahrgang 15, Heft 1. Göttingen: Vandenhoeck & Ruprecht.

Kokkinos, Nikos. 1998. *The Herodian Dynasty: Origins, Role in Society and Eclipse*. JSPSup 30. Sheffield: Sheffield Academic Press.

Kolarcik, Michael. 1991. *The Ambiguity of Death in the Book of Wisdom 1–6: A Study of Literary Structure and Interpretation*. AnBib 127. Rome: Pontifical Biblical Institute.

Kosmin, Paul J. 2014. *The Land of the Elephant Kings: Space, Territory, and Ideology in the Seleucid Empire*. Cambridge, MA: Harvard University Press.

Krauter, Stefan. 2004. *Bürgerrecht und Kultteilnahme: Politische und kultische Rechte und Pflichten in griechischen Poleis, Rom und antikem Judentum*. BZNW 127. Berlin/New York: de Gruyter.

Kreimerman, I, and D Sandhaus. Forthcoming. 'Political Trends as Reflected in Material Culture: A New Look at the Transition between the Persian and Early Hellenistic Periods.' In *Judah and Judeans in the Long Third Century*, ed. Sylvie Honigman, Oded Lipschits, C. Nihan, and Thomas Römer. Winona Lake, IN: Eisenbrauns.

Kreissig, H. 1962. 'Der Makkabäeraufstand zur Frage seiner Socialökonomischen Zusammenhänge und Wirkungen.' *Studii Clasice* 4: 143–75.

Krieger, Klaus-Stefan. 1992. 'Zur Frage nach der Hauptquelle über die Geschichte der Provinz Judäa in den Antiquitates Judaicae des Flavius Josephus.' *BN* 63: 37–41.

Krieger, Klaus-Stefan. 1993. 'Chronologische Probleme in der Geschichte der ersten fünf Statthalter der Provinz Judäa.' *BN* 68: 18–23.

Krieger, Klaus-Stefan. 1994. 'War Flavius Josephus ein Verwandter des hasmonäischen Königshauses?' *BN* 73: 58–65.

Kropp, Andreas J. M. 2009. 'Nabataean Petra: The Royal Palace and the Herod Connection.' *Boreas* 32: 43–59 + 15 tables.

Kropp, Andreas J. M. 2013. *Images and Monuments of Near Eastern Dynasts, 100 BC–AD 100*. Oxford Studies in Ancient Culture and Representation. Oxford: Oxford University Press.

Kugel, James L. 1994. 'The Jubilees Apocalypse.' *DSD* 1: 322–37.

Kugel, James L. 2012. *A Walk through* Jubilees*: Studies in the* Book of Jubilees *and the World of its Creation*. JSJSup 156. Leiden: Brill.

Kugler, F. X. 1922. *Von Moses bis Paulus*. Münster: Aschendorff.

Kugler, Robert A., and Eileen M. Schuller (eds). 1999. *The Dead Sea Scrolls at Fifty: Proceedings of the 1997 Society of Biblical Literature Qumran Section Meetings*. SBLEJL 15. Atlanta: Scholars Press.

Kuhnen, Hans-Peter. 1990. *Palästina in griechisch-römischer Zeit*. HdA, Vorderasien 2, Band 2. Munich: Beck.

Laato, Antti. 1997. *A Star Is Rising: The Historical Development of the Old Testament Royal Ideology and the Rise of the Jewish Messianic Expectations*. University of South Florida International Studies in Formative Christianity and Judaism. Atlanta: Scholars Press.

Laato, Antti. 1998. 'The Apocalypse of the Syriac Baruch and the Date of the End.' *JSP* 18: 39–46.

Lacocque, André. 1999. 'The Different Versions of Esther.' *Biblical Interpretation* 7: 301–22.

Ladouceur, D. J. 1981. 'The Death of Herod the Great.' *Classical Philology* 76: 25–34.

Landau, Tamar. 2006. *Out-Heroding Herod: Josephus, Rhetoric, and the Herod Narratives.* AJEC 63. Leiden: Brill.
Landau, Yohanan, and Vassilios Tzaferis. 1979. 'Tel Iṣṭabah, Beth Shean: The Excavations and Hellenistic Jar Handles.' *IEJ* 29: 152–59.
Lane, Eugene N. 1979. 'Sabazius and the Jews in Valerius Maximus: A Re-Examination.' *JRS* 69: 35–38.
Lange, Armin. 2009. *Handbuch der Textfunde vom Toten Meer, Band 1: Die Handschriften biblischer Bücher von Qumran und den anderen Fundorten.* Tübingen: Mohr Siebeck.
Lange, Armin, Emanuel Tov, and Matthias Weigold (eds). 2011. *The Dead Sea Scrolls in Context: Integrating the Dead Sea Scrolls in the Study of Ancient Texts, Languages, and Cultures.* 2 vols. VTSup 140/1–2. Leiden: Brill.
Lapp, Nancy L. (ed.). 1983. *The Excavations at Araq el-Emir, Vol. 1.* AASOR 47. Winona Lake, IN: Eisenbrauns.
Laqueur, R. 1920. *Der jüdische Historiker Flavius Josephus.* Giessen: Munchow.
Larcher, C., O.P. 1969. *Etudes sur le Livre de la Sagesse.* Etudes bibliques. Paris: J. Gabalda.
Larcher, C., O.P. 1983–85. *Le Livre de la Sagesse ou la Sagesse de Salomon.* 3 vols. Etudes Bibliques, nouvelle série 1. Paris: Gabalda.
Lebram, J. C. H. 1974. 'Perspektiven der Gegenwärtigen Danielforschung.' *JSJ* 5: 1–33.
Lebram, J. C. H. 1975. 'König Antiochus im Buch Daniel.' *VT* 25: 737–72.
Lefkovits, Judah K. 2000. *The Copper Scroll (3Q15): A Reevaluation: A New Reading, Translation, and Commentary.* STDJ 25. Leiden: Brill.
Legrand, Thierry, and Jan Joosten (eds). 2014. *The Targums in the Light of Traditions of the Second Temple Period.* JSJSup 167. Leiden: Brill.
Lehmann, M. R. 1963. 'Studies in the Murabba'at and Nahal Hever Documents.' *RevQ* 4: 53–81.
LeMoyne, J. 1972. *Les Sadducéen.* EB. Paris: Leocffre.
Leszynsky, R. 1912. *Die Sadduzäer.* Berlin: Mayer & Muller.
Levick, Barbara. 2010. *Augustus: Image and Substance.* Harlow, UK: Longman.
Levine, B. A. 1978. 'The Temple Scroll: Aspects of its Historical Provenance and Literary Character' *BASOR* 232: 5–23.
Levine, Lee I. 1975. *Roman Caesarea: An Archaeological-Topographical Study.* Qedem 2. Jerusalem: Hebrew University.
Levine, Lee I. 1981. 'Archaeological Discoveries from the Greco-Roman Era.' In *Recent Archaeology in the Land of Israel*, ed. Hershel Shanks and Benyamin Mazar, 75–88. Jerusalem: Israel Exploration Society; Washington, DC: Biblical Archaeology Society.
Levison, John R. 1994. 'Two Types of Ecstatic Prophecy according to Philo.' *SPA* 6: 83–89.
Levison, John R. 1995. 'Inspiration and the Divine Spirit in the Writings of Philo Judaeus.' *JSJ* 26: 271–323.
Lichtenberger, Achim. 1999. *Die Baupolitik Herodes des Großen.* Abhandlungen des Deutschen Palästina-Vereins 26. Wiesbaden: Harrassowitz.
Lichtenstein, H. 1931–32. 'Die Fastenrolle, eine Untersuchung zur jüdisch-hellenistischen Geschichte.' *HUCA* 8–9: 257–351.
Lightstone, Jack N. 1975. 'Sadducees versus Pharisees.' In *Christianity, Judaism and Other Greco-Roman Cults: Studies for Morton Smith at Sixty*, 3.206–17. SJLA 12. Leiden: Brill.

Lightstone, Jack N. 1983. 'Judaism of the Second Commonwealth: Toward a Reform of the Scholarly Tradition.' In *Truth and Compassion: Essays on Judaism and Religion in Memory of Rabbi Dr. Solomon Frank*, ed. H. Joseph et al., 31–40. Ontario: Wilfrid Laurier University Press.

Lim, Timothy H. 1993. 'The Wicked Priests of the Groningen Hypothesis.' *JBL* 112: 415–25.

Lim, Timothy H., in consultation with Philip S. Alexander. 1997. *The Dead Sea Scrolls Electronic Reference Library, vol. 1*. DSS Electronic Reference Library 1. Leiden: Brill; Oxford University Press.

Lim, Timothy H., in consultation with Philip S. Alexander. 1999. *The Dead Sea Scrolls Electronic Reference Library, vol. 2*. DSS Electronic Reference Library 2. Leiden: Brill; Oxford University Press.

Lim, Timothy H., and John J. Collins (eds). 2010. *The Oxford Handbook of the Dead Sea Scrolls*. Oxford Handbooks in Religion and Theology. Oxford: Oxford University Press.

Lintott, Andrew. 2008. *Cicero as Evidence: A Historian's Companion*. Oxford: Oxford University Press.

Lipschits, Oded, and Oren Tal. 2007. 'The Settlement Archaeology of the Province of Judah: A Case Study.' In *Judah and the Judeans in the Fourth Century B.C.E.*, ed. Oded Lipschits, Gary N. Knoppers, and Rainer Albertz, 33–52. Winona Lake, IN: Eisenbrauns.

Longden, R. P. 1931. 'Notes on the Parthian Campaigns of Trajan.' *JRS* 21: 1–35.

Looijer, Gwynned de. 2015. *The Qumran Paradigm: A Critical Evaluation of Some Foundational Hypotheses in the Construction of the Qumran Sect*. SBLEJL 43. Atlanta: SBL.

Lönnqvist, Minna, and Kenneth Lönnqvist. 2002. *Archaeology of the Hidden Qumran: The New Paradigm*. Helsinki: Helsinki University Press.

Lott, J. Bert. 2012. *Death and Dynasty in Early Imperial Rome: Key Sources, with Text, Translation, and Commentary*. Cambridge: Cambridge University Press.

Lührmann, D. 1987. 'Die Pharisäer und die Schriftgelehrten im Markusevangelium.' *ZNW* 78: 169–85.

Ma, John. 1999. *Antiochos III and the Cities of Western Asia Minor*. Oxford: Oxford University Press.

Maccoby, H. 1989. *Judaism in the First Century*. Issues in Religious Studies. London: Sheldon.

McCown, C. C. 1957. 'The 'Araq el-Emir and the Tobiads.' *BA* 20: 63–76.

Macdonald, John. 1963. *Memar Marqah: The Teaching of Marqah*. BZAW 84. 2 vols. Berlin: Töpelmann.

Macdonald, John. 1964. *The Theology of the Samaritans*. NTL. London: SCM.

Macdonald, John. 1971. 'Samaritans.' *EJ* 14:728–32.

McEwan, G. J. P. 1986. 'A Parthian Campaign against Elymais in 77 B.C.' *Iran* 24: 91–94.

McGing, Brian. 2010. *Polybius' Histories*. Oxford Approaches to Classical Literature. Oxford: Oxford University Press.

Mach, Michael. 1992. *Entwicklungsstadien des jüdischen Engelglaubens in vorrabbinischer Zeit*. TSAJ 34. Tübingen: Mohr Siebeck.

Mack, Burton L. 1973. *Logos und Sophia: Untersuchungen zur Weisheitstheologie im hellenistischen Judentum*. Studien zur Umwelt des Neuen Testaments 10. Göttingen: Vandenhoeck & Ruprecht.

McLay, Tim. 1996. *The OG and Th Versions of Daniel*. SBLSCS 43. Atlanta: Scholars Press.
Magen, Yitzhak. 2002. *The Stone Vessel Industry in the Second Temple Period: Excavations at Ḥizma and the Jerusalem Temple Mount*. JSP 1. Jerusalem: Israel Exploration Society.
Magen, Yitzhak. 2007. 'The Dating of the First Phase of the Samaritan Temple on Mount Gerizim in Light of the Archaeological Evidence.' In *Judah and the Judeans in the Fourth Century B.C.E.*, ed. Oded Lipschits, Gary N. Knoppers, and Rainer Albertz, 157–211. Winona Lake, IN: Eisenbrauns.
Magen, Yitzhak. 2008a. *The Samaritans and the Good Samaritan*. JSP 7. Jerusalem: Israel Antiquities Authority.
Magen, Yitzhak. 2008b. *Mount Gerizim Excavations, Volume 2: A Temple City*. JSP 8. Jerusalem: Israel Antiquities Authority.
Magen, Yitzhak, Haggai Misgav, and Levana Tsfania. 2004. *Mount Gerizim Excavations, Volume 1: The Aramaic, Hebrew and Samaritan Inscriptions*. JSP 2. Jerusalem: Israel Antiquities Authority.
Magen, Yitzhak, and Yuval Peleg (eds). 2007. *The Qumran Excavations, 1993–2004: Preliminary Report*. JSP 6. Jerusalem: Israel Antiquities Authority.
Magen, Yitzhak, and Yuval Peleg (eds). 2018. *Back to Qumran: Final Report (1993–2004)*. JSP 18. Jerusalem: Israel Antiquities Authority.
Magie, D. 1950. *Roman Rule in Asia Minor, to the End of the Third Century after Christ*. 2 vols. Princeton: Princeton University Press.
Magness, Jodi. 1995. 'The Chronology of the Settlement at Qumran in the Herodian Period.' *DSD* 2: 58–65.
Magness, Jodi. 2002. *The Archaeology of Qumran and the Dead Sea Scrolls*. Grand Rapids, MI: Eerdmans.
Magness, Jodi. 2012. *The Archaeology of the Holy Land: From the Destruction of Solomon's Temple to the Muslim Conquest*. Cambridge: Cambridge University Press.
Magness, Jodi. 2013. 'Was Qumran a Fort in the Hasmonean Period?' *JJS* 64: 228–41.
Magny, Ariane. 2010. 'Porphyry in Fragments: Jerome, Harnack, and the Problem of Reconstruction.' *Journal of Early Christian Studies* 18: 515–55.
Mahieu, Bieke. 2012. *Between Rome and Jerusalem: Herod the Great and his Sons in their Struggle for Recognition*. OLA 208. Leuven: Peeters.
Main, Emmanuelle. 1990. 'Les Sadducéens vus par Flavius Josèphe.' *RevB* 97: 161–206.
Marshak, Adam Kolman. 2006. 'The Dated Coins of Herod the Great: Towards a New Chronology.' *JSJ* 37: 212–40.
Mason, Steve. 1988. 'Priesthood in Josephus and the "Pharisaic Revolution".' *JBL* 107: 657–61.
Mason, Steve. 1989. 'Was Josephus a Pharisee? A Re-Examination of *Life* 10–12.' *JJS* 40: 31–45.
Mason, Steve. 1991. *Flavius Josephus on the Pharisees: A Composition-Critical Study*. SPB 39. Leiden: Brill.
Mason, Steve. 1994. 'Method in the Study of Early Judaism: A Dialogue with Lester Grabbe.' *JAOS* 115: 463–72.
Mason, Steve. 1999. 'Revisiting Josephus's Pharisees.' In *Judaism in Late Antiquity, Volume 4, Part II*, ed. Alan Avery-Peck and Jacob Neusner, 23–56. HdO: Erste Abteilung, der Nahe und Mittlere Osten, Bd. Leiden: Brill.
Mason, Steve. 2001. *Flavius Josephus, Volume 9:* Life of Josephus: *Translation and Commentary*. Leiden: Brill.

Mason, Steve. 2007. 'Jews, Judaea, Judaizing, Judaism: Problems of Categorization in Ancient History.' *JSJ* 38: 457–512.
Mason, Steve. 2008. *Flavius Josephus, Volume 1b:* Judean War *2: Translation and Commentary.* Leiden: Brill.
Mason, Steve. 2014. 'The Priest Josephus Away from the Temple: A Changed Man?' *RevQ* 26: 375–402.
Master, Daniel M. (ed.). 2013. *The Oxford Encyclopedia of the Bible and Archaeology.* Oxford: Oxford University Press.
Master, Daniel M., John M. Monson, Egon H. E. Lass, and George A. Pierce (eds). 2005. *Dothan I: Remains from the Tell (1953–1964).* The Excavations of Joseph P. Free at Dothan (1953–1964). Winona Lake, IN: Eisenbrauns.
Mattern-Parkes, Susan P. 2003. 'The Defeat of Crassus and the Just War.' *The Classical World* 96: 387–96.
Mattill, A. J., Jr. 1978. 'The Value of Acts as a Source for the Study of Paul.' In *Perspectives on Luke–Acts*, ed. C. H. Talbert, 76–98. Edinburgh: T. & T. Clark.
Matusova, Ekaterina. 2015. *The Meaning of the Letter of Aristeas: In Light of Biblical Interpretation and Grammatical Tradition, and with Reference to its Historical Context.* FRLANT 260. Göttingen: Vandenhoeck & Ruprecht.
Mazar, Amihai (ed.). 2006. *Excavations at Tel Beth-Shean 1989–1996, Volume 1: From the Late Bronze IIB to the Medieval Period.* Hebrew University Institute of Archaeology, The Beth-Shean Valley Archaeological Project Publication 1. Jerusalem: Israel Exploration Society.
Mazar, Benyamin. 1978. 'Herodian Jerusalem in the Light of the Excavations South and South-West of the Temple Mount.' *IEJ* 28: 230–37.
Mazar, Benjamin, Trude Dothan, and I. Dunayevsky. 1966. *En-Gedi: The First and Second Seasons of Excavations 1961–1962.* 'Atiqot, English Series 5. Jerusalem: Department of Antiquities and Museums.
Mazzinghi, Luca. 2019. *Wisdom.* IECOT. Stuttgart: Kohlhammer.
Meadowcroft, T. J. 1995. *Aramaic Daniel and Greek Daniel: A Literary Comparison.* JSOTSup 198. Sheffield: Sheffield Academic Press.
Meeks, Wayne A. 1967. *The Prophet-King: Moses Traditions and the Johannine Christology.* NovTSup 14. Leiden: Brill.
Meier, Christian. 1995. *Caesar*, trans. David McLintock. London: BCA. ET of Christine Meier, *Caesar*. Berlin: Severin & Siedler, 1982.
Mélèze Modrzejewski, Joseph. 2008. 'Juifs et chrétiens: Bickerman redivivus à propos d'une publication récente.' *Revue historique de droit français et étranger* 86: 245–52.
Mendels, Doran. 1987. *The Land of Israel as a Political Concept in Hasmonean Literature.* TSAJ 15. Tübingen: Mohr Siebeck.
Mendels, Doran. 1993. *The Rise and Fall of Jewish Nationalism.* Anchor Reference Library. New York: Doubleday.
Meshorer, Ya'akov. 1975. *Nabataean Coins.* Qedem 3. Jerusalem: Hebrew University.
Meshorer, Ya'akov. 1982. *Ancient Jewish Coinage, Volume 1: Persian Period through Hasmonaeans; Volume 2: Herod the Great through Bar Kokhba.* 2 vols. New York: Amphora.
Meshorer, Ya'akov. 1986. 'Jewish Numismatics.' In *Early Judaism and its Modern Interpreters*, ed. Robert A. Kraft and George W. E. Nickelsburg, 211–20. SBLBMI 2. Atlanta: Scholars; Philadelphia: Fortress.
Meshorer, Ya'akov. 1990–91. 'Ancient Jewish Coinage: Addendum I.' *INJ* 11: 104–32.
Meshorer, Ya'akov. 2001. *A Treasury of Jewish Coins.* Jerusalem and New York: Amphora.

Metso, Sarianna. 1997. *The Textual Development of the Qumran Community Rule*. STDJ 21. Leiden: Brill.

Metso, Sarianna, Hindy Najman, and Eileen Schuller (eds). 2010. *The Dead Sea Scrolls: Transmission of Traditions and Production of Texts*. STDJ 92. Leiden: Brill.

Meyers, Carol L., Eric M. Meyers, and James F. Strange (eds). 1974. 'Excavations at Meiron, in Upper Galilee. 1971, 1972: A Preliminary Report.' *BASOR* 214: 2–25.

Meyers, Eric M. 1971. *Jewish Ossuaries: Reburial and Rebirth: Secondary Burials in Their Ancient Near Eastern Setting*. BiOr 24. Rome: Biblical Institute.

Meyers, Eric M. 1976. 'Galilean Regionalism as a Factor in Historical Reconstruction.' *BASOR* 221: 93–101.

Meyers, Eric M. 1994. 'Second Temple Studies in the Light of Recent Archaeology: Part I: The Persian and Hellenistic Periods.' *CR:BS* 2:25–42.

Meyers, Eric M. (editor-in-chief). 1997. *The Oxford Encyclopedia of Archaeology in the Near East*. 5 vols. Oxford: Oxford University Press.

Meyers, Eric M., and Mark A. Chancey. 2012. *Alexander to Constantine: Archaeology of the Land of the Bible, volume 3*. The Anchor Yale Bible Reference Library. New Haven, CT: Yale University Press.

Meyers, Eric M., and Carol L. Meyers (eds). 2013. *The Pottery from Ancient Sepphoris*. Sepphoris Excavation Reports. Winona Lake, IN: Eisenbrauns.

Meyers, Eric M., James F. Strange, and Dennis E. Groh. 1978. 'The Meiron Excavation Project: Archaeological Survey in Galilee and Golan, 1976.' *BASOR* 230: 1–24.

Miles, Gary B. 1995. *Livy: Reconstructing Early Rome*. Ithaca, NY: Cornell University Press.

Milik, J. T. 1959. *Ten Years of Discovery in the Wilderness of Judaea*. SBT 26. London: SCM.

Millar, Fergus. 1964. *A Study of Cassius Dio*. Oxford: Clarendon.

Millar, Fergus, and Erich Segal (eds). 1984. *Caesar Augustus: Seven Aspects*. Oxford: Clarendon.

Miller, David M. 2010. 'The Meaning of *Ioudaios* and its Relationship to Other Group Labels in Ancient "Judaism".' *CBR* 9: 98–126.

Miller, David M. 2014. 'Ethnicity, Religion and the Meaning of *Ioudaios* in Ancient "Judaism".' *CBR* 12: 216–65.

Mineo, Bernard, and Giuseppe Zecchini (eds). 2016. *Justin, Abrégé des* Histoires Philippiques *de Trogue Pompée, Tome I: Livres I–X*. Collection des Universités de France. Paris: Les Belles Lettres.

Mineo, Bernard, and Giuseppe Zecchini (eds). 2018. *Justin, Abrégé des* Histoires Philippiques *de Trogue Pompée, Tome II: Livres XI–XXIII*. Collection des Universités de France. Paris: Les Belles Lettres.

Mitchell, Thomas N. 1979. *Cicero, the Ascending Years*. New Haven, CT: Yale University Press.

Mitchell, Thomas N. 1991. *Cicero, the Senior Statesman*. New Haven, CT: Yale University Press.

Mittag, Peter Franz. 2006. *Antiochos IV. Epiphanes: Eine politische Biographie*. Klio Beiheft, N.F. Band 11. Berlin: Akademie Verlag.

Mittwoch, A. 1955. 'Tribute and Land-tax in Seleucid Judaea.' *Bib* 36: 352–61.

Mizzi, Dennis. 2011. '60 Years of Qumran Archaeology.' *Strata: Bulletin of the Anglo-Israel Archaeological Society* 29: 31–50.

Mizzi, Dennis. 2014. 'Qumran Period I Reconsidered: An Evaluation of Several Competing Theories.' *DSS* 22: 1–42.

Mizzi, Dennis. 2017. 'Qumran at Seventy: Reflections on Seventy Years of Scholarship on the Archaeology of Qumran and the Dead Sea Scrolls.' *Strata: Bulletin of the Anglo-Israel Archaeological Society* 35: 9–45.

Mizzi, Dennis, and Jodi Magness. 2016. 'Was Qumran Abandoned at the End of the First Century BCE?' *JBL* 135: 301–20.

Moehring, Horst R. 1959. 'The Persecution of the Jews and the Adherents of the Isis Cult at Rome A.D. 19.' *NovT* 3: 293–304.

Moehring, Horst R. 1975. 'The *Acta pro Judaeis* in the *Antiquities* of Flavius Josephus.' In *Christianity, Judaism and Other Greco-Roman Cults*, ed. Jacob Neusner, 3:124–58. Studies in Judaism in Late Antiquity 12. Leiden: Brill.

Momigliano, Arnaldo. 1934a. 'Josephus as a Source for the History of Judaea.' *CAH* 10:884–87.

Momigliano, Arnaldo. 1934b. 'Richerche sull' organizzazione della Giudea sotto il dominio romano (63 a. C.–70 d. C.).' *Annali della Scuola Normale Superiore di Pisa*, Classe di Lettere 3: 183–221, 347–96.

Momigliano, Arnaldo. 1975. 'The Second Book of Maccabees.' *Classical Philology* 70: 81–88.

Momigliano, Arnaldo. 1982. Review of Gauger, *Beiträge zur jüdischen Apologetik*, *Classical Philology* 77: 258–61.

Montgomery, James A. 1907. *The Samaritans: The Earliest Jewish Sect*. Reprinted with 'Introduction' by A. S. Halkin. New York: Ktav, 1968.

Montgomery, James A. 1927. *A Critical and Exegetical Commentary on the Book of Daniel*. ICC. Edinburgh: T. & T. Clark.

Moore, Carey A. 1977. *Daniel, Esther and Jeremiah: The Additions*. AB 44. Garden City, NY: Doubleday.

Moore, Carey A. 1985. *Judith*. AB 40. Garden City: Doubleday.

Moore, George F. 1927–30. *Judaism in the First Three Centuries of the Christian Era*. 3 vols. Cambridge, MA: Harvard University Press.

Moore, Stewart. 2015. *Jewish Ethnic Identity and Relations in Hellenistic Egypt: with Walls of Iron?* JSJSup 171. Leiden: Brill.

Mor, Menachem, and Friedrich V. Reiterer (eds), in collaboration with Waltraud Winkler. 2010. *Samaritans: Past and Present: Current Studies*. Studia Judaica 53 = Studia Samaritana 5. Berlin/New York: de Gruyter.

Mor, Menachem, Aharon Oppenheimer, Jack Pastor, and Daniel R. Schwartz (eds). 2003. *Jews and Gentiles in the Holy Land in the Days of the Second Temple, the Mishnah and the Talmud: A Collection of Articles*. Jerusalem: Yad Ben-Zvi Press.

Morgan, M. Gwyn. 1990. 'The Perils of Schematism: Polybius, Antiochus Epiphanes and the "Day of Eleusis".' *Historia* 39: 37–76.

Moritya, Akio, and Gohei Hata (eds). 2012. *Pentateuchal Traditions in the Late Second Temple Period: Proceedings of the International Workshop in Tokyo, August 28–31, 2007*. JSJSup 158. Leiden: Brill.

Mørkholm, Otto. 1966. *Antiochus IV of Syria*. Classica et Mediaevalia, Dissertationes 8. Copenhagen: I Kommission Hos.

Mosshammer, Alden A. (ed.). 1984. *Georgii Syncelli Ecloga chronographica*. Leipzig: Teubner.

Mouritsen, Henrik. 2017. *Politics in the Roman Republic*. Key Themes in Ancient History. Cambridge: Cambridge University Press.

Muntz, Charles E. 2017. *Diodorus Siculus and the World of the Late Roman Republic*. Oxford: Oxford University Press.

Murphy-O'Connor, Jerome. 1974. 'The Essenes and their History.' *RevB* 81: 215–44.
Murphy-O'Connor, Jerome. 1976. 'Demetrius I and the Teacher of Righteousness (I Macc., x, 25–45).' *RevB* 83: 400–420.
Murphy-O'Connor, Jerome. 1985. 'The *Damascus Document* Revisited.' *RevB* 92: 223–46. = *Society of Biblical Literature 1986 Seminar Papers Series*, ed. K. H. Richards, 369–83. SBLASP 25. Atlanta: Scholars Press.
Myers, E. A. 2010. *The Ituraeans and the Roman Near East: Reassessing the Sources*. Society for New Testament Studies Monograph Series 147. Cambridge: Cambridge University Press.
Nagy, Rebecca Martin, Carol L. Meyers, Eric M. Meyers, and Zeev Weiss (eds). 1996. *Sepphoris in Galilee—Crosscurrents of Culture*. Winona Lake, IN: Eisenbrauns.
Naveh, Joseph. 1968. 'Dated Coins of Alexander Janneus.' *IEJ* 18: 20–25.
Naveh, Joseph. 1982a. 'An Ancient Amulet or a Modern Forgery?' *CBQ* 44: 282–84.
Naveh, Joseph. 1982b. 'Some Recently Forged Inscriptions.' *BASOR* 247: 53–58.
Negev, A. 1977. 'The Nabateans and the Provincia Arabia.' *ANRW II*: 8:520–686.
Nestle, E. 1884. 'Der Greuel der Verwüstung.' *ZAW* 4: 248.
Netzer, Ehud. 1962. 'Ancient Ritual Baths (*Miqvaot*) in Jericho.' *Jerusalem Cathedra* 2: 106–19.
Netzer, Ehud. 1975. 'The Hasmonean and Herodian Winter Palaces at Jericho.' *IEJ* 25: 89–100.
Netzer, Ehud. 1977. 'The Winter Palaces of the Judean Kings at Jericho at the End of the Second Temple Period.' *BASOR* 228: 1–13.
Netzer, Ehud. 1981. *Greater Herodium*. Qedem 13. Jerusalem: Hebrew University.
Netzer, Ehud. 1999. *Die Paläste der Hasmonäer und Herodes' des Großen*. Sonderhefte der Antiken Welt. Mainz am Rhein: Philipp von Zabern.
Netzer, Ehud. 2008. *The Architecture of Herod the Great Builder*. With new preface; with assistance of Rachel Laureys-Chachy; Paperback ed. Grand Rapids, MI: Baker. TSAJ 117. Tübingen: Mohr Siebeck.
Netzer, Ehud (ed.). 2001. *Hasmonean and Herodian Palaces at Jericho: Final Reports of the 1973–1987 Excavations, Vol. 1: Stratigraphy and Architecture*. Jerusalem: Israel Exploration Society.
Netzer, Ehud, et al. 1981. 'Symposium: Herod's Building Projects.' *Jerusalem Cathedra* 1: 48–80.
Netzer, Ehud, and R. Laureys-Chachy (eds). 2004. *Hasmonean and Herodian Palaces at Jericho: Final Reports of the 1973–1987 Excavations, Vol. II: Stratigraphy and Architecture*. Jerusalem: Israel Exploration Society.
Neubauer, A. 1869. 'Chronique samaritaine, suivie d'un appendice contenant de courtes notices sur quelques autres ouvrages samaritains.' *Journal asiatique* 14: 385–470.
Neuhaus, G. O. 1974. 'Quellen im 1. Makkabäerbuch? Eine Entgegnung auf die Analyse von K.-D. Schunck.' *JSJ* 5: 162–75.
Neusner, Jacob. 1964. 'The Jews in Pagan Armenia.' *JAOS* 84: 230–40.
Neusner, Jacob. 1984. *A History of the Jews in Babylonia: I. The Parthian Period*. 3rd printing with new introduction. BJS 62. Chico, CA: Scholars Press.
Neusner, Jacob. 1971. *The Rabbinic Traditions about the Pharisees Before 70*. 3 vols. Leiden: Brill.
Neusner, Jacob. 1973. *From Politics to Piety*. Englewood Cliffs, NJ: Prentice-Hall.
Neusner, Jacob. 1981. *Judaism: The Evidence of the Mishnah*. Chicago: University of Chicago Press.

Neusner, Jacob. 1988. *The Mishnah: A New Translation*. New Haven, CT: Yale University Press.

Neusner, Jacob, William Scott Green, and Ernest S. Frerichs (eds). 1987. *Judaisms and Their Messiahs at the Turn of the Christian Era*. Cambridge: Cambridge University Press.

Neusner, Jacob, and Clemens Thoma. 1995. 'Die Pharisäer vor und nach der Tempelzerstörung des Jahres 70 n. Chr.' In *Tempelkult und Tempelzerstörung (70 n. Chr.): Festschrift für Clemens Thoma zum 60. Geburtstag*, ed. S. Lauer and H. Ernst, 189–230. Judaica et Christiana 15. Bern: Lang.

Newsom, Carol A. 2014. *Daniel: A Commentary*. OTL. Louisville, KY: Westminster John Knox.

Nickelsburg, George W. E. 1972. *Resurrection, Immortality, and Eternal Life in Intertestamental Judaism*. HTS 26. Cambridge, MA: Harvard University Press.

Nickelsburg, George W. E. 2001. *1 Enoch 1: A Commentary on the Book of 1 Enoch, Chapters 1–36, 81–108*. Hermeneia. Minneapolis: Fortress.

Nickelsburg, George W. E. 2005. *Jewish Literature between the Bible and the Mishnah*. 2nd ed. Minneapolis: Fortress.

Nickelsburg, George W. E. (ed.). 1973. *Studies on the Testament of Moses*. SBLSCS 4. Atlanta: Scholars Press.

Nodet, Étienne. 2018. *The Hebrew Bible of Josephus: Main Features*. Preface by Adrian Schenker. Chiers de la Revue Biblique 92. Leuven: Peeters.

Noethlichs, Karl Leo. 1996. *Das Judentum und der römische Staat: Minderheitenpolitik im antiken Rom*. Darmstadt: Wissenschaftliche Buchgesellschaft.

Noy, David (ed.). 1993. *Jewish Inscriptions of Western Europe. Volume 1: Italy (excluding the City of Rome), Spain and Gaul*. Cambridge: Cambridge University Press.

Noy, David (ed.). 1995. *Jewish Inscriptions of Western Europe, Volume 2: The City of Rome*. Cambridge: Cambridge University Press.

Noy, David, and Hanswulf Bloedhorn (eds). 2004. *Inscriptiones Judaicae Orientis, Volume 3: Syria and Cyprus*. TSAJ 102. Tübingen: Mohr Siebeck.

Noy, David, Alexander Panayotov, and Hanswulf Bloedhorn (eds). 2004. *Inscriptiones Judaicae Orientis, Volume 1: Eastern Europe*. TSAJ 101. Tübingen: Mohr Siebeck.

Oden, Robert A. 1977. 'Ba'al Sāmēm and 'El.' *CBQ* 39: 457–73.

Oegema, Gerbern S. 1998. *The Anointed and his People: Messianic Expectations from the Maccabees to Bar Kochba*. JSPSup 27. Sheffield: Sheffield Academic Press. ET of *Der Gesalbte und sein Volk: Untersuchungen zum Konzeptualisierungsprozeß der messianischen Erwartungen von den Makkabäern bis Bar Koziba*. Schriften des Institutum Judaicum Delitzschianum 2. Göttingen: Vandenhoeck & Ruprecht, 1994.

Ogilvie, R. M. 1965. *A Commentary on Livy, Books 1–5*. Oxford: Clarendon.

Olmstead, A. T. 1937. 'Cuneiform Texts and Hellenistic Chronology.' *Classical Philology* 32: 1–14.

O'Neill, J. C. 1991. 'The Man from Heaven: *SibOr* 5.256–259.' *JSP* 9: 87–102.

Oren, Eliezer D., and Uriel Rappaport. 1984. 'The Necropolis of Maresha—Beth Govrin.' *IEJ* 34: 114–53.

Orlin, Eric M. 2010. *Foreign Cults in Rome: Creating a Roman Empire*. Oxford: Oxford University Press.

Orlinsky, Harry M. 1975. 'The Septuagint as Holy Writ and the Philosophy of the Translators.' *HUCA* 46: 89–114.

Otto, W. 1913. '14) Herodes I.' *PW Supp.* 2:1–202.

Pardee, Dennis. 1972–73. 'A Restudy of the Commentary on Psalm 37 from Qumran Cave 4.' *RQum* 8: 163–94.
Parente, F. 1988. 'The Third Book of Maccabees as Ideological Document and Historical Source.' *Henoch* 10: 143–82.
Parker, Richard A., and Waldo H. Dubberstein. 1956. *Babylonian Chronology 626 B.C.-A.D. 75.* Brown University Studies 19. Providence, RI: Brown University Press.
Parker, Victor L. 2006. 'Judas Maccabaeus' Campaigns against Timothy.' *Biblica* 87: 457–76.
Parker, Victor L. 2007. 'The Letters in II Maccabees: Reflexions on the Book's Composition.' *ZAW* 119: 386–402.
Parker, Victor L. 2008. 'Historische Studien zu den Hohen Priestern der frühen Makkabäerzeit.' *ZDPV* 124: 143–70.
Parmentier, Édith, and Francesca Prometea Barone. 2011. *Nicolas de Damas: Histoires, Recueil de coutumes, Vie d'Auguste, Autobiographie.* Collection Fragments. Paris: Les Belles Lettres.
Parry, Donald W. and Emanuel Tov (eds). 2014. *The Dead Sea Scrolls Reader, Volumes 1 and 2.* 2 vols. 2nd ed., rev. and expanded. Leiden: Brill.
Parry, Donald W. and Eugene Ulrich (eds). 1999. *The Provo International Conference on the Dead Sea Scrolls: Technological Innovations, New Texts, and Reformulated Issues.* STDJ 30. Leiden: Brill.
Pastor, Jack. 1997. *Land and Economy in Ancient Palestine.* London/New York: Routledge.
Pastor, Jack. 2003. 'Herod, King of Jews and Gentiles: Economic Policy as a Measure of Evenhandedness.' In *Jews and Gentiles in the Holy Land in the Days of the Second Temple, the Mishnah and the Talmud: A Collection of Articles,* ed. M. Mor, A. Oppenheimer, J. Pastor, and D. R. Schwartz, 152–64. Jerusalem: Yad Ben-Zvi Press.
Pastor, Jack, Pnina Stern, and Menahem Mor (eds). 2011. *Flavius Josephus: Interpretation and History.* JSJSup 146. Leiden: Brill.
Pelletier, A. 1962. *Lettre d'Aristee a Philocrate.* SC 89. Paris: Cerf.
Pervo, Richard I. 2009. *Acts: A Commentary,* ed. Harold W. Attridge. Hermeneia; Minneapolis: Fortress.
Pestman, P. W. 1967. *Chronologie égyptienne d'après les textes démotiques (332 av. J.-C.–453 ap. J.-C.).* Papyrologica Lugduno-Batava 15. Leiden: Brill.
Petzold, Karl-Ernst. 1969. *Studien zur Methode des Polybios und zu ihrer historischen Auswertung.* Vestigia 9. Munich: Beck.
Poehlmann, William. 1992. 'The Sadducees as Josephus Presents Them, or The Curious Case of Ananus.' In *All Things New: Essays in Honor of Roy A. Harrisville,* ed. A. J. Hultgren, D. H. Juel, J. D. Kingsbury, 87–100. Word and World Supplement Series 1. St. Paul, MN: Luther Northwestern Theological Seminary
Poirier, John C. 1996. 'Why Did the Pharisees Wash their Hands?' *JJS* 47: 217–33.
Popović, Mladen. 2012. 'Qumran as Scroll Storehouse in Times of Crisis? A Comparative Perspective on Judaean Desert Manuscript Collections.' *JSJ* 43: 551–94.
Portier-Young, Anathea E. 2011. *Apocalypse Against Empire: Theologies of Resistance in Early Judaism.* Foreword by John J. Collins. Grand Rapids, MI: Eerdmans.
Porton, Gary G. 1986. 'Diversity in Postbiblical Judaism.' In *Early Judaism and its Modern Interpreters,* ed. Robert A. Kraft and George W. E. Nickelsburg, 57–80. SBLBMI 2. Atlanta: Scholars; Philadelphia: Fortress.
Pritchard, James B. (ed.). 1969. *Ancient Near Eastern Texts Relating to the Old Testament.* 3rd ed. with supplement. Princeton: Princeton University Press.

Pucci Ben Zeev, Miriam. 1993. 'The Reliability of Josephus Flavius: The Case of Hecataeus' and Manetho's Accounts of Jews and Judaism: Fifteen Years of Contemporary Research (1974–1990).' *JSJ* 24: 215–34.
Pucci Ben Zeev, Miriam. 1998. *Jewish Rights in the Roman World: The Greek and Roman Documents Quoted by Josephus Flavius*. TSAJ 74. Tübingen: Mohr Siebeck.
Puech, Emile. 1993. *La croyance des Esséniens en la vie future: Immortalité, résurrection, vie éternelle? Histoire d'une croyance dans le Judaïsme Ancien*: vol. 1, *La résurrection des morts et le contexte scripturaire*; vol. II: *Le données qumraniennes et classiques*. Introduction by André Caquot. Etudes bibliques, nouvelle série nos 21–22. Paris: Gabalda.
Puech, Emile. 1999. 'Le "Fils de Dieu" en 4Q246.' In *Frank Moore Cross Volume*, ed. Baruch A. Levine, Philip J. King, Joseph Naveh, and Ephraim Stern (= *Eretz-Israel* 26; Jerusalem; Israel Exploration Society), 143*–52*.
Pummer, Reinhard. 1976. 'The Present State of Samaritan Studies [1].' *JSS* 21: 39–61.
Pummer, Reinhard. 1977. 'The Present State of Samaritan Studies [2].' *JSS* 22: 27–47.
Pummer, Reinhard. 1979. 'The *Book of Jubilees* and the Samaritans.' *Eglise et Théologie* 10: 147–78.
Pummer, Reinhard. 1982a. 'Antisamaritanische Polemik in jüdischen Schriften aus der intertestamentarischen Zeit.' *BZ* 26: 224–42.
Pummer, Reinhard. 1982b. 'Genesis 34 in Jewish Writings of the Hellenistic and Roman Periods.' *HTR* 76: 177–88.
Pummer, Reinhard. 1987a. *The Samaritans*. IR, Sect. 23. Judaism, Fasc. 5. Leiden, Brill.
Pummer, Reinhard. 1987b. 'Αργαριζιν: A Criterion for Samaritan Provenance?' *JSJ* 18: 18–25.
Pummer, Reinhard. 1988. Review of R. Egger, *Josephus Flavius und die Samaritaner*, *JBL* 107: 768–72.
Pummer, Reinhard. 1989. 'Samaritan Material Remains and Archaeology.' In *The Samaritans*, ed. A. D. Crown, 166–75. Tübingen: Mohr Siebeck.
Pummer, Reinhard. 1997. 'Samaritans.' In *The Oxford Encyclopedia of Archaeology in the Near East*, ed. Eric M. Meyers, 4:469–72. Oxford: Oxford University Press.
Pummer, Reinhard. 2002. *Early Christian Authors on Samaritans and Samaritanism: Texts, Translations and Commentary*. TSAJ 92. Tübingen: Mohr Siebeck.
Pummer, Reinhard. 2009. *The Samaritans in Flavius Josephus*. TSAJ 129. Tübingen: Mohr Siebeck.
Pummer, Reinhard. 2016. *The Samaritans: A Profile*. Grand Rapids, MI: Eerdmans.
Purvis, James D. 1968. *The Samaritan Pentateuch and the Origin of the Samaritan Sect*. HSM 2. Cambridge, MA: Harvard University Press.
Purvis, James D. 1981. 'The Samaritan Problem: A Case Study in Jewish Sectarianism in the Roman Era.' In *Traditions in Transformation: Turning Points in Biblical Faith*, ed. Baruch Halpern and J. D. Levenson, 323–50. Winona Lake, IN: Eisenbrauns.
Purvis, James D. 1986. 'The Samaritans and Judaism.' In *Early Judaism and its Modern Interpreters*, ed. Robert A. Kraft and George W. E. Nickelsburg, 81–98. SBLBMI 2. Atlanta: Scholars; Philadelphia: Fortress.
Raaflaub, Kurt A. 1996. 'Born to Be Wolves? Origins of Roman Imperialism.' In *Transitions to Empire: Essays in Greco-Roman History, 360–146 B.C., in Honor of E. Badian*, ed. Robert W. Wallace and Edward M. Harris, 273–314. Oklahoma Series in Classical Culture 21. Norman: University of Oklahoma Press.

Raban, A. (ed.). 1989. *The Harbours of Caesarea Maritima: Results of the Caesarea Ancient Harbour Excavation Project, 1980–1985, Volume 1: The Site and the Excavations.* Parts i-ii; British Archaeological Reports International Series 491. Center for Maritime Studies, University of Haifa, Publ. No. 3. Oxford: BAR.

Rabin, C. 1956. 'Alexander Jannaeus and the Pharisees.' *JJS* 7: 3–11.

Rahmani, L. Y. 1967. 'Jason's Tomb.' *IEJ* 17: 61–100.

Rahmani, L. Y. 1981a. 'Ancient Jerusalem's Funerary Customs and Tombs: Part One.' *BA* 44: 171–77.

Rahmani, L. Y. 1981b. 'Ancient Jerusalem's Funerary Customs and Tombs: Part Two.' *BA* 44: 229–35.

Rahmani, L. Y. 1982a. 'Ancient Jerusalem's Funerary Customs and Tombs: Part Three.' *BA* 45: 43–53.

Rahmani, L. Y. 1982b. 'Ancient Jerusalem's Funerary Customs and Tombs: Part Four.' *BA* 45: 109–19.

Rajak, Tessa. 1981. 'Roman Intervention in a Seleucid Siege of Jerusalem?' *GRBS* 22: 65–81.

Rajak, Tessa. 1984. 'Was There a Roman Charter for the Jews?' *JRS* 74: 107–23.

Rappaport, Uriel. 1970. 'Gaza and Ascalon in the Persian and Hellenistic Periods in Relation to their Coins.' *IEJ* 20: 75–80.

Rappaport, Uriel. 1976. 'The Emergence of Hasmonean Coinage.' *AJS Review* 1: 171–86.

Ray, John D. 1976. *The Archive of Hor.* Texts from Excavations, Second Memoir. London: Egypt Exploration Society.

Redditt, Paul L. 1999. *Daniel, Based on the New Revised Standard Version.* New Century Bible Commentary. Sheffield: Sheffield Academic Press.

Reese, James M. 1970. *Hellenistic Influence on the Book of Wisdom and Its Consequences.* AnBib 41. Rome: Pontifical Biblical Institute.

Regev, Eyal. 2000. 'Pure Individualism: The Idea of Non-Priestly Purity in Ancient Judaism.' *JSJ* 31: 176–202.

Regev, Eyal. 2013. *The Hasmoneans: Ideology, Archaeology, Identity.* JAJSup 10. Göttingen: Vandenhoeck & Ruprecht.

Regev, Eyal. 2017. 'The Hellenization of the Hasmoneans Revisited: The Archaeological Evidence.' *Advances in Anthropology* 7: 175–96.

Reich, Ronny. 1981. 'Archaeological Evidence of the Jewish Population at Hasmonean Gezer.' *IEJ* 31: 48–52.

Reich, Ronny. 1990. 'The "Boundary of Gezer" Inscriptions Again.' *IEJ* 40: 44–46.

Reich, Ronny, and Eli Shukron. 2007. 'The Yehud Stamp Impressions from the 1995–2005 City of David Excavations.' *TA* 34: 59–65.

Reider, Joseph. 1957. *The Book of Wisdom.* Jewish Apocryphal Literature. New York: Dropsie College.

Reinhold, Meyer. 1988. *From Republic to Principate: An Historical Commentary on Cassius Dio's Roman History Books 49–52 (36–29 B.C.).* American Philological Association Monograph Series 34. Atlanta: Scholars Press.

Reinmuth, O. W. 1948. 'The Ephebate and Citizenship in Attica.' *TAPA* 79: 211–31.

Reisner, G. A., C. S. Fisher, and D. G. Lyon (eds). 1924. *Harvard Excavations at Samaria 1908–1910.* 2 vols. Cambridge, MA: Harvard University Press.

Retsö, Jan. 2003. *The Arabs in Antiquity: Their History from the Assyrians to the Umayyads.* Abingdon/New York: Routledge.

Rich, J. W. (ed.). 1990. *Cassius Dio: The Augustan Settlement (Roman History 53–55.9).* Warminster: Aris & Phillips.

Richardson, J. S. 2012. *Augustan Rome 44 BC to AD 14: The Restoration of the Republic and the Establishment of the Empire*. The Edinburgh History of Ancient Rome. Edinburgh: Edinburgh University Press.

Richardson, Peter. 1985. 'Religion and Architecture: A Study in Herod's Piety, Power, Pomp and Pleasure.' *Bulletin of the Canadian Society of Biblical Studies* 45: 3–29.

Richardson, Peter. 1986. 'Law and Piety in Herod's Architecture.' *SR* 15: 347–60.

Richardson, Peter. 1996. *Herod: King of the Jews and Friend of the Romans*. Studies on Personalities of the New Testament. Columbia, SC: University of South Carolina.

Richardson, Peter. 2004. *Building Jewish in the Roman East*. JSJSup 92. Leiden: Brill; Waco, TX: Baylor University Press.

Rigby, Kent J. 1980. 'Seleucid Notes.' *TAPA* 110: 233–54.

Rigby, Kent J. 1988. 'Provincia Asia.' *TAPA* 118: 123–53.

Rivkin, Ellis. 1972. 'Defining the Pharisees: The Tannaitic Sources.' *HUCA* 43: 205–40.

Rizzolo, Nicolò. 2017. *Pesher: L'interpretazione della Parola per la fine dei giorni: Studio sul genere letterario dei Pesharym*, Etudes Bibliques, n. s. 73. Leuven: Peters.

Rocca, Samuel. 2008a. *Herod's Judaea: A Mediterranean State in the Classical World*. TSAJ 122. Tübingen: Mohr Siebeck.

Rocca, Samuel. 2008b. *The Forts of Judaea 168 BC–AD 73: From the Maccabees to the Fall of Masada*. Illustrated by Adam Hook. Oxford: Osprey Publishing.

Roddy, Nicolae. 1996. '"Two Parts: Weeks of Seven Weeks": The End of the Age as *Terminus ad Quem* for *2 Baruch*.' *JSP* 14: 3–14.

Rodgers, Zuleika (ed.). 2007. *Making History: Josephus and Historical Method*. JSJSup 110. Leiden: Brill.

Roitman, Adolfo D., Lawrence H. Schiffman, and Shani Tzoref (eds). 2011. *The Dead Sea Scrolls and Contemporary Culture: Proceedings of the International Conference Held at the Israel Museum, Jerusalem (July 6–8, 2008)*. STDJ 93. Leiden: Brill.

Roll, Israel, and Oren Tal. 1999. *Apollonia-Arsuf, Final Report of the Excavations: Volume I The Persian and Hellenistic Periods*. Institute of Archaeology Monograph 16. Tel Aviv: Institute of Archaeology.

Roller, Duane W. 1982. 'The Northern Plain of Sharon in the Hellenistic Period.' *BASOR* 247: 43–52.

Roller, Duane W. 1998. *The Building Program of Herod the Great*. Berkeley/Los Angeles: University of California Press.

Rosenfeld, Ben-Zion. 1988. 'The "Boundary of Gezer" Inscriptions and the History of Gezer at the End of the Second Temple Period.' *IEJ* 38: 235–245.

Rosenstein, Nathan. 2012. *Rome and the Mediterranean 290 to 146 BC: The Imperial Republic*. The Edinburgh History of Ancient Rome. Edinburgh: Edinburgh University Press.

Rostovtzeff, M. 1941. *The Social and Economic History of the Hellenistic World*. 3 vols. Oxford: Clarendon.

Roth, C. 1958. *The Historical Background to the Dead Sea Scrolls*. Oxford: Blackwell.

Rowley, H. H. 1935. *Darius the Mede and the Four World Empires in the Book of Daniel*. Cardiff: University of Wales.

Rozenberg, S. (ed.). 2008. *Hasmonean and Herodian Palaces at Jericho: Final Reports of the 1973–1987 Excavations, Vol. IV: The Decoration of Herod's Third Palace at Jericho*. Jerusalem: Israel Exploration Society.

Russell, D. S. 1960. *Between the Testaments*. London: SCM.

Russell, D. S. 1967. *The Jews from Alexander to Herod*. The New Clarendon Bible, Old Testament 5. Oxford: Oxford University Press.

Rutgers, Leonard Victory. 1995. *The Jews in Late Ancient Rome: Evidence of Cultural Interaction in the Roman Diaspora.* Religions in the Graeco-Roman World 126. Leiden: Brill.
Rutgers, Leonard Victory. 1998a. *The Hidden Heritage of Diaspora Judaism.* Contributions to Biblical Exegesis and Theology 20. Leuven: Peeters.
Rutgers, Leonard Victory. 1998b. 'Jewish Ideas about Death and Afterlife: The Inscriptional Evidence.' In *The Hidden Heritage of Diaspora Judaism,* 157–68. Contributions to Biblical Exegesis and Theology 20. Leuven: Peeters.
Sachs, Abraham J. 1952. 'Babylonian Horoscopes.' *JCS* 6: 49–75.
Sachs, Abraham. J., and Hermann Hunger. 1996. *Astronomical Diaries and Related Texts from Babylonia, III: Diaries from 164 B.C. to 61 B.C.* Österreichische Akademie der Wissenschaften, Phil.-hist. Klasse, Denkschriften 247. Vienna: Österreichische Akademie der Wissenschaften.
Sachs, Abraham J., and D. J. Wiseman. 1954. 'A Babylonian King List of the Hellenistic Period.' *Iraq* 16: 202–11.
Sagiv, Nahum, and Amos Kloner. 1996. 'Maresha: Underground Olive Oil Production in the Hellenistic Period.' In *Olive Oil in Antiquity: Israel and Neighbouring Countries from the Neolithic to the Early Arab Period,* ed. David Eitam and Michael Heltzer, 255–92. History of the Ancient Near East Studies 7. Padova: Sargon.
Saldarini, Anthony J. 1986. 'Reconstructions of Rabbinic Judaism.' In *Early Judaism and its Modern Interpreters,* ed. Robert A. Kraft and George W. E. Nickelsburg, 437–77. SBLBMI 2. Atlanta: Scholars; Philadelphia: Fortress.
Saldarini, Anthony J. 1988. *Pharisees, Scribes and Sadducees in Palestinian Society: A Sociological. Approach.* Wilmington, DE: Glazier.
Saldarini, Anthony J. 1992. 'Pharisees.' *Anchor Bible Dictionary* (New York: Doubleday, 1992), 5:302.
Samuel, A. E. 1962. *Ptolemaic Chronology.* Münchener Beiträge 43. Munich: Beck.
Sanderson, Julia. 1986. *An Exodus Scroll from Qumran: 4QpaleoExod^m and the Samaritan Tradition.* HSS 30. Atlanta: Scholars Press.
Sandhaus, Débora. Forthcoming. 'Drawing Borders at the Fringe: The Shephelah from the Fourth to the First Century BCE.' In *The Period of the Middle Maccabees: From the Death of Judas through the Reign of John Hyrcanus (ca. 160–104 BCE),* ed. Andrea M. Berlin. 9th Nangeroni Meeting in Gazzada, Italy.
Sartre, Maurice. 2001. *D'Alexandre à Zénobie: Histoire du Levant antique, IVe siècle avant J.-C., IIIe siècle aprè J.-C.* Paris: Fayard.
Saulnier, Stéphane. 2012. *Calendrical Variations in Second Temple Judaism: New Perspectives on the 'Date of the Last Supper' Debate.* JSJSup 159. Leiden: Brill.
Schäfer, Peter. 1981. *Der Bar Kokhba-Aufstand: Studien zum zweiten jüdischen Krieg gegen Rom.* TSAJ 1. Tübingen: Mohr Siebeck.
Schalit, Abraham. 1962. 'Die frühchristliche Überlieferung über die Herkunft der Familie des Herodes.' *ASTI* 1: 109–60.
Schalit, Abraham. 1967–69. 'Die Eroberungen des Alexander Jannaus in Moab.' *Theokratia* 1: 3–50.
Schalit, Abraham. 1969a. *König Herodes: Der Mann und sein Werk.* Studia Judaica 4. Berlin: de Gruyter.
Schalit, Abraham. 1969b. 'A Clash of Ideologies: Palestine under the Seleucids and Romans.' In *The Crucible of Christianity,* ed. A. Toynbee, 47–76. London: Thames & Hudson.

Schalit, Abraham. 1970–71. 'Die Denkschrift der Samaritaner an König Antiochos Epiphanes zu Beginn der Großen Verfolgung der jüdischen Religion im Jahre 167 v. Chr. (Josephus, *AJ* XII, §§258–264).' *ASTI* 8: 131–83.

Schalit, Abraham. 1989. *Untersuchung zur 'Assumptio Mosis'*. ALGHJ 17. Leiden: Brill.

Schalit, Abraham (ed.). 1972. *Hellenistic Period*. World History of the Jewish People 1/6. New Brunswick: Rutgers University Press.

Schams, Christine. 1998. *Jewish Scribes in the Second-Temple Period*. JSOTSup 291. Sheffield: Sheffield Academic Press.

Schedl, C. 1965. 'Nabuchodonosor, Arpadsad und Darius: Untersuchungen zum Buch Judit.' *ZDMG* 115: 242–54.

Schiffman, Lawrence H. 1984–85. 'The Samaritans in Tannaitic Halakhah.' *JQR* 75: 323–50.

Schiffman, Lawrence H. 1990a. '*Miqsat Ma'aseh Ha-Torah* and the *Temple Scroll*,' *RevQ* 14: 435–57.

Schiffman, Lawrence H. 1990b. 'The New Halakhic Letter (4QMMT) and the Origins of the Dead Sea Sect.' *BA* 53: 64–73.

Schiffman, Lawrence H., and James C. VanderKam (eds). 2000. *Encyclopaedia of the Dead Sea Scrolls*. Oxford: Oxford University Press.

Schlude, Jason M., and J. Andrew Overman. 2017. 'Herod the Great: A Near Eastern Case Study in Roman-Parthian Politics.' In *Arsacids, Romans and Local Elites: Cross-Cultural Interactions of the Parthian Empire*, ed. Jason M. Schlude and Benjamin B. Rubin, 93–110. Oxford: Oxbow Books.

Schlude, Jason M., and Benjamin B. Rubin (eds). 2017. *Arsacids, Romans and Local Elites: Cross-Cultural Interactions of the Parthian Empire*. Oxford: Oxbow Books.

Schorch, Stefan (ed.). 2018. *The Samaritan Pentateuch: A Critical Editio Maior: III Leviticus* (Berlin: De Gruyter).

Schremer, Adiel. 1997. 'The Name of the Boethusians: A Reconsideration of Suggested Explanations and Another One.' *JJS* 43: 290–99.

Schuller, Eileen M. 1956. 'Some Problems Connected with the Supposed Common Ancestry of Jews and Spartans and their Relations During the Last Three Centuries B.C.' *JSS* 1: 257–68.

Schuller, Eileen M. 1990. '4Q372 1: A Text about Joseph.' *RevQ* 14/55: 349–76.

Schunck, Klaus-Dietrich. 1954. *Die Quellen des I. und II. Makkabäerbuches*. Halle[Saale]: Niemeyer.

Schunck, Klaus-Dietrich. 1980. *Jüdische Schriften aus hellenistisch-römischer Zeit: Band I Historische und legendarische Erzählungen: Lieferung 4 I. Makkabäerbuch*. Gütersloh: Gütersloher Verlagshaus Gerd Mohn.

Schuol, Monika. 2007. *Augustus und die Juden: Rechtsstellung und Interessenpolitik der Kleinasiatischen Diaspora*. Studien zur Alten Geschichte 6. Frankfurt am Main: Verlag Antike.

Schüpphaus, J. 1977. *Die Psalmen Salomos: Ein Zeugnis Jerusalemer Theologie und Frömmigkeit in der Mitte des vorchristlichen Jahrhunderts*. ALGHJ 7. Leiden: Brill.

Schürer, Emil. 1973–87. *The Jewish People in the Age of Jesus Christ*. Rev. and ed. Geza Vermes, Fergus Millar et al. 3 vols. in 4. Edinburgh: T. & T. Clark.

Schwartz, Daniel R. 1992. *Studies in the Jewish Background of Christianity*. WUNT 60. Tübingen: Mohr Siebeck.

Schwartz, Daniel R. 2007. '"Judaean" or "Jew"? How Should We Translate *ioudaios* in Josephus?' In *Jewish Identity in the Greco-Roman World*, ed. Jörg Frey, Daniel R. Schwartz, and Stephanie Gripentrog, 3–27. AJEC 71. Leiden: Brill.

Schwartz, Daniel R. 2008. *2 Maccabees*. CEJL. Berlin: de Gruyter.
Schwartz, Daniel R. 2014. *Judeans and Jews: Four Faces of Dichotomy in Ancient Jewish History*. The Kenneth Michael Tannenbaum Series in Jewish Studies. Toronto/Buffalo/London: University of Toronto Press.
Schwartz, Joshua. 1990. 'Once More on the "Boundary of Gezer" Inscriptions and the History of Gezer and Lydda at the End of the Second Temple Period.' *IEJ* 40: 47–57.
Schwartz, Seth. 1989. 'The "Judaism" of Samaria and Galilee in Josephus's Version of the Letter of Demetrius I to Jonathan (*Antiquities* 13.48–57).' *HTR* 82: 377–91.
Schwartz, Seth. 1991. 'Israel and the Nations Roundabout: 1 Maccabees and the Hasmonean Expansion.' *JJS* 42: 16–38.
Schwartz, Seth. 1993a. 'John Hyrcanus I's Destruction of the Gerazim Temple and Judaean-Samaritan Relations.' *Jewish History* 7: 9–25.
Schwartz, Seth. 1993b. 'A Note on the Social Type and Political Ideology of the Hasmonean Family.' *JBL* 112: 305–9.
Schwartz, Seth. 2010. *Were the Jews a Mediterranean Society? Reciprocity and Solidarity in Ancient Judaism*. Princeton: Princeton University Press.
Schwentzel, Christian-Georges. 2013. *Juifs et Nabatéens: Les monarchies ethniques du Proche-Orient hellénistique et romain*. Preface by Bernard Legras; Collection 'Histoire'. Rennes: Presses Universitaires de Rennes.
Scott, James M. (ed.). 1997. *Exile: Old Testament, Jewish, and Christian Conceptions*. JSJSup 56. Leiden: Brill.
Scullard, H. H. 1982. *From the Gracchi to Nero: A History of Rome from 133 B.C. to A.D. 68*. 5th ed. London/New York: Methuen.
Scurlock, Joann. 2000. '167 BCE: Hellenism or Reform?' *JSJ* 31: 125–61.
Seager, Robin. 2002. *Pompey the Great: A Political Biography*. 2nd ed. Oxford: Blackwell.
Seel, Otto (ed.). 1985. *M.Iuniani Iustini Epitoma Historiarum Philippicarum Pompei Trogi*. Bibliotheca scriptorum Graecorum et Romanorum Teubneriana. Stuttgart: Teubner.
Seeman, Chris. 2013. *Rome and Judea in Transition: Hasmonean Relations with the Roman Republic and the Evolution of the High Priesthood*. American University Studies, Series VII Theology and Religion 325. New York: Peter Lang.
Segal, Alan F. 1986. *Rebecca's Children: Judaism and Christianity in the Roman World*. Cambridge, MA: Harvard University Press.
Segal, Michael. 2007. *The Book of Jubilees: Rewritten Bible, Redaction, Ideology and Theology*. JSJSup 117. Leiden: Brill.
Sellers, Ovid R. 1933. *The Citadel at Beth-Zur*. Philadelphia: Westminster.
Sellers, Ovid R. 1958. 'The 1957 Campaign at Beth-Zur.' *BA* 21: 71–76.
Sellers, Ovid R. 1962. 'Coins of the 1960 Excavation at Shechem.' *BA* 25: 87–95.
Sellers, O. R., et al. 1968. *The 1957 Excavation at Beth-Zur*. AASOR 38. Cambridge, MA: American Schools of Oriental Research.
Shackleton Bailey, D. R. 1971. *Cicero*. Classical Life and Letters. New York: Scribners.
Shalom, Nitsan, Oded Lipschits, Noa Shatil and Yuval Gadot. Forthcoming 'Judah in the "Long Third Century B.C.E."—An Archaeological Perspective.' In *Judah and Judeans in the Long Third Century*, ed. Sylvie Honigman, Oded Lipschits, C. Nihan, and Thomas Römer. Winona Lake, IN: Eisenbrauns.
Sharon, Nadav. 2017. *Judea under Roman Domination: The First Generation of Statelessness and its Legacy*. SBLEJL 46. Atlanta: SBL.
Shatzman, Israel. 1991. *The Armies of the Hasmonaeans and Herod: From Hellenistic to Roman Frameworks*. TSAJ 25. Tübingen: Mohr(Siebeck).

Shehadeh, Haseeb. 1989–2002. *The Arabic Translation of the Samaritan Pentateuch*, vols 1–2. Jerusalem: Israel Academy of Sciences and Humanities.

Shehadeh, Haseeb, and Habib Tawa,with collaboration of Reinhard Pummer (eds). 2005. *Proceedings of the Fifth International Congress of the Société d'Études Samaritaines, Helsinki, August 1–4, 2000: Studies in Memory of Ferdinand Dexinger*. Paris: Librairie Orientaliste Paul Geuthner.

Shennan, Stephen J. (ed.). 1989. *Archaeological Approaches to Cultural Identity*. One World Archaeology 10. London/New York: Routledge.

Sherk, Robert K. 1984. *Rome and the Greek East to the Death of Augustus*. Translated Documents of Greece and Rome 4. Cambridge: Cambridge University Press.

Sherwin-White, A. N. 1984. *Roman Foreign Policy in the East, 168 B.C. to A.D. 1*. London: Duckworth.

Sherwin-White, Susan, and Amélie Kuhrt. 1993. *From Samarkhand to Sardis: A New Approach to the Seleucid Empire*. London: Duckworth.

Shutt, R. J. H. 1961. *Studies in Josephus*. London: SPCK.

Sievers, Joseph. 1990. *The Hasmoneans and their Supporters: From Mattathias to the Death of John Hyrcanus I*. SFSJH 6. Atlanta: Scholars Press.

Skeat, T. C. 1961. 'Notes on Ptolemaic Chronology: II. "The Twelfth Year which is also the First": The Invasion of Egypt by Antiochus Epiphanes.' *JEA* 47: 107–12.

Smallwood, E. M. 1967. 'Gabinius' Organisation of Palestine.' *JJS* 18: 89–92.

Smith, Christopher, and Liv Mariah Yarrow (eds). 2012. *Imperialism, Cultural Politics, and Polybius*. Oxford: Oxford University Press.

Smith, Morton. 1956. 'Palestinian Judaism in the First Century.' In *Israel: Its Role in Civilization*, ed. Moshe Davis, 67–81. New York: Harper.

Smith, Robert Houston. 1990. 'The Southern Levant in the Hellenistic Period.' *Levant* 22: 123–30.

Smith, Robert Houston (ed.). 1973. *Pella of the Decapolis, Volume 1: The 1967 Season of the College of Wooster Expedition to Pella*. Sydney: College of Wooster.

Smith, Robert Houston, and Leslie Preston Day (eds). 1989. *Pella of the Decapolis, Volume 2: Final Report on the College of Wooster Expeditions in Area IX, The Civic Complex, 1979–1985*. Sydney: College of Wooster.

Smith, Robert H., and Anthony W. McNicoll. 1983. 'The 1980 Season at Pella of the Decapolis.' *BASOR* 249: 45–77.

Smith, Robert H., and Anthony W. McNicoll. 1986. 'The 1982 and 1983 Seasons at Pella of the Decapolis.' *BASOR, Supplementary Studies* 24: 89–116.

Smith, Robert H., Anthony W. McNicoll, and J. B. Hennessy. 1981. 'The 1980 Season at Pella of the Decapolis.' *BASOR* 243: 1–30.

Sokolovskii, Servey, and Valery Tishkov. 1996. 'Ethnicity.' In *Encylopedia of Social and Cultural Anthropology*, ed. Alan Barnard and Jonathan Spencer, 190–93. London/New York: Routledge.

Sommer, Benjamin D. 1996. 'Did Prophecy Cease? Evaluating a Reevaluation.' *JBL* 115: 31–47.

Spaer, Arnold. 1977. 'Some More "Yehud" Coins.' *IEJ* 27: 200–3.

Sparks, Kenton L. 1998. *Ethnicity and Identity in Ancient Israel: Prolegomena to the Study of Ethnic Sentiments and their Expression in the Hebrew Bible*. Winona Lake, IN: Eisenbrauns.

Spek, R. J. van der. 1997/1998. 'New Evidence from the Babylonian Astronomical Diaries Concerning Seleucid and Arsacid History.' *AfO* 44/45: 167–75.

Sperber, D. 1965. 'A Note on Hasmonean Coin-Legends. Heber and Rosh Heber.' *PEQ* 97: 85–93.

Stacey, David, and Gregory Doudna. 2013. *Qumran Revisited: A Reassessment of the Archaeology of the Site and its Texts*. BAR International Series 2520. Oxford: Archaeopress.

Stadelmann, H. 1980. *Ben Sira als Schriftgelehrter: einer Untersuchung zum Berufsbild des vormakkabäischen Sofer unter Berücksichtigung seines Verhältnisses zu Priester-, Propheten- und Weisheitslehrertum*. WUNT 2/6. Tübingen: Mohr Siebeck.

Starcky, Jean. 1963. 'Les quatres étapes du messianisme à Qumrân.' *RevB* 70: 481–505.

Steck, Odil Hannes. 1993. *Das apokryphe Baruchbuch: Studien zu Rezeption und Konzentration "kanonischer" Überlieferung*. FRLANT 160. Göttingen: Vandenhoeck & Ruprecht.

Steck, Odil Hannes, Reinhard G. Kratz, and Ingo Kottsieper (eds). 1998. *Das Buch Baruch; Der Brief des Jeremia; Zusätze zu Ester und Daniel*. Das Alte Testament Deutsch, Apokryphen 5. Göttingen: Vandenhoeck & Ruprecht.

Steckoll, S. H. 1967–69 'The Qumran Sect in Relation to the Temple of Leontopolis.' *RevQ* 6: 55–69.

Steel, Catherine. 2013. *The End of the Roman Republic 146 to 44 BC: Conquest and Crisis*. The Edinburgh History of Ancient Rome. Edinburgh: Edinburgh University Press.

Stegemann, Hartmut. 1998. *The Library of Qumran: On the Essenes, Qumran, John the Baptist, and Jesus*. Kampen: Kok Pharos; Grand Rapids, MI: Eerdmans. ET of *Die Essener, Qumran, Johannes der Taüfer und Jesus*. Ein Sachbuch, Freiberg: Herder, 1993.

Steinmann, Andrew E. 2009. 'When Did Herod the Great Reign?' *NT* 51: 1–29.

Stemberger, Günter. 1995. *Jewish Contemporaries of Jesus: Pharisees, Sadducees, Essenes*, trans. Allan W. Mahnke. Minneapolis: Fortress. ET of *Pharisäer, Sadduzäer, Essener*. Stuttgart: Katholisches Bibelwerk.

Stemberger, Günter. 1996. *Introduction to the Talmud and Midrash*, trans. and ed. M. Bockmuehl, with a foreword by J. Neusner. 2nd ed. Edinburgh: T. & T. Clark; Minneapolis: Fortress. ET (and revision) of *Einleitung in Talmud und Midrasch*. 8. neubearbeitete Auflage. Munich: C. H. Beck, 1992.

Stemberger, Günter. 2011. *Einleitung in Talmud und Midrasch*. 9. neubearbeitete Auflage. Munich: C. H. Beck.

Stenhouse, Paul. 1985. *The Kitab al-Tarikh of Abu 'l-Fatḥ, Translated into English with Notes*. Mandelbaum Studies in Judaica 1. Sydney: Sydney University Press.

Stenhouse, Paul. 1989. 'Samaritan Chronicles.' In *The Samaritans*, ed. A. D. Crown, 218–65. Tübingen: Mohr Siebeck.

Sterling, Gregory E. 1992. *Historiography and Self-Definition: Josephos, Luke-Acts and Apologetic Historiography*. NovTSup 64. Leiden: Brill.

Stern, Ephraim. 1994. *Dor, Ruler of the Seas: Twelve Years of Excavations at the Israelite-Phoenician Harbor Town on the Carmel Coast*. Jerusalem: Israel Exploration Society.

Stern, Ephraim (ed.). 1978. *Excavations at Tel Mevorakh (1973–1976) Part One: From the Iron Age to the Roman Period*. Qedem 9. Jerusalem: Hebrew University of Jerusalem.

Stern, Ephraim (ed.). 1992. *The New Encyclopedia of Archaeological Excavations in the Holy Land*, vols 1–4. New York: Simon & Schuster; Jerusalem: Israel Exploration Society. *Supplementary Volume*, vol. 5. New York: Simon & Schuster; Jerusalem: Israel Exploration Society, 2008.

Stern, Ephraim (ed.). 1995a. *Excavations at Dor, Final Report: Volume I A Areas A and C: Introduction and Stratigraphy*. Qedem Reports 1. Jerusalem: Israel Exploration Society.

Stern, Ephraim (ed.). 1995b. *Excavations at Dor, Final Report, Volume 1: B Areas A and C: The Finds*. Qedem Reports 2. Jerusalem: Israel Exploration Society.

Stern, Ephraim, and Yitzhak Magen. 2002. 'Archaeological Evidence for the First Stage of the Samarian Temple on Mount Gerizim.' *IEJ* 52: 49–57. ET of 'של השלב הראשון המקדש השומרוני בהר גריזים: עדויות ארכיאולוגיות חדשות [The First Phase of the Samaritan Temple on Mount Gerizim: New Archaeological Evidence].' *Qadmoniot* 33 (2000): 119–24.

Stern, Menahem. 1974a. 'The Greek and Roman Literary Sources.' In *The Jewish People in the First Century: Historical Geography, Political History, Social, Cultural and Religious Life and Institutions*, ed. S. Safrai and Menahem Stern, 1:18–36. CRINT: 1/1. Assen: Van Gorcum; Philadelphia: Fortress.

Stern, Menahem. 1974b. 'Chronology.' In *The Jewish People in the First Century: Historical Geography, Political History, Social, Cultural and Religious Life and Institutions*, ed. S. Safrai and Menahem Stern, 1:62–77. CRINT 1/1. Assen: Van Gorcum; Philadelphia: Fortress.

Stern, Menahem. 1974–84. *Greek and Latin Authors on Jews and Judaism*. 3 vols. Jerusalem: Israel Academy of Sciences and Humanities) = *GLAJJ*.

Stern, Menahem. 1981. 'Judaea and her Neighbors in the Days of Alexander Jannaeus.' *The Jerusalem Cathedra* 1 (1981) 22–46.

Steudel, Annette. 1994. *Der Midrasch zur Eschatologie aus der Qumrangemeinde (4QMidrEschata,b): Materielle Rekonstruktion, Textbestand, Gattung und traditionsgeschichtliche Einordnung des durch 4Q174 ('Florilegium') und 4Q177 ('Catena A') repräsentierten Werkes aus den Qumranfunden*. STDJ 13. Leiden: Brill.

Stocker, Margarita. 1998. *Judith: Sexual Warrior, Women and Power in Western Culture*. New Haven and London: Yale University Press.

Stökl Ben Ezra, Daniel. 2016. *Qumran: Die Texte vom Toten Meer und das antike Judentum*. Jüdische Studien 3. Tübingen: Mohr Siebeck.

Stone, Michael E. 1988. 'Enoch, Aramaic Levi and Sectarian Origins.' *JSJ* 19: 159–70.

Stone, Michael E. 2018. *Secret Groups in Ancient Judaism*. Oxford: Oxford University Press.

Stone, Michael E. and Esther G. Chazon (eds). 1998. *Biblical Perspectives: Early Use and Interpretation of the Bible in Light of the Dead Sea Scrolls: Proceedings of the First International Symposium of the Orion Center for the Study of the Dead Sea Scrolls and Associated Literature, 12–14 May, 1996*. STDJ 28. Leiden: Brill.

Strange, James F. 1975. 'Late Hellenistic and Herodian Ossuary Tombs at French Hill, Jerusalem.' *BASOR* 219: 39–67.

Strange, James F., Dennis E. Groh, and Thomas R. W. Longstaff. 1994. 'Excavations at Sepphoris: The Location and Identification of Shikhin, Part I.' *IEJ* 44: 216–27.

Strange, James F., Dennis E. Groh, and Thomas R. W. Longstaff. 1995. 'Excavations at Sepphoris: The Location and Identification of Shikhin, Part II.' *IEJ* 45: 171–87.

Strugnell, John. 1967. 'Quelques inscriptions samaritaines.' *RevB* 74: 555–80.

Stuckenbruck, Loren T. 2007. *1 Enoch 91–108*. CEJL. Berlin/New York: de Gruyter.

Sussmann, Y. 1989–90. 'The History of *Halakha* and the Dead Sea Scrolls: A Preliminary to the Publication of 4QMMT.' *Tarbiz* 59: 11–76 (Heb.). Partial ET in Appendix 1 of *Qumran Cave 4: V Miqṣat Ma'aśe ha-Torah*, ed. E. Qimron and John Strugnell, 179–200. DJD 10. Oxford: Clarendon, 1994.

Swain, Hilary, and Mark Everson Davies. 2010. *Aspects of Roman History, 82 BC–AD 14: A Source-Based Approach*. Aspects of Classical Civilisation. Abingdon/New York: Routledge.

Swanson, Dwight D. 1995. *The Temple Scroll and the Bible: The Methodology of 11QT*. STDJ 14. Leiden: Brill.

Schwenk-Bressler, Udo. 1993. *Sapientia Salomonis als ein Beispiel frühjüdischer Textauslegung: Die Auslegung des Buches Genesis, Exodus 1–15 und Teilen der Wüstentradition in Sap 10–19*. Beiträge zur Erforschung des Alten Testaments und des antiken Judentums 32. Frankfurt am Main: Lang.

Swoboda, Sören. 2014. *Tod und Sterben im Krieg bei Josephus: Die Intentionen von* Bellum *und* Antiquitates *im Kontext griechisch-römischer Historiographie*. TSAJ 158. Tübingen: Mohr Siebeck.

Syon, Danny. 2006. 'Numismatic Evidence of Jewish Presence in Galilee before the Hasmonean Annexation.' *INR* 1: 21–24.

Syon, Danny. Forthcoming 'The Hasmonean Settlement in Galilee—A Numismatic Perspective.' In *The Period of the Middle Maccabees: From the Death of Judas through the Reign of John Hyrcanus (ca. 160–104 BCE)*, ed. Andrea M. Berlin. 9th Nangeroni Meeting in Gazzada, Italy.

Tabor, James D., and Michael O. Wise. 1994. '4Q521 "On Resurrection" and the Synoptic Gospel Tradition: A Preliminary Study.' *JSP* 10: 149–62.

Taeger, Fritz. 1957–60 *Charisma: Studien zur Geschichte des antiken Herrscherkultes*, vols 1–2. Stuttgart: W. Kohlhammer.

Tal, Abraham (ed.). 1980. *The Samaritan Targum of the Pentateuch: A Critical Edition, Part I: Genesis, Exodus*. Texts and Studies in the Hebrew Language and Related Subjects 4. Tel Aviv: Tel Aviv University Press.

Tal, Abraham (ed.). 1981. *The Samaritan Targum of the Pentateuch: A Critical Edition, Part II: Leviticus, Numeri, Deuteronomium*. Texts and Studies in the Hebrew Language and Related Subjects 5. Tel Aviv: Tel Aviv University.

Tal, Abraham (ed.). 1983. *The Samaritan Targum of the Pentateuch: A Critical Edition, Part III: Introduction*. Texts and Studies in the Hebrew Language and Related Studies 6. Tel Aviv: Tel Aviv University.

Tal, Abraham (ed.). 1994. *The Samaritan Pentateuch edited according to MS 6 (C) of the Shekhem Synagogue*. Texts and Studies in Hebrew Language and Related Subjects 8. Tel Aviv: Tel Aviv University.

Talmon, Shamaryahu. 1958. 'The Calendar Reckoning of the Sect from the Judaean Desert.' In *Aspects of the Dead Sea Scrolls*, ed. Chaim Rabin and Yigael Yadin, 162–99. Scripta Hierosolymitana 4; Jerusalem: Magnes.

Talmon, Shamaryahu. 1970. 'The Old Testament Text.' In *Cambridge History of the Bible, Vol. 1: From the Beginnings to Jerome*, ed. P. R. Ackroyd and C. F. Evans, 159–99. Cambridge: Cambridge University Press. Reprinted in *Qumran and the History of the Biblical Text*, ed. Frank M. Cross and Shemaryahu Talmon, 1–41. Cambridge, MA: Harvard University Press.

Talmon, Shamaryahu. 1975. 'The Textual Study of the Bible—A New Outlook.' In *Qumran and the History of the Biblical Text*, ed. Frank M. Cross and Shemaryahu Talmon, 321–400. Cambridge, MA: Harvard University Press.

Talmon, Shamaryahu. 1986. 'The Emergence of Jewish Sectarianism in the Early Second Temple Period.' In *King, Cult and Calendar in Ancient Israel*, 165–201. Jerusalem: Magnes. Slightly shortened translation of German version in *Max Webers Sicht des antiken Christentums*, ed. E. Schluchter, 233–80. Frankfurt: Suhrkamp, 1985.

Taylor, Joan E. 1998. 'A Second Temple in Egypt: The Evidence for the Zadokite Temple of Onias.' *JSJ* 29: 297–321.
Taylor, Joan E. 2007. 'Philo of Alexandria on the Essenes: A Case Study on the Use of Classical Sources in Discussions of the Qumran-Essene Hypothesis.' *SPA* 19: 1–28.
Taylor, Joan E. 2012. *The Essenes, the Scrolls, and the Dead Sea*. Oxford: Oxford University Press.
Tcherikover, Victor A. 1958. 'The Ideology of the Letter of Aristeas.' *HTR* 51: 59–85.
Tcherikover, Victor A. 1959. *Hellenistic Civilization and the Jews*. New York: Jewish Publication Society.
Tcherikover, Victor A. 1961. 'The Third Book of Maccabees as a Historical Source of Augustus' Time.' *Scripta Hierosolymitana* 7: 1–26. Earlier Hebrew version in *Zion* 10 (1945) 1–20.
Tcherikover, V. A., A. Fuks, and M. Stern. 1957–64. *Corpus Papyrorum Judaicarum*. 3 vols. Cambridge, MA: Harvard University Press; Jerusalem: Magnes.
Tedesche, S., and Solomon Zeitlin. 1950. *The First Book of Maccabees*. Dropsie College Jewish Apocryphal Literature. New York: Harper.
Teeple, Howard M. 1957. *The Mosaic Eschatological Prophet*. SBLMS 10. Atlanta: Scholars Press.
Teicher, J. L. 1951. 'The Dead Sea Scrolls—Documents of the Jewish-Christian Sect of the Ebionites.' *JJS* 2: 67–99.
Thiering, Barbara. 1992. *Jesus & the Riddle of the Dead Sea Scrolls: Unlocking the Secrets of His Life Story*. San Francisco: HarperCollins.
Thompson, Thomas L. 1999. *The Bible in History: How Writers Create a Past* (UK title); *The Mythic Past: Biblical Archaeology and the Myth of Israel* (American title). London/New York: Random House Jonathan Cape.
Tidmarsh, John. 2004. 'How Hellenised Was Pella in Jordan in the Hellenistic Period?' *SHAJ* 8: 459–68.
Tiller, Patrick A. 1993. *A Commentary on the Animal Apocalypse of* 1 Enoch. SBLEJL 4. Atlanta: Scholars Press.
Tilly, Michael. 1997. 'Geographie und Weltordnung im Aristeasbrief.' *JSJ* 28: 131–53.
Tilly, Michael. 2015. *1 Makkabäer*. Herders Theologischer Kommentar zum Alten Testament. Freiburg: Herder.
Timpe, D. 1974. 'Der römische Vertrag mit den Juden von 161 v. Chr.' *Chiron* 4: 133–52.
Toher, Mark. 2003. 'Nicolaus and Herod in the *Antiquitates Judaicae*.' *HSCP* 101: 427–47.
Toher, Mark. 2011. 'Herod's Last Days.' *HSCP* 106: 209–28.
Toher, Mark. 2014. 'Herod, Athens and Augustus.' *ZPE* 190: 127–34.
Toorn, Karel van der, Bob Becking, and Pieter W. van der Horst (eds.). 1999. *Dictionary of Deities and Demons in the Bible*. 2nd rev. ed. Leiden: Brill; Grand Rapids, MI: Eerdmans (= *DDD*2).
Tov, Emanuel. 1976. *The Septuagint Translation of Jeremiah and Baruch: A Discussion of an Early Revision of the LXX of Jeremiah 29–52 and Baruch 1:1–38*. HSM 8. Missoula, MT: Scholars Press.
Tov, Emanuel. 1989. 'Proto-Samaritan Texts and the Samaritan Pentateuch.' In *The Samaritans*, ed. Alan D. Crown, 397–407. Tübingen: Mohr Siebeck.
Tov, Emanuel. 2011. *Textual Criticism of the Hebrew Bible*. 3rd rev. and exp. ed. Assen/Maastricht: Van Gorcum; Minneapolis: Fortress.
Trafton, Joseph L. 1985. *The Syriac Version of the Psalms of Solomon: A Critical Evaluation*. SBLSCS 11. Atlanta: Scholars Press.

Trafton, Joseph L. 1986. 'The Psalms of Solomon: New Light from the Syriac Version?' *JBL* 105: 227–37.
Trafton, Joseph L. 1992. 'Solomon, Psalms of.' *ABD*: 6:115–17.
Trafton, Joseph L. 1994. 'The *Psalms of Solomon* in Recent Research.' *JSP* 12: 3–19.
Tränkle, Hermann. 1977. *Livius und Polybios*. Basel: Schwabe & Co.
Tromp, Johannes. 1993. *The Assumption of Moses: A Critical Edition with Commentary*. SVTP 10. Leiden: Brill.
Tsafrir, Y. 1975. 'The Location of the Seleucid Akra.' *RevB* 82: 501–21.
Tsafrir, Y. 1982. 'The Desert Fortresses of Judaea in the Second Temple Period.' *Jerusalem Cathedra* 2: (1982) 120–45.
Tushingham, A. D. 1987. 'The Western Hill of Jerusalem: A Critique of the "Maximalist" Position.' *Levant* 19 (1987) 137–43.
Tzaferis, Vasillios. 1983. 'New Archaeological Evidence on Ancient Capernaum.' *BA* 46: 198–204.
Tzaferis, Vasillios. 1989. *Excavations at Capernaum, Volume 1 1978–1982*. Winona Lake, IN: Eisenbrauns.
Tzaferis, Vassilios, and Shoshana Israeli (eds). 2008. *Paneas Volume 1: The Roman to Early Islamic Periods Excavations in Areas A, B, E, F, G and H*. IAA Reports 37. Jerusalem: Israel Antiquities Authority.
Tzafrir, Yoram. 1982. 'The Desert Fortresses of Judaea in the Second Temple Period.' *Jerusalem Cathedra* 2: 120–45.
Udoh, Fabian E. 2005. *To Caesar What Is Caesar's: Tribute, Taxes, and Imperial Administration in Early Roman Palestine (63 B.C.E.–70 C.E.)*. BJS 343. Province, RI: Brown University Press.
Ulrich, Eugene C., Jr. 1978. *The Qumran Text of Samuel and Josephus*. HSM 19. Missoula, MT: Scholars Press.
Ulrich, Eugene C., Jr. 1999. *The Dead Sea Scrolls and the Origins of the Bible*. Studies in the Dead Sea Scrolls and Related Literature. Grand Rapids, MI: Eerdmans.
Unnik, Willem Cornelis van. 1993. *Das Selbstverständnis der jüdischen Diaspora in der hellenistisch-römischen Zeit*. AGAJU 17. Leiden: Brill.
Van 't Dack, E., W. Clarysse, G. Cohen, J. Quaegebeur, J. K. Winnicki. 1989. *The Judean-Syrian-Egyptian Conflict of 103–101 B.C.: A Multilingual Dossier concerning a 'War of Sceptres'*. Collectanea Hellenistica 1. Brussels: Peeters.
Van Nuffelen, Peter. 1998–99. 'Le culte des souverains hellénistiques, le gui de la religion grecque.' *Ancient Society* 29: 175–89.
Van Nuffelen, Peter. 2004. 'Le culte royal de l'empire des Séleucides: une réinterprétation.' *Historia* 53: 278–301.
VanderKam, James C. 1977. *Textual and Historical Studies in the Book of Jubilees*. HSM 14. Atlanta: Scholars Press.
VanderKam, James C. 1981a. 'The Putative Author of the Book of Jubilees.' *JSS* 26: 209–17.
VanderKam, James C. 1981b. '2 Maccabees 6, 7A and Calendrical Change in Jerusalem.' *JSJ* 12: 52–74.
VanderKam, James C. 1992. 'The People of the Dead Sea Scrolls: Essenes or Sadducees?' In *Understanding the Dead Sea Scrolls: A Reader from the* Biblical Archaeology Review, ed. Hershel Shanks, 50–62, 300–302. New York: Random House. Originally *Bible Review* 7, no. 2 (1991): 42–47.

VanderKam, James C. 1994a. *The Dead Sea Scrolls Today*. Grand Rapids, MI: Eerdmans; London: SPCK.
VanderKam, James C. 1994b. 'Genesis 1 in Jubilees 2.' *DSD* 1: 300–21.
VanderKam, James C. 1998. *Calendars in the Dead Sea Scrolls: Measuring Time*. The Literature of the Dead Sea Scrolls. London/New York: Routledge.
VanderKam, James C. 2004. *From Joshua to Caiaphas: High Priests after the Exile*. Minneapolis: Fortress; Assen: Van Gorcum.
VanderKam, James C. (ed.). 1989. *The Book of Jubilees: Text and English Translation*. 2 vols. CSCO 510–11, Scriptores Aethiopici 87–88. Leuven: Peeters.
Vaux, Roland de. 1973. *Archaeology and the Dead Sea Scrolls*. Schweich Lectures of the British Academy 1959. London: Oxford University Press.
Vermes, Geza. 1960. 'The Etymology of "Essenes".' *RevQ* 2: 427–43.
Vermes, Geza. 1977. *The Dead Sea Scrolls: Qumran in Perspective*. London: Collins.
Vermes, Geza. 2011. *The Complete Dead Sea Scrolls in English*. Penguin Classics. 7th rev. ed. London: Penguin.
Vermes, Geza. 2014. *The True Herod*. London/New York: Bloomsbury T&T Clark.
Vermes, Geza, and Martin D. Goodman (eds). 1989. *The Essenes According to Classical Sources*. Oxford Centre for Postgraduate Hebrew Studies Textbook 1. Sheffield: JSOT.
Viviano, Benedict T., OP, and Justin Taylor, SM. 1992. 'Sadducees, Angels, and Resurrection (Acts 23:8–9).' *JBL* 111: 496–98.
Volkmann, H. 1924–25. 'Demetrios I. und Alexander I. von Syrien.' *Klio* 1: 373–412.
Vriezen, T. C., and A. S. van der Woude. 2005. *Ancient Israelite and Early Jewish Literature*, trans. Brian Doyle; Leiden: Brill. ET of *Oud-Israëlitische en vroeg-joodse Literatuur*. Kampen: Kok Pharos, 2000.
Wacholder, Ben Zion. 1962. *Nicolas of Damascus*. Berkeley/Los Angeles: University of California Press.
Wacholder, Ben Zion. 1973. 'The Calendar of Sabbatical Cycles During the Second Temple and the Early Rabbinic Period.' *HUCA* 44: 153–96.
Wacholder, Ben Zion. 1975. 'Chronomessianism: The Timing of Messianic Movements and the Calendar of Sabbatical Cycles.' *HUCA* 46: 201–18.
Wacholder, Ben Zion. 1983. 'The Calendar of Sabbath Years During the Second Temple Era: A Response.' *HUCA* 54: 123–33.
Wacholder, Ben Zion. 1984. 'The Beginning of the Seleucid Era and the Chronology of the Diadochoi.' In *Nourished with Peace: Studies in Hellenistic Judaism in Memory of Samuel Sandmel*, ed. F. E. Greenspahn, Earle Hilgert, and Burton L. Mack, 183–211. Homage Series. Atlanta: Scholars Press.
Walbank, F. W. 1957–79. *A Historical Commentary on Polybius*. 3 vols. Oxford: Clarendon.
Walbank, F. W. 1972. *Polybius*. Sather Classical Lectures 42. Berkeley/Los Angeles: University of California Press.
Walsh, P. G. 1961. *Livy: His Historical Aims and Methods*. Cambridge: Cambridge University Press.
Waltke, Bruce K. 1965. 'Prolegomena to the Samaritan Pentateuch.' PhD diss., Cambridge, MA: Harvard University Press.
Waltke, Bruce K. 1970. 'The Samaritan Pentateuch and the Text of the Old Testament.' In *New Perspectives on the Old Testament*, ed. J. Barton Payne, 212–39. Waco, TX: Word.
Warner, Rex (trans.). 1954. *Thucydides, History of the Peloponnesian War*. Penguin Classics; London: Penguin.

Warrior, Valerie M. 1996. 'Evidence in Livy on Roman Policy Prior to War with Antiochus the Great.' In *Transitions to Empire: Essays in Greco-Roman History, 360–146 B.C., in Honor of E. Badian*, ed. Robert W. Wallace and Edward M. Harris, 356–75. Oklahoma Series in Classical Culture 21. Norman: University of Oklahoma Press.

Waubke, Hans-Günther. 1998. *Die Pharisäer in der protestantischen Bibelwissenschaft des 19. Jahrhunderts*. Beiträge zur historischen Theologie 107. Tübingen: Mohr Siebeck.

Weitzman, Steven. 1999. 'Forced Circumcision and the Shifting Role of Gentiles in Hasmonean Ideology.' *HTR* 92: 37–59.

Weitzman, Steven. 2004. 'Plotting Antiochus's Persecution.' *JBL* 123: 219–34.

Weitzman, Steven. 2008. 'On the Political Relevance of Antiquity: A Response to David Goodblatt's *Elements of Ancient Jewish Nationalism*.' *Jewish Social Studies* 14: 165–172.

Welles, C. Bradford. 1934. *Royal Correspondence in the Hellenistic Period: A Study in Greek Epigraphy*. Studia Historica 28. New Haven, CT: Yale University Press. Reprinted Rome: Bretschneider, 1966.

Wellhausen, Julius. 1905. 'Über den geschichtlichen Wert des zweiten Makkabäerbuchs im Verhältnis zum ersten.' *Nachrichten von der Königlichen Gesellschaft der Wissenschaften zu Göttingen*, Phil.-hist. Klasse: 117–63.

Wenning, Robert. 1987. *Die Nabatäer—Denkmäler und Geschichte: Eine Bestandesaufnahme des archäologischen Befundes*. NTOA 3. Freiberg [Schweiz]: Universitätsverlag; Göttingen: Vandenhoeck & Ruprecht.

Wenning, Robert. 1990. 'Das Nabatäerreich: seine archäologischen und historischen Hinterlassenschaften.' In *Palästina in griechisch-römischer Zeit*, by H. P. Kuhnen, 367–415. HdA, Vorderasien 2, Band 2. Munich: Beck.

Wenning, Robert. 1994. 'Die Dekapolis und die Nabatäer.' *ZDPV* 110: 1–35.

White Crawford, Sidnie, and Cecilia Wassén (eds.). 2018. *Apocalyptic Thinking in Early Judaism: Engaging with John Collins'* The Apocalyptic Imagination. JSJSup 182. Leiden: Brill.

Whittaker, C. R. 1978. 'Carthaginian Imperialism in the Fifth and Fourth Centuries.' In *Imperialism in the Ancient World*, ed. P. D. A. Garnsey and C. R. Whittaker, 59–90. Cambridge University Press.

Wiesehöfer, Josef (ed.). 1998. *Das Partherreich und seine Zeugnisse: The Arsacid Empire: Sources and Documentation*. Historia Einzel-Schriften 122. Stuttgart: Steiner.

Wiesehöfer, Josef, and Sabine Müller (eds.) 2017. *Parthika: Greek and Roman Authors' Views of the Arsacid Empire / Griechisch-römische Bilder des Arsakidenreiches*. Classica et Orientalia 15. Wiesbaden: Harrassowitz.

Wilkinson, J. 1975. 'The Streets of Jerusalem.' *Levant* 7: 118–36.

Will, Edouard. 1979. *Histoire politique du monde hellénistique (323–30 av. J.-C.), Tome I*. 2nd ed. Annales de l-Est, Mémoire 30. Nancy: Publications de l'Université.

Will, Edouard. 1982. *Histoire politique du monde hellénistique (323–30 av. J.-C.): Tome II Des avènements d'Antiochos III et de Philippe V a la fin des Lagides*. 2nd ed. Annales de l-Est, Mémoire 32. Nancy: Publications de l'Université.

Will, Ernest. 1982. 'Un Monument Hellénistique de Jordanie: Le Qasr el 'abd d''Iraq al Amir.' *SHAJ* 1: 197–200.

Will, Ernest, and François Larché (eds.) 1991. *'Iraq al Amir: Le Château du Tobiade Hyrcan*. 2 vols. Institut Français d'Archéologie du Proche-Orient, Bibliothèque Archéologique et Historique 132. Paris: Librairie Orientaliste Paul Geuthner.

Williams, David S. 1999. *The Structure of 1 Maccabees*. CBQM 31. Washington, DC: Catholic Biblical Association of America.

Williams, Margaret H. 1995. 'Palestinian Jewish Personal Names in Acts.' In *The Book of Acts in its First Century Setting, Volume 4: The Book of Acts in Its Palestinian Setting*, ed. Richard Bauckham, 79–113. Grand Rapids, MI: Eerdmans.

Williams, Margaret H. 1997. 'The Meaning and Function of *Ioudaios* in Graeco-Roman Inscriptions.' *ZPE* 116: 249–62.

Williams, Margaret H. 1998. *The Jews among the Greeks and Romans: A Diaspora Sourcebook.* London: Duckworth.

Williams, R. S. 1978. 'The Role of Amicitia in the Career of A. Gabinius (Cos. 58).' *Phoenix* 32: 195–210.

Williamson, Hugh G. M. 1979. 'The Origins of the Twenty-Four Priestly Courses: A Study of 1 Chronicles xxiii–xxvii.' In *Studies in the Historical Books of the Old Testament*, 251–68. VTSup 30. Leiden: Brill.

Willrich, H. 1909. 'Zum hellenistischen Titel- und Ordens-Wesen.' *Klio* 9: 416–21.

Wilson, Bryan R. 1973. *Magic and Millennium: A Sociological Study of Religious Movements of Protest among Tribal and Third-World Peoples*. London: Heinemann.

Wilson, Bryan R. 1990. *The Social Dimensions of Sectarianism: Sects and New Religious Movements in Contemporary Society*. Oxford: Clarendon.

Winston, David. 1979. *The Wisdom of Solomon: A New Translation with Introduction and Commentary*. AB 43. Garden City, NY: Doubleday.

Winston, David. 1989. 'Two Types of Mosaic Prophecy according to Philo.' *JSP* 2: 49–67.

Wirgin, W. 1969. 'Judah Maccabee's Embassy to Rome and the Jewish-Roman Treaty.' *PEQ* 101: 15–20.

Wise, Michael O. 1989–90. 'The Teacher of Righteousness and the High Priest of the Intersacerdotium: Two Approaches.' *RevQ* 14: 587–613.

Wise, Michael O. 1997. 'To Know the Times and the Seasons: A Study of the Aramaic Chronograph 4Q559.' *JSP* 15: 3–51.

Wissowa, Georg, and Wilhelm Kroll (eds). 1894–1972. *Paulys Real-Encyclopädie der classischen Altertumswissenschaft*. Stuttgart: J. B. Metzlersche Verlagbuchhandlung.

Wolski, Jósef. 1993. *L'empire des Arsacides*. Acta Iranica 32. 3me Série: Textes et Mémoires 18. Leuven: Peeters.

Wolski, Jósef. 2003. *Seleucid and Arsacid Studies: A Progress Report on Developments in Source Research*, trans. Teresa Bałuk-Ulewiczowa. Polska Akademia Umiejętności Rozprawy Wydziału Historyczno-Filozoficznego 100. Kraków: Polish Academy of Arts and Sciences.

Woude, A. S. van der. 1990. 'A "Groningen" Hypothesis of Qumran Origins and Early History.' *RevQ* 14: 521–42.

Wright, Benjamin G., III. 2015. *The Letter of Aristeas: 'Aristeas to Philocrates' or 'On the Translation of the Law of the Jews'*. CEJL. Berlin/Boston: de Gruyter.

Wright, G. Ernest. 1964. *Shechem: The Biography of a Biblical City*. New York-Toronto: McGraw-Hill.

Yadin, Yigael (ed.). 1962. *The Scroll of the War of the Sons of Light against the Sons of Darkness.* Oxford: Clarendon.

Yadin, Yigael (ed.). 1975. *Jerusalem Revealed: Archaeology in the Holy City (1968–1974).* Jerusalem: Israel Exploration Society.

Yadin, Yigael (ed.). 1983. *The Temple Scroll: Hebrew and English*. 3 vols. in 4. Jerusalem: Israel Exploration Society.

Yalichev, Serge. 1997. *Mercenaries of the Ancient World*. London: Constable.

Yardeni, Ada. 1997. 'A Draft of a Deed on an Ostracon from Khirbet Qumrân.' *IEJ* 47: 233–237.
Yardley, J. C., and Robert Develin (ed. and trans.). 1994. *Justin: Epitome of the Philippic History of Pompeius Trogus*. American Philological Association Classical Resource Series 3. Atlanta: Scholars Press.
Yaron, R. 1960. 'The Murabba'at Documents.' *JJS* 11: 157–71.
Yarshater, Ehsan (ed.). 1983. *Cambridge History of Iran: vol. 3, parts 1–2: The Seleucid, Parthian, and Sasanian Periods*. Cambridge: Cambridge University Press.
Zeitlin, Solomon. 1918–19. 'Megillat Taanit as a Source for Jewish Chronology and History in the Hellenistic and Roman Periods.' *JQR* o.s. 9: 71–102.
Zeitlin, Solomon. 1919–20. 'Megillat Taanit as a Source for Jewish Chronology and History in the Hellenistic and Roman Periods.' *JQR* o.s. 10: 49–80, 237–90.
Zelinger, Yehiel. Forthcoming. 'The Settlements Patterns in the Plain of Sharon during the Hellenistic and Hasmonean Periods.' In *The Period of the Middle Maccabees: From the Death of Judas through the Reign of John Hyrcanus (ca. 160–104 BCE)*, ed. Andrea M. Berlin. 9th Nangeroni Meeting in Gazzada, Italy.
Ziegler, Joseph. 1980. *Sapientia Salomonis*. 2nd ed. Septuaginta, Vetus Testamentum Graecum 12/1. Göttingen: Vandenhoeck & Ruprecht.
Ziegler, Joseph. 1999. *Susanna, Daniel, Bel et Draco*, ed. Olivier Munnich. Foreword by R. Smend. 2nd ed. Septuaginta, Vetus Testamentum Graecum 16/2. Göttingen: Vandenhoeck & Ruprecht.
Zilberstein, Ayala. Forthcoming 'The Hellenistic Sequence from Givati Parking Lot—Ben-Ami and Tchekhanovets Excavations.' In *The Period of the Middle Maccabees: From the Death of Judas through the Reign of John Hyrcanus (ca. 160–104 BCE)*, ed. Andrea M. Berlin. 9th Nangeroni Meeting in Gazzada, Italy.
Zimmerman, Johannes. 1998. *Messianische Texte aus Qumran: Königliche, priesterliche und prophetische Messiasvorstellungen in den Schriftfunden von Qumran*. WUNT 2/104. Tübingen: Mohr Siebeck.
Zlotnik, Yehoshua. 2010. 'Mattathias Antigonus Coins—The Last Kings of the Hasmonean.' Available on Academia.edu.
Zlotnik, Yehoshua. 2011a. 'Alexander Jannaeus' Coins and their Dates.' Available on Academia.edu.
Zlotnik, Yehoshua. 2011b. 'The Beginning of Hasmonean Coinage.' *The Celator* 25, no. 3: 20–28.
Zlotnik, Yehoshua. 2012. 'Minting of Coins in Jerusalem during the Persian and Hellenistic Periods.' Available on Academia.edu.
Zollschan, Linda T. 2008. '*Justinus* 36.3.9 and Roman-Judaean Diplomatic Relations in 161 BCE.' *Athenaeum* 96: 153–71.
Zollschan, Linda T. 2012. 'A Bronze Tablet from the Church of San Basilio in Rome.' *Classica et Mediaevalia* 63: 217–45.
Zollschan, Linda T. 2016. *Rome and Judaea: International Law Relations, 162–100 BCE*. Routledge Studies in Ancient History. London: Routledge.
Zuckermann, B. 1866. *A Treatise on the Sabbatical Cycle and the Jubilee*. Reprinted New York: Hermon, 1974.
Zsengellér, József (ed.). 2011. *Samaria, Samarians, Samaritans: Studies on Bible, History and Linguistics*. Studia Judaica 66 = Studia Samaritana 6. Berlin/New York: de Gruyter.
Zsengellér, József (ed.). 2014. Rewritten Bible *after Fifty Years: Texts, Terms, or Techniques? A Last Dialogue with Geza Vermes*. JSJSup 166. Leiden: Brill.

Index of References

Hebrew Bible/Old Testament

Genesis
1	98
14:18-20	277
17	269
34	203
37	269

Exodus
12	98
32:10-11	266

Leviticus
7–8	279
10:7	279
16	393
21:10–15	420
23:15–16	141
25	99
25:1–7	32, 410
26	232

Deuteronomy
9:20	266
15:1–11	32
28	232

Joshua
12:22	43
15:61–62	179

Judges
17:30	336

1 Samuel
10:1	279
16:1	279
16:13	279
24:7	279

1 Kings
8:34	232
8:46–53	232

2 Kings
17	213, 233, 244
24:8–16	244
25:11–12	232

2 Chronicles
36:20–21	232

Ezra
7	167
7:1–6	167
7:6	167
7:11	167

Nehemiah
4:7	214
6:1	214
6:17–19	215
8	167
12:5	335
12:18	335
13:4–7	215

Psalms
2	279
90:4	287, 288
110:4	277
133:2	279

Proverbs
1–9	109

Isaiah
40:1–11	232
51:9–23	232
51:10–11	102

Jeremiah
23:5	279
24–27	272
25:11–12	288
26:19–21	272
27:19	290
29	102
29:10	288
30:9	279
43–44	234
45:1–6	279
56:3–5	478

Ezekiel
4:4–5	288
4:5	193

Daniel
1–6	89, 90
2:44	273, 275
7–12	89, 90, 137, 273
7:19–27	275, 291
7:21	350
7:23–27	273, 275
7:25	350, 371
8:9	350
8:10	350
8:16	271
8:23–25	275, 291

8:24	350	9:1–8	152	12:12	153
8:25	497	9:11–13	152	12:13	153
9	277, 287–89	9:14	152	12:18–27	153
9:4–19	102	9:32–34	152	12:28	153
9:21	271	11:2–5	278	12:35	153
9:24–27	288	11:7–19	154	12:37–40	153
9:25	277	12:1–2	152	14:3	153
10:13	271	12:9–14	152	14:43–52	154
10:20–21	271	12:38	153, 168		
10:21	271	15:1–3	153	*Luke*	
11–12	350	15:12	153	2:41	263
11	89, 90, 117, 275, 290, 291	16:1–4	153	3:7–9	154
		16:5–12	153	5:17–26	152
		19:3	153	5:21	168
11:25–31	21	21:23–27	153	5:30–32	152
11:28	347	22:15–16	153, 157	5:33	152
11:29–30	347	22:23–33	153	6:1–2	152
11:30	252	22:34–35	153	6:6–11	152
11:31	354, 356	22:41–42	153	7:19–22	278
11:32	252	23:1–12	153	7:30	154, 169
11:33–35	281	23:2	157, 162, 168	7:36–39	153
11:33	350			10:25	153
11:34–35	350	23:13	154	11:14–15	152
11:36	497	23:15	154	11:16	153
11:37–39	350	23:23	154	11:37–39	153
11:39	255	23:25	154	11:39	154
11:40–12:3	273, 275	23:27	154	11:42	154
11:45	89	23:29	154	11:43	154
12:1–3	90, 290	26:6	153	11:44	154
12:1	271	26:47–59	154	11:47	154
12:2–3	273	27:62	154	11:52	154
12:2	281			12:1	153
12:7	371	*Mark*		13:31	154
12:11	356	2:1–12	152	14:1–3	154
		2:16–17	152	15:1–3	154
Nahum		2:16	168, 169	16:14–18	153
2:12	422	2:18	152	17:20–21	154
		2:23–24	152	18:10–11	154
NEW TESTAMENT		3:1–6	152	19:39	154
Q		3:22	152	20:1–8	153
11:39–52	156	7:1–23	168	20:19	153
		7:1–5	153	20:20	153
Matthew		7:14–23	153	20:27–40	153
1:45–46	153	8:11	153	20:41	153
2:16–18	483	8:15	153	20:45–47	153
3:7–10	154	10:2	153	22:47–53	154
5:20	154	11:27–33	153		

John
1:24	155
2:20	466
3:1	155
4:1	155
4:9	215
7:32–52	155
8:3	155
8:13	155
9:1–41	155
9:22–35	157, 162
11:46–47	155
11:57	155
12:19	155
12:42	155, 157, 162
18:3	155

Acts
2:9–11	245
4:1–2	155
4:1	140
5	143
5:17–39	155
5:17	140, 155
5:34	155, 158
22:3	156
22:30–23:10	156
23	156
23:6–10	140
23:6	156
23:8	140, 156
23:9	168

2 Peter
3:8	288

Philippians
3:4–6	152

Jude
9	103, 272

Hebrews
5	277
5:7	277

Revelation
13	291
17	291
20:4	288

APOCRYPHA
Tobit
14:4–7	232

Judith
4:2–3	101
4:6–8	101
4:11–15	101
4:12	101
4:14–15	101
8:6	101
8:21	101
8:24	101
9	100
9:8	101
9:13	101
11:12–15	100
11:13	101
11:14	101
12:1–4	100
12:6–8	100
12:17–19	100
16:16–20	101
16:22	101

Wisdom of Solomon
1:13–15	274
2:23	274
3:4	274
3:7–9	110
4:1	274
8:13	274
8:17	274
8:19–20	274
11–19	109
12:24–13:19	110
15:3	274
15:18–19	110

Ecclesiasticus
10:5	166
24	102
36:20–21	283
38:24–39:11	167
38:24	167
39:1–3	283
44–49	264, 268
46:1	283
48:24–25	283
50:1–24	204
50:25–26	204, 216

Baruch
1:1–14	101
1:15–3:8	101, 102
3:9–4:4	101, 102
4:1	102
4:5–5:9	101

1 Maccabees
1	339, 372
1:10–15	319
1:10	21
1:11	252
1:14–15	332
1:16–63	345, 346
1:16–24	342, 347
1:19	35
1:20–28	21
1:21	249
1:29–40	22
1:29–36	348
1:34	346
1:41–61	497
1:41–51	352
1:41–43	251
1:43	346
1:48	269
1:54–64	22
1:54–61	497
1:54	354–56
1:56–58	352
1:56–57	82
1:59	354, 356
1:60–62	269
1:60–61	351
2	359, 360, 498
2:1–3:9	358

2:39–42	136	5:25–26	223	8	19
2:42–43	359	5:42	166	8:1–32	378
2:42	89, 136, 358	5:65–68	220	8:17–18	378
2:44–48	361	6:1–16	23, 373	8:22–32	19
2:44	362	6:5–7	24	8:23–32	84
2:46	269	6:7	373	8:23–30	379
2:65–66	360	6:17–47	23	8:26	379
2:70	22	6:18–63	300	8:28	379
3	124	6:18–27	374	8:31–32	379
3:1–37	362	6:20	18, 19	9:1–22	377
3:8	361	6:21	328	9:1–3	17
3:10–12	362	6:28	300	9:3	17, 19, 35
3:10	208	6:34	23	9:19	382
3:13–26	363	6:47–54	384	9:23–12:53	389
3:13	363	6:48–54	374	9:23–31	389
3:14	363	6:48–53	34	9:23	328
3:15	328, 363	6:49–50	23	9:24	389
3:25–26	363	6:49	23	9:25	328
3:27–4:25	363	6:53	23	9:27	283, 285
3:27–37	363	6:55–63	24, 374	9:33	390
3:32–37	25	6:57–59	86	9:34	390
3:37–40	364	6:57	300	9:35	223
3:37	22	6:60	300	9:36–42	223
3:38–4:35	22	6:63	300	9:42–49	390
3:38	363	7–9	380	9:43–49	359
3:39	383	7:1–43	17	9:50–53	390
3:57	364	7:1–25	19	9:50	52
4:1–24	365	7:1	17, 19	9:52	58, 397
4:1–15	384	7:5–7	381	9:54–56	390
4:1–2	365	7:5	328, 375	9:54	391
4:3–4	364	7:12–18	382	9:57–73	390
4:3	364	7:12–16	136	9:57	391
4:26–35	365	7:12–14	381	9:58	328, 391
4:28–35	366	7:12–13	167	9:62	390
4:28–59	25	7:13	167	9:66	390
4:28	25, 366	7:14	381	9:69	328
4:36–59	22, 24, 370	7:20–21	382	9:70	393
4:38	370	7:21–22	382	9:73	328, 392, 393
4:42–58	370	7:23–24	382		
4:43–47	356	7:27–32	376	10	20
4:44–46	283	7:29–30	376	10:1–21	17
4:52–59	370	7:33–38	377	10:1–14	393
4:52	35, 371	7:36–38	377	10:1–6	301
4:60–6:63	371	7:39–50	376	10:1	17, 18, 20, 391, 392
5	23	7:39	377		
5:3	220	7:43	19	10:7	393
5:6–7	365	7:50–8:1	378	10:14	393

1 Maccabees (cont.)

10:18–45	124, 126	12:39–53	401	15:10–14	408
10:18–20	84, 394	13:1–16:17	402	15:15–24	405
10:20	393	13:1–30	401	15:15–21	405
10:21	17, 18, 20	13:1–9	402	15:16–24	84
10:22–47	301	13:31	403	15:25–26	408
10:25–45	84, 393, 395	13:33	403	15:27–36	408
10:37	300, 381	13:35–41	406	15:32–36	411
10:61	328	13:35–40	407	15:33–35	233
10:65–66	395	13:27–29	72	15:38–16:10	409
10:65	393	13:36–40	84, 124, 126	15:38–40	54
10:67–89	395	13:36	404	16:2–3	409
10:69	395	13:41–42	403	16:11–17	409
10:73	392	13:41	35	16:11–12	127
10:74–76	52	13:42	92	16:14	34, 36, 409
10:89	393, 397	13:43–16:24	92	16:18–24	409
11	25	13:43–48	54		
11:1–12	396	13:43	407	*2 Maccabees*	
11:9	396	13:49–52	407	1–2	83
11:10	396	13:52	407, 408	1:1–10	84, 85
11:13–19	396	13:53	407	1:1–9 Eng:	85
11:16–17	398	14–15	406	1:7	85
11:23–37	396	14	360, 410	1:9	371
11:25	328	14:1–3	20	1:10–2:18	84, 85, 238
11:28	397	14:1	20, 408	1:10	85
11:30–37	84, 124, 126	14:4–15	404	2:1–17	347
11:38–53	397	14:5	52, 407	2:13–15	82
11:39	397	14:8	126	2:19–32	81
11:54–59	397	14:12	126	3–4	319
11:57	84, 397	14:16–24	405	3	259, 312
11:60–74	398	14:16–18	405	3:2–6	124, 321
11:60	397	14:20–23	84, 407	3:2–3	300
11:61–62	58	14:24	405	3:4–40	300
11:63–74	44	14:27–47	404	3:4–6	334
11:63	43	14:27–45	360	3:4	334, 335
11:73	43	14:27	36	3:11	318
12:1–23	399	14:28	404	4	315, 324, 329, 339, 494
12:6–23	407	14:29–30	360		
12:6–18	84	14:33	58	4:7–34	317
12:6–12	399	14:34	52, 54, 407	4:7–10	319, 322
12:6	394	14:37	408	4:8	124, 319
12:7–23	399	14:38–39	406	4:9	324, 334
12:20–23	84	14:40	406, 407	4:10–15	330
12:24–32	398	14:41	283	4:11	89, 429
12:33–38	398	14:46	404	4:18–20	331
12:33–34	52, 407	15	406, 407	4:19	334
12:35	394	15:2–9	84		
		15:6	76		

Index of References 569

4:21–22	334, 342, 355	7:23	273	12	372
		8:1–7	358, 362	12:2	365, 376
4:23–26	334	8:1	362, 363	12:3–7	52
4:25	336	8:8–36	363, 365	12:8–9	54
4:27–34	336	8:8–9	364	12:10–45	372
4:27–28	347	8:8	349, 363, 383	12:10–12	223
4:32–34	288			12:43–45	273
4:39–42	252, 328, 336	8:9	364, 383	13	300
		8:16	365, 384	13:1–26	374
4:43–44	328	8:20	246	13:1	19
4:45	363	8:22	365	13:3–8	252, 355
5–7	345	8:28	365	13:14	374
5	21, 496	8:30–36	365	13:19–23	374
5:1–26	345	8:30–33	365	13:22–24	374
5:1	342	8:32–33	372	13:22	384
5:5	344	8:33	365	13:23–24	374
5:7	496	8:34–36	365	14–15	380
5:8	223	9:1–29	371	14:3–13	375, 381
5:11–14	349	9:9–27	372	14:3–4	19
5:15–21	342	9:19–29	84	14:4	19
5:15–16	343	9:19–27	85	14:6	136, 137
5:15	355	9:20	373	14:12	376, 382
5:17–20	249	10:1–9	370	14:15–25	376
5:22–23	208	10:1–8	85	14:25	376
5:22	364	10:3	371	14:26–15:36	376
5:23–26	348, 349	10:5	370	14:31–36	377
5:24	348, 362	10:10–12:45	371	14:34–36	377
5:27	358	10:10–11:38	365	14:46	273
6	345	10:14–38	372	15:30–35	377
6:1–11	348, 497	10:24–38	372		
6:1–4	354	11	86, 375	PSEUDEPIGRAPHA	
6:1–2	206, 208, 345, 345	11:1–21	366	*1 Enoch*	
		11:16–21	84, 86, 375	1–36	271, 290
6:2	356, 357	11:17–21	368	10:6	274
6:7	356, 357	11:22–26	84, 86, 87, 375, 376	22	274, 290
6:8	327			37–72	96
6:10–11	352	11:23–26	351, 369	46:6	274
6:10	351	11:24–25	352	51:1	274
6:11	349, 351	11:24	327	61:5	274
6:12–16	249	11:27–33	87	81–84	96
6:18–31	167, 351	11:27–38	351, 352	83–90	96
7	280, 290, 345, 350, 385, 497	11:27–33	366, 375	83–85	96
		11:29–32	338	83–108	96
		11:30	367	86–89	96
7:9	273	11:33	367	89:73–90:5	96
7:11	273	11:34–38	84, 87, 368, 375	90–105	96
7:14	273			90:6–15	96

Index of References

1 Enoch (cont.)

90:33	274
91:10	274
91:12–17	96, 290
92:3–4	274
93	96
93:2–9	290
98:2	97
99:5	97
102:3–104:6	274
102:5–11	97
103–104	97
104:2	97, 274
104:5	274
104:10–12	97
105–7	96
108	96
108:11–12	97

2 Baruch

53–74	290

3 Maccabees

1:1–7	235
1:3	10
1:8–2:24	235
2:25–6:22	235
6:23–29	235
6:30–7:23	235
7:10	10

4 Ezra

7:28	288
11–12	291
13:39–47	233, 244
14:48	288

4 Maccabees

5:4	167

Jubilees

1:29	273
2:25–33	99
3:30–31	333
4:30	288
5:1–11	271
6:17–31	99
6:32–38	99
10:1–14	272
15:1–4	99
17:15–18	272
17:20–31	99
22:1–9	99
22:1–4	232
23:20–22	273, 290
23:22–31	273
23:31	99
30:18–20	99
31:11–17	99
32:27–29	99
34:17–19	99
35–38	232
44:1–4	99
49	99
48:9–19	272
50	99
50:6–13	98

Letter of (Pseudo-) Aristeas

4	234
9–40	105
12–14	234
83–120	105
128–71	105
134–43	105

Liber Antiquitatum Biblicarum

28:6–10	285

Life of Adam and Eve

12–16	272

Psalms of Solomon

1:4–8	107
2:1–14	107, 233
2:2–5	107
2:15–31	107
2:31	107
3:10–12	273
3:11–12	107
4	107
7–18	276
8:1–22	107, 233
8:11–22	107
13:11	273
14:1–5	273
14:3–5	107
14:6–9	273
14:9–10	107
15:12–13	273
17–18	107, 233, 279
17:5–18	107, 233
17:5–15	107
17:21	276
17:22–25	277
17:22	107
17:35	276

Sibylline Oracles

3	279
3:46–63	279
3:75–92	279
3:193	279
3:318	279
3:350–80	279
3:350–64	291
3:489–829	279
3:520–72	275, 291
3:608	279
3:652	279
3:702–31	279
3:741–95	279
4:130–48	291
5:162–78	291

Testament of Abraham

A 19:7	288
B 7:15–16	288

Testament of Levi

5–7	203

Testament of Moses

5:1–6:1	103
6:2–9	102
6:2–6	443
8–9	102
8	351

Index of References

8:1	351	1.4	188	CD	
8:3	351	1.9–11	188	1.1–2.1	191
9	281	2.11	277	1.1–11	193
				1.5–11	288
DEAD SEA SCROLLS		*1QpHab*		1.5–6	193
1QH		2.12	191	1.11–12	274
3.19–22	275	2.14	191	2.18–21	271
3.27–36	275	3.4	191	4.10–5.2	188
6.29	275	3.9	191	4.12–21	271
6.34	275	7.3–5	284	5.17–19	271
11.3–14	275			6.11–20	187
11.12	275	*4Q266*		7.6–7	188
11.19–22	275	2.1–11	193	7.6	186
11.27–36	275			9.10–16	187
14.29	275	*4Q331*		10.10–13	187
14.34	275	frg. 1 col. 2 l. 7	420	10.14–11.18	98, 187
19.3–14	275			11.18–21	187
19.12	275	*4Q332*		12.1–2	187, 188
		frg. 2, l. 4	420	12.19–14.16	186
1QM				12.23–13.1	277
1.2	191	*4Q372*		14.12–16	187
1.4	191	ll. 11–14	203	15.5	188
1.6	191			16.10–12	188
1.9	191	*4Q521*		16.13	187
1.10–11	271	2.II.12–13	278	19.2–3	188
1.12	191	2.II.7–8	278	19.2	186
7.3	188			19.10–11	277
		4QFlor.		20.14–15	289
1QS		frag. 1, II, 3, 24, 5.3			
1.11–12	187		283	MISHNAH	
3.4–5	187			*Ḥagigah*	
3.13–4.26	271	*4QpHab*		2.7	157
4.11–14	275	7.1–6	287		
4.12	271			*Makkot*	
5.1–22	187	*4QpNah*		1.6	157
5.13–14	187	1.5	191		
6.2	187	1.6–7	422	*Menaḥot*	
6.13–23	187	1.7–8	191	10.3	157
6.16–23	187	2.2	191		
6.25	187			*Niddah*	
9.9–11	283	2		4.2	158
9.11	277	2.6–8	289		
7.2–3	187			*Parah*	
7.13	187	*11QMelch*		3.7	157, 159
		2.9	277		
1QSa		2.17–18	277	*Soṭah*	
1.1	274			3.4	157

Sukkah	
4.9	421

Tohorot	
4.12	157

Yadayim	
4.6–8	158, 160

BABYLONIAN TALMUD
Baba Batra	
164a–b	34

Qiddušin	
76a	195

Sukkah	
48b	421

Taanit	
23a	424

Yoma	
26b	421

TOSEFTA
Berakot	
3.25	158

Ḥagigah	
3.35	158, 159

Parah	
3.8	158, 159

Roš Haššanah	
1.15	158

Šabbat	
1.15	158

Sanhedrin	
6.6	158

Soṭah	
15.11–12	158

Sukkah	
3.1	158

Yadayim	
2.20	158, 160

Yoma	
1.8	158

PHILO
De cherubin	
27	284

Legatio ad Gaium	
155–58	244
155–56	243
314–15	241

De migratione Abrahami	
34–35	284

Hypothetica	
11.1	171, 186
11.4–5	171
11.4	187
11.5	187
11.6	171
11.8–9	171
11.11	187
11.12	171
11.14–17	171

Quod omnis probus liber sit	
75–87	170
75	171, 187
76	171, 186
79	171
81	187
84	171
85–86	171, 187
86	187

Quis rerum divinarum heres sit	
259–66	284

De somnis	
2.164–65	284
2.250	233

De specialibus legibus	
1.65	284
4.178	233

De vita Mosis	
1.263–99	284
1.264–68	284
2.187	284
2.188–91	284
2.264–65	284
2.268–69	284

JOSEPHUS
Against Apion	
1.1 §1	288
1.8 §40–41	286
§37–43	95
§42	96
2.7–8	§§79–96
	117
2.21	
§184–87	151
§193–94	151

Jewish Antiquities	
Proem. 3	
§13	288
1.3.9	
§108	94
3.16.2	
§408	425
4.7.2	
§165	284
4.8.1–46	
§§176–314	95
6.5.6	
§359	285
6.6.3	
§115	285
6.12.4–5	
§254	285
§257	285

7.4.1		12.5.5–6.3		13.3.1–3	
§76	285	§§257–84	358	§§62–73	236
8.15.6		12.5.5		13.3.2	
§418	284	§§257–64	92	§70	237
9.14.3		§§258–64	206	13.3.3	
§291	205	§261	208, 362	§72	237
10.11.4		12.6.4–7.2		13.4.3	
§§245–49	284	§§285–97	362	§§87–88	395
10.11.7		12.6.4		13.4.5–9	
§§267–69	284	§286	362	§§103–22	92
§280	284	12.7.1		13.4.6	
11.4.8		§287	208	§§106–8	396
§111	435	§288	363	13.4.7	
11.5.2		§289	363	§§113–14	396
§133	233, 244	12.7.2–4		13.4.9	
11.7.2–8.7		§§293–312	363	§§129–30	397
§§302–47	203	12.7.2		13.5.1	
11.7.6		§§293–94	363	§131	397
§322	284	12.7.5		13.5.3	
11.8.6		§§313–15	365, 371	§143	397
§341	205	12.7.6–7		13.5.4	
12.3.3–4		§§316–25	370	§146	397
§§129–46	311	12.8.1–9.7		13.5.5–7	
12.3.3		§§327–88	371	§§148–62	398
§142	166	12.9.4–5		13.5.6	
12.3.4		§§367–78	384	§154	43
§§147–53	238	12.9.7		13.5.9	
12.4.1		§§383–85	375	§§171–72	139, 147
§156	204	§385	252, 355	13.5.10	
12.4.3		§387	236, 237	§174	398
§168	215	12.10.1–11.2		13.5.11	
§169	214	§§389–434	380	§186	408
12.4.10		12.10.6		13.6.7–7.4	
§§225–27	399	§414	392	§§215–29	402
12.5.1		§419	392	§§213–28	402
§§237–13.7.4 §229		12.11.2		13.6.7	
	92	§434	392	§§215–17	408
§§237–41	316, 317, 319	13.1.1–6.6		§215	407
		§§1–212	389	13.7.1	
§§237–40	334	13.2.3		§218	403
§§237–38	236	§46	393, 394	13.7.2	
12.5.2–4		13.2.4–34		§§223–24	408
§§242–56	345	§§59–79	92	§§223	408
12.5.2–3		13.2.4		13.7.3	
§§242–46	348	§§58–61	395	§§226–27	409
12.5.2		13.3		13.7.4–10.7	
§§242–56	346	§§358–64	58	§§228–300	409

Josephus, *Ant.* (cont.)		13.11.1–3		§9	93, 443
13.7.4–8.1		§§301–19	417	14.1.4	
§§228–35	34	§§318–19	417	§18	224
13.7.6		13.11.1		14.2.1–2	
§214	92	§301	262	§25	432
13.8.1		13.11.2		§21	432
§230	410	§308	417	14.3.1	
13.8.4		§311	172	§§35–36	93
§249	411	13.11.3		14.3.2	
§§251–52	411	§318	72, 225	§41	432
13.9.1		§319	226, 419	14.4.3	
§§254–58	71	13.12.1–16.1		§66	26, 28, 36
§254	413	§§320–406	419	14.4.4	
§§255–56	208	13.12.1		§75	61
§255	413	§§321–22	416	14.4.5	
§§257–58	220, 443	13.12.5		§77	447
§257	59, 70	§338	45	§78	129, 243
§258	413	13.12.6		14.5.1–7.3	
13.9.2		§347	94, 118	§§80–122	435
§§259–66	414	13.13.3		14.5.2	
13.9.3–10.1		§357	466	§85	243
§§267–74	411	§360	224	14.5.4	
13.9.3		13.15.1		§91	434
§269	302	§§387–391	304	14.6.1	
13.10.1		§§389–91	423	§97	431
§273	413	13.15.3–4		14.6.	
13.10.2–3		§§393–97	62, 63	§99	442
§§275–81	208	13.15.3		14.6.3	
13.10.2		§393	62	§101	442
§§275–76	414	13.15.4		14.6.4	
§275	209, 414	§§395–97	423	§103	435
§§276–78	414	§395	54	§104	93, 94, 118, 435
13.10.3		§397	224, 413		
§280	49, 70, 414	13.15.5–16.5		14.7.1	
		§§401–23	148	§§105–6	129
§§282–83	416	13.16.1–6		14.7.2	
13.10.4		§§407–32	424	§§111–118	93
§§284–87	235, 416	13.16.1		14.7.3	
13.10.5–7		§407	442	§121	443
§§288–99	147, 416	13.16.2		14.7.4–9.1	
13.10.5		§409	148	§§123–57	439
§288	161	14.1.1–4.5		14.7.4	
13.10.6		§§1–79	431	§126	439
§§293–98	139	14.1.2		14.8.1–3	
13.10.7		§4	27	§§127–39	239
§299	284, 416	14.1.3		14.8.1	
§300	416	§8	442	§127	439, 442

§§131–32	442	14.10.16		14.16.4	
14.8.2		§234	239	§487	27, 28, 36, 455
§§133–36	439	14.10.18–19			
14.8.5		§§236–40	239	§§489–90	455
§§144–48	405, 406, 440	14.10.20		15–17	94
		§§241–43	239	15.1.1	
§144	442	14.10.21		§3	148
§§148–55	416	§§244–46	240	15.1.2	
§148	440	14.10.25		§§5–9	455
§151	440	§§262–64	239	§§8–10	455
14.9.1		14.10.22		15.3.5–9	
§§156–57	441	§§247–55	415	§§62–87	472
§157	440	14.11.2		§§65–87	457
14.9.2–14.4		§§271–76	129	15.3.5	
§§158–385	444	14.11.3		§65	457
14.9.2–13.2		§277	445	15.3.8	
§§158–329	442	14.11.4		§79	456
14.9.2		§283	442	15.4.1–2	
§158	442, 444	14.11.6		§§94–96	456
14.9.3		§290	445	15.4.2	
§165	440	14.12.2–6		§§96–103	131, 456
14.9.4		§§304–23	240	15.5.1	
§168	440	14.13.9		§110	458
§172	440	§364	59, 70	15.6.2	
§175	486	14.14.5		§168	474
14.10.1–26		§§386–87	452	15.6.5	
§§185–267	238	§386	451	§§183–86	473
14.10.2–8		§389	36	15.6.6	
§§190–216	239	§403	443, 484	§§189–93	459
14.10.2		14.15.3		15.6.7	
§190	440	§408	215, 218	§195	451, 461
14.10.6		14.15.4		15.7.1–4	
§§202–3	128	§413	215, 218	§§202–34	473
§202	462	14.15.6		15.7.3	
14.10.8		§§432–33	453	§217	462
§216–16	240	14.15.10		15.7.9	
14.10.9–10		§450	454	§§253–55	221
§§217–22	239	14.15.14		§254	463
14.10.11–12		§467	215, 218	15.8.1–3	
§§223–27	239	14.16.1		§§276–81	465
14.10.11		§468	454	15.8.1–2	
§224	239	14.16.2		§§267–79	465, 485
14.10.13		§473	28, 29, 33, 455	15.8.5	
§§228–30	239			§§292–93	465
14.10.14		§475	28, 29, 33	§292	465
§§231–32	239			§293	466
				§§296–98	465

Josephus, *Ant.* (cont.)		§145	131, 466	17.11.2	
15.9.1–7		16.6.1–2		§§304–10	483
§§380–425	466	§§161–65	241	17.12.1–2	
15.9.1–2		§§160–61	241	§§324–38	243
§§299–316	486	16.7.1		17.13.2	
15.9.3		§§186–86	93	§342	31, 215, 219
§318	465	16.7.6			
15.9.4		§§220–28	476	17.13.3	
§§323–25	465	§§221–25	485	§§347–48	172
15.9.5		16.9.1–4		18.1.1	
§§326–30	466	§§271–99	469	§§4–8	233
15.9.6		16.10.8–9		18.1.3	
§§331–41	466	§§335–55	469	§§4–23	146
§341	48, 466	17.1.3		§§12–17	151
15.10.1		§20	215, 219	§§15–17	161
§343	462	17.2.1–3		18.1.4	
15.10.3		§§23–32	246, 471	§§16–17	139
§360	462	17.2.1–2		18.1.5	
15.10.4		§§23–28	246	§§18–22	170
§§365–72	486	§§23–27	131	§18	171
§§368–71	149	17.2.4–3.1		§19	171, 187
15.10.5		§§41–47	145	§20	171, 187
§373	172	17.3.2		§21	171
15.11.1		§§52–57	471	§22	171
§380	466, 468	17.4.2		18.1.7	
§385	485	§69	215, 219	§17	162
16.1.1		17.6.3		18.2.1	
§§1–5	463	§156	463	§26	31
§§6–11	474	17.6.4		18.2.2	
16.2.1		§167	29	§§29–30	210
§13	465	17.6.5–8.3		§30	214
16.2.3–7		§§168–99	30	18.4.1–2	
§§166–73	241	17.8.1		§§85–89	211
16.2.3–5		§191	29, 36	18.4.6	
§§27–65	487	17.8.3		§106	31
16.2.5		§199	461	18.5.4	
§§64–65	486	17.9.1–2		§130	420
16.3.3		§§209–10	463	18.6.4	
§86	475	17.9.3		§167	215, 219
16.4.1		§213	29	18.6.10	
§90	475	17.10.2		§225	31
16.5.1		§255	465	19.8.2	
§136	466	17.10.5		§352	131
16.5.2		§271	45	20.5.1	
§§142–43	466	17.10.9		§97	284
§143	465	§289	45	20.5.2	
§144	465			§100	10, 109

Index of References

20.6.1–3		1.2.2		1.7.6	
§§118–36	211	§50	408	§153	128
20.6.1		§§52–53	409	1.8.1–9	
§118	211	1.2.3–8		§§159–82	435
§120	211	§§54–69	409	1.8.3	
20.6.2		1.2.3		§163	243
§129	212	§§50–54	402	1.8.5	
20.6.3		§56	410	§170	434
§136	212	1.2.5		1.8.7	
20.8.6		§61	411	§§175–77	437
§169	284	1.2.6–7		§175	442
20.8.10		§§63–65	208	§178	435
§188	284	1.2.7		1.8.9	
20.9.1		§65	414	§181	443
§199	140	§66	70	1.9.1–10.4	
20.9.7		1.2.8		§§183–203	439
§§219–23	131	§67	416	1.9.2	
§§219–20	466	§§68–69	284	§§185–86	439
§222	131	§68	416	1.9.3	
20.10.3		§69	416	§§187–88	442
§237	392, 394	1.3.1–6		1.9.4	
§238	394	§§70–84	417	§190	442
20.10.4		1.3.1		§§191–92	439
§§243–44	431	§70	262	1.10.3	
		1.33.3		§199	442
Jewish War		§652	463	1.10.4	
1.Pref.2		1.4.1–8		§§201–3	441
§5	233, 244	§§85–106	303, 419	§§202–3	440
1.1.1–2.2		1.4.7		§203	442, 444
§§31–53	92	§§99–102	304, 423	1.10.4–14.4	
1.1.1–4		1.4.8		§§203–85	444
§§31–39	316, 317, 319	§104	62	1.10.4–12.7	
1.1.1–2		1.5.1–4		§§203–47	442
§§31–35	346	§§107–19	424	1.10.5	
1.1.2		1.5.1		§207	442
§§34–35	345	§109	442	1.10.6	
1.1.3–6		1.5.2–3		§§208–9	442
§§36–47	358	§§110–14	145	1.11.1–2	
1.1.3		§110	425	§§218–22	129
§§36–37	360	1.6.1–7.7		1.11.3	
§37	360	§§120–58	431	§223	445
1.1.5		1.6.1		1.11.4	
§§41–46	384	§120	431	§225	446
1.2.1		1.6.2		1.11.7	
§§48–49	389	§123	442	§232	445
		1.6.9		1.15.1–20.3	
		§180	243	§§286–393	451

Josephus, *Ant.* (cont.)

1.18.2		1.26.3		2.8.12		
§351	28, 455	§529	166	§159	172, 285	
1.18.5		1.29.2		2.8.13		
§§361–62	131, 456	§571	145	§160	172	
1.20.1		1.29.3		2.8.14		
§§388–90	459	§§574–77	469, 471	§§162–66	146	
1.20.3–33.9		1.33.8		§§164–66	138	
§§393–673	461	§665	29	2.8.2–13		
1.20.3–4		2.1.2		§§120–61	170	
§§396–400	462	§5	479	2.8.2		
1.20.4		2.1.3		§§120–2	171	
§399	468	§8	463	2.8.3		
1.21.1		§10	29	§122	171, 187	
§401	465, 468	2.12.3–7		§123	171	
§402	465	§§232–46	211	2.8.4		
1.21.2		2.12.3		§124	171, 186	
§403	465	§232	211	§126	171	
1.21.5–7		2.12.6		2.8.5		
§§408–14	466	§§241–42	212	§§128–32	171	
1.21.8		2.12.7		§128	171	
§415	465	§245	212	§129	171, 187	
§416	466	2.17.2–3		§132	171, 187	
1.21.9		§§410–11	147	2.8.6		
§417	465, 466	2.17.4		§135	171	
§418	465, 466	§421	246	§136	171	
1.21.10		2.18.1		2.8.7		
§§419–21	465	§459	43	§§137–42	171, 187	
1.21.11–12		2.20.4		§142	171	
§§422–28	466	§567	172	2.8.8		
1.21.12		2.4.1		§§143–44	171	
§426	93	§56	45	§147	172, 187	
1.22.1		2.5.1		2.8.9		
§§432–33	475	§68	45	§147	187	
1.22.2–4		2.5.2–3		2.9.5		
§§436–44	472	§§72–79	221	§180	31	
1.23.1–27.6		2.6.2		2.13.5		
§§445–551	474	§§84–86	483	§§261–63	284	
1.23.3		2.6.3		2.17.4		
§452	475	§98	54	§421	471	
1.24.3		2.7.1–2		2.19.8		
§479	166	§§101–10	243	§§546–50	363	
1.24.5		2.7.3		3.2.1		
§483	468	§111	31	§11	172	
1.24.6		2.8.10		3.4.2		
§487	476	§150	171	§68	225	
		2.8.11		3.7.1–32		
		§§154–58	171	§§289–315	212	

3.7.32		§9	95	§10–	68	397, 403
§308	212		12	149,	70	304
3.8.3				151		
§§351–53	285	§§10–11	171		Cassius Dio	
4.4.3		§12	95, 149		37.16	26
§236	183	5			37.16.4	28
5.4.1		§21	149		39.55	435, 437
§139	408	11			47.27	445
5.13.1		§§46–61	471		49.22	455
§532	166	38			49.22.4	28
6.5.2		§§189–94	151		49.23.1	27, 33
§§285–87	284	§191	149		53.29	467
6.5.4		39			54.7	467
§311	289	§§196–98	150		54.9	462
§§312–313	289	52				
6.6.2		§269	215, 219		Cicero	
§343	233, 244	76			Pro Sestio	
7.6.2		§§424–25	284		43	436
§§171–77	465					
7.8.3–4		APOSTOLIC FATHERS			Diodorus Siculus	
§§280–303	465	Barnabas			2.48.6–9	113
7.10.2–4		15.4	288		3.43.5	223
§§423–36	236				19.98–99	113
7.10.2		CLASSICAL AND ANCIENT			30.2	341
§423	237	CHRISTIAN LITERATURE			30.15–16	314, 342
7.10.3		Ammianus Marcellinus			31.32a	393
§427	237	22.13.1	354		32.9c–d	395, 396
7.10.4					32.10.1	396
§§433–36	237	Appian			33.3–4a	397
7.11.1–3		Bella civilia			33.3–4	395
§§437–50	284	4.63	445		33.4.1–4	397
15.9.1–7		5.75.319	462		33.28	403
§§380–425	466	5.75.319	27		33.28a	403
16.7.6		13–18	111		34/35.1.1–5	117, 410
§§220–25	470				34/35.1.1–2	410
16.9.1		Mithridatica			34/35.1.3–4	351, 356
§279	470	117	243		34/35.1.3	113
16.10.8		571	243		34/35.1.4–5	410
§343	470				40.2	378, 432
17.1.1		Syriaca			40.3	113
§10	470	8.51	436			
		11.67	393, 395,		Eusebius	
Life			408		Historia ecclesiastica	
1.11		11.68	408		1.7.11	443
§§46–61	246	49	304			
2		66	314		Praeparatio evangelica	
					8	170

Jerome
Commentariorum in Danielum
8.9	354, 357
11.31	354, 357

Justin
34.2.7	314
35.1.6–8	393
35.1.6–24	393
35.1.9	395
35.2.1–4	395, 396
36.1.1–6	408
36.1.7	403
36.3.9	378, 400
38.9.1–3	408
38.9.1	411
39.1–9	302
39.1.1–2	411
39.4	235
40.2.2	304
52	443

Libanius
Oracles
60.12	354

Livy
Perioch
6.147	354
42.29.5–6	314
52	395
55	403

Macrobius
Saturnalia
2.4.11	484

Origen
De principiis
3.2.1	103

Pliny the Elder
Naturalis historia
5.15.74	61
5.73	170
60.28.160	467

Plutarch
Aemilius Paullus
17.7–10	30, 479

Anthony
36	455

Moralia
184E–F	410

Pompeius
45.1–2	243

Polybius
De legat. gent.
5.71.3	61
5.79	383
26.1	249
26.1.10–11	354
26.1a	249
28.1	314, 341, 342
28.18	250
28.20–21	314, 342
28.20	342
29.27	343
30.25.13	353
31.33.1–5	379
32.2.1–3	379
33.3.13	379
33.15.1–2	20, 393
33.18	301
33.18.1–14	20
33.18.6–14	393
33.18.6–13	393

Quintus Curtius
4.8.9–11	203

Strabo
14.5.2	408
16.2.35–37	252
16.2.28–46 §759–65	118
16.2.29	61
16.2.30	118
16.2.34	221, 222
16.2.40	26
16.4.3	467
16.4.8	223

Suetonius
Divus Augustus
76.2	26

Julius
84	243

Syncellus
351.13	408
355	47, 61

Tacitus
Historiae
5.8	250
5.4.2	345
5.8.2	351

Thucydides
1.6.5–6	332

Valerius Maximus
1.3.3	241

OSTRACA
Yaḥad
line 8	183, 184

INSCRIPTIONS
Genizah fragment Cambridge T-S
16.94	203

TAD
C1.1:1	166
C1.1:42	166

Index of Authors

Abegg, M. Jr 176
Abel, F.-M. 79
Adler, E. N. 118, 197, 199
Aharoni, Y. 60
Albani, M. 97
Albright, W. F. 52
Alexander, P. S. 177
Allison, D. C. 482, 483
Alon, G. 205, 206
Alston, R. 440, 450
Altheim, F. 312
Ameling, W. 53, 54, 74
Amitay, O. 398, 400
Applebaum, S. H. 64, 68, 69, 71, 123, 127–32, 464, 465
Arav, R. 41–43, 46–53, 55, 57–62, 66
Archer, G. L. 116, 117
Ariel, D. T. 43, 47, 55, 75–77
Atkinson, K. 106, 275, 402, 403, 408, 409, 417, 419, 424, 431
Aune, D. E. 281, 286
Austin, M. M. 74
Avi-Yonah, M. 41, 461
Avigad, N. 55, 56, 75
Aymard, A. 312

Babota, V. 378, 388, 391, 393, 402, 403, 407
Bagnall, R. S. 74
Baltrusch, E. 241, 242, 414, 424, 429, 449, 457, 480, 483
Bar-Adon, P. 178
Bar-Kochva, B. 13, 15, 17, 19, 20, 22–25, 80, 81, 83, 86–88, 106, 248, 254, 257, 318, 320, 340, 349, 359, 361–66, 371, 373, 374, 376, 377, 380, 383, 384, 389
Bar-Nathan, R. 53
Barag, D. 205, 209, 419
Barclay, J. M. G. 91
Barnes, T. D. 26, 27
Barone, F. P. 114

Barth, F. 5, 8
Bartlett, J. R. 79, 388, 398
Barthélemy, D. 263, 266
Baumgarten, A. I. 134, 143, 173
Baumgarten, J. M. 190
Becker, M. 116, 117, 340, 350, 354, 357
Ben-Dor, M. 55, 464
Ben-Hayyim, Z. 194, 196–98
Benoit, P. 32–34
Bergren, T. A. 79, 83, 85
Berlin, A. M. 41–44, 47, 49, 50, 54, 56, 60, 64, 67–74, 123, 126, 127, 225, 226, 269, 270
Bernegger, P. M. 26, 27, 29
Bernhardt, J. C. 13–17, 32, 79, 236, 237, 248, 249, 251, 310, 321, 335, 340, 350, 352–54, 356–59, 367, 368, 371, 379, 388, 393, 400, 402, 404–407, 414
Berthelot, K. 176, 231, 232
Bickerman, E. J. 13, 14, 16–18, 21, 24, 26, 28, 32, 79, 81, 83, 85, 86, 205–207, 236, 238, 241, 242, 248, 249, 251, 252, 304, 310, 337, 340, 348, 349, 356–58, 378, 389, 393, 398, 399
Biran, A. 43
Bivar, A. D. H. 226, 230
Bleicken, J. 440, 450
Bloch-Smith, E. 7, 8
Bloedhorn, H. 55, 56, 75
Blosser, D. 32
Boccaccini, G. 181, 189
Bohak, G. 5, 236, 238
Bons, E. 107
Borchardt, F. 79
Bowersock, G. W. 220, 224, 225
Bowman, J. 194, 195, 197–200
Braund, D. C. 129, 132, 343, 433, 435, 461
Braunert, H. 341
Braverman, J. 116
Brennan, T. C. 414, 415

Brenner, A. 99, 100
Brett, M. G. 5, 8
Bringmann, K. 13, 14, 17–21, 24, 83, 86–88, 124, 205, 207, 248, 249, 251, 252, 255, 310, 325, 327, 334, 338, 340, 348, 349, 356, 358, 371
Briscoe, J. 113
Brock, S. P. 107, 263, 266, 267
Brodersen, K. 74, 111
Brooke, G. J. 176, 178, 190, 275, 278
Broshi, M. 88, 90, 129, 131, 181, 185, 190, 191
Brown, T. S. 111
Brownlee, W. H. 13, 14, 190, 191
Bruggen, J. van 26, 27, 29, 30, 33
Bunge, J. G. 88, 248, 260, 312
Burgmann, H. 389, 393
Burstein, S. M. 74

Calduch-Benages, N. 108
Callaway, P. R. 176
Campbell, E. F., Jr 51
Cancik, H. 111
Capdetrey, L. 389, 393
Cardauns, B. 398
Cargill, R. R. 176, 180, 185
Cary, M. 429
Cavallin, H. C. C. 272
Champion, C. B. 115
Chancey, M. A. 41
Charles, R. H. 88, 97
Charlesworth, J. H. 176, 275, 276
Chazon, E. G. 176, 178, 190
Cheon, S. 108
Chiat, M. J. S. 482, 485
Chrubasik, B. 298
Chyutin, M. 190
Clarysse, W. 5
Clines, D. J. A. 263, 267
Coggins, R. J. 194, 195, 202–204, 206, 214
Cohen, G. M. 41
Cohen, J. M. 197, 198
Cohen, S. J. D. 5, 7, 91, 92, 134, 135, 143, 268, 482, 485
Collins, A. Y. 165
Collins, J. J. 88, 89, 102, 103, 108, 135–37, 176–78, 181, 201, 203, 234, 235, 276, 278, 281, 340
Cook, J. 263, 266

Cook, M. J. 165, 168, 169
Cotton, H. M. 74
Craffert, P. F. 269, 270
Crane, O. T. 197, 198
Craven, T. 99, 100
Crawford, M. H. 281, 429
Cross, F. M. 176, 181, 183, 191, 263, 265
Crowfoot, G. M. 50
Crowfoot, J. W. 50
Crown, A. D. 194, 195, 197–200
Cryer, F. H. 176, 181, 184

Dabrowa, E. 409, 411, 414, 417, 419, 424, 431
Dagut, M. B. 13, 25, 32
Dalman, G. 32, 33
Danby, J. C. 159
Dancy, J. C. 79
Dar, S. 68, 69, 71, 127
Daube, D. 137, 140, 141, 143
Davidson, M. J. 270
Davies, J. K. 310
Davies, M. E. 429
Davies, P. R. 88, 135, 136, 176, 178, 179, 181, 187, 188, 190, 192, 193, 272, 324
Davies, W. D. 231, 482, 483
Davis, N. 75
Day, L. P. 61
De Groot, A. 55
De Troyer, K. 263, 267
Deines, R. 143, 144
Delcor, M. 205, 207, 236, 237
Dentzer, J. M. 63
Dequeker, L. 55
Derow, P. 74, 115
Develin, R. 114
Dever, W. G. 53
Dexinger, F. 96
Di Lella, A. A. 88
Dimant, D. 176, 177
Doran, R. 79, 80, 83, 97, 98, 201, 208, 318, 324, 328, 333, 340, 357, 367
Dorothy, C. V. 267
Dothan, T. 58
Doudna, G. 179
Drews, R. 111
Driver, G. R. 181, 184
Dubberstein, W. H. 13, 15, 16
Dunayevsky, I. 58

Eck, W. 450
Eckhardt, B. 5, 8, 9, 11, 268
Eckstein, A. M. 115, 304, 306
Edelstein, L. 117
Edmondson, J. 91
Edwards, D. R. 65
Edwards, O. 26, 29, 33
Egger, R. 194, 204–207, 212, 218
Ehling, K. 13, 16, 75, 76, 298, 340, 381, 388, 394–96, 401, 403, 408, 422
Eisenman, R. 181, 184
Elgavish, J. 46
Ellenson, D. 168
Endres, J. C. 97
Engel, H. 108
Eshel, E. 88, 90, 181, 183, 190
Eshel, H. 177, 190, 191

Falk, D.K. 177
Fallon, F. 201
Fantalkin, A. 419, 423
Feldman, A. 83, 177
Feldman, L.H. 398, 399, 482, 483
Fidanzio, M. 177
Fiensy, D.A. 65
Filmer, W.E. 26, 27, 29, 33
Finkelstein, I. 7, 8, 41, 65
Finkielsztejn, G. 75, 205, 209
Fischer, T. 75, 83, 86, 88, 89, 378
Fischer, U. 272
Fisher, C. S. 50
Fisher, G. 220
Fittschen, K. 449
Fitzmyer, J.A. 13, 14, 34, 143, 155, 177
Flint, P. 88, 176, 177
Florentin, M. 197, 198
Focke, F. 108
Foerster, G. 449
Fontanille, J.-P. 75–77
France, R.T. 482, 483
Frerichs, E. S. 276
Frisch, A. 88
Frye, R.N. 226
Funk, R.W. 57

Gabba, E. 129, 130
Gadot, Y. 55
Gafni, I.M. 231, 233, 234
Galor, K. 55, 56
Gärtner, J. 53

Gaster, M. 197, 198
Gauger, J.-D. 83, 389, 394
Geertz, C. 5, 8
Gelzer, M. 112, 429
Georgi, D. 108
Gera, D. 13, 24, 47, 340, 342, 371, 374, 389
Geva, H. 55, 56, 464
Gibson, B. 115
Gichon, M. 65, 464, 465
Gilbert, M. 108
Gilboa, A. 444
Giovannini, A. 405
Gitin, S. 53
Golb, N. 181, 183, 186
Goldingay, J. E. 88
Goldschmidt-Lehmann, R. P. 41, 464
Goldstein, J.A. 13, 17, 19, 23–25, 32, 79–81, 85, 91, 92, 97, 98, 248, 250, 252–55, 310, 315, 333, 340, 357, 358, 388, 390, 391, 397, 399–401
Goldsworthy, A. 440
Goodblatt, D. 5, 226
Goodman, M. 137, 143, 170, 181, 182, 188, 440, 450
Grabbe, L. L. 3, 7, 13, 21, 88, 89, 91, 97, 108, 134, 144, 150, 155, 160, 162, 165, 167, 173, 181, 183, 185, 186, 190–92, 194, 203, 231, 232, 244, 263, 265, 270, 272, 276, 281–83, 285, 287, 288, 290, 318, 326, 328, 337, 356, 419, 423
Grainger, J. D. 341, 344, 388, 395, 411
Gray, R. 281
Green, W. S. 276
Greenfield, J. C. 203, 276
Griffith, G. T. 318, 320
Groh, D. E. 45, 65
Gruen, E. S. 7, 8, 13, 22, 83, 88, 234, 236, 238–40, 242–44, 248, 249, 298, 299, 304, 306, 340, 379, 380, 398, 400, 405–407
Guerra, T. 270
Günther, L.-M. 449
Günther, W. 74

Habicht, C. 79, 83, 86, 87, 112, 248, 250, 310, 315
Hachlili, R. 65, 72
Hackl, U. 222, 223
Hadas, M. 103

Haenchen, E. 241
Hall, J. M. 5
Hall, R. G. 319
Halpern-Amaru, B. 97
Halpern-Zylberstain, M.-C. 41
Hanhardt, R. 13, 20, 24, 25, 335, 373
Hann, R. R. 107
Hanson, J. S. 281
Hanson, R. S. 75
Harnack, A. von 116
Harrington, D. J. 13, 14, 34, 166, 190
Harrington, H. K. 144
Harris, W. V. 305, 306
Harrison, T. 115
Hartman, L. F. 88
Hausmann, J. 231, 232
Hayward, C. T. R. 236, 237
Heichelheim, F. M. 123, 128
Heinemann, I. 248, 252
Hempel, C. 176, 178
Hendin, D. 31, 75–77
Hengel, M. 144, 248, 252, 253, 310, 325, 340
Hennessy, J. B. 62
Hensel, B. 194, 195
Henten, J. W. van 79, 80, 83, 91, 280, 328, 335, 403, 404
Herbert, S. C. 42–44
Herzog, Z. 49
Hirschfeld, Y. 61, 179, 180, 185
Hoffmann, A. 61
Hogan, K. M. 108
Hölbl, G. 296, 388, 395, 411
Holladay, C. R. 201
Holland, T. 429
Honigman, S. 79, 81, 123, 124, 248, 249, 259, 310, 321, 323, 327, 336, 340, 347, 349, 352, 355
Hoover, O. D. 13, 15, 75, 76
Horbury, W. 74
Horgan, M. P. 190
Horowitz, G. 59
Horowitz, W. 13, 24, 371, 374
Horsley, R. A. 281, 286
Houghton, A. 13, 15, 75, 76
Hübner, H. 108
Humbert, J.-B. 179, 185
Humphries, W. L. 88, 89
Hunger, H. 407
Huß, W. 13, 16, 296, 340, 343, 388, 395, 411

Hutchinson, J. 5, 8

Isaac, B. 54, 65, 70, 74
Israeli, S. 42
Isser, S. J. 194

Jacobson, D. M. 59, 449
Jacoby, F. 114
Jassen, A. P. 281
Jeansonne, S. P. 263, 267
Jellicoe, S. 263
Jeremias, J. 166, 168
Jeselsohn, D. 75, 77
Ji, C. C. 63, 70
Ji, C.-H. 63, 64, 70
Jobes, K. H. 263, 267
Johnson, S. R. 234, 236
Jones, A. H. M. 8, 433, 434
Jones, C. P. 399, 400
Jones, S. 5
Jonnes, L. 319, 323
Joosten, J. 196, 197

Kabasele Mukenge, A. 101
Kamp, K. A. 5, 8
Kampen, J. 135, 137, 170, 172
Kanael, B. 32, 33, 433, 435
Kapera, Z. 177
Kaplan, J. 52
Kasher, A. 41, 58, 220, 221, 224, 226, 458, 464, 465
Katzoff, R. 399
Keaveney, A. 226
Keitel, E. 226
Kelso, J. L. 52
Kenyon, K. M. 50
Keyes, C. F. 5, 8
Kidd, I. G. 117
Killebrew, A. E. 5, 8
Kindler, A. 76
Kippenberg, H. G. 123, 125, 132
Klawans, J. 91
Kletter, R. 5, 8, 9, 54
Kloner, A. 59, 65
Kloppenborg, J. S. 166
Knibb, M. A. 97, 177, 276, 328
Kobelski, P. J. 270, 271
Koch, K. 88
Kokkinos, N. 449
Kolarcik, M. 108, 110, 272, 274
Kottsieper, I. 88, 101

Kraay, C. M. 75
Kratz, R. G. 88, 101
Kreimerman, I. 65
Kreissig, H. 123, 125
Kropp, A. J. M. 76, 222
Kugel, J. L. 97
Kugler, R. 13, 18, 20, 176, 177
Kuhnen, H.-P. 41, 42, 65, 66, 70
Kuhrt, A. 227, 298, 299

Laato, A. 276, 287
Lacocque, A. 263
Ladouceur, D. J. 478, 479
Lance, H. D. 53
Landau, T. 449
Landau, Y. 48, 49
Lane, E. N. 241, 242
Lange, A. 177
Lapp, N. L. 63
Laqueur, R. 91, 94, 441, 442
Larché, F. 63
Larcher, C. 108
Laureys-Chachy, R. 53
LeMoyne, J. 137, 140–42
Lebram, J. C. H. 88
Lederman, Z. 65
Lee, J. K. 63, 64, 70
Lefkovits, J. K. 190
Lehmann, M. R. 32, 34
Leszynsky, R. 138
Levick, B. 440
Levine, B. A. 190
Levine, L. I. 41, 48, 464
Levison, J. R. 281
Lichtenberger, H. 275, 276, 464
Lichtenstein, H. 13, 14
Lightstone, J. N. 135, 136, 138, 142
Lim, T. H. 177, 178, 181, 189
Lintott, A. 112
Lipschits, O. 41, 55, 56, 59
Longden, R. P. 226
Longstaff, T. R. W. 45
Lönnqvist, K. 179
Lönnqvist, M. 179
Looijer, G. de 177
Lorber, C. 13, 15, 75, 76
Lührmann, D. 166
Lyon, D. G. 50

Ma, J. 248, 258
Maccoby, H. 134

Macdonald, J. 194, 195, 197
Mach, M. 270
Mack, B. L. 108
Magen, Y. 51, 65, 72, 73, 179, 185, 194, 209
Magie, D. 433, 434
Magness, J. 41, 179–81, 185
Magny, A. 116
Mahieu, B. 26, 27, 29, 31, 33
Main, E. 138
Marshak, A. K. 26
Martínez, F. G. 176–78, 181, 189
Mason, S. 5, 91, 144, 149, 151
Master, D. M. 50
Mattern-Parkes, S. P. 226
Mattill, A. J., Jr 144, 155
Matusova, E. 103, 234, 236
Mazar, A. 48
Mazar, B. 55, 58, 59, 63, 464
Mazzinghi, L. 108
McCollough, C. T. 65
McCown, C. C. 63
McEwan, G. J. P. 226
McGing, B. 115
McLay, T. 264, 267
McNicoll, A. W. 61, 62
Meadowcroft, T. J. 264
Meeks, W. A. 281
Meier, C. 429
Mendels, D. 5, 201, 216, 231, 232
Meshorer, Y. 76, 77, 222
Metso, S. 177, 190
Meyers, C. L. 45, 65
Meyers, E. M. 41, 45, 65
Miles, G. B. 113
Milik, J. T. 33, 177
Millar, F. 112, 440, 450
Mineo, B. 114
Misgav, H. 51
Mitchell, T. N. 112
Mittag, P. F. 13, 15, 248, 312, 313, 340, 353, 354, 364
Mittwoch, A. 123, 125
Mizzi, D. 179, 180, 184
Moehring, H. R. 234, 238, 241
Momigliano, A. 79, 83, 85, 86, 91, 129, 130, 132, 433, 435
Montgomery, J. A. 88, 194, 195
Moore, C. A. 88, 99–101
Moore, G. F. 134
Moore, S. 5

Mor, M. 91
Morgan, M. G. 116, 310, 340, 344
Mørkholm, O. 13, 15, 21, 22, 248, 250, 312, 313, 315, 340, 343, 354, 364
Mosshammer, A. A. 118
Müller, H. 405
Müller, S. 227
Muntz, C. E. 113
Murphy-O'Connor, J. 170, 177, 181, 187, 193, 389, 392, 393
Myers, E. A. 65, 225, 226

Nagy, R. M. 45
Naveh, J. 43, 75, 76, 209, 213
Negbi, O. 49
Negev, A. 222, 225
Nestle, E. 356, 357
Netzer, E. 53, 64, 65, 269, 270, 464
Neubauer, A. 197, 198
Neuhaus, G. O. 79, 80
Neusner, J. 144, 156, 158, 162, 163, 165, 166, 244–46, 276
Newsom, C. A. 88, 89
Nickelsburg, G. W. E. 96, 98, 102, 103, 272, 275
Nodet, E. 91
Noy, D. 74, 75

O'Neill, J. C. 276
Oden, R. A. 356, 357
Oegema, G. S. 275, 276
Ogilvie, R. M. 113
Olmstead, A. T. 13, 20
Oren, E. D. 59
Orlinsky, H. M. 103, 105
Otto, W. 94, 129, 132

Panayotov, A. 75
Pardee, D. 190, 191
Parente, F. 234–36
Parker, R. A. 13, 15, 16
Parker, V. L. 83, 85, 236, 238
Parmentier, E. 114
Parry, D. W. 177, 178
Pastor, J. 91, 123, 127, 129, 130
Peleg, Y. 179, 185
Pelletier, A. 103
Pervo, R. I. 144, 155
Pestman, P. W. 13, 15
Petzold, K.-E. 116

Pinnick, A. 190
Poehlmann, W. 138, 140
Poirier, J. C. 144
Portier-Young, A. E. 248, 258
Porton, G. G. 134
Pouchelle, P. 107
Pucci Ben Zeev, M. 91, 95, 106, 234, 238, 411
Puech, E. 272, 275, 276
Pummer, R. 51, 98, 194, 195, 199, 201–205, 207–13
Purvis, J. D. 194–96, 204, 213, 214

Raban, A. 464
Rabin, A. 419
Rahmani, L. Y. 65, 72
Rajak, T. 91, 95, 409, 410
Rapp, G. Jr 49
Rappaport, U. 59, 76, 177
Ray, J. D. 13, 22, 341, 344
Redditt, P. L. 88
Reese, J. M. 108
Regev, E. 11, 65, 73, 269, 270
Reich, R. 53, 54, 76
Reider, J. 108
Reinhold, M. 112
Reinmuth, O. W. 319, 320
Reisner, G. A. 50
Retsö, J. 220
Rich, J. W. 112
Richardson, J. S. 440, 450
Richardson, P. 449, 464, 482, 483, 485
Ricl, M. 319, 323
Rigsby, K. J. 248, 250, 356, 357
Rives, J. 91
Rivkin, E. 144, 157, 166, 168
Rizzolo, N. 190
Rocca, S. 65, 449, 464
Roddy, N. 287
Rodgers, Z. 91
Roitman, A. D. 177
Roll, I. 49, 66, 67
Roller, D. W. 41, 42, 64, 66, 464
Rosenfeld, B.-Z. 54
Rosenstein, N. 305, 429
Rostovtzeff, M. 310, 324
Roth, C. 181, 184
Rowley, H. H. 88, 89
Rozenberg, S. 53
Rubin, B. B. 226

Russell, D. S. 328, 329, 333
Rutgers, L. V. 272

Sachs, A. 13, 15, 20, 21, 23, 35, 36, 407
Sagiv, N. 59
Saldarini, A. J. 134, 136, 140, 143, 144, 161, 166, 168, 169
Samuel, A. E. 13, 15
Sanderson, J. 265
Sandhaus, D. 65, 66, 70
Sandmel, S. 483
Sartre, M. 298, 340
Schäfer, P. 32, 33
Schalit, A. 102, 123, 128, 129, 131, 132, 205–207, 419, 434, 442, 443, 449, 458, 482, 483
Schams, C. 166, 167
Schedl, C. 99, 100
Schiffman, L. H. 177, 181, 184, 190, 195
Schlude, J. M. 226
Schmitt, H. H. 74
Schneider, H. 111
Schorch, S. 196, 264
Schremer, A. 138, 140, 141
Schüpphaus, J. 107
Schuller, E. M. 177, 203, 399
Schunck, K.-D. 13, 14, 16–18, 24, 79–81
Schürer, E. 14, 80, 88, 94, 98, 99, 101–103, 107, 108, 132, 172, 177, 203, 237, 245, 348, 435
Schwartz, D.R. 5, 6, 80, 83, 85, 166, 168, 244, 246, 340, 347, 348, 357
Schwartz, J. 54, 372
Schwartz, S. 6, 80, 81, 381
Schwenk-Bressler, U. 108
Schwentzel, C.-G. 222
Scott, J. M. 232
Scullard, H. H. 305, 429
Seager, R. 429
Seel, O. 114
Seeman, C. 248, 257, 305–307, 378–80, 388, 399–407, 414, 415
Segal, A. F. 134
Segal, E. 440, 450
Segal, M. 98
Seligsohn, M. 197, 199
Sellers, O. R. 57, 58, 76
Shackleton Bailey, D. R. 112
Shalev, Y. 55
Shalom, N. 66

Sharon, N. 429
Shatzman, I. 340, 361, 362
Shehadeh, H. 196, 197
Shennan, S. J. 6, 8
Sherk, R. K. 75
Sherwin-White, A. N. 227, 298, 299, 433
Shukron, E. 76
Shutt, R. J. H. 91, 114
Sievers, J. 83, 136, 310, 340, 358, 359, 370, 372, 381, 388, 394, 402–406, 410, 411, 414, 416
Skeat, T. C. 13, 21
Smallwood, E. M. 434
Smith, A. D. 5, 8
Smith, C. 116
Smith, M. 134
Smith, R. H. 41, 61, 62
Sokolovskii, S. 6, 8, 9
Sommer, B. D. 281
Spaer, A. 76
Sparks, K. L. 6
Sperber, D. 76, 77
Stacey, D. 179
Stadelmann, H. 166, 167
Starcky, J. 276
Steck, O. H. 88, 101
Steckoll, S. H. 236, 237
Steel, C. 305, 429
Stegemann, H. 177
Steinmann, A. E. 13, 27, 29–31, 33
Stemberger, G. 134, 203
Stenhouse, P. 197, 199, 200
Sterling, G. E. 216
Stern, E. 47, 48, 51
Stern, M. 26–29, 33, 114, 419
Stern, P. 91
Steudel, A. 190
Stiehl, R. 312
Stocker, M. 99
Stökl Ben Ezra, D. 176, 177, 180, 184
Stone, M. E. 134, 176, 178, 203
Strange, J.R. 45, 65, 75
Strugnell, J. 209, 212
Stuckenbruck, L. T. 96
Sukenik, E. L. 50
Sussmann, Y. 144, 165
Swain, H. 429
Swanson, D. D. 190
Swoboda, S. 91
Syon, D. 66, 76

Tabor, J. D. 276, 278
Tal, A. 194, 196, 197
Tal, O. 41, 49, 55, 56, 59, 66, 67, 419, 423
Talmon, S. 134, 263–65, 329, 330
Taylor, J. E. 138, 170, 178, 181, 236, 237
Tcherikover, V. A. 85–87, 103, 234–36, 248, 249, 251–54, 310, 325, 334, 338, 340, 348, 349, 357, 360
Tedesche, S. 80, 310, 341
Teeple, H. M. 281
Teicher, J. L. 181, 184
Thiering, B. 181, 184
Thoma, C. 144, 163
Thompson, T. L. 7, 176, 213, 214
Tidmarsh, J. 62
Tigchelaar, E.J.C. 177, 178
Tiller, P. A. 96
Tilly, M. 80, 104, 105
Timpe, D. 378
Tishkov, V. 6, 8, 9
Tov, E. 101, 102, 177, 178, 196, 264, 265
Trafton, J. L. 107
Tränkle, H. 113, 116
Tromp, J. 102, 103
Tsafrir, Y. 55, 64, 464, 465
Tsfania, L. 51
Tuffin, P. 118
Tushingham, A. D. 55, 56
Tzaferis, V. 42, 44, 48, 49

Udoh, F. E. 123, 126, 129, 130, 132
Ulrich, E. 176, 177, 264, 266
Unnik, W. C. van 232

Van't Dack, E. 419, 420
VanderKam, J.C. 98, 144, 160, 177, 178, 181, 185, 356, 357, 399
Vaux, R. de 179, 188
Vermes, G. 170, 172, 178, 182, 191, 449
Vermeylen, J. 108
Villeneuve, F. 63
Viviano, B. T. 138
Volkmann, H. 14, 20

Wacholder, B. Z. 14, 16, 32–34, 85, 114
Walbank, F. W. 14, 20, 116, 341, 342
Walsh, P. G. 113

Waltke, B. K. 196, 264, 266
Warner, R. 329, 333
Wassén, C. 281
Waubke, H.-G. 144
Weigold, M. 177
Weiss, Z. 45
Weitzman, S. 6, 248, 341, 349, 352
Wenning, R. 222
Whittaker, C. R. 305
Wiesehöfer, J. 227
Wilkinson, J. 55, 464
Will, Ed. 429
Will, Er. 63, 314, 341, 343
Williams, D. S. 80
Williams, M. H. 6
Williams, R. S. 434
Williamson, H. G. M. 329, 330
Wilson, B. R. 134, 135
Winston, D. 108, 281
Wirgin, W. 378, 399
Wise, M. O. 276, 278, 287, 389, 393
Wiseman, D. J. 13, 15, 21, 23, 35, 36
Wolski, J. 227
Woude, A. S. van der 182, 189
Wright, B. G., III 104
Wright, G. E. 51, 53
Wright, G. R. H. 51

Yadin, Y. 55, 190, 191, 464
Yalichev, S. 319, 320
Yardeni, A. 182, 184
Yardley, J. C. 114
Yaron, R. 32, 34
Yarrow, L. M. 116
Yarshater, E. 227
Yoffee, N. 5, 8

Zecchini, G. 114
Zeitlin, S. 32, 80, 310, 341
Zelinger, Y. 66
Ziegler, J. 88, 108
Zilberstein, A. 55, 56, 69
Zimmermann, J. 276, 278
Zlotnik, Y. 76
Zollschan, L. T. 378, 379
Zuckermann, B. 32

Index of Subjects

Aaron 136, 277, 280, 283, 381
Aaronic 199, 426
Aaronite 334, 336
Abaddon 275
Abdera 106, 113, 399
Abila 434
Abraham 99, 198, 234, 269, 288, 399–400
Achiab 481
acropolis 63, 330
Actium 36, 279, 298, 449, 451, 455, 457–59, 467, 473, 487, 488, 506
Adasa 376, 377
Adiabene 229
Adida 398, 401
Adini 245
administration 44, 123, 132, 175, 299, 326, 342, 352, 361, 364, 373, 381, 389, 391, 434, 435, 460–63, 488, 505
administrative 43, 49, 66, 161, 166, 225, 300, 361, 368, 389, 434, 435, 459, 463
administrator(s) 145, 425, 428, 461, 476, 503
Adora 423, 435, 436
Adoraim 69
Aelius 224, 467, 472
Aemilius 30, 190, 479
Africa 41, 57, 438, 439, 441
Africanus 118, 119, 443
afterlife 64, 143, 161, 164, 272, 273, 276, 290
Agathocles 416
agricultural 54, 68, 71, 127, 157, 174
agriculture 33, 68, 71, 115, 171, 172, 225, 327
Agrippa 27, 36, 131, 212, 215, 219, 240, 241, 246, 247, 267, 433, 450, 460, 461, 465, 467–69, 471, 475, 483, 485, 486
Agrippa I 131, 267, 433, 483, 485
Agrippa II 131, 212, 246, 471, 483

Agrippeum 465
Agrippium 466
Ahiqar 105, 166
Ake 260, 353, 412
Akkaron 396
Akko 44, 67, 68
alabarch 10
Alayiq 53
Alcimus 19, 101, 136, 137, 167, 300, 375, 377, 380–82, 386, 389, 390, 392, 394, 498, 499
Aleppo 422
Alexander 10, 14, 17, 20, 21, 41, 46, 49, 51–54, 56, 58, 59, 61–64, 68, 71, 76, 77, 84, 106, 109, 118, 140, 145, 148, 151, 177, 180, 191, 192, 200, 203, 209, 211, 223, 227, 235, 243, 247, 260, 295–98, 301–305, 322, 325, 329, 393–98, 406, 412–14, 416, 418–22, 424, 425, 427, 428, 431, 436, 437, 439, 463, 474–77, 486, 499, 500, 502, 503, 505
Alexander Balas 20, 84, 301, 393, 395, 397, 398, 412
Alexandrium 10, 64, 71, 104, 108, 109, 170, 181, 231, 235, 284, 290, 296, 326, 342–44, 385, 412, 425, 432, 436–38, 451–53, 458, 465, 468, 477, 495
Alexas 479
altar(s) 52, 142, 241, 242, 283, 330, 346, 347, 351, 352, 356, 357, 373, 456, 494, 497
Amathitis 398
Amathus 420, 434
Ammianus 113, 354
Ammon 62, 71
amphitheatre 48, 465, 479
amphora(s) 49, 67, 73, 75, 126, 205
Anafa 42, 68, 74
Ananel 246, 456
Ananias 212, 235, 416, 420

Ananus 138, 140, 151
Andronicus 208, 336
angel(s) 137, 138, 140–43, 156, 162, 171, 270, 271, 274, 275
angelic 191, 270–72
angelology 141, 270, 271
aniconic 484
Anthedon 421, 423, 434, 436, 462, 466
Antigonids 295
Antigonus 16, 31, 76, 77, 93, 209, 223, 228, 247, 341, 414, 417, 418, 420, 436, 437, 439–41, 446, 451–55, 457, 480, 487, 488, 502, 505, 506
Antioch 24, 25, 86, 87, 237, 240, 246, 260, 300, 301, 303, 312, 317, 334, 336, 343, 344, 349, 353, 365–67, 369, 374, 375, 381, 390, 395, 397, 403, 412, 422, 439, 455, 471, 482, 495, 499, 500
Antiochene(s) 103, 280, 324, 331, 334, 337
Antiochus I 22, 250, 322, 496
Antiochus III 51, 58, 60, 124, 225, 227, 235, 246, 250, 296, 299, 306, 307, 311, 313, 326, 329, 341, 383, 493
Antiochus IV 11, 13, 15, 20, 21, 35, 48, 58, 80, 84, 85, 87–90, 101, 113, 116, 124, 190, 191, 205, 206, 209, 217, 222, 223, 236, 237, 248, 250, 258–60, 262, 291, 297, 300, 301, 310–13, 315–17, 319, 321, 340, 341, 351, 354, 357, 366, 368, 369, 371, 372, 374, 375, 380, 385, 386, 388, 393, 400, 413, 493, 497–500
Antiochus V 15, 23, 54, 65, 84, 86, 87, 300, 338, 351, 364, 367, 369, 374–76, 381, 385, 497, 498
Antiochus VI 84, 301, 397, 398, 403, 500, 501
Antiochus VII 50, 54, 117, 227, 245, 301, 302, 320, 408, 410–15, 501
Antiochus VIII 302, 304, 412, 414, 420, 421
Antiochus IX 302, 303, 414, 415, 420, 421
Antiochus X 303, 304, 421
Antiochus XI 303, 421
Antiochus XII 304, 422, 423, 503
Antiochus XIII 13, 75, 304, 308, 309
Antipas 31, 102, 210, 224, 431, 478, 480, 482

Antipater 93, 221, 239, 298, 431, 432, 435–48, 466, 469, 471, 474–78, 480, 487, 503, 505, 506
Antipatris 423, 466
Antistius 445
Antonia 56, 289, 465
Antony 26–28, 112, 115, 129–31, 228, 240, 298, 430, 436, 437, 439–41, 445–48, 450–59, 462, 465, 472–74, 487, 488, 506, 507
Apamea 117, 299, 311, 408, 445
Apameia 313
Apion 91, 92, 95, 117, 297
apocalypse 12, 89, 90, 96, 97, 103, 248, 272, 278, 280, 282, 287, 290
apocalyptic ix 36, 88, 90, 96, 102, 135, 177, 228, 280–82, 285, 290, 371
apocalypticism 36, 134, 176
apocalypticists 282
Apollonia 49, 66, 67, 423, 434, 436
Apollonius 206, 208, 253, 345, 346, 348, 349, 362–64, 368, 395, 396, 414, 496
Appian 27, 111, 243, 303, 304, 313, 314, 393, 395, 397, 403, 408, 436, 445, 462
Aquila 263
Arab 62, 223–25, 397, 398, 422, 432, 439, 461, 469–71, 476, 481, 502
Arabic 196–99
Arabs 41, 220, 221, 223, 225, 227, 229, 398, 422, 423, 449, 458, 463, 464, 467, 469, 472, 503
Arad 70
Arados 46
Aradus 240, 421
Aramaic 6, 13, 14, 43, 51, 134, 172, 176, 177, 194, 197, 203, 264, 267, 279, 287, 400
Araq 63
Arbela 453
archaeological 5, 6, 11, 41, 44, 51, 53, 54, 57–59, 62, 64–67, 71–76, 123, 126, 179, 185, 205, 213, 215, 269, 419, 449
archaeologically 226, 423
archaeologists 56, 179, 270, 417, 423
archaeology 3–5, 7, 8, 41–43, 45, 47, 49, 51–53, 55, 57–59, 61, 63, 65, 67, 69–73, 75, 77, 144, 177–79, 182, 185, 188, 192, 195, 209, 213, 226, 237, 244, 245, 269, 270, 295, 408, 413, 427, 464, 502

Index of Subjects

Archelaus 31, 54, 102, 114, 172, 210, 215, 219, 475, 476, 478, 480, 482
archōn 363
archonship 416
Aretas 223–25, 304, 421, 423, 432, 436, 471, 481, 503
Arethusa 434
Areus 84, 399
Aristeas 103, 104, 234
Aristobulus I 12, 60, 76, 172, 174, 262, 269, 417, 418, 427, 428, 503
Aristobulus II 74, 76, 77, 93, 112, 224, 228, 309, 429, 431, 446, 451, 503
Armenia 226–29, 246, 304, 308, 309, 315, 425, 450
Armenian 229, 246, 303, 335, 432
army/armies 13, 17, 22, 23, 25, 28, 52, 64, 106, 124, 126, 132, 229, 235, 260, 302–304, 306, 308, 309, 316, 318, 320, 340, 342, 344–48, 362–66, 371, 374, 376, 377, 381, 382, 384–86, 389, 392, 393, 395, 397, 400, 401, 409, 412, 414, 416, 420, 421, 423, 425, 432, 433, 436, 437, 439, 440, 445, 452, 454, 458, 470, 480, 481, 495, 496, 498, 500, 501, 504, 506
Arqiah 200
Arsaces I 227
Arsuf 49, 66, 67
Artapanus 105, 219
Artaxerxes 100, 286
Artemis 172
Arubboth 68
Asael 274
Asatir 197, 198
Ascalon 57, 76, 434, 443, 482
Aseneth 236
Ashdod 57, 67, 74, 396, 409
Ashkelon 57, 67, 68, 73, 396, 398, 462
Asia 5, 227, 238–41, 243, 247, 248, 256, 279, 296, 300, 302, 308, 309, 323, 333, 433, 438, 441, 466, 468
Asinius 26, 36, 474
Asochis 45, 420
Asophon 420
Assyria 166, 229, 447
Assyrian(s) 100, 202, 220, 233, 244, 246, 493
Astarte 47
astrologers 241, 242

astronomical 13, 15, 30, 371, 374, 407
astronomically 15
astronomy 15, 115, 117
atheism 12
atheist 12
Athenian(s) 208, 308, 345, 348, 417, 497
Athenion 458
Athenobius 408
Athens 103, 108, 201, 234, 312, 353, 416, 417, 453
Athrogaeus 481
Atlit 46
Atonement 26, 28, 29, 99, 393, 455
Attalus III 307
Augusteum 42
Augustus 48, 50, 57, 93, 108, 111, 114, 118, 228, 234, 241, 243, 244, 247, 440, 449, 450, 459–62, 465–71, 474, 475, 477, 480, 482–84, 487, 488, 507
Auranitis 462, 467, 482
Aurelius 229, 230
Aviv 52
Axidares 229
Ayalon 69
Azariah 372
Azotus 57, 396, 409, 423, 434, 436, 463, 482
Azoun 71

Baal 47, 256, 357, 358
Babylon 15, 16, 18, 20, 23, 131, 200, 229, 246, 374, 443, 456
Babylonian(s) 13–16, 20, 24, 34–36, 100, 230, 234, 245, 246, 254, 258, 319, 371, 374, 443, 493
Bacchides 19, 52, 58, 136, 346, 365, 377, 381, 382, 389, 393, 499
Balâtah/Balâṭah 51
Balgea 335
balsam 53, 127, 131
bandit(s) 135, 281, 444, 453, 505
Bannus 149
Barnabas 288
Baruch 88, 101, 102, 287, 290
Barzaphranes 451
Bashan 462
Baskama 401
Bassus 445
Batanaea 246, 462, 471, 480, 482
Bathyra 246, 471

Beelzebul 152
Beersheba 60
Bel 88
beliefs 11, 72, 73, 99, 105, 138, 141–43, 146, 151, 152, 156, 159, 161, 162, 164, 165, 171, 172, 174, 185, 189, 192, 206, 232, 262, 268, 271, 272, 274, 275, 278, 279, 281, 283, 290, 291, 350
Beliel 271, 275
Bemeselis 422
Ben Sira 102, 108, 166–68, 204, 216, 264, 268, 283, 290
Benjamin 69, 334, 335, 339
Berenice 297, 420, 437, 475
Bethbasi 390, 499
Bethbassi 390
Bethel 52, 69, 390
Bethlehem 69, 482, 483
Bethulia 100
Bilgah 335, 339, 500
Bithynia 308
Boethus 140, 143, 165, 467
Boethusians 137, 138, 140, 142, 157–60, 164, 165
border(s) 60, 62, 64, 66, 67, 70, 71, 126, 221, 225, 229, 232, 269, 297, 342, 397, 398, 400, 410, 418, 447, 463, 465, 488, 501
Bostra 225
Boucolonpolis 46
boulē 323, 324
brigands 135, 246, 453, 462, 470, 471
Brundisium 26, 441, 450, 452, 506
Brutus 115, 239, 440, 441, 445
bulla 75
burial(s) 30, 59, 65, 72, 188
Byzantine 47, 64, 65, 112, 116, 118, 245

Cadmus 399
Caecilius 445
Caesar 33, 77, 107, 111, 112, 115, 118, 123, 128, 129, 146, 228, 239, 240, 243, 244, 247, 298, 406, 416, 429–31, 433, 435, 438–41, 444, 445, 448, 450, 459, 462, 467–69, 471, 477, 478, 480, 482, 505, 506
Caesarea 42, 48, 462, 464, 466, 468, 469, 489, 507
Caesareum 465
Caesarian 240

Caesarion 298, 450
Caiaphas 399
Cairo 48, 203
Calchis 439
calendar(s) 16, 18, 25, 28, 32, 86, 98, 99, 134, 141, 178, 210, 238, 329, 368, 377, 460
Caligula 108, 109
Callimandrus 414
Callinicus 422
Callirrhoe 479
Callisthenes 365
Calpurnius 242
Calvinus 26, 36
Cana 458
Canatha 458
canon 95, 141, 264, 268
canonical 98, 107, 141
Capernaum 44
Cappadocia 308, 468, 475, 476
Caracalla 230
Carmel 67, 68, 414, 424, 451
Carrhae 245
Carthage 305–307, 400
Cassius 26–29, 33, 112, 113, 129, 240, 243, 435, 437, 438, 440, 441, 445, 446, 448, 506
Cato 115
Celer 212
celibacy 189
celibate 172, 175, 187, 189
Celsus 332
Cenaz 285
Cendebaeus 54, 409
Cerealis 212
Cerealius 212
Cestius 362
Chaeronea 115
Charax 245
Chelkias 235, 416, 420
Chiron 378
Chosroes 229
Christian(s) 83, 116, 118, 134, 135, 137–39, 144, 152, 160, 169, 181, 184, 197, 203, 228, 232, 276, 278, 285, 287, 288, 318, 443, 483
Christianity 90, 138, 143, 166, 194, 231, 234, 275, 280, 281, 482
chronograph 287
chronographical 289

chronological 19, 30, 35, 85, 94, 278, 347, 464, 473
chronology 3, 13–16, 26, 30, 32, 70, 75, 81, 82, 179, 213, 304, 370, 410, 449
Cicero 12, 26, 36, 112, 115, 243, 247, 430, 436, 440, 441
Cilicia 156, 303, 308, 403
circumcision 10, 11, 72, 207, 214, 220–22, 226, 252, 256, 257, 268, 269, 316, 332, 333, 351–52, 358, 385, 418, 501, 505
citizen(s) 49, 125, 147, 148, 208, 222, 239, 240, 244, 247, 253, 320, 322–24, 326, 328–30, 334, 336–38, 342, 372, 397, 414, 417, 425, 431, 444, 460, 468, 488, 494, 495, 503
citizenship 231, 243, 319, 320, 440, 494, 505
Claudius 27, 212
Cleopatra I 296
Cleopatra II 297, 343, 412
Cleopatra III 235, 297, 416, 420
Cleopatra VII 57, 279, 298, 438, 506
cleruchies 463
Coele 124, 225, 235, 258, 259, 296, 311, 313, 321, 341, 342, 344, 363, 385, 395–97, 400, 403, 411, 412, 444, 456, 495, 496, 500
coin(s) 4, 13, 15, 17, 26, 31, 33, 42, 43, 45–53, 55, 57–63, 65, 67–69, 71, 73, 75–78, 179, 180, 209, 222, 224, 260, 353, 395, 403, 408, 412, 413, 415, 418, 427, 455, 485, 502
Colchis 308
collegia 244
colonies 296, 463
colony 207, 209, 247, 253, 256, 257, 349, 362, 471
Constantine 41
Constantinople 118, 119
consul(s) 26, 28, 36, 84, 112, 238, 242, 308, 309, 405, 406, 415, 430, 431, 436, 439–41, 460, 461
Coponius 210
Corbulo 228
Corinth 299, 400
Costobarus 221, 474
Cotylas 63

council(s) 77, 101, 145, 146, 211, 261, 323, 324, 327, 337, 366, 394, 434, 435, 477, 478, 480, 495
court 89, 104, 145, 146, 161, 241, 271, 370, 390, 418, 444, 458, 469, 475–77, 493, 503
covenant 176, 252, 256, 271
Crassus 115, 129, 226–28, 430, 431, 435, 437, 438, 448
Crete 244, 395
crucify 145
Ctesiphon 229, 230
cult(s) 22, 35, 42, 51, 54, 61, 62, 83, 95, 96, 101, 109, 134, 138, 161, 173, 187, 195, 201, 205, 207, 208, 213, 216–18, 226, 234, 236, 241, 242, 251, 252, 254–57, 259–63, 270, 290, 325, 327, 328, 330, 334, 336, 338, 339, 345, 347, 350, 352–59, 369, 370, 373, 385, 386, 388, 426, 433, 494, 497, 504
cultic 42, 43, 172, 187, 269, 281, 282, 367, 393, 466
Cumanus 211, 212
cuneiform 13, 15, 20, 21, 246, 373
Curtius 203
Cypros 53, 270, 443, 465, 473, 476
Cyprus 75, 235, 296–98, 302, 416, 420, 475
Cyrenaica 74, 297
Cyrene 81, 92, 372

Damascus 92, 98, 111, 114, 118, 170, 176, 181, 186–88, 190, 222, 224, 271, 277, 288–89, 304, 316, 398, 411, 417, 421, 422, 432, 442–44, 446, 455, 462, 469, 471, 473, 478, 482, 484, 503
Daniel 21, 88–90, 101–103, 116, 117, 135–37, 141, 174, 254, 258, 263, 264, 267, 268, 271, 273, 275, 277, 281, 283, 284, 287–91, 318, 340, 350, 354, 356–58, 371, 386, 497, 498
Daphne 15, 22, 314, 354, 364
dead 69–72, 97, 113, 144, 155, 170, 176–79, 181, 182, 186, 190, 264, 270, 272–76, 278, 290, 302, 329, 401, 419, 421, 457, 479, 480, 499
death 13–15, 18, 22–24, 26, 29–31, 33–36, 45, 53–55, 58, 66, 72, 82, 83, 85, 89, 93, 102, 106–108, 110, 111, 114, 119, 138, 140, 142, 145–48, 151, 155,

161, 193, 197, 198, 224, 227, 229, 231, 239, 241, 244, 247, 256, 269, 272–76, 281, 288, 290, 295, 297, 298, 303, 307, 308, 310, 312, 313, 340, 341, 343, 345–47, 349–51, 353, 355–57, 359–61, 363, 365, 367, 369, 371, 373–75, 377–83, 385, 387–90, 392–94, 396, 401, 403, 408, 409, 411, 413, 415–19, 421, 423–26, 428, 429, 438–41, 445, 446, 449, 450, 456–59, 461, 467, 471–72, 474, 477, 480, 487, 489, 498–500, 502, 507, 508
Decapolis 49, 60–63, 67, 68, 71, 434
Deinaeus 211
Delos 239, 240
Delphi 115
Demetrius I 16, 19, 84, 136, 300, 301, 313, 377, 379–81, 389, 393–95, 397, 499, 500
Demetrius II 20, 44, 60, 84, 227, 301, 302, 395–98, 400, 401, 403, 406, 408, 411, 412, 500, 501
Demetrius III 191, 227, 303, 421, 422, 503
demonic 270, 271
demons 152, 272
diaspora 4, 11, 81, 88, 90, 105, 106, 109, 131, 200, 231–35, 237, 239, 241, 243, 245, 247, 258, 263, 272, 486, 487, 489, 507, 508
Diodorus 113, 117, 223, 313, 314, 341, 342, 351, 352, 356, 378, 393, 395–97, 403, 410, 414, 432
Dionysus 236, 254, 260, 297, 301, 304, 356, 357, 397, 422, 497
Dios 86, 368
Diospolis 458
Dium 423, 434
divination 106, 282
divorce(d) 224, 474, 475, 478
Dolabella 239
Domitian 118
Domitius 26, 36
Dor 47, 48, 55, 67, 68, 389, 408, 464, 501
Dorotheus 406
Dositheans 194
Dothan 50, 58, 71
drachmas 331, 332, 406, 435, 437
dream(s) 96, 172, 274, 285, 286

Drimylus 9, 10
Dura 69, 245
Dystros 86

earthquake 46, 180, 458
East 15, 22, 24, 44, 51, 52, 61, 63, 65, 69, 115, 203, 213, 216, 219, 225, 227, 229, 245, 249, 260, 275, 297, 299–301, 304, 305, 307, 308, 314, 322, 325, 364, 366, 367, 374, 408, 411, 412, 421, 430, 434, 441, 446, 452, 461, 464, 467, 483, 488, 493, 501
economy 123, 126, 129–31, 133, 311, 416
Edessa 229, 245
Edomite 207, 222, 232
educated 91, 95, 109, 156, 285, 302, 329, 463, 478
education 89, 108, 109, 201, 202, 245, 313, 320, 325, 326, 474
Egypt 5, 13, 21, 22, 35, 74, 85, 106, 109, 125, 191, 234–36, 238, 239, 247, 253, 255, 256, 263, 296–98, 302, 307, 313–17, 334, 341–48, 385, 396, 397, 400, 405, 412, 416, 420, 437–39, 447, 450–52, 460, 461, 467, 489, 495, 496, 505, 506
Egyptian(s) 14, 15, 75, 84, 104, 110, 235, 236, 238, 279, 296, 298, 314, 341–43, 344, 347, 385, 412, 419, 493, 495, 505
Ekron 396, 397
Elburz 227
elder(s) 101, 147, 151, 153–59, 162, 170, 186, 229, 282, 297, 327, 337, 366, 394, 396, 398, 404, 425, 503
Eleazar 104, 167, 211, 345, 359, 378
Eleazer 351
elephant 364, 376, 382
Elephantine 234, 247, 255
elephants 23
Eleusis 116, 257, 258, 310, 314, 340, 496
elite 475, 480, 481
elites 226, 355
Elymais 226
Emir 63
Emmaus 25, 363–64, 384, 390, 481
empire 16, 88, 90, 108, 202, 223, 227, 240, 244, 245, 248, 250, 251, 257, 275, 291, 296, 298–300, 302, 304, 305, 307, 311, 313, 314, 320, 321, 343, 352, 357,

364, 373, 378, 382, 388, 395, 398, 408, 411, 426, 429, 438, 440, 441, 447, 450, 460–63, 466, 475, 488, 493, 498, 504, 506
empires 88, 220, 296, 299, 311, 335, 468, 493
Enoch 79, 96, 97, 134, 258, 263, 264, 270, 271, 273, 274, 290
ephebate 258, 319, 320, 494
ephebates 320
Ephesus 239, 241
Ephraim 65, 191
eschaton 275, 291
Essene(s) 134, 135, 137, 141, 144, 149, 164, 165, 170–78, 181, 182, 184, 189, 192, 193, 275, 285, 417, 468
Esther 88, 99, 101, 178, 236, 263–65, 267, 268
ethnarch 77, 239, 440, 448, 482, 505
ethnic 5–10, 12, 37, 207, 214, 216, 218, 232, 238, 305, 502
ethnicity 5–8, 11, 12, 232, 443, 485
Eulaeus 341
Eumenes 312, 313, 319, 323
eunuch 478
Euphrates 25, 87, 228, 233, 309, 364, 450, 454, 456
Eupolemus 89, 91, 201, 202, 219, 232, 326, 329, 330, 378
Europus 245
Eurycles 476
Eusebius 170, 443
Ezechias 106, 481
Ezekias 444
Ezra 165, 167, 168, 176, 177, 180, 184, 202, 232, 233, 244, 263, 269, 287, 288, 290, 291

Fabius 446
Faḥl 61
Fannius 414, 415
farm(s) 68, 71
Fath 197–200
Felix 223, 472
festival(s) 11, 83, 85, 99, 101, 158, 174, 177, 211, 235, 258, 263, 331, 370, 371, 446, 451
fiction 258, 350, 419, 507
fictional 351
fictionalized 112, 124, 321

fictions 234
Flaccus 241, 243, 406
Flavian 91
Flavius 91, 106, 138, 144, 194, 234, 389, 441
florilegium 190
foedus 379
foretell 172, 285, 416
forger 106, 206
forgery 85, 86, 209, 213, 394, 395, 477
fortification(s) 50, 53, 56, 59, 436, 465, 466
fortress(es) 46, 49, 50, 56, 60, 62, 64, 71, 179, 185, 246, 328, 346, 365, 374, 403, 410, 412, 424, 425, 426, 432, 436, 437, 446, 452, 453, 457, 464, 465, 468, 471, 474, 477, 480, 481, 485, 500, 501
freedman/men xv 215, 219, 244
friend 119, 129, 139, 145–48, 214, 215, 219, 222, 247, 327, 331, 381, 389, 393–95, 397, 408, 409, 437, 449, 455, 456, 459, 460, 466, 467, 469, 474, 476–78, 487, 488, 506, 507
Fukhar 44

Gaba 463
Gabinius 49, 58, 298, 433–37, 448, 504
Gabriel 271
Gaius 36, 241, 454
Galaaditis 422
Galatians 246
Gallus 27, 36, 224, 362, 467, 472
Gamala 60, 70, 423, 424, 436
Gamaliel 140, 149, 151, 155–59, 161–63, 174
Garizim 209, 414
garrison(s) 22, 23, 52, 58, 60, 62, 238, 255, 257, 300, 302, 304, 346, 349, 361–63, 369, 370, 374, 375, 384, 385, 390, 391, 395, 398, 401, 407, 410
Gaul 75, 430, 431, 438, 440, 441, 460
Gaulana 423
Gaulanitis 74, 424
Gauls 246, 462
Gaza 16, 58, 67, 68, 76, 118, 220, 224, 398, 407, 420, 421, 423, 434, 436, 462, 474, 482
Gazaca 245
Gazaeans 421
Gazara 390, 397, 407–409, 435

Gedi 58, 66, 170
Geniza/Genizah 203
Gerasa 62, 68, 71, 423
Gerizim 51, 66, 69, 194, 195, 199–202, 205, 206, 208, 209, 211–14, 217, 218, 265, 348, 354, 413, 414, 502
German 117, 326
Germany 115
Geron 208, 345, 348, 349, 497
gerousia 84, 101, 125, 324, 328, 337, 338, 367, 394
Gezer 53, 54, 66, 74, 361, 407, 435, 436
Gibeon 376
Gilead 223, 401, 422, 462
Gittha 454
Givati 55
gladiators 458
Glaphyra 475–77
Gnaeus 36
god(s) 9, 10, 13, 42, 43, 62, 79, 91, 96, 97, 99, 100, 105, 107, 138, 141, 146, 154, 156, 167, 168, 199, 200, 207, 208, 214, 233, 235, 241, 242, 248, 249, 251, 253, 260, 270, 271, 273, 275, 277–84, 286–88, 291, 310, 331, 340, 350, 353, 354, 357, 369, 372, 373, 416, 455, 479
Golan 60, 65, 68, 70, 71, 73, 74, 225, 226, 372
gold 67, 129, 243, 345, 406, 437, 455, 467, 469
Gophna 361, 374
Gorgias 364, 365, 372
gospel(s) 140, 152, 155, 156, 162–66, 168, 169, 231, 276, 278, 482
governor(s) 106, 129, 190, 203, 208, 211, 221, 224, 227, 228, 239, 362–64, 372, 376, 382, 383, 395, 396, 409, 422, 431, 434, 436–40, 444, 446, 448, 454, 461, 462, 470, 472, 474, 476, 477, 487, 496, 503
governorship 130, 210, 435, 437
Govrin 59
Gracchi 305, 307, 429, 430
grain 33, 49, 60, 69, 127, 152, 244, 326, 436, 467
grammateus 166
grapes 23
grave(s) 154, 188, 431
Greece 57, 116, 129, 238, 307, 308, 322, 400, 438, 441, 466

guerrilla 209, 361, 384, 386, 414, 458, 498
Gundashapur 245
gymnasium/ia 258, 316–20, 323–24, 330, 332, 333, 335, 466, 494

Habakkuk 186, 191, 284, 287
hades 289
Hadid 398
Hadrian 118, 229
Hakkerem 69
halakha 144, 160, 377
halakhah 195
halakic 164
Hamath 398
Ḥammah 62
Ḥammat 61
Hananel 456
Hannibal 306
Hanukka 258
harbour(s) 44, 46, 48, 49, 52, 54, 464, 466
harvest 23, 467
Hasidic 89, 253
Hasidim 82, 89, 135–37, 167, 172–74, 253, 347, 348, 358, 381, 382, 498
Hasmonaean(s) 10, 11, 14, 26, 35, 45, 50, 52, 53, 56, 57, 59, 64, 68, 69, 71–74, 76, 77, 80–82, 91, 92, 94, 100, 102, 104, 107, 111–14, 123, 124, 126–28, 130, 132, 133, 151, 174, 178, 185, 190–92, 196, 198, 200, 205, 220–23, 228, 232, 233, 245, 247, 258, 260, 262, 264, 269, 270, 276, 295, 309, 316, 328, 335, 336, 339, 340, 358–61, 370, 388, 389, 391–95, 397, 399, 400–403, 405, 407, 409, 411, 413, 415, 417–19, 421, 423, 425–29, 431, 433, 435–37, 439, 441, 443, 445, 447, 448, 455, 463, 473, 474, 482, 486, 487, 489, 497, 499–502, 504, 505, 507, 508
Hassan 71
Hauran 224
Hawa 225
Hazor 44, 398
heaven 85, 86, 97, 103, 137, 235, 256, 272, 273, 276, 280, 291, 344, 357, 372, 373
heavenly 30, 270, 271, 277, 280, 333

Hebrew 6, 11, 14, 25, 36, 43, 51, 54, 75, 76, 80, 84, 90, 91, 96, 101, 102, 107, 136, 137, 141, 159, 172, 176, 178, 194, 196, 264, 266, 270, 272, 275, 277, 279, 286, 289, 318, 326, 336, 357, 358, 398, 420, 455, 462
Hebron 69, 220
Hecataeus 106, 113, 399
Hegra 224, 225
Heliopolis 236–38, 316, 317
Helios 312
Helix 446
Hercules 47, 331
Hermon 42, 226
Herod 11, 13, 14, 26–31, 33, 36, 41, 42, 45, 48, 53–60, 64–66, 74–78, 93, 94, 102, 112, 114, 123, 127, 129–133, 140, 145, 146, 148, 149, 151, 153, 154, 161, 166, 172, 210, 215, 218, 221, 222, 224, 228, 231, 240, 243–47, 262, 298, 329, 336, 340, 361, 433, 435, 442–449, 451–459, 461–489, 495, 497, 499, 501, 503, 505–508
Herodian(s) 11, 26, 32, 41, 47, 50, 53, 55, 59–61, 65, 72, 75, 77, 106, 113, 114, 129, 132, 151–53, 157, 162, 178, 179, 185, 220, 244, 264, 268, 269, 275, 295, 449, 453, 455, 464, 480, 483, 489
Herodium 30, 64, 452, 464, 465, 468, 485
Heshbon 424, 463
Hesi 67
Hezekiah 106, 444
Hieronymus 116, 117
high priest 17, 19, 30, 75, 77, 79, 84, 101, 104, 106, 123, 128, 136, 139, 140, 143, 147, 150, 151, 155–58, 160–62, 165, 192, 197–201, 204, 212, 236–38, 240, 246, 248, 256, 259, 262, 278, 279, 284, 288, 300, 310, 313, 316, 319, 321, 322, 324, 328, 330, 334–38, 340, 345, 346, 349, 351, 368, 375, 377, 381, 382, 385, 386, 389–94, 397, 402, 404, 406, 410, 415, 416, 418, 420, 421, 425, 426, 428, 431, 432, 434, 436, 448, 452, 455–57, 467, 478, 494–96, 498, 500, 502, 503, 506, 507
Hillel 33, 158, 163, 165, 174
Hilqiyah 200
Hippodamian 46–48, 61

hippodrome 465, 479
Hippolytus 143
Hippos 61
Hippus 434, 462, 482
historian(s) 3, 4, 91, 92, 98, 111–13, 115, 116, 119, 139, 149, 201, 221, 249, 250, 252, 295, 306, 311–13, 315, 361, 383, 392, 418, 449, 469, 472
historical 3–5, 9, 14, 35, 37, 64, 65, 82, 88, 90, 91, 94, 95, 98–100, 103, 107, 112, 113, 115–17, 155, 159, 162–65, 167–69, 181, 184, 185, 190, 191, 195, 196, 200, 202, 204, 210, 217, 223, 227, 234, 245, 258, 266, 267, 276, 278, 281, 286, 311, 318, 325, 329, 336, 350, 355, 357, 359, 419, 461, 463, 496
historicity 200, 201, 379, 400, 424
historiography 165, 216, 287
history 3–8, 10–12, 14–16, 18, 20, 22, 24, 26, 28, 30, 32, 34–36, 42, 44–46, 48, 50, 52, 54–58, 60, 62–64, 66, 68, 70–72, 74–76, 78, 80–84, 86, 88–94, 96, 98–100, 102–104, 106–108, 110–19, 124, 126, 128, 130, 132, 134, 136–38, 140, 142, 144, 146, 148, 150, 152, 154, 156, 158, 160, 162, 164–66, 168, 170, 172, 174, 176–82, 184, 186, 188, 190–96, 198–200, 202, 204–206, 208, 210, 212–14, 216–18, 220, 222, 224, 226–28, 230–32, 234, 236, 238, 240, 242, 244–46, 248, 250, 252, 254, 256, 258, 260, 261, 263–66, 268–70, 272, 274–76, 278, 280, 282, 284, 286–88, 290, 295, 296, 298–300, 302, 304–306, 308, 310, 312–14, 316, 318, 320, 322, 324, 326, 328–330, 332, 334, 336, 338, 340, 342, 344, 346, 348, 350, 352, 354, 356, 358–60, 362, 364–66, 368, 370, 372, 374, 376, 378, 380, 382–86, 388, 390, 392, 394–96, 398, 400, 402, 404, 406, 408–12, 414, 416–20, 422, 424, 426, 428–32, 434, 436, 438, 440, 442, 444, 446–50, 452, 454, 456, 458, 460, 462, 464, 466, 468, 470, 472, 474, 476, 478, 480, 482–84, 486, 488, 493, 494, 496, 498–500, 502, 504, 506, 508
Holophernes 99, 100
Horon 362, 363, 377, 390
horoscope(s) 13, 20
Hortensias 431

Hula 42, 68
Huleh 462
Hyrcania 64, 71, 227, 245, 425, 436, 457, 468, 480
Hyrcanus 12, 34, 49, 50, 52, 55, 56, 59, 60, 66, 70, 71, 74–77, 80, 83, 84, 117, 124, 128, 139, 147, 148, 151, 161, 164, 174, 190, 192, 196, 200, 201, 205, 208, 209, 215, 218, 220–22, 224, 225, 232, 239, 240, 245, 246, 259, 262, 269, 284, 302, 309, 310, 321, 340, 388, 405–407, 409–18, 420, 425, 427–29, 431–37, 439–48, 451, 452, 456, 458, 469, 472, 474, 486, 501–507

Idumaea 27, 53, 59, 67, 73, 74, 220–22, 232, 366, 372, 374, 413, 423, 424, 427, 431, 434, 435, 443, 451–54, 474, 481, 482, 501, 503
Idumaean(s) 10, 12, 27, 41, 70, 72, 209, 215, 220–23, 225–27, 229, 269, 413, 414, 427, 431, 442, 443, 449, 464, 470, 471, 474, 484, 501, 502
Illyrian 132
Illyricum 430
image 76, 101, 102, 105, 110, 146, 167, 251, 271, 273, 275–78, 313, 353, 354, 357, 409, 440, 450, 459, 465, 479, 484, 485
Imalkoue 397
immortal 107, 110, 146, 272, 274
immortality 97, 110, 171, 272–74, 290
intercalary 17, 18, 210, 377
intercalations 25
intermarriage 215, 249
Ionia 240, 247, 469
Ionian 240
'Iraq al-Amir 63, 71
Isaiah 101, 237, 265, 272, 283
Ishmaelites 232
Isis 109, 241
Israel 3–7, 32, 33, 35, 41, 42, 49, 75, 80, 105, 129, 134, 136, 158, 165, 177, 179, 201, 204, 205, 208, 218, 231–34, 244, 249, 253, 269, 275–77, 279–81, 283, 288, 346, 380, 389, 392, 403, 404, 409, 423, 424, 447, 502, 505
Israelite(s) 5, 7, 12, 53, 99, 110, 143, 158, 179, 195, 199, 213, 232, 233, 246, 269, 290, 326, 463, 485, 503

Italian 126, 308, 430, 450
Italy 57, 74, 241, 305–307, 438, 441, 450
Ituraea 72, 418
Ituraean(s) 10, 12, 65, 70, 72, 222, 224–26, 269, 427, 473, 502
Iztabba 48

Jabal 62
Jabel 66
Jacob 99, 158, 159, 203, 213
Jaffa 49, 52, 76
Jamnia 54, 65, 396, 434, 436
Jannaeus 46, 49, 52–54, 56, 58–64, 68, 71, 73, 76–77, 118, 140, 148, 151, 180, 191, 192, 200, 223, 224, 227, 235, 303, 304, 413, 416, 418–25, 427, 428, 431, 432, 463, 486, 502, 503
Januarius 242
Japha 212
Jarash 71
Jason 65, 72, 81, 92, 124, 133, 137, 217, 237, 252, 253, 255–57, 259, 260, 313, 316–19, 321–25, 327–39, 342, 344, 345, 347–49, 355, 372, 378, 381, 385, 406, 414, 494, 496
Jehoiachin 244
Jehoiakim 101
Jerash 62, 71
Jeremiah 85, 88, 101, 102, 234, 247, 266, 268, 288
Jericho 53, 64, 69, 71, 127, 131, 182, 269, 270, 390, 409, 410, 431, 432, 434, 453, 454, 456, 464–66, 479, 480, 501
Jerome 90, 116, 117, 350, 354, 357
Jerusalem 17, 18, 21–23, 26–29, 31, 33, 36, 41, 51, 55, 56, 58, 63–65, 67, 69, 71–72, 74–78, 81, 91, 101, 103, 104, 107, 108, 112, 117, 124, 125, 128, 129, 131, 142, 148–50, 155, 156, 166, 177, 182, 183, 187, 190–92, 199–201, 203, 208–18, 220, 221, 232, 234–38, 240, 241, 243, 244, 246, 249–51, 253–59, 263, 269, 276, 289, 300–302, 311, 313, 314, 316–29, 331–34, 336–38, 342, 344–49, 353, 354, 356, 358, 359, 361, 364, 365, 367, 369, 370, 373–77, 381, 385, 389–94, 398, 404, 405, 408–10, 413, 419, 422, 432–37, 440, 444–47, 449, 451–56, 463–66, 468, 469, 471,

474, 475, 478, 480–82, 484–88, 493–96, 498, 499, 501, 504–507
Jeshanah 454
Jesus 134, 140, 144, 152–57, 162, 165, 166, 168, 177, 181, 184, 263, 278, 281, 288, 316, 317, 467
Jew(s) 3–12, 14, 16, 18, 20–24, 26, 28, 30, 32, 34, 36, 37, 41, 42, 44–46, 48, 50, 52, 54, 56, 58, 60, 62, 64, 66–68, 70–74, 76–78, 80, 82, 84–96, 98, 100, 102, 104–14, 116, 118, 124–34, 136, 138, 140–42, 144–46, 148, 150, 152, 154–56, 158, 160, 162, 164, 166, 168, 170, 172, 174, 175, 178, 180, 182, 184, 186, 188, 190, 192, 194–96, 198, 200, 202, 204–24, 226, 228, 230–36, 238–58, 260, 261, 263, 264, 266, 268–74, 276, 278–80, 282, 284, 286–90, 295, 296, 298–304, 306, 308, 310–12, 314, 316, 318–20, 322–30, 332–34, 336, 338–42, 344–46, 348–56, 358–70, 372–76, 378–86, 388–96, 398–400, 402–404, 406, 408, 410, 412–16, 418, 420, 422, 424, 426–28, 430–40, 442–44, 446–52, 454–56, 458, 460, 462–66, 468–72, 474, 476, 478–89, 493, 494, 496–500, 502, 504–508
Jewish 3–18, 21, 22, 26, 28, 32, 34–37, 41, 43, 45, 46, 52–56, 60, 65–69, 71–76, 79, 81–85, 87, 89–93, 95, 97–101, 103–11, 113, 114, 117, 123, 126, 128, 134, 135, 137, 138, 141, 143, 144, 146, 152, 156, 160, 162, 163, 165–67, 169, 170, 172, 173, 178, 180, 181, 183, 188, 189, 191, 192, 194–97, 199–203, 205–208, 210–22, 225–28, 231–47, 249, 251, 253–58, 260, 262–70, 272, 276, 278, 280, 281, 284, 287, 288, 290, 295, 300, 302, 303, 311, 313–19, 323, 324, 326–29, 337–40, 342, 347, 349–55, 360–62, 364–68, 370, 372, 374, 375, 377, 378, 381, 383–86, 391, 393–95, 397–402, 405–12, 414, 416, 418–20, 425, 427, 428, 432, 434, 436, 442–46, 448, 452, 454, 461, 463–64, 466, 468–70, 476, 481, 483–85, 487, 489, 493, 494, 497, 498, 500–508
Jezer 53
Jezreel 401
Jimmeh 67

Johanan 76, 77
John 12, 34, 49, 50, 55, 56, 59, 60, 66, 70, 71, 75, 77, 80, 83, 84, 91, 117, 139, 147, 151, 152, 154, 155, 157, 161, 162, 164, 172, 174, 177, 184, 190, 192, 194, 197, 200, 201, 205, 208, 215, 220, 232, 262, 269, 281, 284, 302, 310, 318, 326, 328–30, 340, 359, 368, 378, 388, 390, 406, 407, 409, 412, 415–17, 425, 427, 428, 440, 443, 469, 486, 501–503
Jonathan 17, 20, 44, 47, 52, 58, 75–77, 84, 126, 127, 139, 147, 173, 191, 192, 212, 267, 301, 359, 372, 389–403, 406, 407, 409, 426–28, 456, 499, 500
Joppa 52, 67, 128, 396, 398, 407–10, 423, 434, 452, 462, 466
Jordan 62–64, 71, 390
Joseph 136, 176, 181, 199, 203, 204, 206, 214, 215, 236, 278, 372, 394, 452–54, 457, 472–74
Josephus 4, 6, 10, 12, 21, 26–34, 43, 45, 47, 48, 56, 61, 70, 72, 79, 83, 91–95, 106, 109, 114, 117–19, 128, 129, 138, 139, 142–51, 159–66, 168, 170–73, 180–83, 186–89, 192, 194, 200–206, 209–13, 215, 217–20, 222, 225, 226, 233, 234, 236–38, 241, 243, 245–47, 252, 262, 264–66, 272, 274, 276, 280, 281, 284–89, 303, 304, 313, 315–18, 334, 346, 348, 350, 355, 360–62, 366, 374, 384, 389, 392, 394–96, 398, 399, 402, 405–11, 413–19, 421–25, 427, 431, 434–45, 447, 449, 452, 455–57, 459, 464, 468, 472–77, 479, 482–86, 497, 501, 503, 506
Joshua 197, 198, 200, 233, 283, 284, 399
Jotapata 212
Jubilee 32, 98, 99
Jubilees 97–99, 194, 203, 232, 263, 266, 271, 273, 277, 288, 318, 328, 333
Judas 13, 17–19, 22, 23, 25, 34, 35, 52, 54, 55, 58, 66, 79, 81–85, 87, 96, 136, 137, 154, 172, 220, 248, 300, 340, 341, 343, 345, 347, 349, 351, 353, 355, 357–89, 392, 393, 400, 402, 426, 428, 479, 481, 498–500
Jude 103, 272
Judith 99–101, 203
Julius 10, 77, 111, 112, 115, 118, 119, 128, 228, 239, 241–44, 247, 298, 406,

416, 430, 439–41, 443–45, 448, 462, 476, 505
Jupiter 241, 242, 350
Justin 111, 114, 115, 235, 302, 304, 314, 378, 393, 395, 396, 400, 403, 408, 411, 416, 443

Kadesh 398
kaige 266, 267
Kallinikos 302
Kanaf 70
Karaites 141, 143
Kedesh 43, 75
Kedron 409
Kerak 46
Kidron 72
Kifri 245
Kislev 22, 24, 355, 370, 497, 498
Knidos 67
Kokhva 33, 72, 180
Korban 143

Labienus 451
Lacedaemonians 399
Laenas 242, 343
Laenus 400
Lagynoi 126
Laodice 20, 312
Laodicea 239, 446
Lathyrus 297, 420, 421
Latin 6, 26, 31, 79, 102, 109, 113, 115, 117, 119, 238, 305, 335, 337
law(s) 5, 7, 9–11, 65, 72, 82, 91, 95, 99, 100, 104–106, 124, 136, 139, 140, 142, 143, 145, 147, 149, 150, 152, 155–57, 167–69, 174, 175, 207, 208, 211, 214, 220–22, 225, 252, 260, 263, 302, 316, 317, 322–24, 326, 327, 330, 331, 333, 334, 337, 343, 345, 346, 351, 352, 362, 367, 386, 369, 378, 379, 390, 396, 409, 415, 418, 420, 425, 457, 463, 464, 466, 467, 469, 472, 473, 475, 476, 479, 482, 484, 485, 494, 501, 503
Lazarus 155
Lebanon 226, 418, 454, 463
Lemba 424
Lenaeus 341
Lentulus 238, 239, 436
Leontopolis 85, 235–38, 247, 263, 416
Lepidus 441, 450

Lesbos 467
Levant 41, 55, 59, 75, 257, 295, 298, 464
levirate 420
Levites 155, 168, 334
Levitical 336
Leviticus 196, 264, 267, 269
Libanius 354
Licinius 425
limes 64, 65, 464, 465
Livia 469, 478
Livius 113, 116
Lod 69
Lucian 266
Lucianic 265–67
Lucius 238, 405, 406, 425, 445
Lucullus 304, 308, 425
Lydda 54, 453
Lysias 19, 23–25, 84, 86, 87, 300, 364–66, 368–71, 374–76, 381, 384

Maccabaean(s) 22, 41–42, 80, 87, 89, 90, 92, 96, 98, 100, 102–104, 112, 114, 116, 125–27, 173, 174, 220, 249, 251–53, 255, 257–59, 261, 273, 280, 288, 311, 313, 315–17, 319, 321, 323, 325, 327–29, 331, 333, 335, 337, 339, 341, 343, 345, 347, 349, 351, 353, 355, 357–65, 367, 369, 371, 373, 375, 377, 379, 381–83, 385–89, 391, 392, 409, 426, 498–500, 504
Maccabaeus 13, 54, 79, 83, 96, 136, 248, 300, 340, 359, 360, 362, 363, 365, 371, 376, 377, 380, 383, 384, 386
Maccabee 17, 35, 44, 47, 56, 58, 85, 136, 173, 200, 220, 242, 301, 302, 341, 361, 378, 388, 389, 397, 399, 403
Maccabees 4, 5, 10, 11, 13, 16–25, 55, 56, 58, 61, 64–66, 79–86, 90–92, 114, 123–26, 134, 136, 137, 167, 174, 181, 205, 208, 223, 234–38, 244, 245, 248, 249, 252, 258–62, 268, 269, 273, 276, 280, 281, 283, 290, 300, 301, 310, 313, 315–19, 321–22, 324, 326, 328–37, 339–42, 344–51, 354–64, 366–68, 370–84, 386–90, 392, 393, 398, 399, 402–404, 406–408, 433, 464, 494, 496–99, 504
Macedonia 307, 311, 434

Index of Subjects

Macedonian(s) 16, 18–21, 24, 51, 62, 86, 113, 132, 209, 218, 311, 323, 342, 346, 368, 400, 414, 495
Machaeras 454
Machaerus 64, 71, 425, 436, 437, 454
Macrinus 230
Macrobius 484
Madeba 71
magi 483
magistrate(s) 241, 323, 324
Magnesia 300, 311
Maimonides 32
Makmish 49
Malalas 356
Malchos 397
Malchus 452
Malichus 223–25, 436, 445, 446, 458
Malthace 210, 480
Manaemus 172
Manetho 106
Manius 369
mantic 91, 282, 284
Marcellinus 113, 354, 436
Marcellus 211
Marcius 436
Marcus 26, 27, 36, 93, 112, 190, 229, 239, 240, 414, 442, 450, 460, 461, 467, 468, 476
Maresha 59, 67, 70, 74
Mariamme 93, 446, 454, 457, 458, 467, 469, 472–78
Maris 46, 49
Marisa 59, 209, 220, 414, 424, 434, 436
Maritima 48, 464
Marius 430
Mark 26–28, 46, 52, 69, 112, 129–31, 152, 154–57, 162, 163, 165, 168, 169, 185, 224, 228, 240, 298, 299, 332, 377, 394, 430, 436, 448, 465, 488, 506
Markan 168, 169
Marqa 199
martyr(s) 79, 273, 278, 280, 281, 328, 443
martyrdom 81, 83, 89, 90, 103, 136, 167, 261, 280, 281, 345, 350, 385, 497
Masada 64, 66, 71, 170, 180, 446, 452, 458, 464, 465, 485
Masoretes 265
Masoretic 263, 265
Mastema 272

matrilineal 5, 482, 485
Mattathias 22, 76, 83, 136, 269, 310, 340, 358–60, 386, 388, 455, 498
Matthew 152, 154, 162, 168, 482, 483
Matthias 30, 478, 479
Maximus 241, 242
Medaba 390, 413, 424
Megillah 398
Melchizedek 270, 271, 277
Memmius 369
Menahem 149, 184, 461
Menelaus 87, 92, 124, 125, 133, 137, 208, 217, 237, 252–57, 261, 316, 317, 322, 324, 325, 327, 328, 334–39, 342–45, 347–49, 355, 358, 367, 368, 375, 381, 385, 386, 495, 496, 498, 500
menorah 158, 159, 346, 347
mercenary/ies 22, 126, 318–20, 363, 411, 422, 425, 503
meridarchēs 362
Mesopotamia 213, 229, 230, 238, 244–46, 303, 322, 447
messiah 157, 162, 164, 275–80, 283, 288
messiahs 276, 277, 281
Metellius 439
Metellus 431
metempsychosis 274
Mevorakh 47
Michael 103, 271, 272, 277
Michmash 391, 393, 499
midrash 109, 203
midrashic 199, 267
mikva'ot 11, 36, 269, 504
Miletus 240
Milik 33, 34, 177
millennium/ia 5, 62, 134, 179, 265, 279, 288, 433
minas 405, 406
Minim 158
Miqsat 190
Miqva'ot 54, 269, 270
miqveh 60, 270
Mishnah 130, 134, 144, 162–64, 166
Mishnaic 65
Mithradates 20, 227, 408, 422, 425, 430
Mithridates 304, 308, 439
Mitylene 467
Mizpah 364
Moab 223, 224, 419, 421, 422, 424
Modein 359, 361, 374, 382, 401

money 22, 124, 131, 133, 170, 214, 215, 239, 241, 255, 256, 259, 261, 306, 313, 320–22, 331, 332, 335, 336, 344, 347, 365, 401, 411, 432, 437, 452, 467, 469, 485, 494, 495
Mopsuestia 303, 421
Moses 13, 89, 90, 98, 99, 102, 103, 140, 147, 153, 162, 167, 174, 195, 197–99, 272, 281, 283–84, 286, 290, 336, 351, 443, 483
Murabba'at 32
Murashu 246
Murcus 445
Mycenaean 43
Mylae 306
Mysian 345, 346, 348, 362, 496
Mysiarch 348

Nabataea 224, 225, 432
Nabataean(s) 62, 71, 220, 222–25, 421, 423, 432, 436, 458, 485, 503
Nabataeans 62, 63, 71, 78, 220, 222–25, 304, 390, 398, 421–23, 432, 436–37, 457, 458, 465, 471, 485, 503, 506
Nablus 199
naked 333
Namra 225
Narbata 68
Nebuchadnezzar 99–101, 232, 244
necropolis 59
Negev 59, 70, 222, 225, 463
Nehemiah 79, 82, 83, 85, 167, 202, 214, 215, 218, 232, 263, 269, 502
Neofiti 267
Nepotianus 242
Nero 33, 34, 228, 229, 305, 429
Nicator 20, 301, 303, 421
Nicephorium 245
Nicodmus 155
Nicolaus 92–94, 111, 114, 118, 222, 316, 411, 417, 442, 443, 455, 469, 471, 473, 475, 477, 478, 482, 484
Niger 230
Nimra 66
Nisan 16–21, 23, 24, 34, 35, 355, 377
Nisibis 229, 230
Noah 96, 198, 271
Norbanus 27
nude 332, 333
nudity 333

Numenius 405, 406
Nysa 48

oath(s) 146, 149, 171, 172, 183, 377, 468, 477
Obodas 223, 224, 422, 469, 471, 476
occupation(s) 44, 50, 60, 64, 179, 180, 227, 228, 415
Octavian 26, 112, 129, 130, 298, 430, 440, 441, 445, 446, 448, 450–52, 457–62, 473, 487, 488, 506, 507
Odomera 390
olive 48, 59, 67, 70, 333
Olympiad 26–29, 431, 465, 469
Olympic 28, 93, 333
omen 345
Onias I 399
Onias III 124, 237, 249, 253, 255, 259, 288, 319, 321, 335, 336, 494, 495, 497, 499, 501, 503, 505, 507
oracle(s) 275, 279, 282, 284, 286, 287, 289, 291, 473
oral 194, 197, 267
orally 368
Oresa 452
Orient 222
Oriental 105, 127, 201, 251
Origen 103
Orodes 451
orthography 196
ossuaries 65, 72, 73
ossuary/ies 65, 75
ostracon/a 181–83
ovens 50, 60
overseer(s) 171, 208, 348

Pacorus 229, 451
Pagan(s) 22, 29, 97, 106, 195, 199, 201, 202, 213, 214, 218, 260, 332, 333, 336, 348, 351–52, 356, 357, 359, 370, 466, 484, 494, 497
palace(s) 11, 45, 53, 54, 56, 57, 60, 64, 71, 73, 222, 269, 270, 451, 456, 457, 464, 465, 467, 480, 482, 504
Palaestina 465
Palaestinae 53, 64, 74, 75, 464
Palestine xv 4, 12, 33, 37, 41, 64, 73, 74, 82, 83, 87, 105, 106, 108, 116, 118, 123, 124, 127, 169, 195, 203, 204, 225, 228, 232, 234, 244–46, 251, 253, 263, 281,

296, 311, 329, 341, 349, 361, 409, 415, 434, 441, 451, 453, 455, 456, 461, 466, 482, 487, 489, 493, 495, 506
Palestinian 6, 13, 66, 84, 118, 126, 134, 166, 224, 234, 235, 383, 403
palm(s) 127, 131, 170
Pan 42
Paneas 42, 462, 468, 480
Paneion 42
Pappus 454
papyrus/i 5, 15, 48, 75, 203, 238, 247
paradosis 143, 161
Parni 227
Parthia 28, 226–29, 245, 302, 435, 438, 450, 451, 460, 476, 488
Parthian(s) 20, 59, 70, 129, 221, 223–30, 244–46, 299, 301–303, 320, 408, 411–13, 421, 422, 431, 438, 441, 450–57, 465, 487, 488, 501, 504, 506
Passover 29, 30, 99, 210, 263, 432, 480
patris 234
Patroclus 364
Paullus 30, 479
Paulus 13
Pausanias 476
peasant 125, 259, 326
peasants 125, 126, 495
Peitholaus 191, 436, 438
pekod 245
peleg 75, 179, 185
Pella 61, 62, 71, 423, 424, 434
Peloponnesian 329
Pelusion 412
Pelusium 67
Pentateuch 99, 104, 105, 141, 194–98, 216, 264, 265, 502
Peraea 71, 468, 480–82
Perdiccas 62
Pergamum 307, 308, 312, 313, 415, 439
periochae 395
Perseus 342, 343, 400
Persia 213, 271, 300, 372
Persian(s) 41, 43, 44, 46, 47, 49, 51, 53, 55, 57, 60, 65–69, 74, 76, 96, 99, 100, 135, 167, 174, 200–202, 206, 226, 236, 245, 246, 268, 290, 319, 433, 434, 461, 493
Pescennius 230
pesharim 190, 287
pesher 190

Petra 222, 225, 432, 436, 452, 481
Petronius 467
Pharisee(s) 73, 77, 95, 100, 134, 135, 137–66, 168, 169, 173–75, 191, 192, 274, 416, 419, 423–28, 468, 477–79, 503
Pharsalus 438, 505
Phasael 55, 444–47, 451–52, 464, 465, 476, 481, 505, 506
Phasiron 390
Pheroras 145, 146, 453, 468, 475–78
Phiabi 467
Philadelphia 62, 63, 71, 410, 421, 458
Philadelphus 301, 303, 304, 421
philhellene 224, 418
Philip 24, 31, 102, 208, 300, 303, 304, 307, 311, 345, 349, 364, 374, 421, 422, 478, 480, 482, 496, 503
Philip V 307, 311
Philippus 436
Philistia 52, 396, 398
Philo 10, 12, 108, 109, 170–72, 181, 182, 186, 187, 189, 192, 201, 233, 241, 243, 244, 272, 276, 281, 284, 285, 290, 326
Philocrates 103, 104
Philometor 279, 297, 302, 395, 396
Philopator 297, 300, 302, 303, 421, 422
Philos 393
philosopher 116, 117, 252
philosophers 61
philosophical 187, 189
philosophy 103, 139, 142, 160, 161
Philoteria 46
Phineas 360
Phoenicia 42, 44, 124, 258, 259, 313, 321, 341, 357, 363, 364, 423, 456, 466, 470
Phoenician(s) 43, 44, 46–48, 52, 57, 67, 70, 72–74, 126, 207, 224, 251, 357, 399
phoenix 434
Phraates 227, 408, 411, 456
Phrygia 238, 319
Phrygians 208
Pieria 304
Pilate 211
pirates 308
Piso 239, 242
Plato 117
Pliny 61, 115, 170, 172, 182, 186, 189, 467

Plutarch 12, 30, 115, 243, 410, 455, 479
Poleg 67
poleis 250, 321, 323
polis 124, 125, 133, 250, 251, 253, 255, 261, 319, 320, 322, 323, 325–27, 329, 333, 336, 338, 493, 494
politeia 240
Pollio 26, 36, 474
Pollion 148, 149, 161, 468
Polybius 14, 20, 61, 113, 115, 116, 249, 250, 301, 310, 313–15, 340–43, 353–54, 357, 379, 383, 393
polytheism 110, 349
Pompeius 13, 75, 111, 114, 243, 298, 313, 340, 429, 450
Pompey 26–29, 36, 61–63, 73, 74, 107, 112, 113, 115, 128–30, 210, 224, 227, 228, 238, 239, 243, 247, 297, 304, 308, 309, 429–34, 436–40, 445, 447, 450, 451, 455, 504, 505
Pontus 240, 308, 425, 468
Popilius 343
Popillius 242, 400
Porphyrius 116
Porphyry 90, 111, 116, 117, 350, 354, 357
Posidonius 117
praetor(s) 241, 308, 406, 415
praetorship 414
prayer(s) 100–102, 146, 171, 177, 272
prefect 467
price 394
priest(s) 10, 17–19, 30, 48, 75, 77, 79, 84, 91, 95, 99, 101, 104, 106, 115, 123, 128, 136, 139, 140, 142, 143, 147, 149–51, 153–58, 160–62, 164, 165, 167, 174, 181, 184, 190–93, 197–99, 200–204, 212, 213, 217, 218, 236–38, 240, 246, 248, 249, 255, 256, 259, 262, 271, 278, 279, 281, 284, 285, 288, 300, 310, 313, 316, 317, 319, 321, 322, 324, 326, 328, 329–31, 334–40, 345, 346, 349, 351, 368, 370, 375, 377, 381, 382, 385, 386, 389, 394, 396, 397, 402, 404, 406, 410, 415, 416, 418–21, 425, 426, 428, 431–34, 436, 443, 447, 448, 452, 455–57, 466, 467, 478, 486, 494–96, 498
370, 377, 386, 396, 404, 418, 433, 447, 466, 486, 495, 501, 504

priesthood 20, 82, 92, 101, 103, 124, 143, 144, 165, 174, 199, 203, 238, 248, 255, 256, 258, 301, 316, 317, 319, 322, 325, 330, 334, 336, 344, 378, 382, 388, 393, 394, 397, 402, 403, 407, 426, 433, 435, 440, 478, 494, 495, 499–501, 503, 505
proconsul 239, 241, 439
procurator(s) 211, 440, 446, 468, 480
prophecy/ies 90, 96, 237, 238, 279, 281–90, 416
prophet(s) 97, 141, 154, 165, 234, 263, 277, 278, 281–87
prophetic 238, 279, 281–86, 416
protrepticus 109
province(s) 6, 41, 55, 87, 123–25, 128, 133, 195, 210, 223–25, 227, 229–31, 256, 295, 308, 311, 319, 322, 336, 364, 367, 376, 391, 395, 397, 409, 433–35, 444, 446, 450, 460, 461, 463, 482, 487, 497, 500, 507
provincial 461
Psalms 106, 107, 273, 276, 279, 290
Ptolemaic 13, 16, 47, 52, 59, 90, 104, 123, 204, 214, 235, 236, 247, 249, 260, 270, 273, 279, 296, 307, 311, 341–42, 344, 357, 383, 385, 388, 395, 396, 411, 412, 463
Ptolemais/Akko 44
Ptolemy I 16, 106, 234, 296, 341
Ptolemy II 42, 62, 71, 104, 105
Ptolemy III 204
Ptolemy IV 62, 235
Ptolemy V 204, 295, 296, 341
Ptolemy VI 237, 260, 279, 297, 314, 316, 341–43, 346, 347, 385, 395, 396, 500
Ptolemy VII 297
Ptolemy VIII 297, 302, 343, 412, 414
Ptolemy IX 235, 297, 420, 421
Ptolemy X 297
Ptolemy XI 297
Ptolemy XII 297, 437, 438
Ptolemy XIII 57, 298, 438
Punic 43 113, 116, 305–307, 400, 430
Purim 377

Qasr/Qaṣr 63, 64
Qaṣr al-'Abd 64
Qeis 61
Qeiyafa 66
Qôm 67

Quadratus 211–12
quaester 438
Quintilius 478
Quintus 203, 369, 451, 456, 458
Qumran 57, 75, 97, 98, 106, 135, 141, 144, 145, 160, 170, 173, 175–93, 203, 236, 237, 263–68, 270–72, 274–78, 280, 283, 284, 287, 288, 328, 392, 419, 422, 503

Rabbat 71
Rabbath 62
rabbinic 5, 32, 77, 127, 134, 138, 140, 144, 145, 156–60, 162–65, 169, 174, 184, 195, 233, 245, 247, 253, 267, 270, 421, 424, 482
Rabirius 239
rabbis 143, 158, 234
Raḥel 66
Ramat 66
Raphaim 69
Raphia 236, 383, 421, 423, 434, 436
Rebecca 134
religion(s) 6–10, 12, 65, 81, 82, 92, 96, 98, 100, 104, 109, 115, 123, 137, 143, 145, 173, 174, 176, 194, 195, 199–201, 205, 207, 214, 215, 217, 218, 221, 240, 250, 252–58, 260–63, 265, 267–69, 271, 273, 275, 277, 279, 281, 283, 285, 287, 289, 291, 326, 327, 329, 336, 338, 339, 346, 349, 352, 355, 357, 358, 366, 375, 386, 443, 464, 497, 502
religious 6, 7, 9, 11, 12, 72, 73, 81, 82, 87, 92, 95, 96, 100, 109, 125, 126, 135, 141–43, 145, 151, 157, 159, 161, 162, 164, 165, 168, 174, 175, 180, 184, 195, 202, 207, 208, 214, 215, 226, 238, 240, 242, 244, 245, 249–54, 256, 263, 268, 280, 281, 286, 311, 325, 329, 337–39, 349–55, 358, 370, 375, 381, 384, 385, 392, 410, 411, 426, 466, 469, 479, 483, 484, 497
resurrection 72, 73, 90, 97, 99, 110, 138, 140–42, 153, 156, 162, 229, 272–76, 281, 289, 290
Revelation 98, 282–84, 287
rewritten Bible 98
Rhodes 67, 301, 459, 466, 506
Rhodian 50, 57, 75, 205

ritual 11, 42, 45, 143–44, 157, 161–64, 185, 269, 270, 421, 504
romance 472
Rosetta 296
Rubicon 429, 431, 439

Saba 60
Sabaeans 467
Sabazi 241
Sabazius 241, 242
sabbath(s) 26, 28, 29, 32, 34, 98, 99, 101, 136, 141, 142, 152, 157, 158, 162–64, 172, 174, 177, 187, 206, 207, 214, 239, 241–42, 244, 271, 287, 351, 359, 390, 433, 496, 497
Sabinus 480, 481
sacrifice(s) 22, 52, 103, 127, 187, 206, 248, 259, 271, 316, 317, 330–32, 346, 350, 352, 354, 358, 359, 371, 410, 494, 497, 504
sacrificial 330, 433, 454, 504
Sadducean 184, 185
Sadducee(s) 134, 135, 137–44, 147, 148, 150, 151, 153–57, 160–66, 168, 173–75, 182, 185, 191, 272, 290, 416
Salampsio 476
Salome 53, 54, 72, 140, 145, 150, 152, 161, 174, 175, 190, 308, 418–20, 424, 428, 429, 457, 470, 473–80, 482, 485, 503, 507
Samais 148, 149, 161
Samareitikon 196, 197
Samaria 27, 50, 51, 64–66, 68, 69, 71–74, 123, 127, 194–96, 200, 202, 203, 205, 208–10, 213–15, 217, 218, 232, 345, 362, 394, 397, 413, 414, 424, 427, 434, 436, 444, 446, 452–54, 462, 465, 481, 482, 500, 502
Samarian(s) 51, 71, 195, 210
Samaritan(s) 27, 51, 97, 98, 140, 141, 143, 158, 194–219, 207, 209–19, 263–65, 327, 357, 413, 414, 463, 502
Samarkhand 227, 298
Samega 71
Samosata 454
Samuel 13–15, 263, 264, 266–68
Sanballat 202, 215
sanctuary 42, 52, 238, 256, 373, 437
Ṣandaḥanna 59

Sanhedrin 132, 140, 142, 143, 155–57, 162, 165, 166, 318, 337, 444, 445, 458, 463, 486, 487, 506
Sardinia 306, 450
Sardis 227, 241, 298
Sarnoga 413
Sarṭaba 62
Sasanian 226, 227
Sasanians 230
Satan 103, 271, 272, 277
satrap 451
satrapy 364, 367, 373, 408
Saturnalia 484
Saturninus 470, 472
scapegoat 222, 270
Scaurus 190, 224, 432, 435, 436, 448
Scipio 241, 439
scribal 10, 167–69, 237, 282
scribe(s) 101, 134, 136, 152–54, 157, 162, 165–69, 267, 281, 282, 286, 318, 345
scripture(s) 97, 104, 126, 144, 148, 151, 161, 162, 164, 181, 192, 196, 197, 284–86, 289, 419,
Scythopolis 48, 61, 70, 414, 424, 434, 436
Sebastenians 481
sect(s) 11, 12, 91, 95, 100, 106, 134, 135, 137, 139, 141, 143–47, 149, 151, 153, 155, 157, 159, 161–63, 165, 167–75, 177, 178, 181, 186, 190–95, 199, 209, 210, 213, 236, 265, 287, 329, 495, 502
sectarian 12, 134, 168, 169, 173, 175, 176, 178, 180, 181, 184–86, 192, 196, 206, 265, 270, 274, 390, 421
seer 281
Seleucus I 16, 250, 296, 298, 341
Seleucus II 227
Seleucus IV 13, 15, 21, 35, 75, 124, 259, 260, 295, 300, 312–13, 321, 380, 494
senate 20, 112, 239, 300, 301, 307, 309, 337, 342–43, 379, 380, 386, 393, 400, 403, 405, 406, 415, 428, 430, 431, 437, 438, 440, 441, 452, 455, 459–61, 493, 499, 506
senators 307, 441, 460
Sepphoraeus 479
Sepphoris 45, 68, 269, 420, 434, 453, 481
Septimius 230

Septuagint 101, 103, 263
Seron 362–64, 368
Servilius 437
Sestio 436
Severus 230
Sextus 444, 445, 450
Shalshalah 198, 199
Shammai 158, 163, 174
Sharon 66, 69, 429, 433, 466
Shavu'ot 158
Shean 48, 401, 414
Sheba 60
Shechem 51, 66, 69, 76, 196, 199–201, 203–204, 206–209, 213, 215–18, 327, 413, 414, 422, 502
Shechemite 203, 205, 207, 269
Shephela/Shephelah 52, 66, 69, 70, 396, 398
Sheva 60
Shikhin 45
Shiloh 55, 199
Shiqmona 46
Shmittah 410
showbread 346, 347
Sibylline 275, 279, 282, 287, 291, 437
Sidon 43, 128, 240, 243, 403
Sidonian 54, 65, 70, 206, 207, 362
Sigillata 42, 44, 73
Silo 50, 60, 452, 453
Simon 34–36, 52, 54, 56, 58, 69, 71, 72, 76, 81, 84, 85, 114, 124, 126, 127, 149, 151, 153, 159, 161, 163, 172, 191, 192, 200, 204, 242, 255, 301, 302, 316, 317, 321, 334, 335, 359, 360, 372, 376, 390, 391, 396–98, 401–11, 414, 415, 426–28, 467, 478, 481, 500, 501
Simon I 81, 405
Simon II 204
Sisenna 437
slave(s) 171, 204, 243–44, 247, 322, 323, 365, 443, 476, 481
slavery 172, 203, 240, 247, 345, 350, 463, 496
Socrates 12
Soemus 473
Solomon 41, 85, 106–108, 179, 273–76, 279, 280, 290, 404, 447
Soreq 69
Sosius 27, 454, 455

Index of Subjects

Spain 57, 74, 438, 439, 460
Sparta 84, 398–401, 405
Spartan(s) 84, 85, 333, 398–401, 407, 476
Strabo 26, 29, 61, 92–94, 118, 221–23, 226, 235, 252, 408, 418, 419, 455, 467, 472, 502
stratēgos 363, 364, 376, 406, 409, 415, 463
Straton 48, 68, 74, 420, 423, 434, 462, 466
Suetonius 26, 118, 243
suicide 251, 298, 306, 308, 441, 451, 452, 468, 478, 504, 506
Sulla 308, 430
Sultan 53
Susa 245
Susanna 88, 99
Syllaeus 224, 470–72, 476–78
synagogue(s) 44, 45, 60, 82, 154, 155, 162, 165, 196, 241, 242, 244, 262–64, 267, 482, 485
Syncellus 47, 61, 111, 118, 119, 408

Ta'anit 14, 127, 407
Tabbai 158
Tabernacles 17, 18, 141, 142, 394, 410, 421, 456
Tacitus 112, 113, 115, 118, 211, 212, 226, 250, 351, 352
talents 124, 125, 129, 131, 133, 319, 320, 324, 335, 397, 401, 408, 420, 436, 437, 445, 451, 453, 456, 461, 468–70, 475, 481, 482, 494, 496
Talmud 34, 130, 203, 205
Talmudic 204, 221, 234, 247
targum(s) 196, 197, 267
Tarichaeae 243, 438
Tarsus 156
tax(es) 79, 123–26, 128–30, 132, 133, 152, 154, 246, 248, 259, 300, 310, 321, 322, 326, 340, 394, 397, 435, 468, 469, 471, 480, 485, 486, 488, 494, 507
Tekoa 69, 390
temple(s) 4–6, 8–12, 14, 16, 18, 20–26, 28, 30, 32, 34–36, 41, 42, 44, 46–48, 50–56, 58, 60–66, 68, 70, 72–74, 76, 78–80, 82–86, 88–92, 94–96, 98, 100–104, 106–108, 110, 112–14, 116, 118, 124–26, 128–32, 134–36, 138, 140, 142–44, 146, 148–52, 154–56, 158–60, 162, 164–70, 172–75, 178–82, 184, 186–88, 190, 192–94, 196, 198, 200, 202, 204–10, 212–18, 222, 224, 226, 228, 230, 232–38, 240–44, 246–66, 268, 270, 272, 274–76, 278–84, 286, 288–90, 296, 298, 300, 302, 304, 306, 308, 311, 312, 314, 316–18, 320–22, 324, 326–28, 330–32, 334–39, 341–48, 350–60, 362, 364, 366, 368–78, 380, 382–86, 388, 390, 392–94, 396, 398, 400, 402, 404, 406, 408, 410, 412–14, 416–18, 420–22, 424, 426, 428, 430, 432–34, 436–38, 440, 442–44, 446, 448, 450, 452, 454, 456, 458, 460, 462, 464–66, 468–70, 472, 474, 476, 478–82, 484–86, 488, 494–500, 502, 504, 506–508
tetradrachmas 44
tetrarch(s) 77, 447
tetrarchy 468, 478, 480, 482
Thea, Cleopatra 301
theatre(s) 48, 465, 466, 484
theocracy 432, 435, 447
Theodotus 201, 263
Theophanes 119
Theophilus 478
Therapeutae 172
Thracian 423
Thucydides 113, 116, 329, 332
Tiberius 10, 31, 109, 211
Timagenes 226
Timnath 390
Timothy 5, 365, 372
Titius 476
Titus 225, 369
Tobiad 63, 92, 124, 204, 214–15, 249, 252, 254–55, 316–18, 321, 335, 500–501
Tobiah 63
Tobias 316
Tobit 232
Tolidah 197
tomb 43, 62, 65, 72, 154, 411, 469
tombs 43, 59, 64–65, 72, 75, 154
toparchies 463
torah 11, 79, 97, 102, 143–44, 167–69, 190, 195, 233, 253, 263, 334

Tosephta 162–64
Trachanaea 245
Trachonitis 131, 246, 462, 468–71, 480, 482
trade 44, 62, 70, 125, 131, 133, 185, 223, 224, 228, 244, 327, 493, 504, 507
tradition(s) 10, 71, 72, 83, 97, 103, 105, 108, 109, 114, 135, 136, 140, 143, 144, 148, 151, 152, 156, 158, 159, 161–64, 167–69, 174, 177, 194, 196, 201, 202, 205, 211, 213, 216, 219, 228, 234, 238, 242, 258, 263–65, 267, 268, 271, 276, 281, 296, 337, 342, 394, 399, 402, 413, 424, 443, 480, 483, 484, 507
traditional 11, 127, 132, 146, 159, 197, 217, 221, 240, 255, 260, 311, 322, 323, 325, 326, 329, 330, 334, 336, 337, 353, 357, 375, 377, 381, 386, 389, 400, 450, 463, 469, 494, 498
Trajan 111, 212, 225, 226, 229
Transjordan 60, 70, 71, 73, 74, 128, 344, 372, 390, 413, 424, 427, 434, 463, 468, 478, 481, 502
Transjordanian 70, 372, 421
translation(s) 13, 31, 34, 36, 85, 91, 101, 102, 104, 105, 108, 111, 117, 143, 159, 176, 178, 196–99, 201, 204, 208, 238, 252, 263, 265, 267, 284, 310, 332, 333, 442, 446
transmigration 110, 146, 274
treaty 84, 226, 228, 230, 311, 378–80, 386, 399, 401, 405, 410, 415, 425, 428, 441, 450, 452, 493, 499, 500, 502, 506
tribe(s) 105, 170, 208, 223, 225–27, 233, 244, 305, 323, 334, 335, 339, 502
tribune 156, 212
tribute 112, 123–25, 128, 129, 132, 133, 146, 224, 246, 258, 259, 319, 321, 322, 335, 336, 343, 347, 397, 408–10, 413, 427, 433, 435, 436, 441, 445, 457, 471, 486, 494, 495, 501
Trikomia 5
Trogus 111, 114, 115, 313
Tryphaena 303
Tryphon 47, 301, 302, 389, 397, 398, 401–403, 405–408, 426, 500, 501
Tulidah 198–200
Tulul Abu el-'Alayiq 53

Tyre 43, 68, 78, 240, 302, 331, 336, 397, 403, 412, 446, 451, 477, 494
Tyriaion 319, 323, 324
Tyrian 68, 78
Tyrians 44, 240

Ulatha 468
Ummidius 211
urban 52, 324, 325
urbanization 173, 222, 224

Valerius 241, 242, 406
Varro 462
Varus 45, 221, 478, 480–82
Ventidius 211, 452–54
Vespasian 212, 285, 289, 404
village(s) 45, 60, 64, 65, 67–69, 71, 74, 166, 169, 171–72, 186, 189, 211–12, 215, 246, 361, 454, 463, 466, 471, 481
Vipsanius 467
vision(s) 88, 95, 96, 99, 102, 115, 135, 273, 274, 275, 282, 286, 291, 322, 325, 329, 338, 339, 427, 447
Vitellius 211
votive 187, 357, 479, 484

Watchers 271, 273, 290
wavesheaf 141, 142, 157, 164
wheat 467
wife/wives 10, 145, 146, 148, 171, 210, 215, 297, 301–303, 312, 346, 408, 409, 412, 417–20, 424, 425, 428, 431, 446, 450, 457, 469, 472, 475, 478, 480, 502, 503
wine 23, 67, 69, 70, 73, 126
wisdom 89, 91, 101, 102, 104–105, 108, 109, 144, 166, 167, 190, 272, 274, 280, 283, 290, 395
wise 166, 174, 273, 276, 278, 285, 287, 325, 389, 393
woman/women 97, 99, 100, 145, 155, 157, 161, 170, 171, 188, 213, 269, 326, 345, 348, 351, 418, 426, 443, 446, 451, 472, 477
worship 97, 101, 109, 110, 117, 146, 151, 165, 187, 199, 200, 207, 213, 215, 218, 236–38, 253, 255, 256, 260, 262, 263, 269, 325, 337, 347–50, 352, 356, 359, 370, 381, 382, 386, 494, 497, 498

writing 11, 12, 14, 79, 80, 82, 90–92, 94–97, 99, 105–108, 111–13, 116, 117, 138, 141, 145, 151, 156, 163, 164, 167, 171, 172, 174, 178, 182–84, 186, 194, 195, 197, 199, 201, 203, 204, 228, 233, 237, 239, 264, 268, 269, 275, 277, 280–82, 285–88, 290, 291, 319, 320, 324, 331, 337, 350, 357, 373, 375, 407, 474, 494

Xanthikos 87, 367, 369

yahad 184
Yahweh 256
Yannai 49, 419, 423
Yarkon 67
Yarmuk 61

Yavneh 54, 143, 175, 396
Yeraḥ 46
Zabadaean 398
Zabdai 398
Zabdiel 398
Zabinas 302, 412
Zadok 142
Zadokite(s) 181, 236, 336
Zakkai 158
Zamaris 129, 245, 246, 471
Zenodorus 462, 467, 468, 482
Zenon 48, 421
Zeus 48, 51, 61, 62, 206, 208, 251, 252, 256, 260, 327, 350, 353–58, 497
Zoilus 43, 420
Zonaras 112

www.ingramcontent.com/pod-product-compliance
Lightning Source LLC
LaVergne TN
LVHW021609060925
820435LV00017B/155